CAPITALISM IN THE COLONIES

Capitalism in the Colonies

AFRICAN MERCHANTS IN LAGOS, 1851–1931

A. G. Hopkins

PRINCETON UNIVERSITY PRESS
PRINCETON & OXFORD

Published by Princeton University Press
41 William Street, Princeton, New Jersey 08540
99 Banbury Road, Oxford OX2 6JX

press.princeton.edu

Library of Congress Cataloging-in-Publication Data

Names: Hopkins, A. G. (Antony G.), author.
Title: Capitalism in the colonies : African merchants in Lagos, 1851-1921 / A. G. Hopkins.
Description: Princeton : Princeton University Press, 2024. | Includes bibliographical references and index.
Identifiers: LCCN 2023042796 (print) | LCCN 2023042797 (ebook) | ISBN 9780691258843 (hardback) | ISBN 9780691258959 (ebook)
Subjects: LCSH: Capitalism—Nigeria—History. | Merchants—Nigeria—Lagos—History. | Lagos (Nigeria)—Commerce—History. | Nigeria—Economic conditions—History. | Great Britain—Foreign economic relations—Nigeria—History. | Nigeria—Foreign economic relations—Great Britain—History.
Classification: LCC HC1055.Z9 C625 2024 (print) | LCC HC1055.Z9 (ebook) | DDC 330.96690901—dc23/eng/20230913
LC record available at https://lccn.loc.gov/2023042796
LC ebook record available at https://lccn.loc.gov/2023042797

British Library Cataloging-in-Publication Data is available

Editorial: Ben Tate and Josh Drake
Production Editorial: Karen Carter
Jacket/Cover Design: Haley Chung
Production: Danielle Amatucci
Publicity: William Pagdatoon
Copyeditor: Karen Verde

Jacket Image: Ebute Ero market, Lagos, in 1920. The modern building on the left was built by Isaac Cole for G. L. Gaiser in 1911. The passenger lorries in mid-picture belonged to the Anfani Bus Service, which was owned and managed by Charlotte Obasa. Courtesy of Mary Evans / Pharcide.

This book has been composed in Miller

Printed in the United States of America

10   9   8   7   6   5   4   3   2   1

CONTENTS

[v]

CONTENTS [vii]

ILLUSTRATIONS

Figures

Maps

Tables

PREFACE

ALL BOOKS HAVE A story. This one is longer than most. It originated in 1960, when I graduated from the University of London and began research into African history. My interest, crudely conceived and at the time crudely expressed, lay in the development of capitalism in the non-Western world. My specific aim was to test various assumptions, derived from modernisation theory, about the inadequacy of indigenous entrepreneurs. The subject was largely uncharted. Studies of African history were only just appearing; the *Journal of African History* published its first issue in 1960. I decided to focus on Lagos, a substantial port that was home to a busy commercial community. In seeking advice, however, I was warned that it was most unlikely that I would be able to find sufficient material on African entrepreneurs. Accordingly, I retreated from my original aim and produced a safe, pedestrian economic history of the port between 1880 and 1914 for my Ph.D. thesis.[1]

In retrospect, the advice I received was mistaken. At the time, however, it was entirely reasonable because so little was known about the existence of sources that were essential to my original plan. Once I began fieldwork in 1961/62, however, I discovered that the material I needed could be found in official records in Lagos and, with luck and persistence, in private papers as well. By then, however, it was too late to change course. I ended by writing one Ph.D. and gathering material for another. Subsequent visits to Nigeria in 1963–1964 and 1967 enabled me to amplify my information and (with the aid of a car) to travel more easily to neighbouring settlements, with the result that I was able to add a rural dimension to my predominantly urban story.

By then, other aspects of life had intervened. In 1963, I was appointed to an Assistant Lectureship in the new Centre of West African Studies in the University of Birmingham and given the task of teaching a course on the economic history of West Africa. In the ensuing scramble, I had no time to consider how to create a book out of my two mismatched pieces of specialised research, though I did publish several articles on and around the theme of capitalism and imperialism.[2] Shortly after my appointment, a publisher approached me with a proposal for producing a text on the economic history of West Africa. I replied that a book of this scope was premature, given the rudimentary state of research. His next letter suggested that I should assemble some readings and preface them with an introduction instead. As this seemed to be a limited and feasible proposition, I identified some extracts and articles

1. A. G. Hopkins, 'An Economic History of Lagos, 1880–1914'.
2. Several of these are listed in the Sources.

and began work on the introduction. At this point, I committed the first of what were to be several egregious miscalculations during my career: I underestimated the scale of the task I had undertaken. The introduction became the book I said could not be written; the modest time I had initially allocated to it stretched to nearly a decade.

By the time my *Economic History of West Africa* was published in 1973, the study of African history, in all its forms, had become a recognised and substantial undertaking.[3] A new generation of scholars, armed with impressive disciplinary and language training, carried the subject inland and into areas that had been thought to be beyond the reach of historical scholarship. My plan of writing the history of coastal capitalists, which seemed excessively ambitious in 1960, now looked old-fashioned. Moreover, the contextual design I had formulated had already appeared in my *Economic History*. I did not want to repeat myself, and at that time I was unable to think of fresh ideas that would do justice to the subject.

These circumstances suggested that it might be more productive to take a detour. African history was established and in safer hands than my own. Imperial history, however, had become unfashionable. Acting on the principle that the best time to enter a field of study is not when it has reached its peak but when it is at its lowest point, I began to explore ways of reappraising the history of the British Empire. Although a project of this scale was clearly unwise, on this occasion I had the benefit of working with Peter Cain, a colleague and friend whose expertise more than compensated for my own limitations. Nevertheless, hope again defeated experience. We published our first article on this subject in 1980 and our book, *British Imperialism, 1688–1990*, in 1993.[4]

Time and life pass faster than anticipated. In the 1990s, another supposedly small detour led to a book on *Globalisation in World History* (2002).[5] By then, however, I was also spending more time on Africa preparing the long-promised second edition of my *Economic History of West Africa*. Unfortunately, I allowed an international crisis to subvert my intentions. In March 2003, President George Bush ordered the invasion of Iraq. At that time, I was working in the United States and viewing at first hand the debate over this issue, which included various hasty and sometimes alarming assertions about whether the United States was an empire or ought to become one. I felt compelled to set the drafts of my second edition aside to wonder why the leader of the Free World should have engineered such a predictable catastrophe, which has had enduring consequences for political and social stability in the Middle East. My decision to leap into this subject has to be

3. Longman, 1973; 2nd ed. Routledge, 2020.
4. Longman 1993; 3rd ed. Routledge, 2016.
5. Pimlico and Norton, 2002.

classified as being irrational. I knew nothing about the United States between independence in 1783 and Pearl Harbor in 1941. Moreover, I had reached Shakespeare's sixth age of life, that of the 'lean and slippered pantaloon with spectacles on nose and pouch on side'. Optimism again discounted the lessons of experience. Good fortune carried my unwise decision through to completion. *American Empire: A Global History*, was published in 2018.[6] Although the text went far beyond my original purpose, my long-standing interest in the history of capitalism appears in the central theme, which combines domestic and international influences in an explanation of American development.

The preceding account of a scholarly life is more relevant to the present book than might be thought. Of course, some readers might learn lessons from my own wayward trajectory, which has taken me to different parts of the world. Others might resolve to control their time better than I have done. Readers of *Capitalism in the Colonies*, however, need to know not only why so much material has remained buried for so long but also how the book now finally published relates to my original, incomplete enquiries. The answer, in brief, is that the present study contains extensive new research, especially on the period 1851–1880 and from the early 1900s into the 1930s. The few sections that originally appeared as articles have been rethought and revised. The sample of 116 entrepreneurs that supports the key findings has been assembled for the first time; individual biographies have been amplified and corrected.

The oral testimony I gathered from the siblings and children of the great merchants of the period is no longer available; enquiries made today are obliged to rely on the memories of grandchildren and, increasingly, great-grandchildren. Numerous citations throughout the book show how valuable the Supreme Court records have been to my research. The shocking news, reported in 2020, that the civil and criminal records for the nineteenth century had been destroyed adds a special, if also unwanted, significance to those referred to here.[7] Very few scholars have made extensive use of these records; now none will be able to do so. Other sources referred to here, such as the Lands Office records and those of the Lagos Town Council and the Registrar of Companies, remain secure, though still largely unexplored. My commitment to producing this study so many decades after it was conceived is partly explained by the importance of making available information that can no longer be retrieved.

The merits of these motives would be qualified had this study, or one like it, been published during the sixty years that have elapsed since I first became interested in the subject. Yet, remarkable though it may seem, no such work

6. Princeton University Press.

7. Reports claim that 'hoodlums' took advantage of a series of protests against police brutality in October 2020 to destroy the court records. *Premium Times* (Nigeria), 25 Oct. 2020; *The Independent*, 23 Jan. 2021. The full extent of the loss remains uncertain.

has appeared. Fortuitously, the present study still has a valid purpose, which is to underline the importance of entrepreneurs in Africa's long-run development and to reappraise the long-running debate over their fortunes under colonial rule.

I cannot claim that the finished product justifies the embarrassing delay between conception and delivery. I can, however, appeal to the medieval proverb, 'better late than never', which has been worn almost to extinction because it has been used so often by others before me.

ACKNOWLEDGEMENTS

MY GREATEST DEBT IS to the many Lagosians who welcomed me into their homes, offered me hospitality, and provided me with information about the history of their families. Without their contribution, this study would lack the element of individuality that I hope it retains. Acknowledgements to specific families appear at appropriate points throughout the book. However, I would like to record here my particular gratitude to the late Mrs Henrietta Lawson for welcoming me into her compound in central Lagos, where I was able to shelter from the sun, make friends with members of the family, and eat enough 'penny, penny' oranges to boost the local economy. Although evidence relating to all the merchants in my sample underpins the assessment of their fortunes and trajectory, I have been able to present only a limited number of examples for detailed study. This is disappointing for me, as for the families that do not receive the prominence they deserve. I plan to offer some compensation by making my research notes available in Cambridge and Lagos, where other scholars will be able to access them and perhaps produce a *Who's Who?* of great names of Lagos past.

Three institutions have supported my research during its long gestation. The Centre of West African Studies at the University of Birmingham provided invaluable financial assistance for visits to Nigeria in 1963–1964 and 1967. The Stellenbosch Institute for Advanced Study awarded me a fellowship for the first three months of 2020 that enabled me to experiment with various ways of organising the book. Pembroke College, Cambridge, awarded me a travel grant from the Fellows' Research Fund that helped to finance a visit to Lagos in December 2022. Genny Grim and Natalie Kent in Pembroke College Library eased the difficulties of securing material during the dark days when movement of all kinds was inhibited by COVID. Arina Grebneva and James Hudson in Pembroke's IT department demonstrated patience as well as skill in unravelling the continuing mysteries of Windows 10.

Authors routinely rely on the expertise of other scholars as they grind their way towards the finish line. The very early stages of my research benefitted from the expert assistance of Robert Irvine, who explored the Colonial Office documents relating to Nigeria during World War I. Although research assistants in the humanities and social sciences are now unknown, such posts existed in the 1960s, when it was possible to share limited time with other colleagues. I am greatly indebted to James Bertin Webster, who was completing his Ph.D. dissertation when I was beginning mine. I introduced him to James Davies, who has a prominent place in this book; he told me about Jacob Coker, the founder of the African Church. The exchange was unequal: Davies, an

Anglican, had no relevance to Bertin's research, whereas Coker was important to my interests in economic history. It was thanks to Bertin's kindness that I was able to use the Coker Papers, which he had located and begun to assemble.

Kristin Mann, the leading authority on nineteenth-century Lagos, generously supplied some information that I had failed to include, read much of the script, and tolerated an excess of one-sided enquiries. Karin Barber, the noted authority on Yoruba culture and language, read the script and provided valuable comments on several chapters. Gareth Austin contributed not only by reading parts of the script and dealing with some intrusive questions, but also through his illuminating articles on the subject of capitalism in Africa. Alexander Bud checked the chapter on Agege and obliged me to refine some conceptual issues in chapters 1 and 16. Tirthankar Roy contributed far more than he received in answering my questions about comparable studies of Indian merchants. Deji Olukoju devoted much of his time to my visit to Lagos in December 2022 and organised a trip to Ijon, which remained unknown to him, as it does to most Lagosians. On arrival, we found ourselves involved in an unexpected altercation with the *Bale*. Fortunately, Deji's considerable diplomatic skills extricated us from unspecified but possibly unwelcome consequences of our unannounced territorial incursion. His first visit to Ijon will live on in both our minds.

I owe a particular debt to three busy scholars whose motives for helping me are solely the product of their generous natures. Ademide Adelusi-Adeluyi, the expert on historical maps of Lagos, steered me through Penfold's *Maps and Plans in the Public Record Office* and spent time advising on the merits of the short list of candidates under consideration. Liora Bigon provided scans of relevant pages from the *Red Book*, when COVID made access to libraries difficult, and introduced me to the remarkable photography of Edmond Fortier, whose work is represented here in his striking image of the Marina in 1909. Ewout Frankema allowed me to use his extensive series of trade data, took me through various possibilities, and ended by drawing figures 2.1 and 2.2, possibly in response to my suggestion that I should attempt the task myself. Both graphs contain important new information that has not been published before. Their implications are discussed in the chapters that follow.

Dr Simon Russell, my clinical oncologist at Addenbrooke's Hospital, has ensured that I am still around to make mistakes and even to overcome some of them.

It is conventional to absolve those who have contributed to the final product from any adverse consequences of their generosity. I embrace the convention with particular enthusiasm because the time taken to produce this book may have introduced errors of fact and perspective that an author either cannot see or is now too committed to accept.

Orthography

The Yoruba language was first transcribed into English script in the mid-nineteenth century. The presentation of the language in writing and print continued to evolve until 1974, when agreement on a standard orthography was reached, though further revisions have been made subsequently. Today, Yoruba has a range of diacritics that aid pronunciation and clarify meaning. This was not the case in the nineteenth century. Authors of Yoruba-language texts used sub-dots consistently but added tone marks only intermittently, if at all. Authors of English-language texts invariably omitted both sub-dots and tone marks in referring to Yoruba place names or personal names. The sources used in this study rarely used even sub-dots. The town 'Isheri', for example, was commonly spelled with 'sh'; where the 'h' was dropped, the name was regularly presented as 'Iseri' without a sub-dot.

Scholars of Yoruba history face a dilemma. By adding tonal marks, they show respect for the language and improve on the simplicities that characterised it in the nineteenth and early twentieth centuries. This course, however, risks imposing linguistic uniformity on a period that lacked it. I have opted for a pragmatic solution by presenting Yoruba words, as far as possible, as they were written in the sources I have cited. A historical study based on different sources might justifiably reach a different conclusion.

Currency Values

The currency values given in the text are the values current at the time cited. The procedure required to convert them into present-day values is complex and produces variable results. Different measures are appropriate for different purposes. One index of real wages shows that £100 in 1850 would be the equivalent of about $11,000 in 2020. Other indices of real wages that use a different mix of expenditures produce a different result. Comparators of wealth and the value of labour are different again. All these calculations, however, are based on British data. The British Consumer Price Index, for example, is applied to measure trends in purchasing power. Unfortunately, an equivalent price index for Nigeria during the period under review does not exist at present. Evidently, the British CPI cannot be used to chart trends in Nigeria. The multiplier used in the example given here might be broadly indicative of changing values; citing it, however, is risky and open to challenge.

All that can be said at present, unsatisfactory though it is, is that £100 was worth considerably more in Lagos in 1850 than its face value today might suggest. A more definite statement can be made on a particular subject: the exchange rate between sterling and cowries. Local sources provide reliable evidence on changing values and allow examples of equivalents to be given in the chapters that follow.

Weights

Unless otherwise stated, weights are in imperial (long) tons, as defined by an Act of Parliament in 1824: 1 imperial ton = 2,240 lb. For comparison, 1 U.S. (short ton) = 2,000 lb. and 1 metric tonne (1,000 kg) = 2,205 lb.

ABBREVIATIONS

ABC African Banking Corporation

Badadiv Badagri Division (of Provincial Administration) Records

BBWA Bank of British West Africa

CMS Church Missionary Society Records

C.O. Colonial Office Records

CSO Central Secretary's Office Records

DATP David A. Taylor Papers

DCTP Daniel C. Taiwo Papers

Epediv Epe Division (of Provincial Administration) Records

F.O. Foreign Office

HP Holt Papers

IBWP Isaac B. Williams Papers

JHDP Josiah H. Doherty Papers

JKC Jacob K. Coker Papers

JPLDP James P. L. Davies Papers

LAP Letters of Administration and Probate Records

LLOR Lagos Lands Office records

LMB Lagos Municipal Board Records

LSCR Lagos Supreme Court records

LTC Lagos Town Council Records

PJCTP Peter J. C. Thomas Papers

RC Registrar of Companies (Lagos) Records

SHPP Samuel H. Pearse Papers

CAPITALISM IN THE COLONIES

Prologue

A GUNBOAT FOR CHRISTMAS, 1851

CHRISTMAS DAY, 1851, passed peacefully for the crew of HMS *Bloodhound*. Their ship was stationed off Lagos, having arrived in response to an appeal for support from John Beecroft, the itinerant British Consul for the Bights of Benin and Biafra. Beecroft was charged with the task of ending the external slave trade, but his soft power was limited, and his hard power depended on the availability of the British Navy. The day after Christmas, Captain L. T. Jones, RN, ordered the bombardment of Lagos to begin.[1] The defence was resolute and sustained for three days. At the end, Kosoko, the residing ruler (*Oba*), made a hurried exit with most of his leading supporters and set up camp in Epe, a small port on the lagoon about forty miles east of Lagos. Many Lagosians also left the town, some to join Kosoko, others to find refuge on the mainland. Akitoye, the displaced *Oba* and Kosoko's rival, was on board the *Bloodhound*, waiting for the fires sweeping through the town to die down. When he set foot on the island on 29 December, he found that about half the town had been 'reduced to a deserted heap of rubble', in the words of one observer, and that the 'very few inhabitants' who remained 'were living in appalling poverty'.[2] Whatever Akitoye's expectations might have been, he was not greeted, to cite a more recent phrase, with 'sweets and flowers'.[3] Thus

---

1. *Bloodhound* was a 'paddle gun vessel' with an iron hull and three guns (one 18 pounder and two 24 pounders). The most reliable account of the bombardment is in Robert S. Smith, *The Lagos Consulate, 1851–1861*, ch. 2, especially pp. 26–31. See also the occasionally wayward *Memoirs of Giambattista Scala*, chs. 2–4, edited, invaluably, by Robert S. Smith.

2. Brand to F.O., 3 Jan. 1852, F.O. 84/886. The observer was Giambattista Scala, who was in Lagos six weeks after the bombardment. See Smith, *Memoirs*, pp. 13, 22.

3. Kanan Makiya, member of the Iraqi National Congress, advocating the invasion of Iraq at a meeting with President George W. Bush, 10 Jan. 2003. See http://musingsoniraq .blogspot.com/2013/02/we-will-be-greeted-as-liberators-why.html

ended a dramatic episode, one among many in the nineteenth century, known as 'gunboat diplomacy'. Free trade had arrived.

Diplomacy followed the gunboat. At the beginning of January, the newly-restored *Oba* signed a treaty that committed him to abolish the slave trade, guarantee free trade, and protect Christian missionaries.[4] Shortly afterwards, Commander Wilmot directed him 'to put on his kingly robes, mount his horse, assemble all his warriors and ride completely round the town', halting 'every 10 minutes' so that the inhabitants could be encouraged to 'call out "Hurrah for Akitoye"'.[5] In this manner, one more restoration joined those of the grander monarchs who resumed their places in Europe after 1815. Like many formerly displaced kings who were reinstated by force, however, Akitoye found that the crown sat uneasily on his head. He was a reluctant abolitionist. He had approached Britain for support only because he needed an ally in his struggle to regain the throne.[6] Kosoko had been defeated but not dispatched. Moreover, he was popular and capable, whereas Akitoye had limited support and lacked both the personality and the power to increase it. The action that Britain thought would mark an end to one of many stories of abolition turned out to be the beginning of a sustained effort to establish an alternative form of commerce and its supporting institutions. Destruction, as other great powers were to discover, was easy; construction was frustrating, costly, and protracted. What happened to Lagos and its hinterland after 1851 would later be classified as 'mission creep', which eventually incorporated the mainland to an extent that far exceeded the imagination of those who planned the coup and established a modest consulate in the ruined town.

These events were part of Britain's programme for developing the world through the duality of free trade and the civilising mission.[7] Intervention in Lagos had its complements in the Ottoman Empire, Southeast Asia, and China. Free trade was a moral imperative as well as an economic policy. Spiritual and cultural uplift were at the heart of what the Victorians referred to as 'improvement'. Progressive thinkers devised projects of social reform that would uplift alien peoples; dedicated missionaries carried the Word to heathens everywhere. Civilised societies were defined as those that succeeded in

---

4. Smith, *The Lagos Consulate*, reproduces the treaty in appendix A, pp. 135–7. Curiously, his summary on pp. 30–31 does not mention Article 6, which deals with free trade. Akitoye negotiated a financial settlement with the leading merchants to secure an income from customs duties. Campbell to Clarendon, 1 June 1854, F.O. 84/950; Campbell to Clarendon, 14 May 1856, F.O. 84/1002.

5. Wilmot to Bruce, 11 Feb. 1852, F.O. 84/893.

6. Brand to Bedingfield, 27 Jan. 1852, F.O. 84/858.

7. A. G. Hopkins, 'The "New International Economic Order" in the Nineteenth Century: Britain's First Development Plan for Africa', in Robin Law, ed. *From Slave Trade to 'Legitimate' Commerce*, ch. 10. Reprinted in A. G. Hopkins, *Africa, Empire, and World Disorder*, ch. 8.

implanting the twin virtues of progress and order, which were modelled on the values and habits of the colonising power. Progress involved activating underutilised resources; order called for political regimes that accelerated economic growth while avoiding social upheaval. Both were to be achieved by institutional change. Free trade would promote international specialisation, raise incomes to the level needed to lift living standards, and underpin political stability. Eager advocates canvassed schemes for green revolutions in distant lands. Modern property rights were the means of liberating individual enterprise while simultaneously creating an interest in stable government. The propertied citizen, 'the mainspring as well as the foundation of political society', became 'the grand source of civilisation' for the world.[8] Britain's development plan was global in scope and astounding in its ambition. It was a gigantic experiment in what would later be called 'social engineering'. It anticipated many of the assumptions that were codified in modernisation theory, which took practical shape under the aegis of the Pax Americana after World War II.

These spacious aims required the co-operation of indigenous intermediaries who had the skills to straddle two worlds. In Lagos, as in other colonial port cities, merchants were in the vanguard of those bringing light where there was gloom. The means at the disposal of policy-makers, however, rarely matched the ends they desired. Even Palmerston's minimal requirement that states involved in Britain's global experiment should be 'well-kept and always accessible' was not easily attained.[9] When policies of limited intervention failed to produce the expected result, the temptation to secure by force what co-operation was unable to deliver was not easily resisted. The modernising experiment in Lagos entered a new stage in the 1890s. Colonial rule expanded into the hinterland, as it did elsewhere in Africa and Asia during the era of assertive imperialism. Co-operation gave way to intervention. Paternalism supported by supposedly scientific ideas of racial superiority displaced the ideals of cosmopolitanism and equality. The chosen intermediaries were obliged to find their way through the uncertainties this transformation imposed. Some accommodated themselves to the new order; others explored alternatives. Out of dissent came innovations that pioneered the diversification of the economy and organised opposition to colonial rule. These beginnings developed into the nationalist movements that helped to end the imperial version of development.

These considerations provide an opening for the present book, which is a study of the long-run development of capitalism in a colonial setting, as

8. John McCulloch (1789–1864), quoted in S. Ambirajan, *Classical Political Economy and British Policy in India* (Cambridge: Cambridge University Press, 1978), p. 221.

9. Quoted in M. E. Chamberlain, *The Scramble for Africa* (Harlow: Longman, 1974), p. 36. The remark was made to underline Britain's reluctance to take control of Egypt.

seen through the lives of the African entrepreneurs who were the heart (and part of the soul) of the town of Lagos, the leading port city in tropical Africa. Did they have a 'Golden Age'? If so, did it lose its glitter? If it did, when did promise turn into disappointment? Were mercantile fortunes determined by colonial policy, the actions of expatriate firms, internal structural weaknesses, or movements in international trade that were beyond the reach of all parties? An appraisal of these questions ought to improve our understanding of the colonial legacy and the contribution made by indigenous entrepreneurs to the long-run development of Nigeria. The answers suggested in the course of this book should help readers to decide whether the entrepreneurs of Lagos were relegated to subsidiary roles under colonial rule or whether they played an innovative part in economic development, even before the achievement of independence in 1960.

CHAPTER ONE

The Global Meets the Local

THE PRODIGAL HAS RETURNED. Capitalism, once a prominent theme in the study of economic history, was cast out in the 1980s and not welcomed back until after the turn of the present century. Before then, the subject occupied a central place in historical studies. Marx and Engels emphasised a key feature of capitalist development in 1848, when they declared that 'the bourgeoisie, historically, has played a most revolutionary part' in promoting a decisive transformation: the transition from feudalism to capitalism.[1] This proposition generated a series of long-running and influential debates. The 'rise of a middle class' was the focus of one of the great historical controversies of the 1950s and 1960s. The original formulation was later expanded to encompass what became known as the 'general crisis' of the seventeenth century, which included broader questions of state-building, demography, and climate change. Echoes of the debate can been found in the dependency thesis, which claimed that intrusive foreign capitalists undermined Africa's development prospects. Even modernisation theory, though lacking a historical perspective, assumed that indigenous entrepreneurship was central to development and devoted time and ingenuity to remedying its supposed defects.

Historical studies, however, are constantly on the move. Approaches to the subject rise and fall in favour as external influences penetrate ivory towers and the internal ruminations of the occupants reach the point where an infusion of novelty is required.[2] The collapse of the Soviet Union and the preceding decline of Marxist influences on historical studies stimulated a search for appealing alternatives. One result was the rise of post-modernism, which was also a product of the preoccupation with multi-culturalism in the United States. Post-modernists cast doubt on the presumed paramountcy of material

---

1. Marx and Engels, *Manifesto*, p. 46.
2. For an example of these principles in action in the African context, see Hopkins, 'Fifty Years', pp. 1–15.

forces and emphasised instead the importance of representations of claimed realities. Economic history was pushed to one side. By 2000, anyone reviewing the literature on Africa might have supposed that long-standing problems of global poverty had been solved.

An appraisal carried out in 2020 would show, unsurprisingly, that poverty not only remained endemic but had also regained the attention it had once commanded. By then, post-modernism had run its course. At the same time, the Western world was coming to terms with the implications of 9/11, the consequences of the financial crisis of 2008, and the rise of China. New concerns have joined these problems: the realisation that economic development has increased inequality between and within states, the growth of nationalist reactions against globalisation, and the encompassing alarm brought by climate change. Clearly, it is time to take a fresh look at how we got 'from there to here'.

The Revival of Economic History

Today, the study of economic history is thriving.[3] It has attracted a new generation of scholars whose research interests span the continuum from qualitative to quantitative dimensions of the subject. Two illustrations, scarcely known to each other, provide an indication of the renewed vigour of the discipline. In the United States, what is called the 'new history of capitalism' has captured attention and earned an acronym (NHC).[4] The considerable discussion this departure has stimulated cannot be evaluated in the space available here. It is sufficient for present purposes to indicate the direction of travel. NHC takes a position that is critical of both neo-classical economics and Marxism. Proponents of NHC fill a space between these two schools by emphasising the role of political power and its attendant social and cultural institutions in shaping economic affairs. This formulation of political economy sees the development of capitalism as being linked, above all, to the mobilisation and exploitation of labour, especially coerced and slave labour. The wider consequences are manifest in the unequal distribution of wealth that is such a striking feature of developed societies today. So far, these ideas have been applied mainly to US history, but advocates of NHC are well aware that capitalism is a global phenomenon and needs to be treated in ways that transcend state boundaries.[5]

3. For two of many examples, see Neal and Williamson, *The Cambridge History of Capitalism*, Vol. I, Vol. II. Readers of the present study will be particularly interested in the chapters by Morten Jerven in Vol. I and Gareth Austin in Vol. II. Also Kocka and van der Linden, *Capitalism*, which includes an important contribution by Gareth Austin, pp. 207–34.

4. Beckert and Desan, *American Capitalism*; Beckert and Rockman, *Slavery's Capitalism*.

5. See particularly Beckert, *Empire of Cotton*; Beckert and Sachsenmaier, *Global History*.

The second example is very different. During the last twenty years, the economic history of Africa has received an injection of vitality from economists who have been attracted by the apparent failure of many states in the continent to climb the development ladder.[6] Although the resulting initiatives have yet to acquire a formal acronym, they can be referred to collectively as the 'new economic history of Africa' (NEHA). A notable feature of this research has been the recognition by economists that history is an indispensable tool for understanding long-term development problems.[7] The most distinctive contributions so far have applied statistical techniques to data that can now be processed rapidly by computer programmes instead of by hand.[8] The results have included new findings on subjects relating to long-run economic growth, including the slave trade, demography, colonial fiscal policy, real wages, tax burdens, and measures of nutrition and welfare. The renewed interest in poverty, however, has reinvigorated research across an array of other relevant historical issues that are too varied to be summarised here.[9] Although the NEHA makes little explicit use of the term 'capitalism', its central interest is in capitalist forms of development, particularly as mediated by colonial authorities. Its assumptions adopt rational-choice models of behaviour; its priorities include the role of state policies in facilitating or retarding development, the need to install what it takes to be progressive institutions, such as individual property rights, and the importance of mobilising the labour force, whether through wages or by other means.

At this point, there is a prospect of building a bridge between NHC and NEHA, despite some profound differences over the nature of capitalism and its consequences. Both perspectives agree on the importance of the state; both accept that economic life is part of a complex of social and cultural institutions that influence outcomes, even if they often defy precise measurement; both take a spacious view of the subject, recognising that key issues are no longer confined to one locality or even to one country. They also share an important omission: neither school has given much attention to entrepreneurship. The subject readily escapes accounts at the macro-level; its place in the micro-economy is rarely amenable to statistical treatment. So far, NEHA has tended to put research into entrepreneurial history to one side in the belief that it

6. An early statement that helped to focus attention on the problem was Collier, *The Bottom Billion*. The recent revival of the subject is symbolised by the publication of a special issue of the *Economic History Review*, 'The Renaissance of African Economic History', 67 (2014), pp. 893–1112; Frankema and van Waijenburg, 'Bridging the Gap'.

7. The early literature is assessed by Austin, 'The "Reversal of Fortune" Thesis'; Hopkins, 'The New Economic History of Africa'. The examples that follow are taken from the later and current literature, which is less ambitious but more plausible.

8. Fourie, 'The Data Revolution'.

9. The vibrancy of the subject can been seen in the online publication, the *African Economic History Network*.

yields only slim pickings. Other historians have stooped to gather, if not to conquer. In the case of Africa, however, their publications, though numerous and often admirable, tend to focus on individuals or groups scattered across the continent, and their predominantly descriptive quality is not easily assimilated into the current development debate.

Port Cities in History

The embryonic 'bourgeoise' of Lagos occupied an economic environment shaped by the 'port city', a concept that derives from a long and distinguished literature on urban development. The analysis of the relationship between towns and the rural areas around them was pioneered by Johan Heinrich von Thünen in a famous study published in 1826.[10] A century later, Walter Christaller, drawing on von Thünen, advanced what became known as central-place theory to explain the distribution of cities across a region, the circles of activity around them, and the hierarchy of goods and services within the circles themselves.[11] These two contributions set the course taken by studies of modern urban history, which have undergone considerable expansion during the last half century and now span several disciplines, including history, economics, and sociology.[12]

Although the term 'port city' was in use by the 1930s, when Christaller published his celebrated book, it was not until the 1970s that the species began to be seen as a distinctive urban type.[13] In 1971, Andrew Barghardt, a geographer, applied the term 'gateway' to refer to towns that were not central places but entrances (and exits) connecting two or more different regions or zones.[14] Port cities were gateways, though in Barghardt's usage gateways could also be inland towns serving the same function. This was the case in North America, where the frontier of settlement created new gateways as it moved westward. Inland wholesaling centres on West Africa's desert edge performed the same function as gateways to and from the Sahara. Barghardt's contribution made it

10. Von Thünen, *The Isolated State.*

11. Coincidentally, Christaller's *The Central Places in Southern Germany* (1933) also had to wait until 1966 for its English translation. Broeze reviews the development of the subject in 'Port Cities', as does Barnes, 'Notes from the Underground'. There is a large literature on African urban history. The starting point is Coquery-Vidrovich, *Histoire des villes d'Afrique noire.* Recent guides include: Salma and Falola, *The History of African Cities*; Fourchard, 'African Urban History'; Coret, Zaugg, and Chouin, 'Les villes en Afrique avant 1900'.

12. Recent developments in economic geography are covered by Pines, 'New Economic Geography'; see also Fujita and Krugman, 'The New Economic Geography'.

13. For one example, see Anon, 'Port Cities', and the descriptive study that follows: Seeman, 'Seattle as a Port City'.

14. Barghardt, 'A Hypothesis'.

clear that gateways were not merely variations on central places but a different type of settlement requiring separate analysis.

One of the first historians to have had a significant influence on the subject was Edward Fox, whose book on pre-revolutionary France was also published in 1971.[15] Fox contrasted one France that was inward-looking and predominantly agricultural with another that was outward-looking and dependent on trade across the Atlantic. The second France developed port cities that were also gateways, though they lacked the physical mobility Burghardt ascribed to them. Fox went on to argue that the French Revolution brought about the decline of the cosmopolitan, outward-looking France and the consolidation of its inward-looking counterpart.[16] Irrespective of the validity of his conclusion, it is evident that Barghardt's gateways and Fox's outward-looking ports had much in common without being identical.

Since the 1970s, port cities have become big business in the academic world.[17] Research has spread from studies of Europe and North America to encompass most of Asia; the chronological range has extended beyond periods that are immediately accessible to cover the centuries before industrialisation.[18] An awareness that the history of globalisation could inform our understanding of the present and provide a fresh perspective on the past has stimulated an increasingly spacious approach to the subject during the last 20 years. Although accounts of individual ports continue to predominate, there have also been efforts to link ports to each other and to set them in regional contexts shaped by the Atlantic, the Pacific, the Indian Ocean, and the China Sea. This development has not only given port cities greater prominence but has also helped to rescue oceanic islands from the long-standing assumption that their size limited their influence.[19]

Port cities were the bridgeheads (or nodal points) connecting two or more worlds.[20] They fostered informal relations with the interior and with external trading partners. They also served as launching points for conquests that paired political subordination with the 'liberating' power of commerce. They nurtured capitalists whose influence spread throughout the port and into

15. Fox, *History in Geographic Perspective*.

16. On this subject, see now Drayton's important contribution, 'The Globalisation of France'.

17. John Darwin has provided an immensely valuable guide to this now daunting literature in *Unlocking the World*.

18. The following are indicative of a much larger literature: Basu, *The Rise and Growth of Colonial Port Cities*; Broeze, *Brides of the Sea*; Knight and Liss, *Atlantic Port Cities*; Broeze, *Gateways of Asia*; Pearson, *Port Cities and Intruders*; O'Flanagan, *Port Cities of Atlantic Iberia*; Masashi, *Asian Port Cities*; Gipouloux, Hall, and Martin, *The Asian Mediterranean*; Amrith, *Migration*; Bosa, *Atlantic Ports*.

19. For example, Sivasundaram, *Islanded*; Sivasundaram, *Waves Across the South*.

20. Darwin, 'Imperialism and the Victorians'; McPherson, 'Port Cities', in Fawaz and Bayly, eds., *Modernity*, ch. 4.

hinterlands where markets and merchants operated in an economy that had still to embrace capitalism fully.[21] They provided incentives in the form of consumer goods that encouraged societies in the hinterland to develop export crops; their own food demands stimulated local farmers to produce for the urban market. Port cities owed their prominence to locations that had distinct advantages in linking a productive hinterland to the wider world that lay across the oceans. In connecting different regions separated by long distances, port cities created elements of a world society as well as a world economy. In moving goods and channelling investment, they also transported people and ideas, carried exotic flora and fauna to distant continents, and unwittingly helped the spread of deadly diseases. Visitors often became sojourners, who in time could also become permanent settlers. The result was the creation of fluid, mobile, and hybrid societies that were multiplied by the mass migrations that colonised continents beyond Europe in the nineteenth century and Europe itself in our own time. In this sense, to adapt Marx, the early port cities 'showed the face of the future' to the rest of the world.

Lagos, which became a port city during the period covered by this study and remained one throughout the colonial era, exemplified the main characteristics featured in the literature.[22] The town occupied an island that lay close to both the sea and the mainland and was situated, uniquely in West Africa, at a natural breach in the lagoon system. It commanded an extensive system of waterways that ran parallel to the coastline and was joined to its northern hinterland by rivers that, though of modest proportions, provided the cheapest means of inland travel before modern transport facilities became available. Like most other port cities, Lagos was a key point of entry to and exit from large producing regions.[23] Accordingly, its main business was wholesaling, transport, and trans-shipment.

21. Gareth Austin distinguishes clearly between two basic concepts that are easily elided: capitalists are individuals; capitalism is a system. Thus, capitalists can inhabit a non-capitalist society. See 'The Return of Capitalism as a Concept', in Kocka and van der Linden, eds., *Capitalism*, pp. 207–34.

22. Lagos is the name given by Portuguese traders. *Eko*, which is still widely used locally, has several derivations, the most probable dates from the occupation of the island by Benin some time before 1603. Two translations of *Eko* have been advanced: one being that it is the Bini name for a camp; the other that it has a Yoruba derivation and refers to the people from the nearby island of Iddo. Lees to Secretary of State, 28 Feb. 1879, C.O. 806/130; evidence of Obeseke, senior adviser to King of Benin in Re Public Lands Ordinance: Amodu Tijani, Chief Oluwa v. Secretary Southern Provinces, LSCR, Civ. 76, 1915. See also Bigon, 'The Former Names of Lagos'. The authority on the early history of Lagos is Robin Law, whose publications on the subject are too extensive to be listed in this citation but are conveniently grouped in Falola and Childs, *The Changing World of Atlantic Africa*. See also the thoughtful essay by Olukoju, 'Which Lagos?'.

23. McPherson, 'Port Cities', in Fawaz and Bayly, eds., with the collaboration of Robert Ilbert, *Modernity and Culture*, pp. 75–95.

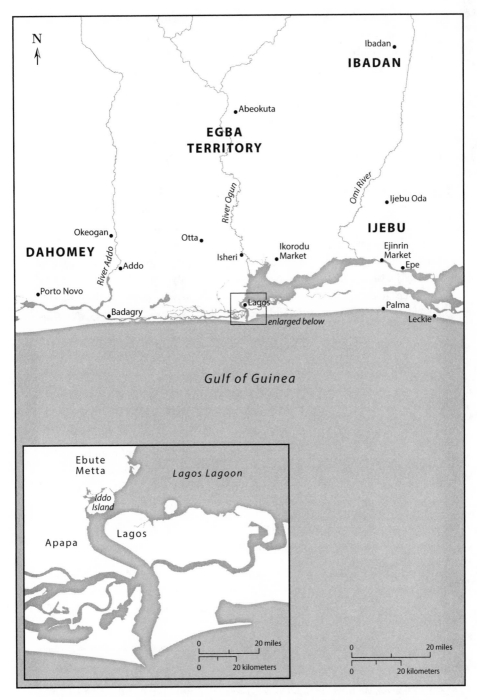

MAP 1.1. Lagos and Its Hinterland in the 1880s. Adapted from 'Route Survey Through Yoruba Country', in PP. LX, 1877, p. 167.

The town exhibited the sense of restlessness that characterised all frontier settlements, where enticing opportunities allied to commensurate levels of risk attracted adventurous spirits. Immigration, accompanied by different shades of ethnic differentiation, filled out the port and filled it up with a high proportion of poor and semi-employed inhabitants. Lagos was typical, too, in having extremes of wealth. Old wealth was attached to chiefs who commanded followers and enjoyed rights of tribute and taxation. New wealth stemmed from trade in the goods that replaced the slave trade. The bulk of the population struggled on limited incomes and had low standards of housing, sanitation, and nutrition compounded by high rates of disease and death.[24] The unsettled way of life in port cities made it difficult to establish a fixed social order. Like its comparators, Lagos experienced an extended contest between advocates of different models of political and social order on the one hand and the fluidity that the needs of commerce demanded on the other. Old chiefs tended to lose ground; new money funded the emergence of an alternative oligarchy, as it did in other port cities.

The features that categorise Lagos as a port city make it possible to place the town in a wider analytical and comparative setting without which its singularities and similarities would remain unknown and its identity would be no more distinct than that of being one large port among many others. Lagos was part of a global transformation in the nineteenth and twentieth centuries. Accordingly, its history needs to be joined to a long chain connecting port cities in other continents if its broader significance is to be understood. Yet, Lagos, like Africa as a whole, is bypassed by comparative studies that begin in Europe, travel west across the Atlantic and east to Asia without touching the continent's shoreline.[25] The present study draws on the literature on port cities to understand the opportunities and constraints that influenced the fortunes of the African merchants who injected the port of Lagos with much of its dynamism. The comparative references noted here should enable future historians to link the port to the much larger world of which it was a part.

The Colonial Port City

Although Lagos clearly qualifies as a port city, significant features of its historical development are obscured if it is bundled with other port cities without further differentiation.[26] Port cities are a generic category; Lagos is one of a

24. The important source for this subject is Bigon, *History of Urban Planning*, which makes an invaluable comparison with Dakar.

25. For some valuable exceptions, see Fawaz and Bayly, *Modernity and Culture from the Mediterranean to the Indian Ocean*; Green, 'Maritime Worlds and Global History'; Darwin's pioneering study, *Unlocking the World*, is the first to integrate the specialised literature. Exceptions in West Africa include Law's exemplary study, *Ouidah*, and Olukoju and Hidalgo, *African Seaports*.

26. The concept of a 'port city' raises questions of classification that cannot be pursued further here. The standard is generally assumed to be the European port city. Yet some

distinct species. Although the term 'colonial port city' makes frequent appearances in the literature, especially in studies of Asia, most historical research on the subject has tended to take the colonial context for granted.[27] The present account has no special insight into this question. Nevertheless, it is important to declare implicit assumptions if the characteristics of the colonial version of port cities are to receive the emphasis they merit.

Colonial port cities differed from port cities in Western Europe in at least two striking ways: they were ruled by a foreign power, and they were imbued with racial discrimination.[28] Decisions taken by imperial and colonial governments were major influences on the shape and fortunes of the port cities they controlled. Imperial political ambitions, sometimes presented as necessities, transformed relations between the port and its hinterland and subordinated previously independent polities. Foreign rule created structures of political control, law, and education that invaded indigenous sources of authority, social customs, and beliefs. Economic policy, which expressed wider imperial priorities, greatly enlarged the market and turned the economy in directions it might not otherwise have taken. Colonial port cities displayed ethnic diversity at its most extreme. White rulers presided over indigenous and immigrant subjects (including in some cases white settlers). A formal political and social hierarchy separated the minority of colonial officials and expatriate merchants from most of the population. Varying degrees of discrimination accompanied these intrusions, stimulating both resentment and innovative reactions. Foreign rule gave content and substance to colonial politics. Questions about the legitimacy of an externally imposed government, the manifestations of the racial supremacy that accompanied it, and disputes over the surviving rights of indigenous political authorities achieved a degree of prominence that was absent from port cities in Western Europe. These were all highly sensitive issues. They came together in the nationalist movements that eventually brought colonial rule to an end.

The location of colonial port cities was determined partly by the transport revolution, which carried the steamship across the world during the second half of the nineteenth century, and partly by the politics of colonial expansion.[29] Larger ships required larger harbours; the cost of improvements

---

European port cities might more appropriately be classified as colonial port cities. Odessa, for example, was subjected to foreign rule in the nineteenth century and its large Jewish population suffered discrimination from at least the 1880s and continuing into the twentieth century.

27. Bosu, *The Rise and Growth of the Colonial Port Cities*, p. xxi, recognises the issue but does not pursue it.

28. Green, 'Maritime Worlds and Global History', emphasises similarities between the two ports he studied. Port cities and colonial port cities do have features in common, but his study explicitly omitted consideration of colonial rule, which is regarded here as a crucial difference.

29. Darwin, *Unlocking the World*, is now the authoritative work.

concentrated shipping on a small number of key ports. Nevertheless, colonial ports were selected for the potential of their hinterlands rather than the quality of their natural harbours. Despite its advantages, the harbour at Lagos had shallow waters and was obstructed by a formidable sandbar; Madras was no more than a roadstead; Calcutta's access to the sea was tortuous. Freetown had one of the largest natural deep-water harbours in the world, but it never developed to the extent that Lagos did because its hinterland was far less productive. Political priorities also determined the location of major ports, which were often chosen to be capital cities of the colony or its provinces.[30] Lagos and Dakar, the two great ports of West Africa, owed much of their eminence to colonial patronage. Favours shown to Lagos reduced competing ports on the lagoon to minor satellites. The preference given to Dakar led to the contraction of St. Louis and Rufisque.[31] Similarly, Takoradi and Conakry displaced smaller rivals, Colombo eclipsed Galle, Singapore displaced Malacca and Penang, and Hong Kong outstripped Canton.[32] Decisions affecting the location of colonial ports had the further consequence of influencing the starting points of the railway lines built during the second half of the century and a corresponding commitment to costly harbour improvements. The outcome was the concentration of business on the fortunate few and the decline of the unlucky.[33]

Notwithstanding these similarities, colonial port cities in tropical Africa had distinctive features that influenced the reception and trajectory of capitalism. Many port cities in Asia were well established before European merchants arrived and had reached an informal accommodation with the foreign presence in advance of the decision to formalise relations. Lagos was different. It was an upstart creation: a fishing village that was transformed into the leading slave port in West Africa during the early decades of the nineteenth century.[34] The contrast between the established economy and the one projected in Britain's development model was exceptionally sharp. The consequences for existing political and economic authorities descended with an alacrity that required rapid adjustment. The emergence of the port's merchant capitalists provides a dramatic example of assisted development at speed. Other changes, of structure and institutions, took time. In 1863, Richard Francis Burton, admittedly a highly opinionated observer, thought that the

30. For one of many examples, see Johnson, *Shanghai*.
31. Hidalgo, 'The Port of Dakar', in Bosa, *Atlantic Ports*, pp. 90–111.
32. Broeze, 'The Ports and Port Systems of the Asian Seas', at p. 78; Goerg, 'La destruction'.
33. The wider aspects of this process are covered by Konvitz, 'The Crises of Atlantic Port Cities'.
34. See Law, 'The Chronology of the Yoruba Wars'; 'Trade and Politics Behind the Slave Coast'. Elements of continuity (that do not focus on Lagos) are traced by da Silva, 'The Slave Trade'; and Saupin, 'The Emergence of Port Towns'.

site of the port was 'really detestable' and the town itself 'squalid and dirty'.[35] Some fifty years later, the acting governor was able to report that 'the town of Lagos itself has rightly earned the reputation of the "Liverpool" of British West Africa'.[36] Its population and trade had experienced huge increases. Its merchants enjoyed unprecedented wealth; like Liverpool, its inequalities had grown commensurately.

The Atlantic slave trade and the intervention that led to its elimination were unquestionably the most distinctive of the differences that marked West Africa's colonial port cities. The slave trade had created centres of power along the coast that converted new wealth into political authority in what were essentially militarised societies. When the Atlantic trade was abolished, many established supply systems were disrupted; those invested in them faced losses of wealth and power; alternative possibilities were uncertain and seemingly less profitable. Asian ports did not experience upheaval on this scale or with comparable rapidity. Merchants in Karachi and Bombay enjoyed a greater degree of continuity than their counterparts in West Africa; the Hongs in China survived the Opium Wars, even though some of them lost influence in ports that became uncompetitive.[37] By contrast, the leading ports in West Africa relied on a new generation of educated African immigrants to help develop what became known as 'legitimate' commerce in non-slave products. The transition was neither straightforward nor swift. After a dramatic start, orchestrated by the Royal Navy, it continued to the end of the century and created problems that became bound up with the decision to partition the region among the major European powers.

Entrepreneurship in a Colonial Context

It is apparent from what has been said so far that port cities have been studied from many angles. Surprisingly, however, indigenous entrepreneurs have yet to achieve a prominent place in current research on colonial port cities, given that their activities were (and remain) central to the lives and livelihood of these pre-eminently commercial centres.[38] Studies of African entrepreneurs were

---

35. Burton, *Wanderings*, pp. 223–24.

36. Boyle, 26 May 1911, enc. in Boyle to Harcourt, 31 May 1911, C.O. 520/103.

37. In one respect, Asian entrepreneurs suffered more than their African counterparts: as shipowners, they were largely eliminated by expatriate competitors. Broeze, 'The Ports and Port Systems on the Asian Seas', p. 81.

38. I am grateful to Prof. Tirthankar Roy for his advice on the relevant literature dealing with India. The most concerted effort I can find is in Bosu, *The Rise and Growth of the Colonial Port Cities*. This collection of abstracts of conference papers contains 21 contributions, of which seven deal with entrepreneurs. Austin has provided an admirable survey of the whole field: 'African Business History', in Wilson, et al., *The Routledge Companion*, pp. 141–58.

undertaken by development economists during the 1960s and 1970s, but their work on tropical Africa has long been neglected.[39] Historians also produced some excellent research on this subject during that period, but their interest, too, waned after the 1980s.[40]

This conundrum calls for an explanation, given that the concept of entrepreneurship was first promoted in the eighteenth century. The subject has long been embedded in schools of business and management and currently supports a range of reputable journals. A survey of seventeen leading journals in the field between 1981 and 2010 has shown that the number of relevant publications has increased substantially since dipping during the 1970s and 1980s.[41] It is telling, too, that Joseph Schumpeter remained the single most cited author, even though his key work was published in 1934.[42] The branch of the subject concerned with history, though much smaller, is also flourishing. The foundation in 1926 of the *Business History Review*, which remains the flagship journal, was an early indication of institutional recognition. Other journals followed: *Explorations in Entrepreneurial History* published its first issue in 1949; *Business History* in 1958. Entrepreneurship, it might be said, has created a thriving academic industry.

Evidently, there is no lack of either interest or outlets. The problem is that nearly all this research relates to North America and Europe. The analysis of citations noted above shows that between 1981 and 2010, hardly any articles ventured outside these familiar confines.[43] The sole contribution given a specific mention was a comparative study in which China shared space with the United States and Europe.[44] Journals focussing on history have done little better. The index to the *Business History Review* identifies only a handful of articles on Africa, none of which deals specifically with indigenous entrepreneurs. A survey of *Business History* produces a similar result. A recent assessment has confirmed that the Western bias remains substantially undisturbed.[45] *Explorations in Entrepreneurial History* took a more spacious view

39. As the valuable survey by Lindsay confirms; 'Biography in African History'. Examples relating to Nigeria include: Kilby, *African Enterprise*; Kilby, *Industrialization*; Nafziger, *African Capitalism*; Hogendorn, *Nigerian Groundnut Exports*; and an important late addition, Forrest, *The Advance of African Capital*.

40. See, for example, Laboratoire Connaissance du Tiers-Monde, *Actes du colloque*, 2 vols.; Ellis and Fauré, *Entreprises et entrepreneurs africains*.

41. Ferreira, Reis, and Miranda, 'Thirty Years of Entrepreneurship'. As always, there are exceptions to generalisations pitched at this level. For example, Ochonu, *Entrepreneurship in Africa*.

42. Schumpeter, *The Theory of Economic Development*.

43. Schumpeter, *The Theory of Economic Development*.

44. Jing, Qinghua and Landström, 'Entrepreneurship Research'.

45. Berquist, 'Renewing Business History'.

THE GLOBAL MEETS THE LOCAL [17]

of the subject but was criticised for claiming more than it could deliver.[46] In 1969, the journal was absorbed by *Explorations in Economic History*, which has a broader remit.

A further difficulty is that there is no ready-made theory of entrepreneurship that fits pre-colonial and colonial economies. Neo-classical economists underplayed the distinctive role of entrepreneurs because they assumed that potential risk-takers had perfect information and would respond readily to demand when opportunities arose. Responses, however, are not automatic. Information flows are far from perfect. Even when they flow freely, other constraints can intervene to prevent supply from matching demand. Schumpeter reacted to this impersonal view of a highly personal world by emphasising the heroic qualities of entrepreneurs, whose distinctive innovating attributes not only created new firms but also shaped the performance of the economy as a whole.[47] His analysis did much to enhance the image of entrepreneurs and raise the profile of the subject. Schumpeter's interest, however, was in the operation of advanced industrial economies, which were far removed from the economic and social structures of typical colonial economies.[48] Heroism, moreover, is characteristic of the few rather than the many. It is not typical of the multitude of small businesses whose founders nevertheless engage in novel and risky activities.

Recent restatements of entrepreneurial theory are far more sophisticated than those of the 1950s and 1960s, but still remain firmly anchored in the Western world.[49] The proliferation of theories there appears to have reached saturation point. The more comprehensive the possible explanations of entrepreneurial motivations are, the harder it is to integrate them satisfactorily, even assuming that coherence is attainable.[50] Over the years, the names of distinguished scholars have been attached to characteristics such as innovation, profit-making, risk-taking, uncertainty, societal values, co-ordinating functions, and marginal groups, among other relevant attributes. Recent contributions have included the economic environment, resource dependence, organisational and educational skills, information flows, and a variety of institutional influences. All these features are undoubtedly relevant in some proportion, but fixing the proportion would seem to be impossible without relating very general variables to specific contexts. The difficulty here is that most closely specified theories have been devised mainly with the United

46. Fredona and Reinert, 'The Harvard Research Center,' unpick the character of academic entrepreneurship.

47. Hagedorn, 'Innovation and Entrepreneurship'.

48. Ebner, 'Schumpeterian Entrepreneurship Revisited' shows how Schumpeter's interests shifted from his European phase to his later American phase.

49. See Brown and Rose, *Entrepreneurship*, especially chs. 2–3; Cassis and Minoglou, *Entrepreneurship*.

50. Valuable syntheses include Casson, *The Entrepreneur*; Casson, *Entrepreneurship*.

States in mind.[51] The literature on organisational strategies and structures, for example, arose in response to the appearance of large industrial companies in North America. The consequent distinction between unitary and multi-divisional types of corporate government is closely related to that setting and has little application to the history of entrepreneurship in Africa.[52]

It is hardly surprising that this assortment of highly general character-istics and diverse applications has led the authors of a survey published in 2017 to conclude that 'research on entrepreneurship remains fragmented' and that 'a lack of conceptual clarity inhibits comparisons between studies'.[53] Although this perceptive review contains a handful of references to the non-Western world, they relate to Western firms and forms and not to indigenous entrepreneurship. In this respect, the geographical focus of the literature remains today much as it was in the eighteenth century. Yet, more than half a century has passed since scholars in the social sciences and humanities began to investigate development problems in Africa and Asia, where indigenous entrepreneurs are plentiful, highly visible, and accepted as being essential to development.

The neglect of the non-Western world is more than a gap waiting to be filled; it also presents the problem of how to fill it.[54] Given the bias of entre-preneurial theory towards societies in Europe and North America, there is little to be gained from trying to squeeze Africa into a model devised for other purposes. One approach is to return to some of the basic propositions put for-ward by the founders of the subject, who described economies characterised by agriculture, commerce, and handicrafts.

Adam Smith is unhelpful in this regard.[55] He warned of the 'pernicious' tendencies of merchants and their monopolistic ambitions. His reference to their being an 'unproductive class' was later removed from its context and became widely generalised. In 1910, a European observer remarked of Free-town that, though it was 'undoubtedly a distributing centre', it was itself 'a non-productive place. It makes nothing and it grows nothing'.[56] Smith had no word for 'entrepreneur' and relied on the invisible hand to draw the factors

51. For an analysis based on this (typically assumed) context, see Low and MacMillan, 'Entrepreneurship'.

52. Austin, Davila, and Jones, 'The Alternative Business History', is a lone and impor-tant exception to this generalisation, but one that deals with large foreign firms rather than with African entrepreneurs, as the authors make clear (n. 45). Verhoef provides a concise survey of the literature in *The History of Business in Africa*.

53. Wadhwani and Lubinski, 'Reinventing Entrepreneurial History'.

54. For some characteristically thoughtful remarks on this subject, see Austin, 'African Business in the Nineteenth Century', in Jalloh and Falola, eds., *Black Business and Eco-nomic Power*, ch. 4.

55. The quotations that follow are from *The Wealth of Nations* (1776, New York: Ran-dom House, 1937), pp. 98, 633.

56. M. B. Gleave, 'Port Activities', p. 267.

of production together.[57] A more positive approach, however, can be found in the work of his near-contemporaries in France, Richard Cantillon (1680s–1734) and Jean-Baptiste Say (1767–1832), who were entrepreneurs themselves before they wrote the pioneering studies that put the term into circulation.[58]

Cantillon and Say regarded entrepreneurs as risk-bearers operating in the conditions of extreme uncertainty that typified pre-modern economies. Businesses in these economies were typically small scale, run by one owner or family, and included many part-time or seasonal occupations. Cantillon was well aware that risks were not confined to business decisions but also included unpredictable hazards, such as war, robbery, and harvest failure. Given that nearly everyone lived in circumstances where the four horsemen of the apocalypse were just around the corner, it followed that entrepreneurship was a widespread attribute deployed to minimise risks as well as to seek profits. For Cantillon, entrepreneurs included everyone who lived on unfixed incomes. Self-employed water carriers, who he called 'petty entrepreneurs', were among those whose costs were known but whose incomes were uncertain.

Say's assessment was similarly broad and included knife-grinders in his list of entrepreneurs. The essential characteristics of entrepreneurship for both writers were access to market information and the exercise of judgement honed by experience. Incomes were rewards for the exercise of skill in taking risks. Cantillon and Say drew a formal distinction between the supply of capital and the operation of a business, but agreed that in practice most entrepreneurs were sole owners who provided their own capital. They were also at one in emphasising the crucial part entrepreneurs played in the wider economy. Cantillon showed that entrepreneurs co-ordinated the flow of resources and goods between different sectors of the economy. Say portrayed the entrepreneur as the linchpin holding different elements of the economy together. Neither made innovation a defining quality, though Say referred to entrepreneurs as being leaders as well as organisers. It was not until the mid-nineteenth century that British writers began to fill a gap in their vocabulary by adopting the French term, which now occupies a familiar place in the Anglo-Saxon literature.[59]

The qualities identified by Cantillon and Say are well suited to many aspects of entrepreneurship in Lagos and its hinterland between 1850 and

57. He referred (sparsely) to 'undertakers', a term that eventually became confined to funeral directors. It is interesting to discover that nineteenth-century translations of both Cantillon and Say substituted 'undertaker' for 'entrepreneur'.

58. Cantillon, *Essaie*; Say, *Traité d'économie politique*. In later life, after he had published his book on entrepreneurs, Say opened a cotton spinning factory. See Brown and Thornton, 'Entrepreneurship Theory'; Koolman, 'Say's Conception'. Murphy, *Richard Cantillon*, and Shoorl, *Jean-Baptiste Say* are two among the very few biographies.

59. John Stuart Mill (1848) distinguished between risk-bearers and managers and emphasised the role of innovation. Marshall (1890) was the first economist to consider entrepreneurship as a fourth factor of production.

1950. Risks were high; returns were uncertain. Entrepreneurs were leaders and organisers who co-ordinated exchanges between local, regional, and international markets. They were typically sole owners who ran modest businesses and provided their own finance. Merchants were among the most prominent 'leaders and organisers', as they were in Cantillon's and Say's time. Contemporaries applied the term 'merchant' to Lagosians who were direct importers and exporters who were also sizeable wholesalers.[60] Some additions are needed, however, to complete the characteristics of the entrepreneurs in Lagos. Their role as innovators needs to be highlighted. As we shall see, they contained Titans as well as minnows. They also operated in an open economy. Cantillon and Say, and many subsequent economists, were concerned with entrepreneurship in one country. Lagos entrepreneurs, however, were situated as intermediaries between the outside world and Africa. They were part of an international system that was central to their existence and the ultimate source of their fortunes. Subsequent chapters will show how the static system described here was made dynamic by external political intervention and fluctuations in international trade that had an immediate effect on commercial fortunes by changing opportunities and stimulating innovation.

This approach, though derived from eighteenth-century sources, is consistent with the claim that Africans understood the profit motive and did not need to convert their values and institutions into an idealised version of supposedly superior Western forms before entrepreneurship could flourish. That battle was fought and won more than fifty years ago, when it became clear that the notion of a 'traditional society' was found more easily in Western minds than in African realities. This position is also compatible with the view that African entrepreneurs had what are referred to here as 'extra-pecuniary' motives. The acquisition of wealth was of primary importance, but it was also a means to other ends: esteem, honour, and status, which were visibly expressed through philanthropy.[61] A complementary analysis has shown that, from the mid-nineteenth century, the Yoruba concept of 'enlightenment' became associated with ideas of progress derived increasingly from external influences, such as world religions, international travel, and education.[62] The merchants who appear in this study exemplified these qualities: their wealth delivered a high standard of living that was accompanied by a strong commitment to religious institutions, to less fortunate members of society, and to the improving force of education.

60. See, for example, the evidence of Ernest Barth, the agent for Rothlisberger in Rothlisberger v. Fabre, 1888. Lagos Supreme Court records (subsequently, LSCR), Civ. 8, 1888. Merchants and brokers are discussed further later in this chapter and in chapter 2.

61. Barber, 'Documenting Social and Ideological Change'.

62. Peel, 'Olaju'.

The Entrepreneurs of Lagos

The vanguard of the new order that landed in Lagos with the British Naval Squadron in 1851 consisted of a group of Westernised former slaves of Yoruba origin.[63] Most of them had been captured by raiders and were intended for a life of slavery in the New World.[64] Unlike many of their less fortunate compatriots, the ships transporting them were intercepted by the British Anti-Slavery Naval Squadron and the slaves liberated and taken to Freetown, Sierra Leone. Many freed slaves returned to their homelands when it seemed safe to do so. They formed a distinctive group that soon acquired a collective shorthand: 'Saro'.[65]

The Saro were ideally placed to provide the intermediary services the Lagos gateway needed. The majority of Saro, and all the leading members of their community, were Christians; most had been educated in mission schools in Freetown and spoke English as well as Yoruba, which was the language of the port and much of its hinterland. They became merchants, joined government service, and entered the Church. The businesses they operated can be classified as 'firms' because they were specialised, unlike households that conducted several tasks or individuals whose activities were seasonal. The typical firm was individually owned and unincorporated. Accordingly, African firms in Lagos can be compared in structure, if not always in scale, with the expatriate firms in the port for most of the period under review. Structural divergence was not apparent until about 1914, when the majority of expatriate firms had adopted limited liability, and became manifest in 1919, when the first wave of significant amalgamations took place.

The Lagos merchants were unique, however, in having dual connections with their regions of origin in the interior as well as with the European mercantile houses and officials who represented the colonial presence in Lagos.[66] They formed a reciprocal relationship with the British that straddled politics as well as commerce. The colonial authorities had a stake in the success of the Saro as agents of the civilising mission and as valuable sources of local

63. Huge credit should be given to the authors of three indispensable studies: Jean Herskovits Kopytoff for her pioneering work, produced at the outset of African Studies, *A Preface to Modern Nigeria*; Kristin Mann for her impressive study of aspects of Lagos life that goes well beyond the Saro community and in doing so conquers some formidable research problems: *Slavery and the Birth of an African City*; and Olukoju, *The Liverpool of West Africa*, which draws together many decades of thorough and invaluable research into this subject.

64. For important explorations of what is now a considerable literature, see Falola and Childs, *The Yoruba Diaspora* ; Falola and Childs, *The Changing Worlds of Atlantic Africa*.

65. Also known as Krio in Sierra Leone and many other parts of the West Coast. See Cole, *The Krio of West Africa*.

66. The relationship between merchants, brokers, and traders, is discussed in chapter 2 of this text.

knowledge. States in the interior regarded them as key representatives in their dealings with the colonial government. The familiarity of the Saro with Yoruba culture, added to their family connections in the hinterland, gave them a competitive edge over the European firms in areas of trade that required local knowledge of market potential. At the same time, a degree of acculturation helped the Saro to enter international trade. Their knowledge of English enabled them to deal with expatriate firms in Britain as well as in the port; their espousal of gentlemanly values made them recognisable beyond the confines of Lagos, generated confidence, and improved their access to commercial credit.

The Lagos Saro were well aware of the value of their singular qualities. Their ethos gave them a sense of mission in spreading beneficial forms of commerce and 'improving' values to Africa; their attributes as intermediaries gave them the means of contributing to these ambitious goals. Inevitably, there were divisions within the group. As merchants, they were commercial competitors; they had loyalties to rival states in the hinterland; they owed allegiance to different branches of Christianity. Yet, they were fortified by common origins and shared values to an extent that generally rose above their differences. A variety of social organisations nurtured familiarity and provided mutual support. A high degree of inter-marriage integrated the group, reinforced its sense of distinctiveness, and gave it a claim on the future. Personal and commercial connections created networks that ran from Government House to family members in the hinterland and extended as far as Manchester.[67] It used to be thought that hybridity produced rootless, unbalanced individuals who spent their lives searching for an identity they never found. It now seems, though it is impossible to be sure, that in general the Saro managed their dual roles capably, if not effortlessly, probably because they were able to strike a balance that produced more benefits than costs.

Other repatriates added to the commercial life as well as to the diversity of the port city. Freed slaves from Brazil, Cuba, and elsewhere in Latin America, known collectively as 'Brazilians' (also called *Amaro* or *Aguda*), began returning to Lagos from the middle of the century, bringing the Portuguese language, and elements of Portuguese-Brazilian styles and ways of life.[68] In addition, they arrived with a different version of Christianity—Roman Catholicism—albeit with added syncretic elements.[69] By this time, too, there was an established Muslim community. Islam entered the port in the late eighteenth century, and its following expanded before and after the British, the

67. On networks, see Hein, *Port Cities*.

68. Amaro: 'those who have been away from home'. For an overview see Omenka, 'The Afro-Brazilian Repatriates'; a detailed study is Rosenfeld, 'Apparitions of the Atlantic'.

69. As Robin Law has pointed out, the term is a generic that includes those who had never been to Brazil but had absorbed elements of Lusophone-Portuguese culture: *Ouidah*, p. 185; Law, 'Yoruba Liberated Slaves', in Falola and Childs, *The Yoruba Diaspora*, p. 350.

Saro, and the Brazilians (some of whom were Muslims) made their appearance. By the 1840s, Lagos Muslims had established a chief imam and a central mosque, which provided a focus for political as well as religious activity.[70] The cosmopolitan character of Lagos was a common feature of all colonial port cities. The Saro had counterparts who acted as intermediaries elsewhere, including (with variations) freed slaves in other ports in West Africa, *métis* in Senegal, Parsees in India, compradors in East Asia, *mestizos* in the Philippines, and members of creole and mulatto elites in Spanish America and the Caribbean.

Cases and Sources

The careers of eminent Saro were among the first topics to attract attention when the study of West African history began its rapid expansion in the 1960s.[71] In those early days, there was considerable uncertainty about what kinds of African history could be written, how far back the past could be traced, and the extent to which the vast interior of the continent could be brought into the story. The first generation of historians of Africa, like the Old Coasters themselves, had good reason to hug the coastline. The Saro were appealing subjects because they counted as being indigenous but were also reasonably accessible through official and mission records. Subsequently, as confidence about the existence of source materials grew, the research frontier moved inland, and the Saro tended to be left behind. The small number of scholars who continued to study creole elites (including Saro) asked new questions and produced penetrating, detailed work on subjects such as multiculturalism and the Atlantic diaspora.[72] Nevertheless, changing priorities becalmed a subject that remains incompletely researched and open to new ideas.

Much of the existing literature includes material on business activities. Relatively few studies, however, have been devoted to entrepreneurial history and most of these concentrate on individuals or particular families. These accounts are products of impressive research and have made important contributions to African history. It is difficult, however, to know how far conclusions relating to specific cases can be applied more generally. A major finding

70. Raifu, 'Intrigues'; Animashaun, *The History of the Muslim Community*. I am grateful to the late *Alhaji* Animashaun for his advice on this subject.

71. The term 'creole' is used here in a cultural rather than in an ethnic sense to refer to Westernised Africans who stemmed mainly from Freetown, Sierra Leone, and spread to other ports on the west coast in the nineteenth century. The term 'Saro', a contraction of Sierra Leonean, is used to refer to creoles (and their descendants) who returned to what became Nigeria (principally to Lagos). These shorthand definitions need expanding, as suggested by Dixon-Fyle, *A Saro Community*, and Falola and Childs, *The Yoruba Diaspora*.

72. See, among other examples, Lindsay, *Atlantic Bonds*.

of many of these studies, for example, is that African merchants in the West Coast ports enjoyed a period of prosperity and matching eminence during the early years of legitimate commerce before entering a long decline towards the close of the nineteenth century.[73] Other themes, however, such as the structure of African businesses, have been neglected. An additional problem with existing studies is that the sample is small, often being confined to one merchant or family, and rarely extends into the twentieth century.

The contribution that comes closest to meeting the necessary criteria is Raymond Dumett's meticulous research on the Gold Coast between 1860 and 1905.[74] Dumett compiled a list of nearly two hundred indigenous traders from which he identified just twenty-five who were large enough to qualify as merchants. He then examined the careers of three prominent individuals in the coastal towns of Ada, Winneba, and Cape Coast. Dumett's analysis provides convincing evidence of the organising and innovative abilities of his subjects, including their awareness of the need for diversification. His comments on 'decline', however, are brief, pending (as he says) further study. He draws attention to the expanding role of the expatriate firms, the rise of racism, and the difficulty of obtaining credit. He qualifies these considerations, however, by noting the 'natural attrition' that accompanied sole ownerships everywhere, the rise of new opportunities following the rapid expansion of the cocoa industry, and the effect of displacement as trade shifted from small coastal towns to new centres, such as Takoradi, which the colonial government had selected to be the terminus to the colony's first railway line. In the absence of the complementary study Dumett hoped to produce, the fate of his sample remains uncertain, not least because it is unclear if it included merchants who were to achieve prominence after his selected terminal date of 1905. Nevertheless, this is a pioneering study that deserves credit for its detailed and objective analysis.

The foregoing comments reaffirm the truism that it is easier to see shortcomings and omissions in the work of other scholars than it is to recognise

---

73. See recent summaries of the literature containing further references in Akyeampong et al., eds., *Africa's Development*, chs. 6–7. For a generally gloomy view of mercantile fortunes, see also Barry and Harding, eds., *Commerce*; Harding and Kipré, eds., *Commerce*. An early general statement of the decline thesis is Amin, *Le monde des affaires sénégalais*. Amin had a sample of five hundred companies but his interest lay mainly in the years after 1945. His treatment of the period before then was far more schematic, though his interpretation was clear: the embryonic bourgeoisie did well during the nineteenth century but its development was retarded during the colonial period. Other sources that set the scene include: Reynolds, 'The Rise and Fall of African Merchants'; Nwabughuogu, 'From Wealthy Entrepreneurs to Petty Traders'; Lynn, *Commerce and Economic Change*, ch. 6; Olaoba and Ojo, 'Influence of British Economic Activity'.

74. Dumett, 'African Merchants', conveniently reprinted in Dumett, *Imperialism, Economic Development, and Social Change in West Africa* (Durham, NC: Carolina Academic Press, 2013), ch. 11.

failings in our own. I can now see that my own early research, though incomplete, was among those that failed to test the hypothesis about the decline of African merchants against evidence that new merchants might have been emerging.[75] Nevertheless, the inherited body of work referred to in this chapter has placed previously unknown evidence in the public domain and set out propositions that provide starting points for subsequent research. Without these contributions, the present book would contain far more weaknesses than it no doubt does.

The sample that forms the basis of this book attempts to meet the criteria suggested above by assembling a list of 116 African entrepreneurs covering a time span that begins with the establishment of the Lagos Consulate in 1851 and ends in 1931 with the onset of the world slump in 1929 and the ensuing financial crisis two years later.[76] One hundred of the entrepreneurs are merchants; the remainder have been classified as planters or as being in finance and other services.[77] Although Saro dominate the list, Muslims are present in increasing numbers. The sample also has limitations. The available source materials are biased towards members of the Saro community, who appear more frequently in official correspondence, missionary records, and Lagos newspapers than other groups do. Saro families also yield occasional golden nuggets in the form of a small number of private papers that have survived. Muslim merchants, those sometimes referred to by contemporaries as 'pagans', and women appear far less frequently in these sources than Saro do, despite their considerable presence in the commerce of the town. Moreover, I was unable to locate business records of any of these groups, assuming that they have survived. The omens are not favourable. Muslim informants assured me that business records had existed but were destroyed on the death of the founder. Nevertheless, a dedicated search might produce results that, however slim, would be a considerable improvement on the present state of knowledge.

Compensation can be found in several sources that remain significantly underused. The Land Registry Archive records crown grants, conveyances, and mortgages from the 1860s. The Supreme Court records deal with civil

75. Hopkins, 'An Economic History of Lagos, 1880–1914'. As explained in the preface, my original idea was to write a history of Lagos merchants, but I was advised that it would be impossible to find enough material for a Ph.D. on this subject. Consequently, I wrote a very general survey of the economic history of the port interspersed with comments about particular merchants. The result has been quite widely cited but in my estimation was an unsatisfactory compromise.

76. See the appendix.

77. See the appendix. Mann's list of 'Educated Elite Males in Lagos Colony, 1880–1915' in *Marrying Well*, pp. 128–32, identifies fifty-five merchants among two hundred names. We agree on all the major figures. Discrepancies arise because my own sample of one hundred merchants covers a longer period and because of inevitable difficulties of classifying marginal characters for whom information is incomplete.

and criminal cases from 1867; the Probate Registry houses wills and letters of administration from the 1880s. The Lagos Town Council archive deals with the affairs of the town from 1900; the records of the Registrar of Companies contain information about limited liability from 1912 onwards. Interviews with family members have provided information that varies from being no more than an outline to supplying vital details that cannot be found elsewhere. Fieldwork can be revelatory, sometimes embarrassingly so. I recall walking around Jacob Coker's estate at Agege with one of his sons and pausing at an elongated clearance to ask what it was. His reply indicated his surprise and, worse, his disappointment at my ignorance. It was, 'of course', the old caravan road running up to northern Nigeria and down to Lagos and, as I belatedly realised, the best possible advertisement for the major new export crop his father had developed: cocoa. Unusual sources can supplement written information. The cemeteries of Lagos may not be on the tourist route, but they provide information about family relationships and a plenitude of dates, even though the latter can include some heroic exaggerations of the life span of great men. In this instance, the requirements of precision overrule approximations that better represent reality.

The resulting list is pragmatic rather than rigorous. It includes almost all the merchants who contemporaries regarded as 'important'. Their subjective judgements have been checked against information in the sources noted above, which contain information about wealth and indebtedness, success and failure. Objective measurements of the performance of African merchants relative to each other and to the expatriate firms are invaluable but correspondingly rare. I have found only three such comparisons for the whole period 1851–1931, each based on contributions to customs revenues made by the leading merchant houses. Inevitably, uncertainties remain. It is clear that Saro represented local Lagos participants in the export trades with reasonable accuracy; the much wider range of merchants involved in the import trades can also be identified with some confidence, at least as far as the most prominent figures were concerned. Merchants who were connected only indirectly to the important export trades or whose activities have been preserved only in outline may well have been under-reported. Nevertheless, when these qualifications have been acknowledged, it remains the case that this sample is larger than any other comparable set of data available on Africa, and the period covered is also longer than that found in existing studies.

Three Shocks

The static analysis presented so far needs a dynamic approach to set its subjects in motion. If history is the past on the move, entrepreneurs need to be given time if their place in the evolving economic environment is to be understood. The period has been divided into three phases, each corresponding to

an external shock that altered relationships among the components of the economic environment: colonial policy, the expatriate firms, African businesses, and
international trade. As these relationships shifted, so too did the opportunities
available to African entrepreneurs and their prospects for achieving profits
or suffering losses. This approach provides a structured way of reassessing
familiar arguments about the rise and fall of their fortunes, their motives for
innovating, and the adequacy of their business structures. The two shocks that
occupy the greater part of the book interacted with internal developments to
produce their effects. Only the third shock, that of the world war in 1914, was
independent of events in Lagos and its hinterland, though its consequences
were felt there as they were in other ports and colonies.

The first shock, in 1851, was transmitted by Britain's decision to end the
slave trade by bombarding the town and establishing a consulate, which
became a colony ten years later. The outcome was decisive in shifting external
trade from exports of slaves to exports of palm oil and kernels. Saro merchants
took advantage of the change to establish their place in Lagos, whether in
business, colonial service, or the Church. The development of legitimate commerce produced the first 'merchant princes' of Lagos, men who made money
but were also motivated by a desire to show that Africans could absorb mid-
Victorian values and carry the civilising mission into the interior.

Saro merchants led these revolutionary changes, which can be summarised
as laying the foundations of the economy that characterised the greater part
of the colonial period. What is not well known is how the creation of the
colony enabled entrepreneurs to adapt business structures to fit new opportunities. A major transformation, known only through the Lands Office and
Court Records, recast property rights. In the 1860s, freehold land became the
basis of credit and, by extension, mercantile fortunes. The surprise here is
how quickly indigenous merchants adjusted to the new system and also piled
into the land market. The change was accompanied by another of fundamental importance, though one that indigenous merchants were slower to adopt:
the emergence of wage labour. This development, which was momentous in
principle if not yet in practice, was initiated by Saro merchants led, as will be
shown, by James Davies.

The second shock hit Lagos in 1892, when the British government decided
to enlarge the colony, which at that time was still confined to the island of
Lagos and a narrow strip on the mainland side of the lagoon. The assessment
of this event begins in the 1880s, when declining terms of trade reduced profits
and caused relations with states in the hinterland to deteriorate. The invasion
of the hinterland was an attempt to restore the fortunes of legitimate commerce. It formed the prelude to subsequent advances that led to the creation
of the Colony and Protectorate of Nigeria in 1914. It did not, however, improve
commercial prosperity. There was no instant recovery; the century ended with
another serious commercial crisis. The advance of the expatriate firms inland

after the turn of the century added to the difficulties faced by African merchants, whose limited capital resources made it hard for them to compete.
Adverse trends extended beyond issues of economic development: increasing
racism destroyed the universal ideals of the mid-Victorian period, reduced the
status of educated Africans, and limited their opportunities for advancement
in the Church and government employment, though not in business.

It is easy to see why many studies of the period conclude that by 1914 the
'Golden Age' enjoyed by African merchants in the West Coast ports had turned
into what might be called an 'Age of Lead'. The interpretation advanced here
suggests that the decline thesis needs modifying. Analysis of a large sample
followed over a long period shows that, though some merchants declined,
newcomers arose to take their place. Moreover, after 1900, African merchants
responded to changing circumstances by innovating. Some developed new
export crops. Others began to diversify the staple import-export economy.
Another group turned from commerce to money lending and property rentals.
Most of these activities took place within business structures founded in the
1850s and 1860s that were characterised by sole ownership. Nevertheless, after
the turn of the century, African merchants recognised the need for change
and began to experiment with new forms of organisation, including limited
liability companies.

The third shock began abruptly in 1914. The war disrupted international
commerce and presented fresh challenges for African merchants. Yet, they survived the conflict, participated enthusiastically in the post-war boom, and suffered correspondingly, if far less enthusiastically, in the slump that followed.
The grim commercial outlook was confirmed by the global economic crises that
struck in 1929 and 1931. Expatriate firms survived by amalgamating. African
merchants responded, though less successfully, by forming limited liability companies in an attempt to increase capital resources while also limiting risks. The
most obvious hypothesis identifies this period as the one that marked the irreversible decline of the merchants who had made such an important contribution to the Lagos economy since 1851. Any assessment of their fortunes between
1920 and 1945, however, has to be speculative because the necessary research
on the period has still to be undertaken. Meanwhile, there are alternative possibilities, discussed in the concluding chapter, which suggest that the file should
be kept open.

Signposts

Treatment of the first two shocks applies a format that descends from the general
to the particular. Each part of this book begins with a contextual chapter, followed by an account of the mercantile scene, and by detailed chapters illustrating the careers of specific merchants. This sequence is an attempt to surmount
one of the most perplexing and enduring problems in writing history: how to

relate the particularities of individuals to the grand events that swirled around them. The space allocated to the three shocks is also unequal. Assessment of the second shock occupies the greater part of the book because the consequences of the invasion of 1892 unfolded over a period that extended to at least 1914. This period is long enough to reappraise judgements that depend on evidence that is confined mainly to the nineteenth century. Expansion into the hinterland after 1900 introduced new challenges and opportunities and increased the volume of material describing them. Extra space is needed to ensure that this evidence is incorporated into the history of the merchant community.

The third shock is treated briefly because it covers a short period and acts as a culminating statement, though one that opens the way for research on the unexplored era that follows. Analysis is confined to two chapters, one giving an account of the context and the fortunes of the merchant community and the other illustrating the career of Peter Thomas, who rose to eminence before being brought down by the sudden post-war slump and the grim years that followed. He struggled through the inter-war period hoping for a revival that never occurred. The discussion in the final chapter reassesses the application of the decline thesis to this period, evaluates the relationship between business structures and mercantile fortunes, and identifies initiatives that provide links with the expansion of Nigeria's economy after 1945.

Before reaching that point, however, I hope readers will pause long enough to enjoy this record of the careers of some of the most colourful and fabled figures in the history of Lagos. Their stories remind us that economic structures have no life of their own until they are animated by the actions of creative individuals.

The Shock of 1851

CHAPTER TWO

Creating a Cosmopolitan Frontier, 1851–1880

BRITAIN'S VIOLENT ENTRY INTO Lagos in 1851 set off the first of the three shocks that were to reverberate through the island and its hinterland during the next seventy years. Once the Royal Navy had withdrawn, Britain's interests were represented by a new consulate, which was expected to be a low-cost means of overseeing the abolition of the external slave trade while encouraging substitutes that had become known as 'legitimate' commerce. The task far exceeded the consul's limited resources.[1] By 1850, Lagos had become the largest exporter of slaves north of the equator.[2] Although the *Oba's* position had been compromised by his agreement with Britain, Lagos was still a sovereign state. Powerful vested interests remained in place that were reluctant to abandon the profitable trade in slave exports. Against these influences, the consul had little more than a stone to throw. The military force at his immediate disposal was barely enough to defend the consulate. His knowledge of the people and resources in the vast and largely uncharted hinterland that stretched northwards was sketchy. Although successive consuls claimed that they needed more power to carry out their mandate, the Foreign Office kept a close watch on tendencies to expand the scope of British authority. The standard response from London during the 1850s was that the immediate objective, suppressing the overseas slave trade, had largely been accomplished and that commerce in legitimate products would duly follow because they were 'more advantageous'.[3] The view from Lagos was rather different.

1. As Consul Brand forcefully stated: Brand to Russell, 9 April 1860, F.O. 84/1115.

2. Mann, *Slavery and the Birth of an African City*, pp. 39–40. In chapter 1 of her book, Mann provides an authoritative account of the history of the port down to 1851.

3. F.O. to Beecroft, 21 Feb. 1851, F.O. 84/858, confirmed by Campbell in 1857: Campbell to Clarendon, 11 May 1857, F.O. 84/1031.

The Expansion of Legitimate Commerce

The performance of the import and export trades was the most important influence shaping the economic context within which Lagos merchants operated. The staple items of trade were similar to those found elsewhere along the West Coast during this period: exports were based on a few primary products; imports consisted of a variety of manufactured consumer goods. The leading export from Lagos was palm oil, which was joined from the 1870s by palm kernels; the main import was textiles, principally cotton goods. At a time when the market was still dominated by barter, the export trade helped to guarantee a return trade in manufactured goods. Predictably, the colony's overseas trade was oriented towards Britain, which dominated both imports and exports.[4] A striking feature of the data, however, was the importance of trade with Germany, which by 1881 had reached about two-thirds of the annual value of the colony's trade with Britain.

The basic trends are clearly marked. Figure 2.1 charts the increase in the volume of exports from British West Africa, which are an indicative proxy for Lagos, between 1850 and 1940. The log scale reveals some of the fluctuations in the broad upward trend that occurred in the nineteenth century; a linear scale would smooth the trend but accentuate the substantial rise after 1900. The log scale reveals a sharp dip in export volumes during the first half of the 1860s and a pause between 1880 and 1887. Palm oil exports from Lagos itself averaged around 4,000 (imperial) tons a year during the second half of the 1850s; the median for the decade 1862–1871 was 6,925 tons, with most of the gains coming in the second half of the decade.[5] Volumes continued to grow during the next decade, though at a lower rate: the median for the period 1872–1881 was 7,463 tons. The total value of imports and exports entering and leaving Lagos also rose between 1862 and 1881, with annual variations showing an approximate correlation between imports and exports.[6]

The upward but fluctuating volumes shown in figure 2.1 are complemented by the data represented in figure 2.2, which present, for the first time, the net barter terms of trade for palm oil and kernels exported specifically from Lagos between 1856 and 1906. The smoothed line follows a rising trend from the mid-1860s to the early 1880s. When combined with increasing export

4. Data from the *Lagos Blue Books*.

5. These figures are drawn from the *Blue Books* and *Annual Reports* for the Colony of Lagos. Figures given in imperial gallons have been converted to imperial tons at the rate authorised by the Weights and Measures Act of 1824, which became effective in 1826. As the figures for the consular period are incomplete, I have cited an approximate average rather than the median.

6. Data drawn from the *Annual Reports* of the Colony of Lagos. The figures reported in the *Annual Reports* for this period include specie and goods in transit. The value of the pound sterling was unchanged during this period; the current values recorded and shown here can also be treated as constant values.

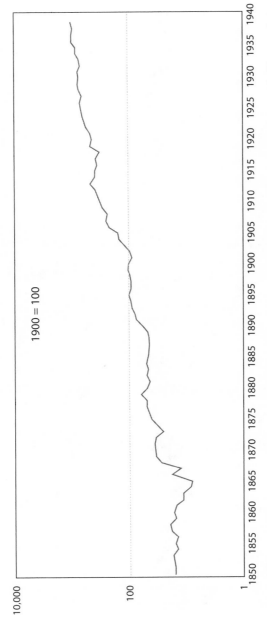

FIGURE 2.1. Volume of Exports from British West Africa, 1850–1940 (log scale). Data and graph provided by Professor Ewout Frankema.

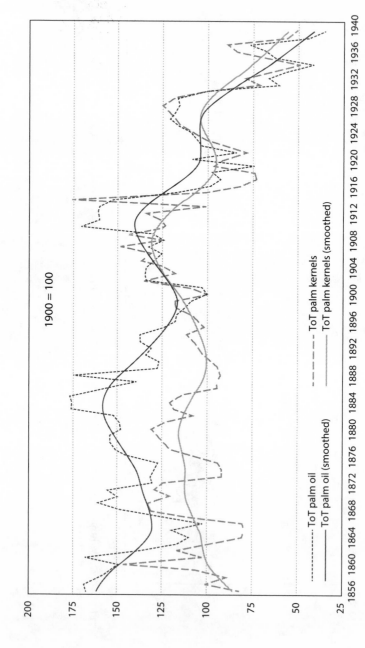

1900 = 100

200 175 150 125 100 75 50 25

1856 1860 1864 1868 1872 1876 1880 1884 1888 1892 1896 1900 1904 1908 1912 1916 1920 1924 1928 1932 1936 1940

- - - - ToT palm kernels
———— ToT palm kernels (smoothed)

- - - - ToT palm oil
———— ToT palm oil (smoothed)

FIGURE 2.2. Net Barter Terms of Trade of Palm Oil and Kernels Exported from Lagos, 1856–1940 (1900 = 100). The data refer to Lagos from 1856–1906 and to Southern Nigeria and Nigeria thereafter. Data and graph provided by Professor Ewout Frankema.

volumes, the upward trend suggests a long period of favourable trade. Ewout Frankema's data for British West Africa as a whole show that the purchasing power of exports grew at an annual average of 4.65 per cent between 1853 and 1885.[7] The income terms of trade are an incomplete index of net gains because they do not allow for changes in productivity, which in the case of West Africa are not easily calculated. Nevertheless, given that agronomic techniques and transaction costs were either (broadly) unchanged or improved (through steamship services), the available evidence indicates that this was a period of prosperity for those involved in West African trade. The upward trend was a manifestation of the mid-Victorian boom: manufacturing and freight costs fell; surging demand in Europe raised import prices and expanded export volumes. This was indeed a time when shrewd merchants could aim for a fortune and make it.

Fortunes, however, were never guaranteed, even during years of prosperity. The broken lines in figure 2.2 reveal the importance of sudden, short-term fluctuations that could catch merchants holding stocks in a falling market or lacking sufficient credit to take advantage of a rising one. Unanticipated and often swift variations underline the risks that faced those engaged in Lagos trade. It should be remembered that the smoothed lines provide retrospective confidence in trends that remained unknown to contemporaries. The broken lines are a more accurate guide to imminent realities. Merchants with important decisions to make were never sure of the state of the market the next month or even the next week. Favourable long-term trends were consistent with significant temporary deviations that played a considerable part in creating and destroying fortunes. Spikes in the terms of trade in 1859–1860, 1868–1871, and 1881–1883 stand out, as do pronounced dips in the mid-1860s and in 1872–1873. From the early 1880s, when the terms of trade turned against West African exporters, entrepreneurial decision-making became even more challenging, as the following chapters will show. At this point, the difference between palm oil and kernels in the smoothed lines becomes apparent, as do the consequences for mercantile fortunes.

The most important decisions merchants had to make lay beyond their control. On the demand side, palm oil and kernels made only a small contribution to the vast oils and fats market in Europe. Their modest share of the market combined with the ready availability of substitutes ensured that producers and merchants in Lagos were price-takers rather than price-makers. When supplies of tallow from Russia sank during the Crimean War, the price of palm oil rose; when peace was restored, the price retreated. The use of mineral oil in lighting caused a drop in palm oil prices in the early 1860s; prices recovered later in the decade, when palm oil was adopted as a flux in the expanding tin plate industry. The most far-reaching change was the creation of a market for palm kernels from the 1870s, when they became an ingredient in

7. Frankema, Williamson, and Woltjer, 'An Economic Rationale', table 3, p. 249.

the manufacture of cattle cake and margarine. Successive shifts in the centres of demand continued to open and close opportunities for primary producers from then onwards. On the supply side they were beset by the unknowable and the uncontrollable: variations in rainfall affected the volume and quality of crops entering the export market; unsettled relations among the Yoruba states hindered or at times halted movement along the trade routes. In 1880, the *Lagos Times* followed a long line of commentors in fretting about four years of 'paralysis' following the 'stoppage of the roads'.[8]

The calculation of mercantile profits arising from these favourable conditions of trade is a step into the twilight. In the absence of records of bank accounts, income tax, corporation tax, and the information required of registered companies, researchers are left with indications rather than systematic statements. Although the price of palm oil in Liverpool is known, indications of the prices paid in Lagos at this time are incomplete. The prevalence of barter was a further complication: the price of goods was increased as a form of insurance to cover possible losses on produce; conversely, an equivalent percentage was deducted when cash was paid for goods.[9] Occasional estimates of profits provide percentages but rarely state whether the figure is gross or net or on turnover or capital. Many costs are now beyond recall. Furthermore, the trade was full of allowances and discounts that were applied to freight rates, bulk purchases and sales, and the quality of produce. Consequently, only the most general and usually indirect indications of mercantile fortunes can be given for the period 1860–1880, though individual cases provide some degree of precision. Fortunately, the evidence for the period 1880–1900 is fuller and allows a more detailed assessment, which will be presented in chapter 7.

Business Uncertainty under the Consulate

The political history of the consulate from this point on has been well told in a meticulous study that makes it unnecessary to reproduce the story in detail here.[10] The assessment offered in this chapter sees the decade as a battle to determine whether the port, the gateway to the interior, would continue to facilitate the shipment of slaves or turn decisively to other, less immediately profitable, exports. The outcome involved a variety of contending interests and remained unresolved until the end of the decade.

Portuguese and Brazilian slave-traders were eager to see the trade continue. In 1853, an Austrian merchant was caught buying slaves; even the

8. *Lagos Times*, 27 April 1881.
9. Evidence in West v. Taiwo and Dawudu, 15 Feb. 1888, LSCR. Civ. 7, 1888. A comprehensive account of the barter trade in the 1880s is in Rothlisberger v. Fabre, LSCR, Civ. 8, 1888. Rönnbäck, 'The Business of Barter', provides a much-needed analysis of the differentials linking prices and goods.
10. Smith, *The Lagos.*

British Vice-Consul, Louis Frazer, was said to favour slaving interests.[11] As hope of resurrecting slave exports began to fade, European merchants competed to increase their share of exports of palm oil and imports of cowries by backing either Akitoye (and his successor, Dosunmu), or Kosoko and his faction.[12] The German firm of Wilhelm O'Swald first favoured Dosunmu, then attempted to join Kosoko's camp, and ended by supporting the consul; the French firm of Régis Frère remained close to Kosoko.[13] The Church Missionary Society used its influence to support the resettlement of the Saro and defend Christian converts, the beacon of the anticipated future, in the Egba capital, Abeokuta. The consul had his own priorities, which involved mobilising support for legitimate commerce among local political and mercantile interests and preserving Lagos itself as the centre of trade and the main source of government revenue. The consul, however, was not lord of what he surveyed. The competing interests seeking to influence him extended beyond Lagos and the lagoon to include, among other states, the Egba, who wanted to keep the port as their main outlet and who favoured Dosunmu over Kosoko. Britain's 'man on the spot' found himself sitting in an uncomfortably hot spot.[14]

Uncertainty and its ally, instability, ran through the decade. Despite Akitoye's formal agreement to co-operate in ending the slave trade, hostility to the new regime continued to bubble. Kosoko was considered to be a permanent threat, even though in 1854 he was persuaded to abandon his claim to rule Lagos and cease trading in slaves in return for financial compensation.[15] Other militant elements menaced the new order. In 1855, the redoubtable Madame Efunroye Tinubu, a political activist, substantial trader, and Akitoye's niece, headed a conspiracy to assassinate the consul and members of the expatriate and Saro communities and place her son, Adele, on the throne.[16] Tinubu's political ambitions were

11. Frazer to Clarendon, 30 May 1853, F.O. 84/920; Campbell to Clarendon, 23 July 1853, 27 July 1853, 19 Sept. 1853, C.O. 84/920; Campbell to Clarendon, 2 July 1857, F.O. 84/1031.

12. Contemporary spellings of Dosunmu's name varied. Modern orthography favours the version used here, though 'Docemo' has been retained where it appears in nineteenth-century quotations. I am indebted to Karin Barber for advice on this matter.

13. Nzemeke, 'Local Patronage'.

14. Lynn, 'Consuls and Kings'.

15. Campbell to Clarendon, 1 Oct. 1854, F.O. 84/950. The episode is covered in detail in Smith, *The Lagos Consulate*, ch. 4. Doubts about Kosoko's new commitment appeared almost immediately and continued during the rest of the decade. See Campbell to Clarendon, 24 Nov. 1854, F. O. 84/950; Campbell to Clarendon, 1 Oct. 1856, F.O. 84/1002; Campbell to Malmesbury, 28 Jan. 1859 and 4 March 1859, F.O. 84/1088; Lodder to Russell, 2 Nov. 1859, F.O. 84/1088.

16. Campbell to Clarendon, 12 Feb. 1855, F.O. 84/976. For fears that Kosoko would mount a counter-coup, see Wilmot to Bruce, 11 Feb. 1852, F.O. 84/893; F.O. minute by Lord Stanley, 2 Aug. 1852, F.O. 84/895; Admiralty to F.O. 26 Aug. 1852, F.O. 84/895; Campbell to Clarendon, 1 Sept. 1853, F.O. 84/920; Campbell to Bruce, 4 Nov. 1853, F.O. 84/954. Tinubu

tied to her commercial commitments because in 1854 she was 'heavily indebted to some merchants' in Lagos and refusing to pay.[17] Although the planned coup failed, Tinubu and some disaffected war chiefs made a further attempt to unseat Dosunmu, Akitoye's legitimate successor, in 1856.[18] The ambitions of the plotters again exceeded their capacity: Tinubu was exiled and took refuge in her Egba homeland. In 1860, she asked to be allowed to return to Lagos, but was refused permission because she owed money in Abeokuta as well as Lagos.[19]

This was by no means the end of the consul's problems. In 1859, several issues combined to underline the precariousness of his position. Oshodi Tapa, Kosoko's senior adviser, passed on information that the former *Oba* had formulated a new scheme to return to Lagos.[20] Soon after, reports came that the French firm, Régis Aîné, was reviving the slave trade at two ports on the lagoon.[21] Even more disturbing news arrived when the Egba, Ijebu, and Ibadan closed the trade routes to Lagos to demonstrate their opposition to legitimate commerce, and reports of spreading hostilities in the interior began to arrive.[22] In the following year, the troubling news about the hinterland was magnified by threats of invasion from the neighbouring state of Dahomey and the associated fear that the French might use the occasion to advance inland from Porto Novo.[23]

Weighty economic considerations underlay these events. The end of the external slave trade struck a massive blow at the specialisation that had become the mainstay of the rulers of Lagos. This trade had remained in their hands, and the distribution of the resulting largesse and jobs was essential to the creation and maintenance of a political following. As Consul Campbell observed of the slave trade in 1854: 'that horrid traffic being confined to the King, his Chiefs and principal people, they were all under the necessity of feeding their numerous slaves and dependants'.[24] It became depressingly clear

---

was married to one *Bada*, who was employed by Dosunmu as his executioner (among other functions). Campbell to Clarendon, 20 Dec. 1854, F.O. 84/950.

17. Campbell to Clarendon, 1 May 1854, F.O. 84/950.

18. Campbell to Clarendon, 26 March 1856, 26 May 1856, F.O. 84/1002. Akitoye died in mysterious circumstances in 1853.

19. Brand to Russell, 25 May 1860, F.O. 84/1115.

20. Campbell to Malmesbury, 4 March 1859, F.O. 84/1088. A report in 1856 that Kosoko was trading profitably in palm oil may have been premature: at the beginning of 1861, he was said to be 'without lands or revenue'. Campbell to Clarendon, 1 Oct. 1856, F.O. 84/1002; Foote to F.O. 9 Jan. 1861, F.O. 4/1141.

21. Campbell to Malmesbury, 28 Jan. 1859, F.O. 84/1088.

22. Campbell to Malmesbury, 5 March 1859, F.O. 84/1088. Not for the first time. See Campbell to Clarendon, 1 Oct. 1855 and 7 Dec. 1855, F.O. 85/976. On war in the interior, see Hand to Russell, 10 Sept. 1860 and 3 Nov. 1860, F.O. 84/1115; McCoskry to Russell, 9 July 1861, F.O. 84/1141.

23. Brand to Russell, 9 April 1860, F.O. 84/1115; Minute by Wylde, 14 Aug. 1860, on Hand to Russell, 8 July 1860, F.O. 84/1115; Foote to F.O., 9 Feb. 1861, F.O. 84/1141. See also Campbell to Clarendon, 3 March 1858, F.O. 84/1061.

24. Campbell to Clarendon, 1 June 1854, F.O. 84/950.

that the new exports, which consisted of palm oil supplemented by raw cotton, were less profitable than the trade in human lives. It was all very well for Beecroft to explain to Kosoko in 1851 that 'by cultivating the soil greater riches would more honourably, and certainly more happily, be attained than slave traffic could possibly issue', but the growth of the new morality was stunted by lower profits, which in turn kept happiness at bay.

The evidence on the relative profitability of the two different exports is primarily qualitative and represents the views of participants who were promoting their own interests.[25] Nevertheless, the commentary runs through the decade, reflects diverse perspectives, and is consistent.[26] The struggle between Kosoko and Akitoye was a battle not only to establish the legitimacy of their dynastic claims but also to control the profits of the slave trade, which sustained their authority. Akitoye abandoned the trade provisionally and only to secure support for his political ambitions. Kosoko and his followers held on because, according to Consul Campbell, it was 'the only commerce that enriches them'.[27] Akitoye's decision to co-operate with the British turned out to be a gamble that threatened to erode his power base and increase his vulnerability. In 1853, two of his war chiefs transferred their support to Kosoko because 'they could not acquire such immense wealth from the Palm Oil trade as from the Slave Trade'.[28] Three years later, Campbell reported that Akitoye and his senior chiefs 'have lost all benefit from the slave trade' and many of them are now 'very poor'.[29] Private traders expressed similar concerns. At a meeting between Lagos and Egba traders in 1855, the latter complained that 'by pleasing the English to abandon the slave trade and take to palm oil trade they had all become poor'.[30] In 1859, Ibadan and Ijebu chiefs lamented, not for the first time, that the 'palm oil trade brings them no revenue and that the Slave Trade enriches them'.[31]

The news was not entirely gloomy. In default of more profitable possibilities, the palm oil trade made modest progress during the 1850s. In 1854, Consul Campbell noted that the 'numerous slaves and dependants of the king and his chiefs' were able to maintain themselves by 'trading in palm oil and other

25. See the admirable summary of recent research on income from the slave trade in Mann, *Slavery and the Birth of an African City*, pp. 59–66.

26. Law, 'The "Crisis of Adaptation" Revisited', in Falola and Brownell, *Africa*, pp. 126–9. Law's study is particularly concerned with the hinterland, where deficiencies of evidence require a more nuanced assessment.

27. Campbell to Clarendon, 10 Sept. 1853, F.O. 84/920.

28. Akitoye to Campbell, 29 July 1853, enc. in Campbell to Clarendon, 19 Sept. 1853, F.O. 84/921.

29. Campbell to Clarendon, 14 May 1856, F.O. 84/1002.

30. Campbell to Clarendon, 2 Oct. 1855, F.O. 84/976.

31. Campbell to Malmesbury, 28 Jan. 1859, F.O. 84/1088; confirmed in Campbell to Malmesbury, 5 March 1859, F.O. 84/1088. See also Campbell to Clarendon, 30 Aug. 1855, F.O. 84/976; Campbell to Malmesbury, 5 March 1859, F.O. 84/1088.

articles'.[32] Two years later, he reported that the palm oil trade was increasing at all the ports in the Bight of Benin, 'and if the revenues derived from it do not satisfy all the old slave-trading chiefs, the profits of the lawful traffic amply compensate the masses of the populations who are now engaged in it'.[33] As the basis of wealth shifted, so did political rivalry. In 1853, Campbell had recognised Kosoko as ruler of the ports of Lekki and Palma in the hope that he would abandon his claims to Lagos.[34] The development of the palm oil trade there, however, also attracted merchants from Lagos and threatened the dominance of Lagos and the revenues it derived from taxes on overseas trade.[35] In 1857, Dosunmu expressed his resentment at this development by burning down the Lagos warehouses of two European firms that had begun to trade with Kosoko's ports.[36] This episode, and concern that revenue might flow eastwards to ports controlled by Kosoko, prompted Campbell to arrange a deal with the former *Oba* that brought him back to Lagos in 1862, this time as a pacific resident.[37]

There were considerable obstacles to the expansion of legitimate commerce, quite apart from profitability and uncertainties arising from political instability in the port and its hinterland. In full accord with the liberal beliefs of the age, the consul supposed that legitimate commerce would ameliorate slavery by giving slaves 'the possession of a little property' of their own.[38] In 1858, he observed that 'the acquisition of property caused by their own labour and industry has naturally led to the desire on the part of many domestic slaves to purchase their own freedom'.[39] In this instance, Campbell's optimism ran ahead of events: he saw the beginnings of a momentous social change, but the end was more distant than he imagined. In the interim, slaves continued to be used in production, transport, and trade.

The success of the new trade required institutional innovation that would establish a secure basis for economic growth. Two related issues were of primary importance and have yet to attract the attention they deserve: a mechanism for dealing with debt and a means of providing security for commercial credit. Both appear to be tangential to the events of 1851 and 1861, which have been seen primarily in political terms.[40] Yet, they not only enlarge our under-

32. Campbell to Clarendon, 1 June 1854, F.O. 84/950.

33. Campbell to Clarendon, 14 June 1856, F.O. 84/1002.

34. Campbell to Clarendon, 1 Oct. 1854, F.O. 84/950.

35. Campbell to Clarendon, 1 Oct. 1854, F.O. 84/950.

36. Nzemeke, 'Local Patronage', pp. 110–13.

37. McCoskry to Russell, 5 Dec. 1861, C.O. 147/2; Freeman to Newcastle, 7 June 1862, C.O. 147/1.

38. Campbell to Clarendon, 14 March 1857, F.O. 84/1031.

39. Campbell to Clarendon, 28 March 1858, F.O. 84/1061.

40. Smith's authoritative study, *The Lagos Consulate*, p. 124, makes little reference to these questions; he notes the addition of the two relevant clauses in the Treaty of Cession but without further comment.

standing of the decision to turn the consulate into a colony but are also central to the history of African entrepreneurs in Lagos throughout the period covered by this study and, as an extension of it would indicate, well beyond it.

The trade of Lagos was based on what was known as the 'trust system', which had been devised to meet the needs of the slave trade. Where slaves were not immediately available, goods and currency (cowries or silver dollars) were advanced in anticipation of the delivery of human beings for export. Credit arrangements depended on personal relations between visiting slave traders and local rulers and on the extent to which rulers and other Big Men could control networks of followers and associates whose activities stretched into the hinterland. Personal relations were supplemented by Yoruba law, which prescribed sanctions for debtors who defaulted.[41] The system was inherited by the pioneers of legitimate commerce, who soon found that its limitations inhibited their progress.[42] The new merchants, Saro as well as expatriates, stood outside the system they had taken over. They were Big Men in their own way, but they lacked extensive followings and they relied on local authorities and indigenous law to police indebtedness. Sanctions, however, were not easily applied. Debtors could abscond; impersonal forms of security were not readily available; imprisonment did not produce money that had been lost. Furthermore, the increased numbers of traders involved in legitimate commerce made it certain that the incidence of bad debts would also rise.

Obtaining payment for commercial debts was a serious and persistent problem that featured prominently in various trade agreements the merchants negotiated with Dosunmu during the consular period. The first agreement, reached in 1852, provided for the recovery of commercial debts.[43] This seemingly promising start proved disappointing, and in 1854 a new agreement was reached that reinforced the position of creditors and included provisions allowing a debtor's house or other property to be sold.[44] In the following year, the Saro merchants formed a tribunal with the aim of exerting greater direct control over debtors, and in 1859 a further agreement was made with Dosunmu to ensure that creditors received payment.[45] By the end of the decade, however, it was clear that none of these measures was satisfactory. Under Dosunmu's jurisdiction, enforcement remained uncertain; at the same time, the consuls lacked the authority to adjudicate matters of debt.[46] The ultimate solution was to install effective means of policing the credit system and to create transferable security in the form of land. These moves, however, required a

41. Moore, *Laws and Customs*, pp. 58–62.

42. *Lagos Times*, 10 August 1881.

43. Bruce to Admiralty, 1 April 1852, F.O. 84/894.

44. Campbell to Clarendon, 1 June 1854, F.O. 84/950.

45. Campbell to Clarendon, 2 Aug. 1855, F.O. 84/976; Campbell to Clarendon, 25 Sept. 1856, F.O. 84/1002; Newbury, 'Credit and Debt', p. 92.

46. Campbell to Clarendon, 1 June 1854, F. O. 84/950.

more radical transformation of indigenous law and institutions than was possible under the consular regime.

The introduction of impersonal forms of security, above all land, to underpin commercial credit was to be a momentous development that transformed Lagos, and eventually Nigeria, in ways that can justly be called revolutionary.[47] This claim does not rely on the assumption that pre-colonial society was static and resolutely conservative. By the 1840s, the expansion of the slave trade had increased the population of Lagos and generated claims over land rights.[48] Nevertheless, the changes that followed involved radical institutional reform. As early as 1863, a group of Lagos chiefs had already glimpsed the future: 'It is a fact not to be controverted', they stated, 'that the wealth and opulence of a European consists of money, land etc., and that of the Black is by far the reverse, which is of slaves and wives'.[49] In the 1850s, Yoruba land law, which also applied to Lagos, did not recognise regular land sales; dispossession of land was possible but only in rare circumstances.[50] Chief Daniel Taiwo, who was a prominent and well-informed figure in Lagos in the 1850s, summarised customary practice as follows: 'Before the cession of Lagos land was of no value: if you gave a bottle of rum and kola nuts you could get land, and at the end of the year you gave corn or yam, or some of the fruits of the land'.[51]

The allocation of land was primarily in the hands of the *Idejo* chiefs, who had jurisdiction over different parts of Lagos. Their rights, however, were not exclusive and were shared with the *Oba* and several other families that had inherited or acquired rights over land.[52] The outlines of a struggle between the *Oba* and his chiefs appeared in the 1850s and 1860s, when the allocation

47. Hopkins, 'Property Rights and Empire-Building'. Mann, *Slavery and the Birth of an African City*, pp. 144–50, 238–58, 262–67, goes beyond my own work in including the fortunes of slaves and former slaves. Where we overlap, we are in broad agreement.

48. Mann, 'African and European Initiatives', in Saliha Belmessous, ed., *Native Claims*, pp. 223–48.

49. Petition of Lagos chiefs to Governor Glover, 8 Sept. 1863, C.O. 147/43. The chiefs were aggrieved that they had incurred debts from buying slaves who were being emancipated without their owners being compensated.

50. See, for example, Odibo v. Salako, LSCR, Civ 5. 1882; Moore, *Laws and Customs*, pp. 9–18.

51. Evidence of D. C. Taiwo, in Eshugbiyi v. Odunyi, 15 May 1900, LSCR, Civ. 24, 1900. Taiwo was one of the chiefs who signed the petition referred to in n. 49. His account was confirmed by two White Capped Chiefs, Obanisoro and Aromire, in 1904. Eshugbiyi Oloto v. Dawudu & Ors, LSCR, Civ. 34, 1904. See also Odibo v. Salako, LSCR, Civ. 5, 1882.

52. The *Idejo* were one of four categories of Lagos chiefs. For further information on their role and rights, see Mann's nuanced account in *Slavery and the Birth of an African City*, pp. 238–49. For examples of the *Oba* allocating land rights, see Coelho v. Pereira, Chief Magistrate's Court, LSCR, 1864; evidence of Abari in Fanojora v. Kadiri, LSCR, Civ. 3, 1881; evidence of Soguro, messenger to Akitoye and Dosunmu, in Taiwo v. Queen's Advocate, LSCR, Civ. 9, 1889; and the further discussion in Amodu Tijani, Chief Oluwa v. Secretary, Southern Provinces, LSCR, Civ. 76, 1915.

of land rights became a major political issue. The belief that the *Idejos* had exclusive rights was a tradition that was to some extent invented later to suit various political and legal interests.[53] Moreover, the *Idejo* had no authority to sell land.[54] Their rights were confined to the allocation of usage on nominal terms.[55] Gifts made in exchange for rights of occupancy were acknowledgements of fealty, or duties of service, and not rents paid for an economic resource. They were primarily a means of settling followers and building up a power base of dependants, both free men and slaves, by attaching them to the entourage of the chief concerned. Tenure was the right to beneficial use subject to the payment of tribute; dispossession was permitted only if these obligations were not met or in cases of persistent 'bad behaviour'.[56]

The expatriate firms and Saro merchants were aware that the existing system did not fit easily with free-market capitalism. Dosunmu co-operated by helping them and the 'Brazilians' to secure unoccupied land outside the Old Town.[57] However, Dosunmu and his successor, Akitoye, did not see themselves as agents of capitalism: their aim was to give others a stake in their own political future. After Kosoko was expelled from Lagos in 1853, Dosunmu immediately 'sent round his bell man saying that anyone who wanted possession of unoccupied land could take it', which they did.[58] The agreements made between the *Oba* and the merchants during the 1850s included the 'right to erect stores', and to 'choose their own place of residence in any spot previously unoccupied or which they may purchase from a previous occupant'.[59] The reference to purchase clearly indicates that the merchants expected guaranteed security with rights of alienation; whether the *Oba* understood the word in the same way is unlikely, given that the allocations were not money-making ventures. In addition to these agreements, Dosunmu and his chiefs issued about seventy-six land grants, mostly to newcomers, between 1853 and 1860.[60] The form of the grants varied and the ambiguity of some of the wording was to propagate court actions

53. Animashaun, 'Benin Imperialism', claims that the *Idejo* had exclusive rights before 1850, but his evidence, though valuable in many ways, does not refer to the relevant primary sources for the nineteenth century cited by Mann, *Slavery and the Birth of an African City*, pp. 238–49, or, more briefly, here.

54. Evidence of Faro, a White Cap Chief, in Ajose v. Efunde & Ors, 1 July 1892, LSCR, Civ. 12, 1892.

55. See, for example, Evidence of Soguro, messenger to Akitoye and Dosunmu, in Taiwo v. Queen's Advocate, LSCR, Civ. 9, 1889.

56. This was not easily proved. See the judgement given for the defendant in Modele Onilegbale and Anor, LSCR, Civ. 25, 1900.

57. The term, 'Brazilians', is defined in chapter 1.

58. Coelho v. Pereira, Chief Magistrate's Court, LSCR, 1864; evidence of Abari in Fanojora v. Kadiri, LSCR, Civ. 3, 1881.

59. Bruce to Admiralty, 1 April 1852 and enclosure, F.O. 84/894; Campbell to Clarendon, 1 June 1854, F.O. 84/950.

60. Report by J. J. C. Healy in Denton to Chamberlain, 4 Oct. 1898, C.O. 147/135.

that in some cases lasted for generations.[61] In this instance, too, it seems likely that Dosunmu and his chiefs intended to grant rights of occupancy and use virtually without constraints on function or limits of time rather than to confer a freehold that could then be alienated without reference to the grantor.

Nevertheless, however unintentionally, written grants were a large step towards codifying land rights and marked the growing importance of a new form of property. Disputes about rights of occupancy and boundaries quickly followed. The most prominent, and the most acrimonious, lasted for several years and involved the head of the Church Missionary Society (CMS) in Lagos, the Reverend Charles Gollmer, the consul, and the mercantile community.[62] Gollmer, for whom the phrase 'muscular Christian' might have been invented, moved with the speed of a sprinter in 1852 to obtain a grant of a large stretch of river frontage known as Water Street, so called because it was flooded at high tide. It later became prime land, known as the Marina, but in 1858, Water Street was not a road but a route that people could use at low tide.[63] Gollmer, who was also a risk-taking entrepreneur, took a chance while others hesitated in case Kosoko returned and brought retribution to supporters of the restored regime. Akitoye, whose cause Gollmer had supported, 'made over' five plots of land 'without condition' and 'free of expense and without limit of time'.[64] The merchants, realising that they had been out-thought, rushed to object; the consul, realising that a fine site for a new consulate building had just disappeared, joined them.

The long wrangle that followed reached a conclusion only after the consul refused to register the *Oba*'s grant. Gollmer was then obliged to give up a large part of his acquisition, which duly became the commercial centre of Lagos and the home of the consulate.[65] The episode showed that, if the stakes were high enough, Britain's representative was prepared to rescind Akitoye's grants, even though he had no right to interfere in a matter that lay within the jurisdiction of what was still a sovereign state. The consul's intervention indicated that the future had almost arrived.

Founding a New Colony

By the close of the decade, advocates of the 'civilising mission' were convinced of the need for further action if the conversion to legitimate commerce was not to falter or perhaps even founder. European firms, Saro merchants, and

61. The principal decisions are outlined in Park, 'The Cession of Territory'.

62. Malmesbury to Vice-Consul Frazer, 20 Dec. 1852, F.O. 84/1886; Frazer to Malmesbury, 11 March 1853, F.O. 84/920; Campbell to Clarendon, 20 Sept. 1853, F.O. 84/920; Clarendon to Gollmer, 1 May 1854, F.O. 84/950; Campbell to Clarendon and enclosure, 28 May 1855, F.O. 84/976.

63. Evidence of T. W. Johnson and W. A. Allen in Att. Gen. v. John Holt and Att. Gen v. McIver, LSCR, Civ. 55, 1909.

64. Campbell to Clarendon, and enc., 28 May 1855, F. O. 84/976.

65. For the wider context, see Darch, 'The Church Missionary Society'.

the CMS voiced persistent complaints about the dangers to 'life and property' in Lagos and the costs of the interruptions to trade resulting from warfare in the hinterland.[66] In April 1860, Consul Brand summarised the current anxieties and advanced a solution: 'The increase of trade, of civilised ideals, and European interests and habits demand that there should be such an administration of Government as to give an efficient protection of property'.[67] At present, he continued, 'there is no effective protection to property, no mode of enforcing the payment of debts applicable to Europeans'.[68] In the following month, he reinforced the case for action: 'year after year a feeling of insecurity is raised in the minds of those who have property exposed here and their plans for turning that property to best account are upset by doubts as to the amount and certainty of the protection they have to expect'.[69]

Unforeseen developments added weight to the consul's sense of urgency. Palm oil exports had begun to decline in volume and value from a peak reached in 1858–1859.[70] The setback led to serious trade stoppages, and to rumours, some of which had substance, that the slave trade was being revived at nearby ports.[71] The appearance of French naval vessels in the vicinity of Lagos heightened the feeling that Britain's position there was becoming increasingly precarious.[72] Coincidentally, distant sounds of imminent warfare in the United States generated pressures from Manchester manufacturers for the development of alternative supplies of raw cotton.[73]

The accumulation of difficulties culminated in an abrupt shift in British policy. The consul's representations chimed with fortuitous changes in the composition of the British government that returned Lord Palmerston to power as Prime Minister in 1859 and increased the influence of a group of assertive officials in the Foreign Office. The tone of policy altered: action replaced caution. In July 1860, the Foreign Office recommended that the

66. Brand to Edmonstone, and enclosure, 24 April 1860, F.O. 84/1115; F.O. Minute by Wylde, 14 Aug. 1860, on Hand to Russell, 8 July 1860, F.O. 84/1115; McCoskry to Russell, 9 July 1861, F.O. 84/1141. The principal conflict at this time, now known as the Ijaiye War (1860–65), was between Ibadan, on the one hand, and an alliance formed by Ijaye, Egba, Ijebu, and Ilorin on the other, and ended with the victory of the former. The authoritative statement is Law, 'The "Crisis of Adaptation" Revisited', in Falola and Brownell, *Africa, Empire and Globalization*, ch. 6.

67. Brand to Russell, 9 April 1860, F.O. 84/1115.

68. Brand to Russell, 9 April 1860, F.O. 84/1115.

69. Brand to Edmonstone, 1 May 1860, F.O. 84/1115.

70. Newbury, *Western Slave Coast*, p. 57, and figure 2.2 for the sharp fall in the terms of trade.

71. Campbell to Malmesbury, 28 Jan. 1859, and 4 Feb. 1859, F.O. 84/1088; Brand to Russell, 28 Jan. 1859, F.O. 84/1088; Hand to Russell, 8 July 1860, F.O. 84/1115; Foote to F.O. 8 Jan. 1861, F.O, 84/1141.

72. Foote to F.O., 9 Jan. 1861, and minute by Palmerston, 3 March 1861, F.O. 84/1141; Foote to F.O., 9 Feb. 1861 and minute by Palmerston, 20 March 1861, F.O. 84/1141.

73. Gavin, 'Palmerston's Policy', pp. 224–31.

only solution lay in 'taking possession of Lagos'.[74] The advice was repeated in the early months of 1861; Consul Foote acted as cheerleader; Palmerston turned sympathy into substance. In June, the decision was made to convert 'this anomalous protectorate' into a colony to 'complete' the suppression of the slave trade and give 'aid and support to the development of lawful commerce'.[75] In July, Consul McCoskry 'sounded the English residents and the Sierra Leone emigrants', and with 'a few exceptions' among the last, 'found them favourable [to the idea]'.[76] 'Most of them,' he added—in case there was any doubt—'have reason to complain of the want of protection of property under the rule of Docemo [*sic*]'.[77]

Initially, Dosunmu refused to transfer sovereignty, which he felt, correctly, was being forced upon him.[78] His position was supported not only by the *Idejo* chiefs but also by a group of Saro, who sent petitions to the Foreign Office and to Queen Victoria protesting the annexation. Their pressure succeeded in extracting amendments to the draft treaty. Dosunmu remained a reluctant donor, but he signed after two key articles were added.[79] One allowed the *Oba* to continue to adjudicate disputes between Lagosians, subject to their consent and their right to appeal to British laws.[80] This was a modest concession to the wide powers that accompanied colonial status, which allowed expatriate firms to pursue local debtors in courts under British jurisdiction for the first time. The other article, which followed pressure from the *Idejo* chiefs, who feared that they would lose their rights over the allocation of land, confirmed that the *Oba*'s stamp on documents respecting land transfers remained valid proof that 'there are no other native claims upon it, and for this purpose he will be permitted to use it as hitherto'.[81] Dosunmu appears to have understood that he had ceded political sovereignty, with some reservations, but retained control over the allocation of land.[82] While there was a measure of truth in his interpretation, subsequent developments were to transfer important land rights without reference to the *Oba* or the *Idejo*s. The expansion of the port

74. Wylde, minute, 14 Aug. 1860 on Hand to Russell, F.O. 84/1115.

75. F.O. to Foote, 23 June 1861, F.O. 84/1141.

76. McCoskry to Russell, 7 Aug. 1861, C.O. 147/2.

77. McCoskry to Russell, 7 Aug. 1861, C.O. 147/2.

78. Contemporaries provided different accounts of the sequence of events leading to the treaty and the inclusion of two additional clauses. See Mann, *Slavery and the Birth of an African City*, pp. 101–02; Elebute, *The Life of James Pinson Labulo Davies*, pp. 115–23.

79. The Treaty is reproduced in Smith, *The Lagos Consulate*, pp. 140–41. See also McCoskry to Russell, 7 Aug. 1861, C.O. 147/2.

80. McCoskry to Russell, 5 Oct. 1861, C.O. 147/2; McCoskry to C.O. 15 Oct. 1861, C.O. 147/2; Freeman to Newcastle, 5 March 1862, C.O. 147/1.

81. Article 3, in Smith, *The Lagos Consulate*, p. 141.

82. The complexity of ownership and use rights ensured that they remained controversial for many decades. See, for example, the substantial Colonial Office memo on the subject (including Herbert Macaulay's assessment), Aug. 1912, C.O. 520/120.

and the growth of the mercantile community took precedence over other claims from this time onwards.

Annexation was completed on 6 August 1861, and Lagos formally became a colony on 5 March 1862.[83] The cession was 'carried somewhat against the will of Docemo [*sic*]'; senior chiefs and several prominent Saro were also reluctant to accept that sovereignty had been transferred.[84] The *Idejo*, who were not required to be signatories to the treaty, retained serious doubts about the security of their property rights and continued their protests for several months.[85] Henry Freeman, the first governor of Lagos, explained that the cession did not abolish their rights over land and claimed (in ways he left unspecified) that they would gain from the settlement.[86] The *Idejo* were unconvinced but in the end were obliged to accept the new reality. Dosunmu became a pensioner. His supporters remained reluctant subjects of the Crown and slipped to the margins of the new export trades. Kosoko acknowledged that his time had passed and was allowed to return to Lagos, where he accepted a title and an annual pension of £500.[87] Members of his inner circle, headed by Oshodi Tapa and Taiwo Olowo, had already indicated their willingness to co-operate with the British and profited substantially from their decision.[88] In 1862, when Oshodi Tapa saw steamships in the harbour, he knew that power had shifted irrevocably. 'This is no longer a native town', he observed, 'it is a white man's. We could never do this'.[89]

From the standpoint of this study, the annexation is interesting for revealing not only the importance of property rights in moving the British to act but also for what it says about the attitude of leading members of the Saro community. The first generation of nationalist historians tended to criticise them for being submissive to British interests. Saro leaders were undoubtedly keen

83. McCoskry to Russell, 3 Sept. 1861, C.O. 147/2; Minute, 18 Sept. 1861 on McCoskry to Russell, 7 Aug. 1851, F.O. 84/1141; F.O. to McCoskry, 23 Sept. 1861, F.O. 84/1141.

84. McCoskry to Russell, 7 Aug. 1861, C.O. 147/2. On continuing opposition, see McCoskry to Russell, 3 Sept. 1861 and 5 Oct. 1861, C.O. 147/2; Freeman to Newcastle, 5 March 1862, C.O. 147/1.

85. Freeman to Newcastle, 5 March 1862, C.O. 147/1. The treaty was signed by Dosunmu and four chiefs who gave their names but not their titles. This is a contentious issue. For contrasting views, see Elias, *Nigerian Land Law*, pp. 11–15; Coker, *Family Property*, pp. 182–204.

86. Freeman to Newcastle, 5 March 1862, C.O. 147/1.

87. Freeman to Newcastle, 7 June 1862, C.O. 147/1; Berkeley to Administrator in Chief, 24 May 1873, C.O. 147/27. Kosoko died in Lagos in 1872.

88. Campbell to Malmesbury, 4 March 1859, F.O. 84/1088; McCoskry to Russell, 5 Dec. 1861, C.O. 147/2. Oshodi Tapa had helped the acting governor deal with an attempt to set fire to the town in 1862 and departed (unsurprisingly) 'leaving the best impression'. Edmonstone to Admiralty, 20 Jan. 1862, C.O. 17/2. Mann, *Slavery and the Birth of an African City*, pp. 106–07.

89. McCoskry to Russell, 7 Jan. 1862, C.O. 147/2.

to promote 'civilisation and commerce', the Bible and the plough. They had risked a good deal in returning to Lagos at such an uncertain moment and were understandably anxious to see that 'lives and property' were secured.[90] Their view, however, was that this goal could be achieved without annexation. Governor Freeman portrayed them, in his characteristically exaggerated prose, as being 'that class of Sierra Leone people whose motto is "Africa for the Africans"' and who would 'rejoice to see their benefactors and supporters, the English, either swept from the Coast or subjected to the dominion of the blacks'.[91] Far from being 'lackeys of imperialism', the Saro showed considerable courage in making a stand against 'their benefactors'. The context clarifies their perspective. The first generation of Saro grew up when the universal principles of the Enlightenment pervaded both government policy and missionary activity.[92] Africans were to be civilised so that they could assume the responsibility of running their own affairs in ways that met the Victorian ideal of 'improvement'. The assertive measures that led to annexation were a departure from these assumptions that shocked several influential Saro into opposition. The world of the late nineteenth century, with its pervasive racist ideology, was already in sight, even though only its outlines could be discerned in 1862.

The creation of the Colony of Lagos confirmed changes initiated during the Consulate but also significantly extended them. Colonial status was a guarantee of last resort: from this point on, Britain was obliged to defend the colony from internal subversion and external threats. The new colonial government faced an immediate challenge in 1863, when Dosunmu, drawing on French support, attempted to overturn British authority, but the plan was frustrated. The *Oba* suffered the humiliation of a fine and was deprived of his pension for several months.[93] Thereafter, the colonial government had sufficient authority to maintain political stability in Lagos and its environs. Anxiety was never far from Government House, especially during the Ajasa crisis in the mid-1880s, but attempts of the kind made by Kosoko and Tinubu in the 1850s to unseat the *Oba* and consul were not repeated.

Nevertheless, the reach of the administration remained limited, as did the number of colonial officials. The governor of the new colony was expected to oversee the development of Lagos trade, but had no power to influence independent states in the hinterland, which produced the port's exports and

90. Petition requesting naval presence, 3 Feb. 1859, in Campbell to Malmesbury, 4 Feb. 1859, FO 84/107; petition dated 24 April 1860 in Brand to Russell, 9 April 1860, F.O. 84/1115.

91. Freeman to Newcastle, 31 Dec. 1863, C.O. 147/4; Freeman to Newcastle 9 April 1864, C.O. 147/6.

92. The early history of the efforts to create an 'African middle class' is covered by Everill, *Abolition and Empire*, ch. 2.

93. Cole, *Modern and Traditional Elites*, p. 28.

consumed most of its imports. When Governor Freeman sought permission to conquer Dahomey in 1862, anxiety in the Colonial Office switched to alarm and was speedily translated into a firm rebuke.[94] The authorities in Lagos were also under persistent pressure to increase the revenues of the colony, which came entirely from customs duties, and to extend their influence among the Yoruba states to prevent interruptions to trade. Under the cautious guidance of the Duke of Newcastle (1859–1864), however, the Colonial Office returned to a policy of restraint.[95] Newcastle consistently expressed his 'disapproval of the meddling policy on the coast of Africa'.[96] The orthodoxy of the time held that Lagos should 'be a centre of British influence without being the nucleus of an increasing dominion'.[97] When successive governors resorted to unilateral action to secure control of the small ports scattered along the lagoon, their actions were received with a mixture of resignation and reprimands.[98] Such episodes caused officials in London to wring their hands. 'Lagos is a deadly gift from the Foreign Office', minuted one official.[99] Newcastle concurred.[100]

Although Palmerston remained Prime Minister until 1865, he was preoccupied with larger issues, including the American Civil War, the creation of nation states in Europe, and relations with China and Latin America. The Report of a Select Committee of the House of Commons in that year confirmed the policy of non-intervention.[101] Palmerston's adventurous policy died with him. The plan, to the extent that there was one, was for Lagos to attain by influence what could only be achieved by coercion. In these circumstances, the colonial government relied on local networks to transmit its policies and to help enforce them. As far as diplomatic methods were concerned, the governor followed the tradition of the Obas who preceded him, except that he could also call upon tailor-made intermediaries in the Saro community. The shock

94. Newcastle to Freeman, 22 Aug. 1862, C.O. 147/1; Freeman to Newcastle, 26 Feb. 1863, 2 March 1863, 30 March 1863 and minute by Newcastle, 2 April 1863, C.O. 147/3.

95. Freeman to Newcastle, 10 Dec. 1863, C.O. 147/4; Freeman to Newcastle, 9 March 1864, C.O. 147/6; F.O. to McCoskry, 20 Aug. 1861, F.O. 84/1141; Freeman to Newcastle, 9 Jan. 1864, and minute by Newcastle 17 Jan. 1864, C.O. 147/6. The Colonial Office was taken aback when the War Office produced the first map of the new colony and officials realised that their responsibilities extended to parts of the lagoon beyond the island. C.O. minutes on Freeman to Newcastle, 7 Feb. 1863, C.O. 147/3.

96. Newcastle minute, 18 Jan. 1862, on Burton to F.O. 20 Nov. 1861, C.O. 147/2.

97. Minute by Fortescue, 10 Sept. 1863 on Russell to C.O. 5 Sept. 1863, C.O. 147/5.

98. Newcastle to Freeman, 22 Aug. 1862, C.O. 147/1; Freeman to Newcastle, 26 Feb. 1863, 2 March 1863, 30 March 1863 and minute by Newcastle, 2 April 1863, C.O. 147/3; Glover to Newcastle, 8 August 1863, C.O. 147/4; and the discussion that ensued in Glover to Newcastle, 6 Nov. 1863, C.O. 147/4.

99. C.O. minute, 22 April 1864, on Freeman to Newcastle, 9 Jan. 1864, C.O. 147/6.

100. Minute by Newcastle, 17 Jan. 1864, on Freeman to Newcastle, 9 Jan. 1864, C.O. 147/6.

101. Hargreaves, *Prelude*, pp. 65–90.

administered to Lagos between 1851 and 1861 set the boundaries of policy until 1892, when British forces invaded Yoruba country.

Colonial status finally gave entrepreneurs the confidence they needed to invest in the future of the port. Some changes were already under way before the 1850s in response to Britain's efforts to suppress the slave trade.[102] Slave-traders began to establish permanent bases on shore to speed turnaround; increased sailings, aimed at avoiding interception, allowed smaller traders to hire cargo space. Inevitably, however, many improvements still lay ahead. The sandbar remained a frustrating and shifting obstacle that restricted entry to ships with a shallow draft and limited capacity.[103] Land transport was unchanged until railway construction began at the close of the century. Trans-actions were still conducted by a combination of barter and cowries until the 1880s; modern banking was deferred until the 1890s. Yet the changes that occurred in the 1850s and 1860s went a long way towards reducing the costs and boosting the volume of the import and export trades.

One of the most important, and certainly the most familiar, of the novel-ties affecting business prospects was the advent of steamship services, which began in the 1850s but became more frequent and reliable from the 1860s.[104] Large vessels still had to anchor outside the harbour and trans-ship freight across the bar, which was a costly procedure. Nevertheless, steamships brought about a fundamental change in the organisation of business. They separated shipping from commercial functions, increased freight capacity, reduced sail-ing times, and cut costs.[105] Individual merchants could lease cargo space that approximated their needs. Firms in Europe were able to appoint local com-mission agents to receive manufactured goods and ship produce.[106] These developments stimulated competition. Small firms that lacked the financial

102. See Kristin Mann, *Transatlantic Lives: Slavery and Freedom in West Africa and Brazil* (forthcoming), ch. 3. See also the complementary study by Ojo, 'Organization of the Atlantic Slave Trade'.

103. Rees to Secretary of State, 28 Feb. 1879, C.O. 806/130, stated that vessels of 400 tons could cross the bar when towed by steam tugs. The new governor, Henry Freeman, reported his experience of 'the terrors of the bar' when he first arrived. Freeman to Newcas-tle, 10 Feb. 1862, 147/1. Access to the harbour remained a constant problem throughout the century. Correspondence on the subject took up acres of space in the official records. See, for example, Coode & Matthews, to Crown Agents, 21 April 1892, enc. in C.A. to C.O., 25 May 1892, C.O. 147; Egerton to Crewe, 17 May 1910, C.O. 520/93; Mary Kingsley recorded her uncomfortable experience crossing the bar in *Travels in West Africa*, p. 77.

104. For an overview see Olukoju, 'The Port of Lagos', in Bosa, *Atlantic Ports*, ch. 6; Davies, *The Trade Makers*, chs. 1–3; Lynn provides a detailed account in *Commerce and Economic Change*, ch. 6, though his evidence relates more to the Delta than to Lagos.

105. In the seventeenth century, the voyage from London to West Africa took about three months. By the middle of the nineteenth century, the time had been cut to 35 days; by 1920, it was down to 14 days. McPhee, *The Economic Revolution*, p. 129.

106. The variety and evolution of the system are examined by Chapman, 'Agency Houses'.

resources needed to invest in sailing ships could enter the import and export trades for the first time. Business shifted decisively from ships and wharves to permanent warehouses, known locally as factories. Some barracoons were adapted to store puncheons of palm oil instead of slaves; new buildings, typically with shops attached, housed imported goods.

Contemporaries understood the implications of these developments. In 1870, the Liverpool firm of Kidd McCoskry wrote to Daniel Taiwo, the Lagos merchant, to solicit his business: 'The facilities now offered by the frequent and regular visits of steamers to your port induces [*sic*] us to call your attention to the great advantages to be derived by shipping your produce to us direct and entrusting us with the execution of your orders for goods'.[107] This was the moment when small firms in both locations had an unprecedented opportunity to participate directly in international trade.

Settling In: The Town and Its Inhabitants

The inhabitants of Lagos were a cosmopolitan group. Diversity was evident long before the cession of Lagos, but colonial status attracted immigrants by improving security, reducing fears of enslavement, and creating opportunities in legitimate forms of commerce. The number and variety of migrants from the hinterland and more distant regions continued to increase during the rest of the century. From the 1850s onwards, the most visible newcomers were Europeans, Saro, and Brazilians, whose numbers were small but whose influence was considerable. Even so, it is worth emphasising that immigrants from the interior, though largely unrecorded and unheard, accounted for most of the port's rapid growth. A report on the port's mixed population in 1879 listed 'Yorubas, Binis, Ijebus, Egbas, Ifes, Effios, Tapas, Hausas, Ketus, Awories, and Popos', among many others.[108] This degree of mobility raises questions about the term 'indigenous', which is frequently used but not easily defined. It will be applied here to refer to long-established Lagosians whose families were settled before the colony was established. The alternative of confining the term to lineages or families that were present since the foundation has commendable purity but faces insuperable difficulties in establishing claims to such great antiquity.

Lagos continued to grow during the 20 years that followed the creation of the colony. In the absence of an official and well-conducted census, population figures are no more than guesswork. Giambattista Scala, who visited the town

107. Kidd McCoskry to Taiwo, 24 Oct. 1870, Taiwo Papers (TP), Lagos Affairs, 1870–1902.

108. Lees to Secretary of State, 28 Feb. 1879, C.O. 806/130. I have been unable to identify 'Effios' or possible variants among the 371 ethnic groups in Nigeria. 'Yorubas' was a term often used at that time to refer to Ibadans.

in 1851, guessed that the total was around 20,000; in 1863, Richard Burton put it between 20,000 and 30,000.[109] An official estimate recorded the total for the 'town and island' as 35,000 in 1868 and drew attention to the large numbers of people who were constantly moving in and out of the town.[110] The first government census, conducted in 1872, arrived at a total of 36,005, though the figure covered Lagos 'and its vicinity'.[111] Of this number, eighty-two were Europeans (seventy-seven males and five females). The census of 1881 put the total at 37,452, though subsequent enquiry showed that this figure was almost certainly an overstatement.[112] The census of 1881 also provided a breakdown of occupations, which showed, unsurprisingly, that 'merchants, trades, agents, clerks, and shopmen' were easily the largest single group, reaching a total of 11,049.[113] Growth had also propelled change. Elite occupations expanded after the colony was established: by 1881, there were 399 'civil servants' and 348 members of the 'professions'. Since the white population was listed as numbering 117, some of whom were in business, it is evident that the majority of the civil servants and professionals were Africans who had a command of English, namely the Saro. Islam was already outstripping Christianity. In 1863, Burton guessed that there were about eight hundred Muslims in the town. This was an understatement. A Chief Iman and a central mosque were already present by the 1840s; the census of 1881 estimated that 36 per cent of the population were Muslims.[114]

Foreign visitors were not impressed. John Whitford, who first visited Lagos in 1853, thought it 'very primitive . . . a filthy, disgusting, savage place'.[115] Robert Campbell, a West Indian who would later settle in Lagos, recorded a calmer impression of the town following a visit made in 1859:

> In African native cities there are no streets such as would be called so in
> a civilized country. The houses or compounds are scattered according
> to the discretion or taste of their owners; lanes, always crooked, and

109. Smith, *Memoirs of Giambattista Scala*, p. 13; Richard Francis Burton, *Wanderings*, Vol. 2, p. 225. All population figures for this period should be treated as orders of magnitude. The population was permanently mobile, especially during the trading season, and there was no effective census. In 1863, the governor estimated the population to be around forty thousand, Freeman to Cardwell, 4 July 1864, C.O. 147/6. A similar caution applies to estimates of religious affiliations. In 1853, Frazer estimated that three-quarters of the population were Muslim. Frazer to Malmesbury, 11 March 1853, F.O. 84/920. If later figures are preferred, Frazer's estimate becomes an exaggeration.

110. Glover to Kennedy, 14 Sept. 1868, C.O. 147/14.

111. Lees to Secretary of State, 28 Feb, 1879, C.O. 806/130.

112. Enc. in Moloney to Kimberley, 6 June 1882, C.O. 147/49; *Lagos Times*, 28 Sept. 1881. See also chapter 5.

113. The census listed the second largest group as 'trades, manufacturers, mechanics, and artisans' (5,173), though without explaining why 'trades' should appear in two categories.

114. *Lagos Times*, 14 Sept. 1881.

115. Whitford, *Trading Life*, p. 87.

frequently very narrow, being left between them. These dwellings are sometimes very large, including in many instances accommodations for from twenty to two hundred inmates, especially in those of some of the wealthier chiefs, which are sometimes tenanted by over three hundred people.[116]

Burton, a remarkable linguist and a perceptive, if also prejudiced, commentator, recorded his opinion in 1863 that 'the site of the town is really detestable'.[117] The Consulate was 'a corrugated iron coffin or plank-lined morgue containing a dead consul once a year'.[118] The town itself, with its clay houses, narrow lanes, and thatched roofs, was 'squalid and dirty', though redeemed to some extent by trees and greenery.[119] Lagosians fared little better: 'this mangy people appeared to me a merry race of pagans'.[120] Even so, Burton preferred 'natural' Africans to those who seemed set on assimilating Western ways. Many of the Saro, he thought, were 'indebted to the natives', owned slaves and were occasional slave-dealers.[121] Hutchinson, who visited Lagos shortly before Burton did, took a more indulgent view of the town and its inhabitants, noting the sandy streets lined with trees, whitewashed houses made of sun-dried mud bricks, the 'impressively arranged' goods in the shops, and the flowing robes of the people.[122] Whitford, who returned to the town in 1875, acknowledged that improvements had been made but nevertheless concluded that 'it is not a pleasant place, for you can tell in which direction it lies, long before seeing it'.[123]

Whitford listed the changes he observed since his first visit to Lagos in 1853, nearly all of them appearing since Burton's time there at the start of the 1860s.[124] Some of the developments he described can be seen in map 2.1, which shows the northwestern tip of the island in 1883. A more complete map, based on that of 1883, was drawn two years later and shows that spaces in the middle of the island that were left empty in 1883 in fact contained streets and settlements. Unfortunately for present purposes, nineteenth-century maps were designed to be spread out on a table and lose detail if they are compressed to fit the pages of a modern book. Faced with a choice between accuracy and legibility, I have opted for the latter because the map drawn in 1883 clearly shows the areas that were at the centre of the new enterprise of legitimate commerce.

116. Quoted in Brown, 'Public Health in Lagos', p. 338.
117. Burton, *Wanderings*, Vol. 2, p. 212.
118. Burton, *Wanderings*, Vol. 2, p. 213.
119. Burton, *Wanderings*, Vol. 2, p. 223.
120. Burton, *Wanderings*, Vol. 2, p. 224.
121. Burton, *Wanderings*, Vol. 2, p. 215.
122. Hutchinson, *Impressions of Western Africa*, p. 75.
123. Whitford, *Trading Life*, p. 87.
124. Whitford, *Trading Life*, pp. 86–106.

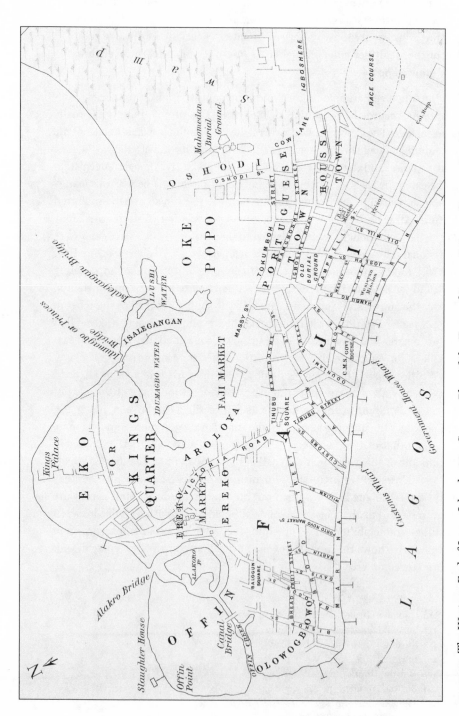

MAP 2.1. The Western End of Lagos Island, 1883. Source: Plan of the Town of Lagos, C.O. 700/Lagos 9/1, with permission of the National Archives, U.K.

The permanence and heightened visibility of the colonial presence were evident in novelties such as Government House, the court house, customs house, barracks, a prison, racecourse and cemetery, and the creation of a police force to oversee the new establishment.[125] The Marina and Broad Street had been reclaimed and laid out. Churches and mosques had sprung up. Large walled compounds, known as factories, had been built with one entry point, which was guarded by a policeman, a trading store at the front with living accommodation above, a courtyard with workshops inside for coopers, carpenters, and blacksmiths, and space for processing palm oil, packing palm kernels, ginning cotton, and receiving visiting traders.[126] Whitford also remarked on how 'industrious' the women of Lagos were.[127] They performed 'most of the hard work', 'tilling the soil and buying and selling in the markets'.[128] In an observation that has proved to be timeless, he recorded how the formidable traders of the future were formed, beginning with the little girl who learned to carry heavy loads by balancing 'an empty bottle on her head'.[129] The population included numerous ethnicities and an increased number of Muslims, some of whom, he noted, wore green turbans to signify that they had made the pilgrimage to Mecca.[130]

Alfred Ellis, who visited Lagos in 1880, also reported on the town in terms that contrasted with descriptions given 20 or more years earlier.[131] After crossing the bar, Ellis could see that the town had 'quite a business-like appearance'.[132] By this time, the Marina, 'with its trees and white houses', extended along a 'frontage of some two miles'.[133] Prosperity had produced an elite of 'haughty aristocrats' who had migrated from Sierra Leone and other parts of the West Coast. Wealthy merchants kept horses and traps, though sandy roads confined their outings mainly to the Marina. An exclusive club, the 'Flower of Lagos', brought members of the elite together for social occasions, including concerts and balls, which displayed their conformity to Victorian etiquette. The civilising mission had struck roots.

---

125. At this date, the buildings were not as imposing as they were to become. Writing in 1873, the Administrator in charge of the colony referred to the prison as 'a collection of miserable mud huts with thatched roofs', while Government House and the Court House were 'both in a state of decay', with leaking roofs and 'defective drains'. Strahan to Administrator in Chief, 18 Nov. 1873, C.O. 147/28.

126. Whitford, *Trading Life*, pp. 90–91.

127. Whitford, *Trading Life*, p. 92.

128. Whitford, *Trading Life*, p. 92.

129. Whitford, *Trading Life*, p. 92.

130. Whitford, *Trading Life*, p. 90.

131. Ellis, *The Land of Fetish*. Ellis joined a long line of commentators in disparaging the Victorian Saro.

132. Ellis, *The Land of Fetish*, p. 73.

133. Ellis, *The Land of Fetish*, pp. 75–8.

Residents, unlike visitors, had additional insights. In 1878, the smallpox epidemic then 'raging' prompted a petition from forty Saro asking for measures to improve the 'defective sanitary arrangements'.[134] Some parts of the town, they claimed, 'are so offensive that it is hardly possible to get through without a painful effort. The olfactory nerves are shocked by the stench from decayed vegetable matter, water used for dyeing and other purposes, and from dead animals in a state of decomposition'.[135] This problem, combined with the consequences of a large fire in the same year, provided an incentive to improve sanitation and widen roads to create firebreaks.[136] Costs ensured that these works remained 'in progress' for many years to come.[137]

Little is known about the social distribution of purchasing power in the town, but the indications are that the dualism that distinguished the Old Town from the New was reinforced during this period rather than eroded. Evidence of the spread of land sales and mortgages to sections of Lagos well outside Olowogbowo and the Marina indicates that change was under way, but it is impossible to say at present how far the trend was linked to improvement, to the confirmation of existing rights, or to expropriation favouring wealthy landowners. Meanwhile, the arrival of migrants and refugees increased the pressure on resources and may have held down potential increases in average living standards.[138] As the area around the Marina developed, the Old Town continued to suffer from overcrowding, contaminated water, and disease, while the numerous fires that caught hold of the thatched roofs were partly deterred from reaching New Lagos by Broad Street and the large stretches of swampland that separated the two sections of the island.[139] One fire in 1871 destroyed 'several hundred houses'; another, shortly afterwards, ruined 'nearly one sixth of the town'.[140] The problem persisted until the early twentieth century, when thatched roofs were replaced by corrugated iron.[141] As purchasing power expanded, the range of imports—from building materials to 'boots and shoes'—grew commensurately, but most of these were found in New Lagos. There were few brick buildings in the Old Town; horses and traps were unknown; most feet were unshod; Europeans were rarely seen.[142]

134. Petition, 21 Jan. 1978, enc. in Dumaresq to Freeling, 9 Feb. 1878, C.O. 147/35.

135. Petition, 21 Jan. 1978, enc. in Dumaresq to Freeling, 9 Feb. 1878, C.O. 147/35.

136. Bigon, *History of Urban Planning*, part I, chs. 1–2.

137. Dumaresq to Freeling, 9 Feb. 1878, C.O. 147/35; Moloney to Lees, 8 March 1879, C.O. 147/37.

138. These speculations are offered to encourage others to investigate the history of inner Lagos in greater detail.

139. C. Onyeke Nwamunobi, 'Incendiarism'.

140. Glover to Kennedy, 18 Oct. 1871, C.O. 147/21.

141. See also Banner Bros to Board of Trade, 6 April 1863, C.O. 147/5; Banner Bros to C.O. 8 Nov. 1864, C.O. 147/7; Moloney to Granville, 23 Aug.1886, C.O. 147/54; *Lagos Times*, 28 March 1883.

142. Even as late as 1961, when I first made my way on foot through Odunfa to the Old Town, I was greeted with amazement by children, many of whom ran away crying, and

The leading import and export merchants established warehouses and shops in a discontinuous line stretching along the Marina southwards from Olowogbowo.[143] In 1860, the development extended for about one mile; by 1880, it was closer to two miles. Figure 2.3, though incomplete, provides a sense of this development in the 1870s. By then, too, many gaps that were present in 1860 had been filled: some of the smaller swamps had been reclaimed; other unoccupied land had been taken up, notably by government buildings. The warehouses built by substantial merchants took the form of self-contained compounds of the kind described by Whitford in 1875; smaller merchants erected two-storey brick houses with display counters at the front.[144] Numerous short piers had been constructed to allow small boats and canoes to tie up where goods could be off-loaded close to the Marina and carried to warehouses at minimal risk and cost.

Contemporary accounts inevitably expressed the personalities of individuals and the values of their time and should be treated with care, as should similar views expressed by many colonial officials. Visitors also recorded more information about what might be called New Lagos than about the Old Town (*Isaleko*), where most Lagosians lived and few Europeans ventured. The imbalance reflected a growing divergence between the two. The Old Town was located in the northeast of the island, faced the mainland, and remained unchanged in layout and structure, which consisted of networks of family compounds joined rather than separated by narrow streets, the whole having evolved in what has been appropriately termed 'Yoruba freestyle'.[145] By contrast, New Lagos was in the northwest, looked towards the harbour, and was the centre of a construction boom that began in the 1860s (and has continued ever since) that aimed at bringing the formality of English and Brazilian urban styles to the tropics.[146] Stretches of swampland divided the two; unmade streets, tracks, and scattered housing ensured that they remained in communication.

Like many other port cities, the attractions of Lagos were functional rather than aesthetic. Although the island covered just under four square miles, the

---

with some concern by adults who thought I might be a tax collector. This experience, after a century of British rule, left me with an enduring insight into the character and reach of the colonial government.

143. Except where otherwise notified, the information in the following five paragraphs is drawn from a wide variety of sources that cannot be listed in full at this point but will be referred to in detailed examples in this and the following chapter. Sources that should be mentioned here include the John Holt Papers, Lagos newspapers, and court records. Among specific references are: *Lagos Times*, 23 March and 27 July 1881; West v. Taiwo and Dawudu, LSCR, Civ. 7, 1888; Rothlisberger v. Fabre, LSCR, Civ. 8, 1888; Rylands & Sons v. J.S.B. Cole, LSCR, Civ. 23, 1899.

144. Whitford, *Trading Life*, pp. 86–106.

145. Bigon, 'Sanitation and Street Layout', p. 254.

146. Based on right angles (formally known as orthogonal).

FIGURE 2.3. View of the Marina Looking Northwest, 1870s. Engraving by an unknown artist; permission from Mary Evans Picture Library, ID 10225310.

population was concentrated in the Old Town, which occupied less than one-third of the area. Much of the rest of the low-lying, sandy island was taken up by mangroves, swamps, and creeks. The water was brackish; sanitation was primitive; malaria and poverty were endemic. Yet, adjusting for latitude, underlying conditions in British ports at that time were scarcely superior. Subsequently, the colonial government directed most of its limited resources towards new settlements that were located well outside the Old Town, which remained largely unchanged, except in size, for the rest of the century.[147] Development accentuated the contrast between the two sections of the town. New Lagos was supposed to be a beacon for the civilising mission. The inhabitants of the Old Town could see the light; following the way was a far harder and not an entirely appealing task.

The Saro Draw Lines in the Sand

The Saro community in Lagos began to take shape as these events were unfolding. They were well placed to capitalise on the opportunities that followed the decision to establish a consulate in Lagos. In their eyes, proximity to their Yoruba homeland and the promise of British protection easily outweighed the strikingly unattractive features of the town. Repatriation began as early as the 1830s, when a band of freed slaves left Freetown and returned to Abeokuta, the Egba capital, which was regarded as a more promising base for advancing the 'civilising mission' than the slave-trading port of Lagos.[148] Once the consulate had been established, the flow of newcomers increased. In 1853, Campbell reported that 'many' Saro had arrived in Lagos. These, he said with satisfaction, were 'the better class of Africans . . . who have attained correct notions of right and wrong'.[149] Several of the European firms, however, expressed their opposition to a development that was likely to increase competition in what was still a new and experimental trade.[150] Their anxiety was well founded. Larger numbers of repatriates followed in 1861, when the consulate became a colony.

The Saro were a mixed group.[151] The self-defined elite among them commended themselves to the British by their education, their adherence to Christianity and their acceptance of Victorian values. A few had already earned money from trade; most made their start after they arrived. Others used their education to enter government service, the Church, and, before long, the legal and medical professions. Many other members of the community remained

147. Bigon, 'Sanitation and Street Layout', pp. 247–69.
148. Forbes to Admiralty, 10 April 1852, F.O. 84/893.
149. Campbell to Clarendon, 11 Aug. 1855, F.O. 84/1002.
150. Campbell to Clarendon, 2 June 1857, F.O. 2/50.
151. Mann, *Marrying*, ch. 1; Mann, *Slavery and the Birth of an African City*, pp. 124–5.

poor, had little knowledge of the English language, and experienced few of the advantages that the British claimed would flow to the new order. The best available assessment indicates that Saro accounted for almost three-quarters of the Lagos elite in 1880.[152] Nearly 60 per cent of this number were merchants, 20 per cent were civil servants, and 11 per cent were in the professions. About 60 per cent had received secondary or more advanced education. In these ways, the Saro acquired a rare and invaluable resource: the skills needed to negotiate a path to and through the new British order and privileged access to information in the highest reaches of government. This advantage complemented their knowledge of Yoruba and their connections with their homelands. At this time, too, they held an asset denied to most expatriates: they had greater immunity to tropical diseases. Their inherited defence gave them greater longevity and, in principle, the advantages that accompanied continuity in both business and politics.

One hundred and thirty families of 'self-emancipated Africans from the Brazils' also reached Lagos in 1853.[153] Few of them had much capital, but a handful of individuals prospered in trade with Bahia. The wider community became well known as builders and skilled craftsmen. Permanent settlement began in 1847, following a visit to Brazil made by Oshodi Tapa, who was acting on the authority of Kosoko.[154] In 1853, Consul Campbell offered repatriates from Brazil protection and issued them British passports, even though they were not British citizens.[155] Official support encouraged more Brazilians to settle; more than six hundred newcomers arrived from Bahia during the 1870s; by 1887, their numbers had risen to 3,221.[156] They created a distinct community bound together by the Portuguese language, Roman Catholicism, Afro-Brazilian spiritual practices, and the proximity fostered by living in their own quarter, which was located between the Marina and the Old Town and grouped around what became Campos Square.

The Saro established their headquarters on a modestly 'elevated and airy part of the waterside', known as Olowogbowo.[157] Their choice was determined

152. The evidence here and in the next two sentences is from Mann, *Marrying Well*, pp. 25–34.

153. Most were Yoruba from Egba country. Campbell to Clarendon, 4 May 1854, F.O. 84/950.

154. Moloney to Holland, 20 July 1887, C.O. 147/59.

155. Campbell to Clarendon, 28 Dec. 1853, F.O. 84/920. See also the overview by Lindsay, '"To Return to the Bosom of Their Fatherland"', pp. 26–7; Omenka, 'The Afro-Brazilian Repatriates'.

156. Castillo, 'Mapping', pp. 51–2; Law, 'Yoruba Liberated Slaves', in *The Yoruba Diaspora*, p. 356.

157. The name has a common derivation and some minor variations. The most authentic is that given by T. W. Johnson, who was able to recall the early settlement from his own experience. His account translates as 'the water claims his money from the debtors', which is evidence of the commercial character of the area and of its susceptibility to flooding

mainly by the fact that the area was unoccupied and had become one of the town's rubbish dumps.[158] Some of Kosoko's entourage had settled there in the 1840s, but they made a hurried exit with their leader after the failed coup of 1852. Akitoye had already allocated land there to Daddy Savage, the senior figure among the early returnees, in recognition of the support he and his followers had shown him. Savage then distributed plots to other members of the small Saro community.[159] In 1854, Gollmer, the head of the CMS, appealed to Akitoye's successor, Dosunmu, on behalf of the Saro, but the new *Oba* did not need persuading to see the advantage of placing a new set of potential supporters on land previously occupied by some of his opponents.[160] Reciprocally, the Saro, like the Brazilians, acquired a solid reason for backing Dosunmu and the British, who had become the ultimate guardians of political stability. At this time, Lagos had some of the attributes of the Wild West, where law and order were not guaranteed and the uncertain frontier carried risks that matched its opportunities. The merchants of Olowogbowo who were beginning their careers did not enjoy the immediate rewards of a 'lucky strike' of gold or oil. They were close to the harbour but pursuing an uncertain trade in palm oil, lacking roads, and relying on canoes and porters, while also trying to prevent their rudimentary houses and stores from catching fire or being flooded.

By the mid-1850s, a few Europeans had also taken sites along the nearby waterfront, which ran for 'at least a mile' and was unoccupied.[161] This, too, was an adventurous act. Essentially, it was a gamble on the ability of the consul to maintain stability in the face of a former *Oba* who hoped to recover his throne and a restored *Oba* who hoped to regain his independence. Europeans also faced the even greater risk of an early death at a time when tropical diseases had not yet been brought under control.[162] It was only after the declaration of colonial status that confidence rose to investment point and put land values on an almost permanent upward trajectory.

Difficulties arose because Dosunmu's grants were inconsistently worded, and the boundaries they referred to were inaccurately drawn. 'Underhand dealing', as Freeman put it, combined with incompetence, created disorder and led to

---

at high tide. Evidence of T. W. Johnson in Att. General v. John Holt & Co. Ltd., and Att. General v. McIver & Co. Ltd., LSCR, Civ. 55, 1909. Deniga has a similar interpretation, though from different sources: Deniga, *Notes on Lagos Streets*, p. 4. The area is also called Apongbon, which is said to be a quasi-Yoruba reference to Consul McCoskry's red beard.

158. Deniga, *Notes on Lagos Streets*, pp. 4–5.

159. Evidence of Isaac H. Willoughby, who had lived in Lagos since 1852 and was Superintendent of Police under Governor Glover, 1860–72, in David Macaulay v. Christie & Co., LSCR, Civ. 5, 1882.

160. See, for example, Campbell to Clarendon, 1 June 1854, F.O. 84/950.

161. Campbell to Gollmer, 1 May 1854, F.O. 84/950; Campbell to Clarendon, 27 July 1853, F.O. 84/920.

162. Quinine was only just beginning to be used at this time as a defence against malaria. On this subject, see Curtin, *Disease and Empire*.

disputed claims.[163] After the cession of Lagos, Dosunmu's grants were called in and a new form of authorisation, known as a crown grant, was issued in 1863 to occupiers whose plots had been surveyed and their claims to possession substantiated. Although the Commissioners made a start, they were unable to remove all the inconsistencies, and in 1869 an ordinance was passed to settle outstanding claims and give validity to possessory titles.[164] The main provision allowed anyone who had been in possession of land for a period of three years before the date of the ordinance to apply for a crown grant under a simplified procedure. To accelerate the transition, the ordinance required claimants to obtain a valid grant within six months or risk having their land revert to the crown. Consequently, Dosunmu's remaining grants were converted to crown grants with unusual speed. In this way, Yoruba land law was adapted to fit British concepts of property rights, with consequences that still reverberate today.

Crown grants were permeated by ambiguities. The formal position, accepted subsequently by the Lagos Supreme Court, was that the *Oba's* land rights were transferred to the crown when his territories became a British colony.[165] The principle, however, left room for uncertainties over the extent of Britain's jurisdiction and raised complex issues, such as inheritance and the disposition of family land, that became apparent as disputes were brought before the courts.[166] The key distinction that Governor Glover and *Oba* Akitoye appear to have had in mind was between unoccupied land, for which crown grants could be issued, and occupied land, which they assumed would remain under Yoruba law. Crown grants issued for occupied land became the subject of innumerable court cases right through the colonial period.[167] Nevertheless, though crown grants covered just over half of the inhabited land on the island, they applied to virtually all the previously unoccupied land in New Lagos, the burgeoning commercial centre, where the most valuable

163. Fenn to Newcastle, 16 April 1863, C.O. 147/5; Freeman to Newcastle, 9 Oct. 1862, C.O. 147/1; Freeman to Newcastle, 3 June 1863, C.O. 147/5; Freeman to Cardwell, 9 July 1864, C.O.147/6.

164. The ordinance and its history are discussed in Denton to Chamberlain, 4 October 1898, C.O. 147/135. The ordinance was suspended for a while in 1870. C.O. to Kennedy, 30 Oct. 1870, C.O. 147/16.

165. See, for example, the Chief Justice's ruling in Ajose v. Efunde & Ors, 1 July 1892, LSCR, Civ. 12, 1892. The judgement included the statement that, after 1861, those with vested rights and in possession for 30 years could claim a crown grant. The ruling was confirmed definitively by the Judgment of the Privy Council in deciding the Appeal in Attorney General of Southern Nigeria v. John Holt & Co., 9 Feb. 1915.

166. Omoniregun v. Sadatu, LSCR, Civ. 8, 1888; In the Matter of the Estate of Hotonu, Deceased, LSCR, Civ. 9, 1889.

167. Denton to Chamberlain, 4 Oct. 1898, C.O. 147/135. It is also the case that many transactions were confirmed by verbal agreement or written documents other than crown grants.

plots were located. The all-important consequence was that land individually acquired became treated as if it were held in fee simple. Once this step had been taken and accepted, the way was clear for individuals to deploy land to guarantee credit, repay debt, or sell for a profit. Dosunmu had hoped to use land to secure followers; after 1862, the followers became owners who, in a sense, dispossessed him.

A total of 3,438 crown grants were issued between 1863 and 1891 (inclusive).[168] Contrary to reasonable expectations, the rate of issue did not gather pace with the passage of time but accelerated during the early years of the colonial period and dwindled thereafter. No fewer than 2,914 grants were issued between 1863 and 1873. Dosunmu's grants accounted for seventy-six of the total; an additional but unknown number were grants issued by the British consul and exchanged as a result of the incentives offered by the ordinance of 1869. Although precision is not to hand, evidence of a great land rush during the decade after the creation of the colony is incontestable. An analysis of the names of the grantees given in the index covering crown grants issued between 1863 and 1882 suggests that, of the total of about 3,500, approximately one hundred grants were issued to European merchants and missionaries, 1,100 to Christian Africans, and the rest, roughly 2,300, to indigenous Lagosians.[169] The last figure stands out because it is unexpected. Evidently, indigenous landholders were quick to see the merit of acquiring land and attributing property values to themselves, even though they lacked the advantages that gave the Saro a head start. As palm oil began to bring democracy to the export trade, crown grants started to carry the concept of freehold land down the social order and eventually into the hinterland as well.

The examples that follow are just a small sample of the vast and still largely untapped records of land transactions in Lagos. They have been selected to indicate the social diversity, geographical range, and frequency of property deals in the early days of the colony.[170] Taken together, they provide evidence, which is normally hidden from sight, of the start of the profound transformation that was to sweep through the whole town during the second half of the century.

The first volume of the Lands Office records, which covers the year 1862, provides evidence not only of the number of transactions but also of their variety and rapid turnover.[171] These features can be explained by the ubiquitous use of the term 'mortgage', which was applied, not to long-term house purchase, but

168. Denton to Chamberlain, 4 Oct. 1898, C.O. 147/135. Although Denton was writing in 1898, his evidence was taken from a survey made in 1891.

169. Calculated from the Lands Office records in Lagos.

170. To the best of my knowledge, only two historians, myself and Kristin Mann, have sampled these records. Although our focus is different, there is sufficient overlap to suggest that our conclusions are similar.

171. Lagos Lands Office records (LLOR), Lagos, Vol. 1, 1862.

to short-term credit for commercial purposes. At the top end of the scale, Isaac Willoughby, a Saro merchant and colonial official, mortgaged three houses in 1862 to William McCoskry, the former consul turned trader, to secure a debt of £151 and a new advance of £291 at an annual interest rate of 10 per cent.[172] At the foot of the scale, Hannah Cooper, a peddler, owed Thomas Cole, a Saro merchant, seven bags of cowries (£12) but was unable to pay the debt. She then assigned her land and house to Cole on condition that they would be returned to her if she settled the debt within three months.[173]

Outright sales were also common, especially, it seems, in the early years of the colony, when desirable land was still readily available. In 1862, for example, Korowo, 'a native of Lagos', sold 'all his right and title to and possession of the premises' at Olowogbowo to Banner Bros., a British firm, for thirty bags of cowries (£49).[174] Presumably, Korowo, who was illiterate, understood the essence of the transaction, even though he may not have grasped all the legal niceties of 8 & 9 Vict, cap.199, 'an act to facilitate the conveyance of real property', which appeared routinely in most of the property sales in Lagos. Banner Bros. continued to trade, but the business failed in the 1880s, and at that point the firm sold a crown grant it had held since 1863 to the colonial government, which needed additional office space on the Marina. The crown grant cost nothing; in 1887, the government paid the firm £8,000 for the property.[175]

By the 1870s, land sales had spread well beyond the Marina, Broad Street, and the most favoured parts of Olowogbowo and also far down the social scale. In 1862, for example, Henry Robbin, who was instrumental in developing exports of raw cotton, purchased land at Balogun Street from two farmers, Abracca and Brimah, for 190 heads of cowries. Although there was no mention of a crown grant, the owners claimed to be 'seized and well possessed' of the land.[176] In 1868, James W. Cole, then only twenty-four years old and at the outset of his career, bought a crown grant covering land at Balogun Square from a carpenter named J. W. Davies for £38.[177] Subsequently, Cole became a Big Man in every sense and acquired the nickname 'Cole Bamba'.

It was in the 1870s, too, that J.A.O. Payne, a Saro who was appointed Chief Registrar in 1867, began to formalise and extend the list of street names in the town.[178] Novel names mingled with local ones to mark the spread of habitation in the large area between Old and New Lagos. These included Alli Street,

172. LLOR, 1/205, 1862.

173. LLOR, 1/20, 1862.

174. LLOR, 1/2, 1862.

175. Evans to Holland, 11 March 1887, C.O. 147/58; C.O. to Banner Bros., 11 Feb. 1887, C.O. 147/62. The firm had improved the plot since acquiring it. but it is impossible to know if the premises were an asset to the government.

176. LLOR, 1/77, 1862.

177. LLOR, 5/126, 1868.

178. Deniga, *Notes on Lagos Streets*.

Apongbon Street, Balogun Square, Bishop Street, Breadfruit Street, Odunfa Street, Oluwole Street, Tinubu Square, and Victoria Street. Among many other names were those of prominent merchants, such as Davies Street, Osodi Street, and Taiwo Street. The process was extended in the 1870s and 1880s to the island of Iddo and the nearby mainland at Ebute Metta. Government agencies benefitted from having these fixed identities. Private interests also gained, not least in the assurance it gave to property transactions.

Lagosians other than Saro were active in developing the land market outside prime sites. Prominent merchants, such as Sumanu Animashaun and Brimah Apatira, acquired substantial portfolios from the 1860s onwards, covering a wide area of Lagos. In 1872, for example, Animashaun bought land at Oluwale Street from one Momu (who held a crown grant), for 60 bags of cowries (£37. 10s.). Relatively small sums were regularly covered by mortgages. In 1873, Idowu Yeyeju owed Apatira 240 heads of cowries (£15), which he was unable to pay. His father, Gbasi, came to the rescue by mortgaging a crown grant he held for a plot in Alli Street. The debt was paid later in the year and the property released to its owner. In 1876, Fagbemi (whose family reappears later in this study under the name Dawodu), bought land in Apongbon Street from Charles Forsythe, the Saro lawyer, for £200.[179] Otherwise unknown Lagosians were also busy buying and selling property. When Chief Oshodi Tapa died in 1868, his slaves claimed possession of the twenty-one compounds they occupied in Epedeto and quickly acquired crown grants for them.[180] In 1871, one Ayorinde bought land at Idunshagbe Street from Thomas Lewis, 'a labourer', for £130.[181] How a labourer came to own property worth £130 and how the obscure Ayorinde acquired the money to buy it are intriguing but now unanswerable questions.

The creation of crown grants and freehold tenure entailed complementary reforms in the procedures for dealing with debt. Successive commentators were quick to deplore the 'irresponsible' lending and widespread indebtedness that characterised the commerce of Lagos.[182] However, the credit 'system', as it was known, was a commercial necessity in a market where capital was scarce, business was conducted through chains of intermediaries, and turnover was slow. Without credit, the volume of business would have been much smaller. Yoruba law dealt with the repayment of debt by securing credit on livestock, personal belongings, rights to produce, and pledges of labour, but these sanctions were of little use to expatriate firms and of slight value to Saro merchants. Where credit was based on personal relations and effective

179. LLOR, 25/89, 1876.
180. *Representations of the Oshodi Chieftaincy Family*, p. 15. Nigeria, *The Epetedo Lands*, p. 15.
181. LLOR, 13/102, 1871.
182. *Lagos Times*, 10 Aug. 1881; *Lagos Standard*, 'The African Trader', 15 Nov. 1899, 22 Nov. 1899; 13 Dec. 1899.

sanctions were limited, default was an option and one that grew as the scale of trade and the number of traders expanded.

The efforts made to overcome these problems during the consular period foundered on the twin difficulties of devising negotiable forms of security and agreeing effective means of enforcement.[183] The colonial government treated the issue as a priority but also struggled before finding an adequate solution. In 1866, the administration passed a key ordinance 'for giving relief to Creditors Against Debtors Absconding or out of the Settlement to avoid Process'.[184] Both parties recorded the debt, specified the security, and empowered the creditor to realise the estate of the debtor to the amount claimed should he default on the debt. Legal process, however, required efficient administrative machinery, which was lacking. In the 1860s, a series of new courts was formed and reformed, each with different names and modified mandates, and it was not until 1876 that the Supreme Court was established with comprehensive powers to deal with civil and criminal cases.[185] Gaps remained. Defaulters could abscond to the hinterland, which extended beyond the reach of the colonial authorities. Legal reforms in England that limited the liability of shareholders (1855), allowed traders to file for bankruptcy (1861), and abolished imprisonment for debt (1869), did not apply to Lagos and were adopted long after they had become relevant to business in the colony.[186]

Chapter 3 and subsequent chapters will draw on the Supreme Court and Lands Office records to reconstruct the development of the land market from the mid-nineteenth century onwards. It would require several volumes to display the wealth of the civil cases adjudicated by the Supreme Court, which contain invaluable information about the family history of particular litigants and witnesses, the evolution of the law relating to inheritance, and testimony about the history of chieftaincy and of Lagos itself.[187] Similarly, the Lands Office records provide precise information about land transactions and often add personal details about the parties concerned. Taken together, the two

183. McCoskry to Russell, 5 Oct. 1861, C.O. 147/2.

184. Ordinance No. 6, 4 Oct. 1866.

185. Elias, *Nigerian Land Law*, chs. 3–4. The Supreme Court's powers were supplemented by divisional and local courts. Examples of legal experiments to deal with debt are in Glover to C.O., 1 Feb. 1865, C.O. 147/8; Glover to Cardwell, 9 April 1866, C.O. 147/11; Blackall to Carnarvon, 18 Oct. 1866, C.O. 147/11.

186. The attempt to introduce a bankruptcy law in 1899 aroused so much opposition among the Saro elite and leading chiefs that the government decided to withdraw the bill it had prepared. Denton to Chamberlain, 1 April 1899, 8 April, 14 April, C.O. 147/12.

187. The criminal cases are equally important and contain material for several Ph.D. dissertations on subjects such as the character and causes of crime in Lagos, the history of the litigants, and the political battles of the period. Since writing this encouraging note, I have discovered that many of the Supreme Court records have been destroyed. Further details are given in the preface.

sources provide evidence on matters of credit, debt, and the fortunes of the mercantile elite that is not available from other, more familiar, records.

The New Order Established

The sequence of events that led to the creation of the consulate and its transformation into a colony a decade later has usually been treated as an example of the interaction between British diplomacy and domestic politics in Lagos. A wider angle of vision places the episode in the context of Britain's global development plan, which carried the Victorian conception of 'civilising mission' and its complement, 'law and order', across the world. Few bounds were set on Fowell Buxton's vision of 'bringing forth into the market of the world some scores of millions of customers who may be taught to grow the raw material which we require, and who require the manufactured goods which we produce'.[188] Attempts to implement this spacious conception, however, produced unforeseen complications. British settlers, who appeared to be fitted by birth to be natural agents of the modernising mission, discovered that regions such as Canada, South Africa, Australia, and New Zealand were not, as they assumed, *terra nullius*, but lands that were already claimed and would be defended. Elsewhere, as in India, Africa, and China, where the development plan had to engage with densely populated societies and substantial states, Britain needed indigenous intermediaries who had to be identified and then persuaded or cajoled into co-operating.

Lagos was in this second category, which Palmerston referred to as encompassing the 'half-civilised governments', but it presented the additional challenge of possessing a thriving trade in slaves that had to be eliminated before a 'fully civilised' form of commerce could be established.[189] The Foreign Office, in collaboration with the Royal Navy, took the view that this aim was to be achieved by diplomacy supported by what Palmerston called 'a sharp dressing down' if negotiations needed stiffening.[190] This policy led to the bombardment of Lagos and the establishment of a consulate in 1851. Beyond this point, the Foreign Office was guided by two principles: the need to avoid additional costly extensions of power, and the belief, later shared by Mr Micawber, that good things would somehow happen. It seemed self-evident that 'legitimate commerce', being morally superior to the slave trade, would also be more

188. Buxton to Normanby, 30 April 1839, C.O. 2/21, quoted in Gallagher, 'Fowell Buxton and the New African Policy', p. 45.

189. Palmerston's well-known comment, made in 1850, defined 'half-civilised governments' to include China, Portugal, and South American republics. Minute by Palmerston, 29 Sept. 1850 in F.O, 17/173. Quoted in Lynn, 'British Policy, Trade and Informal Empire', in Porter, *The Oxford History of the British Empire*, Vol. 3, p.108.

190. Lynn, 'British Policy, Trade and Informal Empire', in *The Oxford History of the British Empire*, Vol. 3, p. 108.

profitable than the 'pernicious' trade in human beings. This belief turned out to be mistaken. The old trade was more profitable than the new; vested interests resisted change; the Foreign Office found itself drawn into experiments with what would be called, much later, social engineering to create effective alliances and provide them with a secure institutional base.

The view from the Foreign Office needs adjusting to take account of conditions on the ground. The experiment in modernisation began by identifying potential allies among the ruling elite and offering them inducements to support the civilising mission. The Saro were the qualified and willing agents of Buxton's vision of the future world order. They formed the vanguard of the ambitious venture and made Lagos their frontier outpost. Matters, however, were not as simple as they seemed from the distant comfort of a London office. The consuls entrusted to carry out Britain's spacious aims soon found themselves embroiled in local politics. They had the status of chiefs but suffered from the disadvantage of being newcomers among the established Big Men. As Britain's representatives made their way through the mangrove forests of Lagos politics, they were used by local rivals and other vested interests at least as much as they made use of them.

Although the bombardment of Lagos ended the external slave trade, the consulate was unable to guarantee the success of legitimate commerce. As the decade advanced, it became clear that a deal confined to high politics was insufficient to give legitimate commerce the boost it needed. Expatriate and Saro merchants, though essential to the success of the new trade, lacked the confidence to commit to long-term investments in the port unless fundamental institutional changes were forthcoming. The restored *Oba* and his senior chiefs, though in need of British support, were unwilling to add to the concessions they had already made, and the consul lacked the power to persuade them. At this point, the Foreign Office agreed that greater certainty was required to prevent the experiment from foundering. The new colony was created to facilitate the changes that would secure the future of legitimate commerce by arranging a happy marriage between profitability and morality.

It is tempting to follow contemporary opinion and conclude that the story is one of progressive forces grappling with and defeating a backward regime. Closer inspection, however, provides a more nuanced assessment of the economic revolution that began in the 1850s. The slave-trading economy, pernicious though it was, met many of the criteria of an efficient business. The Big Men who managed the trade in Lagos minimised transaction costs (within the technical constraints of the time) and dealt with principal-agent problems by organising and rewarding networks of followers, some of whom were family members and others, dependent slaves. Moreover, some features of slave-exporting survived the abolition of 'that horrid traffic'. Networks adapted; barracoons that housed slaves became stores for puncheons of palm oil before purpose-built warehouses were constructed. Slave-traders, however, recycled profits by increasing their following and augmenting their power. They lacked opportunities to invest capital in more productive ways. Slaves were later employed in export production in the hinterland, but that development depended on the anterior intervention that established British rule in Lagos.

Continuities, however, were matched and soon overtaken by institutional changes. Action taken by the new colonial government in response to pressure from merchants who were trying to develop the new exports opened the way for the creation of freehold tenure and the effective policing of debt. Evidence presented in this chapter has emphasised an unfamiliar dimension of the history of Lagos: the key part played by land sales, credit, and its complement—debt—in the life of the port. A thriving property market arose as soon as land became a resource that could be defined and alienated. Once land acquired value, prices rose, sales increased, and credit could be secured in a form that was independent of personal relations. The influence of these far-reaching institutional innovations extended well beyond commerce. Property was used to raise and repay capital for constructing houses, churches, and mosques, to fund marriages, funerals, and education, and to lubricate political activities.

Saro merchants pioneered these changes, which were vital to their own commercial success. They founded singly-owned businesses that were more specialised than those run by slave-traders. Consequently, they lacked the networks that allowed the most powerful slave-traders to achieve degrees of horizontal and vertical integration. The Saro adapted by offloading some transaction costs, especially protection costs, to the colonial government and dealt with principal-agent problems, notably those arising from debt, through the new colonial court system. These innovations were accompanied by another of fundamental importance: the development of a wage-labour force. Although this theme is not a central feature of this study, it will appear in subsequent chapters in connection with both urban and rural labour. Taken as a whole, it is no exaggeration to say that the creation of the land market and the transformation of the terms on which labour was employed amounted to a socio-economic revolution. Put another way, it can be said that the pioneers of legitimate commerce were capitalists who established capitalism in Lagos and later helped to spread it to the rest of what was to become Nigeria.

From this time onwards, the island, though barely above water, was kept afloat on a raft of paper, which was fashioned out of crown grants, mortgages, and promissory notes. These developments allowed trade to expand in the decades ahead. The enterprise of the mercantile community, whose history is the subject of the next three chapters, ensured that it did. The Saro drew lines in the sand, but they also made sure that they were not washed away.

CHAPTER THREE

The Mercantile Community

THE SHOCK THAT struck Lagos in 1851 and culminated in the shift to colonial status a decade later set the geographical and institutional boundaries
of commerce until the 1890s. At that point, a second shock, the invasion of
the hinterland, modified and greatly enlarged the economic environment
and altered the opportunities open to entrepreneurs. Oscillations, however,
occurred within the structure established in 1862 that had a profound effect
on mercantile fortunes. Lagos merchants enjoyed broadly favourable conditions for most of the 1860s and 1870s. When they receded in the 1880s, the
difficulties that followed prepared the way for the second great shock: Britain's
decision to take control of Yorubaland in 1892.

The New Commercial Environment

As noted in chapter 2, before Britain outlawed the Atlantic slave trade, sailing
ships anchored offshore, business was conducted on board, and goods and
slaves were ferried to and from designated points on shore. After 1807, the
intervention of the Royal Navy forced slave-traders to adapt to avoid being
intercepted. One tactic was to establish onshore bases where slaves could be
held pending shipment and ships could be turned around quickly. This innovation, however, should be seen as a response to the increasing difficulties of
pursuing the illegal trade rather than as an anticipation of the business structures needed to conduct legitimate commerce. There were some continuities.
For example, in the early years of the palm oil trade, before the 1850s, puncheons of oil were sometimes stored in barracoons, which were used primarily
to hold slaves pending shipment. However, many barracoons were destroyed
when Lagos was bombarded in 1851, and those that remained were located
elsewhere rather than on the Marina.[1]

1. Ford Fenn to Newcastle, 16 April 1863, C.O. 147/5.

The warehouses erected to handle the new trade were purpose-built and differed considerably in structure as well as in function from the old barracoons.
The permanence of the new Marina establishments was both an expression of
confidence in the security symbolised by colonial rule and a practical response to
the needs of legitimate commerce. In the mid-1850s, puncheons of oil were still
rolled and carried to 'one spot on the beach' before being trans-shipped to ocean-
going vessels.[2] From the 1860s, however, piers were built to serve the warehouses
on the Marina and cargo was ferried from there to ships anchored in deeper
waters. Steamships complemented these land-based developments. After an
experimental start in the 1850s, steamships provided regular and increasingly
frequent services, as well as offering expanded freight capacity and reduced
freight rates. These improvements allowed trade to grow and seasonality to be
smoothed.[3] By 1870, steamships had overtaken sail in the palm-oil trade; by
1880, they were responsible for 90 per cent of the total tonnage in the trade.[4]

Permanent establishments required permanent staff. The expansion of
steamship services encouraged the growth of commission houses in Europe,
which shipped goods and received produce through local agents in Lagos and
other West African ports. These firms made their money by charging commission, which at that time was around 2.5 per cent on imported produce
and 1.5 per cent on exported goods.[5] Some European firms sent out their own
representatives. Others appointed local agents, most of whom were Saro. Representatives and agents in turn employed book-keepers and stock-keepers,
who were generally drawn from Saro families. The independent agents were
almost exclusively resettled Saro merchants: only a few Europeans managed
their own businesses in the port and their number diminished later in the
century, when increasing competition eroded profits. Representatives were
allowed considerable discretion in daily business decisions and had the same
freedom as independent merchants in negotiating prices and deciding the
quantities of produce they would buy. Delegation was essential because there
was no speedy means of transmitting prices to and from Europe until the submarine cable reached Lagos in 1886. Before then, 'it took two to three months
to communicate with Europe'.[6] Timing (and considerable luck) was vital in the
produce trade, where short-term price variations were common; the import
trade was steadier and required less capital. Import merchants ordered goods

2. Campbell to Clarendon, 14 May 1856, F.O. 84/1002.

3. Seasonality was determined manly by the palm produce harvest, which occurred in
December–April (main) and August–September (minor). Inspector of Produce to Comptroller of Customs, 1 June 1910, CSO 14/2/3.

4. Lynn, *Commerce and Economic Change*, table 5.1, p. 110.

5. This was the rate paid by James O'Connor Williams to his commission house. LLOR,
14/250, 1899.

6. Evidence of G. Montaignac, general agent for Fabre & Cie, in Shitta v. Fabre, LSCR,
Civ. 7, 26 March 1888.

from Europe (principally from Manchester and Hamburg) from firms they represented or had established good relations with. Prices were either fixed by the head office or offered on a 'sale or return' basis, which gave local representatives greater freedom of action. Orders for both imports and exports were accepted against credit, which placed a premium on good standing and the availability of tangible security.

There were no banks in Lagos during the early colonial period and specie was often in short supply. Until the last quarter of the century, British policy conformed to the prevailing currency zones in different parts of the world. The predominant currencies in Lagos were an exotic mixture of Spanish American dollars, a handful of other silver currencies and, above all, cowries. Sterling silver was of minor importance. Although cowries were essential for transactions in Lagos and its hinterland, they were not legal tender in Europe and were accepted by expatriate firms only for recirculation locally. The problem of making remittances to Europe was partly solved by the prevalence of the barter trade, which reduced the need for cash transactions, though, reciprocally, barter limited the size of the market by reducing competition and the availability of cash for other expenditures. External accounts were settled by bills of exchange drawn on banks in Europe, by borrowing from merchants who had sufficient liquidity in acceptable currencies, by issuing 'cheques' for produce that could be redeemed at a later date, and, as a last resort, by selling produce originally bought for shipment to other exporters.[7] At times of acute shortage, even the colonial government was obliged to borrow cash from local merchants.[8] Lack of liquidity was less of a problem for Saro merchants, who had greater opportunities to recirculate cowries, though they too needed convertible currency to settle bills in Europe and ultimately to serve as a store of value.

Contemporaries applied the term 'merchant' principally to Lagosians who were direct importers and exporters and performed wholesaling functions on a sizeable scale.[9] The definition, however, was flexible rather than rigorous, and wisely so. Although merchants typically sold some of their imported goods on their premises, the bulk of the import trade and the whole of the export trade depended on local brokers (also known as barracooners). Brokers did not import or export directly, but delivered produce to compounds on the Marina, negotiated sale prices, and purchased consumer goods in bulk for distribution to traders with whom they had close connections. Consul Campbell reported that there were three hundred brokers in 1855, but that figure should be regarded as

7. Christie & Co. v. Escherich & Co., LSCR, Civ. 3, 1881. Overdue balances owing to houses in Europe at this time (1860–80) were charged at an annual rate of about 5 per cent.

8. Mann, *Slavery and the Birth of an African City*, p. 147. The problem persisted: Griffith to Assistant Collector and Treasurer, 15 Oct. 1880, enc. in Ussher to Kimberley, 26 Nov. 1880, C.O. 806/184.

9. See, for example, the evidence of Ernest Barth, the agent for Rothlisberger in Rothlisberger v. Fabre, 1888. LSCR, Civ. 8, 1888.

being broadly indicative rather than solidly based.[10] Brokers were of key importance to the functioning of the commercial system. Without their trading networks, the market would have been confined to a small radius. European firms would have struggled to create connections outside Lagos, and even the Saro would have been at a disadvantage because their ties with the hinterland were neither as extensive nor as strong as those developed by brokers. Contemporaries acknowledged that brokers ranked among the Big Men of the town and that their influence extended far beyond commerce and into politics.

The distinction between merchants and brokers was primarily one of function and was not necessarily correlated with the scale of business operations.[11] Many of the leading brokers owed their positions to inherited or acquired titles and the political leverage that accompanied them. To stay ahead of keen competition, however, brokers also had to demonstrate that they possessed the managerial qualities needed to control complex networks run by relays of followers who often spanned different ethnic groups. The networks supplied palm oil and kernels and distributed consumer imports. Produce was accumulated in successive stages of increasing bulk; imports were broken down in the same way until they reached petty traders in the streets of Lagos and villages in the hinterland. The system was composed of many moving parts and was vulnerable to internal strains and external political events. Yet, trading networks proved their flexibility and resilience. They survived the crises that occurred in the nineteenth century, the wrenching changes brought by colonial rule in the twentieth century, and the criticism directed at them by colonial official and expatriate firms, who were inclined to think that they burdened an otherwise efficient commercial system.

Brokers and even some traders who conducted businesses on a substantial scale might also be referred to as 'merchants' as a mark of esteem. The broader definition will be adopted here. Although it dilutes precision, it has the merit of capturing the variety of mercantile activities connected to overseas trade and allows for changes to individual businesses brought by time. Most merchants started as traders; some combined wholesaling with retailing; others diversified their businesses away from staple imports and exports and developed new lines of trade. The flexibility afforded by the enlarged definition has the advantage of reflecting the shifting realities of commerce in the port.

Property Becomes Big Business

As described in chapter 2, the expansion of commerce depended on the growth of credit, which in turn was linked to the creation of acceptable security. Crown grants and other legal instruments confirming the inviolability of

10. Campbell to Clarendon, 14 May 1856, F.O. 84/1002.
11. As discussed in chapter 2.

freehold tenure sealed the new deal. Governor Freeman, unlike some subsequent commentators, realised how vital the credit system was to the success of legitimate commerce. 'Credit', he observed in 1863, 'is the great genius of the African trade'.[12] The argument advanced here is not that personal relations became redundant, but that impersonal security was an essential precondition of the expansion of legitimate commerce. Trust based on personal relations remained important among the networks managed by brokers, within families, and among friends. It was the new, impersonal system, however, that gave vitality to the business of the port and allowed credit of all kinds to expand.[13]

The detailed evidence contained in the Lagos Lands Office and Court Records, though immensely informative, does not provide figures covering total lending of the type currently supplied by banks and mortgage companies.[14] Nevertheless, the two sources in combination reveal the main trends that emerged from the 1860s onwards and provide an insight into an otherwise invisible but vibrant undercurrent of history that influenced the fortunes of the whole of Lagos society.

Two cautionary remarks should be made at the outset. First, as noted earlier, the term 'mortgage' in this context refers not to a loan for house purchase spread over many years, but typically to a short-term advance of between six months and one year. The same arrangement was often repeated in the following year, which suggests that borrowing was timed to coincide with the trading season. The system allowed for flexibility: in rare circumstances, contracts could be agreed for two years and even for five. Second, debt is the obverse of credit and not an index of disaster. Chains of indebtedness, where a debtor settled his obligation by borrowing from someone else, were common.[15] Such chains snaked through society, forming bonds between creditors and debtors in ways that each knew only in part. The test was repayment. Successful merchants secured credit, were able to repay the money they borrowed, and reclaimed their collateral (typically property). The records sound an alarm when the repayment period had to be extended, when a further loan had to be negotiated to repay the first one, when default prompted the

12. Freeman to Newcastle, 9 March 1864, C.O. 147/6.

13. The commercialisation of land was taking place across the expanding empire during the second half of the nineteenth century. For a rare (and welcome) comparative study within Africa, see Wayne Dooling, 'The Making of Private Property: Comparing the Cape and Lagos'. I am grateful to the author for allowing me to cite his unpublished paper.

14. The Lagos Lands Office records date from 1862 and are identified here by the abbreviation LLOR followed by volume and page numbers. The records housed in the Supreme Court date from 1861. Unpublished records of civil and criminal cases are complete from 1876. Cases are cited here with the abbreviation Civ. followed by the volume number and the year.

15. For a more detailed discussion, see Mann, *Slavery and the Birth of an African City*, pp. 144–50.

surrender of security, and when additional land had to be sold under duress. At that point, the game really was up.

The most important trend was the substantial rise in property prices, which were the basis of the credit system and increasingly of private wealth, not only from trade but also from rental incomes and capital gains from property sales. Land values jumped as soon as the treaty of cession was signed. 'The value of waterside lots', Consul McCoskry observed at the close of 1861, 'is daily becoming higher'.[16] Two years later, Governor Freeman confirmed the progression, commenting that a land scramble was taking place as Saro and Brazilians claimed 'any unoccupied plots they could lay their hands on'.[17] The upward movement scarcely paused until the 1930s, before resuming after 1945. The gains from rising land values accrued largely to Saro, who obtained the most desirable plots. Many other Lagosians were quick to join the great land rush, though the land they acquired was generally at the cheaper end of the property market. The fortunes of Lagos merchants and their successors were derived, almost literally, from turning sand into gold.

The European firms did not leap in with the same enthusiasm. They were free to purchase land in Lagos and several of them did so. An early example is provided by the British firm of Banner Bros., which in 1862 bought land in Olowogbowo from an illiterate Lagosian, Korowo, for thirty bags of cowries.[18] At this time, however, many expatriate firms preferred to rent suitable property, even if the buildings required extensive renovation.[19] Firms with headquarters in Europe may have hesitated to place long-term investments in immovable property in what was still a frontier town. Legal complications may also have encouraged them to pause. The intersection between Yoruba and English land law was being worked out with legal slowness throughout the second half of the century and beyond. Meanwhile, claimed rights of freehold were open to challenge in cases where, for example, families asserted that an individual holding was family land that could not be alienated at will.[20] It was only after about 1900 that European firms began to negotiate long leases of ten, twenty, and occasionally even more years.

Future research might be able to generate a time-series of property prices for this period. Unfortunately, the data are not in a form that can be assembled easily or allow comparisons to be made over a period of years. The size of plots was frequently altered by additions and subtractions in ways that cannot be related to values with any confidence. Property sales rarely distinguished the value of land from the cost of buildings. In 1887, for example, the colonial

16. McCoskry to Russell, 30 November 1861, F.O. 84/1141.
17. Freeman to Newcastle, 29 June 1863, C.O. 147/5.
18. LLOR, 1862.
19. Moseley to Chamberlain, 1 Oct. 1902, C.O. 147/182.
20. Oyero and Anor v. Edun and Anor; Oyero and Anor v. Taiwo and Anor, LSCR, Civ. 39, 1905.

surveyor reported that the property occupied by Oil Mills on the Marina covered 6,992 square yards, which he valued at 2s. per square yard, producing a notional total value of £699.[21] The same report valued Lesi's smaller plot of 3,318 square yards, also on the Marina, at 1s.3d. per square yard, which was worth a total of £207. It is impossible to deduce a common value per square yard from this evidence. Several variables may have been at work: Lesi's land might have occupied a less advantageous position on the Marina; the buildings on one site might have been far more valuable than those on the other.

The compromise adopted later in this chapter, and in subsequent chapters, is to examine specific examples of plots that retained their essential features over periods long enough to allow major changes in value to appear plausible. Meanwhile, it is important to bear in mind that all increases in the value of crown grants from the 1860s onwards were from a zero base because they were issued virtually free of charge. Accordingly, any sums realised from sales were net gains after the cost of building and maintenance had been deducted.

Land that was purchased appears to have been financed from savings derived from commercial profits or by borrowing from other merchants. The first generation of merchants either secured crown grants without payment or bought land from indigenous Lagosians for cowries. In 1862, for example, Joseph Wey, a Saro merchant, secured land in Faji from Faseye, a farmer, for nineteen bags of cowries. Faseye, who was illiterate, nevertheless claimed to be 'seized in his demesne as of fee; or otherwise well and sufficiently entitled to the inheritance'.[22] Evidently, lawyers were present in Lagos at a very early date. Saro who bought land with a statement of title in legal language but without official recognition, speedily acquired crown grants for their purchases. In 1862, when James George, a substantial merchant, bought land at Olowogbowo from Samuel B. Williams for £300, he lost no time in converting his uncertain paper title into a crown grant.[23] Some purchases suggest investment for capital gain rather than for trade credit. In 1867, John Ezzidio, a Freetown merchant who conducted no business in Lagos, sold a crown grant he had obtained for a plot on the Marina to a Lagos merchant, Henry Robbin, for £425.[24] In 1876, James Cole, a wealthy Lagos merchant, bought land on the nearby island of Iddo, which was only just beginning to develop, from one Mumuni for the modest sum of £11.[25] Land was also purchased or assigned to safeguard family fortunes. It was in this spirit that James George gave land 'in Lagos' to his adopted son, John, in 1866.[26]

21. In the Matter of Public Lands Ordinance of 1876, LSCR, Civ. 7, 1887.

22. LLOR, 1/13, 1862.

23. LLOR, 1/18, 1862; LLOR 3/149, 1864.

24. LLOR, 51/183, 1867.

25. LLOR, 25/22, 1876. Iddo was designated the main railway terminus in 1899 and joined to Lagos by the Carter Bridge in 1901.

26. LLOR, 4/75 1866.

The great majority of civil cases coming before the Supreme Court dealt with the linked issues of debt and land. The Lands Office records confirm that mortgages and cases involving debt proliferated in the second half of the century. Many more loans and pledges of security were negotiated outside official institutions. The courts used sterling as the official currency, though cowries predominated in Lagos. The court's practice of reporting the sterling value of cases that were presented in cowries provides a valuable guide to exchange rates and confirms evidence from other sources that cowries ceased to be the preferred local currency by the close of the 1880s and were rarely mentioned in the following decade. Claimants who kept accounts, and who therefore were either literate or employed literate clerks, had an advantage in cases where evidence was disputed because the court accepted written records as the gold standard of reliability. Until 1900 at least, most mortgages and cases of debt involved sums of less than £100 and nearly all, with a few spectacular exceptions, were for less than £500. It must be remembered that these figures were current at the time and need increasing to bring them up to date.[27] Seen from this perspective, the stakes were much higher than they would otherwise appear to be and explain why court cases involving seemingly small amounts were, in fact, dealing with substantial sums that justified the court fees and legal costs.

Interest rates on money loaned on the security of mortgages were finely tuned and indicated that the market was incorporating risk efficiently. Rates generally ranged from 5 per cent to 12 per cent annually. In 1876, a Lagosian named Brimah mortgaged a crown grant on land at Victoria Street to secure a debt of £22 (in cowries) he owed another Lagosian named Fagbemi.[28] As the crown grant was solid security and the debt relatively small, he was charged an annual rate of 5 per cent. Isaac H. Willoughby, a Saro merchant, was not so fortunate. He was already in debt to William McCoskry (the consul turned merchant) and was charged an annual rate of 10 per cent, when he took out a further loan on the security of three houses in 1862.[29]

Although the incidence of debt cannot be treated as a proxy for impending business failure, clusters of debt, especially when associated with sales and foreclosures, provide a surer guide to commercial difficulties, and one that cannot be found in other sources. Two examples, both involving Jacob Leigh, a prominent Saro merchant, convey the flavour of some of the debt cases adjudicated during the early colonial period. In 1868, a luckless trader named Bada owed Leigh 242 heads of cowries (about £15).[30] Bada was unable to pay and

27. See the note on currency values in the front matter.
28. LLOR, 24/86, 1876. Fagbemi, the son of Mabinuori (d.1874), was a successful merchant and founder of the house of Dawodu, whose fortunes are discussed later in this study.
29. LLOR, 1/205 1862.
30. LLOR, 6/345, 1868.

was imprisoned before being rescued by a benefactor named Akilagun, who agreed to settle the debt in exchange for Bada's release. As security, Akilagun gave Leigh authority to sell his house and land at Ereko (a district in Olowogbowo) if the debt was not paid in time. To complete the agreement, Akilagun affirmed that 'any deed or instrument executed by the said Jacob S. Leigh to the purchaser of the said premises shall be sufficient to pass the estate to such purchaser'. A codicil by one Ogunfunwa certified that 'the foregoing house and land is part of our father's property which we inherited since his death, and that I am the elder brother of Akilagun and that I was present at the execution of the foregoing instrument and I hereby give my assent thereto'. Further details are lacking, but it is plausible to assume that the three men were linked by kinship because Yoruba custom gave the family responsibility for the debt of a member who was unable to discharge his obligation. It is likely, too, that the case is a very early example of the assignment of family land, which, unlike acquired land, was rarely alienated.[31]

The second example had its origins in 1881 and involved one Brimah Baya, who was unable to settle a debt of £186.[32] The court ruled in Leigh's favour, but Baya was still unable to settle the debt and was imprisoned for nine months. When he was released, the court ordered him to repay Leigh at the rate of £3 a month. The unrelenting procedure illustrates the consequences of the absence of legislation covering bankruptcy and insolvency in the colony. Ordinance 6 of 1866 'For Giving Relief to Creditors' gave Leigh an additional weapon by ensuring that absconding debtors could be compelled to surrender their property and allow their creditor to sell it.[33] Baya was unable to trade and was housed at the expense of the government on the assumption that punitive treatment would be an effective deterrent.

Baya, however, was more fortunate than Yesufu Bada, who in 1884 owed money to the German firm of Voigt & Co.[34] Although Bada was a British subject, the company took action against him in Porto Novo, which was under the jurisdiction of the King of Porto Novo. Justice was rough and swift. Bada was seized, beaten, and imprisoned; his property was confiscated; his wife was sold into slavery. Even this comprehensive outcome did not satisfy Voigt, which then tried to enforce payment in the Lagos Supreme Court. Justice Smalman

31. On the differences between acquired and family land and rights of inheritance, see Omoniregun v. Sadatu, LSCR, Civ. 8, 1888; Eletu Ijebu (White Capped Chief) in the matter of the estate of Hotonu (decd.), LSCR, Civ. 9, 1889; Rayner's judgement in Re Ayorinde, 3 Aug. 1899, LSCR, Civ. 23. 1899; Lewis v. Banjoko, 12 Nov. 1908, LSCR, Civ. 52, 1908; and C. J. William Nicoll's judgement upholding Yoruba law in Sumonu Alugo v. B. F. Damazon & Anor., LSCR, Civ. 33,

32. J. S. Leigh v. Brimah Baya, LSCR, Civ. 25, 1900.

33. In 1868, J.P.L. Davies moved swiftly to sell property owned by George Johnson in settlement of a substantial debt of £499. LLOR, 10/53, 1868.

34. Voigt & Co. v. Yesufu Bada, LSCR, Civ. 5, 1884.

Smith, however, condemned the firm for treating a British subject 'according to the usages of a barbarous state'.[35] Judgement was given in favour of the defendant with costs on the grounds that he had already 'satisfied his creditors'. The case was a reminder that Lagos was the gateway to a still turbulent frontier where 'the rule of law' was understood in a variety of ways.

These cases, though dramatic, were in a minority. Merchants were well aware of the risks entailed in Lagos trade and did their best to distinguish between problems caused by mismanagement and shortages of liquidity caused by unpredictable commercial fluctuations. They preferred to allow debtors additional time rather than go to court immediately, incur costs, and perhaps lose the chance of securing repayment, even if the court ruled in their favour. A striking illustration occurred in 1873, when James Cole was indebted to Andrew Charles, a broker in Birmingham, for the considerable sum of £9,974.[36] Cole had mortgaged seven properties to cover the advance, but these turned out to be worth less than one-quarter of the sum owing. Cole was a prominent figure and Charles, the creditor, was not in a strong position. He agreed to accept £3,000 in immediate settlement with the right to claim the full amount if the balance owing was not paid within two years. It is unclear what other resources Cole could draw on to pay the balance, but it is evident that he could end up in prison if he failed to comply. Fortunately for his reputation and comfort, Cole managed to settle the debt in 1875 and his property was restored to him.

This assessment is incomplete because it does not deal with the rental market. The omission is not deliberate, but results from a lack of systematic information. Substantial merchants acquired property that was beyond their immediate needs. Admittedly, their needs were often extensive. Polygynous households required houses for wives and extended families; Big Men, like Taiwo, provided accommodation for their followers. When these allowances have been made, however, it remains the case that merchants who were either monogamous or did not have a large corps of retainers to support owned property beyond their requirements. Saro who fell into this category used freehold property as security for commercial credit, but also had the prospect of earning rental incomes. Logic suggests that a rental market began to develop from the 1850s and 1860s.

Empirical evidence, however, is limited. Colonial records have little if anything to say on the subject; newspapers were rare and transient until the 1880s; cases involving defaulters rarely came to court because the sums involved were generally too small to justify the cost.[37] All that can be said

35. (Sir) John Smalman Smith (1847–1913) served in Lagos between 1883 and 1895, and was Chief Justice between 1889 and his retirement in 1895.

36. LLOR, 18/96, 1873.

37. Mann, *Slavery and the Birth of an African City*, p. 267, gives three examples of rental arrangements before 1870.

with confidence is that a rental market using cash payments had its origins in the early colonial period but remained largely invisible until the close of the century.

Winners and Losers

There is no wholly reliable way of identifying the leading merchants in Lagos, whether indigenous or not, during this period. The only procedure available is to combine information gathered from contemporary opinion with evidence from the limited number of official records that contain measurable data about the rank order of firms and individuals. The first piece of systematic evidence is contained in the consular trade report for the calendar year 1855.[38] At that time, taxes were derived from customs duties on exports, chiefly palm oil and ivory, which were the most important sources of government revenue.[39] The report listed the total number of puncheons of palm oil (one puncheon=120 gallons) exported and the number shipped by each firm. Of the total of 6,687 puncheons, 77 per cent was attributed to six European firms, the most important being the Hamburg firm of O'Swald, which alone shipped 44 per cent of all the puncheons exported from Lagos. Nineteen Saro merchants exported 1,362 puncheons, which was just over 20 per cent of the total. The ten leading Saro were responsible for 98 per cent of this figure, which amounted to slightly more than 17 per cent of all puncheons shipped from Lagos.

The word 'approximate' should be placed before each of these totals. The report revealed that some firms escaped paying duty by failing to declare the full content of the puncheons they shipped; two Saro names were counted twice; one or two other names on the list are not found in other sources; minor exports were omitted. Moreover, the report excluded the import trade, though the consul added an enigmatic note stating that there were seven, presumably European, importers and three Saro, 'who trade solely with their own imports'.[40] It is also possible that 1855 was an exceptional year in a decade full of instability. However, there is no evidence that unusual influences affected the customs figures at this time. Information on minor exports, such as ivory, might alter the picture. Yet, the value of palm oil was so much larger than that of other exports that it is difficult to see that the inclusion of other exports would change the weighting significantly. Although exports cannot be used as an exact proxy for imports, the prevalence of barter undoubtedly gave the main exporters a grip on the import trade and provides a broad measure of the relative importance of different groups of merchants.

38. Campbell to Clarendon, 14 May 1856, F.O. 84/1002.
39. The 2 per cent duty on exports was replaced by a 4 per cent duty on imports in 1863.
40. Campbell to Clarendon, 14 May 1856, F.O. 84/1002.

The dominance of the European firms is evident. So, too, is the marked element of concentration: the top three European firms and the leading ten Saro merchants were responsible for about 83 per cent of all puncheons of oil shipped from Lagos in 1855. Had the share of the import trade held by Saro merchants matched their share of exports, they would have accounted for about 20 per cent of total overseas trade. It is possible that their share of imports exceeded their share of exports; equally, it might have been lower. Had the proportion been significantly higher, however, it probably would have prompted contemporary comment. There is no evidence in other sources that this was the case. In 1863, Governor Freeman added his opinion that foreign firms constituted 'the majority of the large houses' in Lagos.[41]

The qualifications to these estimates seem insufficient to disturb the broad conclusion that, at the mid-point of the consular period, the bulk of the import and export trade was in the hands of European firms and that the remainder was handled by Saro merchants. This finding appears to contradict the familiar assumption that African merchants occupied a pre-eminent position in the new trade at this time. There are grounds, however, for pausing before confirming this conclusion. Conditions in the mid-1850s still favoured large firms. Wilhelm O'Swald, the leading house in Lagos, enjoyed the considerable advantage of a near-monopoly of imports of the main local currency, cowries, which it shipped from Zanzibar. The prevalence of barter further limited competition by tying import and export trades together. In addition, steamships were only just beginning to compete with sail and the service was still infrequent and unreliable. Most Saro merchants were young in the 1850s and just beginning to build their careers. As trading conditions evolved, the performance of different mercantile groups may well have changed. With caution on this occasion coming before a prospective fall, a more confident assessment will be postponed until the evidence for later periods has been assessed.

Although diversity was a permanent feature of the mercantile community, the contrast between inherited and novel characteristics was particularly marked during the first decades of the colonial period, when former slave-traders either disappeared from the scene or adapted to the new trade in legitimate goods and Saro immigrants were beginning to make their presence felt.

As noted in the previous chapter, the fortunes of Dosunmu and his senior chiefs suffered from the commercial transition, despite supporting the British presence. In 1856, Consul Campbell reported that the king and his 'aged Caboceers' had lost all benefits from the slave trade 'and are many of them very poor'.[42] Five years later, Consul McCoskry stated that the 'native chiefs cannot compete either on mercantile or agricultural pursuits with the emigrants

---

41. Freeman to Newcastle, 10 Feb 1863, C.O. 147/3.
42. Campbell to Clarendon, 14 May 1856, F.O. 84/1002.

from Sierra Leone, Brazil, and Cuba'.[43] The development of the land market appears to confirm their failure to adapt.[44] The *Oba* and the *Idejo* chiefs had been reluctant to agree to the treaty of cession, fearing that it would deprive them of their land rights and encourage their slaves to seek emancipation.[45] Their predictions proved to be correct. The *Oba* relinquished his right to trade on his own account in exchange for an annual pension of £1,000.[46] In 1866, Dosunmu petitioned the governor for additional support, claiming that he and his chiefs were in 'the most miserable position'.[47] He stated that, before the cession, he drew an income of about 2,000 bags of cowries a year (approximately £2,000), and additional unspecified sums from court fines and import duties on tobacco and cowries, as well as 'extensive presents' from merchants. His chiefs were even worse off, having 'no source of maintenance' because their rights to a tariff on cloth and palm oil brought from the mainland had been abolished. The *Idejo*, however, were free to participate in the new economy and were well placed to capitalise on the embryonic land market, but few did so, at least directly, and none with marked success.[48]

Kosoko and his followers, who had long opposed abolition, were more successful. Their support for the new British administration was officially recognised in 1865, when Glover presented the former *Oba* and his chief lieutenant, Oshodi Tapa, with ceremonial swords of honour to mark their loyalty.[49] The following year, the governor increased Kosoko's pension by £100 to acknowledge his services in 'reconciling his people in the outlying districts with the Queen's Government'.[50]

The *Oba*'s chiefs, however, were not proxies for the indigenous commercial community. Their prominence in accounts of the period may be enhanced because more is known about them than about less visible Lagosians. Other sources of privileged wealth were not swept aside after 1862. The *Oba*'s court system co-existed with the new British courts and continued to bring in fees and fines. The *Baba Isale* system that authorised certain Lagos chiefs to act as patrons of important local markets on the mainland provided an

43. McCoskry to Russell, 7 June 1861, F.O. 84/1141.
44. Although appearance seems to match reality, certainty will have to await a study of the financial history of the Lagos chiefs.
45. McCoskry to Russell, 5 Oct. 1861, C.O. 147/2; Freeman to Newcastle, 5 March 1862, C.O. 147/1; Chiefs to Glover, 8 Sept. 1863, C.O. 147/3.
46. As far as I am aware, only one member of the royal house traded in a noticeable way. This was Prince Alfred Ibikunjle Akitoye (1871–1928), whose career is outlined in chapter 11.
47. Dosunmu's Petition, 1866 (no day or month given) in C.O. 147/12.
48. Possible explanations of the failure of the *Idejo* Chiefs to take out crown grants for themselves are discussed in Mann, *Slavery and the Birth of an African City*, p. 254.
49. Glover to Cardwell, 7 July 1865, C.O. 147/9.
50. Glover to Kennedy, 18 Jan 1869, C.O. 147/15.

expanding source of income and power.[51] There are enough glimpses of other figures to suggest that those who showed themselves to be adaptable could also become successful brokers and large traders, even if they did not trade directly with Europe. Among them are names that are familiar to specialists, such as Sumanu Animasaun, Brimah Apatira, Jacob Ogunbiyi, Fasheke Olukolu, Akinpelu Possu, Oshodi Tapa, Daniel Conrad Taiwo, and Madame Tinubu. There is sufficient evidence to provide brief biographies of the most prominent and to confirm that they were also buying, selling, and mortgaging property, but rarely enough to support an account of their business activities beyond generalisations that they traded 'on a substantial scale'. The story of Daniel Taiwo, whose career will be followed in some detail in the next chapter, is a fortuitous exception.

The absence of women is striking but unsurprising. It is customary for studies of Lagos and even of Nigeria as a whole to fill the gap by citing the example of Madame Efunporoye Tinubu (c.1805–1887), the remarkable trader and political activist.[52] She is undoubtedly an attractive subject, so much so that many treatments of her life have been influenced by a desire to celebrate her claimed nationalist and feminist credentials. Irrespective of the validity of this approach, it has not contributed significantly to our knowledge of her business career. The fullest evidence of her life refers to her political influence from the time of her marriage to *Oba* Adele at some point in the 1830s to her exile from Lagos in 1856 and, though in less detail, her activities in her Egba homeland thereafter. Apart from broad statements attesting to her substantial involvement in both the slave and palm oil trades, insufficient evidence has survived to enable a history of her business dealings to be written.[53] It is for this reason that this 'woman of masculine intrepidity', as an obituarist described her, has been omitted from extended treatment here.[54]

Tinubu, however, is the exception who proves the rule. Many, probably most, wives and daughters in Lagos traded, but the majority did so on a small scale and others, with larger businesses, have passed into obscurity. Elite Saro families followed the Victorian ethic that prescribed 'ladylike' activities for women, though those whose aspirations were tempered by pragmatism often helped in shops owned by their husbands and some managed the business

51. Cole, *Modern and Traditional*, pp. 23–9, remains the most informative source.

52. See S. Biobaku, *Eminent Nigerians of the Nineteenth Century* (Cambridge: Cambridge University Press, 1960), pp. 33–41; Losi, *History of Lagos*, pp. 25, 28; Yemitan, *Madame Tinubu*. Scala, who met Tinubu, emphasised her 'feminine charms' and involvement in politics: Giambattista Scala, *Memoirs* (Oxford: Oxford University Press, 2000), pp. 29–40, 51–52, 80–84. Her first name is often shortened to 'Efunroye'.

53. I am grateful to Mr A.Y.S. Tinubu and other members of the family for confirming that, as far as they are aware, no private papers exist.

54. *Lagos Observer*, 3 and 7 Dec. 1887. Also known as the 'Boadicia of Lagos'. *West Africa*, 25 June 1921.

when their husband travelled or was ill.[55] The Yoruba, by contrast, understood marriage as a union that joined economic functions and served dynastic purposes. Tinubu exemplified the Yoruba formula: no other female in her time integrated economic and political activities more successfully than she did. Her career also illustrates one of the ironies of 'modernisation', whereby supposedly backward societies were encouraged to make progress in ways that elevated social status above economic efficiency.

Men of the Marina

The two examples that follow have been chosen because they illustrate features of the indigenous commercial community that might otherwise be overlooked: the rapidity with which individuals could move from slave to free status, the importance of trade with parts of the interior in commodities that did not enter Atlantic commerce, and the increasingly visible presence of Islam and its commercial ties with co-religionists.

Oshodi Tapa is an example of a slave, a slave-trader, and a war chief who converted to legitimate commerce and established a direct link with the new generation of European firms by becoming the main agent for W. O'Swald, the most important foreign firm in Lagos in the 1850s and 1860s.[56] Oshodi's given name was Landuji but he was called 'Tapa' when he came to Lagos because he was originally from Nupe; Oshodi, a title added later, became the family name. Oshodi, as he may now be called, came to Lagos when he was still young as a 'domestic' of *Oba* Osinlokun in the 1820s.[57] Osinlokun sent him to Brazil to learn Portuguese with the aim of solidifying his connections there and expanding his knowledge of the international aspects of the slave-trading business. After Osinlokun's death, Oshodi attached himself to his successor, Ojulari, and then to his son, Kosoko, who authorised him to conduct trade and collect tolls on his behalf, and dispatched him to Brazil in 1847 to encourage repatriation.[58] Oshodi prospered and rose to become one of Kosoko's key advisers. As noted in chapter 2, he accompanied Kosoko when he went into exile at Epe in 1851 and was influential in persuading him to return to Lagos in 1862.

---

55. All scholars of West African history are greatly indebted to Kristin Mann for her meticulous and illuminating study of this subject: *Marrying Well*.

56. I am grateful to *Alhaji* B. D. Oshodi, grandson of Oshodi Tapa, for discussing the history of the family with me on 15 and 25 Feb. 1962 and 7 June 1964. See also Losi, *History of Lagos*, pp. 103–05; Akintan, *Epetedo Lands*; Akintan, *Awful Disclosures on Epetedo Lands*. Decker and Balogun have provided a summary biography (based on secondary sources) in 'Landuji Oshodi Tapa in the Eye of History', in Oyeweso, ed., *Eminent Yoruba Muslims*, pp. 142–61.

57. The alternative spelling, Eshilokun, has gained currency in recent years.

58. Moloney to Holland, 20 July 1887, C.O. 147/59.

Oshodi's political astuteness was confirmed by several contemporaries, including Commodore Bruce, who reported in 1854 that he was 'a man of more than ordinary sagacity'.[59] His skill and connections were evident in the help he offered the consuls and in his close relationship with Governor Glover, who depended on local Big Men to develop a power base in the Lagos community, very much as the *Obas* had done before him. In return, Glover arranged for Oshodi to receive an annual pension of £200.[60] Communication between the two was helped by the fact that Oshodi had picked up some English as well as Portuguese on his travels. The connection was personal as well as instrumental: Glover arranged to have one of Oshodi's sons, Fatusi, educated in England, where he was baptised and adopted the name Henry Glover Oshodi.[61] Oshodi himself remained what was then called a 'pagan'. Henry was among several sons who became Christians. On returning to Lagos, Henry traded in cotton goods and later became a prominent member of the United African Church in the 1890s, when some members of his cosmopolitan family were embracing Islam. When Oshodi Tapa was dying, he asked to see Glover, who came to him and held his hand during the final hours.[62] Glover organised a public funeral, which was 'universally attended'.[63]

Oshodi Tapa was one of the pioneers of the palm oil trade, which he entered in the 1840s, while still dealing in slaves.[64] According to Momadu Awu, one of his slaves, he was the only Lagosian exporting palm oil before the Saro arrived.[65] In the 1860s, he expanded his activities along the lagoon ports to include raw cotton, ivory, and a variety of imported goods, and was said to conduct a 'large' trade, especially at Palma.[66] His business offers a rare example at that time of vertical integration: he employed numerous slaves to produce and deliver much of the palm oil he then exported. Oshodi's position in Lagos and his close ties with Glover also helped him in 1862 to acquire a large slice of land that became known as Epetedo ('those who came from Epe'). The area was large enough to accommodate twenty-one compounds, which housed Oshodi's own family and numerous slaves.[67] In the 1840s, Kosoko had given Oshodi land in what became Olowogbowo, which he cleared and settled many

59. Bruce to Admiralty, 25 Jan. 1854, F.O. 84/954.

60. Glover to Kennedy, 18 July 1868, C.O. 147/14.

61. (?1853–1923). *Nigerian Pioneer*, 17 April 1931.

62. Glover, *Life of Sir John Hawley Glover*, p. 116.

63. Glover to Kennedy, 18 July 1865, C.O. 147/14.

64. Evidence of Momadu Awo, Aina, and Ajayi, Chief Ojora, Att. Gen. v. John Holt and Att. Gen. v. McIver, LSCR, Civ. 55, 1909.

65. See n. 66.

66. Memo by Brand, 5 May 1860, F.O. 84/1115.

67. Braimah Seidu Seriki & Ors v. Faye, LSCR, Civ. 85, 1919; *West Africa*, 1 March 1930, 19 July 1930, 27 June 1936; *Lagos Daily News*, 13 April 1931. It should be added that the extensive legal dispute over Epetedo land produced claims on both sides that are not always easily verified.

of his followers, but he was forced to abandon the site when he joined Kosoko in exile. The allocation in Epetedo was compensation for the land he had lost and a gesture by the *Oba*, encouraged by Glover, to secure the support of his formidable former opponent. Ironically, the land he had occupied in Olowogbowo included a prime site that would soon become Wilberforce House, the mansion built by the Saro merchant, J. J. Thomas.

Oshodi was unusual among his successful contemporaries in deciding not to obtain crown grants for the land he had been allocated in Epetedo. In this matter, he remained loyal to Old Lagos. He was confident that his tenure was secure under Yoruba law because the land had been allocated by Aromire, the White Cap Chief with authority over the area. Evidently, too, Oshodi did not need to use the land as security for commercial credit. In the 1860s, he still retained many slaves, though by then his business was said to be 'not so prosperous' and owed money to a European firm.[68] When he died in 1868, however, his slaves did not hesitate to show their preference for the new property rights. Within a year, they had joined the emerging propertied class by taking out crown grants for the land they occupied—and unsuspectingly created a legal dispute that ran far into the twentieth century.[69] Meanwhile, three of Oshodi's sons, who became property dealers, began by selling off some of the land their father had acquired and that, accordingly, they had the right to alienate. If Oshodi was in debt at the time of his death, he also retained a good deal of credit.

By the time Oshodi died, Mohammed Shitta was still in the middle of a career that continued until shortly before his death in 1895.[70] In formal terms, Mohammed Shitta was a Saro. He was born in Waterloo, Sierra Leone, in 1824, the son of liberated slaves from Yorubaland.[71] The typical Saro story, though, is one of Christian repatriates, whereas Mohammed, like his parents, was a Muslim. Islam had already spread to Ilorin, his father's home town, by the early nineteenth century.[72] In his early years, Mohammed also answered to the name William, probably because it had been assigned to him by the Christians, who were the predominant influence in Sierra Leone's community

68. Akintan, *Epetedo Lands*, p. 8.

69. For example, James Jones v. Alli Agiri, LSCR, Civ. 51, 1908.

70. I am grateful to Mr Sulu Shitta, Mohammed's son, for interviews on 5 Dec. 1961, 6 Dec. 1961, and 10 Jan. 1962, and to Mrs P. O. Bucknor, Mohammed's granddaughter, for an interview on 1 Dec. 1961. Additional information from Losi, *History of Lagos*, pp. 110–12; Deniga, *African Leaders*, Vol. 2, p. 7. Oyeweso has provided a brief account (based on secondary sources) in *Across Three Centuries*.

71. His obituarist entered Shitta's date of birth as 'around 1830', *Lagos Weekly Record*, 6 July 1895. I have preferred Losi's fuller account, which gives the date as 1824. Losi, *History of Lagos*, p. 110.

72. I finally found this information in evidence given by his son, Sani, in Lemomu Abasi et al. v. Tijani Noibi et al. LSCR, Civ. 103, 1924.

of freed slaves.[73] He returned with his parents to Yoruba country in 1844 and settled in Badagri, where his father became the imam of the Muslim community, a position he held until his death in 1849. Mohammed moved to Lagos with his new wife and his mother in 1853, shortly after the consulate was established.[74] He rose to become the most prominent and wealthiest Muslim in Lagos, cementing his memory in history by building the mosque there that bears his name. The cost was estimated to be between £4,000 and £5,000; the opening ceremony in 1894 was a notable event.[75] Governor Carter presided, Abdullah Quilliam, a convert and the leading Muslim in Britain, represented the Sultan of Turkey, who awarded Shitta the prestigious hereditary title of Bey.[76]

Mohammed Shitta was one of a small number of Lagosians who made most of his money in trade with regions that lay beyond Lagos and its hinterland, though his headquarters remained in the port itself. He enjoyed a considerable advantage over Saro merchants in his ability to connect easily with co-religionists in the north. He began trading in Lagos, and in 1864 extended his activities to the Niger, which became an increasingly important part of the business during the next twenty years.[77] He had a base in the Niger Delta, where he entered an association with Miller Bros., but rapidly extended the business to the middle reaches of the Niger. He built a factory at Egga, some 400 miles (about 650 km) inland, owned a steamer that operated between there and the Delta, and also organised caravans that travelled between Yorubaland and the Bida Emirate about 80 miles (130 km) north of Egga, where he was said to have 'great influence'.[78] He sold European cloth and beads, among other manufactured goods, imported kola nuts from the Gold Coast, and bought local cloth, ivory, and potash for sale in Lagos, where he established a connection with the British firm of J. D. Fairley. Business trips in this pioneering trade were lengthy and often gruelling expeditions.[79] Shitta was helped by his brother, Yesufu, but was himself sometimes away

73. The name 'William' also appears occasionally in the 1870s and 1880s in connection with colonial formalities (e.g., jury service and some court cases).

74. Avoseh, *A Short History of Badagri*, p. 106.

75. Carter to Ripon, 9 Jan. 1895, C.O. 147/98. Shitta had already funded the reconstruction of the Central Mosque in Victoria Street in 1873. Animashaun, *The History of the Muslim Community*. Edward W. Blyden was present and recorded some interesting observations of the event in *West Africa Before Europe*, pp. 111–12.

76. Carter to Ripon, 9 Jan. 1895, C.O. 147/98. Shitta paid Quilliam's travel expenses. On Quilliam and the wider context, see Greaves, *Islam in Victorian Britain*; Singleton, '"That Ye May Know Each Other"'.

77. *Lagos Weekly Record*, 6 July 1895.

78. Welsh to Holt and Cotterell, 16 March 1888, Holt Papers 27/2. At this time, Egga referred to a place. Today, Eggan is used in a broader sense to refer to a locality and its people.

79. *Lagos Times*, 9 Nov. 1881. See, more generally, Falola, 'The Yoruba Caravan System'.

FIGURE 3.1. The Opening of the Shitta Mosque, 1894. Seated: Edward Wilmot Blyden (diplomat, educator, Pan-Africanist). Standing: From left Mohammed Shitta Bey (merchant) wearing a turban; James Pinson Labulo Davies (merchant and planter); Jacob Samuel Leigh (merchant); Richard Beale Blaize (merchant). Copied by Paramount Photographers Lagos.

from Lagos for a year at a time. He kept detailed accounts in Arabic but these, a historian's gold mine, have now been lost.

In 1885, Shitta ceased trading with the Niger and from then on remained in Lagos. Although his retirement coincided with the monopoly of Niger trade being established by the precursors of the Royal Niger Company, it is unlikely that this development prompted his decision. Indeed, Shitta became 'the company's right-hand man in the upper river' in 1888, and helped the firm negotiate a treaty with the Bida Emirate, a decision the Emir soon regretted.[80] His obituarist appears to have been correct in stating that success enabled him to retire.[81] He was undoubtedly wealthy when he closed all his trading activities in 1889 and was said to have become 'to some extent a financier' as well as a merchant.[82] The Crown Grants Index for 1863–1882 shows that he was buying land in the 1850s, obtained numerous crown grants, and continued to purchase property in Lagos into the 1880s.[83] In 1884, he was able to lend the struggling French firm of Fabre & Cie the substantial sum of £7,200, without risking the capital needed to fund the construction of the mosque that bears his name.[84] He was a noted philanthropist who supported both secular and religious causes. In 1893, Acting Governor Denton described him as being 'a very influential and rich member of the Mohammedan community'.[85] After he died, his wealth was distributed among the family according to Yoruba and Muslim custom.[86] His brother, Yesufu, and other members of the family continued to trade but did so independently. By then, however, the conditions that had enabled Mohammed Shitta to make his fortune on the Niger were no longer present to favour his successors.

As might be expected, information about the Saro during the early period of colonial rule is more abundant than it is for other merchant groups. Even so, in most cases records have been lost and with them the details needed to give precision to their business fortunes. Some fifteen to twenty names can be counted as representative of the Saro merchants during the early colonial period, among them Richard B. Blaize, Joseph S. Bucknor, James W. Cole, Thomas F. Cole (Daddy Alade), James P. L. Davies, Charles J. George, Thomas Hoare, Thomas Joe, Jacob S. Leigh, Cornelius B. Moore, Harry Pratt, Henry Robbin, Josiah A. Savage, James J. Thomas, James. J. Turner, and Isaac H.

80. Shitta v. Fabre & Co., LSCR, Civ.7, 1888; Welsh to Holt and Cotterell, 16 March 1888, Holt Papers 27/2.

81. *Lagos Weekly Record*, 6 July 1895.

82. *Lagos Weekly Times*, 11 Oct. 1890, reporting on the Privy Council's decision in William [*sic*] Shitta v. Fabre & Co.

83. See also Shitta v. Macaulay and Osborne. LSCR, Civ. 3, 1880.

84. In 1888, he obtained judgement against Fabre for the principal and interest (£7,200). See also Welsh to Holt, 16 March 1888, Holt Papers, 27/2.

85. Denton to Ripon, 1 May 1893, C.O. 147/90.

86. Sani Shitta and Anor, v. Ashiata, LSCR, Civ. 58, 1910; details of the distribution of the estate, which was 'sworn at under £25,000', are contained in LAP I, 384–8, 1895.

Willoughby.[87] Not all of these merchants can be allocated the space they deserve without turning the present study into an encyclopaedia, which is not its purpose. Information about some (such as Thomas F. Cole, Thomas Joe, and Harry Pratt) remains sketchy. Several others who were at the outset of their careers and made their mark later will appear in subsequent chapters. James P. L. Davies, whose eminence made him the most royal of the merchant princes, will be discussed at length in the next chapter.

As already indicated, 'Brazilian' returnees had few representatives among the leading merchants at this time. Laotan's authoritative study of the 'Old Families' of nineteenth-century Lagos lists only two merchants of substance: João da Rocha and Manuel de Sant Anna.[88] One or two others could be added but would not alter the minor position the group occupied in the rankings. Nevertheless, trade with Brazil helped to sustain family and cultural connections as well as having economic importance for the community in Lagos and should not be bypassed. Accordingly, the subject will be carried forward to chapter 7, which deals with the period 1880–1900, when more information is available.

Broadly speaking, the Saro merchants fit the characteristics enumerated earlier in this study: they were returning ex-slaves or their children; most had received education at mission schools, had become Christians, taken English names, and absorbed Victorian values, styles, and ways of life. Behind these generalisations, however, lie the particularities of real people and with them the details that both enlarge and qualify summary statements. The two examples that follow reveal some of the variety within apparent uniformities that exist because of limited information about the group as a whole.

Charles Joseph George is a prime example of the archetypal Saro.[89] His obituary notice, published in the *Lagos Weekly Record* in 1906, spiced the usual encomiums with some remarks that reflected the paper's increasingly anti-government stance.[90] George was an 'intelligent conservative' who assumed an attitude of 'passive acquiescence'. He was a member of the

87. Two of the group (Henry Robbin and C. B. Moore) maintained stores in Lagos but conducted much of their business in and from Abeokuta.

88. Laotan, *The Torch Bearers*, pp. 8–18. The total rises to three if Lourenço A. Cardoso, who began as a teacher and ended as an auctioneer, is included.

89. I owe a particular debt to John Oluwole George, son of John Olawumi George and nephew of Charles, for his considerable help, including access to his uncle's will, the family tree, and some of his letters (interview Oshoba Compound, Abeokuta, 29 Dec. 1961; and to James T. George, a grandson of Charles, Yaba, Lagos, 20 and 29 Feb. 1962). See also Macmillan, *The Red Book*; Deniga, *African Leaders*, pp. 13–14.

90. *Lagos Weekly Record*, 15 Sept. 1906. The paper was edited by the American-Liberian, John Payne Jackson (1848–1915), who moved to Lagos at the beginning of the 1870s and began working for the prominent merchant, Jacob Leigh. Jackson then began trading on his own but was forced out of the Niger by European competition in the 1880s in circumstances that may have fostered the anti-colonial stance that characterised his subsequent career in journalism. See Omu, 'Journalism'.

Legislative Council for nearly twenty years, yet never ventured to initiate changes to ideas that were based on 'past times and past policies', when 'native interests were little affected'. The colonial government certainly thought well of him and with good reason because, in addition to his business commitments, George was tireless in serving on an almost limitless number of boards and committees, which he fitted in between acting as a Justice of the Peace and his duties as Harbour Master, while spending time and money promoting the Wesleyan mission.[91] Charles and his father were also active in advancing Egba interests in Lagos; Charles played a notable part (with his friend Jacob Leigh) in persuading the governments in Abeokuta and Lagos to co-operate in heading off anticipated French incursions into Egbaland in 1888.

Charles George had an advantageous start. He was born about 1840 in Murray Town, Sierra Leone.[92] His grandfather, Thomas (alias Masinka), was an Egba slave who was freed and settled in Hastings, Sierra Leone, where he married, and eventually returned to Lagos in 1852.[93] His father James, an Egba named Osoba, was educated in Freetown and began trading there before being appointed as the Lagos agent for a leading Sierra Leonean merchant, William Lewis. In the 1850s, James built up a substantial business that included running his own sailing ships between Freetown and Lagos.[94] His large portfolio of property in Freetown, capped by the impressive residence he built in one of the most favoured parts of the town, attested to his status.[95] In the mid-1850s, James decided to transfer much of his business to Lagos. By then, Charles, his first son, who had been educated at the Grammar School in Freetown, had begun to look after his father's business affairs in Sierra Leone. In 1862, he joined the family in Lagos and three years later married Isabella Will, the daughter of James Will, a former Yoruba slave who had settled permanently in Freetown, where he became one of the most prominent merchants of his generation.

In 1864, James and Charles registered a formal partnership, known as George & Son, which is the earliest agreement of its kind in Lagos.[96] It was not unusual for family members, especially brothers, to trade together informally, but a formal partnership between father and son was different because it envisaged the prospect of continuity that was a departure from Yoruba (and Muslim) traditions of inheritance. In doing so, the partnership foreshadowed

91. *Lagos Standard*, 19 Sept. 1906. See also Denton to Chamberlain, 24 Nov. 1896, C.O. 147/107; Denton to Chamberlain, 28 Sept. 1898, C.O. 147/135.

92. Different sources give Charles's date of birth as 1839, 1840, and 1841. As there is no means of choosing between them, I have opted for the middle one.

93. Evidence of J. A. Roberts in Allen v. Holloway. LSCR, Civ. 77, 1916.

94. Fyfe, *A History of Sierra Leone*, pp. 257, 317–18; Lewis to Glover, 12 Sept. 1863, C.O. 147/7.

95. Fyfe, *A History of Sierra Leone*, p. 317.

96. Articles of Partnership, LLOR, 3/165, 1864; *Anglo-African*, 12 Nov. 1864.

trends that were to appear early in the twentieth century in response to the need to adopt impersonal forms of business organisation. James contributed stock, land, premises, and boats worth £6,000; Charles put in £300. Both parties agreed to work 'to the utmost of their skill and cunning' entirely for their 'joint interest', to share profits and losses equally, and to keep 'perfect, just and true Books of Account'. Shortly afterwards, James fulfilled his ambition to return to his homeland. He settled in Abeokuta, the Egba capital, where he managed the branch of the partnership established there. Charles stayed in Lagos and oversaw the firm's two stores on the Marina and in Olowogbowo. By the time James died in 1876, he had become the *Lisa* of *Oba*, a senior title in the influential *Ogboni* society that both recognised his prominence and added to it. His last will, dated 1871, split his share of the partnership into three: one-third went to Charles, one-third was divided between his second son, Josiah, and his eldest daughter, Harriet; the last portion was held in trust (by Charles) for the remaining children.[97] Charles also inherited property on two prime sites: in Broad Street and the Marina. Other real estate in Lagos, Abeokuta, and Freetown was divided among the remaining children.

George & Son imported a variety of dry goods, notably cotton textiles and hardware, and exported palm oil and raw cotton, some of which was produced in the vicinity of Abeokuta by James's numerous slaves. After his father's death, Charles continued the business and kept its name, but ran it as the sole partner with the assistance of James's adopted son, John Oluwole George, who managed the branch in Abeokuta.[98] The big decision Charles felt constrained to make at this time was to disband his father's slaves, though this appears to have been done in stages. Emancipation reduced the firm's competitiveness and eventually its participation in the produce trade. Nevertheless, the business was still prosperous in the 1880s and was ranked among the top ten African importers measured by the value of duties paid from 1881 to 1885 (inclusive).[99] Unfortunately, the 'perfect, just and true' account books have not survived, and it is impossible to comment further on the profitability of the firm. Indirect evidence, however, attests to Charles's considerable affluence. He built an impressive residence, known as Pacific House, on the Marina; had a rickshaw, one of the status symbols of the time; made frequent trips to England; educated some of his children there, as well as in Lagos and Freetown; and donated generously to religious, educational, and other 'good causes'.[100]

97. The basis of the valuation and its effects on the business remain matters of speculation.

98. Evidence of John O. George before the Trade Commission of 1898, 24 March 1898, in Denton to Chamberlain. 25 May 1898, C.O. 147/132.

99. Moloney to Granville, 11 April 1886, C.O. 147/55.

100. According to one contemporary source, the otherwise puzzling name given to George's house had nothing to do with the ocean but was an expression of his pacific personality and values. *Lagos Weekly Record*, 15 Sept. 1906.

Charles's health began to decline in the late 1890s. The business may have contracted too, though Charles was still wealthy when he died in 1906. The assets listed in his last will dated 1895 (with subsequent codicils) included money in his account with the Bank of British West Africa (BBWA), investments in London, and a life policy worth £500.[101] His wife, Henrietta, had died in 1882 (aged thirty-five) and his adopted brother, John, had left the firm to become Treasurer of the United Egba Government in Abeokuta before joining Radcliffe & Durrant in 1889 as their agent in Lagos. Charles bequeathed to his son, Charles Will George, all his stock 'should he be in business with me at the time of my death', Pacific House, and property in Abeokuta. His two daughters, Harriet and Hannah, were to inherit a second property and adjoining land on the Marina. The remaining personal property and real estate in Lagos, Abeokuta, and Freetown was to be shared equally between these three surviving children. Charles's funeral was a considerable public event: government offices were closed for part of the day, flags were flown at half-mast, and large numbers of the public joined the funeral procession.

Charles George was unusual among Lagos merchants because he benefitted from his father's early start and did not depend on landed assets to secure credit. Nevertheless, the credit was there if it were needed, and that knowledge increased the confidence of business associates in his standing. He was typical of successful merchants, however, in being able to give his children more than a head start in life. His son, Charles Will George, continued the business. He withdrew from the risky produce trade, but still ran into difficulties, as did many others, during and after World War I. Nevertheless, the business was still active in the 1930s, though it operated on a much-reduced scale. Charles retired in 1935; when he died in 1940, he was said to have 'hardly any means'.[102] It was common for businesses run by Lagos merchants to end when they died. The George family is exceptional because their business lasted for three generations and spanned a period of seventy years.

The subsequent history of the two principal properties that became 56 and 58 Marina illustrates the importance of real estate to Lagos merchants and their families, the advantages accruing to those who obtained crown grants in the 1860s, and the way in which property acquired in the early days of colonial rule supported subsequent generations through difficult times. The history of the two properties is not easily unravelled. In the early years of the colony, boundaries were uncertain, land surveys were in their infancy, and the results were often unreliable. In essence, however, it can be said that 56 Marina was the product of crown grants given to James George & Son in 1868

101. Last will, 1895, LLOR, 2787, 1895; LAP II/424–34, 1906.
102. Peter J. C. Thomas to C.J.K. Macfoy, 6 Feb. 1940 (Private Papers of P.J.C. Thomas).

and the purchase of an adjoining plot from Thomas Joe in 1872 for £200.[103] 58 Marina, which became Pacific House, arose from two crown grants, which James obtained in 1863 and 1864.[104] Both properties were passed down to family members as specified in the wills executed by James and Charles.

By 1906, when Charles James George died, his son Charles Will had already begun to lease land on the Marina and in Broad Street to Miller Bros.[105] In 1914, he mortgaged 58 Marina (Pacific House) to BBWA to cover an overdraft of £400, at an annual interest rate of 5 per cent, which he increased to £600 in the following year and extended yet again to secure an overdraft of £1,000, this time at a rate of 10 per cent.[106] The financial position continued to deteriorate and in 1920, Charles and his siblings sold property they had inherited joining Broad Street to the Marina to McIver & Co. for £16,000.[107] The adverse trend could not be halted, however, and in 1927, Pacific House was sold to the African & Eastern Trade Corporation for £8,575, which was a substantial sum at the time.[108]

Number 56 (which eventually became 56 and 57), was owned jointly by Charles James's two daughters and stayed within the family rather longer. It had long been leased to a succession of African and expatriate merchants to provide an income for Charles's daughters.[109] In 1942, it was leased to the London & Kano Trading Co. for five years at an annual rent of £250 and then mortgaged to the Lagos Building Society in 1948 to cover a loan of £5,000 at 12.5 per cent.[110] The mortgage was repaid in 1950, and in the following year the property was leased once more to London & Kano for 15 years at a rent of £500 p.a.[111] The lease was cut short in 1956, when the National Bank of Nigeria stepped in and bought the freehold for £25,000. These examples reveal a previously hidden yet vital element in the Lagos economy: the growing importance of rental incomes during the colonial period and of the capital gains accruing from sales of real estate, especially after World War II. Property had served the family well. No commercial investment could match the value of a crown grant secured in the 1860s.

Jacob Samuel Leigh, who also achieved commercial success during the early colonial period, was an almost exact contemporary of Charles J.

103. Evidence of James O. George, in Att. General v. John Holt & Co. Ltd and Att. General v. Miller & Co. Ltd., LSCR, Civ. 55, 1909.

104. LLOR 1981, 1862.

105. LLOR 82/14, 1913, 82/229, 1915.

106. LLOR 1981, LLOR 83/400, 1914; 86/349, 1915.

107. LLOR 2202.

108. LLOR 1981.

109. LLOR 47/202, 1907.

110. LLOR, 605/9, 1942; 728/24, 1947.

111. LLOR 896/53, 1951.

George.[112] He was born in Sierra Leone in 1837 and died in Lagos in 1907.[113] Like George, Leigh was an Egba and a Wesleyan. His father, Sodeinde Sodipe, was a slave who was liberated by the Royal Navy's anti-slavery squadron and taken to Freetown, where he was converted to Christianity and took the name Leigh. Jacob's mother, who was originally called Efubemi, became Susannah Turner before her marriage. In 1853, the family decided to return to Lagos, where Jacob entered the new Christchurch School to complete the education he had begun in Freetown.[114] Jacob's father was a trader, though not on a scale that matched Charles George's father, and Jacob began to earn his living as an apprentice cooper under one of the great figures of the day, James P. L. Davies.

By 1862, Leigh had moved to Abeokuta and started a small trading business. He had done well enough by 1866 to return to Lagos, where he entered the import and export trade, selling palm produce and raw cotton to European firms in exchange for dry goods, such as textiles and hardware. He never dealt in alcohol, which was opposed to his Wesleyan principles. He opened a store on the Marina and kept a shop in Broad Street, where he also lived. In 1879, the business expanded to Porto Novo, where Leigh opened a branch, and to the Niger, where in 1879 he joined a group of Lagos merchants, notably Daniel C. Taiwo, Mohammed Shitta Bey, and the Crowther brothers (Josiah and Samuel), in developing legitimate commerce.[115] By the close of the 1870s, Leigh had about five stations and a steamboat on the river.[116] His headquarters were at Akassa in the delta; other branches were opened on the Niger as far as the great market centre of Onitsha, beyond which point navigation by steam-tugs became difficult. Leigh did not employ family members, but had two Saro clerks, George A. Williams, who looked after the business in the Delta, and John P. Jackson, who oversaw affairs on the Lower Niger.[117]

112. I am grateful for information supplied by Francis E. Leigh, Jacob's only surviving child, Surulere, Lagos, 14 Dec. 1961. The *Lagos Weekly Record*, 27 July 1907, provides the fullest obituary. Jacob Leigh appears in the photograph in figure 3.1.

113. The *Lagos Standard*, 24 July 1907, gave Leigh's date of birth as 1836. I have preferred 1837 because it was cited by the *Lagos Weekly Record*, which appeared a few days later (27 July 1907) and is the date accepted by the family.

114. Kenny & Others v. Col. Sec., LSCR, Civ. 5, 1884. I prefer this date of return to others because the evidence in the case was by Leigh himself.

115. David Macaulay v. Leigh, LSCR, Civ. 4, 1882; *Lagos Times*, 9 Aug. 1882.

116. By 1885, the National African Company was buying up European competitors on the Niger and pushing out Africans. (*African Times*, 1 Sept. 1885; 1 July 1886). Expatriate and African merchants protested against the Royal Niger Company's monopoly (*Lagos Observer*, 26 May 1888). Moloney estimated that the Lagos-Niger connection was worth about £60,000. p.a. He listed forty-five 'persons' trading to the Niger before the RNC charter was granted, including seventeen small-scale female traders. Molony to Granville, 19 April 1886, C.O. 147/55; Moloney to Knutsford, 9 Oct. 1888, C.O. 147/66. For opposition in Lagos to the RNC, see *Lagos Weekly Record*, 19 Feb. 1891.

117. Evidence in Savage v. Macfoy, LSCR, Civ. 53, 1909; Evidence in Glassie v. Leigh, LSCR, Civ. 5, 1884.

The business concentrated on buying palm produce, ivory, and local cloth and selling a variety of dry goods.

Jacob Leigh kept accounts but, as in the case of Charles George, these have now been lost. Indirect evidence, however, points to his success in the 1860s and 1870s. He secured a crown grant for land that had a pier on the Marina, had at least two other Marina properties, bought land in Broad Street from one James H. Gooding, a carpenter, in 1865 for 120 bags of cowries (about £75), acquired other property in Breadfruit Lane, Wesley Street, Brook Street, and elsewhere in New Lagos. In the 1870s, his status was manifested in symbols of public display: a horse and carriage to take him along the Marina, where the road could support wheeled traffic, and a boat to traverse the lagoon. In 1871, he made the first of several visits to England, partly for commercial reasons but also to accompany the return of his wife, Sarah, and one of his daughters, Sabina, who had been educated there. Another daughter, Aureola, and a son, Alfred, were also educated in England. Both daughters became teachers in Lagos; Alfred (later Sodeinde Leigh-Sodipe) qualified as a doctor in 1892 and was one of only eight Nigerians to do so in the nineteenth century.[118] Leigh gave generously to the Wesleyan Church, including the land on which Tinubu Church was built, helped to establish Wesleyan Boys High School, which opened in 1878, and was active as a preacher and class leader.

Leigh was also a well-known figure in the confined sphere of Lagos politics. He was Secretary of the African Commercial Association, which representatives of different Yoruba groups formed in 1863 in a bid to forestall hostilities in the interior. Although the initiative failed, Leigh soon acquired a reputation as 'one of the more reasonable advisers of the Egbas'.[119] However, his decision to ship raw cotton from Abeokuta during the embargo imposed by Glover in 1865 prompted the governor to report that his 'entire behaviour was most uncourteous and disrespectful'.[120] His claim for compensation for losses he declared he had suffered as result of the closure of trade routes was dismissed as a ploy designed to persuade the government to lift the embargo.[121] Leigh had more success in 1888, when he joined other Egba Saro (including Charles George) in urging the *Alake* of Abeokuta to strengthen ties with Britain as a means of neutralising French ambitions.

Leigh continued to sign various petitions and memorials, which were the standard means of informing the colonial government of elite opinion, but he remained more critical of government policies than most Saro were. For this

118. Adeloye, 'Some Early Doctors'; *Lagos Standard*, 8 May 1901. Dr Leigh-Sodipe (1865–1901) died at the early age of thirty-six, having succumbed to a 'malignant fever'.

119. Glover to Cardwell, 6 Oct. 1865, C.O. 147/9.

120. Glover to Cardwell, 6 Oct. 1865, C.O. 147/9.

121. Hilbery to Cardwell, 11. Dec. 1865, C.O. 147/10; Leigh to Cardwell, 5 Sept. 1865, C.O. 147/10; Blackall to Cardwell, 5 April 1866, C.O. 147/11.

reason, and in contrast to Charles George, he was never appointed to serve on the Legislative Council. Governor Carter passed judgement on him in 1894: 'he is one of the few disloyal natives in Lagos and was formerly known as a meddlesome intriguer with the Egba government'.[122] Governor McCallum, whose mishandling of a serious labour dispute in 1897 prompted opposition from Leigh among others, shared Carter's opinion. Nevertheless, he endorsed Leigh's appointment as Liberian consul in Lagos. The position not only prevented Leigh from attending political meetings but also ensured consular oversight of the welfare of Kru seamen, who were vital to the maritime trade of the port.[123] The nomination arose from Leigh's friendship with Edward Blyden, the Liberian educator, writer, and diplomat. Leigh sympathised with Blyden's advocacy of African unity, which raised questions about where Saro loyalties should lie. It was left to John P. Jackson, Leigh's former clerk, who had become Editor of the *Lagos Weekly Record* and a critic of the government, to write an obituary notice that called attention to Leigh's 'patriotism'.[124]

Leigh's story did not end happily. In 1872, he mortgaged some of his Lagos property to Callender, Sykes & Mather (CSM), a substantial Manchester textile firm, to secure advances of goods.[125] This was a regular procedure for Lagos merchants and in Leigh's case the debt was settled, and the properties were released. Further advances in 1874 and 1878 were also discharged by the due date.[126] In 1882, however, Leigh lost his Niger steamer, the *White Rose*, in a collision on the river.[127] Although he planned to re-enter the trade with two purpose-built steamers, his hope was never realised. Leigh's former clerk on the Niger later alleged that he was also being cheated by another firm.[128] His timing was as unfortunate as his luck. Unlike Shitta Bey, who was already well established on the Niger, Leigh entered when the predecessors of the Royal Company were already pushing out African competitors, so his future on the river was not promising.[129] Whatever the precise combination of circumstances, Leigh closed his stations on the Niger in 1884. His business in Lagos also suffered from losses incurred there on palm oil. From then on, as the *Lagos Weekly Record* put it, he traded 'with indifferent success for several

122. Carter to Rippon, 19 Dec. 1894, C.O. 147/94. See also Carter to Knutsford, 18 March 1892, C.O. 147/84.
123. McCallum to Chamberlain, 3 Sept. 1897, and enc. from Leigh to McCallum, 31 Aug. 1897, C.S.O 1/1/19. See, more generally, Brooks, *The Kru Mariner*.
124. *Lagos Weekly Record*, 27 July 1907.
125. LLOR, 15/102.
126. LLOR, 21/31, 24/338.
127. *Lagos Times*, 27 Dec. 1882.
128. John Payne Jackson, *Lagos Weekly Record*, 27 July 1907.
129. The United African Company (1879), National African Company (1882), Royal Niger Company (1886). See Pearson, 'Economic Imperialism'.

years'.[130] He was still placed fifth on the list of African importers in Lagos in 1881–1885, but he was unable to sustain that position.

In an ominous move, Leigh felt obliged to lease his Marina premises to Williams Bros. in 1883 and transfer his business to the lower floor of his house in Broad Street.[131] In 1885, he owed Callender, Sykes & Mather £1,300, which he was unable to procure. He agreed to repay the sum plus interest at an annual rate of 5 per cent by 1890 and offered two Marina properties (at the corner of Davies Street and Apongbon Street) as security.[132] Following a court action in 1892, he managed to pay the balance of the debt (£1,096) and regain his mortgaged property.[133] His temporary liquidity was made possible by a loan of £1,000 from the Saro merchant, Richard B. Blaize. In exchange, Leigh immediately remortgaged the newly released property to him and agreed to an annual interest rate of 10 per cent. Leigh repeated the exercise in 1893, this time borrowing £2,500 at 5 per cent interest and contracting to repay the sum by 1901. In 1895, in an obscure deal, Leigh sold his Marina property at the corner of Davies Street for £3,250 to James J. Thomas, a wealthy Saro merchant. The property was speedily rented to Holt & Welsh for £280 p.a.[134] The sum Leigh received from the arrangement with Thomas probably enabled him to repay Blaize. In 1903, Thomas sold the property to the rising Saro merchant, David A. Taylor, for £3,750. Leigh had retained an unknown stake in the property, but only part of the proceeds was credited to him.

The sale brought Leigh's ownership of a key Marina property to a close. His afflictions, however, lived on. His long-standing relationship with the British firm, Ollivant, deteriorated. Between 1886 and 1892, Leigh shipped a total of 1,500 casks of palm oil to Ollivant in accordance with an agreement made with them in 1885.[135] Unfortunately for Leigh, the market remained persistently weak, and the consignments were sold at a loss. He halted shipments in 1892, but by then he owed Ollivant £3,112. Leigh made a new agreement to repay the debt out of profits on future sales or remittances from other sources. By 1899, however, payment had not been forthcoming and Ollivant received a court judgement in their favour for £2,875 plus costs. Leigh appealed and the court reduced the amount he owed to £1,875. Leigh was then driven to take a second mortgage on his property in Broad Street, undertook to repay the first mortgage (to the Saro financier, Isaac B. Williams) within twelve months, and to settle his debt to Ollivant's in annual instalments of £250. By 1902, he had been able to repay

130. 27 July 1907.

131. Notice in the *Lagos Times & Gold Coast Advertiser*, 25 July 1883, 12 Sept. 1883.

132. LLOR, 3/198.

133. This matter rumbled on until at least 1896. *Lagos Standard*, 1 April 1896.

134. Welsh to Holt, 18 March 1888, 23 March 1888, Holt Papers, Liverpool 27/2. Leigh had already rented his pier to Holt & Welsh in 1888 for £50 p.a.

135. Ollivant v. Leigh, LSCR, Civ. 22, 1899, continued in Civ. 27, 1902, and Civ. 28, 1903. Leigh also owed BBWA £677 in 1896: LSCR, Civ. 19, 1897.

no more than £500 of the capital and £25 in interest, at which point Ollivant again went to court to enforce the judgement they had received. By then, Leigh had few assets left, apart from the security he had mortgaged, and finally had to surrender.[136]

Leigh's other properties had also been sold or burdened by debt. In 1893, he sold a modest property on the Marina (at Bishop's Street) for £550 to the Société des missions africaines. In 1896, he mortgaged his Broad Street property (originally a crown grant obtained in 1871) to Isaac B. Williams for £600. Property in Breadfruit Lane followed the same path in 1897, when it was mortgaged to Blaize to raise £400. In these desperate circumstances, it is unsurprising to find that Leigh had almost no income after 1900. He had long given up the produce trade and was technically a commission agent dealing with imported goods but without any business to transact. He had tried to diversify but his farms at Badagri and Ota, being close to the lagoon, were too saline to suit tree crops, such as coffee and cocoa, which were being grown more successfully a few miles inland.[137] His final years were spent in a room, which he rented for £3 a month, in Isaac Williams's house in Broad Street. The merchant princes of Lagos were engaged in a risky business. The heights they could reach were matched by the depths to which they could fall.

Taking Stock

It is difficult now to recapture events that, at the time, were little short of astounding to participants and observers alike. The dramatic intervention by the British in 1851 overturned established economic and political relationships and brought considerable uncertainty about the future of what was to be a new order. Assurance came only with time and the comfort of retrospection. Contemporaries, however, were obliged to adjust to risky and imperfectly understood novelties. As with all revolutions, continuities helped to anchor change. The *Oba* and his chiefs remained in place; slavery itself was not abolished but was used in the production of palm oil. Elements of legitimate commerce were already developing within existing commercial institutions: trading networks purchased and transported palm oil; barter continued to be the main method of completing transactions.

Nevertheless, there was a revolution, even if it did not revolve immediately. Legitimate commerce replaced the overseas slave trade. Material considerations aided morality: the steamship combined with favourable terms of trade

136. I have not followed the subsequent history of Leigh's real estate in detail. The only substantial property the family retained or regained was one in Broad Street (a crown grant obtained by Leigh in 1871), which his children, who were his beneficiaries, mortgaged to BBWA in 1910 (at a rate of 10 per cent p.a.) to secure a loan of £800.

137. C. O. Leigh v. Taiwo and Yesufu, 13 Sept. 1909, Epediv, 4/3, 1909–10.

boosted exports and, reciprocally, imports during the consular and early colonial periods. A new generation of European and Saro merchants took advantage of new opportunities; some slave-trading Big Men adapted; many others faded into obscurity. New Lagos arose; the Old Town lost much of its previous centrality. Responses to price incentives, however, were not automatic. Appropriate institutions were needed to bridge the gap between agency and achievement. Innovative rights to private property in land provided security for credit, which was vital to the expansion of trade. The individual examples cited in this chapter demonstrate how wide-ranging the ramifications of this departure were, affecting not only the founding businesses but also the fortunes of whole families over several generations and embedding values that were to become norms in the twentieth century.

Answers generate fresh questions. This chapter has touched on several key issues relating to entrepreneurial behaviour and performance: the relative importance and Saro and European merchants; the extent to which the size of firms was limited by their structure, which typically depended on the ability of a sole proprietor; the tendency of businesses to dissolve upon the death of their founder. These questions will be carried forward to enable short-run trends to be considered against the evidence of a longer period.

CHAPTER FOUR

Chief Daniel Taiwo
and His Network

THE PREVIOUS CHAPTER described the striking differences between the Old Town and the New. One looked towards the mainland and contained the *Oba*'s residence, the dwellings of his senior chiefs, and the closely packed, modest homes of the majority of the town's citizens. The other looked towards the sea, was the favoured location of the Europeans and Saro, and sported a number of imposing brick properties that proclaimed the arrival of new wealth. The contrast was heightened by the area in between, which contained stretches of marshland and was more sparsely populated. Yet, necessity ensured that there were important connections between the two centres. New Lagos attracted traders and labourers, some of whom commuted from the Old Town; Saro merchants had dealings with local brokers; reciprocally, Government House extended its reach, if often uncertainly, from the Marina to the *Oba*'s domain.

Despite these qualifications, it remains the case that studies of the Saro have long focussed on features that distinguished them from indigenous Lagosians. The emphasis is undeniably accurate, but if left without qualification slips readily into mischaracterisations of the kind once familiar in the contrast between 'modernity' and 'tradition'. The purpose of this chapter is to reconstruct the career of Daniel Conrad Taiwo, an illiterate former slave who became one of the greatest merchants and political 'influencers' of the period. Although his eminence is well attested, few details of his life have found their way into print. Fresh evidence, based on his private papers and the Lagos Court and Lands Office records, makes it possible to construct an expanded, if still incomplete, account of his extraordinarily wide-ranging activities.

Taiwo began his career when the Lagos slave trade was at its height, but speedily converted to legitimate commerce as soon as the opportunity arose and adopted the new institutions it required, from freehold tenure to British silver coin. He also aligned himself with British rule, though less as a subordinate than as a power broker who offered a service that the colonial government was unable to provide for itself. In these ways, he was progressive in promoting forces of change, while deploying his established authority as head of an existing network that connected Lagos to its hinterland. In straddling two worlds, both contained in Lagos, Taiwo established close relations with a number of eminent Saro, including James Davies, the king of the merchant princes. Taiwo was not alone. Other indigenous Lagosians followed his example and established business and personal relations with members of the Saro community. From this perspective, the most useful categorisation of Lagos society during this period is less between Old and New Lagos than between those who adapted to the new conditions and those who did not.

Becoming a Lagosian

There are different accounts of Taiwo's early life, as is often the case where written sources are incomplete or uncertain.[1] According to Losi's standard history of Lagos, Taiwo was the grandson of the *Olofin* (equivalent of *Oba*) of Isheri, a town on the mainland some 15 miles north of Lagos.[2] He owed his affiliation and subsequent rank to his mother, Ishokun, who was a daughter of the *Olofin*; his father, Oluwolo, who was also from Isheri and distantly related to the *Olofin*, held a chieftaincy title in Jiga, a nearby town in Egbado territory.[3] Governor Moloney referred to Taiwo as being 'by birth an Egbado of Iseri', but the designation is incorrect because Iseri (more commonly known then as Isheri) is in neighbouring Awori territory.[4] The two are connected but distinct. The distinction is important for understanding Taiwo's affiliations and the location of his authority on the mainland.

Moloney was in good company in failing on this occasion to match individuals and origins precisely. Yorubaland was in a state of prolonged fluidity in the nineteenth century, following pressures arising from the fall of the Oyo

1. In addition to the sources in the citations that follow, I would like to record my gratitude to members and associates of Taiwo's family for their generous assistance, especially Chief Gabriel A. Taiwo, Taiwo's grandson, Lagos, 15 Feb. 1962, 3 March 1962. Chief Taiwo kindly gave me permission to use and cite documents in his possession (identified here as Taiwo Papers, abbreviated as TP). The headings in the citations are my own provisional ordering of the records. The family were to decide whether the papers would continue to be held by them or deposited with the University of Ibadan or elsewhere. Additionally, my thanks go to: *Oba* Samuel Ayodele II, his secretary, Chief S. A. Folarin, the *Alaiyeluwa Olofin* of Isheri, Chief R. O. A. D. Fashina, the *Aro* of Isheri, the *Oganla* of Isheri, Lagos, for a meeting on 3 March 1962.

2. Formally, *Olofin* was the title given to the founder of Awori but came to be used as the equivalent of *Oba*.

3. Rebecca Lyide Taiwo v. Odunsi Sarumi, LSCR, Civ. 64, 1912; Ali Delokun (the *Otun* of Abeokuta), to Taiwo, 9 Aug. 1898, TP, Lagos Affairs, 1870–1902.

4. Moloney to Granville, 21 June 1886, C.O. 147/55.

Empire in the north and the sporadic but ever-threatening predatory incursions from the kingdom of Dahomey in the west. Refugees and other migrants were driven south and east, creating or expanding states like Ibadan and Egba, and putting pressure on established smaller polities, such as the Egbado and Awori. These states occupied uncertain and contested borderlands, especially where, as in the case of the Awori, they possessed a town like Isheri, which was located on the lower reaches of the River Ogun and commanded access to both Lagos and the Egba capital of Abeokuta.[5] The Egba, who could deploy more firepower than the Egbado and Awori, claimed that Isheri was an Egbado town that paid tribute to Abeokuta and that the Egbado themselves, being Egba Odo ('Egbas by the side of the river') were extensions of the Egba state.[6] Governor Glover denied that the Egba had legitimate claims over Isheri but accepted that the town was not formally part of British territory, despite falling under the influence of Lagos during the period of the slave trade.[7] Rival claims to Isheri and the other borderland towns stoked disputes to the point where hostilities were common.[8]

There are at least two versions of how Taiwo became a Lagosian. One states that he 'very often' accompanied his father on visits to Lagos when he was still a boy and moved there during the reign of Osinlokun, after his father died.[9] This account places his arrival at some point in the 1820s. A second version claims that he came to Lagos around 1848 through the influence of Jacob Ogunbiyi, a prominent trader in the port.[10] Evidence now available adds weight to the first version but does not eliminate the second. Taiwo himself said that he was a small boy when his father took him to Lagos and that he remembered seeing Osinlokun when he was *Oba*, which was during the 1820s. A respected authority stated in 1898 that Taiwo's father sent his son to Lagos 'fearing that he might be enslaved' at a time when hostilities threatened the security of Isheri.[11] This is plausible because we know that *Oba* Osinlokun ensured Taiwo's safe passage and arranged his initial lodging. If this were the case, Taiwo would have been living in Lagos before his father's death, which occurred when Idewu Ojulari was *Oba* in the early 1830s. However, this account is still consistent with the involvement of Ogunbiyi, who became one of Taiwo's close friends, and even with the date of 1848, if it is assumed that

5. Tijani, 'The Lagos-Awori Frontier'.

6. Rebecca Lyide Taiwo v. Odunsi Sarumi, and Willoughby-Osborne's judgement, 19 Sept. 1912, LSCR, Civ. 12, 1914. See, more generally, Biobaku, *The Egba and Their Neighbours*.

7. Glover to Blackall, 17 Jan. 1868, C.O. 147/14.

8. For insight into some of the intricacies, see Folarin, 'Egbado to 1832'.

9. Losi, *History of Lagos*, pp. 105–09. I follow Law's chronology for the dates of the *Oba*'s reign: Law, 'The Dynastic Chronology of Lagos'.

10. *Lagos Weekly Record*, 23 Feb. 1901.

11. Ali Delokun (*Otun* of Abeokuta) to Taiwo, 9 Aug. 1898. TP, Lagos Affairs, 1870–1902.

Taiwo did not settle on what became his permanent base as soon as he arrived. Taiwo's own recollection is consistent with Losi's in stating that the land was granted by 'my friend', Jacob Ogunbiyi, acting on behalf of Chief Ashogbon, who in turn sought permission from the Faji family shortly after the Omira War of 1845.[12]

A firmer judgement can be made about Taiwo's age. His memorial in Lagos states, with the enduring confidence of solid stone, that he was 120 years old when he died in 1901, which means he was born in 1781 and was in his forties when he first came to Lagos in the 1820s. Clearly, not everything set in stone is accurate. If Taiwo was a boy when he came to Lagos, he was born shortly before or after 1815. A contemporary obituary notice gave his age at death as eighty-seven, which fixes his birth date to the year 1814.[13] The basis of the calculation is unknown but since it fits with the reasoning advanced here, it can be regarded as the most reliable date currently available. Although the memorial perpetuated a chronological error, it was entirely accurate in fixing the substantial plot of land (in the area that became Taiwo Street) where Taiwo spent the rest of his days.

All that can be said of Taiwo's early life in Lagos is that it was modest rather than privileged, despite his high-ranking family connections. He seems to have begun as a basketmaker before graduating to become a small trader. Taiwo's social status matched his start. In 1864, he signed a letter (with Ogunbiyi and several other prominent former slaves) stating that he had once been a slave.[14] In 1891, however, he gave evidence to the effect that he had been a 'follower' of the *Ashogbon* but not his slave.[15] Both statements suited the purpose of the moment. Both also have merit if it is allowed that slave status could be an evolving condition and one that covered a variety of occupations and positions in society.

From Kosoko to Glover

Taiwo's early career as a trader remains equally sketchy. He joined Kosoko's following in the late 1840s as a junior associate of Oshodi Tapa and Jacob Ogunbiyi, and left Lagos with them after the bombardment of the port in 1851. In the 1850s, he helped to promote the palm oil trade in the lagoon ports from Badagri in the west, Epe and Palma in the east, and Lekki in the south, though he abandoned Badagri in 1853, when a struggle between Porto Novo

12. As Kristin Mann notes, the procedure appears to have circumvented Chief Aromire, the relevant *Idejo*: *Slavery and the Birth of an African City*, p. 244.

13. *Lagos Weekly Record*, 23 Feb. 1901.

14. Mann, 'The Rise of Taiwo Olowo'.

15. Evidence in Chief Ladega Ashogbon v. Queen's Advocate and Efunde, LSCR, Civ. 11, 1891.

and Abeokuta for control of the port damaged its trade.[16] Avoseh claims that Taiwo then returned to Lagos.[17] Although this is possible, it is more likely that, as a Kosoko loyalist, Taiwo shuttled between Lagos and the lagoon ports, at least during the early 1850s. The survival of a small account book, which records his dealings with Régis Aîné during 1858–1859, shows that he remained active in trade, mainly exchanging palm oil for cotton goods.[18] Although Régis had a base in Lagos, they put much of their effort at that time into developing trade with the eastern lagoon ports in association with Kosoko.

The turning point came in the mid- to late 1850s, when Oshodi Tapa, Kosoko's senior adviser, and Taiwo, Oshodi's younger associate, decided that the British were neither going to leave Lagos of their own accord nor be dislodged and that an accommodation was necessary.[19] By 1859, if not before, Oshodi had opened confidential negotiations with the consul in Lagos and indicated his willingness to co-operate with the British.[20] A deal suited both parties. Once Kosoko had been persuaded to abandon his increasingly unlikely chances of regaining the *Oba*-ship, he and his followers would be free to return to Lagos and could take full advantage of the new commercial opportunities that had begun to appear there. They could also count on the consul's support. For his part, the consul would acquire a set of powerful new allies to offset Dosunmu and his camp, who were still reluctant to accept British control. In addition, the move would also prevent the eastern lagoon ports from becoming rivals to Lagos. The deal was done and sealed with the cession of Lagos in 1861. According to Consul Brand, it was Oshodi's 'judicious advice' that kept Kosoko from 'foolish' action.[21]

The arrangement worked well. Kosoko returned in 1862 but had spent most of his vitality by then, and Oshodi became effective leader of the former *Oba*'s party. Oshodi died in 1868 and Kosoko in 1872, at which point the government estimated that his following still numbered 20,000 and was the most powerful in Lagos.[22] Taiwo, the heir apparent, took over in 1872 and retained the leadership for the rest of his life. By then, Jacob Ogunbiyi, once Taiwo's

16. Avoseh, *A Short History of Badagri*, p. 106. I am grateful to the late Mr Avoseh for giving me copies of some of his publications and for his advice on this and associated subjects. The wider issues are well covered by Sorensen-Gilmore, 'Badagri, 1784–1863', ch. 9.

17. Avoseh, *A Short History of Badagry*, p. 106.

18. D. C. Taiwo Account Books, 1858–59. See n. 1.

19. See chapter 3 in this text.

20. Campbell to Malmesbury, 4 March 1859, F.O. 84/1088.

21. Brand memo, 5 May 1860, F.O. 84/1115.

22. Berkeley to Administrator in Chief, 24 May 1873, C.O. 147/27. Cole, *Modern and Traditional Elites*, p. 28. This study remains indispensable nearly fifty years after it was published.

mentor, had become his business partner as well as his close friend. It was Ogunbiyi's influence that led Taiwo to convert to Christianity in 1867, when he was baptised at Holy Trinity Church in Ebute Ero and took the name Daniel Conrad.[23] Taiwo's rising importance and acceptance of the new, however, was matched by his continuing investment in the old. In 1868, he was installed, with customary ceremony, as *Olofin* of Isheri.[24] He had inherited the title 'six or seven years' earlier but for unknown reasons decided to postpone his formal acceptance.[25] It was around this time, too, that he was accorded the popular Yoruba title of *Olowo*—a wealthy man. Taiwo's position in Isheri came with new obligations but also rewards in taxes, court fines, property, and above all, control of one of the key market towns on the River Ogun. Although Taiwo never made Isheri his home, he exercised power there effectively from his base in nearby Lagos.

The accord between Glover and Oshodi underlines the importance of the ties between business and politics in the history of Lagos. Behind the voluminous official dispatches that stand at the centre of histories of the port lay innumerable private letters, notes, discussions, deals, and compromises that were responsible for maintaining political stability, fostering commerce, and influencing the distribution of wealth. As the governor of the colony became *Baba Isale* of the expatriate community, and was known to Lagosians as Obba Golobar, so Taiwo assumed the headship of a complex network of traders and chiefs that made him *Baba Isale* of Lagos and Isheri, and ensured that he wielded considerable influence along the lagoon and deep into the hinterland.[26] Glover helped Taiwo with local commercial disputes and introduced him to the most important firm in Lagos, G. L. Gaiser. Taiwo reciprocated by supporting Glover in his dispute with Dosunmu, exerting his influence among the hinterland states on the government's behalf, and performing innumerable small services, from catching criminals to guaranteeing safe passage for government emissaries. The relationship constituted a form of corporate commercial capitalism in a colonial setting. It fell short of monopoly status but was nevertheless the most powerful component in an oligopoly that competed with other networks for control of business and government.

Taiwo was an established trader before he forged a close connection with Glover, whose support gave his career a further boost. In 1873, Glover

23. *Lagos Weekly Record*, 19 Feb. 1901.

24. A subsequent allegation casting doubt on Taiwo's right to be installed was met by the information that he travelled to Isheri on the government steamer and was accompanied by Glover and Dosunmu's official representatives (Oshodi and Asogbon). *Lagos Standard*, 21 Oct. 1896.

25. Evidence of Osu, a chief of Isheri, in Rebecca L. Taiwo v. Odunse Sarumi, LSCR, Civ. 64, 1912.

26. Glover, *Life of Sir John Hawley Glover*, p. 106.

FIGURE 4.1. Chief Daniel Conrad Taiwo. Copied by Paramount Photographers Lagos, with permission of Chief Gabriel A. Taiwo (grandson).

provided a rare, if also brief, insight into Taiwo's personality and standing, describing him as 'a strong supporter of the British government and its civilising policy. Added to an independence of character and fluency of speech, he is a handsome man of commanding stature and his birth and station give him a consideration with the natives both within and beyond the territory'.[27] Shortly after Glover left the colony, George Berkeley, the Administrator, commented on the proposal to appoint a successor to Kosoko by saying that the idea was not supported either by the government or the 'more intelligent and influential members of his party, among whom may be reckoned the somewhat celebrated Chief Taiwo, who has long held a prominent position as leader of a powerful section of the Yoruba tribe'.[28] Berkeley was a newcomer to Lagos and his reference to the Yoruba was an unintended exaggeration resulting from his uncertain grasp of the people and states in the hinterland. Nevertheless, he confirmed Glover's appraisal of Taiwo's power and high standing. As for Taiwo himself, he inherited Kosoko's large following without the complications that would have followed had he been appointed formally as Kosoko's successor.

In the 1880s, forty years after starting as a small trader, Taiwo's energy and influence were undiminished. In 1879, a group of traders asked him to approve a set of regulations designed to fix produce prices in the lagoon market of Ejinrin, 'you being the head of all the markets in the Colony'.[29] He continued to trade in produce, though in the 1880s his correspondents reported that it was becoming hard to make a profit on oil and kernels unless payment was made in goods rather than in cash.[30] His status remained consistently high. In 1889, Witt & Busch invited him to renew his account in the New Year, assuring him that 'new credit will always be opened to you'.[31] Taiwo remained active in dealing with debtors and supplicants, exercising his influence to remove or control competitors, settling disputes, nourishing his connections with the British administration and governments in the interior, and helping to keep trade routes clear. His efforts to reopen the roads following the British expedition against the Ijebu in 1892 were greeted with relief and followed by praise from his connections on the mainland.[32]

27. Glover to Kimberley, 27 March 1873, C.O. 147/29.

28. Berkeley to Administrator in Chief, 24 May 1873, C.O. 147/27.

29. Idowo and Others to Taiwo, 11 March 1879, TP, Abeokuta and Interior Affairs, 1865–1900.

30. Sorunke, *Jaguna* of Abeokuta, to Taiwo, 7 Dec. 1889, TP, Abeokuta and Interior Affairs, 1865–1900; Bode Olori to Taiwo, 26 Aug. 1887, TP, Abeokuta and Interior Affairs, 1865–1900.

31. Witt & Busch to Taiwo, 20 Nov. 1889. TP, Lagos Affairs, 1870–1902.

32. Edward Bickersteth to Taiwo, 26 Oct. 1892, TP, Abeokuta and Interior Affairs, 1865–1900.

'The Head of All the Markets in the Colony'

Taiwo conducted business from his headquarters in Lagos, where he had a large compound in what became (and remains) Taiwo Street, and a warehouse on the Marina.[33] He also maintained a branch in Abeokuta and employed agents in other key market towns from Isheri to Ibadan. During his career, Taiwo had dealings with most of the leading expatriate firms in Lagos. His longest relationships were with Régis Aîné, which began in the 1840s and lasted until the early 1880s, and Gaiser, which ran from the 1860s to the beginning of the 1890s. Additionally, he dealt with some of the substantial Saro and Lagosian merchants, including James Davies, Richard Blaize, Jacob Leigh, Mohammed Shitta, and Sumanu Animashaun, all of whom he counted as friends.

Taiwo's shrewdness in business, which was attuned to his astute political judgement, had already elevated him to Kosoko's inner circle. Since Taiwo was illiterate, it may seem odd that we know more about him than about many eminent Saro who were both literate and fluent. Although Taiwo spoke Yoruba, it is unclear whether he could read it, and he admitted that he could neither read nor write English or any other language.[34] He circumvented the problem by employing a team of Saro clerks who were literate in both Yoruba and English and trained in book-keeping. Taiwo dictated outgoing letters and signed them with a bold stamp that read simply: 'Taiwo'. Incoming correspondence was translated and read to him. Fortune has been benign in permitting a substantial sample of his papers to survive. The archive of sixty-two account books and about a thousand letters is larger than the records of any other merchant in this study, with the possible exception of Jacob Coker. Literacy might have improved Taiwo's efficiency but was a less important ingredient than business acumen, which he possessed in abundance.

Among the remaining documents are account books spanning the years 1858–1886. Despite being incomplete, they provide valuable information about business practices during the period of transition to legitimate commerce, when barter was moving to cash payments. The ledgers are detailed and meticulous; the presentation follows the principles of double-entry accounting. A separate account book covering a long period (1872–1884) records credit notes issued to Lagosians between 1872 and 1884 and shows that Taiwo added money lending to his trading activities. Accounts were kept in English with two minor exceptions, one in French for the period 1858–1859 and another in Portuguese covering the years 1872–1881. Taiwo may have been illiterate, but he was cosmopolitan in his business dealings.

33. It is uncertain whether Taiwo retained land he may have held in the northwest tip of the island or whether, on his return to Lagos, he depended on a grant authorised by Governor Glover.

34. Taiwo's evidence in Taiwo v. Ifawe, LSCR, Civ. 4, 1882.

The custom at the outset of the period was to debit traders with goods and credit them with either produce (valued in cowries) or solely in cowries, the price in produce being higher than the price given in cash. The problem of handling a large volume of cowries, which historians have identified as being a drawback, was overcome by the simple device of issuing cheques. Currency conversions with local European firms were made by trading cowries for sterling bills of exchange. In the 1850s, all figures were entered in cowries. In the 1860s, some sterling exchange rates were given and in 1874, one ledger recording business with British firms in Lagos was kept entirely in sterling. With this exception, the account books continued to list transactions in cowries throughout the 1870s. In the 1880s, as cowrie inflation took hold, the records were kept in either cowries or sterling; a few mixed the two. From 1884, most accounts were in sterling, and by 1887–1888, almost all were. In the 1890s, cowries rarely appeared. Taiwo's account books reflect, with great precision, the timing of the rise and fall of cowrie currency all along the West Coast.

Unfortunately, annual balances have not survived, and it is impossible to determine the profitability of Taiwo's business. Some indications of scale, however, can be discerned. A set of monthly accounts listing creditors and debtors shows that in August 1871, the business was owed 24,441 heads of cowries and itself owed 18,655 heads. At that time (before the great cowrie inflation), the exchange rate between cowries and sterling stood at about £16 for every head, which put Taiwo's debtors at £391,056 and his own debts at £298,480.[35] Although the monthly figures give an indication of the size of Taiwo's turnover, it would of course be misleading to extrapolate an annual total from them and equally unwise to infer profitability from Taiwo's net credit for the month of 5,786 heads (£92,576). What is indisputable, though, is the considerable size of his trading operations and the extensive volume of floating credit that kept the business (and Lagos itself) above water. The implied risks attending this vast sea of credit hover just behind the figures.

The inventory of trade items in Taiwo's ledgers reflects the diverse character of the markets he dealt with. Palm oil and kernels headed the export list, while ivory was the most important of the supplementary exports to Europe. Many other products, such as potash, shea butter, local cloth, mats, slippers, hats, calabashes, and Kankanbia beads, were imported from different parts of the country for sale in Lagos. The import trade was infinitely varied. A small personal account with the *Balogun* of Ojo (some 22 miles east of Lagos), for the years 1875–1880 listed his annual purchases as birdshot, gunpowder, dane-guns, twine, rum, gin, 'silk velvet', 'croydons', 'fancy red prints', and cowries. Taiwo's Niger agent held a more substantial stock list, which for the calendar year 1880–1881 included: Madras cloth, Belgian brocade, silk Alayan,

---

35. The exchange rate is calculated from Taiwo's records and the Supreme Court records.

damasks, green, yellow, and red velvet, satin, white, red and spotted prints, grey bafts, croydons, a variety of cotton, lace, and silk stripes, green and white yarn, copper and brass rods, salt, and two packs of Japanese padlocks! Taiwo was also a big arms dealer, supplying both Egba and Ibadan, but this item does not appear in the regular trade ledgers.[36]

It is convenient for historians to summarise West Africa's overseas trade by referring to its leading components, which in the case of Lagos were palm produce and cotton goods. The additional details listed above, however, are more than mere elaborations. They reveal two important features that are otherwise easily overlooked. The first identifies a connection between regional and international trade. Export growth increased purchasing power in Lagos and among hinterland producers, and expanded demand for local products as well as for imported goods. The size of the consequent multiplier effect merits further consideration in studies assessing West Africa's long-run development. The second feature serves as a reminder that the profitability of individual merchant houses relied heavily on their ability to tailor stocks to local demand. Taiwo was adept at assessing and supplying the needs of different markets, which may explain why his cotton goods carried the generic name 'Taiwo Olowo Cloth'. In both cases, African entrepreneurs were far ahead of the expatriate firms because they had the information and connections that success in regional trade required.

Taiwo was quick to see the potential of the new property rights that came with the British Colony in 1862. In 1863, he obtained one of the first batch of crown grants that gave him two prime sites on the Marina.[37] He never looked back. He acquired a number of high-quality sites, including a third property on the Marina, and owned numerous other properties throughout the town. By any of several possible measurements of his multifarious property transactions in Lagos, Taiwo conducted a larger number of registered land transactions than any other individual in the town during the second half of the century, including the prolific James Davies. Between 1863 and 1892, the date of his last registered purchase, Taiwo bought at least forty-six properties in Lagos, without counting unregistered land in the town or real estate in the hinterland.[38] Between 1870 and 1899, he also sold sixteen properties. As in the case of his trading accounts, it is impossible to estimate the profitability of his land transactions. What can be said is that almost all his disposals occurred after 1870 and none appears to have been driven by debt

36. Cole, *Modern and Traditional Elites*, p. 31.

37. Crown Grant Index, I, p. 208, 1863; LLOR, 1209, 1863.

38. Mann, 'The Rise of Taiwo Olowu', p. 100. It is with gratitude and some relief that I can thank Kristin Mann for this meticulous piece of research. Her conclusion coincides with my own earlier findings but is more thoroughly based.

or otherwise forced on him except by a growing concern to prepare for his own demise.

Despite having to provide housing for his extensive family and followers, Taiwo's portfolio was large enough to enable him to add to his income by renting property. Details of this feature of his business activities remain sparse until the 1880s, when a few examples appear in his private papers. In 1884, he leased a property on the Marina to the German firm of Luderitz for three years at £250 p.a.[39] Two years later, he wrote to A. C. Campbell reminding him to settle a debt of £60 he owed for renting another property on the Marina from 1883 to 1886.[40] Taiwo's most expensive single purchase, 49 Marina, which he bought from Benjamin Dawodu in 1886 for £1,000, paid off handsomely in the rents it subsequently yielded.[41] Lagos real estate served Taiwo very well.

Negotiable property was a vital component of Taiwo's trading activities as well as a means of capital accumulation. Like other merchants and brokers, Taiwo advanced goods on the security of property that could be alienated. Between 1868 and 1890, he registered at least eighty-two mortgages with the Lands Office. Twenty-one were repaid; fifteen debtors defaulted and had to surrender their property; the fate of the remaining forty-six is unknown.[42] Taiwo also mortgaged some of his own real estate in exchange for cash to buy palm oil and other produce.

In 1867, he made the largest agreement of its kind recorded in Lagos during the second half of the nineteenth century, with the sole exception of the spectacular deal executed by James Davies a few years later. During the 1860s and 1870s, Taiwo was in partnership with his former mentor, Jacob Ogunbiyi, who was also involved in the agreement. The pair undertook to supply Régis Aîné with forty thousand gallons of palm oil in exchange for money and goods valued at £3,333, which were secured by no fewer than seventeen properties.[43] Ogunbiyi contributed two properties, which were covered by crown grants; Taiwo provided the remainder. The agreement allowed the partners to sell the goods and use the money without having to supply palm oil before the due date. In the interim, Taiwo and Ogunbiyi had an opportunity to profit in other ways. The deal was repeated in 1868 and 1869 with minor modifications. In 1868, however,

39. Agreement 22 Dec. 1884, TP Lagos Affairs, 1870–1902.

40. Taiwo to Campbell, 8 Sept. 1886, TP Lagos Affairs, 1870–1902. In 1868, Taiwo had leased the land to Robert Campbell for £18 p.a. Mann, *Slavery and the British of An African City*, p. 266.

41. LLOR, 10/287, 1886; 52/13, 1906; 81/283, 1913; 151/9, 1921; 376/63, 1933; 376/63, 1941; 589/39, 1945.

42. Mann, 'The Rise of Taiwo Olowu', pp. 95–96. My own estimate, taken from the Index of Crown Grants, is that the number of registered mortgages (essentially loans) was even higher at 112, but I would again prefer Kristin Mann's figures to my own.

43. LLOR, 4/247, 1867.

Taiwo had to offer security worth £4,674 rather than £3,333 because he had failed to complete the previous year's order. The debt was carried forward and eventually settled. Not all borrowers in this high-risk trade were so astute or so lucky.[44]

Although Taiwo's business was based in Lagos, its offshoots extended far beyond the port and its hinterland. To the west, Taiwo had branches and agents in Badagri, Porto Novo, Little Popo, and even as far as Bahia. To the east and beyond lagoon ports, such as Epe, he maintained several agents on the Niger. To the north, his activities took him as far as Bida and through numerous markets in between, the most important of which was Abeokuta, the Egba capital.

A segment of Taiwo's surviving correspondence relates to his outposts in the 1870s and 1880s.[45] As noted earlier, he traded with Badagri at the beginning of his career but was compelled to abandon the town in 1853. A handful of incoming letters, which run from 1877 to 1888, show that Taiwo had returned to the port, maintained a house and an agent there, and was buying palm oil in exchange for a variety of cottons and other consumer goods.[46] Politics, always close to hand, was a frequent intruder. Correspondents appealed to him for help in resolving local trade disputes, looking after witnesses who were travelling to Lagos to give evidence, and interceding with the governor to restore escaped slaves.[47] Badagri was also a meeting point for Taiwo's allies and lawyers in the case of Hotonu's estate, which lingered through 1887 and 1888.[48] Taiwo and a friend, Fagbemi (also known as Benjamin Dawodu), had agreed to stand surety for a local trader, Hotonu, for the considerable sum of £5,000. In 1887, the administrator of the recently deceased Hotonu's estate approached the pair for payment. In a private letter to his lawyer, Taiwo admitted that he had signed the agreement without having it read to him.[49] His lawyers were able to whittle away his obligation and forestall the disaster that might have attended his uncharacteristic lack of concentration on business affairs.[50] This episode, among many others, illustrated one of Taiwo's most

44. Régis Aîné may not have profited greatly, if at all, from the arrangement. The firm began to struggle from this time onwards, greatly reduced its business in the 1880s, and left Lagos in the 1890s.

45. I sorted these, provisionally, under the title Taiwo Papers: Badagri Correspondence, 1877–1900.

46. For example, Konu to Taiwo, 25 May 1877; Ajosseh to Taiwo, 3 March 1883, both in TP, Badagri Correspondence, 1877–1900.

47. Tickel to Taiwo, 3 June 1877, Sale to Taiwo, 12 Aug. 1877, Ada and Others to Taiwo, 19 March 1884, in TP, Badagri Correspondence, 1877–1900.

48. Taiwo to Mobee, 22 March 1888, Ajosseh to Taiwo, 29 Nov. 1888, 6 Dec. 1888, in TP, Badagri Correspondence, 1877–1900.

49. Taiwo to Hebron (Freetown), 10 Feb. 1887, TP, Lagos Affairs, 1870–1902.

50. West v. Taiwo and Dawodu, LSCR, Civ. 1887.

valuable assets: his ability to hire qualified lawyers from among the limited number of those available in Lagos.[51]

Relations with Porto Novo and its king, Toffa, were of a different order.[52] Porto Novo was a major commercial centre and Toffa a formidable ruler. In 1875 (when the correspondence begins), Taiwo's business in the port was managed by one Momo Alawusa, who was buying palm kernels and supplying cotton goods, especially velvets. Commercial expansion, however, required Toffa's support and Taiwo took care to cultivate him after he became king in 1874. The pair established a close relationship and agreed to a mutual-aid pact. Taiwo acted as mediator for Lagos traders in Porto Novo; Toffa called on Taiwo for help in Lagos. Taiwo approached Toffa with a degree of humility he rarely showed other rulers, praising his policies and offering himself as a 'faithful friend' in Lagos.[53] When Mohammed Shitta's agents got into trouble in Porto Novo, Taiwo settled the matter.

In 1883, when it was Taiwo's turn, he asked Toffa to intervene to ensure that a Saro trader named David Macaulay repaid a debt owing to one of Taiwo's female traders in Porto Novo.[54] Toffa responded with enthusiasm. In June that year, Taiwo's agent in Porto Novo reported that the king had tried his 'very best' and pressed Macaulay so hard that he had even asked the king to intercede with the European firms there to obtain credit so that he could pay his debts by trading.[55] The proposal was either rejected or unsuccessful because in 1884, further pressure from Toffa led to the sale of Macaulay's servant into slavery. As these events were unfolding, Taiwo wrote some incautious letters about Macaulay that led the aggrieved debtor to bring an action for libel in 1884.[56] The letters were judged to be 'inflammatory and damaging' to Macaulay's 'character and business' and he was awarded damages of £150 plus costs. It is unclear if Taiwo recovered the money he originally sought. However, he acted against Macaulay primarily to assert his authority, and in this he succeeded. Macaulay never recovered from the losses he suffered; indebtedness followed him; he died in what are referred to conventionally as 'modest circumstances'.[57] Few gained from trying to obstruct Taiwo's will.

51. Among them Nash Williams and Charles Forsythe.

52. Toffa (1850–1908; ruled 1874–1908; contemporary spelling Tofa). Porto Novo came under French protection in 1863 and was incorporated into the new colony of Dahomey in 1883.

53. Taiwo to Toffa, 28 Aug. 1882, TP, correspondence with Porto Novo, 1875–97.

54. David Macaulay (1842–1914), younger brother of T. B. Macaulay and uncle of Herbert Macaulay. Both brothers were traders; both struggled; both were imprisoned at different times for debt. David makes a further appearance in chapter 5.

55. Eba Ewumi to Taiwo, 26 June 1883, TP, correspondence with Porto Novo, 1875–97.

56. Macaulay v. Taiwo, LSCR, Civ. 5, 1884; Moloney to Granville, 21 June 1886, C.O. 147/55, and enclosures.

57. Macaulay v. Leigh, LSCR, Civ. 5, 1884; Savage v. Macaulay, LSCR, Civ. 7, 1887 and Civ.13, 1893; O'Connor Williams v. Macaulay, Civ. 10, 1890.

Tshubi of Bashua
                    To
                         D. C   Taiwo   Dr.

1871
June 23 To His note of hand due 23rd Decr 1871 Mds   5½ 6
1872
         For 1 House Taiwo street £40   640 0 0
July 11 50 Ins salt omitted 26 March 1872 2306 0 0
Octr 12 16 Months house due as per
1880   Agreement @ 8/4 - £6.8.0   102 20 0
July 31 " 50 pcs corded Grey Bafts @ 11   550 0 0
         " 5 Escherve's cheques 120 - 5 Wills 130 250 0 0
1881   " Mortgage deed drawn   33/6
June 28 " Cowries from Majogun   50 0 0
         " Cowries from Fabiyi   19 20 0
Octr 15 " Cowries from Nelly Oyinkan   120 0 0
         " Cowries from Majogun   100 0 0
         " Cowries from Oshun kalude   53 0 0
         " Cowries from Taiwo   37 0 0
     20 " Cash paid Lawyer   33/-
         Total Equal Hds 47/17-40 and £3.66 @ 1 Hd for 1½ " " " £ 239 4 3

1872
July 11 By cheques of C. S. Meyers   1293 35 0
Decr 24 " My order to pay Jones   84 0 0
     27 " Cowries paid Sundress   156 0 0
     30 " Cowries paid C. F. Meyers Ch   518 0 0
     31 " My order to pay Modele   26 0 0
         " My order to pay Isani for   0 0 0
                   Walsh Bros cheques   54 10 0
1873
Jan 1   " My order to summons for C. F. Meyers Ch 69 0 0
1874
June 27 " 1 House debited to him June 23 1874   0 0 0
         and returned the account not   0 0 0
         being in time as per agreement   640 0 0
         By House rent & age debited to him   0 0 0
         Oct 10 1875 + 6000 Bricks @ 25 - 150   252 20 0
1882   By 1 empty pipe rum   4 0 0

Taiwo's connections with Little Popo and Bahia were either limited or under-represented in the surviving evidence. A handful of letters between 1884 and 1886 suggest that his business in Little Popo was a new venture that was managed by one of his sons, Emmanuel Oyasonya, who was dealing mainly in rum and cloth. Emmanuel certainly spoke with the freedom of a family member in advising Taiwo not to tangle with the 'Sierra Leone people', who were against him, and to 'draw nearer to God' now that he was getting old.[58] The connection with Bahia went back to the 1840s, when Taiwo was dealing with Brazilian slave-traders. In the 1880s, his business there was managed by a nephew, Andrew Costa Luna, who in the new era was importing rum and tobacco in exchange for local cloth and kola nuts.[59] There are hints of wider dealings involving, inevitably, credit and debt. One merchant in Bahia, who owed money to Taiwo in Lagos, wrote to Taiwo, giving him permission to sell several houses there in settlement.[60] It is a miniscule episode but one that underlines both the international dimension of Lagos's overseas trade and the remarkable degree of trust that sustained it.

Information about Taiwo's Niger trade, though incomplete, covers the period 1874–87 and tends, understandably, to dwell on problems rather than successes. During the early 1880s, Taiwo traded in all the products listed in the ledgers above and employed several agents who were based at points between Brass and Egga, where he built a factory (named 'Bethlehem Lodge') on an island commanding the trade routes.[61] The chief clerk between 1880 and 1884 was Ephraim Vincent, who was responsible for producing annual accounts and sending interim reports to Lagos listing produce bought, goods sold, stock in hand, and expenses.[62] Taiwo's former business partner, Jacob Ogunbiyi, visited the branches on his behalf; his friend, Mohammed Shitta, assisted by using his influence in Egga and Bida.[63]

The course of commerce did not run smoothly. Taiwo had several years of trouble with Crowther Bros., the firm run by Bishop Samuel Crowther's two sons, Samuel and Josiah.[64] Whether the brothers were unlucky or inexpert is unclear, but it is certain that their Niger ambitions exceeded their resources soon after they launched their venture in 1879.[65] In 1882, Taiwo had to take

58. Oyasonya to Taiwo, 18 July 1884, TP, correspondence with Little Popo, 1884–86.

59. Andrew Costa Luna, to Taiwo, 10 Sept. 1886, 18 March 1887, April 1887, TP, Bahia correspondence, 1886–87.

60. Pompero Campo Grande to Taiwo, 27 Feb. 1886 and 19 Sept. 1887, TP, Bahia correspondence, 1886–87.

61. Bada et al. to Taiwo, 31 June 1883, TP, Niger Affairs, 1874–87.

62. T. W. Tonge & Co. v. D. C. Taiwo, LSCR, Civ. 24, 1900.

63. Ogunbiyi to Taiwo, 15 March 1882, TP, Niger Affairs, 1874–87.

64. Kopytoff, *A Preface to Modern Nigeria*, pp. 168, 285–86.

65. Bad luck was undoubtedly present. The brothers had been agents on the Niger for the West African Company but lost their positions in 1879, when the company was

legal action to recover 818 heads of cowries he had allowed as credit against the sale of cotton goods. In the same year, Crowther Bros. incurred an additional debt of £500, which Taiwo and Sumanu Animashaun had advanced for purchasing the ill-fated 'Southams Trader'.[66] Samuel and Josiah, who needed an additional £800 to complete their purchase of the steam-tug, invited the two creditors to become part owners in the venture. Taiwo, however, was warned against the deal, and declined.[67] He then pressed Crowther Bros. for security for payment of the outstanding £500, which had been advanced on the strength of the high standing of the Crowther family. Taiwo imposed an interest charge on the sum outstanding and underlined his intentions by threatening to take 'severe measures'.[68]

With alarm bells ringing, Crowther Bros. responded by offering the steamer, which they claimed was worth £4,000, as security.[69] At this point, however, Jacob Leigh chartered the ship and Samuel and Josiah mustered sufficient funds to be able to send Taiwo £300 towards the £500 they owed.[70] By 1883, when Leigh had become the owner of the vessel, the brothers were able to send Taiwo a further £100.[71] Matters then stalled while the partners tried to raise £360–400 from the sale of their factory in Onitsha. In 1884, after Shitta had intervened on their behalf, Taiwo replied that he had granted the brothers another six months' grace 'because of your faithful dealings with me'.[72] Even so, the money was not forthcoming and the heavyweight presence of Bishop Crowther himself was needed to plead for clemency. The matter dragged on and remained unsettled in 1887.

Staff problems were an added anxiety. In 1884, Taiwo replaced Vincent, whom he suspected of deception and mismanagement, and pursued him through his favoured procedure: court action.[73] This case, too, had a protracted history and remained unresolved in 1889.[74] By then, Taiwo had to deal with the much larger problem of the Royal Niger Company, which enforced its new monopoly by imposing punitive duties and setting prices that undercut

---

absorbed into the group that eventually became the Royal Niger Company. TP, Niger Affairs, 1874–87.

66. Crowther Bros. to Taiwo, 3 May 1882, TP, Niger Affairs, 1874–87.

67. J. G. Barstow to Taiwo, 8 May, 1882, TP, Niger Affairs, 1874–87.

68. Taiwo to Crowther Bros., 12 Aug. 1882, TP, Niger Affairs, 1874–87. Property on the Marina provided security.

69. Crowther Bros. to Taiwo, 22 Aug. 1882, TP, Niger Affairs, 1874–87.

70. Taiwo to Ogunbiyi et al. 22 Aug. 1882, TP, Niger Affairs, 1874–87.

71. S. Crowther to Taiwo, 4 Feb. 1884 and 27 Feb. 1884, TP, Niger Affairs, 1874–87.

72. Taiwo to Shitta, 23 Sept. 1885, TP, Niger Affairs, 1874–87.

73. W. Ashley to Taiwo, 11 Dec. 1883; Taiwo to Rev. N. Johnson, 29 July 1884, TP, Niger Affairs, 1874–78.

74. E. G. Vincent v. D. C. Taiwo, LSCR, Civ. 5, 1884; D. B. Vincent to Taiwo, 9 Jan. 1889, TP, Niger Affairs, 1874–87.

its competitors.[75] In 1887, Taiwo's agents proposed selling the Niger stores and returning home.[76] They stayed on, at least until 1888, but Taiwo's trade on the Niger dwindled and by the end of the decade his business there had closed.[77]

Business and Politics

Business and politics were joined in an indissoluble union. This theme is present in all the illustrations cited so far but reached exceptional prominence in the two great crises of Taiwo's career: one involved the Egba authorities in Abeokuta following the *Ifole* ('housebreaking') in 1867; the other took place in Lagos, when Taiwo and his rival, Ajasa, the *Apena*, locked horns in 1884. Both examples are well known to specialists; the contribution made here sees them from Taiwo's perspective, as revealed in his private correspondence.

In the mid-nineteenth century, the Egba state was still a recent foundation and the location of authority within it remained uncertain and contested.[78] Abeokuta, the capital, was linked to Lagos, 60 miles to the south, by the River Ogun and by a road through the forest. In 1867, the town was said to consist of 120–130 'aggregated villages' with a total population of about 50,000, which included 2,000 Saro and some 1,500 Christian converts.[79] The *Ifole*, which consisted of a riot and some damage to property, led to the expulsion of Christian missionaries from Abeokuta in 1867 and the exodus of a large number of Saro, many of whom settled in Lagos.[80] In general terms, the crisis was a manifestation of developing tensions within the embryonic Egba state, the complications that followed the intrusion of Christian missionaries, and the assertive policy of Governor Glover.[81] A battle for power between competing factions in Abeokuta during the 1860s led to boundary disputes with neighbouring states, including Lagos Colony, and competition to control trade routes and markets.[82] Taiwo had already shown himself to be a key intermediary between all parties and, remarkably, was trusted by the most

---

75. Momodu to Taiwo, 1 Oct. 1886, 30 Oct. 1886, 31 March 1887, TP, Niger Affairs, 1874–87.

76. Momodu to Taiwo, 19 July 1887, TP, Niger Affairs, 1874–87.

77. Momodu to Taiwo, 11 Dec. 1887, TP, Niger Affairs, 1874–87.

78. The standard work is Biobaku, *The Egba and Their Neighbours*. See particularly ch. 7.

79. Yonge to Buckingham, 25 Oct. 1867, C.O. 147/13.

80. The problem of housing refugee Saro in Lagos was met partly by settling them on Ebute Metta on the nearby mainland. Glover to Yonge, 18 Nov. 1867, C.O. 147/13.

81. Most of the official correspondence on the episode is in C.O. 147/11–14.

82. For example, Freeman to Newcastle, 4 July 1864, C.O. 147/7. Glover to Cardwell, 23 Jan. 1865, and 8 May 1865, C.O. 147/8; Bashorun and Chiefs to Blackall, Feb. 1866, C.O. 147/11; Patey to Cardwell, 9 June 1866, C.O. 147/11; Merchants to Cardwell, 22 Jan 1866, C.O. 147/12.

important of them.[83] The *Ifole*, however, was his biggest test as *Olofin* of Isheri. The disruption caused by the event prevented Taiwo from collecting debts in Abeokuta and from settling his own obligations there and in Lagos.[84] In addition, in 1867 one of the factions in Abeokuta claimed the right to levy taxes at Isheri on behalf of the Egba, thus posing a direct challenge to Taiwo's authority as *Olofin*.

Taiwo faced an awkward situation. Governor Glover, with whom he had a close relationship, had adopted an assertive policy that aimed to reduce the power of the Egba and the influence of their numerous Saro supporters in Lagos and open new trade routes to Ibadan instead.[85] Other contending parties in Abeokuta wanted to control Isheri, marginalise Taiwo, and regain rights of taxation. Faced with this challenge to his authority, in 1867 Taiwo formed an alliance with his uncle, Sorunke, the *Jaguna* of Igbein township in Abeokuta. As Igbein claimed certain rights of administration over Isheri's trade, Taiwo hoped that his uncle would support his bid to remain the effective power in Isheri and that their combined efforts would overcome their rivals in Abeokuta.[86] Taiwo, his uncle, and his friend Jacob Ogunbiyi, who was also *Ologun* of Igbore in Abeokuta, assembled a coalition of friendly chiefs, including the *Parakoyi* (who managed trade), and members of the *Ogboni* and *Oparun* societies to ensure that Isheri and the Ogun maintained its position as a centre of trade.

The more difficult problem was to persuade Glover to moderate his policy. Taiwo's friends knew that his instinct for action rather than reflection was not well suited to the task. In May 1869, his allies in Abeokuta wrote to him urging patience in case his threat to close the Isheri market united all the Egba against him.[87] Taiwo responded with characteristic assertiveness, announcing that he would block the Ogun unless his debts were paid 'by the next market'.[88] His debtors, he added, know that he is master of the river: 'it is God who gave me the river from above and nobody else'.[89] Influential friends

83. Glover to Cardwell, 24 June 1865, and enc. memo of a meeting of interested parties, 13 July 1865, C.O. 147/9. Taiwo's intervention in ending the siege of Ikorodu in 1865 earned him bonus points with the colonial government.

84. Taiwo explained that some of his difficulties arose from the Ikorodu war of 1865, which prevented him from fulfilling a contract for palm oil in Lagos. He claimed that his debtors in Abeokuta were preventing him from meeting his obligations in Lagos. Taiwo to Chiefs of Abeokuta, 18 June 1869, TP, Abeokuta and Interior Affairs, 1865–1900.

85. See, for example, Glover to Cardwell, 8 Jan. 1866, C.O. 147/11.

86. Rebecca Lyide Taiwo v. Odunsi Sarumi, LSCR, Civ. 64, 1912.

87. Solanke, Balogun, to Taiwo, May 1869; Chief *Jaguna* to Taiwo, 7 June 1869, TP, Abeokuta and Interior Affairs, 1865–1900. A later source refers to Solanke as being Taiwo's brother: Rowe to Derby, 30 May 1883; Moloney to Knutsford, 31 July 1888.

88. Taiwo to Chief *Jaguna*, 15 June 1869, TP, Abeokuta and Interior Affairs, 1865–1900.

89. Taiwo to Chiefs of Ibore, 16 June 1869, TP, Abeokuta and Interior Affairs, 1865–1900.

in Lagos, headed by James Davies and Mohammed Shitta, were persistent in urging caution on a man who was always ready to take risks.[90] Fortunately for Taiwo, Glover had begun to retreat from his own assertiveness. The prospect of far-reaching commercial dislocation combined with the alarm expressed in the Colonial Office over the wider consequences of destabilising an already unsteady political situation prompted him to compromise.[91] Moreover, Glover recognised that Taiwo was a loyal ally whose assistance deserved some reward.

Towards the end of 1869, with Glover's co-operation, Taiwo blockaded the Ogun to put pressure on his debtors, reassert his authority in Isheri, and confirm that the river was the best trade route to the northern hinterland.[92] New allies appeared. Early in 1870, Madame Tinubu entered the dispute, asking Taiwo to allow her fifteen canoes (with more to follow) to travel to Lagos and assured him that, in return, she would call on the chiefs in Abeokuta to ensure that Taiwo's debts were paid.[93] By then, the Egba were keen to resume trade because they needed arms to defend themselves against an imminent threat from Dahomey. Governor Glover used his influence to persuade Taiwo's creditors in Lagos to allow him three years to settle his debts there. In 1870, Taiwo's coalition extracted various promises of payment from his debtors in Abeokuta.[94] The Governor in Chief, Arthur Kennedy, raised the blockade in 1871–1872, and in 1872 Glover helped Taiwo to collect the money he was owed. He was then able to pay Gaiser, his main creditor in Lagos.[95] In exchange, Taiwo allowed his uncle, the *Jaguna* of Igbein, to levy tolls at Isheri.[96] Although the Egba closed the roads in protest, the worst of the crisis was over.

Promise and performance took different directions. Taiwo was still collecting old debts from Abeokuta in 1895 and generously (as he saw it) accepting payment in depreciated cowries.[97] In other respects, however, he confirmed his control of Isheri and resumed 'business as usual'.[98] Although Taiwo lost

---

90. Anon to Taiwo, 9 Feb. 1870; Shitta to Taiwo, 13 Feb. 1870; Taiwo to Ogunbiyi, ?1870; Brimah Apatira to Taiwo, 1 April 1870. All in TP, Abeokuta and Interior Affairs, 1865–1900.

91. Glover's policy and its complex ramifications are dealt with by Phillips, 'The Egba at Ikorodu', pp. 23–35; Biobaku, *The Egba and Their Neighbours*, chs. 6–7.

92. *Lagos Weekly Record*, 23 Feb. 1901.

93. Madame Tinubu to Taiwo, 13 Feb. 1870; Philip Jose, Lagos, to Taiwo, 22 Jan. 1870, TP, Abeokuta and Interior Affairs, 1865–1900.

94. Anon to Taiwo, 28 Jan. 1870; Anon to Taiwo, 26 March 1870; Anon but 1870, note to the effect that the *Parakoyi* had arranged for debtors to pay by a certain date. All in TP, Abeokuta and Interior Affairs, 1865–1900.

95. Cole, *Modern and Traditional Elites*, p. 31.

96. Oyero v. Edun and Oyero v. Taiwo, LSCR, Civ. 38, 1905.

97. Taiwo to Odunya Asawo, 27 May 1895, TP, Abeokuta and Interior Affairs, 1865–1900. The Egba's debts were still being settled in 1897: Odunya Asawo to Taiwo, 12 July 1876, TP, Lagos Affairs, 1870–1902.

98. Sorunke, *Jaguna*, to Taiwo, 8 Sept. 1887, 7 Dec. 1889; Taiwo to Chief *Parakoyi*, 27 Aug. 1887; Wadere and Boda of Ijeja to Taiwo, 25 Dec. 1892; Ogubejun, Adlee and *Apena* to

his exceptional connection with the Lagos government when Glover left Lagos in 1872, he made himself useful to his successors by acting as an intermediary with the Egba and guaranteeing safe passage for their emissaries.[99] Taiwo's alliance with his uncle in Abeokuta remained firm and was strengthened by the assistance he gave the Egba government in their dealings with Lagos, Ibadan, and Dahomey, and in recapturing escaped slaves.[100]

The transition from Glover to his successors began in the turmoil that followed the appointment of the Governor in Chief, John Pope Hennessy, a man for whom the phrase 'new broom' might have been invented. Pope Hennessy arrived after Glover's departure in 1872 with fixed ideas and a determination to see them implemented as speedily as possible. He set about replacing Glover's pro-Ibadan, anti-Egba policy with one that favoured non-interference in the belief that this was the best way to keep the trade roads open. His policy was warmly supported by the European merchants and won approval in London for its apparent adherence to principles of free trade. Within a year, however, it became clear that the new policy was no more capable of settling differences among Yoruba states than the old one, and before long Pope Hennessy found himself threatening the Egba with a blockade.[101] At this point, he moved on to become Governor of the Bahamas, leaving his successors to deal with the consequences of the rapid shifts in policy he had so confidently initiated.[102]

The counterpart to the turmoil in British policy was a struggle for supremacy among the rival supporters of Glover and Pope Hennessy that divided the administration as well as the mercantile community. Glover's recall in 1872 led to an attempted purge of his key allies, including Taiwo, whose alliance with the Administrator had long been a matter of public knowledge. Resentments quickly surfaced. There were rumours later in the year that Taiwo was planning to mount an armed uprising against the Acting Administrator and his allies (headed by a group of European merchants), who were determined to prevent Glover from returning to Lagos.[103] To some extent, Taiwo had brought

Taiwo, 17 Dec. 1898, TP, Abeokuta and Interior Affairs, 1865–1900; Moloney to Knutsford, 31 July 1888, C.O. 879/355.

99. I. H. Willoughby to Taiwo, 2 June 1884, TP, Abeokuta and Interior Affairs, 1865–1900.

100. Sorunke, *Jaguna*, to Taiwo, 7 Dec. 1889; *Jaguna* of Igbein to Taiwo, 3 Nov. 1892, TP, Abeokuta and Interior Affairs, 1865–1900. Chief *Parakoyi* and Elders to Taiwo, 7 Feb. 1891, TP, Abeokuta and Interior Affairs, 1865–1900. *Jaguna* of Igbein to Taiwo, 20 April 1884; King Oluwora to Taiwo, 6 May 1884; Chiefs of Igbein to Taiwo, 12 Nov. 1883, TP, Abeokuta and Interior Affairs, 1865–1900.

101. Pope Hennessy to Kimberley, 1 July 1872, C.O. 147/23.

102. Berkeley to Kimberley, 8 May 1873, C.O. 147/27. Pope Hennessy had been appointed to the post before becoming interim Governor in Chief of the West African Settlements.

103. Charles L. Clare to C.O. 18 Dec. 1872, enc. Turton to Clare, 15 Nov. 1872, C.O. 147/25.

retribution on himself. In 1871, for example, he and his 'boys' had become involved in a dispute with another merchant's employees that led to fighting and ended with both parties appearing in court.[104] Taiwo asked Glover for additional magistrates on the grounds that the presiding magistrate, an expatriate, was prejudiced against him (and also against Glover). Glover obliged and Taiwo won the case. Taiwo then organised a petition signed by 157 of his loyalists criticising the chief magistrate, who was forced to apologise. Glover called for the magistrate's removal, at which point the Colonial Office decided that revenge had gone far enough and declined the request.

Other parties also had Taiwo in their sights. The *Alake* of Abeokuta and his supporters were quick to take advantage of Pope Hennessy's arrival to claim that Taiwo had struck a bargain with Glover and would 'do his best to frustrate' Pope Hennessy's 'good wishes' towards them.[105] Pope Hennessy himself lost no time in placing Taiwo in his line of fire. In 1873, he claimed that 'Tywo, who is a native trader of great influence, has been further supported by this government, on many occasions, to the detriment of independent trade here'.[106] As an example of Taiwo's sponsored lawlessness, Pope Hennessy reported that he had held eighteen pawns in shackles in Isheri since 1870 pending the payment of debt, and moreover had done so with Glover's approval.[107] Alarm bells sounded in the Colonial Office, which was sensitive to any issue that touched on slavery, and could envisage questions being raised in Parliament.

Glover responded by compiling the longest letter he had ever directed to the Colonial Office, defending himself, his policies, and Taiwo from the attacks by Pope Hennessy and others.[108] With regard to the pawns held in shackles, Glover pointed out that pawning was an accepted part of Yoruba law and custom, that Isheri was not in British territory, and that the hostages were not 'seized' by Taiwo, but delivered by the Egba as security against the payment of outstanding debts. Glover went on to draw attention to the ambiguities in British policy arising from the problem of categorising the variety of limits on individual freedoms that were grouped under the heading 'slavery'. His defence of Taiwo ended by observing that he and others had 'suffered heavy fines and persecution' during Pope Hennessy's administration.

With some qualifications, the Colonial Office accepted Glover's defence and his standing in official circles rose above Pope Hennessy's criticism.[109] Thereafter, Taiwo's relationships with public officials were more circumspect

104. Kennedy to Kimberley, 27 Nov. 1871, C.O. 147/21.

105. Pope Hennessy to Kimberley, 6 July 1872 and enc. from *Alake*, 26 June 1872, C.O. 147/22.

106. Pope Hennessy to Kimberley, 30 April 1873, C.O. 147/23.

107. Pope Hennessy to Kimberley, 27 March 1873, C.O. 147/29.

108. Glover to Kimberley, 27 March 1873, C.O. 147/29.

109. Glover (1829–85) was knighted in 1874 and became Governor of Newfoundland in 1875.

but no less productive.[110] In 1878, the Acting Administrator, Alfred Moloney, conferred with him about relations between the Egba and Ibadan.[111] In 1882, the Governor of the Gold Coast and Lagos, Samuel Rowe, consulted him about the Ibadan-Ijesha conflict and reported that the conversation had been 'very instructive'.[112] 'Taiwo', he said, 'was one of the most influential men in Lagos and a man of high local rank'.[113] Rowe, like Glover, was inclined to vigorous action. Taiwo agreed. In his view, mediation and gifts were futile. Providing the Egba and Ijebu concurred, he thought that the government should 'use its authority' and 'back it'. Having survived the onslaught mounted by Pope Hennessy and his supporters, Taiwo remained ready to do battle with anyone who stood in his way.

The opportunity arrived with what became known as the Ajasa case, which was a contest between two leading factions in Lagos: Ajasa, who held the title of *Apena* (essentially the *Oba*'s first minister), and Taiwo, the *Olofin* of Isheri and leader of Kosoko's supporters. The Governor of Lagos Colony, who was effectively the *Baba Isale* of the expatriate community and its Saro supporters, was also drawn into the dispute, which at its height tested Britain's ability to maintain civil order in the port.[114] The conflict between the two Big Men was the last significant episode in the long-running struggle for paramountcy between Dosunmu's followers and those of Kosoko. Ajasa, who was energetic and ambitious, expanded his power after he was appointed *Apena* in 1872. He then used the position to accumulate additional titles, the most important being the headship of the *Ogboni*, the body that, formally, stood between the *Oba* and the people. Political acquisition and commercial accumulation were close allies. During the 1870s and into the mid-1880s, Ajasa and Taiwo wrestled for control of the lagoon markets and carried their dispute into the court room.[115] Taiwo and other wealthy Lagosians had previously deployed British law to punish or discipline errant followers and opponents.[116] They now mobilised the technique to sway the outcome of a major power struggle in Lagos politics.[117]

110. He next surfaced in the correspondence between Lagos and the Colonial Office in 1878, when he provided Alfred Moloney, the Acting Administrator, with information on the state of hostilities between the Egba and Ibadan. Moloney to Lees, 3 Oct. 1878, C.O. 147/36.

111. Moloney to Lees, 3 Oct. 1878, C.O. 147/36.

112. Rowe to Kimberley, 3 Feb. 1882, C.O. 147/49.

113. Rowe to Kimberley, 3 Feb. 1882, C.O. 147/49.

114. The best account remains Cole, *Modern and Traditional Elites*, pp. 29–44.

115. C. A. Monnier to Taiwo, 14 April 1884, TP, Lagos Affairs, 1870–1902; Ikorodu Traders to Governor, 22 Sept. 1884, TP, Abeokuta and Interior, 1865–1900.

116. Examples are given in Mann, *Slavery and the Birth of an African City*, pp. 302–12.

117. Evidence of continuing commercial rivalry is in: C. A. Monnier to Taiwo, 14 April 1884, TP, Lagos Affairs, 1870–1902; Ikorodu Traders to Governor, 22 Sept. 1884, TP, Abeokuta & Interior, 1865–1900.

Conflict between the two parties became more intense during the early 1880s, when Ajasa was thought in some quarters to be positioning himself to succeed Dosumnu as *Oba*. In 1882, Brandford Griffith, the Deputy Governor, judged Ajasa to be 'a clever, ambitious and intriguing individual, turbulent, possessing fluency of speech and audacity of manner. He exercises considerable influence over poor King Docemo [*sic*], a harmless and inoffensive man'.[118] In case his judgement left room for uncertainty, Griffith added that the dispute with Taiwo had encouraged Ajasa to develop 'a mischievous manner' that amplified his 'unscrupulous and wily' character. A man so programmed to create trouble, Griffith thought, ought to be deported, a recommendation that the Colonial Office declined to accept. Not everyone agreed with this interpretation. Beyond Government House, voices on the other side were raised to criticise Taiwo's activities in court as well as the supra-legal action he took to enforce his interests.[119]

The rivalry produced several episodes of violence. One instance occurred in 1883, when a group of Lagos traders sought Taiwo's approval for a produce pool, which they had organised at the large Ejinrin market without consulting Ajasa, who claimed that the proposal ought to have been cleared with him.[120] As the dispute gained momentum, established political allegiances became strained. Although Ajasa's rise to prominence had boosted Dosunmu's standing, it had also created an over-mighty subject. The *Oba*'s son and presumed successor, Oyekan, was too young to be a major participant but had already shown his displeasure at what he saw as Ajasa's attempt to take over the House of Dosunmu. In 1883, Dosunmu, 'inoffensive' though he was, considered his position sufficiently perilous to take the dramatic step of abandoning the *Apena* and forming an alliance of convenience with Taiwo in a bid to remove Ajasa's titles and end his dominance. Ajasa's reaction to this blatant but crafty treachery demonstrated the material power of symbolism: he destroyed the *Ogboni*'s drums, a gesture that was both a rejection of the *Oba*'s authority and an act of sacrilege. In doing so, Ajasa also destroyed his career. The *Ogbonis* united against the *Apena*, their leader, and Taiwo secured the support he needed to overcome his rival. Faced with the loss of his offices and power, Ajasa retaliated in 1884 by appealing in person to the Colonial Secretary. When this tactic failed, Ajasa brought an action against Taiwo alleging that

118. Griffith to Kimberley, 18 Dec. 1882, C.O. 147/52; also Moloney to C.O., 11 Dec. 1892, C.O. 147/52.

119. The most prominent of the public opposition was expressed in the *Eagle & Lagos Critic*.

120. *Eagle & Lagos Critic*, p. 35. In addition to the pool that was formed in 1884, Taiwo's papers contain a document dated 11 March 1879, which shows that a group of his traders had compiled a similar set of rules for trading at Iworo market. TP, Abeokuta and the Interior, 1865–1900.

he had engaged in slave-trading.[121] A rumour circulated that, if Ajasa won his case, he would call for a revolt that would remove Dosunmu, kill Taiwo, and make himself *Oba* of Lagos. Against expectation, however, Taiwo was cleared and Ajasa was defenceless against the retribution that was to follow.

At this point, Captain Knapp Barrow, the lieutenant governor, arrested Ajasa and sent him for trial in Accra, where in 1884 he was convicted of conspiracy to overthrow the British government and given a prison sentence. Taiwo and his followers provided Ajasa with an unwanted celebration, including a parade, to mark his departure from Lagos.[122] The way was clear for Taiwo to re-establish his dominance, which he did by ending his alliance with Dosunmu, taking punitive action against his opponents, and regaining control of the Lagos political scene and the disputed markets along the lagoon. Taiwo's triumph demonstrated that his alliance with the British was more powerful than Ajasa's alliance with the *Oba*. At the same time, his success prompted a reaction. Indeed, one of the motives for releasing Ajasa early, in 1885, and allowing him to return to Lagos (with a gratuity of £50) was to provide a counterweight to Taiwo.[123] Governor Moloney also warned him not to act as if he decided the laws of Lagos.[124] By then, however, Ajasa's power had been broken beyond repair. *Oba* Oyekan, who succeeded his father in 1885, was only fourteen years old and was not in a position to lead a revival of the House of Dosunmu.[125] From then on, as far as Lagos politics was concerned, Taiwo ruled supreme.[126] His position in Isheri was equally secure. In response to an enquiry from a visiting government official, one of the chiefs there stated in 1890 that 'Taiwo was their King, and that he was a friend of the Governor, that they looked to the Governor through him for protection'.[127]

Taiwo's surviving correspondence clarifies important aspects of the dispute between the two heavyweights. The exceptional pressure placed on established loyalties is evident in the split that ended the relationship between Taiwo and Jacob Ogunbiyi, his sometime trading partner and long-time friend. Both had benefitted from the patronage of the *Asogbon* when starting their

121. Moloney to Granville, 8 July 1886 and 6 Aug. 1886, C.O. 147/56; Evans to Granville, 17 Sept. 1886, C.O. 147/57; Mann, 'The Rise of Taiwo Olowo', p. 99.

122. *Lagos Observer*, 25 Dec. 1884.

123. *Lagos Observer*, 8 Oct. 1885; Moloney to Granville, 8 July 1886, C.O. 147/56. The Colonial Office also thought that Ajasa had been treated with more severity than the evidence warranted. See also Evans to Granville, 17 Sept. 1886, C.O. 147/57.

124. *Eagle & Lagos Critic*, 17 Sept. 1885, 19 Nov. 1885.

125. Initially, the Colonial Office opposed the appointment of a successor to Dosunmu. On reflection, the Office relented but reduced his pension of £1,000 p.a. to a nominal sum (£200, later increased to £400) to be paid to his successor in an attempt to prevent the issue from becoming a cause of conflict. Moloney to Griffith, 11 Dec. 1882, C.O. 147/52.

126. Ajasa's last years remain obscure. A biography of his career is overdue and would make a valuable contribution to Lagos history.

127. Haddon Smith to Acting Inspector General of Constabulary, 24 June 1890, CSO 8/5/6.

careers, though Ogunbiyi's connection was closer than Taiwo's. The *Asogbon's* association with the *Oba* and Ajasa made contradictory demands on Ogunbiyi's affiliations.[128] He supported his friend until August 1885, when he provided evidence in court claiming that Taiwo was persecuting Ajasa's followers. Taiwo lost the case, which he had brought to extract retribution from Ajasa's defeated supporters.[129]

During a related trial, also in 1885, Ogunbiyi and other witnesses stated that Taiwo was both an *Ogboni* and a member of an associated fraternity, the *Osogbo*. Both organisations were formally under the control of the *Apena*, who had used them to exert pressure on debtors and political opponents.[130] Although Taiwo denied the claim, the Chief Justice found that he had 'lied and manufactured evidence' and gave judgement against him. Taiwo was so incensed with the decision that, in an extraordinary move, he organised a petition to have the Chief Justice removed on grounds of 'oppression and one-sided justice'.[131] Private correspondence, in which Taiwo was addressed as '*Ogboni*', confirms that he was a member of the society.[132] The relationship between Taiwo and Ogunbiyi continued to deteriorate. At the end of the year, Ogunbiyi denounced Taiwo's behaviour in a letter to the *Eagle & Lagos Critic* and confirmed, in effect, that their friendship was at an end.[133] Shortly afterwards, Ogunbiyi asked Taiwo to declare that Moronkeji (Ogunbiyi's wife), who had been one of Taiwo's slaves, had been redeemed by him when she was very young. Otherwise, he said, he would take 'strong measures'.[134] Taiwo's reply, if he gave it, has not survived. Ogunbiyi died a few months after writing this letter.[135] It is possible that the two old friends were reconciled. Given the strength of two powerful and conflicting characters, however, the probability is not high.

Taiwo's political ambitions extended to infiltrating the upper reaches of the colonial government. Patrick Cole speculated that Knapp Barrow, the Lieutenant Governor (who was also Colonial Secretary of the Gold Coast), was biased in Taiwo's favour.[136] Evidence in Taiwo's correspondence falls short of establishing collusion but shows that the relationship was indeed close. The *Lagos Observer*, which admittedly favoured Ajasa, claimed, quite openly, that Taiwo was

128. Mann, *Slavery and the Birth of an African City*, p. 299.

129. The *Lagos Observer*, which was hostile to Taiwo, reported on the case (Lawani & Ors v. Taiwo) on 6 Aug. 1885. For the wider context, see Mann, *Slavery and the Birth of an African City*, pp. 299–300.

130. B. Oreke v. Taiwo, LSCR, Civ.6, 1885,

131. This was a step too far: the Chief Justice survived. Moloney to Granville, 6 Aug. 1886, C.O. 147/56.

132. Iba to Taiwo, 13 Sept. 1877, TP, Badagri Correspondence, 1877–1900; W. E. Cole to Taiwo, 22 April 1889, TP, Correspondence with the Lagos Government, 1879–92.

133. *Eagle and Lagos Critic*, 22 Oct. and 5 Nov. 1885.

134. Ogunbiyi to Taiwo, 19 Nov. 1885, TP, Lagos Affairs, 1870–1902.

135. On 16 April 1886.

136. Cole, *Modern and Traditional Elites*, pp. 38–9.

organising public support in the hope of boosting Barrow's chances of becoming Governor.[137] Taiwo undoubtedly took care to cultivate Barrow, who was keen to irrigate his promotion prospects, and tried to enlist his support in the dispute with Ajasa.[138] In 1883, when Barrow was about to leave for England, he wrote to Taiwo with the hope that he would 'continue' in his 'loyalty and good services for the government'.[139] In 1886, a contact in Accra forwarded a message to Taiwo from 'our friend' the Colonial Secretary saying that he might be sent to Lagos to replace Governor Moloney, who wanted a transfer.[140] Although the transfer did not take place, Barrow wrote to Taiwo in 1887 saying that he looked forward to seeing him again and would call at Lagos on his way to take up a position as Acting Consul for the new Oil Rivers Protectorate.[141]

Barrow's hope was transmitted through Andrew Hethersett, a Saro who was Chief Clerk in the governor's office, served as an official translator, and was also deployed as a messenger and assistant on various missions to the warring hinterland states.[142] He was a good man to know, and Taiwo knew him very well. In 1884, Hethersett wrote to Taiwo asking him to 'start me in life and make me as one of your children'.[143] The 'start' included his hope for 'a better house'. Taiwo obliged: Hethersett got his house and thereafter was indebted to Taiwo both personally and financially. In 1889, he expressed alarm at the news that he had upset Taiwo because, as he put it, 'I consider myself a son—or if you like your protégé'.[144] His loyalty was well attested. He shuttled between Taiwo's compound and Government House delivering and conveying messages that were evidence of Taiwo's special relationship with the upper ranks of the colonial service.[145] The connection was one of reciprocity. The government relied on the

137. *Lagos Observer*, 5 Feb. 1885, 5 March 1885, 2 April 1885, 6 Aug. 1885.

138. Jinadu Shomade to Deputy Governor, 30 Oct. 1885, TP, Correspondence with the Lagos Government, 1879–92.

139. Hethersett to Taiwo, 3 May 1883, TP, Correspondence with the Lagos Government, 1879–92.

140. M. B. Davies to Taiwo, 18 Dec. 1886, TP, Correspondence with the Lagos Government, 1879–92.

141. Barrow to Taiwo, 30 Dec. 1887, TP, Correspondence with the Lagos Government, 1879–92. The Protectorate was formed in 1885.

142. Hethersett entered government service in 1871 as Chief Clerk to the Harbour Master. He was promoted to 2nd Clerk and Interpreter in the Administrator's Office in 1876, became Chief Clerk and Interpreter in 1879, and was appointed Chief of the new Aborigines Department in 1895. He died in 1896. See *Lagos Standard*, 26 June 1895 and examples of his activities in Hethersett to Moloney, 22 March 1881, enc. in Griffiths to Kimberley, 14 April 1881, C.O. 147/49.

143. Hethersett to Taiwo, 2 July 1884, TP, Correspondence with the Lagos Government, 1879–92.

144. Hethersett to Taiwo, 12 Oct. 1889, TP, Correspondence with the Lagos Government, 1879–92.

145. Taiwo to Hethersett, 13 Jan. 1885, 6 Oct. 1886, 25 Aug. 1887, TP, Correspondence with the Lagos Government, 1879–92.

services Taiwo provided to resolve disputes in the lagoon markets, recapture escaped slaves and criminals, and accommodate emissaries from the hinterland states. Taiwo, who received privileged information from Government House, took care to stroke the hand that fed him. 'And whatever His Excellency desires me to do', he purred, 'I am quite ready at all times to do it'.[146] His access to the governor of Lagos remained in place until at least 1895.[147]

Far below these high-level exchanges, Taiwo's correspondence was full of begging letters and supplicatory addresses. Typical examples include a plea from N. G. Thomas, one of his former clerks, who wrote from the debtors' prison in Lagos in 1874 appealing for a reasonable settlement of his debt of £32.[148] Others with nothing to lose took a chance: 'I am but a prodigal repenting for all my offences', wrote one; 'I pray you in the name of God the Father to forgive me all my debts and I will ever be a servant to you as I was before in your house'.[149] Saro of standing wrote in the lofty prose that matched their status. In asking for easy terms for the loan of £100 he had already contracted, Joseph Haastrup almost made it appear that he was doing Taiwo a favour: 'My Dear Sir,' he began,

> We are in the world where we are to depend on each other and where all elderly men are not big men, for big men are those men who render an immediate help to one in time of pressing need; and I believe you are one of those men; for without flattery you are a great boon to the community and I hope the Lord will spare your valuable life and bless you abundantly.[150]

Chiefs of some standing wrote grovelling apologies when they learned that they might have offended the great man. Anxiety drove Kakanfo, the *Are* of Abeokuta, to flourish his rhetoric in defence of his loyalty: 'If I am mad, I believe I shall never forget your countless favours and special acts of kindness and they will be my madman's songs night and day'.[151] How could he be ungrateful, he continued, 'when it was you who took me to the Governor and recommended me to him as your constituted *Are*? When the enemies and opposers of Captain Glover in this Lagos rose up against me twice, and I was fined five pounds on each occasion, who paid the five pounds each time but you?' These extracts, which are no more than samples of many others, provide an indication of the range of Taiwo's network and the measures he took to ensure that loyalties did not waver.

146. Taiwo to Hethersett, 25 Aug. 1887 (and similar sentiments in Taiwo to Governor, 24 June 1885), TP, Correspondence with the Lagos Government, 1879–92.

147. Hethersett to Taiwo, 10 Sept. 1895, C.S.O. 8/7/5a.

148. N. G. Thomas to Taiwo, 4 Dec. 1874, TP, Lagos Affairs, 1870–1902.

149. Alawusa to Taiwo, 21 Oct. 1879, TP, Lagos Affairs, 1870–1902.

150. J. P. Haastrup to Taiwo, 23 July 1883, TP, Lagos Affairs, 1870–1902.

151. Kakanfo to Taiwo, 25 March 1879, TP, Lagos Affairs, 1870–1902.

Taiwo's private correspondence, incomplete though it is, also provides an insight into his personality. It is evident that he was ambitious, ruthless, and energetic beyond normal measure, but so were many other Big Men who reached the top through achievement rather than inheritance. Additionally, Taiwo's attitude during crises reveals a determination to prevail that some-times alarmed his friends, even though they were familiar with the robust qualities needed for success in Lagos commerce and politics. Taiwo held his nerve and triumphed, whether by luck or judgement, in the big battles he fought. Amid the continual and often conflicting demands that accompanied his success, he was also able to keep his close friends, Sumanu Animashaun, Mohammed Shitta, James Davies and, until the last moment, Jacob Ogunbiyi, for the greater part of his life. His religion, too, was a meaningful support rather than simply an instrumental device. He became a loyal supporter of the Anglican church at Ebute Ero, made a 'substantial' donation to finance the native pastorate and a 'generous' contribution to the cost of building the CMS Collegiate Institute in Lagos.[152] He built a church at Isheri shortly after he became *Olofin*, paid the salary of the pastor there, and contributed financially to the Anglican churches at Oyo, Iseyin, and elsewhere.[153] In 1867, he donated £50 (the second highest contribution after that of James Davies) to help fund a new building for the CMS Grammar School.[154]

The Closing Years

Taiwo's last battle ended in 1901. He grappled with illness during the clos-ing years of the decade and died just as the new century was beginning. He had already reduced his trading activities in the 1890s by leasing 40 and 49 Marina to other firms. The *Lagos Weekly Record* judged that he 'wielded greater influence than any other individual in Lagos'.[155] The number of fol-lowers who attended his funeral was proof that the claim had credibility. For someone whose reflex action was to call in his lawyers, it is strange to discover that Taiwo died intestate. He had already assigned his two Marina properties to his eldest son, Alfred, who continued to trade in association with two of his sisters, Rebecca and Sarian, until his death in 1909. By then, the business was operating on a much-diminished scale. The sisters reduced it further by abandoning the produce trade and concentrating on retailing cotton goods.

152. *Lagos Times*, 26 Sept. 1883; Samuel Pearse to Taiwo, 2 April 1888; Taiwo to Revd. W. Morgan, 31 Aug. 1887; James Johnson to Taiwo, 28 May 1895, TP, Church Affairs, 1884–1900.

153. Charles Marke, Freetown, to Taiwo, 31 Aug. 1888; Samuel Pearse to Taiwo, 21 Feb. 1893; A. F. Foster to Taiwo, 13 Jan. 1897; TP, Church Affairs, 1884–1900; Rebecca Taiwo v. Odunsi Sarumi, LSCR, Civ. 64, 1912.

154. Herskovits, *A Preface to Modern Nigeria*, p. 365, n. 87.

155. 23 Feb. 1901.

Intestacy brought the lawyers into court, despite Taiwo's reluctance, on this occasion, to request their presence. His children challenged the distribution of his estate, which the administrator had divided among all ten, apart from Alfred, who had already received most of his share in the form of the Marina properties.[156] In 1908, the court upheld the distribution made in 1905, and by 1911, the most important of the legal challenges was over.[157]

This was by no means the end of the story. Even though Taiwo's great trading operation had ceased by the time he died, his wealth lived on through his children and grandchildren. Alfred leased 49 Marina to Lagos Stores in 1906 for fifteen years at a rent of £250 per annum.[158] His daughter, Sabina Sholabomi, who inherited the property, renewed the lease in 1913 for 30 years at an annual rent of £650.[159] In 1933, she mortgaged the property to the Lagos Building Society for £2,000 at an annual interest of 10 per cent. The loan was repaid and then renewed in 1941 and repaid again in 1945. The property remained in her hands until the end of colonial rule, if not longer. The house at 40 Marina passed to Sabina, who leased it to the African Oil Nuts Co. in 1925 for twenty-one years at a rent of £600 a year.[160] The lease was renewed until the 1940s and the property was rented in 1945 to Nigerian Properties Ltd. for sixty years at £600 a year. In the following year, Nigerian Properties made Sabina an offer she could not refuse: she sold 40 Marina to them for £19,500. The history of the two Marina properties reflects a much wider trend as the families of many of the Big Men of the nineteenth century became rentiers rather than traders.

Conclusion

Although Taiwo is one of the great names in nineteenth-century Lagos, details of his long life and extensive interests have long been lacking. The survival of some of his private papers, however, has allowed a fuller account of his career to be assembled than was possible previously. The result, presented in this chapter, is not only to enlarge a life but also to illuminate features of the port's history that have been either obscure or unknown.

The main story is that of the adaptation of 'indigenous Lagos' to legitimate commerce. Although the Saro were selected to be the ideal agents of progress, it is evident that most of Lagos joined in. In this respect, the reluctance of

156. Rebecca Taiwo v. Alfred Taiwo, LSCR, Civ. 51, 1908.
157. A complementary dispute concerned the nature of Taiwo's marriage and its implication for rights of inheritance. Rebecca Taiwo v. Alfred Taiwo, LSCR, Civ. 29, 1903; Ephraim Taiwo v. Taiwo, LSCR, Civ. 61, 1911.
158. LLOR, 52/13.
159. This transaction and the others cited here can be followed in LLOR, 81/283, 151/9, 376/63, 589/37, 589/39.
160. Sabina's transactions can be followed in LLOR, 1204/1412. Taiwo had transferred the property to his son, Alfred, in 1898. LLOR, 1209/1412.

the *Idejo* (white-cap chiefs) to participate in the new economy was untypical. Numerous other non-Saro traders, including some, like Sumanu Animashaun, Jacob Ogunbiyi, and Oshodi Tapa, became wealthy as a result of their willingness to adjust to new opportunities and their ability to do so. Even more telling, as chapter 3 showed, was the speed with which the concept of freehold tenure and the value derived from it spread among ordinary Lagosians. Placed in this wider context, Taiwo's career suggests that what remains at present largely unknown has the potential to shift, and perhaps even transform, our understanding of Lagos history during this period.

Taiwo, as we have seen, jumped in head-first. Having helped to persuade Kosoko that the old days based on supplying slaves for export had passed and could not be recalled, Taiwo set about building a fortune on the new trade in association with the German firm, G. L. Gaiser, and by investing much of his capital in property. His records reveal the impressive scale and geographical reach of his business, which extended from the Niger to Bahia. Taiwo, the illiterate trader, was an active participant in the process of globalisation that was under way at that time. Equally significant, his records demonstrate the importance of coastal and regional trade to his business. The evidence does not dislodge standard approaches, which focus on export-led growth, but it does suggest that the role of the internal market has been underestimated.[161] Many products imported from the Niger (and elsewhere) were sold in Lagos and not exported to Europe. Although purchasing power derived from export crops was an incentive for buying imported goods, profits from local trade might well have been an additional source of import demand, while producers of palm oil and kernels might also have been motivated by the prospect of acquiring local products. This proposition cannot be determined here, but it can be put on the agenda for future researchers.

The familiar link between trade and politics is also apparent throughout Taiwo's life. To this extent, circumstances favoured the opportunities open to him, even though it needed initiative to take them. Before the expansion of British rule in the 1890s, Lagos Colony was small and depended heavily on local allies, such as the Saro, and others who were connected intimately with the Yoruba states. Taiwo fitted the bill. As *Olofin* of Isheri, he had a power base that was independent of his position in Lagos; as an entrepreneur managing a large network that was connected to similar networks, he stood at the head of an extensive chain of command and information that no colonial governor could match and all of them could benefit from. Taiwo's exercise of power was eclectic: he employed inherited means, such as sanctions and force, where needed, but also had the resources to enforce his authority through the courts the British had established. By the time he died in 1901, these conditions had

---

161. Klas Rönnbäck, one of the 'new' economic historians, is pursuing this theme and achieving illuminating results: 'Climate, Conflicts', pp. 1065–88.

given way to a larger colonial state and an expanded set of expatriate officials, and intimacy of the kind Taiwo had enjoyed with Glover was no longer
possible.

A further aspect of Taiwo's multi-dimensional life was his connection with
the Saro community and with James Davies in particular. The chapter on
Davies that follows provides some obvious contrasts with Taiwo's world. But
the juxtaposition of the two chapters has more in common than the fact that
they were the two greatest figures in the town in the early colonial period.
They were also friends, a fact that, once known, raises the possibility that ties
between the Saro elite and other prominent Lagosians might have been closer
than their apparent social differences suggest.

CHAPTER FIVE

James Davies, King of the Merchant Princes

JAMES PINSON LABULO DAVIES IS one of the best-known figures in nineteenth-century Lagos.[1] His story continues to appear in newspapers, journal articles, and books, and is the subject of a rarity in this context—a book-length biography.[2] His life, with its mixture of exotic and romantic qualities, and his status as a king among merchant princes, has proved irresistible; his reconstructed image as the archetypal Saro gentleman of the high Victorian era ensures that he remains fashionable long after his time. Most commentators focus on his distinctive education and training and his unique link with British royalty forged by his equally unusual marriage. Once these matters have been covered, interest generally fades and the rest of his life is told, if told at all, in the barest outline.

Adeyemo Elebute's valuable study is exceptional in providing a careful account of Davies's activities as a public figure, notably his philanthropic contributions to education and the Christian missions, and an outline of his political interests.[3] Nevertheless, important aspects of Davies's life are still hardly known, even among specialists. Little has been written about his

---

1. I am most grateful to three of James Davies's grandchildren: Mr John Romanes Adewale Randle (better known as Jack), Mrs L. Beckley, and Mrs Catherine Olabisi Eshugibyi, for their considerable help reconstructing their grandfather's life. Interviews in Lagos, 28 Jan. 1962, 29 Jan. 1962, and 12 April 1964.

2. Elebute, *The Life of James Pinson Labulo Davies*. Professor Elebute (1932–2019) deserves the gratitude of all specialists on Lagos for producing such an impressively researched study, not least because he wrote his book in retirement after a distinguished career as a surgeon and health-care provider.

3. Elebute, *The Life of James Pinson Labulo Davies*. An earlier source that is consistent with Elebute's is Onabolu, 'Mrs Randle', which records a long interview with Jack Randle, Victoria's son and James Davies's grandson.

business as a merchant, which was the foundation of his prosperity. His intimate connections beyond Saro society have also been neglected. Almost nothing is known about his pioneering role in founding the Nigerian cocoa-farming industry, a contribution that is explored in chapter 9. These large omissions are less matters of choice than the result of a shortage of information. Although literate Saro kept records, few have outlasted the various upheavals brought by the passage of time. Paradoxically, there is more information about Taiwo, who was illiterate, than about Davies, who wrote with fluency, and more information about Davies the farmer, who is unknown, than about Davies the merchant, who is. Good fortune, however, has allowed some of his private papers to survive. These, combined with the Lands Office and early court records, can be used to fill some of the gaps left by reliance on Colonial Office correspondence, missionary records, and newspapers.

A Saro Story—With Royal Connections

Davies's early life was part of the standard Saro story.[4] His date of birth, 14 August 1828, is uncontested. The location, however, is uncertain. The consensus agrees on Freetown, but without firm evidence. One source states that he was born on the Gold Coast and later moved with his parents to Sierra Leone.[5] Fortunately, there is no doubt about his parents, who were both freed Yoruba slaves, James Labulo Davies and his wife, Nancy Charlotte. The couple also had a second son, Samuel, and at least four daughters.[6] The family's precise origins were for long uncertain, but it can now be established that James's father was an 'an Owu man' and that his mother, Nancy Charlotte, came from Ogbomosho in Oyo.[7] The Owu were displaced and dispersed following the break-up of the Oyo Empire in the 1820s and 1830s.[8]

4. Unless otherwise stated, I follow here Elebute's and Onabolu's treatment of the better known parts of the Davies's life (n. 3).

5. Newman, 'The Davies Chronicles', p. 15. Newman does not give a source for this claim. However, his dissertation is exceptionally well researched, so the possibility should not be dismissed.

6. Elebute, *The Life of James Pinson Labulo Davies*, p. 1, notes that the 'rest of their children . . . were daughters'. The family Bible and associated sources list eight children out of an estimated total of fourteen. Several died in infancy; some remained in Sierra Leone. Among the others, there were two brothers, Samuel, who died at sea in 1857, and Edward Albert Labulo Davies, who died at Davies's farm, Woodland Estate, in 1890. James's mother and two sisters settled in Lagos: his mother traded independently before she died in 1887; Nancy married J. A. Savage, a Lagos merchant; Martha married J.A.O. Payne, the Chief Registrar of the Colony. Information kindly supplied by Mrs Eshugbiyi, J.P.L. Davies's granddaughter, Lagos, 4 Feb. 1862.

7. James Davies, evidence in Adoluju & Ors v. Davies & Ors, LSCR, Civ. 33 and 34, 1904.

8. Mabogunje and Omar-Cooper, *Owu in Yoruba History*.

Different groups resettled in various parts of Yorubaland, one large settlement being in Abeokuta. In time, the Owu came to identify as Egba, while still retaining a sense of their own distinctiveness. James followed the trend. In his adult years, he too came to identify as an Egba. As their names indicate, the family became Christians, and the two boys followed an established route in being educated at the CMS Grammar School in Freetown. They were fortunate to have this opportunity. Their father died while they were still young, and Christopher Taylor (formerly Agidimoh) volunteered to act as their guardian.[9] Taylor, who was among the early group of Egba slaves landed at Freetown, had become a prosperous merchant. Evidently, he was also generous of heart as well as pocket.

From this point, the story departs from the familiar pattern. On leaving school, James and his brother did not return to Lagos and enter trade, the Church, or one of the secular professions. Instead, they were chosen in 1851 to be the first participants in a novel and imaginative experiment. They were assigned to HMS *Volcano*, which was part of the Royal Navy's West Africa (Anti-Slavery) Squadron, for training in navigation and seamanship. Both boys had impressed their teachers and deserved their chance. The opportunity itself, however, arose from an initiative taken by Henry Venn, the active and influential Secretary of the Church Missionary Society (CMS).[10] Venn's aim was to produce what he termed an 'indigenous Church' that would be 'self-extending' and 'self-supporting'.[11] The Bible and the plough were key partners in this endeavour. Spiritual uplift could not be sustained without nourishment fed by economic progress. James and Samuel were to acquire technical skills. Others, like Henry Robbin, were sent to England to learn about cotton processing. Others still, like Samuel Crowther, who was the first African to become an Anglican bishop in West Africa, were to spread the Word. These influences, of opportunity and equality, shaped the two young brothers. James would live long enough to see them applied and then abandoned.

James and Samuel received encouraging reports from their seniors on HMS *Volcano*, and at the close of 1851 James was promoted from cadet to lieutenant. *Volcano* was classified as a paddle sloop, which enabled the brothers to learn how to manage steam as well as sail.[12] James would carry this experience through his career, as his application of new technology to old problems would show. The *Volcano* was present at the bombardment of Lagos in 1851; the brothers were on

9. Little is known about Taylor, who died in 1870. See Fyfe, *A History of Sierra Leone*, pp. 292, 356, 378.

10. 1796–1863; Honorary Secretary for more than 30 years and a key figure in the evangelical revival of the mid-nineteenth century.

11. Ajayi, 'Henry Venn'.

12. Campbell to Clarendon, 14 Aug. 1854, F.O. 84/950.

board and James was slightly wounded during the engagement.[13] Involvement in the 'imperialist project' was once seen to run counter to nationalist interests and was criticised accordingly. Considered from their perspective, the brothers were advancing the cause of African emancipation by helping to eliminate the slave trade and preparing the way for subsequent progress, spiritual and secular. It is anachronistic to interpret their participation as evidence of disloyalty to a nationalist movement that had yet to be invented, especially because they, too, were sensitive to African interests and rights.

James and Samuel left the Royal Navy in 1852, having completed their training, and began independent careers captaining ships owned by Free-town merchants that ran along the West Coast.[14] This was a risky business. Most of the ships were in poor condition; some were unseaworthy. In 1855, one such vessel sank off Lagos in a storm, while James was onshore meeting the owner.[15] After this alarming episode, James decided to find his feet on land. In the following year, he settled in Lagos and was joined by his mother and sisters. This decision was wiser than James realised. In 1857, his brother, Samuel, died at sea while serving as captain of one of James George's ships.[16] Unnerving though James's experience at sea must have been at times, it afforded him an unrivalled knowledge of the coastal ports and opened his mind to possibilities that would not have occurred to him had he remained in one place.

It was at this point that James began his career in commerce as an agent for a London firm with connections in the West Indies. The firm consigned manu-factured goods to him in its ships and received palm oil, cotton, and small quantities of ivory in return.[17] James quickly established himself and opened his own business in 1857. He owned several ships, which he used mainly in the palm oil and cotton trades, and a steamer, the SS *Niger*, which he employed to develop a branch of his business on the Niger. He also had agents in Abeokuta, the Egba capital, and Porto Novo. In 1861, a difficult year for trade, he made a profit of more than £300.[18] In the following year, he reported that the last seven years had been 'very profitable'.[19] Many years later, he described a typi-cal set of exchanges in the days before cash transactions were introduced: 'I used to sell cotton goods, spirits, etc. on credit and the purchaser, the trader,

13. *Lagos Weekly Record*, 5 May 1906.

14. Fyfe suggests that James and Samuel left the Royal Navy because they were too old to qualify as naval captains. This seems unlikely, given that James was only 24 and his brother was younger. Fyfe, *A History of Sierra Leone*, p. 318.

15. *Lagos Weekly Record*, 5 May 1906.

16. Fyfe, *A History of Sierra Leone*, p. 318. For James George and his son, Charles, see above, chapter 3.

17. *Lagos Weekly Record*, 5 May 1906.

18. Newman, 'The Davies Chronicles', p. 17.

19. Newman, 'The Davies Chronicles', p. 19.

would take them to the markets and bring back produce and I would credit them [*sic*] with their value'.[20]

Abeokuta was a priority, not only because of Davies's Egba affiliations but also because he was the main financial support behind the cotton-growing venture the CMS sponsored there during the 1850s. He was fully committed to the purpose of the enterprise, which was to provide an alternative to the slave trade by giving material support to Christian converts. Principle joined 'the Bible and the plough'; Davies helped to make it a reality. Henry Robbin, another of Venn's disciples and one well known to Davies, managed the cotton project in Abeokuta under the name of H. Robbin & Co. Davies, however, supplied the capital and ran the commercial side of the business, as Robbin generously acknowledged in 1858: 'Captain Davies is the person to whom much is owed for all the cotton shipped at Lagos, he commands several English canoes and boats and has shipped on board his vessel the "Saltern Rocks" some hundred bales of cotton when there was no ship to take them and when he could have shipped oil instead'.[21]

Davies's business in Lagos was well organised. He employed a chief clerk, William Alfred Allen, who was paid an annual salary of £150, to supervise and co-ordinate a series of account books that began with 'waste' books and went on to cash books, cowrie books, and day books before the entries finally reached the ledger.[22] Traders entered their transactions in passbooks that were brought to the main office every month, adjusted with reference to the ledger, and balanced.[23] Davies provided some indication of the scale of his activities in 1861, when he listed his total of 133 employees comprised of 8 clerks, 11 carpenters, 10 coopers, 4 shipwrights, 4 bricklayers, 13 sawyers, 42 canoe-men, 20 Kroomen, 20 labourers, and 5 grammar-school boys, adding, with justifiable pride, that there was not 'one slave among them'.[24] He was probably the largest employer of wage labour in Lagos at that time, including the colonial government. Davies underlined the point two years later, when he reported to Henry Venn that he had used 'free children' to help run the business since 1856 and found the experience to be 'very profitable'.[25] Davies's

20. Davies, 'Testimony Before the Trade Commission of 1898', 20 April 1898, enc. in Denton to Chamberlain, 25 May 1898, C.O. 147/132. The typed report of his evidence gives the date, erroneously, as 1896.

21. Robbin to Clegg, 2 March 1858, CMS, CA 2/080. The original is quoted correctly in Herskovits, *A Preface to Modern Nigeria*, p. 98. I have here corrected some very minor slips in the written script.

22. Halliday v. Soguro, LSCR, Civ. 3, 1881. Allen, a Saro and fellow Egba, held this position from 1858 to 1863 and again from 1869 to 1975. He joined Davies on his farm in Ijon in 1882 and remained there as his manager and clerk until the 1890s, when he took a post with the Egba government in Abeokuta.

23. Halliday v. Animashaun, LSCR, Civ. 3, 1881.

24. Davies to Venn, 10 May 1861, CMS CA 2/033.

25. Davies to Venn, 6 July 1863, CMS CA 2/033; for further evidence of his commitment to the anti-slavery movement see *Anglo-African*, 7 Jan 1865.

innovative abilities found early expression in the oil mill he established on the Marina in the late 1860s to process palm fruit. Unfortunately, little if anything is known of this pioneering venture apart from the claim, made some years later, that the 'plant and machinery' cost 'about £10,000', which, if accurate, was an astronomical sum at that time.[26] The existence of the enterprise is commemorated in Oil Mill Street, which is adjacent to the Marina and retains its name today. Davies undoubtedly took his role as a champion of legitimate commerce very seriously.

Unfortunately, little more is known of Davies's commercial activities at this time, even though it was during the first decade or so of his business career that he became very wealthy and made his largest philanthropic contributions. The rapidity with which Davies acquired his wealth raises several questions. Consul Campbell's list of leading exporters of palm oil does not help because it refers solely to 1855, which was just before Davies entered the export trade.[27] Although cotton exports appear to have been modestly profitable, the CMS decided that they were losing money and began withdrawing from the venture in 1858 before closing it in 1863.[28] Davies helped by buying the boat they used for transporting cotton to Lagos for 'a good price'.[29] Although he continued to export raw cotton, there is no indication that the trade brought spectacular returns. He also had to deal with the misfortunes that accompanied a pioneering, frontier business. In 1861, he lost stock and materials worth £1,000 when his store was blown down; in the following year, he alleged that Charles Macaulay had 'robbed and squandered' an advance of nearly £2,500.[30]

One possible explanation of his exceptional wealth is that branches of his business, such as his shipping activities, which combined navigation with commerce, and his trade on the Niger, both of which went largely unrecorded, were highly profitable. There are hints that his four years employed as an independent captain in the merchant marine might also have delivered substantial profits.[31] Evidence is lacking, but the speed of Davies's rise to eminence so soon after he arrived in Lagos suggests that the pump had already been primed. It is also possible that he received help from his affluent

26. Davies v. Colonial Secretary, LSCR, Civ. 9, 1889. This matter needs further investigation. Writing in 1919, Adeoye Deniga suggested that it was a 'European', Robert Campbell, who installed a 'large oil machine'. Deniga, *Notes on Lagos Streets*, p. 6. Existing sources, however, refer to Campbell's enterprise, including founding the *Anglo-African* newspaper, but make no reference to his role in establishing the oil mill. Campbell was a Jamaican of European and African descent.

27. Campbell to Clarendon, 14 May 1856, F.O. 84/1002.

28. Kopytoff, *A Preface to Modern Nigeria*, pp. 97–8, 120.

29. Kopytoff, *A Preface to Modern Nigeria*, p. 330, n.46.

30. Davies to Venn, 10 May 1861. CMS, CA 2/033.

31. Davies to Venn, 3 Sept. 1856; Davies to Wright, 26 Sept. 1873, both in CMS, CA 2/033.

guardian, Christopher Taylor. A more general consideration is the likelihood that merchants who were astute, bold, and well organised could collect windfall gains at the outset of legitimate commerce, when high risks stemming from uncertainty were offset by market imperfections that allowed wide profit margins. His small fleet of ships may also have given him an advantage over his competitors. These conditions were whittled away towards the close of the century, when improved shipping services and the transition to cash payments increased commercial competition.

Whatever the precise explanation, evidence of Davies's wealth is well attested. His property transactions provide a reliable indication of capital accumulation. He was particularly active during the 1860s, when the market had just begun to benefit from the security provided by the reform of crown grants.[32] Davies conducted a larger number of transactions in crown grants between 1863 and 1882 than any other individual in Lagos, except possibly Daniel Taiwo.[33] He obtained a crown grant in 1863 for 50 Marina, a prime site that had a warehouse and a pier, and made a series of additional purchases in New Lagos throughout the decade.[34] He profited in 1864 from selling another plot on the Marina to Governor Freeman, who wanted suitable land for a new Government House.[35] Davies had obtained a crown grant for the land; he sold it for the considerable sum of £550. Even so, in 1871, he still owned three sites on the Marina, a tally that placed him ahead of all other merchants.[36] He was also active in the mortgage market, lending money for commercial advances and sometimes for personal expenditure, and indirectly helping to speed the development of freehold tenure. In 1867, when one Olubode mortgaged land at Tinubu Square that was not covered by a crown grant, he undertook to 'convey the land absolutely' should he fail to repay the loan.[37] In 1870, Davies's business was considered 'by all here' to be 'one of the safest commercial houses in Lagos and his commercial relations with Europe are known to be on a solid basis'.[38]

It is Davies's philanthropy, however, that is evidence not only of his wealth but also of his generous public spirit. His energy and money led in 1859 to the founding of the CMS Grammar School in Lagos, which was to become one of the best-known schools in West Africa.[39] He contributed to the expansion of

32. For example, LLOR, 2/355, 1864; 3/574, 1865; 3/571, 1866; 4/295, 1867; 4/345, 1867.

33. Estimated from LLOR, Index of Crown Grants, 1863–82.

34. LLOR, 39 (50 Marina) and, for example, LLOR, 2/355, 3/574, 4/345, 3/571, 4/295, 5/100, 10/252, 15/141, 16/20, 19/107.

35. John Brown to Cardwell, 11 Sept. 1864, C.O. 147/7.

36. Glover to Sheppard, 5 Aug. 1871, C.O. 147/21.

37. Olubode mortgage to Davies, LLOR, 5/100, 1867.

38. Forsyth to Simpson, 29 Aug. 1870, enc. in Simpson to Kimberley, 29 Aug. 1870, C.O. 147/18.

39. Elebute, *The Life of James Pinson Labulo Davies*, ch. 6.

the school in 1867 and assisted with a complementary development, the building of a town library in 1872. Davies was equally prominent in supporting the Anglican Church.[40] He was the leading benefactor of another famous Lagos institution, St Paul's Breadfruit. He was the moving force behind the decision in 1869 to rebuild the church, and headed the subscription list in 1874 with £104.[41] His resolve helped to see the project through to completion in 1880. In addition, he contributed generously to Christ Church, Faji, which was to become the Anglican cathedral in Lagos. His commitment to both Africa and universal development, which Victorians referred to as 'improvement', was expressed in his support for the Rev. James Johnson and his plans to develop a 'native pastorate', and more generally in his contributions to charities and relief funds.[42]

By the early 1860s, Davies was moving in the highest circles. He was consulted by both the consul and Dosunmu over the king's reluctance to accept the cession of his kingdom.[43] In 1862, he travelled to Abeokuta and Ibadan with representatives of the missionary societies in an attempt to end the Ijaye War.[44] In the following year, he became treasurer of the African Commercial Association, which was formed to represent the interests of African merchants in Lagos.[45] His public presence reached its apex in 1873, when he became the first African to be appointed a member of the Legislative Council of the West African Settlements, an honour that added to his distinction of being the first African Justice of the Peace in Lagos. With 'Honourable' before his name and 'J.P.' after it, Davies was about to rise into rarefied air far above his sea captain's rank.[46] In recommending him for these positions, John Pope Hennessy, the Acting Governor-in-Chief of the West African Settlements, wrote that 'Captain Davies is a wealthy native—well-educated, highly intelligent, and most honourable in all his dealings'.[47] The governor also referred to Davies's wife, 'a protégé of Her Majesty,' adding that 'as the leading people in Lagos, in all charitable undertakings and in Society, they are both worthy of the many kind favours the Queen has graciously bestowed upon them'.[48]

James and Samuel Davies were exceptional in being the first West Africans to receive training in seamanship and navigation. But James's wife,

40. Elebute, *The Life of James Pinson Labulo Davies*, ch. 5.
41. He also offered to donate the land needed for the construction. Lucas, *Lecture*, pp. 8, 16.
42. Herskovits, *A Preface to Modern Nigeria*, pp. 236–40.
43. *Anglo-African*, 6 June 1863, 29 Sept. 1863.
44. Herskovits, *A Preface to Modern Nigeria*, p. 187.
45. *Anglo-African*, 10 Oct. 1863.
46. The title was within his grasp but his appointment was provisional, pending confirmation that was withheld when he was declared bankrupt.
47. Pope Hennessy to Kimberley, 28 Nov. 1872, C.O. 147/18.
48. Pope Hennessy to Kimberley, 28 Nov. 1872, C.O. 147/18.

Sarah (formerly Aina), gave exceptionalism an entirely new meaning.[49] She was born about 1843 in the Egbado village of Oke-Odan and was among the captives taken by Dahomeans who raided the village in 1848.[50] Oke-Odan was destroyed and Aina's parents were killed, among many others. Aina, then only about five years old, found herself in the custody of Gezo, the formidable King of Dahomey whose raiding expeditions were feared by all the smaller states on his borders. Fate, however, offered compensation for her desperate situation. In 1849–1850, Commander Frederick Forbes, who captained HMS *Bonetta*, one of the ships in the Royal Navy's anti-slavery squadron, visited Dahomey with the aim of persuading the king to abandon the slave trade. His mission failed, but among the parting gifts presented to him was Aina. Forbes was unprepared to receive such an unusual present but resolved the dilemma by transporting the girl to Badagri, where she was placed in the care of the CMS, who baptised her and named her Sarah Forbes Bonetta. Forbes, however, was still responsible for whatever future lay before his small charge. Faced with continuing uncertainty, he decided to take her with him on his return voyage to England. After they landed in September 1850, Forbes informed the Admiralty that he had acquired a young female and asked Their Lordships to convey the news to Queen Victoria. Henry Venn supported, and may have suggested, the initiative in the hope of adding impetus to the anti-slavery movement as well as giving Sarah an exceptionally privileged start to her young life.

The queen responded in November by inviting Sarah to Windsor Castle, where she began what became a life-long connection with the royal family. Fate had also decided that Sarah was well above average intelligence, especially talented in languages and music, and had a congenial personality that made her a popular companion for the young royals. The queen entrusted Sarah's education to the CMS with the ultimate aim of enlisting her as a missionary in Henry Venn's army of Christian soldiers. In 1851, aged about eight, Sarah began her formal education in Freetown. Unpredictability, however, had yet to end its influence on her fortunes. In 1855, the illness and death of the two missionaries who were looking after her prompted the queen to recall Sarah to England. She was lodged with another missionary family and continued her education there. She fitted in with her congenial hosts and reports suggest that she was happy there, despite the many upheavals that had marked her short life. The queen kept in touch with Sarah and arranged for her to resume her visits to the royal household.

49. I follow here Elebute, *The Life of James Pinson Labulo Davies*, ch. 2, which is the most reliable of the numerous, and often varied, accounts of Aina's early life. Contemporary spelling often referred to her as 'Ina'.

50. Although Aina is often given the title 'Princess', evidence of her exact status is missing. Unlike some authors, Elebute is very careful on this point: *The Life of James Pinson Labulo Davies*, pp. 36–7.

FIGURE 5.1. James and Sarah Davies, London, September 1862. Photo by
Camille Silvy, with permission from the National Portrait Gallery, London.
Image No. 11699. Image ID: Ax61382. © National Portrait Gallery, London.

The next big event in Sarah's life was her marriage to James Davies. James had married Matilda Bonifacio Serrano in 1859, but she died unexpectedly only a few months later. In November 1860, James proposed to Sarah, who demonstrated her independence by refusing him. It is unclear how and how well the couple knew one another at that time. In 1860, however, Sarah was only about seventeen and at the age of thirty-two James must have seemed elderly. The queen was not amused by the refusal and Sarah was sent away to reflect on her decision. Time, aided by Henry Venn, must have imparted perspective because Sarah changed her mind. In August 1862 the couple were married in Brighton in a sumptuous and appropriately regal ceremony that required a police presence to keep the crowds at a distance.[51] What we know of the relationship between James and Sarah indicates that their marriage was a happy one.[52] Only a few personal letters have survived, but they reveal both the seriousness and the tenderness that James brought to their relationship and the importance of religion in their lives. In 1867, on the eve of Sarah's departure for London with their daughter, Victoria, James wrote as follows:

> I will always commend you in my prayer to our Heavenly Father to grant you the spirit of wisdom and understanding; the spirit of counsel and right. The eyes of the Lord are in every place. He will watch over and keep you from the evil that is in the world and will make you living members of Christ and the true household of faith . . . however fatigued you may be during the day never turn in without prayer and teach our beloved daughter, Victoria, the way she should go now while she is in tender years.[53]

Subsequent letters reveal glimpses of greater intimacy. 'I value my life', James wrote in 1875, 'especially when I have you and the children to look after'.[54] Other affectionate letters are scattered throughout the correspondence.[55] Their marriage exemplified the principles, including monogamy, that Anglicans were expected to uphold in mid-Victorian England. When practised in Lagos, it set a course towards profound social changes that were to reverberate throughout and beyond the colonial period.[56]

It seemed to be the best of times, and so it was, while it lasted. In 1912, Davies's daughter, Victoria, stated in court that 'in 1876 my father said his income was £5,000 a year'.[57] Although the accuracy of her retrospective view

51. For full details, see Elebute, *The Life of James Pinson Labulo Davies*, pp. 52–60.
52. Mann, *Marrying Well*, p. 116.
53. James Davies to Sarah Davies, 1 July 1867, Coker Papers (CP) 2/3.
54. James Davies to Sarah Davies, 6 Dec. 1875, CP, 6/2.
55. For example, James Davies to Sarah Davies, 27 April 1877, Coker Papers (read before being classified).
56. See the authority on this subject, Mann, *Marrying Well*, pp. 116–27.
57. Evidence in Victoria Randle v. James George & Ors., LSCR, Civ. 66, 1912.

cannot be tested, it is evident that Davies's income was sufficient to allow him to pay frequent visits to England, beginning as early as 1859, and to educate his two daughters, and later his young son, there. James and Sarah began married life in Davies Cottage in Davies Square, which was where their daughter, Victoria Matilda, was born in 1863. A son, James Arthur, followed in 1871, and a second daughter, Stella Forbes, in 1873. Victoria's christening in October 1863 was followed by 'one of the most brilliant *soirées* which has ever enlightened . . . the life of the elite of Lagos'.[58] The queen, who had agreed to be Victoria's godmother, presented her with a suitably inscribed gold cup and salver, which were proudly displayed for the guests to admire.[59] After Sarah died of tuberculosis in 1880, when she was still in her late thirties, the queen adopted Victoria, gave her a life-long annuity, and organised and paid for her education at Cheltenham Ladies' College. Following the birth of their third child, the family moved to a much larger house in Broad Street, which became one of the acknowledged centres of social life, a busy location for dinners, parties, recitals, and the venue for even grander occasions. Evidence of this kind is no more than indicative, but it is consistent with the view that, by the early 1860s, Davies had emerged as the most impressive of the Big Men of Lagos.

Davies and Taiwo: An Unexpected Alliance

The story of Davies's high life as a Saro merchant prince is in line with Herskovits's broad conclusion in her pioneering study that during this period: 'Sierra Leonean entrepreneurs were seen and saw themselves as part of the group of European merchants'.[60] Elite Saro lived in the same quarter of Lagos, inter-married, organised their own exclusive social events, embraced the values enshrined in Christianity and Western education, and worked closely with British officials, missionaries, and merchants. Yet, some of them established bonds with local Lagosians that extended beyond essential professional or business relationships. The problem is that the information needed to explore these connections is usually missing. Its absence illustrates the principle that history is what we know now rather than what was happening at the time. By exceptional good fortune, the survival of some of Taiwo's papers (and a few of Davies's) make it possible to glimpse a hitherto unknown aspect of a personal relationship that lasted almost 40 years.

Taiwo's records reveal that Davies was both a close friend and a trusted adviser. The origins of the relationship between the two are unknown, but it was clearly established by the early 1860s and was strong enough to survive the

58. *Anglo-African*, 3 Oct. 1863.

59. *Anglo-African*, 7 Jan 1965; *Lagos Times & Gold Coast Advertiser*, 25 May 1881.

60. Herskovits, *A Preface to Modern Nigeria*, pp. 96–7.

differences between them that arose over Governor Glover's anti-Egba policy. Davies was an Egba and Taiwo an Awori, though with strong Egba connections. Both conducted important business with Abeokuta.[61] Davies, however, could give the Egba unqualified support on both business and political grounds, and accordingly was highly critical of Glover's policy of 'interference', which he judged was not the best way of spreading civilisation in Africa.[62] In 1863, he went so far as to call the British administration in Lagos 'despotic'.[63] Davies's critical attitude extended to the CMS, which he thought was beginning to distance itself from the Africans it was supposed to be serving. In 1872, he was one of the founders of the Association for the Promotion of Religion and Education in Lagos, which embraced Venn's ambition of creating a self-supporting and self-sustained native pastorate.[64] Taiwo's position required him to balance his Egba affiliations with the need to protect the centre of his power in Isheri. This imperative led him to co-operate with Glover while also allying with sympathetic elements in Abeokuta who would profit from his continuing dominance of Isheri. Differences in tactics also reflected their personalities. Taiwo preferred action to inaction, whereas Davies's advice was for him to 'go gently' in case he offended the governor and prompted a damaging reaction.[65]

These issues surfaced in 1866, when Glover imposed an export tax on Egba produce sent down to Lagos in an attempt to coerce the authorities in Abeokuta into adopting a more open trade policy.[66] This was a risky strategy, not least because Egba returnees were the most numerous and most prominent of the Saro in Lagos. Glover's precipitate action provoked 'violent opposition' among the Egba Saro, who objected to his 'interference' in the affairs of an independent state.[67] A small group of them met in the house of the 'well-known' James Davies to co-ordinate resistance to the governor's measure. The governor responded by calling on the 'plotters' to take the Oath of Allegiance, on the assumption that Davies, whose loyalties were divided between the queen and the Egba, would find it impossible to decline the invitation. The result, the governor calculated, would be to damage Davies's standing 'in the estimation of his faction'.[68] The ploy worked: Davies and his colleagues (with one exception)

61. Davies had 'premises' in Abeokuta for collecting and storing palm oil and several cotton gins. *Anglo-African*, 7 Jan. 1865.

62. *Anglo-African*, 7 Jan. 1865.

63. Davies to Venn, 9 March 1863, CA 2/033, quoted in Newman, 'The Davies Chronicles', p. 21.

64. Ayandele, *Holy Johnson*, pp. 91, 95–6.

65. Apatira to Taiwo, 1 April 1870, TP (Taiwo Papers), Abeokuta and Interior Affairs, 1865–1900. Also Glover, *Life of Sir John Hawley Glover*, p. 129.

66. Bashorun and Chiefs to Blackall, Feb. 1866, C.O. 147/11; Glover to Cardwell, 8 Jan. 1866, C.O. 147/11. This paragraph (and the next two) summarise Davies's perspective on events already discussed from Taiwo's viewpoint (see above, chapter 4).

67. Glover to Cardwell, 8 Jan. 1866, C.O. 147/11.

68. Glover to Cardwell, 8 Jan. 1866, C.O. 147/11.

took the Oath and the 'plot' collapsed.[69] Nevertheless, shortly afterwards, Glover felt obliged to cancel the export tax.[70]

Tensions among the interested parties remained during and after the upheaval that followed the *Ifole* in 1867 and reached a crisis in 1869, when, with Glover's approval, Taiwo shut the River Ogun at Isheri to exert pressure on his debtors in Abeokuta.[71] Taiwo's allies in Abeokuta urged him to be patient. Patience, however, was not a quality Taiwo had in abundance; he repeated his demands and added a deadline for them to be met.[72] Davies, who was referred to as 'one of our companions', was called on to mediate with Glover, the governor.[73] Shortly after the meeting, Glover instructed the European merchants in Lagos to allow Taiwo three years to settle his debts.[74] At this price, Taiwo would reopen the Ogun, which connected Isheri to Lagos. The deal was accepted, though Davies's and Taiwo's other friends remained anxious that his impatience might provoke another confrontation.[75] The dispute, however, did not end there. Glover's blatant favouritism offended many European merchants in the port; his unauthorised blockade of Porto Novo in 1872 enraged John Pope Hennessy, the new Governor-in-Chief of the West African Settlements, whose arrival in the same year led to Glover's transfer and the reversal of his policies. Glover's departure was the signal for a purge of his allies, the leading figure among them being Taiwo. Henry Mills (of Child Mills) arrived in 1872 and presented a statement to Pope Hennessy that was highly critical of Glover's policy and Taiwo's association with it.[76] Mills's own incentive lay in getting trade moving again so that merchants like Davies could pay their debts.

Taiwo survived the crisis, though his relations with Davies remained strained. Davies's opposition to Glover's anti-Egba policy encouraged Pope Hennessy to recommend him for appointment to the Legislative Council, whereas Taiwo's commitment to Glover remained unqualified and characteristically assertive.[77] In 1873, the pair came close to confrontation when Davies

69. The unnamed exception served two months in prison.

70. Glover to Cardwell, 10 March 1866, C.O. 147/11.

71. Biobaku provides the context for these developments, though his account is less African-centred than it would be if it were being written today: *The Egba and Their Neighbours*, ch. 7.

72. Solanke, Balogun (Abeokuta) to Taiwo, May 1869, TP, Abeokuta and Interior Affairs, 1865–1900; Taiwo to Chiefs and Elders of Ibore, Abeokuta, 16 June 1869, TP Abeokuta and Interior Affairs, 1865–1900.

73. Anon to Taiwo, 9 Feb. 1870, TP Abeokuta and Interior Affairs, 1865–1900.

74. Anon to Taiwo, 26 March 1870, TP Abeokuta and Interior Affairs, 1865–1900.

75. Brimah Apatira to Taiwo, 1 April 1870, TP Abeokuta and Interior Affairs, 1865–1900.

76. Pope Hennessy to Kimberley, 30 April 1872, C.O. 147/23.

77. Pope Hennessy to C.O. 20 Dec. 1872, C.O. 147/24; C.O. to Pope Hennessy 28 Dec. 1872, C.O. 147/24; C.O. minute, 20 Dec. 1872, C.O. 147/25; Pope Hennessy to Kimberley, 6 July 1872, C.O. 147/22.

sent an agent to Isheri to enquire about the welfare of the son of one of his traders, who was being held in prison by Taiwo. Pope Hennessy tried to use the situation to charge Taiwo with unlawful imprisonment, and possibly slavery; Glover, writing from his retreat in England, saved the day by offering a persuasive explanation of Taiwo's actions.[78] Nevertheless, at this point Taiwo and Davies were, in Glover's words, 'at feud'.[79] Whether as a provocation or in retaliation, Taiwo had insisted that Davies should settle a debt for which he stood security.[80] The obligation fell on Davies just at the moment when his own finances were entering what was to be the defining crisis of his career.

Yet, the relationship between the two Big Men not only survived but also remained strong and became closer with the passage of time. Davies was one of Taiwo's key supporters in the mid-1880s, when he was grappling with the Ajasa crisis.[81] This episode concerned Lagos politics and did not contain the divisive elements that Glover's policy towards the Egba had entailed. In 1883, Davies again urged Taiwo to 'go carefully'.[82] Ajasa, he said, has 'undone himself' and there was no need to organise a public demonstration against him. A few years later, Taiwo consulted Davies about the difficulty he found himself in as a bondsman in the court action arising from Honotnu's estate.[83] Davies also helped in other ways: in 1883, for example, he asked his agent in Brass to take supplies up the Niger to assist Taiwo's clerk at Eggan.[84] Davies's advisory role continued through the 1890s, when both men were suffering the illnesses of old age. After Taiwo had wound down his trading affairs, he consulted Davies over the disposition of some of his Lagos property and sought his help in managing his farm at Ebute Metta.[85]

Commercial ties were solidified by institutional loyalties and personal sympathies. Taiwo himself was an *Ogboni*, though he denied in court being a member.[86] It is also clear from a letter written by Jacob Ogunbiyi that Taiwo,

78. Pope Hennessy to Kimberley, 5 March 1873, and enc. by Davies, C.O. 147/26; Glover to Kimberley, 27 March 1873, C.O. 147/29.

79. Glover to Kimberley, 27 March 1873, C.O. 147/73.

80. Glover to Kimberley, 27 March 1873, C.O. 147/29.

81. See above, chapter 4.

82. Davies to Taiwo, 28 May 1883, TP, Corres. with J.P.L. Davies, 1870–1894.

83. Anon to Taiwo, 9 Feb. 1870, TP, Abeokuta and Interior Affairs, 1865–1900.

84. Davies to ?Auphrey (Brass), 6 Oct. 1883, TP, Corres. with J.P.L. Davies, 1870–1894.

85. Davies to Taiwo, 5 April 1887; Jackson to Taiwo, 24 Jan. 1894, TP, Corres. with J.P.L. Davies, 1870–1894.

86. Evidence of Ogunbiyi in Oreke and Ors v. Taiwo, LSCR, Civ. 6, 1885; Cole to Taiwo, 22 April 1889. The letter begins, 'Ogboni', and ends 'I am, *Ogboni*, Yours Truly . . .'. This is, by definition, a difficult area of research. If, as one source claimed later, all chiefs were *Ogboni*s, it is odd that Taiwo should have denied his membership. Evidently, the term 'chief' needs closer definition before the claim can be evaluated. The same source added the complication that 'all *Ogboni*s need not have titles'. Evidence in Taiwo v. Sarumi, LSCR, Civ. 64, 1912.

Davies, and he were members of an affiliated fraternity, the *Oparun*. The letter, which was marked 'Top Secret', dealt with the affairs of the society, including the provision of guns, and ended with the instruction that Taiwo should keep the communication secret or he would 'go blind'.[87] This chilling warning accompanied correspondence of a much warmer kind. In the 1880s, Davies sent Taiwo some informal, almost chatty, letters reporting progress with his new farming venture, detailing the hard work involved, and saying how much he enjoyed living on his estate.[88] In 1885, he invited Taiwo to have dinner on New Year's Eve with him and his daughter, Victoria, at Woodland Estate.[89] Two years later, after his only son, Arthur, died aged seventeen, Davies wrote to Taiwo from his farm, thanking him for his letter of sympathy and replying as only the closest of friends would do:

> God only knows how He gives me the strength to bear this, the greatest of all my troubles and bereavements. To tell you the truth, I forgot everything and did not know what I was about. I only knew that I was speaking in the day-time! When the night came, I felt as if I was dying and crying and groaning all night long in my room. Of course, I cannot put an end to my own life which the good God gave me because I lost my only son at this time of my life. Thanks be to our Heavenly Father that since my arrival here I feel better day by day and when I am well enough, I shall return to *cruel* Lagos.[90]

Incomplete though the surviving correspondence is, it nevertheless provides insights that cannot be obtained from standard sources. Much remains unknown. It is unclear, for instance, what if anything Davies received in return for his services, though Taiwo supported him in court on at least one occasion, and as *Olofin* of Isheri was well placed to protect Davies's farming venture at Ijon.[91] It is evident that the ties between them, being personal as well as commercial, had a highly individual quality. Yet this does not mean that they were unique. Other Big Men from different social groups had an interest in using the colonial government to advance their own purposes and may have

87. Ogunbiyi to Taiwo, 24 Jan. 1870. TP Abeokuta and Interior Affairs, 1865–1900.

88. Davies to Taiwo, 31 Dec. 1886, TP, Corres. with J.P.L. Davies, 1870–1894. There is a similar letter, dated only 1888, in the correspondence.

89. Davies to Taiwo, 30 Dec. 1885. TP, Corres. with J.P.L. Davies, 1870–1894.

90. Davies to Taiwo, 9 Aug. 1887, TP, Corres. with J.P.L. Davies. James Arthur Taylor Davies (1870–87) died on the return voyage from England, where he had been educated at Maidstone Grammar School and then trained in ceramics (though he had previously expressed a wish to become a lawyer).

91. Taiwo evidence, 19 Sept. 1874, in E.A.L. Davies, T. G. Hoare, and J.P.L. Davies v. Callender, Sykes and Mather, LSCR, Civ. 7, 1887; on Isheri's link with Ijon, see Davies's evidence in J.P.L. Davies v. Olorunfemi and Ors, LSCR, Civ. 25, 1900; and in Aduloju and Ors v. Davies, LSCR, Civ. 33, 1904.

formed similar alliances. Taiwo's world view was narrower than his international business connections. His priority lay in defending his fiefdom, which ran from Lagos to Isheri with an extension to Abeokuta. Davies's attitude was necessarily more complex because he was a Victorian gentleman, as well as a Lagosian with Egba affiliations. These characteristics help to explain the differences between them over Glover's anti-Egba policy. Self-interest operated in both cases, but Davies's opposition to Glover included his belief that the governor was departing from the ideal of co-operative development and racial equality that were core values of the first generation of Saro.

From the Heights to the Depths

Few, if any, reversals of fortune in Lagos can match either the rapidity or the magnitude of the fall that carried James Davies from the heights to the depths. In 1872, in a commitment that was so large as to be breathtaking, Davies mortgaged 'all his property in West Africa' to the Manchester firm of Child, Mills & Co. to secure an advance of £60,000.[92] The mortgage listed a portfolio of fourteen properties (later increased to fifteen) in Lagos. No other transaction in Lagos matched the scale of this one until 1919, when P.J.C. Thomas mortgaged the bulk of his property to secure credit of £150,000.[93] Davies was unable to repay the advance and was called on to forfeit most of his property in Lagos. He was declared bankrupt in 1876 and spent the next fifteen years trying to retain as much of his property as he could in a series of court actions that brought more reversals than triumphs. Legal records provide far more material on this subject than on any other episode in Davies's life. Yet, answers to key questions remain elusive. Davies was used to entrepreneurial risk but was not known to be a speculator. There is no apparent reason, commercial or otherwise, why he should have staked 'all his West African property' to secure this one, huge advance when he was under no evident compulsion to do so. It is possible, however, to see why he ran into difficulties so quickly.

Current explanations of Davies's downfall cite the expansion of Sir George Goldie's monopolies on the Niger and the depression that affected West African trade in the late nineteenth century.[94] The effect of Goldie's activities, however, was felt several years after Davies had defaulted on his huge loan, and the timing of the trade depression needs specifying if it is to fit the disaster that overtook him. What was once called the 'great depression' of the late nineteenth century is now seen as a discontinuous series of events that had their origins in two connected banking crises, one in Vienna in May 1873 and the other in New York in September of that year. Davies's financial difficulties

92. LLOR, 15/141, 1872; 16/20, 19/107, 1873.
93. See chapter 15.
94. Elebute, *The Life of James Pinson Labulo Davies*, p. 101.

date from the end of 1872 and therefore cannot have been prompted by the banking crises that followed. A more likely cause can be found in a temporary but acute downturn in the fortunes of the palm oil trade. As the broken line in figure 2.2 shows, the net barter terms of trade of palm oil fell abruptly between 1869 and 1874; volumes also dropped in 1872–1873. Additionally, the closure of the hinterland trade routes for long spells in 1872 and 1873 limited the ability of merchants to settle their trade advances. It is highly likely that Davies was exposed to these adverse trends because palm oil was his main export. It is probable, too, that his ability to settle the debts he had incurred was made more difficult by the damage to confidence that resulted from the series of international banking crises in 1873.

There is one cause, however, that qualifies as being necessary and might even be sufficient: the failure of Child, Mills & Co. This Manchester firm, about which little is now known, appears to have added a new form of business in West Africa.[95] Instead of tying advances directly to sales of goods and produce, they advanced money on the security of property and relied on merchants to repay the advance (plus interest) from trading profits. The firm's connection with Davies dates from 1870, when he began shipping produce to them.[96] Two years later, as noted earlier, Henry Mills was in the port stirring up opposition to Glover's anti-Egba policy in an attempt to keep trade moving.[97] His contract with Davies, which was executed on 18 March 1872, was probably signed while he was visiting Lagos. Child, Mills was not in obvious difficulties at that time. On the contrary, in August of that year, Mills and Davies were among a small group of merchants who advanced £4,500 to the government to relieve its short-term liquidity problems.[98] Yet, only a few months later, the firm suspended payment of the £60,000 advance and went into liquidation at the end of the year.[99] In January 1873, Charles Leigh, a Manchester merchant, wrote to the Colonial Office to complain about the 'state of the colony' and queried the appointment of Davies to the Legislative Council. 'This gentleman is I believe seriously involved with the late failure of Child, Mills and Co., his property being mortgaged to this firm'.[100]

95. I am grateful to Prof. Robin Pearson, University of Hull, for confirming that the history of this firm remains obscure.

96. Glover to Kimberley, 29 Aug. 1870, C.O. 147/18; Kennedy to Kimberley, 2 Oct. 1870, C.O. 147/18.

97. Pope Hennessy to Kimberley, 30 April 1872, C.O. 147/23.

98. Pope Hennessy to Kimberley, 31 Aug. 1872, C.O. 147/23.

99. Charles L. Clare to Kimberley, 18 Dec. 1872, C.O. 147/25. In the Matter of Child, Mills & Co. and E. P. Bousfield & Co., Bankrupts, LSCR, Civ. 1, 1877. Bousfield & Co. were textile merchants.

100. Charles L. Clare to C.O. 14 Jan. 1873, C.O. 147/29. The Colonial Office left Davies's appointment to the governor, who postponed a decision. In the end, Davies's provisional appointment to the Legislative Council was allowed to lapse. Berkeley to Kimberley, 13 Nov. 1873, C.O. 147/28.

It was the failure of Child, Mills so soon after issuing the loan that put Davies under sudden and extreme financial pressure. Henry Mills seems to have been the primary speculator. He had raised money on the strength of optimistic expectations about the rate of return on West African trade, the interest that borrowers would pay, and the security of newly-established freehold property there. His presence in Lagos and active involvement in the agitation to prevent Glover returning to Lagos and pursuing his anti-Egba policy demonstrated his concern that interruptions to trade would damage his business commitments.[101] His firm was almost certainly over-extended and had no defence against a commercial downturn or the disruption of trade. He must also have been a persuasive salesman. For his part, Davies may have thought that, short of walking on water, his previous record of success had made him invulnerable, whereas it may just have made him unwary. Yet, the deal offered by Mills was sufficiently plausible to attract other established merchants, such as Jacob S. Leigh, Jacob Ogunbiyi, and Charles Cole, and prominent figures such as James Forsythe, the lawyer, and even *Oba* Dosunmu. All had signed deals with Child, Mills and owed substantial sums as a result of the firm's failure, though none came close to the scale of Davies's commitment.[102] Without further evidence, we are left with the speculation that the terms Mills offered were more attractive than those available from rival firms in Lagos but were sufficiently well-judged to appear realistic. Nevertheless, the business had no defence against adversity and fell apart when its optimistic assumptions met the realities of the moment.

The consequences of the collapse of Davies's business reverberated throughout Lagos and beyond. Davies and others, who were also creditors of traders in Lagos and the hinterland, began court proceedings to recover the money they had advanced. The most important case Davies brought was against Isaac Olusi Coker, a merchant in Abeokuta who was supplying him with palm oil and cotton in exchange for advance payments made in goods (and possibly cowries).[103] Davies claimed that Coker owed him £5,075. Although the case appeared to be strong, Davies was non-suited because his claim was barred by the Statute of Limitations. There were also Saro creditors of Child, Mills, including merchants, such as Harry Pratt, Thomas Joe, and Thomas Hoare, who applied to be included in the settlement administered by

101. Charles L. Clare to C.O. 18 Dec. 1872, enc. Turton to Clare, 15 Nov. 1872, C.O. 147/25.

102. Leigh's career is discussed in chapter 3. Forsythe owed about £7,000 for a debt originally contracted in 1873, though Sykes & Mather claimed the debt was £16,783. See Sykes & Mather v. Forsythe, LSCR, Civ. 1, 1877 and 1878; Civ. 3, 1880 and 1881. James Cole owed £10,000. Dosunmu defaulted and his security (39 Marina) passed to CSM, who sold it to Joseph Haastrup in 1891 (LLOR, 1461).

103. Davies v. Coker, LSCR, Civ. 7, 1887. Isaac Coker was not related to the Coker family studied here and represented chiefly by Jacob K. Coker, though the two families knew each other. See also Davies v. Coker, LSCR, Civ. 9, 1887; Davies v. Coker, LSCR, Civ. 9, 1889.

the Trustee in Bankruptcy.[104] Their appeal was rejected because Child, Mills did not own property in Lagos.

In April 1873, Child, Mills dispatched an agent to Lagos to negotiate with the firm's debtors there.[105] With equal speed, Davies applied for leave from his duties on the Legislative Council because 'business of an important nature rendered my presence in England necessary'.[106] He left the town in April, estimating that he would be away for three months. Simultaneous negotiations in Manchester resulted in the debt being bought by a new firm, Callender, Sykes & Mather (CSM), which was also based in Manchester. The suspension of Child, Mills's business implied that Davies might not have received all the advance he had negotiated, which was good news. At the same time, he now faced the problem of dealing with an unknown firm whose primary interest was in securing repayment from Child, Mills's debtors. Davies's liabilities were estimated at £43,324, less the value of his securities and the outstanding debts owing to him. Shortly after arriving in England, Davies reached an accommodation with CSM.[107] They agreed to be his agents and to negotiate a favourable settlement whereby creditors would be compensated at the rate of 6 shillings in the pound. In return, Davies undertook to consign produce to them, which they would then sell through a broker, and to receive partial payment in goods. At the close of 1873, Davies wrote to his wife, Sarah, saying, 'I have sold my fortune to strangers'.[108]

At this point, clouds descended over the proceedings. In 1874, CSM advanced £20,000 to Davies on the security of 50 Marina, which included his warehouse and pier.[109] It is unclear why Davies needed, or at least accepted, such a large additional debt. At all events, he soon became dissatisfied with the arrangement and in September 1874 tried, unsuccessfully, to cancel it.[110] Relations quickly deteriorated. In 1875, Davies went to London to engage lawyers and wrote an optimistic note to Sarah in September, saying that he had 'defeated' CSM.[111] In the same year, CSM sent an agent to Lagos to enquire further into Davies's affairs. The presence of the investigator further damaged confidence

104. In the Matter of Child, Mills & Co. and E. P. Bousefield & Co. (Bankrupts), LSRC, Civ. 1, 1877.

105. Berkeley to Administrator in Chief, 17 April 1873, and enc. from Davies, 1 May 1873, C.O. 147/27.

106. Berkeley to Administrator in Chief, 17 April 1873, and enc. from Davies, 1 May 1873, C.O. 147/27.

107. E.A.L. Davies, T. H. Hoare, J.P.L. Davies v. Callender, Sykes and Mather, LSCR, Civ. 7, 1887.

108. Davies to Sarah Davies, 28 Nov. 1873, quoted in Newman, 'The Davies Chronicles', p. 55.

109. Sykes and Mather v. Davies, LSCR, Civ. 1. 1877.

110. E.A.L. Davies, T. G. Hoare, and J.P.L. Davies v. CSM, LSCR, Civ. 7, 1887.

111. Davies to Messrs Davies and Allen, 13 May 1875, CP, 6/2; Davies's Trustee v. M. J. Brown, LSCR, Civ. 2, 1880; Davies to Davies, 17 Sept. 1875, CP, 6/2.

in Davies's business and remaining assets. Meanwhile, Davies had missed a repayment of £20,000 in July 1874 and failed to pay a further £10,000 a year later.[112] CSM then abandoned the hope that Davies would be able to make the payments needed to redeem his property through trading profits or by any other means and decided to take legal action to claim the property he had mortgaged in Lagos. These ominous developments culminated in the outcome Davies had hoped to avoid: in August 1876, he was declared bankrupt. The report was widely publicised in Lagos and was 'the subject of universal talk and surprise'.[113] Although his humiliation seemed to be complete, events were to make his fall a harrowing experience that would accompany him, like an unwelcome guardian, for the next fifteen years.

In March 1877, CSM purchased Davies's assets and the debts owing to him from the Trustee in Bankruptcy for the modest sum of £550.[114] At that point, the creditors were judged to have a 'proven claim' for £27,480, less securities worth £8,000 that they already held, leaving a net balance owing of £19,480.[115] The bad news became worse. In 1877, the Manchester Court directed the Lagos Supreme Court to act as an auxiliary under the Bankruptcy Act of 1869, giving the Court 'full powers' to act on behalf of the Trustee and CSM.[116] The measure, which was intended to assist the creditors without extending the Act itself, encouraged CSM to appoint a local agent, namely Jacob Leigh, a merchant and fellow Egba who knew Davies well. The authority helped the trustee's agent to seize Davies's family house in Broad Street in 1880 and sell it (to Zachariah Williams) in the following year. In 1889, Davies brought an action to recover the property on the grounds that the Bankruptcy Act of 1869 did not apply to Lagos. Although the Lagos court initially favoured Williams, the full court ruled that the Act did not apply. Williams appealed to the Privy Council, which ruled in 1891 that the Act did apply, though it was not until 1897 that Williams secured a final order implementing the judgement.[117]

The power granted to the Supreme Court in 1877 gave Davies little room for manoeuvre. There followed a series of acrimonious and gruelling court actions in which CSM tried to secure and sell Davies's assets.[118] CSM pressed Davies

112. Sykes & Mather v. Davies, LSCR, Civ. 1, 1977.

113. Evidence of Leigh in Halliday v. Apatira, LSCR, Civ. 2, 1880.

114. Moloney to Holland, 31 Aug. 1887, CO 147/60.

115. Sykes and Mather v. Davies, LSCR, Civ. 1, 1877.

116. In the Matter of the Goods and Estate of J.P.L. Davies, a Bankrupt, LSCR, Civ. 2, 1880. A subsequent ruling made it clear that the powers conferred on the court in 1877 did not alter the fact that it had no jurisdiction in bankruptcy. In the Matter of the Goods and Estate of J.P.L. Davies, a Bankrupt, LSCR, Civ. 3, 1881. Also *Lagos Weekly Record*, 22 Aug. 1891.

117. *Lagos Standard*, 24 March 1897.

118. For example: Sykes & Mather v. Davies, LSCR, Civ. 1, 1877; Sykes & Mather v. Davies and Davies, LSCR, Civ. 1, 1877; Re J.P.L. Davies, a Bankrupt, ex parte Samuel S.

by taking court action in Lagos; Davies tried every possible means to evade the long arm reaching out to grasp everything he possessed. He disputed boundaries; he collected some debts that had not been declared; his agents trespassed on what was judged to be property that he had ceased to own. His main defence, though, lay in the claim that several properties were held in trust or owned by other members of the family and therefore were immune from forfeiture. The claim undoubtedly had merit: some property was in his wife's name and some was in the name of his mother, though in both cases he had free use of the houses and premises. Davies had some confidence that his case could withstand Sykes's lawyers: 'it is no easy job for him', he wrote in 1877, 'to collect debts and sell properties'.[119] The disadvantage of this defence was that it placed Sarah under considerable stress and drew his elderly mother into the intensely adversarial proceedings.[120] Moreover, the realisation that Davies might have raised money on property that, technically, he did not own added to the resolve of his creditors to extract every penny he possessed.

A review of the case in 1880 determined that fifteen pieces of land were involved. The court held that CSM had a 'clear title' to eleven of them, ownership of one was disputed, and three properties had not been disclosed to the creditors. The judgement delivered by Justice Macleod did not spare Davies. 'This is a matter', he concluded, 'that will bring discredit and shame upon men who have hitherto borne an honourable name'.[121] Victorian values could scarcely have descended with greater weight on one who had spent his life trying to uphold them. Moreover, following Macleod's ruling, Davies's creditors were permitted to remove him to Accra, where he was tried in 1880 for receiving money from his debtors while still bankrupt.[122] On this occasion, justice, and perhaps a slice of luck too, were with him: the trial was a 'miserable fiasco' and he was acquitted.[123] It is unclear whether the case against Davies was inherently weak or whether, as he alleged, Sykes had bribed witnesses and members of the judiciary and been found out.[124] Sykes did not read the signals of defeat. He persisted in his attempts to secure Davies's property but was unable to touch freehold land that was held in the names of

---

Davies, LSCR, Civ. 2, 1878; In re J.P.L. Davies ex parte Callender & Ors, LSCR, Civ. 1, 1877; In re J.P.L. Davies ex parte Sykes & Mather, LSCR, Civ. 1, 1877.

119. Davies to Sarah Davies, 16 June 1877, quoted in Newman, 'The Davies Chronicles', p. 56.

120. Sykes & Mather v. Davies and Davies, LSCR, Civ. 1, 1877.

121. In the Matter of the Goods and Estate of J.P.L. Davies, a Bankrupt, LSCR, Civ. 2, 1880.

122. Herskovits, *A Preface to Modern Nigeria*, p. 211; Elebute, *Life of James Pinson Labulo Davies*, p. 106.

123. *Lagos Times & Gold Coast Advertiser*, 23 Feb. 1881, 27 April 1881.

124. Newman, 'The Davies Chronicles', p. 68, makes the case for corruption, but the evidence he cites is inconclusive.

family members. In 1883, further representations from CSM led to a warrant for Davies's arrest to enforce a payment the court had approved.[125] Davies was able to make the payment and escape imprisonment. Yet, like hounds who never lose a scent, CSM kept going. As late as 1887 they consulted the Colonial Office about having Davies arrested and brought to England to stand trial.[126] By then, however, the Houdini of Lagos had made his escape.

Davies took what appears to be a huge and unjustified risk in mortgaging virtually all his property to a firm whose soundness he seems to have taken at face value. Having done so, however, he entered a maze that was further complicated by the uncertain and changing status of bankruptcy law. Although Davies had been declared bankrupt in Manchester, the Bankruptcy Act of 1869 did not extend beyond England without the explicit agreement of other jurisdictions.[127] As the Colony of Lagos was not covered by the Act, creditors in England who needed to realise assets located elsewhere were obliged to apply to local courts and pursue their claims on a case-by-case basis. Foreign creditors, however, had no effective means of securing redress in Lagos until 1876, when the Lagos Supreme Court was established, and 1877, when the Supreme Court was authorised to act on behalf of the court in Manchester.

The English Bankruptcy Act satisfied neither creditors nor debtors.[128] It strengthened the hands of creditors by giving them the power to appoint trustees, but weakened it in cases where creditors failed to co-operate. It favoured debtors by reducing the power of courts to imprison them, but limited the reform by retaining imprisonment for those who were judged to be concealing assets that could be used to settle their debts, while still requiring them to pay the money they owed. Had the Act applied to Lagos, Davies might have been able to file for bankruptcy himself (assuming he could face doing so), thus protecting his assets from summary seizure and guarding his future earnings from claims arising from past debts. Had he traded as a limited company, protection would have been more certain. Apart from the novelty of the device, however, there was no provision at the time for registering companies in Lagos. As matters stood, his personal as well as his business assets were liable to be forfeited. Moreover, imprisonment for debt remained a standard recourse under the law applying in Lagos. In the circumstances, he was shrewd in placing property that he had bought in the names of members of his family.

125. Eshelby v. Davies, LSCR, Civ.5, 1883.

126. Callender Sykes to C.O., 12 July 1887, C.O. 147/62.

127. Halliday v. Apatira, *Nigerian Law Reports*, I, 1880, p. 1; In the Matter of J.P.L. Davies, a Bankrupt, LSCR, Civ. 3, 1881; Moloney to Holland, 31 Aug. 1887, C.O. 147/60. See also *Lagos Weekly Record*, 22 Aug. 1891. On the reform see Chaplin, 'The Origins of the 1885/6 Introduction'.

128. The anomalies arising from the Act of 1869 were not resolved until a new Bankruptcy Act was passed in 1883.

The Privy Council's ruling in 1891 that the English Bankruptcy Act did apply, after all, to Lagos, prompted considerable discussion in the town and led some commentators to call for an Insolvency Act for Lagos modelled on the English Bankruptcy Act of 1883.[129] At present, the argument went, debtors were at the mercy of creditors. English firms were protected; African merchants were hounded and could not even use business losses to mitigate their position. The issue was still being discussed in 1912 with reference to Child, Mills, CSM and Davies.[130] Davies's career was characterised by innovation. Even in defeat, he contributed, however unwillingly, to the clarification of corporate law in ways that legal experts have yet to recognise.[131]

In 1884, the first encouraging news since 1873 arrived: Davies was discharged from bankruptcy.[132] He went to England for the occasion and had a 'satisfactory and amicable' interview with Sykes.[133] Once freed from his status as a bankrupt, Davies took legal action to recover some of his losses.[134] There was no disguising the extent of the disaster that struck him in 1873. Nevertheless, the worst of his ordeal was over. He had survived and saved some of his property, though he was far poorer than he had been in 1872. CSM appeared not to have gained substantially from their efforts over many years, even though they had sold most of the assets they were entitled to.[135] The clear winners, unsurprisingly, were the lawyers, who had enjoyed far more than their 'day' in court.

Davies held his head up throughout the protracted and very public reverses he suffered. He drew comfort from the loyalty of his friends in Lagos who stood by him, among them being the weighty presence of Daniel Taiwo. He found solace, too, in the 'kindness' the queen and members of the royal family continued to show his daughter, Victoria, and his late wife, Sarah, 'in times of my distress'.[136] Lagos opinion seems to have taken the view that it was bad

129. *Lagos Weekly Record*, 11 June 1898, 14 Jan. 1899, 10 June 1899, 6 June 1903.

130. *Nigerian Chronicle*, 5 April 1912.

131. *Lagos Weekly Record*, 22 August 1891. The issues of insolvency and bankruptcy resurfaced at the close of the century, when sections of Lagos opinion urged the case for a local bankruptcy ordinance, emphasising the inequality between European firms that could claim protection and Africans who could not. See *Lagos Weekly Record*, 11 June 1898, 14 Jan. 1899, 6 June 1903; Lagos Standard, 15 Nov. 1899, 22 Nov. 1899, 29 Nov. 1899, 13 Dec. 1899; *Nigerian Chronicle*, 5 April 1912, citing the case of CSM v. Davies. No ordinance was passed. Even today, there are considerable difficulties in applying bankruptcy legislation in Nigeria.

132. *Manchester Guardian*, 25 April 1884.

133. Adoloji & Ors v. Davies, LSCR, Civ. 34, 1904; Mannering to Davies, 6 June 1884, CP, 2/3.

134. For example, E.A.L. Davies, T. G. Hoare, and J.P.L. Davies v. CSM, LSCR, Civ. 7, 1887; Davies v. Coker, LSCR, Civ. 7, 1887; Davies v. Cole, LSCR, Civ. 7, 1888; Davies v. Colonial Secretary, LSCR, Civ. 9, 1889; Victoria Randle & Anor. v. George & Ors, LSCR, Civ. 61, 1911.

135. Moloney to Holland, 31 Aug. 1887, CO 147/60.

136. Davies to H.R.H. Princess Beatrice, 31 March 1884, CP, 2/3.

luck or deception rather than mismanagement that had caused his downfall. The popularity he had earned through his philanthropy survived his misfortune. The action brought against him in 1880 for breaking the conditions of bankruptcy was moved to Accra because the court in Lagos judged that no jury would convict him there, irrespective of the evidence.[137] He remained a welcome guest in elite circles in Lagos and retained sufficient funds to contribute to 'good causes', though not with the munificence that marked his philanthropy in the 1860s. 'All honour', reported his brother-in-law, J.A.O. Payne, in 1879, 'to Mr and Mrs J. P. L. Davies! This is the seventh fashionable wedding that has taken place in their house during the last fifteen years. A band was in attendance and played lively airs'.[138] His talented daughters, Victoria and Stella, no doubt helped the family's standing by being in demand for social and cultural gatherings. In 1881, James gave a moving address on the occasion of Archdeacon Henry Johnson's departure from Lagos, thanking everyone who had supported him during the 'sorest trials of his life'.[139]

Behind the public presence, however, lay a story of humiliation and distress heightened by the family's celebrated connection with royalty and its exceptionally high standing in Lagos.[140] The stress of the disgrace brought by bankruptcy and the seemingly unending court proceedings contributed to the deterioration of Sarah's health. Her early death in 1880 was a heavy blow to Davies and his young family.[141] In the 1880s, Victoria and Stella spent several years in England, partly to escape the atmosphere in Lagos. Their stay reinforced their Anglophilia. Their younger brother, Arthur, joined them but died on the return journey in 1877. Davies himself became more introspective and inclined to believe that Manchester, if not the world, was conspiring against him.

Returning to Business

Bankruptcy did not debar Davies from business. On the contrary he was obliged to keep trading, mostly shipping palm oil, palm kernels, and cotton to CSM as part of his debt settlement. This arrangement ended in 1874, and the business dwindled in 1875, when he was in England, and in 1876, when he

---

137. Herskovits, *A Preface to Modern Nigeria*, p. 211, quoting John Wood, a CMS missionary in Lagos.

138. Payne, *Payne's Lagos*. Payne, the Chief Registrar of the Colony of Lagos, was married to Davies's sister, Martha.

139. *Lagos Times & Gold Coast Advertiser*, 25 May 1881.

140. The reactions of the family, and Davies himself, are covered in Newman, 'The Davies Chronicles', ch. 3.

141. Sarah died in Madeira from tuberculosis on 15 August 1880. She was buried in Funchal in an unmarked grave. A few years ago, a campaign in Britain and Madeira raised funds for a gravestone, which is now in place.

was still making alternative arrangements.[142] During this difficult period, he kept afloat by absorbing '£5,000 and more' from his late wife's marriage settlement.[143] After he had been made bankrupt, he made an arrangement with the London firm of Christie & Co. that enabled him to trade without transgressing the bankruptcy rules. He became their commercial agent in Lagos and in 1878 received authorisation in the form of a power of attorney that gave him wide powers of action.[144] According to Davies's own testimony, given in 1896, he ceased to trade 'on a large scale' in 1878 or 1879.[145] The evidence suggests that, twenty years on, his memory on this matter may have been approximate rather than precise. Other sources indicate that his business activities were on a modest scale soon after 1873, when his world crashed around him.

Nevertheless, Christie's business extended its range during the 1880s from being shipping agents to becoming general merchants. Davies continued to export produce (mainly palm oil but also some palm kernels) in modest quantities, but the expanding branch of the business was in imported manufactures, building materials, and spirits. The average value of Christie's imports (measured by customs duties paid in Lagos) during the five years 1881–1885, placed the firm fourth on Governor Moloney's list of 'African' importers and fifth on the list that included English (but not foreign) firms.[146] The firm moved with the times: in the early 1880s, transactions were conducted in dollars and cowries; by the close of the decade, silver coin predominated.[147] The value and distribution of the firm's profits are unknown, but Davies's benefits were limited because he was an agent and not a partner. The contract ended when Christie ceased trading in or shortly before 1892.[148] During the 1880s and 1890s, Davies also conducted business in the name of Davies Bros., who were auctioneers and small-scale importers.[149] Changes to his self-description tracked his trajectory. He referred to himself as a merchant in 1879, an auctioneer in 1886, and a 'gentleman' in 1897.[150]

142. E.A.L. Davies, T. G. Hoare, and J.P.L. Davies v. CSM, LSCR, Civ. 7, 1887; Davies's Trustee v. M. J. Brown, LSCR, Civ. 2, 1880.

143. E.A.L. Davies, T. G. Hoare, and J.P.L. Davies v. CSM, LSCR, Civ. 7, 1887.

144. Evidence in Davies v. Colonial Secretary, LSCR, Civ. 9, 1889.

145. Davies, 'Testimony Before the Trade Commission of 1898', 20 April 1898, enc. in Denton to Chamberlain, 25 May 1898, C.O. 147/132. The typed report of his evidence gives the date, erroneously, as 1896.

146. Moloney to Granville, 19 April 1886, C.O. 147/55. The German firms would have been at the top of the list had they been included.

147. Christie & Co. v. Escherich & Co., LSCR, Civ. 3, 1881.

148. Evidence of Samuel Sogunro Davies in Victoria Randle & Anor v. James George & Bros., LSCR, Civ. 61, 1911.

149. Adolujo & Ors v. Davies, LSCR, Civ. 34, 1904.

150. Evidence in Cole v. Davies, LSCR, Civ. 2, 1879; evidence in Mary Davies v. Charlotte Davies and J.P.L. Davies, LSCR, Civ. 6, 1886; evidence in Asalu v. Taiwo, LSCR, Civ. 19, 1897.

During the 1880s and 1890s, Davies was often away from Lagos and his commercial affairs there were handled by his long-standing clerk, assistant, and eventually manager, Samuel Sogunro Davies.[151] Samuel was the adopted son of Sogunro, a senior official in the *Oba*'s administration, and (according to one source) a cousin of Davies's late wife, Sarah.[152] He was brought up and educated by Davies, took his name, and remained in his employment in Lagos from 1873–1892, when he left to start his own business.[153]

A diary Samuel kept from October 1883 to January 1884 provides a glimpse of the routine followed in the shop and warehouse in Broad Street.[154] During this period, Davies was shipping palm oil and potash, selling cotton goods and other imported manufactures, and managing auctions. The shop had variable hours but usually opened between 5.30 and 6.00 a.m., closed for 'breakfast' at 11.00 or 11.30, and reopened at 1.15 p.m. until 5.00 or 6.00 p.m., when Samuel made up the books and corresponded with 'the Captain', as he called him. Christmas Day was a welcome break from the confining regimen and long hours, and gave Samuel a chance to enjoy himself:

> Woke at 5. Shop opened at 6. Mrs Duncan came as usual to make tea. Closed shop at 9 and dismissed the men with a tot of grog. Gave some of them their money in advance of service. Attended Breadfruit Church, felt sleepy during the service, left for the purpose of sleep at 11.30. Service never break off till 12.30. Left house at 3 pm for Balogun Square for Cricket Match and left there at 3.30 to Tinubu Square for the Athletic Sports which last place I left at 5 and went to see Mr Martins and returned about 9 pm and went to bed.[155]

By the 1880s, morning tea, a lengthy sermon, cricket, and even athletics were pleasing signs to its earnest advocates that the Victorian Christmas had been installed in Lagos.

Halfway

Davies is both representative and exceptional. His rise to eminence reflected the conditions prevailing between the mid-1850s, when he started his business, and the early 1870s, when disaster fell on him. His Christian convictions

---

151. James's brother, Edward, helped in the business in Lagos and elsewhere. Davies's Trustee v. Brown, LSCR, Civ. 2, 1880.

152. Halliday v. Soguro, LSCR, Civ. 3, 1881.

153. Samuel died following an accident in 1911. His son, Samuel V. Davies, changed the family name to Akinsemoyin. See Randle & Anor. v. George & Ors., LSCR, Civ. 61, 1911; Elebute, *The Life of James Pinson Labulo Davies*, p. 81.

154. I am grateful to Mrs Eshugbiyi, granddaughter of J.P.L. Davies, for allowing me to read and cite this diary.

155. See n.154.

and belief in progress were values that other educated Saro of his generation shared. These raw, frontier days offered opportunities to make generous
profits from the new trade in legitimate goods, but also carried considerable
risks stemming from political and commercial uncertainties that were largely
beyond the control of colonial officials and Lagos entrepreneurs alike. It was
a time when the adoption of universal principles offered the prospect of a co-
operative and equal partnership in development. The Saro occupied a special
place in this programme because the small colonial government depended on
the services and connections that they alone could supply. Taken as a whole,
this was the 'Golden Age' of the Saro, and James Davies exemplified the
achievements it made possible. At the same time, his story, being necessarily
individual, has exceptional qualities. The extent of his wealth, the scale of his
generosity, and his unique connection with British royalty, were unmatched.
Yet, these special qualities arose from origins shared by many Saro, and set
an example that others could follow, even if they did not extend to royal
patronage.

   This chapter has given prominence to features of Davies's life that so far have
received little attention. His business activities can be reconstructed, at least in
outline, to illustrate his commitment to legitimate commerce and abhorrence of
slavery. The phase of his career that began when disaster struck in 1872, the long
and agonising legal battles that followed, and his cautious return to business
in the 1880s, have been assembled in this chapter for the first time. The story
relates external circumstances to individual choice; the context is that of global
connections that functioned across imperfectly co-ordinated borders. Davies
left no record of his reaction to the invasion of Yorubaland in 1892, but, given
his opposition to Glover's assertive policy, he is likely to have opposed it and
to have seen it as irrefutable evidence that the era of co-operation and equality had passed. Other Saro, such as Richard Blaize, struggled to reconcile two
worlds—one African, the other British. Davies occupied both. He wore his top
hat and carried his status as a Victorian gentleman when he was in Lagos, and
embraced rural life, including farm work, when he was on his estate at Ijon. His
accommodation with the new colonial order seems to have suited him. He was
sixty-four years old when Governor Carter invaded Yorubaland. It was time for
a new generation to define a different way forward.

   The other dimension of Davies's life uncovered here reveals a glimpse of
connections outside the Saro community. The strong ties that bonded the Saro
should not be seen, as they often have been, as evidence that they formed an
exclusive commune. At first sight, it seems unlikely that Daniel Taiwo, the illiterate *Olofin* of Isheri, and James Davies, the educated sea captain with connections to royalty, would have anything in common apart from their Christian
beliefs. Yet the two established a friendship that lasted for some forty years
until Taiwo's death in 1900. Although they fell out over Glover's policy towards
the Egba, they reunited after he left Lagos, and became closer as they grew

older. The relationship between the two most prominent merchants of the day had obvious mutual advantages. Davies gave Taiwo valuable links to the Saro community and the colonial government; Taiwo provided Davies with connections in Old Lagos and the hinterland. Co-operation did not reduce existing affiliations; it multiplied the sources of influence and information available to both men. The relationship was more than just instrumental; Taiwo and Davies respected and liked each other. The example of this 'odd couple' poses the question of whether this was an exceptional case or whether it hints at the emergence of a super-elite of Big Men whose influence on Lagos has still to be revealed.

There is more to come. Davies's career did not end with his modest business as an agent of Christie & Co. in the 1880s. It entered a wholly new phase that remains uncharted yet formed the most enduring of his contributions to the history of Lagos and of the world beyond it. This phase will be examined in chapter 9.

PART II

The Shock of 1892

CHAPTER SIX

Crisis and
Transition, 1880–1900

LAGOS WAS HIT by a second shock during the last twenty years of the nineteenth century. The first shock had led to the creation of the consulate and then the colony; the second threatened the development of legitimate commerce, prompted the invasion of the hinterland, and ended by greatly enlarging the boundaries of the colony. The resolution of these problems emerged through political decisions made in London. They were driven partly by international rivalries and changing relations with hinterland states, but they also had a substantial and related economic component, which is the main concern of this study. The shock was cumulative rather than instant. In 1861, the British government was reluctant to authorise the move from a small consulate to a permanent colony, but local circumstances forced its hand. Thus far, was the feeling, but no further. From the early 1880s, however, an accumulation of commercial difficulties intersected with political considerations to produce a reversal of government policy, which was manifested dramatically in 1892, when Governor Carter invaded the Ijebu state. The outcome gave Britain effective control of Yorubaland. It also marked the beginnings of the state that was to become Nigeria.

This chapter describes the commercial environment that shaped the opportunities available to the mercantile community during the last two decades of the nineteenth century. The period was one of exceptional economic and political turbulence that has long been seen as marking the decline of African merchants and middlemen from the heights reached during the 'Golden Age' that characterised the first two decades of the colony's history. The discussion that follows will identify the issues involved in analysing this question and prepare the way for the sequel in chapter 7, which uses new material to reassesses a familiar interpretation.

The Commercial Outlook

Trade in legitimate products remained the most important index of the state of commerce during this period, as it had been since the 1850s. Exports provided much of the purchasing power that drove the import trade, which in turn paid the customs duties that funded the colonial government. Taken together, the overseas trade of Lagos reflected its continuing development as a typical colonial satellite, which exported agricultural raw materials and imported a range of consumer goods.

The composition of the export trade, though still dominated by palm produce, underwent an important change as palm kernels (which were jointly produced with palm oil) increased their share of exports. The development of a process that transformed kernel oil into an edible product boosted Europe's new margarine industry, expanded the range of animal foodstuffs, and gave palm kernels a substantial export market for the first time. During the 1880s, palm oil and kernels accounted for an average of 84 per cent of the value of all exports from Lagos. By then, kernel exports exceeded the value of oil; thereafter, their predominance increased further. Cotton textiles remained the principal import, accounting for an average of 43 per cent of the value of all imports in the 1880s; spirits were in second place with 22 per cent of the total. The remaining items on the import list reflected the gradual diversification of the market, as consumer demand widened and government requirements expanded. Britain continued to be the main source of imports and the chief destination of exports. Germany stayed in second place but increased its share of total trade and made significant gains in exports of produce because German firms dominated the trade in palm kernels. Kernels met a growing demand for animal feed in Germany, and kernel oil was re-exported to the Netherlands, which was the leading producer of margarine. The market for kernels in Britain was small and slow to develop. France was in third place but had only a small share of exports from Lagos and made only a minuscule showing in the import trade.

Frankema's new indices show that West Africa as a whole enjoyed a trade boom from the 1830s to the mid-1880s, when export values and volumes rose and the net barter terms of trade favoured primary producers.[1] Thereafter, however, though volumes continued to increase, the terms of trade turned against African exporters from the mid-1880s to 1940. This overview provides a valuable guide to broad trends but also allows room for variations that reflect particularities of produce, place, and timing.[2]

1. Frankema, Williamson, and Woltjer, 'An Economic Rationale'.
2. In what follows, I have deliberately treated the data as being indicative only. Different official sources give different figures, even where they include/exclude goods 'in transit', specie movements, and items on the 'government account'. The basis of customs valuation also changed from FOB to CIF in 1893. Nevertheless, consistency remained elusive.

A closer look at the main exports from Lagos during the period leading to the occupation of the hinterland in 1892 reveals that the volume of palm oil exports continued to increase during the 1880s from an average of 4,595 tons in the three years from 1880 to 1882 to an average of 8,136 tons in 1888–1890. The volume of palm kernel exports also rose, though more slowly, from 26,341 tons to 38,567 tons during the same two periods. What is striking, however, is that the average value of palm oil exports fell from £166,723 to £149,249 during the two periods, whereas the value of kernel exports increased from an annual average of £276,322 to reach £291,382. Lagos reflects the general direction of palm oil prices in London and Liverpool, which were also on a downward trend from the early 1850s and touched their lowest points in the nineteenth century between the mid-1880s and mid-1890s.[3] Palm-oil producers and the predominantly British merchants and their African associates were earning less for supplying more. German merchants and the African merchants connected to them who traded in palm kernels were more fortunate: they were exporting more and earning more.

These trends are reflected in the terms of trade for the period, which have now been computed specifically for Lagos and include data on palm kernels, the leading export, for the first time (see figure 2.2). The net barter terms of trade for palm oil reached a peak in the early 1880s and then fell until the close of the century. Palm kernels, however, performed differently, declining in the 1880s, but beginning to rise at the close of the decade and continuing until 1907. As in the period 1856–1880, the broken lines in figure 2.2 indicate sharp variations within these general trends that identify the uncertainties facing decision-makers at the time.

As noted earlier, Lagos merchants were price-takers rather than price-makers.[4] Palm produce entered the international oils and fats market, in

---

See C.O. minute 21 Jan. 1903, on MacGregor to Chamberlain, 13 Jan. 1903, C.O. 147/165; and customs fraud continued to have a (largely unquantifiable) effect on the trade data. See the series of deceptions recorded between 1900 and 1912 in Moseley to Lyttelton, 21 July 1904, C.O. 147/171; Egerton to Lyttelton, 23 Oct. 1904, C.O. 147/171; Egerton to Lyttelton, 17 Dec. 1904, C.O. 147/172; Egerton to Lyttelton, 19 Jan. 1905, C.O. 147/174; Attorney General v. Pickering and Berthoud, 13 Sept 1909, LSCR, Civ. 55; Crown Agents to C.O. 14 March 1912, C.O. 520/1118, regarding the prosecution of John Holt; Fox to Harcourt, 11 Nov. 1912, C.O. 520/1120, regarding the prosecution of Ashton Kinder. It will require a forensic mind and an insatiable appetite for work to produce an accurate time series for the period through to World War I.

3. Frankema et al., 'An Economic Rationale', p. 242. See also Latham, 'Palm Produce from Calabar, 1812–1887', in *Figuring African Trade*, graph VIII.1, p. 283. The trend is confirmed by the *Annual Report for the Colony of Lagos*, No. 32 (1890), and was similar in neighbouring Dahomey, as Hélène d'Almeida-Topor has shown: 'Les termes de échange du Dahomey, 1890–1914', in Liesegang et al., *Figuring African Trade*, ch. 11.

4. For reasons of convenience, this paragraph covers material that accompanies figure 2.2 in chapter 2.

which it competed with substitutes as well as with identical produce from other sources. The market price was determined both by specific industries that used palm produce in the manufacturing process and by broader demands that reflected the state of the national economy. Needless to say, neither of these determinants took account of the interests of merchants in Lagos. Consequently, estimates of the demand for Lagos produce, which occupied a minute place in the international market, were as hazardous as they were complex. Unpredictability flourished on the supply side as well. The quantity of palm produce available was partly a function of rainfall, which could vary markedly from season to season. In the absence of quality controls, produce could be adulterated or poorly processed. These circumstances not only affected the price produce could command but also made forward contracts difficult and a futures market impossible. Political priorities among the hinterland states were an additional consideration that continued to influence the volume of produce available for sale. Local prices were highly sensitive to all these considerations and fluctuated, sometimes markedly, not only from season to season but also from day to day.

The great mid-Victorian boom was generated by rising demand for raw materials, falling transaction costs (notably freight rates), and lower manufacturing costs. During the last quarter of the century, the rate of growth of world trade slowed and demand for tropical produce slackened.[5] Volatility also increased: there was only one occasion between 1871 and 1905 when a sequence of positive rates of growth of GDP in Europe lasted for five years, whereas there were thirteen years when the rate of growth was negative. These trends had repercussions throughout the world: profit margins were squeezed; indebtedness increased; governments applied interventionist remedies. It should be no surprise to find that Lagos fitted a pattern that was reproduced in other colonial port cities in and beyond Africa.

An analysis confined to time series derived from the trade data is incomplete unless matched by experience on the ground. Admittedly, business commentary also needs to be used with care. Businessmen are more likely to advertise their problems than their profits; colonial officials can infuse information with the prejudices of the time. In this case, however, local commentary was unanimous in testifying that the decade leading to Britain's decision to occupy the hinterland was one of unrelieved gloom.

The litany of pessimistic assessments began as soon as the decade opened. In 1881, the *Lagos Times* reported on the 'anxious crisis' facing the colony as a result of the 'universal depression' caused by the 'interior difficulties'.[6] In

---

5. There is now a vast literature on what used to be called the 'Great Depression' of 1873-96, which is no longer seen as a period of unrelieved economic decline. The view summarised here is stated at greater length in Hopkins, *American Empire*, pp. 255-61.

6. *Lagos Times*, 26 Jan. 1881.

further comments, the newspaper noted the narrowing profit margins and the 'universal paralysis' of trade following the 'stoppage of the roads', and urged the government to deal with the problem by devising a package of treaties and subsidies.[7] In the same year, the large expatriate firms tried to bypass the brokers by eliminating their commission.[8] This expedient failed because the brokers were indispensable intermediaries between exporters in Lagos and producers in the hinterland. In two other assessments, the *Lagos Times* provided a detailed analysis of rising costs and falling profits.[9] The paper repeated the demoralising news in 1883, adding that 'competition mania' had led to imports being sold at 'cut prices'.[10] The *African Times* joined the chorus, reporting the 'depression in all branches of trade in 1885', and noting the record low prices reached for palm oil in 1886.[11] The *Eagle & Lagos Critic* went even further, predicting in 1886 that 'the days of the palm oil and kernel traffic seem about to be numbered'.[12]

The count-down continued. In 1887, the *African Times* judged that trade was even worse than in the previous year.[13] The acting governor concurred, reporting that disputes over low produce prices had led to the closure of inland markets.[14] In 1888, William Welsh, John Holt's trading partner and agent in Lagos, found the fall in palm oil prices 'disheartening' and lamented that profit margins on produce and cotton goods were 'very slim'.[15] The following year, the depressed conditions brought one of several deputations to the governor's door.[16] In 1890, the *Lagos Weekly Times* reported that firms exporting produce had again abolished the commission paid to brokers in an attempt to stabilise their own shrinking profit margins.[17] In the following year, the *Lagos Times* underlined what by then had become obvious: 'the days of making money easily and even with small investments have passed away'.[18] In 1892, shortly before the invasion of Yoruba country, John Holt confirmed that 'trade all round is bad'.[19] By then, no one believed that an invisible hand would restore the 'Golden Age' that memory assigned to the early years of the colony.

7. *Lagos Times*, 23 Feb. 1881, 27 April 1881.
8. Letter from 'Mercator', Liverpool, *Lagos Times*, 23 March 1881.
9. *Lagos Times*, 23 March 1881, 27 July 1881.
10. *Lagos Times*, 10 Oct. 1883.
11. *African Times*, 1 Sept. 1885, 1 Dec. 1885, 1 Jan. 1886, 1 Feb. 1886, 1 March 1886.
12. *Eagle & Lagos Critic*, 31 Dec. 1886. Also *Lagos Observer*, 3 March 1886, urging the government to end the depression by ending the war.
13. *African Times*, 2 Jan. 1887.
14. Evans to Holland, 11 May 1887, C.O. 147/59.
15. Welsh to Holt, 16 March 1888, 18 March 1888, Holt Papers (HP), 27/2.
16. Deputation to Denton 23 Sept. 1889, C.O. 806/334.
17. *Lagos Weekly Times*, 3 May 1890, 10 May 1890.
18. *Lagos Times*, 13 June 1891.
19. Holt to Welsh, 31 May 1892, HP, 19/4.

Business Uncertainty under the Colony

Producers responded to falling prices for palm oil and kernels by increasing the volume of exports, though the rise was insufficient to restore returns to boom levels. Moreover, expanded output was accompanied by rising costs of harvesting, processing, and transporting produce.[20] Additional expenditure might have been offset by productivity gains, but there is no sign that these were achieved during the crucial period before the invasion of Yorubaland, or indeed before 1914.[21] There were no economies of scale in the production of oil and kernels at this time. Reports of 'plantations' refer not to centralised management and systematic planting but to 'big men' who commanded a large labour force, whether slave or free. Most expansion took place on the extensive margin by applying additional labour to new land. Volumes grew but without cutting unit costs. By the 1880s, too, the most striking gains from cheaper manufacturing costs and lower freight rates had been achieved. Further substantial cost reductions awaited the construction of the railway, which began at the close of the 1890s, following the decision to annex Yorubaland.

The innovations that occurred during this period of adversity reduced transaction costs but also increased competition. The first major change transformed the media of exchange that had been used in Lagos since the 1850s. Spanish dollars and cowrie shells, the two most important of several currencies circulating in the port, were effectively demonetised during the 1880s.[22] Neither reform was planned; both were resisted by interested parties. The Spanish silver dollar became legal tender in 1869 and its exchange rate against sterling fixed formally at 4s.2d. in 1875. In 1879, however, the fall in the gold price of silver enabled agile traders to buy dollars in Britain for 3s.6d. and ship them to Lagos, where they could be exchanged to pay customs duties at the official rate of 4s.2d. One estimate indicates that the German firm of Gaiser, which had the largest share of this risk-free trade, was able to make a net profit on the transaction of more than 10 per cent.[23] The cost was borne by the colonial government, which rapidly accumulated weighty losses. The reaction was swift, if also precipitate. The Spanish dollar was demonetised in 1880 without recompense and with hardly any time allowed for redemption.[24] Some prominent African merchants who

20. Far from being simple and quick, these tasks were arduous and time-consuming. See Millson, 'Notes on the Preparation of Lagos Palm Oil'; and the admirable account given by Maier, 'Precolonial Palm Oil Production'.

21. See Inspector of Produce to Comptroller of Customs, Lagos, 6 Oct. 1910, CSO 14/2/3. Assistant Director Royal Botanic Gardens to Colonial Office, 27 Aug 1908, C.O. 520/71. Billows and Beckwick, *Palm Oil and Kernels*, pp. 13–21.

22. Rowe to Hicks-Beach 27 March 1880, C.O. 879/18; *Lagos Times*, 10 Nov. 1880.

23. Ussher to Hicks Beach, 27 Aug. 1879, CO 806/184.

24. After the event, the Treasury acknowledged that the matter had not been handled well. Treasury to C.O. 13 Dec. 1880, C.O. 806/184.

kept stocks of dollars incurred considerable losses. One estimate suggested that six merchants, who were said to own property in Lagos worth £100,000, held silver dollars valued officially at £20,000.[25]

The consequences spread far beyond a small number of wealthy merchants. Demonetisation created a liquidity crisis because it coincided with the depreciation of the cowrie. The discovery of new sources of supply had stimulated a substantial increase in imports of cowries and led to a dramatic fall in their value.[26] In 1867, to cite one reliable source, eighty heads (one head = 2,000 cowries) exchanged for £5; in 1879 they exchanged for £4; by 1889 the rate had dropped to ten shillings (half of £1).[27] The colonial government considered replacing cowries with metallic coin as early as 1865, but judged that reform would be premature (and would also deprive the administration of revenue from the import tax levied on cowries).[28] The decline of the cowrie was not as dramatic as the sudden demise of the dollar but was nevertheless striking and irreversible. Cowrie imports fell rapidly in the course of the 1890s, and had dwindled to unimportance by 1900, though they continued to circulate inland during the early years of the new century.[29] These unforeseen developments created a pressing demand for a sound alternative currency, which was supplied by British silver coin. By the close of the 1880s, most local transactions involving Lagos merchants were conducted in cash in the form of British silver currency.[30] Specie imports rose during the 1880s and expanded rapidly in the 1890s.[31] Daniel Taiwo's account books for the decade, provide an apt illustration of the intersection between the decline of the cowrie and the rise of silver currency.[32]

The increasing prevalence of cash payments eliminated barter as a means of exchange. Merchants offered higher prices for produce that was exchanged for goods and hoped to profit from both transactions.[33] In the 1880s, 20 per cent was added to the price of goods to cover possible losses on produce.[34] Cash payments not only circumvented the prospect of securing a double profit but also gave recipients a chance to spend their money elsewhere. Barter remained

25. Brandford Griffith to Ussher, 13 May 1880, C.O. 806/184.The merchants listed were: T. F. Cole, J. J. Thomas, J. W. Cole, J. P. Haastrup, and D. C. Taiwo.

26. Hieke, *G. L. Gaiser*, pp. 14–18; Hopkins, 'The Currency Revolution', table 6.5, p. 475. The authoritative study is Hogendorn and Johnson, *The Shell Money of the Slave Trade*, ch. 4.

27. The District Commissioner's Court Record book for Badagri has a detailed list of exchange rates from 1865 to 1898, Badadiv 1/1, vol. 1; 1/2 vols. 1–3.

28. Glover to C.O., 7 June 1865, C.O. 147/9.

29. *Colonial Annual Report*, No. 32, Lagos, 1890.

30. Moloney to Knutsford, 7 Oct. 1887, C.O. 147/62.

31. *Lagos Blue Books*, 1878–1905.

32. See above, chapter 4.

33. *Lagos Times*, 10 Aug. 1881; *Lagos Observer*, 1 Oct. and 29 Oct. 1886.

34. West v. Taiwo and Dawodu, 15 Feb. 1888, LSCR, Civ. 7, 1888.

as a means of dealing with shortages of specie but ceased to be standard business practice by the close of the 1890s, soon after the African Banking Corporation (ABC), the first modern bank in Lagos, established a branch there in 1891. Although the ABC fell short of expectations, it was replaced in 1894 by the Bank of British West Africa (BBWA), which turned the opportunity into a success and remained in Lagos throughout the colonial period.[35] BBWA had the substantial backing of Sir Alfred Jones, who controlled Elder, Dempster, the leading shipping company serving Lagos.[36] Far from welcoming the appearance of this agent of modernity, the large expatriate commercial firms campaigned against the bank's effective control of specie imports because it cut into their own trade in shipping silver coin to Lagos.[37]

The end of the barter system added to the problems of profitability facing large merchants and brokers by making prices more transparent and competitive. Greater liquidity attracted new entrants and provided openings for African traders at the lower end of the trading hierarchy. The first clear evidence that local traders gained from the currency revolution, however, appeared in the mid-1890s following the arrival of the new banks, which reduced interest rates on small loans and helped African exporters by advancing up to 75 per cent of the value of the produce shipped.[38]

The second significant development was the arrival of the undersea cable, which reached Lagos in 1886.[39] The cable was transformative in reducing the time taken to transmit messages between Europe and the West Coast. Contemporaries recorded their astonishment at the extent to which time had suddenly been discounted. In 1892, the *Lagos Weekly Record* observed that twenty years ago, communication by sail took two to three months, whereas messages from Lagos to England could now be sent and answered within a few hours.[40] Although the cost of the service was the subject of complaints that persisted into the new century, the immediate response to the new facility was entirely positive.[41] What today would be referred to as globalisation had significantly increased the degree of integration in international trade.

35. Elder Dempster to C.O. 20 April 1894, C.O. 147/93.

36. The authoritative studies are: Davies, *The Trade Makers*, and Davies, *Sir Alfred Jones*.

37. See, for example, Lagos Warehouse Co. to Knutsford, 4 Feb. 1892, C.O. 147/88; F.O. to C.O. 3 Aug. 1895, C.O. 147/102. The Liverpool and Manchester Chambers of Commerce also joined the protest. See Manchester Chamber of Commerce to C.O., 3 March 1893, C.O. 147/92, and Liverpool Chamber of Commerce to C.O., 22 March 1893, C.O. 147/92. Memo by M. F. Ommaney, on C.O. to Carter, 9 Feb. 1892, C.O. 147/81.

38. Denton to Ripon, 1 April 1893, C.O. 147/89; evidence of G. W. Neville and J. A. Hutton in Denton to Chamberlain, 4 June 1898, C.O. 147/133.

39. *Lagos Observer*, 7 Aug. 1886. A new facility, a cable office, was built on the Marina in 1885.

40. *Lagos Weekly Record*, 7 May 1892; and *Lagos Observer*, 7 Aug. 1886.

41. *Lagos Observer*, 2 Oct. 1886; *Lagos Weekly Record*, 24 July 1897.

Judgements about the effects of the cable on the port have to be provisional because the subject has yet to be researched.[42] One possibility, that African merchants were disadvantaged by access or even cost, can be discounted because they were quick to join the expatriate firms in urging the governor to protect the confidentiality of the messages processed by the telegraph company.[43] What seems inescapable is that the cable improved information and reduced risk, with the result that it also sharpened competition in the port and reduced profit margins.[44] Once produce prices were cabled to and from head offices in Europe and Lagos, local agents became managers who had less scope for exercising their own initiative and less need for doing so. The development of forward contracts and futures market would have favoured large firms that had the capital to buy in bulk, but these advances depended on palm produce meeting international standards of quality, which it was far from achieving.

Nevertheless, in the short run these changes added to the problems Lagos merchants faced in the period immediately before the invasion of Yorubaland.[45] The struggle to preserve profits drove producers, traders, and merchants to adopt measures that ranged from the defensive to the desperate. One line of defence drew the large expatriate merchants together in an attempt to stabilise the market by buying produce at agreed prices.[46] In the late 1880s, Gaiser took the lead in fixing the buying price of palm kernels; Lagos Warehouse Company did the same for palm oil.[47] A similar effort was made to agree on uniform prices for the main imported goods.[48] None of these schemes appears to have been successful. The continuing pressure on profits encouraged an increase in fraudulent practices. British firms were among those that initiated the practice of short-folding imported cloth, with the result that thirty folds equalled twenty-eight yards instead of thirty.[49] Imported liquor was diluted as it made its way to consumers.[50] Producers retaliated by adulterating palm

42. The subject would be an excellent topic for a Ph.D. dissertation. I am most grateful to Gervase Clarence Smith and Alexander Engel for helpful exchanges on this subject. On futures markets, see Engel, 'Buying Time'.

43. Acting Govr. Evans to Granville, 29 Dec. 1886, C.O. 147/57; also *Lagos Observer*, 6 Nov. 1886. This comment applies to merchants whose trade was large enough to justify the cost of using the cable service.

44. *Lagos Weekly Record*, 7 May 1892.

45. See the evidence given by William Findlay, McIver's agent, and C. B. Moore, Ollivant's agent, enclosed in Denton to Chamberlain, 25 May 1898, C.O. 147/132.

46. Welsh to Holt, 23 March 1888, HP 27/2.

47. Welsh to Holt, 20 March 1888, HP 27/2.

48. *Lagos Weekly Record*, 3 May 1890.

49. Moloney to Knutsford, 15 Oct. 1887, C.O. 147/6; Denton to Knutsford, 17 Sept. 1889, C.O. 147/72; *Lagos Times*, 17 Jan. 1891, 19 March 1891; 17.1.91. Denton to Ripon, 3 June 1893, C.O. 147/90.

50. *Lagos Observer*, 3 and 24 Sept. 1887; Moloney to Holland, 15 Oct. 1887, C.O. 147/61; Denton to Knutsford, 17 Sept. 1889, C.O. 147/72.

produce.[51] Kernels were soaked to add weight; shells were added to increase bulk; oil was watered down.

What commentators saw as a sustained crisis of legitimate commerce also prompted the colonial government to explore alternatives to the current export staples.[52] In 1881, the *Lagos Times* was among the first to recommend agricultural diversification as an alternative to poor returns to the trade in palm produce.[53] Thoughtful commentators in the port had been advocating agricultural diversification since the early 1880s to reduce the dependence of Lagos on faltering staples, especially palm oil.[54] These ideas did not become official policy until Moloney became governor and persuaded the Colonial Office to approve his proposal.[55] Other supporters added their voices to the suggestion in the course of the decade. But it was Alfred Moloney, who served as governor of Lagos from 1886 to 1891, who turned the idea into reality. Moloney's initiative led in 1887 to the opening of a Botanic Station at Ebute Metta, which was the first of its kind in West Africa.[56] The Station, which stood on the mainland just opposite Lagos, grew a variety of plants, including a small amount of cocoa, but devoted most of its efforts to the production of coffee and cotton. These crops were not the successes the governor had hoped for.[57] Nevertheless, Moloney was a pioneer, and like many others, was ahead of his time. After he left Lagos, interest in the Botanic Station dwindled. In 1897, the Director of Kew Gardens expressed his disappointment that much energy was being expended to provide decorative plants for Government House.[58] Two years later, the Annual Report for the colony acknowledged that the station was in decline and that the curator had little to occupy his time.[59] The

51. *Lagos Times*, 24 Nov. 1880, 12 Jan. 1881, 9 March 1881; Moloney to Knutsford, 27 Feb. 1889, CO 147/69; Denton to Ripon, 8 July 1890, C.O. 147/90; Rohrweger to C.O., 7 Sept. 1896, C.O. 147/106. The practice survived until stricter controls were introduced: Egerton to Lyttelton, 26 May 1905, C.O. 147/175.

52. Previous experiments aimed at providing alternatives to the slave trade included raw cotton and groundnuts, though these were overtaken by the success of palm oil and kernels. Glover to Cardwell, 10 April 1866, C.O. 147/11.

53. 24 Aug. 1881.

54. *Lagos Times*, 25 Oct. 1882; *Lagos Observer*, 16 March 1882; *Eagle & Lagos Critic*, 25 July 1885; *Lagos Observer*, 1 and 29 Oct. 1887.

55. There was 'no official information on botanical matters', before then. Griffith to Ussher, 1 April 1880, C.O. 147/40.

56. Omosoni, 'Alfred Moloney'. A fuller account of the Botanic Station is provided in chapter 9.

57. Moloney to Knutsford, 25 Feb. 1889, C.O. 147/77; McNair to Royal Gardens, Kew, 8 Oct. 1888, C.O. 147/73; Moloney to Knutsford, 16 May 1890, C.O. 147/149. The station also produced kola and various dyes that may have been more successful but are not relevant to the present study.

58. Kew Gardens to C.O. 23 Feb. 1897, C.O. 147/126; Kew Gardens to C.O. 31 Dec. 1897 and 24 Aug. 1898, C.O. 147/139; Kew Gardens to C.O. 26 Nov. 1900, C.O. 147/153.

59. *Annual Report*, Lagos No. 321, 1899.

early history of the Botanic Station was far from being synonymous with the story of agricultural innovation. As chapter 9 will show, African entrepreneurs had already begun experiments that were to transform the agricultural exports of Western Nigeria during the colonial period.

Expanding the Colony

Britain's default position on the West Coast remained one of non-intervention.[60] Traditional policy was reinforced by the Parliamentary Select Committee of 1865, which recommended that the West African settlements should be consolidated both to save money and to restrain colonial officials from further expansion. Between 1866 and 1874, Lagos Colony was placed under the governor of West Africa Settlements based in Sierra Leone, and in 1874 transferred to the jurisdiction of the Gold Coast.[61] Annexations were modest and confined to the coast. In the case of Lagos, territorial expansion was restricted to establishing a few small protectorates along the lagoon to determine the western and eastern boundaries of the colony. In the 1880s, however, the mood changed. Fears of French expansion and the consequent loss of markets and revenue were especially alarming at a time of commercial depression. Pressure from the Manchester and Liverpool Chambers of Commerce, and from Lagos merchants who were dissatisfied with the way the joint administration had represented their interests, deluged the Colonial Office.[62] In 1886, Lagos regained its autonomy and with it the hope that direct representation would enhance its influence in policy-making circles in London.

Relations with the hinterland states were a nagging problem that had preoccupied colonial officials from the time of the consulate onwards. Yorubaland was in a fluid and unstable condition as a result of the collapse earlier in the century of the Oyo Empire to the north and the irregular but continuing incursions from Dahomey in the west.[63] New states and statelets were being created; citizens were being formed out of a mobile population that contained many immigrants, refugees, and slaves; boundaries were established, disputed, and redrawn. The state of the country mattered because it supplied the palm oil and kernels that were the basis of the export trade from Lagos and consumed most of the manufactured goods imported in return. By mid-century, Ibadan had emerged as the predominant power with an ambition

60. C.O. minute by Anderson, 10 Sept. 1886, on Evans to Granville, 2 Aug. 1886, C.O. 147/56.

61. Newbury, *Western Slave Coast*, ch. 4.

62. Newbury, *Western Slave Coast*, p. 95; Moloney to S of S, 27 Feb. 1886, C.O. 147/54.

63. For the considerable literature on this subject and further references, see Falola and Oguntomisin, *The Military*; Falola and Oguntomisin, *Yoruba Warlords*; Law, 'The "Crisis of Adaptation Revisited"', in *Africa, Empire, and Globalization*, ch. 6.

to control the whole of Yoruba country.[64] In reaction, states to the east, such as Ekiti, Ijesha, and Ife, and those to the south, such as Egba and Ijebu, responded by defending their independence. The conflict was discontinuous, but it was renewed in 1877 and ran on, with pauses, throughout the 1880s.

The relationship between these wars and Britain's decision to invade Yorubaland has been the subject of a long and productive discussion since the 1960s.[65] An early formulation positing a 'crisis of adaption' argued that slave-supplying states faced significant problems in adapting to the end of the overseas slave trade.[66] The new trade in palm oil was less profitable than the export of slaves and also allowed small, competitive producers to enter the export market for the first time. The resulting clash of interests between large producers using slaves and a new generation of export producers and traders using household labour played an important part in the political conflict that intensified among the Yoruba states in the 1880s, when the transition to legitimate commerce experienced mounting difficulties. The wider conclusion was that the modern economic history of Lagos, and West Africa generally, dates from the second half of the nineteenth century, when the main features of the export economies that were to characterise the era of colonial rule first appeared. Colonial rule did not 'modernise' West Africa, as was once thought. Its role was to accelerate a process that was already under way.

This thesis has been both amplified and modified by research that deserves more space than can be assigned to it here. The most recent assessment of developments in Yorubaland by Robin Law, the authority on the subject, emphasises important features that received insufficient attention in the original argument: the intricacy of the relationship between economic and political motives; the role of internal slave-raiding as a major means of adjusting to the end of the overseas slave trade; the importance of 'war-boys' as well as 'big men' in instigating slave-raiding expeditions; the difficulty of finding 'clear evidence' of conflicts between large and small producers.[67] Nevertheless, Law's analysis provides broad support for the original argument. Palm oil was not as profitable as slave-trading; adaptation by producing and trading oil by means of slave labour did not shield slave-producers from the adverse terms of trade that characterised the 1880s; hostilities among Yoruba states were exacerbated by efforts made by traders and producers to use state agencies to shift the burden of falling profits to shoulders other than their own. The ultimate

64. The fundamental study is Falola, *The Political Economy of a Pre-Colonial State*.

65. See particularly Law, ed., *From Slave Trade to "Legitimate" Commerce*; Law, Schwarz, and Strickrodt, eds., *Commercial Agriculture*; and the recent references given in Law's essay cited in n. 63.

66. Hopkins, 'Economic Imperialism in West Africa'; Hopkins, 'The Lagos Strike of 1897'; Hopkins, *An Economic History of West Africa*, pp. 23–30 and ch. 4.

67. Law, 'The "Crisis of Adaptation Revisited"', ch. 6, and the further references given there. The quotation is from Law, '"The Crisis of Adaptation Revisited"', p. 137.

conflict was between the continued dominance of Yoruba military interests and the development of the full potential of 'legitimate' commerce.

The military response to the crisis brought by the end of the external slave trade was clearly incompatible with the needs of the new international economy. Adaptation through intensified slave-raiding interrupted production and trade, created insecurity, and brought devastation to unlucky communities. Moreover, the absence of economies of scale in the production of oil and kernels at this time obliged large-scale producers to rely on compulsory labour, which was acquired through costly wars. These non-market, military supports were removed when peace descended. That large producers existed is beyond dispute; evidence of their importance, however, is currently beyond reach. Reports of small-scale production, using free and slave labour, are widespread but equally hard to quantify. A careful contemporary estimate suggested that 15 million palm trees were needed to produce the volume of palm oil shipped from Lagos in 1891.[68] All that can be said about the division of shares at present is that the size of the export trade left plenty of room for both large and small suppliers. The new economy was struggling to emerge before the expansion of British rule into what became Nigeria but required fundamental institutional change for its potential to be realised. In the end, as Law concludes, the crisis of adaptation was posed and ultimately settled by the increasing pressure Britain exerted to resolve problems of integration that had exceeded the scope of informal influence.

As soon as Alfred Moloney, the new governor, arrived in Lagos in 1886, he made a sustained effort to identify the interests of the competing states and the power structures within them.[69] His report to the Colonial Office included statements from the warring parties and informed observers, including the Rev. Samuel Johnson, a Saro cleric with the Anglican mission.[70] 'It is heart-rending', Johnson wrote, 'to think of the effects of this unfortunate war. Many families have been ruined. . . . The distress in the country is general'.[71] The officials in Lagos also tried to identify what they took to be the culprits among the several suspects. This exercise brought them into close contact with local politics and with the Saro, who acted as informal agents of their Yoruba homelands. There followed a contest of competing images as representatives of different hinterland interests advertised their cause in ways that were calculated to appeal to the British.

Moloney's central concern was the deterioration in the trade of the port, which affected government revenues as well as private incomes. The history

68. Millson, 'Notes on the Preparation of Lagos Palm Oil', pp. 203–08.

69. Moloney to Granville, 23 June 1886, C.O. 147/ 56.

70. See Falola, *Pioneer, Patriot and Patriarch*.

71. Samuel Johnson to Governor Rowe, enc. 11 in Moloney to Granville, 23 June 1886, C.O. 147/ 56.

of the peace negotiations that occupied the 1880s are not the concern of this study. Essentially, they formed a catalogue of failed efforts to secure a lasting settlement of the disputes among the Yoruba states. They were prompted by the renewal of hostilities, the closing of trade routes and markets, disputes between Lagos traders and those in the hinterland, dissatisfaction with the prices paid for palm produce, accusations about adulteration and short-folding, and requests for the return of slaves who had escaped to Lagos where, formally speaking, slavery had been abolished.[72] By the close of the decade, Moloney and his Colonial Secretary, Alvan Millson, had decided that the main problem stemmed from the actions of the Ijebu and Egba, who were impeding their northern neighbours from securing access to the coast.[73] This interpretation cast the assertive Ibadans as aspiring free-traders and their southern neighbours as parasitic middlemen collecting largely unearned income.[74] As commercial profits continued to fall, both officials emphasised the huge potential of the market for Manchester's cotton goods once peace was restored and barriers to free movement removed.[75]

Manchester was eager not only to listen but also to act, as was Liverpool. In 1884, the Liverpool Chamber formed an African Section. In 1892, one hundred Manchester firms with substantial interests in West Africa secured two designated members to represent their interests on the board of their chamber. Both organisations were linked directly to Lagos in 1888, when the port established its own Chamber of Commerce.[76] The UK chambers were connected, in turn, to central government through an influential group of members of parliament. As the depression deepened and commercial profits sank, lobbying became more frequent and increasingly strident.[77] The turning point came in March 1892, when the Acting Governor reported that the Egba and Ijebu had set aside their differences and formed an alliance to defy the Lagos

72. See, among numerous possible citations, Evans to Holland, 11 May 1887, C.O. 147/59; Seidu Olowu, interview at Government House, 27 Nov. 1889, C.S.O. 8/7/2; Willoughby to Acting Governor, 27 Nov. 1889, C.S.O. 8/7/2; Millson to Col. Sec. 14 Feb. 1890, C.S.O. 8/7/3; Moloney to Col. Sec. 29 March 1890, C.S.O. 8/5/5; Peel to Col. Sec. 13 May 1891, Badadiv 5/3/90–2; Lagos Weekly Times, 3 May 1890; Milson to Col. Sec. 25 May 1890, C.S.O. 8/7/3; Smith to Col. Sec. 28 March 1892, Epediv 5/2.

73. Moloney to Knutsford, 13 March 1890, 5 April 1890 and encs. C.O. 879/33; Millson, 'The Yoruba Country'.

74. The stereotype gained currency, though Moloney realised that reality was more complex. In the case of Ijebu, he thought that the large traders controlled the routes whereas the king favoured more open roads. Moloney to Knutsford, 30 April 1890, C.O. 879/33.

75. Moloney, 'Cotton Interests'; Millson to Colonial Secretary, 14 Feb. 1890, C.S.O. 8/7/3.

76. Moloney to Knutsford, 17 June 1890, C.O. 879/33; African Times, 1 Feb. 1892; Hopkins, 'The Lagos Chamber of Commerce, 1888–1903'.

77. African Times, 1 Oct. 1892.

government.[78] The Chambers of Commerce flooded the Colonial Office with protests and demands for action.[79]

The records of the Liverpool firm of John Holt provide an exceptional insight into the way external pressure was exerted on Parliament and Whitehall. In January 1892, Holt informed his Lagos partner, Thomas Welsh, that 'Lord Salisbury is troubled by the agitation of the commercial classes'.[80] Three weeks later he reported that 'We are doing what we can to urge the Government to move towards the interior,' adding that the Colonial Office was 'having a bad time of it'.[81] On hearing in February that the roads had been closed, Holt noted that, 'if true, we shall have to bring measures to bear upon the Colonial Office to bring the Egbas to reason'.[82] When confirmation arrived, Holt said that he and others 'will get to work' on the Secretary of State.[83] By March, he was confident that the government was 'ready to act'.[84]

Commercial agitation coincided with increased French activity on the western edge of the colony, which threatened, or was thought to threaten, Britain's interests. Any advance inland from Porto Novo, which France had annexed in 1883, could reduce Lagos to being a port without a hinterland and a colony whose circumscribed boundaries would also limit or even reduce the revenue from the customs duties that kept the government afloat.[85] A series of reports from Moloney in 1887 convinced the Colonial Office that Britain would have to move at speed.[86] 'If we do not do so', Lord Onslow minuted in agreement, 'we shall soon have nothing left'.[87] In a break with tradition, Moloney was given permission to negotiate treaties with states on the mainland to prevent them from ceding territory to France.[88] The arrival of a French expedition at Abeokuta in 1888 prompted Moloney to collect a series of agreements with states in western Yorubaland that served the immediate purpose

78. Denton to Knutsford, 3 March 1892, C.O. 879/36.

79. *African Times*, 1 Oct. 1892.

80. Holt to Welsh, 1 Jan. 1892, HP, 19/4.

81. Holt to Welsh, 22 Jan. 189, HP, 19/4.

82. Holt to Welsh, 16 Feb. 1892, HP, 19/4.

83. Holt to Welsh, 17 Feb. 1892, HP, 19/4.

84. Holt to Welsh, 29 March 1892, 14 April 1892, HP 19/4. Nevertheless, Holt opposed war as a means of settling the dispute with the hinterland states partly because it would interrupt trade. Holt to Welsh, 7 March 1892, HP 19/4.

85. Tickel to Acting Col. Sec., Lagos, 5 May 1886, Badadiv 5/3/1885–87; *African Times*, 1 July 1889; Moloney to Knutsford, 21 Feb. 1889, C.O. 147/69.

86. Moloney to Holland, 1 June 1887, and minutes by Hemming and Onslow, C.O. 147/59; Moloney to Holland, 10 June 1887, C.O. 147/59; Moloney to Holland, 12 June 1887, and minute by Hemming, 13 June 1887, C.O. 147/59.

87. Minute by Onslow, 13 June 1887, C.O. 147/59.

88. Moloney to C.O., 19 June 1887, and minutes, C.O. 147/59.

of halting French penetration.[89] In 1889, Britain and France reached agreement on the western boundary between Lagos Colony and Porto Novo that kept most of Yorubaland within Britain's sphere of interest.[90] The agreement, however, did nothing to halt the westward flow of trade, which was attracted by the lower duties levied at Porto Novo, or to end repeated Dahomeyan raids into western Yorubaland, which had been common during the 1880s and recurred in 1890 and 1891.[91]

After 1889, the western boundary was regarded in London as an irritant rather than a pressing issue. The Foreign Office judged that it did not merit further action and left the matter to the local colonial administration to manage as best it could.[92] The agreement with France freed the Lagos administration to focus on remedies for the hinterland war. A failed attempt to negotiate a settlement in 1890 ended with the Lagos administration blaming the Egba and Ijebu 'middlemen'.[93] Moloney then offered representatives from Ijebu Ode and Abeokuta some blunt advice: 'France is out of the question now— you cannot play between this government and the French now'.[94] Unless the roads were opened, he added, 'the time may soon come when they will have to be opened by force'.[95] A co-ordinated response from the Chambers of Commerce endorsed this view and urged the government to authorise the most senior official in Lagos to undertake a tour of the hinterland.[96] Acting Governor Denton's mission in 1891 precipitated the final crisis.[97] He established several protectorates in western Yorubaland to reinforce the boundary agreement with France, but in doing so offended the Egba, who saw his action as a threat to their own independence and closed the trade routes to Lagos in protest.[98] Denton's visit to Ijebu, accompanied by a large military escort, was even less

89. Moloney to Knutsford, 23 May 1888, 11 June 1888, C.O. 147/64; Moloney to Knutsford, 21 Aug. 1888, and minute by Hemming, 26 Sept. 1888, C.O. 147/65; on the alarm expressed by Liverpool merchants, see *African Times*, 1 July 1889.

90. Agreement, 10 Aug. 1889 and minute by Hemming, 15 Dec. 1889, C.O. 147/73.

91. Abeokuta chiefs to Moloney, 16 June 1890, CSO 8/7/3; F.O. to Egerton, 4 Feb. 1892, C.O. 147/87.

92. F.O. to C.O., 9 May 1890, and minute by Hemming, 12 May 1890, C.O. 147/78; F.O. to C.O. 12 May 1891.

93. Alvin Millson to Col. Sec. Lagos, 14 Feb. 1890, 7 March 1890, 26 March 1890, C.S.O. 8/7/3.

94. Moloney interview with representatives from Ijebu Ode and Abeokuta, 7 May 1890, CSO 8/7/3.

95. Moloney interview with representatives from Ijebu Ode and Abeokuta, 7 May 1890, CSO 8/7/3.

96. Lagos Chamber of Commerce to Col. Sec., Lagos, 2 Dec. 1890, enc. in Moloney to Knutsford, 10 Dec. 1890, C.O. 147/77; Manchester Chamber of Commerce to Knutsford, 31 March 1891, C.O. 147/83; Liverpool Chamber of Commerce to Knutsford, 31 March 1891, C.O. 147/83.

97. Denton to Knutsford, 28 Aug. 1891, C.O. 806/344.

98. Johnson, *History of the Yorubas*, pp. 606–07.

successful. The authorities there concluded that war was intended and refused Denton's offer of a subsidy in exchange for abolishing the tolls they levied on trade.[99] On his return to Lagos, Denton reported to London that 'nothing short of armed compulsion will, I am convinced, induce the Jebus to relinquish their lucrative position of middlemen'.[100]

The atmosphere of suspicion and hostility remained to greet the arrival of the new governor at the close of 1891.[101] Gilbert Carter was determined not to repeat his experience in the Gambia, where he had seen French assertiveness and British indifference combine to truncate the boundaries of what had become a colony in miniature. However, Carter's attempt to reach a negotiated settlement joined the list of failures.[102] At the beginning of 1892, the Ijebu and Egba put aside their differences and presented a united front against British expansion.[103]

The Colonial Office was rapidly overwhelmed by representations from chambers of commerce and associated shipping interests, which criticised the supine character of British policy towards West Africa and demanded action to reopen the trade routes. MPs were mobilised; Lord Salisbury's Conservative government was bombarded with appeals for action; a deputation descended on the Liberal leader, William Gladstone. Governor Carter deplored delay and advocated coercion. The expatriate firms trading with Lagos went the extra mile and agreed to an increase in import duties to pay for a military expedition.

In the face of this sustained assault, government ranks wavered and finally broke. The thin red line in Whitehall was not as steady as it had been. A younger generation of officials, such as Augustus Hemming, were less committed to the universal ideals that had inspired an earlier generation and had absorbed some of the strident beliefs publicised by Charles Dilke.[104] In March 1892, Hemming advised that it was time to 'take the bull by the horns'.[105] A week later, the decision was made: a military expedition was approved.[106] The Colonial Office explained to the War Office that 'the closing of the roads has completely paralysed the trade of the Colony and is causing much anxiety and impatience on the part of merchants in this country. Great pressure has been brought to bear on this department by the Chambers of Commerce'.[107]

99. *Lagos Times*, 23 May 1891.

100. Denton to Knutsford, 22 May 1891, C.O. 806/357.

101. Moloney had been transferred, at his own request, to British Honduras.

102. Carter to Knutsford, 10 Dec. 1891, C.O. 147/82.

103. Denton to Knutsford, 16 Feb. 1892, 18 March 1892, C.O. 147/84; Johnson, *History of the Yorubas*, p. 618.

104. Augustus Hemming (1841–1907); subsequently governor of British Guiana and then Jamaica.

105. Hemming, C.O. minute, 11 March 1892, C.O. 147/84.

106. Carter, 18 March 1892, C.O. 147/84.

107. C. O. to W.O., 23 March 1892, C.O. 147/84.

The expedition left Lagos in May. The Ijebu forces, some seven to ten thousand strong, made a brave stand but were defeated. The way was then clear for British troops to enter the capital, Ijebu Ode.[108] Carter next threatened to send troops to Abeokuta, even though his mandate did not extend to using force against the Egba. Luck, however, marched with him. The Egba, having observed the fate of the Ijebu, capitulated and agreed to reopen the trade routes.[109] Early in 1893, Carter undertook an extensive tour of the hinterland.[110] Treaties were made with Ilorin, Oyo, and Ibadan that ended the long war and guaranteed freedom of passage for traders.[111] By the close of the year, protectorates had been established with most of the Yoruba states, though the Egba were able to retain their independence in return for signing a treaty of 'trade and friendship'.[112] Variations in legal status, however, did not alter the new reality: most of the Yoruba states were now under British control. No more inter-state wars would be fought; no more roads would be closed.[113] Times had changed. Carter's action realised Glover's ambition. This was free trade, not with an invisible hand, but with a strong arm.

The Commercial Consequences of Colonial Expansion

The dramatic events that transformed the history of Lagos and its hinterland in 1892–1893 had far-reaching consequences. The political effects were apparent immediately; the economic effects were postponed until the turn of the century. Influences transmitted by international trade were more powerful than forces at the disposal of governments. There was a marked increase in the value of Lagos's external trade, which was an average of 65 per cent higher between 1893 and 1899 than it had been between 1880 and 1899.[114]

108. *The African Times*, 4 July 1892; Johnson, *History of the Yorubas*, pp. 618–22.

109. Carter to Ripon, 31 Oct. 1892, C.O. 147/86; Johnson, *History of the Yorubas*, pp. 624–25.

110. Carter to Ripon, 11 Oct. 1893, Cd.7227, P.P. LXII, 1893.

111. Carter to Knutsford, 15 July 1893, C.O. 147/90.

112. See Newbury, *Western Slave Coast*, pp. 138–9.

113. In 1896, Governor Carter made an ill-judged attempt to exert pressure on the Emirate of Ilorin by imposing a blockade on trade with Lagos. Opposition in Lagos and evidence of the counterproductive consequences of his action caused the governor to withdraw. (Although Ilorin was a Yoruba state, it had not been incorporated into the hinterland of Lagos.) Rohrweger to Chamberlain, 6 Oct. 1896, C.O. 147/106; Denton to Chamberlain, 16 December 1896, C.O. 147/107.

114. As already noted, official statistics at this time should be treated as orders of magnitude. In this case, too, the figures were inflated by a change in the basis of valuation. From 1893, the value of imports into Lagos was calculated after docking at the port and included the invoice value, freight, and insurance; exports valued similarly at port of shipment (CIF value). Before then, the valuation was termed 'free on board' (FOB) and excluded freight charges. Customs duty continued to be charged on the invoice value only. *Colonial Annual Report, Lagos*, No. 58, 1891; Carter to Knutsford, 26 March 1892, C.O.

Although palm produce remained the leading export, kernels extended their lead over oil during the 1890s. Export volumes also rose during the two periods of comparison (1880–1889 and 1893–1899), though not in unison: palm-oil exports increased by an average of about 8 per cent; palm kernels by just over 50 per cent. The growth of trade was reflected in the number and tonnage of ocean-going steamers entering the harbour.[115] A total of 270 steamships with a total tonnage of 162,650 arrived in 1880; in 1900, the figures were 537 and 535,708, respectively. The corollary was the decline of sailing vessels. In 1880, ninety-six sailing ships entered the harbour; in 1900, the figure had dropped to one. The tonnage fell accordingly from 28,090 to 383. In this development Lagos joined the rest of the world in bringing the great age of sail to a close.

The expansion of trade was not matched by a general rise in profitability. As figure 2.2 shows, the net barter terms of trade for palm oil continued to decline during the 1890s. Palm kernels, however, performed significantly better. Unsurprisingly, complaints came from the British firms, which were committed to palm oil and had little stake in the kernel trade. In 1896, George Neville, the manager of BBWA in Lagos, stated that 'at no period during my experience of over sixteen years here has a greater or more general depression existed'.[116] Frederick Osborne, who had fifteen years' experience of Lagos trade and was the agent for Paterson Zochonis, spoke for most of the expatriate representatives when he stated in 1898 that capital ought to make 'an average of 10 per cent' and that 'in olden days much more was made'.[117] The agents also agreed that no firm was achieving that figure in current conditions. Holt & Welsh's agent reckoned that 'as things go now' 5 per cent would be a 'fair average' return on capital. If the evidence the agent provided for the Lagos Stores is accepted, even that figure was ambitious because few firms 'have been making money recently'. The Lagos press had no doubt that times were exceptionally challenging. Several papers lamented the difficulties faced by 'civilised'

147/84. The increase in reported values after 1893 does not affect the broad conclusion that there was a considerable expansion of overseas trade after the decisive political intervention in 1892. Figures are calculated from the *Lagos Blue Books* for the years in question. I have excluded 1890, 1891, and 1892 from the comparison because the returns were affected by the political crisis.

115. *Lagos Blue Books*, 1880–1900.

116. Neville to Rohrweger, 20 Sept. 1896, C.S.O. 7/1/3. George William Neville (1852–1929) was a major figure in West African trade between 1874 and 1899. He began as the agent for Sir Alfred Jones's steamship companies in Bonny and Lagos, became manager of the successor company, Elder, Dempster & Co., in Lagos, manager of the ABC and effectively founder as well as manager of BBWA in 1894. He became a director of the Bank in 1899. See *West Africa*, 30 Nov. 1929, p. 1628.

117. This quotation, and those that follow in this paragraph, are taken from evidence to the Commission of Enquiry into Trade Conditions enc. in Denton to Chamberlain, 25 May 1898, C.O. 147/132.

African merchants, who faced increasing competition from European firms.[118] In 1899, the *Lagos Standard* claimed that 'development' had driven trade into the hands of a few large 'European capitalists' and concluded, mournfully, that the 'days of large businesses and big profits are over for Africans'.[119] The remedy, which was not immediately at hand, was for Africans to increase their capital resources by combining.

The information needed to test these generalisations is scattered and incomplete, not least because profit figures, where given, commonly fail to state whether the recorded rate applies to turnover or capital, and cover such a wide range that either possibility is credible.[120] In 1896, when conditions appear to have been even worse than in the 1880s, margins on imports were said by one merchant to be 10 per cent and by another to range from 5 to 10 per cent.[121] James O'Connor Williams, a broker who had been in business in Lagos since the late 1860s, provided an additional piece of evidence in 1898, when he stated that '30 years ago merchants were making 25 per cent profit; now they make barely 5 per cent'. While these figures are in line with the evidence given by the European agents, it is also apparent that the experience of individual businesses could vary considerably. Claudius Oni, for example, provided confidential evidence showing that between 1887, when he began trading, and 1891, when he stopped dealing in produce, he earned 30 per cent on capital. In 1897, however, he suffered a loss, even on his trade in imported goods.

The search for alternatives to the traditional staples led to a sudden boom in exports of wild rubber, which rose from zero in 1894 to a peak of 38 per cent of the value of all exports from Lagos in 1896 before falling into insignificance in (and after) 1900.[122] A similar boom in hardwood began in 1897, reached a high point of 8 per cent of total exports in 1900, and then shrank rapidly.[123] The demand for timber led to the mass felling of suitable trees and to the predictable result that the resource, being finite, was soon exploited to extinction. The rubber bounce came at the expense of palm oil, which declined in volume to levels not seen since the 1860s. Evidently, price incentives shifted labour out of oil and into rubber, but had far less effect on exports of kernels. Since both were jointly harvested, the presumption must be that men transferred their

118. *Lagos Standard*, 30 Sept. 1896; *Lagos Reporter*, 18 July 1899.

119. 21 June 1899.

120. 21 June 1899.

121. Evidence of G. A. Williams and S. H. Pearce, in João da Rocha v. Egerton Shyngle, LSCR, Civ. 18, 1896.

122. Carter to John Holt, 21 Nov. 1894, HP 12/7; Denton to Chamberlain, 9 Feb. 1897, C.O. 147/112; Denton to Chamberlain, 28 June 1898, C.O. 147/133; Denton to Chamberlain, 6 Jan. 1899, C.O. 147/141; Egerton to Lyttelton, 31 May 1905, C.O. 147/175.

123. *Lagos Blue Books*, 1890–1905; McCallum to Chamberlain, 19 Aug. 1897, C.O. 147/116.

labour from gathering palm produce to tapping rubber, while women, who were in charge of processing, opted to process kernels rather than oil because the returns were higher. Moreover, the incentive to concentrate on kernels increased in years such as 1898, which followed poor rainfall in 1897, because the yield from the pericarp (oil) was reduced more than from the endocarp (kernels).[124] This reasoning is the start rather than the end of an untold story. Other considerations, such as the return of peaceful conditions, the demobilisation of the 'war-boys', and the decline of internal slavery were also involved in the expansion of the land and labour harnessed to export production during the 1890s.

Conditions continued to deteriorate. Looking back on the concluding years of the century, the Collector of Customs commented: 'I can confidently say that I have never, in the ten years I have been here, seen the Lagos trade in such a depressed and unsatisfactory state'.[125] In 1898, Governor McCallum reported on the widespread complaints about diminishing profits during the last ten years and took the exceptional step of recommending that a commission of enquiry be established to examine the problem.[126] The commission was the first of its kind since the foundation of the colony and indicated the seriousness of commercial conditions in the port. It consisted of five members, two of whom (Richard Blaize and James Thomas) were African merchants, held nineteen meetings, and heard forty-one witnesses. Although McCallum's initiative was taken with the depressed trade of 1897 in mind, conditions worsened in 1898, when the commission finally heard evidence and compiled its report, and deteriorated further still in 1899.[127]

The commission's promising start led to a disappointing finish. The commissioners concluded that 'for some time past there has been an almost total lack of profit upon the business done'.[128] They identified the fundamental cause as being 'reckless competition', but were unable to offer a persuasive solution. Their suggestion that the remedy lay 'in the hands of the merchants and not through legislation' was a tame return on the effort expended.[129]

124. The low output of oil in 1898 helped the authorities to work out the relationship between rainfall and yield and subsequently to show that record export volumes followed exceptionally high rainfall in 1901: *Colonial Annual Report*, Lagos, No. 400, 1903.

125. *Lagos Customs Report*, 1900, enc. in *Lagos Annual Reports*, 1899–1905.

126. McCallum to Chamberlain, 15 Jan. 1898, C.O. 147/129; and the confirmatory comments made at the end of the year by the *Lagos Reporter*, 12 Dec. 1898.

127. The report and evidence are in Denton to Chamberlain, 25 May 1898, C.O. 147/132.

128. Denton to Chamberlain, 25 May 1898, C.O. 147/132.

129. The quotations are from the commission's report as cited in the previous note. The commission made several other recommendations, including the need for a Department of Agriculture, measures to deal with defaulting debtors outside the bounds of the colony, legislation to cover insolvency, tighter controls over adulterated produce and goods, and the need to diversify the export trade.

The commission failed to distinguish between immediate supply-side causes, such as lack of rainfall, and long-term trends in demand, notably the falling share of West African palm oil in the European oils and fats market.[130] The recommendation that merchants should collaborate to control competition was a strange prescription to apply to a colony that was supposed to be bringing the benefits of free trade to Africa. Some of the expatriate firms had already begun to experiment with pooling arrangements, but these were symptoms of depression and not a remedy for it. Commercial conditions did not improve. In 1899, the *Lagos Reporter* ended its gloomy assessment by affirming that the days of big profits lay well in the past.[131] John Holt's letters to his partner in Lagos in 1900 confirm that trade remained 'unsatisfactory' and that profit margins were tight.[132] Following comments from various chambers of commerce, the Colonial Office shelved the report in 1899.[133]

Two of the interested parties in Lagos that came through the 1890s better than others are worth mentioning here because they have not received the notice they deserve. One clear winner was the colonial government, which emerged from the successful invasion of Yoruba country with its standing and power greatly enhanced. As commercial profits fell, government revenues boomed. Between 1880 and 1889, official revenues averaged £47,000 annually; between 1893 and 1899, the figure was £145,000.[134] Expenditure followed suit and with it the reach of government. The increase was mainly the result of the growth in the value of external trade and the consequent rise in customs duty, which supplied almost 90 per cent of all government revenue between 1893 and 1899. The rates of import duty had also risen, following the increase agreed with the merchants to fund the Yoruba expedition. The rapid growth of government altered its ties with the Saro repatriates, who lost much of the intimacy that characterised the relationship at the outset of the colonial period, when necessity obliged the colonial authorities to turn to members of the Lagos community for assistance in managing the affairs of state.

The German firms, headed by Gaiser, survived the period in far better condition than most of their English counterparts did.[135] Gaiser and Witt

130. The *Customs Report* for 1900 gave as contributory causes: heavy rainfall, which flooded rivers and impeded communication; scarcity of labour owing to the Asante War; the failure of the Egyptian cotton crop, which doubled the price of cotton goods in Lagos; and the uncertainty caused by the Anglo-South African War. *Lagos Annual Reports*, 1899–1905.

131. 12 Dec. 1898, 21 Jan. 1899.

132. Holt to Welsh, 6 March 1900, 20 March 1900, 3 April 1900, HP 19/4–5.

133. Denton to Chamberlain, 9 March 1899, and minute by Mercer, 15 March 1899, C.O. 147/141.

134. *Lagos Blue Books*, 1880–1899.

135. See Hieke, *G. L. Gaiser*, pp. 38–45, 63–8; Gaiser hoped conditions would improve but, unlike the British firms, did not make representations to the colonial government. McCallum to Chamberlain, 15 Jan. 1898, C.O. 147/129.

& Busch had long been the principal firms in Lagos and in 1896 controlled almost 50 per cent of the port's overseas trade.[136] They had profited from the cowrie boom, then from imports of silver coin, and even more from their dominance of the trade in palm kernels, which had become the leading export. In 1891, John Holt noted that the British firms were suffering more than their German rivals because kernel prices had held up better than oil prices.[137] The trade went to Hamburg, he added, because there was very little demand in Britain for kernel cake and, accordingly, no crushing centre in Liverpool. The success of the German firms was broadly based. They operated their own steamers, which cut their freight costs; some of their imports, such as hardware and even some cotton goods, were cheaper than their British equivalents; their relations with local brokers and traders were congenial as well as profitable.[138] In 1897, Governor McCallum commented to John Holt that 'the Germans, you will be sorry to learn, are much more go ahead'.[139]

The pressure to intervene in the political affairs of the hinterland came largely from British firms. While this was understandable, given that the colony was British, it was also a reflection of the British firms' commitment to the palm oil trade, which was less profitable than the trade in kernels. Gaiser remained quietly prosperous. It is tempting to see in this example a sign of deeper problems of productivity and competitiveness that were beginning to confront British companies across the world and were to leave a long-term legacy.

The Port and Its People

Lagos continued to grow, despite the difficulties that hampered commerce during the last twenty years of the century.[140] Estimates of the town's population must be regarded as approximations, despite the assurance conveyed by official censuses, which presented the figures with misleading precision. The population was highly mobile and its size also varied with the trading seasons. Moreover, the early enumerations were incomplete and supplemented by guesswork. The population was recorded as being 37,452 in 1881, 32,508 in 1891, and 42,847 in 1901. The census of 1891 reported that the population had not fallen but had been over-estimated in 1881.[141] If it is accepted that the

136. Carter to Chamberlain, 29 May 1896, C.O. 147/195.

137. Holt to Welsh, 25 Dec. 1891, HP. 19/4.

138. Carter to Chamberlain and encs., 29 May 1896, C.O. 147/195.

139. McCallum to Holt, 11 Sept. 1897, and 9 Dec. 1897, HP 17/2.

140. *Lagos Times*, 28 Sept. 1881; Moloney to Kimberley, 6 June 1882, C.O. Library, London; *Lagos Annual Report*, 1891; MacGregor to Chamberlain, 20 Nov. 1901, C.O. 147/157; 'First Annual Report on the Town of Lagos', *Lagos Annual Report*, 1904, C.O. 149/5; Egerton to Crewe, 30 Nov. 1909, C.O. 520/83.

141. Following a misguided decision to pay enumerators according to the size of their count.

figure for 1881 was under 32,000, the increase between 1881 and 1901 was more impressive than the stated figures suggest. Since births were also matched by deaths, growth was the result of immigration, as a mixture of fortune hunters, refugees, fugitive and freed slaves made their way from the hinterland to the town. The occupational structure remained unchanged: employment in commerce and associated crafts and services continued to predominate. A differentiated view shows that a small number of skilled services, including lawyers, government officials, and the first doctors had also appeared, providing opportunities for a new generation who were largely the children of Saro repatriates. Europeans remained a minute proportion of the total population: they numbered 117 in 1881 and 301 in 1901. In 1881, most of the Europeans were in business; by 1901, employment in the administration, following the expansion of government, had taken the lead. Nevertheless, the number of European residents was still restrained by considerations of health.

There are no reliable figures for the number of repatriates from Sierra Leone or the 'Brazils' in Lagos. According to the census of 1872, the former numbered 1,533, and the latter, 1,305.[142] A subsequent estimate put the total Brazilian residents at 3,221 in 1887.[143] More repatriates arrived than remained because an unknown number made their way to their homelands in the interior. Net migration from Sierra Leone appears to have remained at low levels from the 1880s onwards. Immigration from Brazil may have risen as manumission increased in response to the tightening of restrictions on the Atlantic slave trade. It then seems to have tailed off after 1888, when slavery in Brazil was abolished, and it almost ceased in the 1890s, when the seaborne connection with Lagos ended.[144] Despite the absence of firm figures, it is clear that Saro and Brazilians combined accounted for a small and diminishing share of the port's growing population. The Saro elite retained a special advantage in being prominent among the small number of Lagosians who could read and write English. This facility continued to provide access to European firms and to some extent to the colonial government. Nevertheless, their relative decline as a proportion of the total population was one consideration, among others, in reducing the visibility they had enjoyed at the outset of the colonial period.

The increase in the number of inhabitants was an incentive to filling in swampland, but also a recipe for rising rents and overcrowding.[145] Drainage on an island where the highest elevations (in Olowogbowo and near the *Oba*'s palace) were little more than twenty feet above sea level was particularly

142. Lees to Secretary of State, 28 Feb. 1879, C.O. 147/130.
143. Castillo, 'Mapping'; Law, 'Yoruba Liberated Slaves', p. 356.
144. Lees to Secretary of State, 28 Feb. 1872, C.O. 806/130; Kopytoff, *A Preface to Modern Nigeria*, p. 171.
145. Moloney to Granville, 28 March 1886, C.O. 147/54; Evans to Stanhope, 4 Feb. 1887, C.O. 147/58.

difficult. Water was drawn from private wells and was unfiltered; there was no refuse collection; piped sewerage was a miracle that lay in the future. Consequently, disease was part of everyday life, though exceptional outbreaks, like the smallpox epidemic in 1878 and the yellow fever threat in 1881, attracted considerable local publicity.[146] In 1882, an anonymous Saro correspondent complained that, even on the Marina, the odours formed 'one continuous smell the whole way of the most villainous kind'.[147] Five years later, the *Lagos Observer* commented that 'fetid pools, swamps and marshes, rubbish and rank vegetation, permeate the island'.[148] Matters did not improve: in 1897, Governor Carter reported that 'the native portion of the town can only be described as a huge cess pit'.[149] The inadequate water supply had the additional consequence of making it hard to quench fires, which spread easily across the town's thatched roofs.[150] The undoubtedly unhealthy, potentially dangerous, and generally unattractive features of the town need to be seen in their contemporary context.[151] Lagos was by no means exceptional. Towns in Europe and the United States also reflected the primitive state of scientific and technical knowledge in the area of public health. Facilities that are taken for granted today did not exist in the nineteenth century.

The governor's residence and most other administrative buildings were clustered on the less crowded southern section of the Marina (between Odulami Street and the Race Course), which was also where the first new European residences appeared. The commercial centre of the town remained in the northwestern section of the Marina between Hamburg Street and the original Saro settlement at Olowogbowo. Most of the leading business establishments occupied this stretch of the Marina or one of the short, connecting streets to Broad Street, which ran parallel to it. These were large, two-storey or occasionally three-storey buildings that served as shops, warehouses, and residences. Some were renovated versions of old barracoons; others were new buildings in various styles imported by 'Brazilian' craftsmen, copied from the houses of notable Manchester merchants, or amalgamated from a variety of architectural influences, including elements of Gothic revivalism.[152] Among them were the houses of successful Saro merchants, including Liverpool House and Raymond House (Isaac Williams), Manchester House (Zachariah Williams), Pacific House (Charles George), and Caxton House (Richard Blaize), which was named to reflect the owner's publishing interests. Other

146. Brown, 'Public Health in Lagos'.

147. *Lagos Observer*, 4 Feb. 1882, quoted in Brown 'Public Health in Lagos', p. 340.

148. *Lagos Observer*, 17 Dec. 1887, quoted in Brown, 'Public Health in Lagos', p. 341.

149. *Lagos Weekly Record*, 26 June 1897, quoted in Brown, 'Public Health in Lagos', p. 349.

150. *Lagos Times*, 28 March 1883.

151. Brown, 'Public Health in Lagos', makes the point admirably.

152. Faluyi, 'Migrants', traces the evolution of Brazilian architecture in the town.

prominent private developments during this period included several impressive religious buildings, notably the Anglican church, St. Paul's Breadfruit
(1880), the Roman Catholic Pro-Cathedral (1881), and the grandest of them
all, the mosque sponsored by Mohammed Shitta Bey that was opened in
1894.[153] All were major undertakings funded largely by donations from the
merchant community.

It was appropriate that Shitta Bey's mosque was also the most impressive
religious building in the town at that time. The majority of studies of Lagos,
including the present one, have viewed the town from a Western or at least a
Christian viewpoint partly for reasons of training and partly because of the wide
range of records available in British and other European languages.[154] The bias
may often be subconscious but it can easily present a warped picture of important aspects of the port's history. Although Islam in Lagos is not the subject of
this book, it is important to note that in 1891 about 45 per cent of the population was Muslim and about 26 per cent Christian.[155] In the early 1880s, there
were no fewer than twenty-one mosques (and thirty-nine Koranic schools) in
the town, compared to fifteen Christian churches of various denominations.[156]
Until the Koranic schools began to introduce elements of Western education, the first being in 1896, educated Christians, led by the Saro, continued
to hold their privileged position as intermediaries between rulers and ruled
and between Lagos and Manchester.[157] The expansion of Islam nevertheless
diminished the relative importance of Christianity and its Saro leaders in the
religious life of the town.

It is also the case that, after 1893, the Saro lost their position as brokers
between the colonial government and the hinterland states. During the 1880s,
they were active intermediaries in the effort to secure a negotiated settlement
of the desultory but disruptive war in the hinterland.[158] Unsurprisingly, the
Saro were advocates of a peaceful settlement. Unity about ends, however, was
not matched by agreement about means. Saro from Ibadan were inclined to

153. Lucas, *Lecture*, pp. 22–23; Laotan, *The Torch Bearers*, pp. 20–21; On the Shitta Bey
mosque, see above, p. 89.

154. I am indebted to *Alhaji* Adamu Animashaun for his considerable help and particularly for his generous gift of a copy of his *History of the Muslim Community of Lagos
and the Central Mosque*.

155. Lagos Census, 1891, *Lagos Annual Reports*, 1891.

156. *Lagos Times*, 14 Sept. 1881.

157. Elements of Western secular education were first provided by a Koranic school
in Lagos in 1896 (with government support). 'An important point has been gained by the
establishment of this school, and it is indeed a new era in the history of Lagos when the
most conservative element of the Muslim population have concluded to enter into competition with the Christians in their efforts to acquire Western learning'. *Lagos Annual
Report*, No. 219 (1896).

158. See Correspondence on the Stoppage of Trade Routes at Lagos, C.O. 806, African
West No. 428, 1893.

view that state as a proponent of free trade that was denied free access to the coast by unproductive middlemen; Saro from Egba and Ijebu saw Ibadan as a predator that was disrupting legitimate commerce. Nevertheless, all parties agreed that a solution should be achieved by negotiation.[159] The outcome, which was realised by force, caused consternation in the Saro community. The Saro were seen by their European sponsors, and saw themselves, as pacific agents of the civilising mission. Civilisation at gunpoint was a contradictory concept that shook the Saro's understanding of their role and their value in the new colonial order. Previous scholars have studied the political and cultural consequences of the dramatic events of 1893. Chapters 7 and 11 will explore an aspect of the expansion of British rule that has received far less attention: the relationship between the new colonial order and the entrepreneurial opportunities available to the Saro.

Furthermore, the Saro stood in the margin of the two big disputes that divided the town during the 1880s and 1890s. One, which expressed the growing importance of the Muslim community, was a dispute between different factions within Sunni Islam that began in 1876, when a new group, known as the Koranic Party, challenged established orthodoxy.[160] Theological differences rapidly became entwined with a power struggle that set two wealthy Muslim merchants against one another: Mohammed Shitta Bey, who defended orthodoxy, and Alli Balogun, a younger man who carried the dispute into the twentieth century.[161] The other disruptive event, the crisis prompted by the ambitions of Ajasa, the *Apena*, in the mid-1880s, was resolved without the mediation of the Saro.[162] Daniel Taiwo, who was one of the leading protagonists, was a prominent merchant but not a Saro. His intervention was one of the last occasions, if not the last, when an individual African merchant could pull strings at the top of the colonial government in an effort to influence the outcome of a major political event in the town.

Whether despite or because of the dispiriting developments that characterised the 1880s and 1890s, the small Saro community continued to uphold the Victorian values that defined them. Church attendance did not falter; education remained an unquestioned priority. Clothes designed for the British climate oppressed African bodies in the clammy heat of Lagos. Social and cultural events displayed fashions and advertised attainments. The 'Flower of Lagos' club and occasional 'grand balls' were prominent meeting places

159. See, for example, *Lagos Times*, 27 April 1881, 27 Dec. 1882; *Lagos Observer*, 3 April 1886. The official correspondence for the period contains numerous attachments expressing the views of Saro on the war and its resolution.

160. Animashaun, *History of the Muslim Community of Lagos*.

161. See Momodu Tiamiyu Bashorun et al. v. Kasumu Ekemode, LSCR, Civ. 75, 1915; Buraimo Ogunro v. Momo Dabiri et al., LSCR, Civ. 85, 1919; Alliu et al. v. Dabiri, LSCR, Civ. 99, 1923; Lemomu Abasi et al. v. Tijani Noibi et al., LSCR, Civ. 103, 1924.

162. See above, p. 126–128.

for those Ellis termed Saro 'aristocrats' and their companions.[163] Literary clubs and debating societies honed the talents of future journalists and politicians. Musical events extended beyond religious compositions to include performances of Gilbert and Sullivan's operettas.[164] The Lagos Bachelors' Cricket Club promoted the characteristic English game and encouraged it in schools. In 1885, a Wesleyan High School team demonstrated Africa's development potential when, having scored fifty-four runs, they dismissed their opponents, a European 11, for the exceptionally low score of nine runs.[165] All victories are celebrated; some are sweeter than others.

By the close of the century, however, conformity was being challenged, especially by a younger generation who were children of repatriates but born in Lagos.[166] The world that had shaped their parents was being transformed. The new generation was exposed to the doctrines of 'scientific' racism, which eroded the universalism that had inspired mid-Victorians represented by Henry Venn and their protégés in Lagos, the Saro elite, such as James Davies. The shock of the invasion of Yorubaland changed the balance of power and shook the assumptions that underlay the original concept of the civilising mission. Signs of a departure from mid-Victorian orthodoxy appeared in Lagos during the 1880s, when the newspapers began to discuss the merits of exchanging English names and dress for their Yoruba equivalents.[167]

Behind these manifestations of uncertainty lay a concern about how to achieve 'progress' if emulation, which implied equality, no longer had British support. After the invasion of Yorubaland, the balance began to shift away from a model based on imitation and towards an alternative that included a larger African component. Some Saro explored Yoruba history and customs. A few members of the elite began to adopt Yoruba names and dress. In 1896, the *Lagos Standard* felt able to remark that 'the days when the educated African aspired to European names are gone—or going'.[168] The Protestant Church also paid a price for collaborating with racism. One schism led to the creation of the United Native African Church in 1891; another to the foundation of the African Church in 1901. These changes, in association with the commercial difficulties of the period, had a profound effect on entrepreneurial opportunities, as subsequent chapters will show.

Amid these multiple difficulties, the Saro and increasing numbers of Lagosians of all kinds were still able to cling to one solid asset: property. A survey conducted in 1891 showed that just under half of the island was inhabited and

163. Ellis, *The Land of Fetish*, pp. 75–8. Ellis attended one such occasion in 1880.
164. Echeruo, *Victorian Lagos*, chs. 2–4; Adedeji, 'The Church'.
165. *Lagos Observer*, 8 Jan. 1885.
166. Echeruo, *Victorian Lagos*, pp. 36–44.
167. *Lagos Observer*, 31 Aug. 1882. Examples of the reversion to African names are given in the *Lagos Standard*, 1 April 1896.
168. *Lagos Standard*, 18 March 1896.

that slightly under half of this figure was secured by a total of 3,438 crown grants.[169] Two-thirds of the total had been issued by 1873 and the remainder by 1891. An important (and unstudied) late development followed an ordinance passed in 1877, which allowed crown grants to be given to reclaimed swampland. By 1891, 165 such grants had been issued, many of them to eminent Saro merchants such as James Davies and Zachariah Williams.[170] By 1880, if not before, virtually all the prime sites in the commercial centre around Olowogbowo and along the Marina were held under crown grant. Consequently, the price of land in this favoured area was protected by its scarcity value.

The other occupied area was mostly held under Yoruba land law and was inconveniently located for transacting business with Europe. The unoccupied parts of the island were deemed unsuitable for building and accordingly provided no outlet for the demand for property. Even so, the declining profitability of overseas trade might have pushed down land values and rents had countervailing influences not intervened. Property values were supported by the influx of newcomers from the hinterland and by increased commercial competition, which was attracted by improved steamship services, the advent of the submarine cable, the shift to cash payments, the provision of banking services, and the greater security offered by the expansion of the colonial government after 1893. The data needed for accurate comparison are lacking, but evidence compiled by Acting Governor Denton in 1898 suggests that land on the Marina that had been acquired for virtually nothing in the 1860s had increased in value by 500-700 per cent by the close of the century.[171]

The original crown grants were issued to occupants of unoccupied land, principally in New Lagos, to provide favoured newcomers, such as the Saro, the 'Brazilians', and European merchants and missionaries, the security they needed. From the 1860s, the concept of freehold tenure spread to occupied land in Old Lagos. However, the creation of freeholds there lacked the contractual uniformity that characterised the areas held under crown grant and inhibited the liquidity of the market. In 1898, Acting Governor Denton instituted a review of what Chief Justice Rayner called the 'confused mass of English and native law' in Lagos and the 'surrounding districts'. New rules for freehold grants were agreed in the following year.[172]

---

169. Denton to Chamberlain, 4 Oct. 1898, C.O. 147/135. See also chapter 2.

170. Moloney to Knutsford, 17 May 1888, C.O. 147/64; Denton to Chamberlain, 4 Oct. 1898, C.O. 147/135; also Denton to Ripon, 13 May 1895, C.O. 147/99.

171. Denton to Chamberlain, 4 Nov. 1898, C.O. 147/136. Denton estimated the price of land on the Marina to be between 5s. and 7s.6d. per square yard. In 1876, property on the Marina (at Oil Mills St.) was valued at 2s. per sq yard; Lewis's land, 1s.3d. per sq yard. In the matter of the Public Lands Ordinance No. 7, LSCR, Civ. 7, 1887. Detailed study of the Lands Office records may produce a representative time series of changing land prices.

172. Denton to Chamberlain, 4 Oct. 1898, C.O. 147/135 and enc. memo by Rayner. See also McCallum to Chamberlain, 4 Aug 1897, C.O. 147/116, and 3 Jan. 1898, 147/98; Denton

Anomalies, as seen from the perspective of English law, remained and deserve more attention than is possible here.[173] In 1908, Acting Chief Justice Speed declared that 'native ideas as to the ownership of property were utterly unsuited to modern requirements' and were in any case 'dying a more or less natural death'.[174] Speed, however, was ahead of himself. Family land was not easily transferred by sale, which meant that potential lenders were reluctant to accept it as security. As Chief Justice Rayner put it in 1898: 'many trading firms refuse to take houses or land as security because though the individual may hold in fee simple this is often family land and attempts to realise on the security often mean litigation'.[175] Indeed, as Kristin Mann has shown, in some respects Yoruba land law was being strengthened after the turn of the century, when policies of indirect rule influenced the courts to rule in favour of 'traditional' customs of land-holding and inheritance.[176] Denton's summary of the position in 1898 that 'the native has grasped and appreciated the idea of handing property to his children unburdened in any way' was both correct and incomplete.[177] The law on matters of tenure and inheritance remained a medley of confusion. In 1902, the lawyer, Kitoyi Ajasa, asked a witness when these customs had changed. The answer was telling, despite its imprecise chronology: 'when the lawyers came'.[178]

Nevertheless, important changes were under way. One consequence of the development of the land market was the adoption of the English law of descent. Under customary law, the property of a deceased man passed to his younger brother.[179] By the close of the century, it was increasingly common for the children of the elder brother to inherit and, among the Saro, for the first son to receive a substantial share of the estate's assets. Muslim families, however, continued to distribute assets among the children of the deceased, with preference given to sons. Inheritance of assets, whether by a brother or an eldest son, increased the chances of a business being continued after the founder's death. Whether or not it did so will be examined in chapter 16.

---

to Chamberlain 18 March 1899, C.O. 147/141, and 6 June 1899, C.O. 147/143; MacGregor to Chamberlain, 7 July 1899, C.O. 147/143.

173. Mann, *Slavery and the Birth of an African City*, ch. 7, provides a meticulous and authoritative account of this subject.

174. Lewis v. Banjoko, LSCR, Civ. 52, 12 Nov. 1908.

175. T. C. Rayner, 'Land Tenure in West Africa', in Denton to Chamberlain, 4 Oct. 1898, C.O. 147/135.

176. Mann, *Slavery and the Birth of an African City*, ch. 7. Interesting cases include: Omoniregun v. Sadatu, LSCR, Civ. 8, 1888; Eletu Ijebu, Lagos, in the Matter of the Estate of Hontonu (decd.), LSCR, Civ. 9, 1889; Ayorinde v. Asiatu and Ors, LSCR, Civ. 23, 1899; Paula Santos v. A. O. Taiwo & Ors, LSCR, Civ. 28, 1900.

177. Denton to Chamberlain, 4 Oct. 1898, C.O. 147/135. See also the important judgement of Chief Justice Rayner in re Aorinde, LSCR, Civ. 23 1899.

178. Paula Santos v. O.A. Taiwo & Ors., LSCR, Civ. 28, 1902.

179. In the matter of the Estate of Hotonu, LSCR, Civ. 9, 1889.

Reverberations

By the 1890s, the conditions that had nurtured the 'civilising mission' since the creation of the colony had lost their impetus. Adverse terms of trade and increased competition reduced the profitability of the export staples; the invasion and subjugation of Yorubaland destroyed the ideal of an equal partnership in the development of Africa. The two were sequential but also causally connected: waning prosperity generated pressures that produced the decision to move inland. The result was the second great shock to hit the port. Established commercial and political institutions were challenged either to adapt or to accept decline and eventual elimination.

Detailed research has uncovered many of the complexities underlying this basic formulation. The debate over the causes of the hinterland wars has revealed the difficulties the Yoruba faced in consolidating new states while adapting to the end of the external slave trade. A form of economic dualism developed in which palm oil and kernels were produced by both slave and free labour. The relationship was contradictory rather than harmonious. As there were no economies of scale attached to the production of the staple exports at that time, Big Men who controlled a large labour force did so by supporting slave-raiding. The outcome was insecurity, destruction, and the creation of 'no-go' areas that became unsettled wastelands. These conditions inhibited the free expansion of small-scale producers. The net result was to constrain the economic potential of the region.

Merchants in Lagos also had to adjust to innovations that removed imperfections in the market but also increased competition. Other institutions put in place after the creation of the colony, notably those dealing with property, security, and credit, remained essential to the conduct of business but had no part to play in solving the problems that arose in the 1880s and 1890s. A pacific solution depended on a revival in the prosperity of international trade, which was far beyond the reach of anyone in Lagos, and a reduction in transaction and production costs. By the 1890s, transaction costs had been lowered by means of the introduction of silver currency, telegraphic communication, and falling freight rates. Further improvements could be made only by ending the conflict in the interior and reducing the cost of land transport. Experiments to diversify production were considered and some were applied. Where they were successful, however, the beneficial results lay in the future.

Persuasion remained the policy of choice, but compulsion had become an acceptable option if 'reasonable' requests were refused. Notions of equality that predominated in the mid-century had lost ground to novel certainties based on ideas of racial supremacy. By the late 1880s, a generation of assertive civil servants and politicians had come to the fore in London. They were complemented by an infusion of eager young missionaries who provided a spiritual blessing to the new ethos. Chambers of Commerce in Britain added their influential voices. Further institutional change was necessary to maintain international competitiveness. Recalcitrant polities had to be brought under control and the British version of law and order established. Only then could the great hope of the nineteenth century, the railway, be run through the interior, cut transport costs, and expand the market.

Beyond these interests lay wider considerations. This was the age of 'new imperialism'. Britain had to keep pace with international competition, not only from the old rival, France, but also from newcomers, especially Germany and the United States. If France remained the main competitor for international status, Germany and the United States had become major commercial rivals by penetrating Britain's market and protecting their own. The loss of desirable markets in these and other countries helped to push Britain into more difficult regions in Africa and Asia. The decline in Britain's competitiveness could be seen in microcosm in Lagos, where the success of the German firms prompted Governor McCallum's rueful reflection in 1897 that they were 'much more go ahead'.[180]

The focus of this book, however, is on the colonial port city and the fortunes of its African merchants. As the next chapter will show, some eminent Saro merchants were felled by the depression that afflicted Lagos during the closing years of the nineteenth century. Their fate was widely advertised and caused consternation in the town. The key question, however, is whether these and other examples represented a general trend or whether their demise was offset by countervailing developments that have yet to receive the attention they deserve.

180. McCallum to Holt, 11 Sept. 1897, and 9 Dec. 1897, HP 17/2.

CHAPTER SEVEN

The Mercantile Community

THE SHOCK TRANSMITTED by the invasion of Yoruba country in 1892 had swift and far-reaching political consequences. Contrary to expectations, however, the invasion did not lead to an immediate improvement in the port's commercial fortunes, which were governed by even more powerful influences transmitted by international trade. The economic effects became apparent only after the turn of the century. Consequently, as chapter 6 showed, the last twenty years of the century were a time of great difficulty for all parties engaged in overseas trade. Accordingly, it is understandable that historians have identified the period as marking the demise of the entrepreneurial elite that helped to pioneer legitimate commerce in the 1850s and 1860s. The 'Golden Age' of the early colonial years is readily contrasted with the barren times that followed. African merchants undoubtedly lost the visibility they enjoyed during the early decades of the colony's existence; whether the slow drift towards obscurity is evidence of decline, however, is one inference among others and needs to be demonstrated. The issue is a controversial one because it relates to the much wider question of whether Europe underdeveloped Africa by appropriating its resources and limiting opportunities for its entrepreneurs.

The Consequences of the Invasion of Yorubaland

All generalisations about the effects of the depressed conditions of trade on African merchants in Lagos are based on incomplete evidence. Various lists of prominent merchants can be found in official and private sources, but they usually lack detail and some express personal preferences rather than objective evidence. The assessment that follows is based on the sample of 116 entrepreneurs listed in the appendix, which expands available lists and supplements them with information derived from newspapers, Supreme Court and Lands Office records, family testimony, and, where available, private papers. The result is still incomplete and open to question, but it should mark an advance on what is currently available.

Contemporaries were not short of opinions on the subject, and commentaries became more numerous as the depressed 1880s gave way to the disappointing 1890s and culminated in a calamitous year in 1898. In 1895, the *Lagos Standard* gave its opinion that 'the middleman system, which has done good service in the days of yore has been relegated to the limbo of forgetfulness'.[1] In the following year, the paper judged that the 'civilised African' was losing ground to both European merchants and interior producers.[2] In 1899, it seemed that the game was up: 'The days of large businesses and big profits are over for Africans' because 'increased competition has driven the trade into the hands of a few large capitalists, almost exclusively Europeans'.[3] In a parallel comment in the same year, the *Lagos Reporter* claimed that European firms were now monopolising even the retail trade.[4] This mournful commentary was qualified by those who saw grounds for optimism. In 1887, the *Lagos Observer* listed seven African merchants who were 'competing and rivalling' some of the European firms.[5] In 1896, the *Lagos Standard* referred to two members of a new generation of 'rising merchants' (David Taylor and Claudius Oni), who were about to visit Europe.[6] As for the middlemen, Gaiser's agent, reflecting in 1898 on his experience of the 1890s, thought that they 'are the same in number as they used to be'.[7] There is no doubt that the middleman 'system' was shaken up by the invasion of Yorubaland and increasing competition in the 1890s. Nevertheless, the networks that joined merchants to brokers and to Lagos traders, who dealt with hinterland traders at the lagoon markets, survived.[8]

Rare testimony from George W. Neville, the manager of the BBWA, provides an insight into the bank's policy towards African merchants and brokers.[9] From the mid-1890s, BBWA provided support for African importers and exporters and also reduced interest rates on small loans.[10] The bank allowed importers to order goods from Europe by paying only 25 per cent of the invoice value and settling the balance when the consignment arrived. The

1. *Lagos Standard*, 13 May 1895.

2. *Lagos Standard*, 30 Sept. 1896.

3. *Lagos Standard*, 21 June 1899.

4. *Lagos Reporter*, 18 July 1899.

5. Richard B. Blaize, James W. Cole, Charles J. George, Thomas G. J. Hoare, Jacob S. Leigh, James J. Thomas, and Zachariah W. Williams, *Lagos Observer*, 1 and 29 Oct. 1887.

6. *Lagos Standard*, 6 May 1896.

7. Emil Holtman, evidence in Denton to Chamberlain, 4 June 1898, C.O. 147/133.

8. On the survival of brokers/barracooners see the evidence of Seidu Olowo, Edmund Joseph, and James O'Connor Williams, in Denton to Chamberlain, 4 June 1898, C.O. 147/133.

9. Evidence of G. W. Neville (manager of BBWA in Lagos) in Denton to Chamberlain, 4 June 1898, C.O. 147/133. See also evidence of J. A. Hutton in P.P. (1909), Cd.4685.

10. Denton to Ripon, 1 April 1893, C.O. 147/89.

bank paid for the goods in advance and collected the sum due from the customer in Lagos. Similarly, BBWA helped small exporters by advancing up to
75 per cent of the value of produce as soon as it had been shipped. Neville's
general judgement was that 'Lagos is going through a process that all new
countries have to go through. The capitalist is losing ground and the smaller
trader is coming in and the struggle between the two is at present rather
upsetting trade generally'.[11]

Neville's testimony received independent support from Claudius Oni and
David Taylor, who confirmed in 1898 that they used credit authorised by
BBWA to order goods from Europe. Frederick Osborne, the agent for Paterson Zochonis, agreed. He judged that there were about seventy native traders who were 'competing with us—importing to themselves direct. And owing
to their expenses being smaller than ours they are to that extent in a better
position'.[12] The agent for Holt & Welsh had a similar view: 'Lately a large number of natives have sprung up who import on their own account. Formerly,
they bought off the merchants. Their doing so has had a detrimental effect
on the trade'.[13] Matthew Brown, the agent for Lagos Stores, confirmed this
assessment: 'the Bank has been the means of giving facilities that formerly
did not exist to native traders starting [out]. In my opinion', he added grimly,
'we could do without the bank'.[14] Gaiser saw self-interest in operation: in their
view, BBWA supported African traders to help fill the ships of its related company, Elder Dempster.[15] Adam Smith might have replied that in this case self-
interest conferred wider benefits.

Acting Governor Denton, writing in 1898, was clear about the consequences of the bank's policy on 'small traders, a large and influential body in
Lagos', who 'have become an important factor in our commerce' now that they
can obtain 'advances at a moderate rate of interest'.[16] In a separate report,
also written in 1898, Denton, who knew Lagos well, summarised the transformation he had witnessed in the following way: 'Some twenty years ago
the trade of this colony was practically in the hands of a few large firms' . . .
but 'the establishment of telegraphic and regular steamship communication
with Europe and the introduction of a gold and silver currency in place of
the old and cumbersome barter system have enabled many native traders of
small means who formerly dealt with the large firms to become importers
themselves', with the result that 'they are now formidable competitors' of the
European firms.[17]

11. Evidence of G. W. Neville in Denton to Chamberlain, 4 June 1898, C.O. 147/133.
12. Frederick Osborne, evidence in Denton to Chamberlain, 4 June 1898, C.O. 147/133.
13. Donald McLaren, evidence in Denton to Chamberlain, 4 June 1898, C.O. 147/133.
14. Matthew Brown, evidence in Denton to Chamberlain, 4 June 1898, C.O. 147/133.
15. Gaiser memo, 5 July 1895, enc. in F.O. to C.O., 3 Aug. 1895, C.O. 147/102.
16. Denton to Chamberlain, 6 Nov. 1898, C.O. 147/136.
17. Denton to Chamberlain, 25 May 1898, C.O. 147/132.

Where opinions vary so widely, it becomes difficult to determine the direction of travel. Such judgements can form the basis of a hypothesis but cannot be treated as being conclusive. The only record that qualifies as being systematic and objective dates from 1886, when Governor Moloney compiled a list of independent 'native merchants' based on 'the social position they occupy and their transactions with the customs' as part of a less than comprehensive assessment of individuals who might qualify to serve on the Legislative Council.[18] Between them, the leading eleven African merchants provided a median value 15 per cent of total customs revenue (which was levied on imports) from 1880 to 1885 (inclusive). Instead of falling, as might be expected, given the difficulties of the time, the share accounted for by African importers increased from 10.1 per cent to 16.4 per cent during the period covered by Moloney's report. Since the eleventh merchant on the list (T. G. Hoare) paid an average of only £75 annually in duty, it is evident that only very minor importers were omitted from Moloney's list.

The list, however, excluded those who were deemed not to qualify as 'native gentlemen' and accordingly were considered to be unsuitable candidates for membership of the Legislative Council. Muslims were not on the list; nor were women. Anyone who lacked literacy in English was eliminated. Moloney also stated that the African merchants on his list dealt 'almost entirely in dry goods', which covered all commercial imports, apart from alcohol. Since spirits accounted for about 22 per cent of the value of imports during the 1880s, Moloney's list understated the share of imports taken by African merchants. Although the true rate cannot be ascertained, it is reasonable to suggest that, had spirits been included in his report, they would have raised the median value of 15 per cent he attributed to African merchants to a level that was at least similar to the share they had in 1855. Had the duties paid by those who were not 'native gentlemen' been counted, the total would undoubtedly have exceeded 20 per cent.[19]

Moloney implied that Africans had little stake in the direct export trade. Thomas Welsh, who had considerable experience with Lagos trade, confirmed this assessment in 1888, when he commented that 'produce buying in Lagos is largely in the hands of Europeans'.[20] The position was different in 1855, when the Saro were actively involved in the export trade and were importing goods from Europe as well. By the 1880s, the risks of dealing in produce and the increasing use of British silver currency, which released the import trade from its ties with exports, encouraged Saro merchants to concentrate on the import

18. Moloney to Granville, 19 April 1886, C.O. 147/55.

19. See chapter 3 above.

20. Welsh to Cotterell, 20 March 1888, HP. 27/2. A month later, he reinforced his comment by reporting that 'all the natives have gone out of the produce trade'. Welsh to Holt, 7 April 1888, HP 27/2.

trade, which was not only steadier but, being more diverse, also allowed individual traders to create a niche for themselves. Nevertheless, the information on individual merchants presented in this study shows that African merchants remained active in the export trade, even though some of them varied their commitment in response to changing prices. Incomplete data hamper a precise conclusion. The most that can be said is that, if Saro merchants imported more than they did in 1855 but exported less, their share of total trade in the 1880s may not have changed dramatically.

The next substantial piece of evidence dates from 1898, when the Lagos government established a Commission of Enquiry to examine trading conditions following complaints from merchants of falling profits during the past decade.[21] Although the commission gathered valuable information, it made no attempt to provide a systematic account of the division of overseas trade between African and European firms. There is solid evidence, however, from both African and European sources showing that BBWA was helping African merchants to re-enter the export trade and expand their import businesses after 1894. The evidence lacks statistical precision, but is sufficiently robust to suggest, minimally, that fortunes in the late nineteenth century showed signs of revival as well as of decline.

The evidence so far has focussed on the Saro and omitted references to the Brazilian community. This is not an oversight. Members of the Brazilian community hardly featured in discussions of mercantile affairs during this period. The number of Brazilians in Lagos increased slightly during the 1880s, rising from 2,732 in 1881 to reach 3,221 in 1888.[22] Governor Moloney hoped that larger numbers would wish to return after slavery was abolished in Brazil in 1888, and in 1890 he persuaded Elder Dempster to operate a trial shipping service between Lagos and Rio de Janeiro.[23] Although the experiment failed, the trial showed that those seeking to return were elderly Yoruba rather than members of a new generation who were eager to build careers.[24] The Brazilian community in Lagos remained tightly knit and vibrant but expressed itself in ways other than high commerce.[25] It produced notable craftsmen and architects, and maintained an active cultural life, which revolved around the church, music, literary clubs, friendly associations, and sport. At the same time, it remained largely isolated from the rest of Lagos society: Roman

21. McCallum to Chamberlain, 15 Jan. 1898, C.O. 147/129. The commission is analysed in chapter 6.

22. Moloney, 'Cotton Interests', pp. 268–71.

23. Moloney to Holland, 20 July 1887, C.O. 147/59; Moloney to Holland, 4 Aug. 1887, C.O. 147/60; Moloney to Knutsford, 23 Dec. 1888, C.O. 147/67.

24. *Lagos Times*, 16 Aug. 1890, 6 Sept. 1890; Hemming, C.O. minute, 'Steam Service to Brazil', 10 June 1891, C.O. 147/83.

25. Laotan, *The Torch Bearers*. I am also grateful to the late Mr Laotan for a series of valuable discussions in February 1962.

Catholicism and the Portuguese language cemented group solidarity but also hindered interaction with the Protestant, English-speaking sections of Lagos.

Commerce and shipping between Lagos and Brazil declined during the period under review. This was a niche where Lagos Brazilians held a competitive advantage, which they used to import tobacco, rum, salted meat and fish in exchange for Yoruba cloth and kola nuts. In 1880, trade between Lagos and the 'Brazils' was worth £52,159, which amounted to 5.5 per cent of the total overseas trade of Lagos.[26] The business then slumped in the late 1880s and in 1892 was worth only £8,517, which accounted for no more than 0.9 per cent of the total trade of the port. The trade dwindled further in the 1890s, as did seaborne communication, which had almost died out by 1900. There was one last flourish in 1899, when the brig *Allianca* arrived from Bahia with sixty-one passengers, 'a large proportion of them' being 'old and worn out people whose desire it was to return to die in this country'.[27]

The connection had been maintained mainly by Manoel Joaquim de Sant Anna, one of the community's few prominent merchants.[28] He owned a sailing vessel that conducted trade and passengers between Lagos and Brazil, and a steamer that ran between Lagos, Badagri, and Porto Novo.[29] However, when his ship, the *Bento de Freitas*, was wrecked on the harbour bar in 1894, his business went down with it and the connection with Bahia and Rio was virtually severed.[30] In the following year, Santa Anna was sued successfully for a debt of £2,382; he responded by escaping to Porto Novo, where he died shortly afterwards.[31] It was the end of an era that had begun more than half a century earlier, when Kosoko's initiative reinvigorated the connection with the 'Brazils'. The leading Brazilian merchant in the 1890s was João da Rocha, but he made his money in Lagos rather than in trade with the Americas. He has a place in chapter 11 in conjunction with his son, Candido, who became even more prominent than his father in the business life of Lagos.

Lagosians themselves continued to produce numerous prominent traders. The pre-colonial elite that had dominated the slave trade retained its status and a degree of political influence in Lagos affairs but lost ground, in every sense,

26. Calculated from *Lagos Blue Books*, 1880–1900.

27. MacGregor to Chamberlain, 25 Oct 1899, C.O. 147/145.

28. According to Laotan, *The Torch Bearers*, p. 14, Sant Anna was of 'mixed parentage'. Two other merchants deserve to be mentioned here: Joaquim Francisco Branco (1852–1924) and Walter Paul Siffre (?–1923), who imported goods such as tobacco and spirits from Brazil.

29. Welsh to Holt, 23 June 1888, 26 June 1888, HP 27/2.

30. Carter to Rippon, 21 Sept. 1894, C.O. 147/95. Sant Anna's downfall had consequences for others: the business run by Lazaro Borges da Silva (1856–1928) was badly affected by the disaster. I am grateful to Mrs Sophia Morelawa da Silva (daughter) for information about her father: Lagos, 7 Feb. 1862.

31. Plus interest at 5 per cent: Johannes Schubach v. M. J. Sant Anna, LSCR, Civ. 15, 1894; Denton to Chamberlain, 9 Oct. 1895, C.O. 147/100.

economically. In 1911, the Commissioner for Lands reported that 'for evidence of the completeness and rapidity with which the loss of control over land results in the loss of all prestige and power, we have only to turn our eyes to the degraded condition of the Lagos White Cap chiefs'.[32] Others connected to the royal house rarely appear in evidence dealing with commercial affairs. The only example worth mentioning is Alfred Akitoye (1871–1928), the son of Prince Fasiro Aki-toye, grandson of *Oba* Akitoye, brother to Prince Eshugbayi Eleko, and eventually head of the House of Dosunmu.[33] He was educated at the CMS Grammar School, became a Christian, began as a book-keeper and transferred to the civil service before joining J. Nathan & Co., a Manchester firm specialising in cotton goods, in 1900. Akitoye acted as Nathan's local representative for about twenty-five years before becoming *Oba* of Lagos in 1925. His eminence stemmed from his inherited status, which far exceeded the modest scale of his business activities.

Beyond the Saro and royal circles, Lagosians with far less status and visibility also operated substantial businesses. Their relative obscurity means that estimates of contributions made by different sections of the population to the port's overseas trade that are based on businesses conducted by Saro merchants almost certainly underestimate the proportion supplied by all Africans in Lagos. Unfortunately, the share is unknown and cannot even be guessed. Among the prominent figures, established and new, in the 1880s and 1890s, were Seidu Olowu, Claudius Oni, Abibu Oke, Braimah Ajao (Abibu Oke Balogun), Idris Olaniyan, Fasheke Olukolu, and the greatest of them all, Alli Balogun, whose career will be considered in chapter 11. Information about these businessmen is sketchy and relies heavily on oral testimony, which is valuable in broad terms but lacks the detail needed to give precision to adjectives such as 'substantial' and 'influential'. As a generalisation, it can be said that these merchants and brokers all dealt with imports and that a more limited number handled produce. Profits were reinvested in trade and property, which was used to secure credit. These businesses died with the founder in nearly every case; their estates were usually divided between the children according to either Yoruba or Muslim law. Sons had some opportunities depending on their education; daughters invariably became traders who dealt mainly in cotton goods. Although evidence about their lives is even more limited than it is in the case of men, some examples of successful female traders will be provided in chapter 10.

Failure and Success

The list of eleven leading merchants provided by Governor Moloney in 1886, combined with additional information relating to the period 1880–1900 as a whole, provides the best available guide to the scale of businesses conducted

32. Enc. in Egerton to Harcourt, 20 May 1911, C.O. 520/103.
33. Macmillan, *The Red Book*, pp. 112–13; *West Africa*, 25 Aug. 1928.

by Saro who were engaged in the import–export trades.[34] Eight of the eleven names on Moloney's list appear in this or other chapters. Sketches of Jacob Leigh and Charles George were given in chapter 3; James Davies receives extensive treatment in chapters 5 and 9; Richard Blaize and Isaac Williams occupy chapter 8. Three others, Nathaniel Shepherd (1830–1909), Joseph Bucknor (1840–1890), and Thomas Hoare (1824–1889), can be discounted. Shepherd owed his presence entirely to an exceptional volume of trade in 1885 and was better known for his equally exceptional criminal record. Bucknor had been prosperous but his business was fading by the mid-1880s. Hoare was last on the list of eleven names and no longer conducted trade on any great scale. That leaves the three who are portrayed here and who had in common the fact that the foundation of their wealth lay in the prosperous years before the 1880s. They also had distinctive qualities: Zachariah Williams was prob-ably the most prosperous of the merchant princes in the 1880s, James Thomas illustrates the enduring connections between the Saro and their Sierra Leone origins, and James Cole's life shows that, by the 1890s, even first-generation returnees were ready to sever some of their Victorian roots.

By all accounts, Zachariah Archibald Williams was the greatest of the Lagos Saro merchants during the last quarter of the century. 'All accounts', however, remain sketchy. In the absence of private papers and business rec-ords, it is hard to follow the career of the 'Native Napoleon of West African Commerce', as the *Lagos Standard* called him, beyond readily accessible infor-mation, which tends to treat his life as an unqualified success story.[35] The fol-lowing reconstruction remains incomplete in many respects but adds enough details to outline his early years and record the hitherto unrecognised disas-ters that marred the closing decades of his life.[36]

Zachariah was the second son of Samuel Ladipo Osanyintade Williams (popularly known as Daddy Sam), an Egba from Abeokuta who was enslaved and then freed and taken to Freetown. He adopted the name Williams on becoming a Christian, received education from a CMS mission school, and began his life as a trader. He married Ajayi, also a Yoruba freed slave, who took the name Lucy, and had three children in Sierra Leone, the first being James O'Connor (1843–1906), who became a close business associate of his brother, Zachariah; the second was Eliza Sabina (1848–1886), who later married the merchant, Cornelius Moore; the third was Zachariah (1851–1912).[37] Samuel

34. Moloney to Granville, 19 April 1886, C.O. 147/55.

35. *Lagos Standard*, 7 Aug. 1895.

36. I am immensely grateful to Mrs Adelphine Lande Williams, daughter-in-law of Zachariah, for an interview on 30 Jan. 1962, and to Zachariah's grandson, Chief Frederick Rotimi Alade Williams, the celebrated lawyer popularly known as 'Rotimi Bamba', for an interview on 29 Jan. 1962.

37. *Lagos Observer*, 3 April 1886. Some sources give Zachariah's date of birth as 1850. I have preferred 1851, which is the date given by Mrs A. L. Williams (see n.36 above) and is also given on Zachariah's marriage certificate.

and his wife returned to Abeokuta shortly after the CMS established a mission there and began shipping raw cotton, which the mission was promoting as an alternative to the slave trade. It was there that the family became associated with Cornelius Moore, who was also heavily invested (via James Davies) in the cotton venture.[38] Samuel then moved to Lagos, began trading in palm oil and cotton goods and started to invest in property, shrewdly obtaining a crown grant in 1869 for land on the Marina.[39]

Zachariah was educated at the newly-established mission school in Abeokuta and in 1870 formed a partnership with his older brother, James. The pair began trading under the name Williams Bros., specialising in raw cotton and cotton goods.[40] In 1877, the interruptions and uncertainty caused by the conflict in the hinterland prompted Zachariah to transfer the business to Lagos. By then, he had already achieved considerable success, having accumulated, according to one account, as much as £5,000.[41] This sum was more than enough to enable him to 'marry well', and he did.[42] In 1879, Zachariah married Eleanor Cole, the daughter of a substantial Lagos merchant, Thomas Francis Cole (Daddy Alade), who contributed to their happiness by giving them a house in Apongbon.[43] Williams Bros. adjusted to the end of the brief cotton boom by exporting palm oil and importing cotton goods and a variety of other consumer manufactures. There are no details of the relationship between the brothers, though it is clear that Zachariah was the senior partner.[44] Other family members were also involved, though not as partners. One brother, Jacob Taiwo Williams, was the firm's agent in Porto Novo; another, A. T. Faro Williams, was a clerk in the Lagos office. The wives of the partners also provided crucial support, as will become clear.

Zachariah's fortunes received a further boost in 1880, when he made his first visit to England and agreed on behalf of Williams Bros. to use the Manchester firm of John Walkden as his sole agent for both produce and consumer goods.[45] By this time, Williams was installed on the Marina in a mansion appropriately called 'Manchester House', which he used to secure an annual credit of £5,000 advanced by Walkden. He had bought the house from James Davies's creditors for £850 in 1881 and rebuilt it at a cost of £5,000, which

38. See above, p. 139.

39. LLOR, LO 2819, 1899.

40. *Lagos Standard*, 1 Nov. 1899.

41. *Lagos Observer*, 3 April 1886.

42. I borrow here the highly appropriate title of Kristin Mann's book, *Marrying Well*, which lists the connections between these families and many others on pp. 95–8.

43. I am grateful to Samuel Alade, nephew of Daddy Alade, for this information. Interview, Lagos, 29 Jan. 1962.

44. 'I am the senior partner in the firm of Williams Bros. & Co'.. Evidence given by Zachariah Williams in D. H. Taylor v. Williams Bros., LSCR, Civ. 6, 1886.

45. *Lagos Standard*, 7 Aug. 1895; Indenture, 3 Sept. 1883, enc. in deed of conveyance in L.O. 0039, 1883.

FIGURE 7.1. Zachariah Archibald Williams. Copied by Paramount Photographers, Lagos, with permission of Chief Frederick Rotimi Alade Williams (grandson).

exceeded the sums spent by any of the other eminent Saro merchants, including Richard Blaize and James Thomas, on their Marina properties.[46] The opening of the renovated property was a great event that was attended by Governor Moloney and the elite of Lagos.[47]

There was more to come. Moloney's ranking of mercantile houses showed that Williams Bros. paid far more in import duties between 1881 and 1885 (inclusive) than the other ten African merchants listed combined, and also more than all the English firms, apart from Lagos Warehouse Company.[48] In addition to the import trade, Williams was exporting palm oil, kernels, and ivory. He had several stores in Lagos, branches in Abeokuta, Ijebu Ode, Porto Novo, and other hinterland towns, and employed approximately twenty clerks and numerous Kroomen.[49] In 1886, two English clerks arrived to help manage his extensive business.[50] By 1883, according to one assessment, he had made a fortune of £30,000; in the following year, his turnover was said to have reached £60,000.[51] Williams's lifestyle advertised his success. He was one of the best dressed men of the day and always wore a frock-coat and top hat.[52] He visited Government House in a barge rowed by uniformed oarsmen. He was a regular attendant and generous supporter of Christchurch, the most prestigious Anglican church in Lagos. He continued to visit England, principally to see John Walkden in Manchester.

Everything fell apart in 1887. Until then, Zachariah had been in a 'large way of business'.[53] The first sign of possible difficulties came in 1886, just as the two English clerks were arriving. At the end of October, only a few weeks after they had landed in Lagos, the partnership between the brothers was dissolved and the business became solely Zachariah's, though continuing under the name Williams Bros.[54] The reasons for the cancellation of an association that had lasted for sixteen years are unclear. A clue to the timing of the sudden shift from expansion to contraction, however, can be found in Porto Novo. Zachariah had long traded with the port, where his brother was his main representative. In 1884, Williams Bros. bought premises there with the aim of expanding the business. However, trade was slack because goods had been priced, erroneously, at 10 per cent above prices ruling in Lagos.[55] Early

46. *Lagos Standard*, 27 March 1895.
47. *The Service* (Lagos), 11 March 1961, p. 9.
48. Moloney to Granville, 19 April 1886, C.O. 147/55.
49. *Lagos Standard*, 27 March 1895.
50. *Lagos Observer*, 18 Sept. and 2 Oct. 1886.
51. *Lagos Observer*, 18 Sept. and 2 Oct. 1886.
52. Akinsanya, 'Dandies of the 1900s'.
53. Z. A. Williams evidence in Williams v. Ollivant, LSCR, Civ. 14, 1894.
54. *Eagle & Lagos Critic*, 31 Oct. 1886, 12 and 31 March 1887.
55. D. H. Taylor v. Williams Bros., LSCR, Civ. 6, 1886.

in 1886, Williams began to close one of two small branches and planned to add Porto Novo to the list.

By the beginning of 1888, Zachariah was actively seeking to dispose of his premises in Porto Novo and sell a launch and two barges, which he was no longer using.[56] Early in 1890, he transferred the Porto Novo business to the Liverpool firm of Holt & Welsh, who rented his premises there.[57] The situation in Lagos was even worse. By 1888, Zachariah had to reach a private accommodation with Walkden because he was unable to repay the advance he had received.[58] He began to sell property in 1887; sales continued for more than a decade until there was little left to surrender.[59] Like other successful merchants, he had accumulated a substantial portfolio of properties in Lagos. Between 1870 and 1886, he bought prime sites in the town, swampland, which had considerable development potential, and houses and farmland in the hinterland.[60] The high point was the purchase of Manchester House in 1881; his last purchase occurred as late as 1886, when he bought a property at the corner of Broad and Martins Street.[61]

Thereafter, the disposals accelerated and the debts mounted. Between 1890 and 1893, Zachariah disposed of at least five properties in prime sites in Lagos and two nearby on the mainland at Ebute Metta for a total of £2,503, and in 1899 he sold a prime site near the Marina to the Colonial Government for £800, which the Director of Public Works judged to be 'a decided bargain'.[62] Additionally, he was compelled to raise several loans to meet a debt of £4,000 to John Walkden, his principal creditor, the largest being for £1,634 (at 7.5 per cent), which he borrowed from the newly established African Banking Corporation.[63] A further setback occurred in 1894, when he failed in a claim against G. B. Ollivant, his agent in Manchester at the time, for a loss of £740 on the sale of palm oil in 1890.[64] His biggest battle, however, took the

56. Welsh to Holt, 23 Feb. 1888, HP 27/2. The launch and barges had been ordered from the UK and delivered only '15 or 16 months ago'. Holt & Welsh opened their business in Lagos under the name Thomas Welsh in 1887 and changed it to Holt & Welsh in 1889. The partnership was dissolved in 1899, but John Holt continued the business under the name of Holt & Welsh. Memo of Agreement, 29 Dec. 1887 and 19 Dec. 1889, HP 19/4 19/5.

57. Welsh to Holt, 11 April 1890, HP 26/3a.

58. Welsh to Holt, 6 Feb. 1888, HP, 27/2.

59. Conveyance of land on the Marina to Josiah Savage for £425. LLOR, 16/335, 1887.

60. LLOR, Vendee Index provides a guide to his purchases. Specific examples are given in the disposals that follow.

61. Conveyance from Charlotte Davies, LLOR, 3/215, 1886.

62. LLOR, Lagos Properties: 16/335, 1887; 16/16 1890; 15/402, 1890; 16/66, 1890; 16/74, 1890. Ebute Metta: 18/402, 1892; 22/114 (1893). Tomlinson & Co. v. Williams, LSCR, Civ. 10, 1891; Denton to Chamberlain, 6 April 1899, C.O. 147/142.

63. LLOR, 14/436, 1892.

64. Williams v. Ollivant, LSCR, Civ. 14, 1894.

form of a prolonged rearguard action to retain Manchester House, which was both mortgaged and leased, but finally remained in his name.[65]

Indebtedness, however, had become a way of life. Zachariah was still struggling to repay creditors at the end of the century. The pioneering Saro doctor, John Randle (who was James Davies's son-in-law), took Zachariah to court for a debt of £81 in 1897; his long-standing friend, Richard Blaize, began legal action in 1902 to recover a debt of £900.[66] Evidently, the *Lagos Standard's* portrait of the 'Napoleon of West African Commerce' published in 1895, was economical with the truth.[67] By then, Zachariah had met his Waterloo. He had been forced to leave Manchester House and move to more modest premises in Broad Street. In 1891, he was already a 'retired merchant' who currently had 'no occupation'.[68] In 1897, he stated that he had 'nothing that I can call my own in Lagos' and was living on £6.5s. a week.[69]

Zachariah's rapid and precipitous reversal of fortune remains a puzzle. One possibility, referred to in some sources, is that the business experienced a disastrous fire that destroyed stocks at the end of the decade.[70] Fires were common in Lagos at this time. The firm's Marina stores were broken into and burned in 1883 and some branch stores suffered a similar fate in 1884.[71] Fortunately, the properties were covered by insurance, so the setback, though unwelcome, was unlikely to have been disastrous. In 1890, a serious fire in Porto Novo brought 'great loss' to traders but occurred subsequent to the decision to close the firm's branch there.[72] A promising alternative lies in the difficult trade conditions of the time, which reduced profit margins and made the produce trade particularly risky. While these are contributory considerations, they are unlikely to have been direct causes. Had they been significant, it is likely that contemporary sources would have identified them as prime sources of the downfall of such an eminent merchant, and that is not the case.

There is a third, unpublicised possibility that can be culled from the Supreme Court records: Zachariah was seriously ill. Giving evidence under oath in October 1891, he stated that he had been 'very ill for the past four years'.[73] In the following year, he confirmed that he had been 'suffering from

65. The main transactions are in LLOR, 14/436, 1891; 18/358, 1892; 25/289, 1895; 39/440, 1905; 66/285, 1910; 81/449, 1913.

66. Randle v. Williams, LSCR, Civ. 18, 1897; Davies & Williams v. Blaize, LSCR, Civ. 27, 1902.

67. *Lagos Standard*, 7 Aug. 1895.

68. LLOR, 3/345, 1891; Wright v. Williams, LSCR, Civ. 11, 1891.

69. Randle v. Williams, LSCR, Civ. 18, 1897.

70. Notably in Mrs A. L. Williams's detailed testimony. The comments here are not intended to deny the possibility but to note that evidence of the connection is not easily found in the contemporary records.

71. *Lagos Times*, 10 Oct. 1883; Payne, *Almanack*, 1885, p. 140.

72. B. A. Coker, 'Historical Notes of Porto Novo', n.d., in Holt Papers, 7/4.

73. Evidence in Wright v. Williams and Walkden, LSCR, Civ. 11, 1891.

mental depression since May 1887' and had been obliged to give up his business 'in consequence'.[74] In 1896, again speaking in court, he said that he was
ill in 1883, 1886–1887, and in 1895 as well.[75] These statements are consistent,
given that the third statement is an elaboration of the first two. The picture
is one of an illness that first appeared in 1883 and became steadily more serious. Indeed, Thomas Welsh, reporting to John Holt on Zachariah's voyage to
England in 1888, wrote that 'I heard he had attempted at Accra to commit sui-
cide onboard but failed'.[76] Admittedly, this was hearsay, but it fits with what is
known of Zachariah's condition. Dr John Randle provided a medical diagnosis
in 1892, when he stated in court that in 1891 Zachariah was 'suffering from a
species of mental depression which rendered his conduct very uncertain'.[77]
Illness is the explanation closest to the chronology of the collapse of the business and its likely cause, which lay in erratic decision-making at a time when
the finest of judgements were needed to keep a large undertaking from being
submerged under adverse trading conditions.

As these bouts of illness grew more serious, Zachariah became increasingly
dependent on his wife, Eleanor, not only for personal care but also for her business experience. She had traded on her own account for many years, though using
his shop and sometimes his credit too. During two critical years, 1886–1887 and
1890, she managed the whole enterprise, negotiating with creditors while securing
advances that enabled her to keep the business afloat.[78] Zachariah struggled on,
without employment and with little income, until his death in 1912. The *Nigerian
Chronicle's* sad but accurate conclusion was that 'notwithstanding life's misfortunes, he kept up his gentlemanliness to the last'.[79] Under the terms of his will,
his remaining assets passed to his wife and children, the prize being Manchester
House. The former mansion was leased to Lagos Stores Ltd., which generated an
income for his widow, though little for the education of his remaining children.[80]
Following Eleanor's death in 1928, the family decided to sell the house, which
was bought by Nigerian Properties Ltd., for £10,000.[81] The original crown

74. Evidence in Wright v. Williams, LSCR, Civ.11, 1891–92.
75. Evidence in Walkden v. Williams, LSCR, Civ. 17, 1896.
76. Welsh to Holt, 11 June 1888, HP, 27/2.
77. Evidence in Wright v. Williams, LSCR, Civ. 11, 1891–92.
78. Evidence in Tomlinson & Co. v. Williams, LSCR, Civ. 10, 1891; Evidence in Walkden
v. Williams, LSCR, Civ. 17, 1896.
79. 5 March 1912.
80. Zachariah hoped that his son, Josiah Folarin Williams (later known as Adebesin
Folarin), would become a lawyer, but lacked the money to support his studies. Josiah began
as a clerk to a commercial firm before starting a successful business in the Cameroons. He
used his savings from trade to fund his studies in London. He was called to the Bar in 1913
and became a highly successful lawyer (*Lagos Weekly Record*, 10 July 1920). One of Zachariah's sons, Frederick Rotimi Williams, became a noted lawyer and politician; Rotimi's
brother, Akintola Williams, was Africa's first qualified chartered accountant.
81. LLOR, LO 039, 50 Marina.

grant, which was virtually costless when issued to James Davies in 1863, and worth £850 when Zachariah bought the house in 1881, had proved to be a fine investment, though not one that Zachariah himself lived to see.

James O'Connor's career was a less dramatic version of his younger brother's story. James had begun trading before entering the partnership that became Williams Bros. in 1870, but was never as successful as his brother and was unable to stay in credit long enough to accumulate substantial capital.[82] The dissolution of the partnership in 1886 opened the way to further difficulties, which began in 1888, when Zachariah sued him for £120.[83] Success continued to elude him. His career as an independent commission agent and barracooner remained on a small scale and was scarcely profitable throughout the 1890s. From 1889 onwards, he was in debt to Gaiser, McIver, and Witt & Busch, among others, and was making a modest living from his farm at Agege.[84] During these challenging years, James depended heavily on his wife, Sarah, whose earnings from trade and property kept the family afloat. In 1889, she mortgaged land she owned at Apongbon to secure a debt of £548, which James was unable to pay.[85] In 1891, she agreed to mortgage property in Broad Street that was jointly owned to guarantee a line of credit for him from Walkden; in the following year she agreed to sell land in Market Street that was also owned between them.[86] After she died in 1895, James sold the Broad Street property to Jacob Coker for £705.[87] The sale brought only temporary relief: in 1896, he was threatened with prison for non-payment of debt.[88] By then, he had mortgaged or sold his property in Lagos and leased his farm at Agege as well.[89] When he died in 1906, there was little left for the family to inherit—or to dispute.[90]

James Jonathan Thomas's career provides a more encouraging example of continuing success during the challenging years at the close of the century. Thomas was the archetypal first-generation Saro who conformed to all the stereotypes of the Victorian African gentleman. In 1894, Governor Carter

82. For James's early trading activities, see his evidence before the Commission on Trade in Denton to Chamberlain, 25 May 1898, C.O. 147/132; LLOR, 10/182, 1870; 12/189, 1871; 15/315, 1872; 18/33, 1872; 18/108, 1873; 17/280, 1873; Welsh Bros. v. Williams, LSCR, Civ. 1, 1878.

83. Williams Bros. v. O'Connor Williams, LSCR, Civ. 8, 1888.

84. Gaiser v. O'Connor Williams, LSCR, Civ. 9, 1889; Gaiser v. Williams, Civ. 9, 1890; Witt & Busch v. Williams, Civ. 9, 1890; Witt & Busch v. Williams, Civ. 10, 1890; Witt & Busch v. Williams, Civ. 13, 1893; McIver v. Williams, Civ. 13, 1893; McIver v. Williams, Civ. 14, 1894; Coker v. Williams, Civ. 17, 1896.

85. LLOR, 14/1, 1889.

86. LLOR, 14/250, 1891; 19/260, 1892.

87. LLOR, 27/416, 1895.

88. Coker v. Williams, LSCR, Civ. 17, 1896.

89. To Rufus Wright: Wright v. McIver, LSCR, Civ. 18, 1896.

90. He died intestate. His estate was assessed at less than £35. LSCR, Letters of Administration & Probate, III/33, 1906.

FIGURE 7.2. The Hon. James Jonathan Thomas, 1905, member of the Legislative Council, Sierra Leone, being received by King Edward VII at St. James's Palace, London. Copied by Paramount Photographers Lagos, with permission of Jacob Olumide Williams (friend of the family).

recommended his appointment to the Legislative Council with the following endorsement: 'Thomas', he reported, 'is a well to do native merchant of good repute . . . a loyal subject of the government' who 'may be relied upon not to offer any factious opposition'.[91] He worked tirelessly on numerous committees, commissions, and boards, and received a further endorsement in 1898 from Carter's successor, Governor MacGregor, who commented that Thomas 'has at all times, both in his public and private capacity, proved himself a thoroughly loyal and reliable servant of Her Majesty'.[92] The final accolade came in 1908, when he was appointed a CMG, which was only one step short of a knighthood.[93] He was just the person an undemocratic government needed, and also someone who is easily disparaged today.

Distinction came after a long struggle. Thomas was born in Wellington, Sierra Leone, in 1850. Little is known of his ancestry. His parents were freed Egba slaves from Yorubaland; his father, also named James, was a small farmer and fisherman.[94] James, his son, had a brief spell as a printer's apprentice, but decided to make his way in Lagos once the colony had been established and security improved.[95] He arrived there in 1867 and was fortunate enough to be taken on by Thomas Joe, a merchant who was also an Egba repatriate.[96] James's family were Christian converts and staunch Wesleyans, and James had received enough education to begin his career as a junior clerk. Within a few years, he decided to start his own business and in 1873, he married Thomas Joe's daughter, Patience, who was also a committed Wesleyan.[97] Although 'marrying the boss's daughter' is a route to riches that has become a cliché, there is no evidence that Thomas gained financially from his new family connection. His business was entirely separate from that of his father-in-law and had its own sources of success.[98]

Despite James's subsequent prominence in Lagos, very little information about his business has survived. He was involved in the produce trade and was shipping palm kernels to Europe in the 1870s, but his principal source of profit appears to have come from the import trade, where his ingenuity gave him a competitive advantage. According to an account given by the *Sierra Leone News*, James had noticed that several combinations of the colours in

91. Carter to Ripon, 7 March 1894, C.O. 147/94.

92. MacGregor to Chamberlain, 17 April 1900, C.O. 147/148.

93. In the arcane but still vibrant British honours system, CMG is the abbreviation of Companion of the Order of St. Michael and St. George.

94. I am grateful to Dr M.C.F. Easmon of Freetown for his assistance and to Thomas's nephew, Willie Cookson, also of Freetown, for supplying this information in correspondence in May 1962.

95. Fyfe, *A History of Sierra Leone*, p. 536.

96. Little is known about Joe. He died in 1888 aged about seventy-seven according to the gravestone in the Campos Graveyard; other sources offer the alternative age of seventy.

97. *Lagos Times*, 27 June 1891.

98. It is possible that Thomas gained indirectly from whatever his wife inherited from her father's death in 1888, but James's business was well established by then.

Manchester cotton goods were especially popular in Lagos and among hin-terland traders.[99] He used watercolours to sketch some new patterns that he thought would attract customers and sent them to his Manchester agents, who had the designs registered. James ordered a trial quantity that sold well and the business expanded. James kept ahead of his rivals by continuing to add fresh designs to his stock. In 1881, he shrewdly decided to shift to a 'ready money system' and cut back on both cowries and credit.

Like other merchants, James was buffeted by the headwinds that affected Lagos in the 1880s and 1890s. In 1888, for example, when falling produce prices reduced purchasing power, he was forced to sell ten thousand pieces of imported cloth at auction at a 'considerable loss'.[100] Nevertheless, he adjusted better than some of his rivals. He was placed third (behind Zachariah Wil-liams and Richard Blaize) on the list of leading African importers between 1881 and 1885, and was regarded as 'one of the largest retail men in Lagos in the 1880s'.[101] There are indications that Thomas reduced his import–export business in the 1890s. He rented his main premises to T. E. Tomlinson, Walk-den's representative, in 1889, when he was said to be 'retiring, temporarily anyway'.[102] In 1898, he left Lagos to accompany his wife, who was ill, to Free-town. His absence became permanent in 1900.[103]

Whether falling profits made trade unattractive or for other reasons besides his wife's health, Thomas's decision to close his business was not an indication of declining fortunes. He remained prosperous throughout the 1890s. His status as a 'merchant prince' stayed with him.[104] He was said to be 'one of the most outstanding of the best dressed men'.[105] He had a horse and carriage and made frequent trips to England. Instead of having a house con-structed in 'the current Lagos style', he visited Manchester to arrange for an exact replica of the mansion owned by 'his friend, John Walkden', to be built in Lagos, including its marble-lined interior walls.[106] The house was erected in Broad Street in the late 1880s at a cost of about £3,500. It had twenty-three rooms spread over three storeys, a tennis court, and stables. The name, Wilberforce House, paid tribute to one of the inspirational figures in his life. James Thomas had arrived and his status shone from every window.

99. As reported in *West Africa*, 3 Jan. 1920.

100. *Lagos Times*, 9 March 1881; Welsh to Holt, 15 July 1888, H.P. 27/2.

101. Moloney to Granville, 19 April 1886, C.O. 147/55. The quotation is from Welsh to Holt, 5 Feb. 1888, HP 27/2.

102. Welsh to Holt, 6 Sept. 1889, HP 19/5.

103. *African Times*, 6 June 1900.

104. The accolade was given by the *Lagos Standard*, 12 Nov. 1919, which listed him with Zachariah Williams, James W. Cole, and Richard Blaize.

105. This quotation and the next one are from Akinsanya, 'Dandies of the 1900s'.

106. *Lagos Standard*, 27 March 1895; Akinsanya, 'Dandies of the 1900s', *Sunday Express* (Nigeria), 27 Aug. 1961.

Thomas's continued prosperity rested increasingly on income from property bought from past commercial profits. Like other merchants of his generation, he was an early participant in the embryonic property market, securing crown grants and buying what were to become prime sites on the Marina and in Broad Street. The Lands Office records show that he was an active purchaser, who rented rather than sold the property he owned and rarely, if ever, required a mortgage. He sustained this pattern of investment during the difficulties of the 1880s and 1890s, when he offered mortgages (essentially loans) to other merchants, some of whom were struggling to stay afloat. The names of those who borrowed from him (at rates of 5–10 per cent) during this period would have been familiar to contemporaries: Jacob Williams (1883), Samuel Crowther (1887), Benjamin Dawodu (1887), Alfred Campbell (1888), James O'Connor Williams (1891), and Joseph Haastrup (1896).[107] Among his acquisitions in the 1880s and 1890s were premises in Broad Street, which he bought from Samuel Pearse in 1887 for £425, and a substantial property on the Marina, which he purchased from Jacob Leigh in 1895 for £3,250.[108]

Thomas did not dispose of any of his real estate until after he retired to Freetown in 1900. Rather, like other successful merchants, he continued to draw a retirement income from property he retained in Lagos. He sold one property on the Marina to David Taylor for £3,750 in 1903 and another to Bishop Tugwell for £1,600 in 1908.[109] His next and final transactions in Lagos occurred in 1914, when he sold Wilberforce House and substantial adjoining land to Walkden, his long-standing agent in Manchester, for £7,000, and in the following year, when he leased another Marina property to a British firm, H. B. W. Russell, for five years at a rent of £52 per annum. In making these dispositions, Thomas may have been deliberately 'putting his house in order'. In 1915, he was well into retirement; he died in Freetown in 1919 at the age of sixty-nine.

The other indication of Thomas's wealth lay in his philanthropy. His life-long commitment to the Wesleyans was apparent in the financial support he gave the mission as well as in his personal contribution as a preacher and class leader.[110] His retirement from business in 1898 did not curtail his generosity. In 1900, it was noted 'on reliable authority' that 'there are over a hundred paupers in Freetown . . . who are weekly recipients of his bounty'.[111] In 1906,

---

107. LLOR, 3/41 1883; LLOR, 3/308, 1887; LLOR, 3/328, 1887; LLOR, 3/394, 1888; LLOR, 14/320, 1888; LLOR 42/205, 1896. The last transaction was registered as a sale but in effect was a mortgage or loan for £2,500. Haastrup redeemed the property in 1903 (LLOR, 42/205) and sold it to Joseph H. Doherty in the same year (LLOR, 42/205).

108. LLOR, 12/165, 1887; LLOR, 27/161, 1895.

109. LLOR, 42/380.

110. *African Times*, 6 June 1900.

111. *African Times*, 6 June 1900.

he presented the people of Sierra Leone 'with a decent and costly library'.[112] His business ceased when he closed his Lagos premises. He had one daughter and a son with his wife, Patience, who died in 1891.[113] Their son, however, suffered from a mental disability and remained dependent on his parents. In 1896, James married Rhoda, a sister of the noted Freetown lawyer, Abraham Hebron, but she suffered from ill health and it was her condition that hastened his decision to close the Lagos business and retire to Sierra Leone in 1898.[114]

James William Cole's career was similar to Thomas's, but added an element of nonconformity that anticipated some of the strains the Saro were to feel under colonial rule. Cole was born in Freetown in 1834.[115] His parents, Thomas and Hannah Cole, were Egba slaves from Abeokuta who had been freed and settled in Freetown. Although they remained poor, James was fortunate to receive elementary education from a school run by the Wesleyan mission. While still 'in his youth', he decided to make his way in Lagos, where the newly established Consulate offered the prospect of combining political stability with new commercial opportunities.[116] He arrived in Lagos in 1853 and was taken on by James George (Daddy Osoba), a fellow Egba and father of the merchant, Charles George, whose career was featured in chapter 3. James began as a trainee cooper, but in 1862, a British merchant named David Chinnery gave him the chance to become his agent in Badagri and Porto Novo. He shuttled between these ports and Lagos for several years, supplying cotton goods, iron bars, and gin in exchange for palm oil, and did well enough to set up his own business and buy a motor launch, which was one of the first to operate on the lagoon.[117]

In the late 1860s, James disposed of his business in Porto Novo and settled in Lagos, where he remained for the rest of his life.[118] His commercial activities, in common with those of most of his Saro contemporaries, are known only in outline; details, such as can be collected, have to be inferred from

112. *Lagos Weekly Record*, 11 Aug. 1906. Deniga, *African Leaders*, p. 7, gives the date (incorrectly) as 1907.

113. *Lagos Times*, 27 June 1891; *African Times*, 6 July 1891.

114. MacGregor to Chamberlain, 11 April 1900, C.O. 147/148 and enc.

115. I am particularly indebted to Mr Georgius Cole, William's nephew, for his detailed and careful account of his uncle's life given in two meetings in Lagos, 7 Nov. 1961, and 20 Feb. 1962. Cole's date of birth is sometimes given as 1840. All three obituary notices in the Lagos newspapers, however, give the date as 1834, which is consistent with him obtaining a land grant from Dosunmu in 1855. For this reason, I have also opted for 1853 as the date of his arrival in Lagos rather than 1858, as suggested by the *Lagos Weekly Record*, 27 March 1897. See also *Lagos Standard*, 31 March 1897.

116. Oke, *A Short History of the U.N.A.*, pp. 15–16.

117. Akinitan v. Singbo, Badadive, 1/1, 15 Oct. 1870; LLOR, 25/22, 1876.

118. In 1868 William encouraged his mother, Hannah, then a widow, to return to Lagos, where she settled until her death in 1885. The dates are taken from the gravestone in the Campos Cemetery, Lagos.

indirect evidence, notably property dealings and court cases. He continued to trade in palm oil and cotton goods, owned a sailing vessel, and was influential in introducing John Walkden to Lagos. He became their representative in the port and travelled to England on several occasions to solidify the business relationship. Globalisation before the telephone, let alone the internet, took time. Success brought Cole private wealth and public prominence. He owned a house and stores in Broad Street and had his main residence, Porto Novo House, on the Marina, where he kept a horse and carriage and a complement of stewards. He was a member of the Lagos elite, mixed with the big names of the day, and was particularly close to John Payne, the Registrar of the Colony, to the point of acting as his bondsman.[119] In accordance with his status, James was a prominent public figure, serving on the Legislative Council, assisting the Hussey Charity, and giving generously to the Wesleyan Mission.

These worthy activities were typical examples of the Saro community's commitment to the public good. Cole's decision to join the United Native African Church (UNA) at its foundation in 1891, however, was a marked departure from convention. Moreover, Cole was the most influential member of the UNA and its chief financier from then until his death in 1897. He purchased Phoenix Hall, which he bought from Daniel Taiwo for £160 in 1891, donated it to the UNA, and funded its conversion into a church.[120] Thereafter, he was the main figure supporting the church, meeting its running costs, and maintaining its new school. The UNA represented lay discontent with the performance of the existing Christian missions, which had lost impetus, allowed Islam to advance, and had failed to confront the problems of relating the Christian message to African culture.[121] Polygamy was one issue, but so too was the need to secure respect in an increasingly racialised world and the desire to see Africans spreading the Christian Word. The movement was led by laymen who were reformist rather than revolutionary; Cole's standing in the eyes of the colonial government did not suffer from his defection from the Wesleyans. Nevertheless, the UNA marked a departure from the mid-century values and institutions that had guided the first generation of Saro repatriates and was the precursor of a more radical secessionist movement that had far-reaching economic as well as spiritual consequences, as will become clear in chapter 13.

Like most successful Lagos merchants, James Cole experienced setbacks. The most notable occurred in 1873, when he was sued by Andrew Charles, a Birmingham merchant, for the substantial sum of £9,974.[122] An assessment

119. J.A.O. Payne to Chief Justice, 21 July 1898, enc. In Denton to Chamberlain, 21 July 1898, C.O. 147/135.

120. LLOR, 18/191, 1891.

121. Needless to say, this is a complex matter that cannot be explored here, but it has been examined in James Bertin Webster's pioneering account: *The African Churches Among the Yoruba*.

122. This episode is covered in LLOR, 17/190, 1873; 18/97, 1875.

of James's assets concluded that his real and personal wealth would not cover a quarter of this amount. A compromise was arranged whereby Charles agreed to settle for £3,000 on the surety of seven properties, which would be forfeited if payment were not made within two years. The origins of the crisis are obscure. It might have been connected to the fate of his sailing ship, which was wrecked on the notorious Lagos sandbar in 1873, with the loss of the captain and a clerk.[123] Alternatively, or additionally, the debt may have been related to the closure of the trade roads for part of this time or indirectly to the international banking crisis of that year. At first sight, an assessment that fixed Cole's total wealth at less than £2,500 appears inconsistent with his status as a leading merchant. It has to be remembered, though, that this was a considerable sum in the mid-nineteenth century. It is also possible that the assessment might not have captured everything that Cole possessed. At all events, the debt was settled in 1875 and Cole regained his property.

Cole experienced no further losses of comparable importance, and in 1897 was still ranked as 'one of the wealthiest natives of the community'.[124] It is impossible even to guess at the relative importance of trade and property to his success, but it is clear that property in Lagos was an increasing source of wealth, and for many others besides Cole, not least because it provided a degree of stability that commerce lacked. The Crown Grants and Vendee indexes show that Cole was acquiring and buying land in Olowogbowo, Balogun Square, and Broad Street for relatively small sums in the 1860s and 1870s. The largest single purchase was a property in Broad Street, which he bought for £300; the most adventurous was some land on the nearby island of Iddo, which he bought in 1876 from one Mumuni for the modest sum of £11.[125] At that time, Iddo was scarcely developed, but in 1899 it was designated the main railway terminus for Lagos and in 1901 was joined to Lagos by the Carter Bridge. It was probably the best investment Cole ever made.

Cole continued to advance money and make selective purchases in the 1880s and 1890s. Among his more important transactions were loans to Joshua B. Benjamin of £1,600 in 1880, of £700 to Edwin Williams in 1894, both on the security of property they owned, and the purchase of two properties on the Marina from the Crowther family in 1887 and 1892.[126] The properties originally formed one crown grant, which was issued to Samuel Crowther (the son of the bishop) in 1866 and subsequently divided. In 1887, Cole bought 43 Marina, which stayed in the Cole family until 1932, when it was sold for £4,150 to Ferris George, who then sold it to A. G. Leventis for £10,000 in 1943.

123. Payne, *Payne's Lagos*.

124. *Lagos Weekly Record*, 27 March 1897.

125. LLOR, 25/22, 1876.

126. Welsh Bros. v. Benjamin, LSCR, Civ. 5 1882; LLOR, 20/368, 1894. The history of the Marina properties can be followed in LLOR, 2854, 0543, and 21/18, 1892.

Cole's second purchase, 44 Marina, for £800 in 1892 remained in the family until it was sold by the Curator of Intestate Estates to Candido Da Rocha for £4,000 in 1932.

James Cole was known as Cole 'Bamba' because of his girth, which defied standard furnishings and obliged him to have chairs specially made to fit his frame. Any suggestion of a Falstaffian image, however, is misleading. Cole's personal life was permeated by tragedy. His only legitimate son, Alfred (1866–1915), suffered from mental illness; his wife, Mary Jemima (neé Sawyer), whom he married in 1864, also developed mental health problems and needed special care for the last twenty years of her long life, which ended in 1931.[127] The deterioration of the marriage during the 1880s was an additional cause of Cole's decision to join the UNA. Husband and wife were both committed Christians and Cole thought it would be hypocritical for him to take another wife while remaining in the Wesleyan Church.

Cole himself was in poor health before his death and lived increasingly in seclusion. He died intestate in 1897, at which point his estate was valued at 'upwards of £20,000', of which £8,545 was held in the National Bank in Manchester.[128] Cole's brother, Abraham, continued the business, as William had instructed, but when he died in 1904, the enterprise was wound up. Harmony had ended long before then. William's death led to what became the *locus classicus* of customary rules of inheritance, when Abraham challenged the right of Alfred, William's son, to inherit, arguing that customary law should apply, even though William's marriage had followed Christian rites.[129] The decision that English law should prevail did not end the matter, not least because the two beneficiaries, mother and son, were both permanently ill. It was not until after Mary's death that further proceedings culminated in the escheat of the estate to the crown and the distribution of the remaining assets among Abraham's children and James's natural children. The two Marina properties realised £8,150 and there were some additional assets. There were also numerous beneficiaries, all of whom gained something, though none became rich through inheriting the wealth that remained from William Cole's enterprise.

The End of a Golden Age?

The biographies of Zachariah Williams, James Thomas, and James Cole introduce an element of individuality into generalisations about mercantile fortunes, and in doing so draw attention to the range of possible causes of

127. *Nigerian Pioneer*, 13 Nov. 1931.

128. Denton to Chamberlain, 12 June 1899, C.O. 147/143; Payne v. Cole, LSCR, Civ. 21, 1898.

129. Elias, *Nigerian Land Law*, p. 255, and further references in chapter 10. On the first judgement, which favoured William's brother, Abraham, see A. B. Cole v. M. J. Cole, LSCR, Civ. 21, 1898.

business success and failure. Standard views assume that African merchants suffered from a combination of hostile colonial policies, competition from expatriate firms, and adverse trading conditions. This interpretation ignores other considerations that play a part in the real world of business experience. These include mismanagement, luck, and natural events such as illness and old age. A disaggregated view of the mercantile community underlines the diversity of causes of success and failure.

A group of established merchants survived and even prospered during the last two decades of the century, though some had retired before 1900 for reasons related to age and family obligations. Of the eleven merchants on Governor Moloney's list of leading exporters during the first half of the 1880s, seven remained either prosperous or afloat during this period (Richard Blaize, Joseph Bucknor, James Cole, James Davies, Charles George, James Thomas, and Isaac Williams), and an eighth (Thomas Hoare) remained in business until his death in 1889. Three (Zachariah Williams, Jacob Leigh, and Nathaniel Shepherd) suffered significant reversals. Most members of the first group have either been discussed already or will appear in subsequent chapters. Members of the second group require further comment because the causes of their difficulties varied. As suggested earlier, Williams's business was almost certainly brought down by his illness. Shepherd was a maverick and speculator whose high-risk activities landed him in prison as well as in court, where he was sued successfully for considerable sums of money during the 1800s and 1890s. Leigh made his fortune in the 1870s, but his business suffered a series of calamitous misfortunes in the 1880s and 1890s, first on the Niger and then in Lagos. In this case it seems clear that the Niger Company's aggressive application of its monopoly rights was an important cause of Leigh's downfall.

Other prominent figures who were not on Moloney's list also struggled during the 1880s; some who traded into the 1890s succumbed to the commercial crisis that enveloped the port during the last three years of the century.[130] As shown earlier, James O'Connor Williams (1843–1906) incurred weighty debts in the 1880s and 1890s. Samuel and Josiah Crowther (trading as Crowther Bros.) were active without ever being successful. Their Niger trade lost money and the brothers accumulated significant debts in the 1880s and 1890s.[131] Benjamin Dawodu (1860–1900) gave up the produce trade at the close of the 1880s, became an auctioneer, but remained heavily indebted for the rest of his life.[132] Josiah A. Savage (1849–1920), a 'native merchant of

130. Space compels me to abbreviate the biographical notes and references that follow. The assessments are made on far more material than can be cited here.

131. Samuel (1829–1900), Josiah (1839–1910). They owed much of their visibility to being sons of Bishop Samuel Crowther (c.1806–1891).

132. Interview with Babalola Dawudu (Benjamin's son), Lagos, 22 Jan. 1962; *Lagos Weekly Record*, 16 and 30 June 1900.

some standing', was laid low by the deep depression that struck in 1898.[133] Seidu Olowu (c.1850–1921) was successful during the 1880s, lost money on produce during the 1890s, was over-committed during the rubber boom, and never recovered.[134] Claudius Oni (1861–1932) shifted from produce to cotton goods in the 1890s, suffered during the depression of 1897–1900, took employment with Miller Bros., but was unable to regain his former position.[135] Again, however, the causes of failure varied. James O'Connor Williams, the Crowther brothers, and Benjamin Dawodu were not good businessmen and would probably have failed whatever the circumstances. Josiah Savage, Seidu Olowu, and Claudius Oni were struck by a combination of bad luck and unwise business decisions. As subsequent chapters will show, several of the early cocoa farmers were also merchants and brokers who were adversely affected by the difficult trading conditions of the 1880s and 1890s.

There were other substantial merchants who did not appear on Moloney's list of importing firms. These included a small number of produce exporters and a larger number of sizeable barracooners and brokers, who, as defined here, also counted as merchants. The leading African merchants who exported on their own account in the 1880s were also among the principal importers and are covered by Moloney's list. Imports were the permanent staple of their business and they moved in and out of the riskier export trade according to their judgement of the market. The two most important brokers (who had the status of merchants) were Daniel Taiwo and Mohammed Shitta Bey, whose careers were discussed in chapters 3 and 4. Both remained prosperous, though age prompted them to retire from business in the 1890s. Many less prominent produce brokers survived. Some, like Fasheke Olukolu (c.1841–1906), prospered by lending money to less successful traders during the 1890s.[136] An even larger number of importers beyond the ranks of the Saro lasted throughout this period and some, such as Alli Balogun, prospered well beyond it. Unfortunately, there is insufficient information to fill the space they deserve.

This is not the end of the story, however. It is important to note that, as some merchants sank, others rose. Some, like Alli Balogun, were already making their mark but expanded their businesses further after 1900. Others, such as Josiah Doherty, Samuel Pearse, David Taylor, David Akerele, Seidu Jabita Williams, and Philip Henryson Williams, entered business during the testing

133. Denton to Chamberlain, 18 Sept. 1898, C.O. 147/135.

134. I am grateful to Mr R. A. Olowu and H. I. Olowu, Seidu Olowu's sons, and Dr A. O. Olowu, grandson, for information they supplied on 5 Jan. 1962. See also *African Mail*, 2 June and 18 Aug. 1921; *Nigerian Pioneer*, 19 Aug. 1921; *Lagos Weekly Record*, 19 Aug. 1921.

135. Interview with Mr Olagunju Oni, brother of Claudius, Lagos, 26 Nov. 1961; *Lagos Daily News*, 11 Feb. 1932; *Nigerian Daily Times*, 11 Feb. 1932.

136. I am grateful to Mr N. A. Olukolu and Madame N. S. Olukolu, son and daughter of Fasheke, for helping to reconstruct their father's career: interview, Lagos, 13 Jan. 1962. Court records for the 1890s attest to his success.

1890s and survived to become prominent figures after the turn of the century. These are just a few examples of a larger group of Lagos entrepreneurs who became successful after 1900, despite the onset of colonial rule. Selected examples, chosen to illustrate the scale and the range of the businesses founded by Lagosians, appear in the chapters that follow.

An instructive way of assessing the diverse record of African merchants during the last twenty years of the century is to compare it with the performance of the expatriate firms in Lagos during the same period. It is telling to discover that only two companies lasted the course and remained sound. The leading firms in the port, G. L. Gaiser (1869) and Witt & Busch (1876), retained their positions throughout the period, helped by their dominance of the booming trade in palm kernels. The record of the British firms, which accounted for the great majority of the European firms, was far less impressive. Lagos Stores was a rare survivor that began in 1882 as T. E. Tomlinson, became Lagos Ready Money Stores in 1889, and acquired the name Lagos Stores & Tomlinson in 1894, when it absorbed Tomlinson's business. In 1898, the firm had not paid a dividend since 1893 and was reported to be losing money every year, despite increasing its turnover.[137] Lagos Stores struggled on and achieved better results after the turn of the century.[138]

British firms suffered, as did African merchants, from increased competition and falling profits. Banner Bros., which established its business in Lagos in 1853, ceased trading in 1887. Swanzy's closed their business in 1896.[139] Henry Dunkley arrived in 1873 and was taken over in 1881 by a newcomer, Lagos Warehouse Company, which in 1891 paid no less than 23 per cent of the entire customs revenues of the colony, but was wound up in 1898 and absorbed by John Holt in the following year.[140] The firm conducted a large business, but its profits fell consistently during the decade, mainly because it was slow to adjust to changing trading conditions.[141] Hutton and Osborne failed in 1896 following heavy losses on shipments of produce.[142] J. D. Fairley started in 1882, left Lagos in 1892, while keeping an agent there, and closed the business in 1899, having lost money dealing in produce. Charles McIver, founded in 1875, invested heavily in rubber and was bankrupt in 1900, when the boom ended.[143] Radcliffe Son & Durant and H. B.W. Russell failed in the

137. Isaac B. Williams to I. T. Palmer, 26 Nov. 1898, IBWP; evidence of M. Brown enc. in Denton to Chamberlain, 4 June 1898, C.O. 147/133.

138. C. A. Birtwistle to Acting Col. Sec. Lagos, 8 May 1902, enc. in MacGregor to Chamberlain, 7 July 1903, C.O. 147/166.

139. *Lagos Standard*, 5 Aug. 1896.

140. *Lagos Reporter*, 26 Sept. 1898; *Lagos Weekly Record*, 15 July 1899.

141. Evidence of J. Bradley, enc. in Denton to Chamberlain, 4 June 1898, C.O. 147/133.

142. Evidence of F. G. Osborne, enc. in Denton to Chamberlain, 4 June 1898, C.O. 147/133.

143. Holt to Gardner, 31 July 1900, HP 26/3a.

same year, though the latter firm was resuscitated with outside help.[144] The partnership of Holt & Welsh, which was formed in 1887, was dissolved in 1897, owing John Holt & Co. £53,000.[145] It was this failure that prompted Holt to set up his own business in Lagos in 1899. Welsh's correspondence with Holt, which began in the late 1880s, is a persuasive record of the grinding effort merchants made to stay afloat in adverse circumstances.[146]

The two leading French firms also failed to last until the end of the century. Régis Aîné, which arrived in Lagos in 1854, sold its property to the colonial government, alleging that it had been affected by competition from African merchants, and left Lagos in 1894.[147] Cyprian Fabre, founded in 1866, was badly managed, lost money, and sold its premises to the government in 1897.[148] Even the German firms were not immune to the pressure of the times. Voigt Schabert took over Julius Escherich in 1880 and was itself taken over in 1889 by M. Konigsdorfer & Co., which, in turn, had disappeared by the end of the century.

It is evident that African and expatriate firms had broadly similar experiences of success, failure, and renewal during the period under review. The exact rates of survival and failure cannot be calculated precisely because African firms were part of a large but unquantifiable pool, whereas the number of expatriate firms is known with some accuracy. However, the evidence does allow one important conclusion to be drawn: the structure of African businesses was not a cause of the difficulties they faced at the close of the century. African merchants managed businesses characterised by sole ownership that had been put in place in the 1850s and 1860s. Capital resources were accumulated from past profits; credit was advanced on the security of landed property, which had either been acquired as a crown grant or bought from business profits. Sole ownership did not place African merchants at a relative disadvantage at this time because most expatriate firms were also run by individuals or partnerships and their survival rate between 1880 and 1900 was no better than that of their African competitors.

The explanation of commercial fortunes, individual cases apart, should focus instead on the circumstances they had in common, namely depressed produce prices, increased competition, and reduced profits. Given that Lagos could not alter world prices, the solution to these problems lay in fresh innovations on the supply side and reduced transaction costs. Reforms in property rights, credit arrangements, and ocean transport had driven the expansion of legitimate commerce from the 1860s. The reduction in transaction costs

144. On Radcliffe, see Richard Blaize to John Holt, 8 Aug. 1900, HP.
145. Articles of Partnership, 1897–99, HP, 1/1.
146. The Holt Papers are now held in the Bodleian Library, Oxford.
147. Moloney to Knutsford, 9 Oct. 1888, C.O. 147/66.
148. Welsh to Holt, 16 March 1888, 18 March 1888, HP.

brought by silver currency and the submarine cable in the 1880s and 1890s, though essential to expansion and efficiency, had the short-term consequence of increasing competition in a difficult market. The invasion of Yorubaland signalled the start of far-reaching political changes, but effective occupation and its accompanying juggernaut, the railway, did not take effect until after 1900. Enterprising Africans were trying to diversify the export economy by experimenting with new crops, but these, too, made their mark only after the turn of the century. Until then, supply-side costs were unchanged and productivity in the export sector remained static.

'Decline' in Context

It has long been established that the closing decades of the nineteenth century saw the end of the mid-Victorian boom and the onset of structural and cyclical problems in the international economy. It is equally well known that the period witnessed the partition and occupation of Africa. This demanding setting provides a favourable basis for the hypothesis that these years also marked the end of what had been a 'Golden Age' for Saro repatriates. The hypothesis is attractive. As far as Saro merchants are concerned, however, the evidence cited to support it is fragmentary and lacks a representative sample of relevant cases. The summary that follows does not claim to supply the missing evidence but only to offer a considered advance on current knowledge.

African merchants undoubtedly increased the value of the trade they conducted with Europe in absolute terms. With regard to the proportion of overseas trade, a cautious conclusion suggests that, in the mid-1880s, local merchants held on to their share of imports and almost certainly increased it. At the same time, they accounted for a reduced share of exports, with the result that their share of total trade experienced some decline relative to their European competitors. Given that African merchants were far from holding a majority position, even during the 1850s, the decline was modest and limited rather than sudden and dramatic. Moloney's data refer to the outset of the period of depression. A firmer judgement needs to consider the position in the early 1900s, when conditions of trade had begun to improve. As no rigorous comparison is available after the one conducted by Moloney, evidence of changing fortunes has to be qualitative and indicative until after the turn of the century.

Fortunately, reliable statements from African and European sources show that BBWA helped African merchants to re-enter the export trade and expand their import businesses after 1894, when it opened its business in Lagos. The evidence is sufficiently plausible to suggest, minimally, that the fortunes of African merchants showed signs of reviving at the close of the century, despite hostile trading conditions. Moreover, a survey of mercantile careers shows that a number of merchants continued to trade successfully during this period and that many failures were the result of mismanagement, bad luck, retirement, and death, as they were in all other business communities. A comparison of African and European business outcomes leads to the striking conclusion that the rate of attrition was very similar. Finally, it is important to note that the decline thesis counts failures without also counting newcomers whose prominence lay in the future. Without this dimension of the subject, the analysis is significantly incomplete.

It is still possible to generalise about the 'Golden Age' of the Saro, providing the statement is phrased to incorporate the complexities identified here. There remains a sense in which the 'Golden Age' was reaching its conclusion in the 1890s. From then on, the Saro progressively lost visibility. The rapid growth of the Lagos population dwarfed their modest numbers; the spread of Islam diluted their predominantly Christian influence; the expansion of the colonial government reduced their value to the authorities; the rise of racism lowered their status and their ease of access to the white elite.[149] Changes within the Saro community reinforced these tendencies. The abandonment of the universal principles that had both guided and united the community obliged them to rethink their role as colonial subjects. The outcome of this process led them to take different directions in the economy, religion, and politics. This trend fused with another. By the 1890s, the first generation of repatriates had mostly passed on and many of their children were ageing. The generation of Saro growing up at the close of the century were obliged to adjust to the new order they saw arising around them. Their worldview, however creative, was inevitably very different from that of their forebears.

The file, however, cannot be closed just yet. The fact that the Saro as a community lost visibility is not to be equated with a loss of entrepreneurial endeavour and achievement. On the contrary, as the next chapters will show, a new generation of Saro led the way in pioneering innovations that had a profound effect on the economy of Lagos and its expanding hinterland throughout the colonial period. Once this dimension of their enterprise is given the recognition it deserves, it will become apparent that judgements about their fortunes need to extend beyond the conventional, and limited, focus on their role in external trade. There is a much larger and more important story to be told.

149. Bickford-Smith, 'The Betrayal of Creole Elites'.

CHAPTER EIGHT

Merchants as Money Lenders

RICHARD BLAIZE AND ISAAC WILLIAMS

Context

It is well known that merchants and various forms of banking go together and have done in all parts of the world since distant times. Historians of pre-colonial Africa have shown that the needs of commerce, especially regional trade, encouraged the development of loans that were issued against securities, such as cattle, crops, and pledges of people, as well as reliance on personal trust. Yet, the relationship between new ways of raising money on the security of land, the consequent accumulation of capital, and the larger history of economic development has yet to be explored. The argument advanced here is that the money lenders of Lagos laid the foundations of a capital market that was impersonal and rested on the solid security provided by freehold land. Inherited business institutions were more efficient in collecting debts through the exercise of moral and physical sanctions than they were at mobilising capital in excess of profits from trade. Lagos merchants were money lenders rather than bankers. They were capitalists who raised money from their own resources, whereas modern banks are intermediaries that mobilise capital subscribed by shareholders and perform additional functions, such as holding money on behalf of customers. Nevertheless, Lagos money lenders acquired property portfolios that were independent of trading profits and enabled them to advance money to third parties who could offer adequate security. It is worth noting that money lenders have often evolved into bankers, which is why the term 'merchant bank' is still current in major financial centres, such as the City of London.

Previous chapters have shown that a business in loans expanded rapidly in Lagos from the 1850s once negotiable property became accepted as security. The current chapter tells the first part of an unwritten story that begins with specialised money lending, continues with the foundation of the National

Bank of Nigeria in 1933, and develops further with the growth of commercial banking after 1945 and the foundation of a stock exchange in Lagos in 1960. In doing so, the chapter also argues that generalisations about changing mercantile fortunes that exclude this dimension of business activities are bound to be incomplete and accordingly may also be misleading. It is apparent that lending and rental businesses underwent considerable development towards the close of the century, when international trade lost some of its attraction, and expanded further after 1900, as population growth met finite land resources. After that, rentiers never looked back.

These themes connect two well-known Lagos merchants: Richard Beale Blaize and Isaac Benjamin Williams, who had much in common as merchants, as Saro, as Egba, as Christians, and as members of the same generation. Blaize and Williams make an appropriate pairing because they both developed an extensive business in loans. New evidence, however, makes it possible to identify distinctive features in their careers. Both were successful merchants, though Blaize was undoubtedly the more eminent when judged by the scale and longevity of his business and estimates of his wealth. Blaize, however, combined trade with money lending, whereas Williams took the decisive step of abandoning commerce in mid-career, when his business was still profitable, to become a full-time financier. The fortuitous survival of some of his private papers makes it possible to trace his evolution from being a merchant to becoming a money lender who also became a rentier drawing an income from property he leased. Both entrepreneurs were active before and after the shock of 1892 and had to adjust to the new order that accompanied the invasion of Yorubaland. Blaize was greatly troubled by the abandonment of the principles of universalism he had grown up with. Williams lived a private life, was less involved with the politics of the day, and, like many others, accommodated himself to the inevitable.

Richard Beale Blaize: Beginnings

Richard Beale Blaize was one of the great figures of nineteenth-century Lagos and one of the most eminent of the Saro merchants. His name was distinctive, too, being the only one of its kind in the town and possibly of French origin.[1] As in so many other cases, however, the family records have been destroyed or

---

1. In his early years, the name was sometimes rendered as 'Blaise'. A possible connection is suggested by a note that a European, one Richard Blaize, opened a 'tavern' in Freetown in the 1820s. Fyfe, *A History of Sierra Leone*, pp. 144–45. The merit of the name for historians is that there is no risk of muddling this family with others, as there is with names such as Williams, Thomas, Cole, and Coker. I am grateful to Richard's two surviving sons, Charles Olayemi and Ernest Olufemi, for candid interviews on 18 Dec. 1961, 28 Jan. 1962, and 2 April 1964.

lost and it is no longer possible to reconstruct the detail that his prominence deserves.[2]

Blaize's father, Ojelabi Olapajuokun, came from Ake, Abeokuta.[3] He was captured by Dahomeyan raiders around 1844 and sold to Portuguese slavers. The ship carrying him across the Atlantic was intercepted by the Royal Navy, and the slaves were taken to Freetown where they were freed, placed in the care of missionaries, and the majority baptised as Christians. Shortly afterwards, Ojelabi married a slave who had been on the same ship and came from Igbore, Abeokuta. Her original name has been lost but on being baptised she took the name Maria, while Ojelabi became John Blaize. Their only son was born in Freetown on 22 November 1845 and christened Richard Beale Blaize, though his parents added the Yoruba name, Olamilege. Little more is known about John and Maria, except that they spent the rest of their lives in Freetown and that John was a moderately successful trader who died in 1881. Richard received an elementary education in Freetown at a school sponsored by the Church Missionary Society and was then apprenticed as a compositor to Alexander Harleston, a newspaper proprietor who had previously held the post of official Government Printer.

In 1862, at the age of seventeen, Richard Blaize made the first of two important decisions.[4] He decided to leave Freetown and seek his fortune in Lagos, joining other newcomers who hoped to make their way under the protection of the new colonial government. Shortly after his arrival, he was engaged as a printer by Robert Campbell, the owner and editor of the *Anglo-African*, the first newspaper to be published in the town.[5] In 1863, Blaize left the paper to join the newly established government printing press, where he rose to become Head Printer, a post he held for ten years. In 1865, he was awarded the silver medal at the Sierra Leone Industrial Exhibition for the best printing work in British West Africa.[6] Circumstances favoured Blaize because technical skills were in short supply. Success, however, depended on ability and commitment, and Blaize had already demonstrated that he possessed both qualities.

2. Information provided by Charles Olayemi Blaize, Richard's eldest surviving son, 2 April 1964. Richard Blaize's papers passed into the possession of Mrs Charlotte Obasa, the eldest surviving child, and were destroyed on her instructions after her death in 1952.

3. Interview with Charles O. Blaize, 18 Dec. 1961; Denton to Chamberlain, 24 Nov. 1896, C.O. 147/107. Blaize's wife, Emily, as well as his mother, were both Egba. The obituary notice in the *Lagos Weekly Record*, 24 Sept. 1904, is puzzling because it stated that Blaize's father was a member of the Olapini clan of Oke Apini, Oyo. It is possible to see how these accounts could be reconciled but there is no means now of doing so.

4. Blaize interview with the *Liverpool Courier*, reported in the *Lagos Standard*, 27 Oct. 1897.

5. *Anglo-African*, 26 Aug. 1865. See also Echeruo, *Victorian Lagos*, pp. 3–4.

6. *Lagos Standard*, 28 Sept. 1904.

FIGURE 8.1. Richard Beale Blaize. Copied by Paramount Photographers, with permission of Charles Olufemi Blaize (son).

Blaize made his second big decision in 1873, when he left his post with the government and entered commerce.[7] While working as a printer, and with government approval, he had begun to sell a limited number of imported consumer goods on a part-time basis.[8] By 1873, he had saved £20, which encouraged him to venture fully into the world of commercial risk. He started by opening a store in Breadfruit Street, near the main centres on the Marina and Broad Street, which became his home. It was common practice among merchants and many brokers to combine the two functions: a shop and store on the ground floor and living accommodation above. Only the grandest merchants could afford to separate the two.

At first, Blaize concentrated on retailing a variety of imported goods, such as textiles, haberdashery, hardware, tobacco, and a novelty of the time—tinned provisions. The only staple import he did not stock was liquor, which he refused to sell as a matter of principle. Textiles were the core of the business and Blaize soon won a reputation as a supplier of rich cloths, such as damasks, and less luxurious lines, such as everyday cottons. His shrewdness in copying indigenous designs and having them printed in Manchester appears to have given him a competitive edge over his numerous rivals. His inventiveness may have been guided by his training as a printer, which suggested technical possibilities that others did not see. By the close of the 1870s, he was placing regular orders with suppliers in Manchester and had added wholesaling functions to his retail business. During the first half of the 1880s, he was ranked second (behind Williams Bros.) on Governor Moloney's list of African importers.[9] Moreover, the value of his imports increased from 1881 to 1885, as indicated by his payments of duty on imports, which rose from £71 in 1881 to £1,417 in 1885. Most of the other ten leading merchants struggled to maintain their level of imports during this period; some were in evident decline.

By about 1880, Blaize had also entered the export trade, handling cotton, palm oil, and palm kernels. He acted both as a broker, buying from itinerant traders and selling to firms who exported directly to Europe, and as a direct exporter himself. By this time, he had become an important figure in Lagos commerce. He owned shops in Victoria Road and Davies Street as well as on

7. The obituary in the *Lagos Weekly Record*, 24 Sept. 1904, gives the date as 1875. However, the Lands Office records show that Blaize recorded his occupation in 1873 as 'trader', having given it in 1866 as 'printer'. See LLOR 4/71, 1866. By 1876 he was referring to himself as a 'merchant'. In following this evidence, I have also adjusted the date for the time he spent as Head Printer (noted in the preceding paragraph) from twelve to ten years.

8. Blaize to Glover, 19 Aug. 1869, enc. in Glover to Kimberley, 11 Feb. 1870, C.O. 147/17. Blaize reported that he was earning 'very little' from his trade activities. The colonial government allowed African employees in certain positions to supplement their salaries by undertaking a limited amount of outside work.

9. Moloney to Granville, 19 April 1886, C.O. 147/55. Moloney's list, which ranked merchants according to the duty paid on imports, is discussed in chapter 7 above.

the Marina, employed clerks and labourers, and had become an acknowledged public figure.[10] When the first Lagos Chamber of Commerce was founded in 1888, Blaize was one of four African merchants who were invited to become members.[11] Two years earlier, he had moved from his modest premises in Breadfruit Street to a prime site on the Marina, where, at the substantial cost of £4,500, he built a three-storeyed house containing a shop with two show-rooms and extensive residential accommodation.[12] In tribute both to the origins of his career and to his continuing interest in the printed word, he named the new building Caxton House. The opening ceremony, which took place in the presence of the governor and the educated elite of the town, was a major event. Blaize had arrived, and the solidity of his new house symbolised his expectation that he would remain.

Remain he did, despite the increasingly difficult trading conditions at the close of the century. In 1888, Thomas Welsh, who was in partnership with John Holt and lived next door to Caxton House, reported that 'Blaize seems to do a big cash trade; He has a landau and a pair of greys, with which he drives out occasionally, footman and coachman on the box'.[13] Welsh also reported that it was difficult for him to compete with Blaize, who not only imported directly from England but also sold cotton goods at a price he could not match.[14] Blaize remained in the export trade during the 1880s, supplying palm kernels to Gaiser and sending palm oil to Liverpool. Kernel prices held up much better than oil prices but Blaize, like others, was buffeted by the deterioration of the oil market. In 1888, Welsh observed that 'if old Blaize had held on to his oil in store then he would not have come out so badly. His agents acted up to their judgement and if by storing they had made money for him he would not have objected'.[15] In the absence of a futures market, Blaize and other produce exporters were still dependent on prices at the time of delivery. The submarine cable reduced risk by providing information at the point of purchase in Lagos, but uncertainty remained until shipments reached their destination.

Blaize continued to trade profitably until his death in 1904. It is unclear if he exported produce beyond the 1880s, but he remained 'a large importer' of cotton goods in the mid-1890s.[16] In celebration of his fiftieth birthday in 1895, he donated a total of £2,200, divided between the Lagos Native Pastorate

10. Blaize entered Payne's list of 'Principal English Commercial Houses' in 1876. Payne, *Payne's Lagos*.

11. Hopkins, 'The Lagos Chamber of Commerce'.

12. *Lagos Observer*, 18 Sept. and 2 Oct. 1886; *Eagle & Lagos Critic*, 25 Sept. 1886; *Lagos Standard*, 27 March 1895.

13. Welsh to Holt, 23 Feb. 1888, HP, 27/2.

14. Welsh to Holt, 1 May 1888, 3 May 1888, HP, 27/2.

15. Welsh to Holt, 14 Dec. 1888, HP, 26/3a.

16. *Lagos Standard*, 20 March 1895.

FIGURE 8.2. Caxton House, 54 Marina (1886) in 1964. Paramount Photographers Lagos.

Mission (£1,000), a new technical department to be attached to the Lagos Grammar School (£1,000), the Wesleyan Missionary Society (£100), and the Society's support for the poor (£100).[17] In 1896, Acting Governor Denton reported that Blaize's assets stood at around £150,000, and Governor Carter added that this figure made him 'undoubtedly the wealthiest native merchant in Lagos'.[18] In 1900, Sir Alfred Jones, the shipping magnate, who knew affluence well, referred to Blaize as being 'a man of very considerable wealth', a judgement that the *Lagos Standard* endorsed, calling him 'one of the wealthiest of the native merchants here today'.[19] In 1902, when the colonial

17. *Lagos Standard*, 27 Nov. 1895.

18. Denton to Chamberlain, 24 Nov. 1896, C.O. 147/107; Carter to C.O., 30 Dec. 1896, C.O. 147/110.

19. *Lagos Standard*, 8 Aug. 1900.

government was considering the prospects of raising a loan locally to fund railway-building, Governor MacGregor consulted Blaize because he was 'the wealthiest man in this country' and any loan would depend largely on the amount he would be prepared to subscribe.[20]

Diversification: Property and Money Lending

In 1897, Blaize confirmed what other evidence suggests, namely that the biggest commercial profits were made during the early years of the colony. Reflecting on the beginning of his career, Blaize observed: 'I could make from 50 to 80 per cent, and I have even gone as far as 150 per cent, but now it is difficult to make 5 per cent. Competition practically did not exist in those days'.[21] He also realised that African merchants would have to adapt their businesses and had plans for forming an African business combine, which was intended to provide serious competition for the European houses. He shared with James Davies an interest in modern technology and was keen to provide the new generation with opportunities to learn the skills that were necessary for participating in the industrial world. The scheme for organising a commercial combine was too ambitious for its time, but Blaize gave generously in founding the first technical training school in Nigeria.

Blaize was also concerned to diversify his own interests and started a bank (the Marina Bank) in 1882.[22] Although the bank operated only briefly, Blaize provided some informal banking functions by lending money on the security of property. He was not alone in extending his business activities in this way: all successful merchants bought and sold property and a small number, such as Daniel Taiwo, James Thomas, and James Cole, conducted a regular business in loans. Since Blaize was probably the most active of this first generation of merchant-financiers, it is worth taking a closer look at the operation of this branch of his business. Although there is no way of judging the relative importance of trade and property to Blaize's prosperity, his standing as a merchant was widely attested, though with few precise details, whereas his property business was never mentioned by officials or newspapers. Nevertheless, despite the absence of private papers, far more information about his property transactions than about his trading activities has survived because the former are preserved in the Lagos Lands Office and Supreme Court records.

A total of forty-four transactions were recorded in Blaize's name between 1866, when his first official entry appeared, and 1903, when the last one was

20. MacGregor to Chamberlain, 21 March 1902, C.O. 147/160.

21. Blaize interview with the *Liverpool Courier*, reported in the *Lagos Standard*, 27 Oct. 1897.

22. *Lagos Times*, 9 Nov. 1881.

made.[23] Blaize may have conducted other property deals outside the official records, but it is unlikely that these, assuming they existed, were substantial. Blaize confined nearly all of his agreements concerning land to crown grants because they provided the best guarantee of legal tenure. His transactions were spread unevenly over thirty-seven years. The entries were few and modest during the early years when his resources were limited. He made just two purchases and one sale from 1866 to 1876, all for sums ranging from £17 to £175 and none in prime sites.[24] Nevertheless, they confirm that property was being bought and sold in the vicinity of the Marina and Broad Street at an early date and that the parties involved were not confined to Big Men.[25]

The remaining forty-one transactions took place between 1878 and 1903 and were on a much larger scale. Eleven of these were purchases, five were sales, and twenty-five were loans. There was also one gift (of a house in Breadfruit Street), which Blaize made to his daughter, Charlotte, on the occasion of her marriage in 1902.[26] Most acquisitions occurred during the first half of the 1880s, which suggests that Blaize was funding his purchases from trading profits rather than from his previous (limited) property deals. In 1878, he bought a prime site on the Marina for £700 and two more properties in 1882, one in Breadfruit Street for £600, the other in Tinubu Street for £550.[27] A few smaller purchases of between £100 and £200 also appear, but these were mostly disposals of property from debtors in default.[28] It is hard to assess the motives behind the five sales, except to say that they were unforced decisions that appear to have been based on estimates of the likely return to holding and selling stock. Blaize's most valuable disposal was a site in Olowogbowo, which he sold to Lagos Stores in 1899 for £400.[29] Two others, in Broad Street, fetched £375 and £150 in 1896, and one in Garber Street was sold at auction for £350 the following year.[30]

Precise comparisons of prices during the whole period are beyond reach, but it is clear that Blaize's transactions were an accurate reflection of the general increase in property values during the second half of the century. In the absence of price inflation, the explanation has to lie in the expansion of trade and population, which pushed up the value of prime sites, while also

23. Most of the evidence that follows is drawn from the Lagos Lands Office records. I am most grateful to Kristin Mann, who has generously allowed me to supplement my research with her own notes on these records.

24. LLOR, 4/71, 1866; 17/30, 1873; 23/33, 1876.

25. See above, chapter 3.

26. LLOR, 39/32, 1901.

27. LLOR, 33, pp. 356, 1878; 35, pp. 105, 1882; 35, pp. 111, 1882.

28. For example, LLOR, 31, pp. 268, 1880; 35, pp. 192, 1885; 29/2, 1896.

29. LLOR, 36/42, 1899.

30. LLOR, 28/73, 1896; 29/11, 1896; 29/107, 1897.

expanding the property market beyond them. In Lagos, as elsewhere, location was everything.

The most striking feature of the Lands Office records is the evidence they provide about Blaize's involvement in the loans market. No fewer than twenty-five of his forty-one transactions after 1878 were loans. They began in 1879, when he advanced £700 to Thomas F. Cole, also a Lagos merchant, on the security of property in Breadfruit Street, and £600 to one Sojeh that was secured by a crown grant on land in Olowogbowo.[31] The largest advance Blaize made was in 1893, when he loaned £2,500 to the troubled merchant, Jacob Leigh, guaranteed by his property on the Marina.[32] Most loans, however, were for smaller amounts, ranging from £150 to £500. Interest rates remained at 5–10 per cent per year throughout the period, depending on the length of the loan and Blaize's estimate of the risk attached to his debtors, though he occasionally varied the term to suit special cases.[33] Jacob Leigh, who was a friend-in-need, was given exceptional terms in 1894, when he borrowed £2,500 at 5 per cent and was allowed until 1901 to repay the debt.[34] The usual repayment period was one year or occasionally, two. Most debtors met the repayment date, though two formerly eminent merchants, Jacob Leigh and Zachariah Williams, were unable to extricate themselves from large debts incurred through business difficulties.

It appears that most credit was granted to assist business expansion, though some was applied to repay other outstanding debts, and the smaller sums may also have been used to fund personal expenditure. It is interesting to find that just one transaction involved leasing a property. This contract was made in 1895 between Blaize and the expatriate firm of F. & A. Swanzy, which leased premises in Tinubu Street for three years at an annual rent of £84.[35]

Success in commerce made Blaize one of the most important figures in Lagos during the last quarter of the nineteenth century. His public activities and those of his family, especially his two daughters, were given prominent notice in the newspapers that appeared in the 1880s and 1890s. He was on close terms with successive governors of the colony. When he visited Sierra Leone and England, which he did on numerous occasions, he moved in circles that extended to the royal family. Wealth enabled him to pursue a range of interests that extended well beyond business matters, notably the Church, the press, and politics. No interest, however, was greater than his family, which stood at the centre of his life and his hopes for the future.

31. LLOR, 29/33, 1879; 29/47, 1879.
32. LLOR, 20/32, 1893.
33. See A. W. Thomas, v. Antonio Oke & Anor., LSCR, Civ. 36, 1905.
34. LLOR, 29/33, 1879. This is the loan referred to in n.31.
35. LLOR, 27/29, 1895.

A Family Man

Richard Blaize's family ties illustrate the closeness of the relationships among the Lagos Saro.[36] In 1871, Blaize married Emily Cole, the daughter of Thomas Francis Cole (Daddy Alade), a merchant who made his mark in Sierra Leone before returning to Lagos in 1859.[37] Cole had two daughters: Eleanor married one famous merchant, Zachariah Williams; Emily married another, Richard Blaize. According to one source, Daddy Alade gave his new sons-in-law a good start by providing Zachariah a house in Apongbon and Richard a house in Breadfruit Street.[38] Emily, who was born in 1852, was 'highly educated', having been through schools in England and France, as well as Freetown and Lagos.[39] She was also 'an exemplary Christian who took a prominent part in improving society'. By all accounts, the marriage was a happy one.[40] Although Emily was a committed Wesleyan and Richard an Anglican, each contributed time and money to support both denominations. Their Christian principles also led them to avoid alcohol.

The couple had ten children but only six, two sons and four daughters, survived to adulthood.[41] Another measure of Blaize's wealth, as well as an insight into his and his wife's ambitions, is provided by the fact that all six children were educated in England as well as in Lagos, and some stayed abroad for several years. Blaize had received only an elementary education, but he was a thoughtful man who took care to educate himself, as far as his busy life allowed. He was a regular visitor to England and was often accompanied by Emily. On one such visit, undertaken in 1895 'for the benefit of her health', she became ill and died at the early age of forty-three.[42] Blaize never remarried.

Philanthropy was an expression of the couple's Christian values, which held that moral and material progress were essential companions. It is impossible now to aggregate their numerous contributions, but some examples will give an indication of the range of their interests. Blaize contributed 'freely' to the construction of St. Paul's Church, Breadfruit, which was completed in 1880, and to

36. The definitive account of this subject is Kristin Mann's detailed study, *Marrying Well*.

37. Thomas F. Cole (c.1812–1890) settled in Oke Olowogbowo (on the site now known as 4 Alade Lane). He came from Obo in Ekiti country. He was a keen Wesleyan. He and his wife, Sally, had two daughters and a son (Rotimi Cole, who changed his name to Alade), who studied in London and became a lawyer. *Lagos Weekly Times*, 12 July 1890; 20 Sept. 1890. I am also grateful to Samuel Alade (formerly Cole), a nephew of Thomas Cole, for providing information about the history of the family. Interview, 29 Jan. 1962.

38. Information from Samuel Alade, 29 Jan. 1962.

39. Deniga, *African Leaders*, Vol. 1, pp. 4–5; see also *Lagos Standard*, 10 Jan 1895.

40. Mann, *Marrying Well*, p. 83.

41. I am again grateful to Charles Olayemi Blaize for information relating to the family tree. See n.1 above.

42. *Lagos Standard*, 10 Jan. 1906; *Lagos Weekly Record*, 24 Aug. 1895.

the Glover Memorial Hall, which was opened in 1887. Emily was noted for her work in assisting the poorer members of the Wesleyan congregation. After her death in 1895, Blaize commemorated her memory by donating £100 to extend the commitment she had made. In the same year, he donated £2,000 to the CMS to support the expansion of the native pastorate.[43] Two years later, he contributed £500 to start a technical school at Abeokuta.[44] Like his wife, Blaize spent time as well as money on good causes. In 1899, for example, he took two young children, recently freed from slavery, into his care.[45] Blaize also looked to the wider world as a source of progress. He donated £500 to the new Liverpool School of Tropical Diseases in 1900, gave 'generous' support to the Royal African Society at the time of its foundation in 1901, and presented £250 to the British Cotton Growing Association in the following year.[46]

Newspapers and Politics

Two other large and related interests occupied Blaize's attention: newspapers and politics. Both were expressions of his understanding of 'progress' and how it should be achieved. At first sight, his position might seem to be contradictory, for he was both an imperialist and an African patriot. At the time, however, it was common across the empire for the two to exist in combination. An obituary, published by the Royal African Society in 1904, commented that he was 'a strong imperialist', believing that the empire was the best means of 'knitting together . . . the races of the world in a league of peace and commerce', but equally an advocate of advertising the 'character, capabilities and aspirations of the negro'.[47] Although the comparison may not readily come to mind, Blaize's stance was very similar to that of Jan Christian Smuts, who was both an imperialist in believing that the British Empire was a force for world progress, and an Afrikaner nationalist, who held that the process should be co-operative and respectful of the rights of the colonised. Smuts was thinking primarily of white settlers, but Blaize and many others across the empire thought that the principle should be applied irrespective of race, colour, or creed. He became increasingly critical of the way policy was being implemented, especially after the second 'shock' of 1892, when Britain shifted from co-operation to coercion in bringing Yorubaland under effective control.

Although Blaize left printing for commerce, he remained interested in the press all his life. In 1878, he bought a commercial printing press, and two years

43. CMS Archives, Y1/7, No.7, 1895.

44. *Lagos Standard*, 27 Oct. 1897 and 8 Aug. 1900.

45. Badadiv (Records of the Badagri Divisional Office, 1865–1900), 4/1, 2 Aug. 1899.

46. *Royal African Society Journal*, 4 (1904), pp. 149–50; *Lagos Standard*, 1 Aug. 1900; *Journal of the African Society*, 2 (1902), p. 102. Blaize was also a member of the Council of the RAS.

47. *Royal African Society Journal*, 4 (1904), pp. 149–50.

later produced a pioneering newspaper, the *Lagos Times & Gold Coast Colony Advertiser*. The paper appeared fortnightly until 1883, when Blaize decided that he could no longer support the experiment. The paper lost money, but this was unsurprising because all Lagos newspapers were unprofitable at this time. The problem in this case was that the editor, John Payne Jackson, an immigrant from Liberia and a former book-keeper in Blaize's shop, combined considerable talent with an equally impressive capacity for alcohol.[48] Although Blaize was a teetotaller, his main objection to Jackson was less on personal grounds and more because it led the business to be conspicuously and disastrously mismanaged.[49] The paper was relaunched briefly as the *Weekly Times* in 1890, still under Jackson's editorship, but hope could not overcome experience and the venture soon closed. In 1891, Jackson parted from Blaize and launched the *Lagos Weekly Record*, the paper that was to make his name.[50] Blaize was reluctant to involve himself in further newspaper ventures, which he found 'too arduous', though he did become the principal backer of the *Echo*, which appeared in 1894 and disappeared soon afterwards.[51]

Evidently, Blaize did not enter the newspaper business to make money. Rather, as one commentator observed, he regarded newspapers as a means of advancing what he saw as his 'racial and religious duty'.[52] His opposition to Governor Gilbert Carter's assertive actions and other infringements of 'native rights' encouraged him to advocate alternatives that would allow Africans greater participation in the government of the colony and ensure that officials were accountable to those they ruled. This was radical thinking for its time, and it placed Blaize on a route that led to Home Rule and ultimately to independence. Blaize saw the process as one of evolution rather than revolution and supported policies that favoured co-operation over coercion. Although his relations with Carter were strained, he established close ties with his successor but one, William MacGregor, whose attitude and policies, particularly his advocacy of what was to become known as indirect rule, were close to Blaize's own views.[53] It was Blaize who recommended Eshugbayi, a prospective candidate, to MacGregor, who recognised him as *Oba* in 1901.[54] Blaize's assessment of the British presence extended beyond the political arena. Like

48. Omu, 'Journalism'. More generally, see Sawada, 'The Educated Elite'.

49. *Lagos Times*, 20 Dec. 1890.

50. It is to Jackson's great credit that, despite the failure of the partnership, he wrote a generous appraisal of Blaize in the *Lagos Weekly Record*, 24 Sept. 1904.

51. *Lagos Weekly Record*, 24 Sept. 1904.

52. *Lagos Standard*, 27 Oct. 1897.

53. Blaize to Holt, 8 Aug. 1900, HP 22/1. MacGregor was a remarkable man. If what is now seen as being old-fashioned imperial history ever returns to favour, he would be an excellent subject for a biography.

54. Cole, *Modern and Traditional*, p. 183. Cause and consequence were not entirely fused, as Cole points out, p. 270, n.23.

other Saro Christians, he was concerned about the rapid spread of Islam and censured the Anglican Church, to which he belonged, for failing to appoint and promote sufficient numbers of African clergy.[55]

Blaize's efforts to find a middle way between colonial rule and African rights explain why he both welcomed and criticised the British presence in Lagos and Yorubaland. His positive view of the British Empire encouraged him to support the effort to forestall the French in 1888, when it was thought that they had designs on Abeokuta.[56] The defects of imperial rule led him to deplore Britain's response to the Asante revolt of 1900, which the governor of the Gold Coast had provoked, and to speak out against the treatment suffered by Africans in the Congo.[57] Similarly, as an Egba patriot he denounced the colonial government's interference in Egba affairs and in 1903, was a leading figure in the vocal opposition to the abolition of internal tolls, which were an important component of state sovereignty.[58] At the same time, Blaize helped the colonial government to find solutions to sensitive issues, such as the allocation of land for the railway at Abeokuta, where he thought that the outcome would be beneficial. Governor MacGregor, who had a high opinion of Blaize, reported that he had received 'loyal and useful assistance' in the matter.[59] When the Alake Bridge was opened in Abeokuta in 1903, Blaize accompanied MacGregor in celebrating the occasion, as he did at other major events involving the governor and the *Alake*.[60]

The administration recognised Blaize's value as an intermediary, but was reluctant to bestow political favours on him. He was never appointed to the Legislative Council, though his name was put forward and it was agreed that he was well qualified for the position. In recommending him for the appointment in 1896, Acting Governor Denton wrote that he was a 'man of independent spirit and has considerable intelligence. He takes a keen interest in all matters connected with the affairs of his country and is possessed of large means'.[61] The Colonial Office noted that 'the independent spirit might prove embarrassing' and consulted Governor Carter, who was on leave in England.[62] Carter did not like the idea, commenting that Blaize's independent spirit had 'in times past taken the form of hostility to the Government'.[63] After listing examples, Carter concluded that 'more recently he has been the main support of a scurrilous

55. *Lagos Standard*, 19 Jan. 1898.

56. Moloney to Knutsford, 12 May 1888, C.O. 806/288.

57. *Lagos Standard*, 8 Aug. 1900; 29 Sept. 1904. Blaize knew E. D. Morel and supported his views. Blaize to Holt, 8 Aug. 1900, HP 22/1.

58. *Lagos Weekly Record*, 4 July 1903. Blaize resigned from the Lagos Chamber of Commerce over the issue. On this subject generally, see Falola, 'The Yoruba Toll System'.

59. MacGregor to C.O., 9 June 1903, C.O. 147/166.

60. *Lagos Weekly Record*, 22 August 1903; *Lagos Standard*, 24 Oct. 1900.

61. Denton to Chamberlain, 24 Nov. 1896, C.O. 147/107.

62. C.O. minute, 23 Dec. 1896, on Denton to Chamberlain, 24 Nov. 1896, C.O. 147/107.

63. Carter to C.O., 30 Dec. 1896, C.O. 147/110.

newspaper known as the *Echo*. To confirm his condemnation, Carter added that Blaize 'possesses . . . a stammer of so pronounced a character that it is painful to converse with him'. This was a low blow. Blaize did indeed have a stammer, but it did not prevent him from being an effective intermediary, from appearing on various public platforms, such as the Commission on Trade in 1898, or from 'conversing' with notables such as Sir Alfred Jones, E. D. Morel, and Mary Kingsley.[64] The Colonial Office, however, had heard enough: the nomination was dropped.

Blaize took a different view of the Legislative Council, claiming that it was 'a farce and unofficials are ciphers', adding that he had declined the invitation 'several times'.[65] He thought that Denton and MacGregor were doing their best to govern 'on the right lines' but were hampered by the inherently 'autocratic' nature of the colonial system.[66] Governor MacGregor, who was an enlightened administrator, knew Blaize well, thought highly of him, and probably considered him for the Legislative Council.[67] By the turn of the century, however, Blaize had ruled himself out by both his outspoken comments and his long absences from the colony.

During the closing years of his life, Blaize became increasingly dissatisfied with his formulation of a middle path though colonial rule. Fortuitously, his search for a route to the future gained clarity and impetus from Edward Blyden's presence in Lagos. Blyden visited Lagos on several occasions between 1891 and 1894 and spent a year there in 1896–1897 as the government's Agent for Native Affairs.[68] Blyden's concept of the unity of the African race (as he called it) and his claims regarding the pre-colonial achievements of Africans resonated with many thoughtful Saro, including Blaize, as did his belief that European education had a distorting influence on African minds. In 1897, Blaize gave a notably frank interview with the *Liverpool Courier* that revealed the extent to which his vision for Africa had evolved.

> Civilization has its advantages and disadvantages, but on the coast when weighed in the balance it is always disadvantageous to the African race. It is easier to copy the vices than the virtues of civilization. Our people in their first passion for everything European imitated the European style of dress, mode of living and general habits. These were

64. Jones and Blaize got on particularly well and met regularly during Blaize's frequent visits to England. In 1900, Blaize reported that he was suffering from indigestion, having had dinner with Jones at his club and at the Cafe Royal the previous evening! Blaize to Holt, 8 Aug. 1900, HP 22/1.

65. *Lagos Standard*, 8 Aug. 1900.

66. *Lagos Standard*, 8 Aug. 1900.

67. For MacGregor's appreciation of Blaize's help, see MacGregor to Chamberlain, 22 May 1902, C.O. 147/161, and MacGregor to Chamberlain, 9 June 1903, C.O. 147/166.

68. There is a substantial literature on Edward Wilmot Blyden (1832–1912), though much of it is scattered in journal articles. The pioneering modern study is Lynch, *Edward Wilmot Blyden*.

not suitable for us. It would have been far wiser if we had blended the two—retained so much of our old customs as was suitable to our climate and physique, and utilized anything in your methods that would have been beneficial to us. I am glad, however, to notice signs of a change for the better. Instead of becoming Europeanised Africans we want to become native civilized Africans.[69]

Coming from such an established public figure, Blaize's outspoken remarks created a 'great sensation' in Lagos.[70] Although the response was generally favourable, Herbert Tugwell, the Anglican bishop and an expatriate, whose middle name might well have been 'Stolid', denounced Blaize from the pulpit of Christchurch. His reaction illustrated the extent to which expatriates and Africans, including Saro, had drifted apart, because Blaize was a loyal Anglican who thought that the CMS was failing in its duty of spreading Christianity. The dispute died down, but did not disappear. Blaize's assessment not only reveals a good deal about the evolution of his own values and aspirations but also stands as a proxy for the dilemma the Saro faced at the close of the century. The way forward, as we shall see, took several routes. Blaize, however, did not have time to find a practical compromise that would meet his own requirements because he died in 1904 at the age of fifty-nine. Although he had been suffering from ill health for some years, his demise came suddenly. He was taken ill in September with acute entero-colitis, underwent an operation, but died a few days after leaving hospital. It was said by those who knew him that, had he lived much longer, he would either have left Africa and retired to England, or given up his cosmopolitan life in Lagos and moved to Abeokuta, his parents' hometown.[71]

Blaize's Legacy

Blaize's estate was valued at 'under £60,000'.[72] His will, dated 1904, instructed his executors to sell the stock in his shop and warehouse and close the business. The proceeds and the residue of the estate were to be divided between an investment in British government securities (primarily consols) and an account with London & Westminster Bank with the aim of accumulating capital that could be 'handed down from generation to generation'. Caxton House was to be leased and the family house relocated in Tinubu Street. Blaize made a number of specific bequests, among them £500 to the Princess Christian

69. Reproduced in the *Lagos Standard*, 27 Oct. 1897. The inconsistent use of the letters 'z' and 's' is in the original.

70. *Lagos Standard*, 19 Jan. 1898, 27 Oct. 1898.

71. *Lagos Weekly Record*, 24 Sept. 1904. Confirmed by his son, Charles Olayemi Blaize, who believed that his father would have gone to England. Interview, 18 Dec. 1961.

72. LAP (Letters of Probate and Administration), II, pp. 341–46.

Hospital in Freetown, £150 to the Royal African Society, and £100 to the Aborigines Protection Society.

With regard to his six surviving children, Blaize left an immediate sum of £1,000 to his eldest child, Charlotte Olajumoke (Obasa), and £500 to each of the others. The daughters were already married into prestigious families and were independent. They had all been educated in England and were active in Lagos affairs. Charlotte Obasa (1872–1952) was the most prominent.[73] She was one of the pioneers who introducd the motor car in Nigeria, as well as gaining visibility through her marriage to Orisadipe Obasa, who was both a doctor and political activist.[74] The three other sisters used their education to good effect in promoting schooling for girls and providing training for midwives. Blaize made elaborate plans for his sons. Charles Olayemi was to become an engineer and Ernest Olufemi a doctor who was to devote his career to 'attendance on the sick poor'. Although both sons spent considerable time training in England, neither followed the course prescribed for them.[75] The aspirations of parents are often transmitted to their children and often have unintended consequences.

Blaize also bequeathed £3,000 (to supplement the £500 he had given in 1897) to establish an institute at Abeokuta to train young men in skilled crafts. The location in Egba territory rather than in Lagos was significant. Blaize was an Egba patriot who was keen to help the Egba retain their precarious independence. The foundation, which became known as the Blaize Memorial Institute, was opened by Sir Walter Egerton, the Governor of Southern Nigeria, in April 1908.[76] Work had begun in the previous year, when six apprentices had been accepted. By 1910, there were twenty apprentices, each serving a term of four years and receiving training in carpentry and other crafts. At the end of their training, they were given a set of tools worth £6, and were then free to seek employment wherever they chose.[77] In 1960, at the close of the colonial period, there were fifty resident apprentices taking courses extending to five years and ending with one of several trade certificates.[78] By then, the Institute and the qualifications it offered were widely recognised and

73. Minor variations on these dates are readily found. I have followed the dates that appear on the tombstone in Ikoyi Cemetery.

74. Charlotte Obasa's innovative bus service is discussed in chapter 11.

75. Caxton House was used by Blaize's daughters for their own business activities and was not leased until 1919, following a review of the estate and Justice A. R. Pennington's judgement that the funds Blaize had allocated in his will, especially those relating to his two sons, were insufficient to carry out the detailed instructions he had given. Judgement in Charles O. Blaize v. Charlotte O. Blaize in Re R. B. Blaize (deceased), LSCR, Civ. 84, 1919.

76. *Southern Nigeria Civil Service List*, 1909, pp. 29–30; *Southern Nigeria Handbook*, 1912, p. 18.

77. *Lagos Weekly Record*, 22 Feb. 1908.

78. I am grateful to Mr G. S. Neil-Dwyer, Superintendent of the Blaize Memorial Institute, Abeokuta, for providing verbal and written information about the Institute. Ibara, Abeokuta, February 1961.

applications for apprenticeships far outweighed the number of places available. In accordance with its innovative origins, the Institute began to diversify its interests during the Second World War and became a well-known producer of high-quality fruit drinks. The Institute remained entirely self-financing and active into the 1970s. It closed not because it had failed but because additional, larger technical training facilities had become available. For half a century, the Institute stood as a monument to the memory of a man whose vision was for an Africa that was both developed and self-supporting.[79]

Other provisions of the will did not survive so well. Caxton House was used by Blaize's daughters for their own business activities and was not leased until 1920, following a review of the will by Justice A. R. Pennington, who found that the funds Blaize had allocated, especially those relating to his two sons, were insufficient to carry out the detailed instructions he had given.[80] The official trustee, acting on behalf of the six surviving children, leased Caxton House for twenty-five years at a rent of £1,375 per annum to Charlotte Obasa, who sublet part of the property to the African Oil Nuts Company for twenty years at £480 per annum, increasing to £600 per annum.[81] In 1928, that part of the property was rented for ten years to K. Chelleram & Sons. After World War II, Caxton House passed to new owners and is currently in the possession of Wema Bank, which took over a small bank in 1969 and is today the largest indigenous bank in Nigeria with more than 150 branches and nearly two thousand employees.

Caxton House has now been replaced by the twenty storeys of Wema Towers, though the number '54' is still emblazoned on the entrance to the building. The current occupants may not know that the original owner was one of the great merchants and financiers of the nineteenth century. Nevertheless, we may guess that Richard Blaize would have been pleased to see that his dilemma about choosing between English and African cultures has found a cosmopolitan solution, and that his commercial legacy has been perpetuated by African entrepreneurs in the era of independence.

Isaac Benjamin Williams: Early Life

Although Isaac Williams was a prominent merchant, he is known to only a handful of specialists, and even then more in name than in detail.[82] He avoided publicity and limited his profile as a public figure. The survival of some of his

79. The Institute deserves to have its history written. Much depends on the fate of its records after it closed. An enquiry should not be arduous and might well be productive.

80. Judgement in Charles O. Blaize v. Charlotte O. Blaize in Re R. B. Blaize (deceased), LSCR, Civ. 84, 1919.

81. LLOR, 0062, 54 Marina. As the text suggests, this was a complex matter that ran on for some years and was reviewed again by the Supreme Court in 1937.

82. I am greatly indebted to Jacob Olumide Williams, Isaac's favourite nephew, for numerous discussions about his uncle held in the first-floor front room of Raymond

papers, however, makes it possible to reconstruct his career with a degree of detail that is unavailable for merchants, such as Richard Blaize and Zachariah Williams, who conducted larger businesses. What emerges is not just the familiar story of a Lagos import merchant, but an insight into a major departure that led to the foundation of a class of rentiers who were to populate the Lagos economy in the twentieth century.

Unfortunately for researchers, there are numerous families in Freetown and Lagos with the family name of Williams. Some are related; some are not. It is sufficient here to note that Isaac Benjamin Williams was unrelated to any of the other well-known families in Lagos with the same family name. He became the most prominent member of his own Williams family, though his younger brother, Jacob Sylvanus Williams (1849–1933), acquired a greater public presence, first as the Anglican pastor of St. Jude's Church in Lagos, then as one of the founders of the African Church in 1901, and later still as Superintendent of its Bethel Church.[83]

Isaac Williams was born in Aberdeen, Sierra Leone, on 28 August 1846.[84] His father, Robert, an Egba from Yorubaland, had been sold as a slave, exported from Lagos, intercepted by a British naval patrol, and delivered to Freetown. There, he was freed, baptised, given an elementary education by Methodist missionaries, and provided with an English surname, which in this case was that of his teacher. In 1851, the family moved to Wilberforce, Sierra Leone, but Isaac's father died shortly afterwards, leaving his widow, Nancy, three sons, and a daughter. In this difficult situation Isaac was placed temporarily in the care of an aunt, who looked after him while he attended King's School in Freetown. A year or so later, Isaac's mother married one John Scott, about whom almost nothing is now known. Evidently, however, this was a moment for reconsidering the family's future because in January 1857, Isaac, his younger brother Jacob, his mother, and his stepfather landed in Lagos, where they joined others who had been tempted to return following the establishment of a British consulate in 1851 and the increasingly successful efforts to stamp out the slave trade.

Once in Lagos, the family settled in the Saro quarter in Olowogbowo, and Isaac resumed his education by attending Olowogbowo Day School until October 1859, when, aged thirteen, he was apprenticed to a local carpenter,

House, where we used to sit in the shade, like Isaac before us, and watch the people in the street pass by. Meetings included: 10 Nov. 1961, 13 Nov. 1961, 24 Nov. 1961, 28 Nov. 1961, 7 Dec. 1961, 2 Feb. 1962.

83. See the indexed entries in Webster, *African Churches*.

84. The biographical information that follows is drawn principally from: Dada Adeshigbin, *Almanack* (Lagos, n.d.); Anon., 'Outline of the Life of I. B. Williams', (Unpublished paper in the possession of Jacob Olumide Williams); Akinsanya, 'Dandies of the 1900s', p. 6; interviews with Jacob O. Williams, Isaac's nephew and oldest surviving relative, Lagos 1961–62.

FIGURE 8.3. Isaac Benjamin Williams. Copied by Paramount Photographers Lagos, with permission of Jacob Olumide Williams (nephew).

J. L. Baptiste, who had premises on the Marina.[85] The early years of Isaac's career remain sketchy and are unlikely now to be amplified. However, it is clear that he started his own business as a carpenter in the late 1860s and was able to buy a property in Martin's Street, which he converted into a workshop. He also began part-time trading, buying small quantities of imported consumer goods and selling them to visiting traders from the hinterland. He did well enough to purchase additional properties in the 1870s in Broad Street and Lower Martin's Street. In retrospect, it is apparent that buying property in the area of Broad Street and the Marina was as close as anyone in Lagos could get to striking oil. At the time, however, the purchase of swampland in a small port with an uncertain future may well have seemed both risky and costly, irrespective of the price. Williams, however, placed a winning bet on the combination of freehold tenure and the stability that followed British rule.

The Import Trade

By the mid-1870s, Isaac decided that his trading venture had expanded to a level that enabled him to give up carpentry and become a full-time businessman.[86] Evidently, he prospered, because he was said to have carried on 'a very large business' in the 1880s and to have joined the ranks of the 'merchant princes' of Lagos, as the commentators of the day called them.[87] He was placed tenth on Moloney's list of leading African importers, which covered the years 1881–1885, but was only just behind James George & Son and James W. Cole, and, like them, was expanding his business during this period.[88]

In 1886, Williams moved a short distance from his Martin's Street workshop to Broad Street, where he built an imposing house, named Raymond House, on the corner with Martin's Street. Raymond House, which was Isaac's home for the rest of his life, was constructed in the fashionable Brazilian style at a cost of about £1,600; the interior was equipped with the latest Victorian furniture, including a piano and sets of crockery inscribed with his initials.[89]

85. The location was well suited to the work, which consisted mainly of boat-building and repair and extended to the construction of piers and minor harbour works.

86. Looking back on his career, Williams gave the date as 1875: Williams to Walkden, 11 April 1904. Another family document specified 1870. Anon, 'Outline of the Life of I. B. Williams'.

87. Denton to Chamberlain, 28 Sept. 1898, C.O. 117/135.

88. Moloney to Granville, 19 April 1886, C.O. 147/55. The amount of customs duty Williams paid from 1881 to 1885 fits quite well with the duty he recorded in his own accounts for the years 1882–1885. The match is imperfect because I have had to calculate his duty on the basis of invoice value plus freight, which produces a higher figure.

89. *Lagos Standard*, 27 March 1895. I have been unable to identify the inspiration for the name. The only (very tenuous) connection I can find is with an American missionary, William Raymond, who was in Freetown in the 1840s (where he died in 1847), and who had good relations with the Wesleyan Methodists. Fyfe, *History of Sierra Leone*, pp. 223, 247.

From the mid-1880s, he kept a horse and carriage and employed several servants, as well as a cook. In 1891, he ordered a small boat for use on the lagoon,
stipulating that 'it must be splendid'.[90] Like other members of the Saro elite,
he dressed in the style of an English gentleman and had suits made from 'the
very best cloth' shipped from England.[91] A later survey of the Lagos elite classified him as being among the 'dandies' of the 1900s.[92] He took private lessons to improve his English, and subscribed to *The Times Weekly*, *Illustrated
London News*, *The Liverpool Courier*, and the *Review of Reviews* (as well as
Sylvia's Home Journal for his wife), to ensure that he kept up with trends in
what was then the pace-setting metropolis.

Williams's private papers, though incomplete, are one of the very few col-
lections of Saro business records to have survived from the nineteenth century.
They consist of two letter-books containing copies of more than a thousand
outgoing letters. One deals with his business with the Manchester firm of John
Walkden & Co. between 1882 and 1919; the other records some of his business
transactions with different parties between 1889 and 1919. There is also an
account book with John Walkden covering the period 1881–1919, and a 'memo
book' containing copies of other business letters sent between 1914 and 1916.[93]
The papers have limitations: the outgoing letters are mostly routine, repetitive
orders; there are almost no incoming letters; the surviving ledgers record purchases only; there is no sales ledger; balance sheets, assuming they were compiled, have disappeared. Nevertheless, the records add detail and precision to
what would otherwise be a brief and highly generalised account. Moreover,
they are the main source for revealing what Isaac did after he ceased trading
in 1889.

Isaac Williams never touched the produce trade, which was the riskiest
branch of the import–export business, and, as a committed Wesleyan, he
never sold alcohol. He concentrated, instead, on a miscellany of imported
goods, which included hardware, corrugated iron and zinc sheets, flatware,
nails, rat traps, mirrors, earthenware, yarn, thread, clay pipes, needles, hooks,
matches, soap, umbrellas, candles, paper, boots, buttons, cotton goods, cotton
balls, and packaged foodstuffs such as biscuits, rice, tea, sardines, and sugar.
The scope pointed towards the department store; the scale was that of a sizeable corner shop.

Isaac began ordering goods from John Walkden's catalogue in 1877. Walkden, a Manchester firm, had begun a mail-order business—then a novel means
of trade—in 1868. In 1887, the firm claimed to be agents for one hundred firms

90. Williams to Walkden, LBJW, 19 August 1891. See n. 92 below.
91. Williams to Walkden, LBJW, 5 August 1886.
92. Akinsanya, 'Dandies of the 1900s'.
93. The Williams papers (IBWP) have been subdivided as follows: LBJW (Letter Book
John Walkden, 1882–1919), LBMisc. (Letter Book Miscellaneous, 1889–1919), A/CJW
(Account Book John Walkden, 1881–1919), and MB (Memo Book, 1914–16).

of 'native traders' and to have shipped goods to the value of £100,000 to the West Coast in that year.[94] Williams's correspondence with Walkden reveals a pattern of orders and an accompanying set of regular payments that were timed to fit with the steamship service, which left Liverpool for Lagos twice a month. It is evident that Williams had a keen business eye: his orders were precise, reflecting a mixture of quality considerations and consumer demand, and he was quick to point to superior products and lower prices when he found them among his competitors. In 1882, for example, he reported that he was 'very much grieved at the cotton balls I mentioned last. You generally send the best quality to Mr Z. A. Williams. But you have sent me inferior quality and not a few'.[95] The nagging continued. In 1888, Williams began a three-and-a-half-page letter saying, 'I have many complaints to make', and concluded, after a host of details: 'Really, Mr. Walkden, I can assure you that I can get this cheaper elsewhere'.[96]

Payment was also a perennial problem. Lagos was shifting from barter to cash in the 1880s, and before 1884 Williams sometimes settled transactions in Spanish silver dollars.[97] There was no bank in Lagos until 1894, and British silver coin was often scarce. Williams regularly made payment in bills of exchange drawn mainly on local expatriate firms, and in bankers' drafts, which were met from his account with the National Provincial Bank in Manchester. Occasionally, he had to ask Walkden to supply silver coin to maintain liquidity in the Lagos market. Produce traders could still exchange palm oil for imported manufactures, but import merchants were obliged to convert to cash sales.

Williams ordered exclusively from Walkden, and in the early days took great care to establish his credentials: 'I should like you to trust me', he wrote in 1882, 'as I trust you; rest assured that if I owe you 1d. you are sure to get it again'.[98] In 1884, following an exchange about non-payment, he wrote: 'it is high time for you to believe that I am determined not to swindle any man'.[99] For his part, Williams tried to ensure that Walkden offered him the best terms possible by making the firm aware that he could take his business elsewhere. He reported an approach by the Lagos Warehouse Co. in 1885, concluding that

94. Walkden to Foreign Office, 16 April 1888, in F.O. to C.O. 28 August 1897, C.O. 147/124.

95. Williams to Walkden, LBJW, 16 December 1882.

96. Williams to Walkden, LBJW, 16 April 1888.

97. Large quantities of 'comparatively spurious' dollars purporting to be from South America were manufactured in Birmingham and shipped to Lagos to take advantage of the official exchange rate, which was fixed in 1843—long before the fall in the price of silver. The resulting profiteering led the Gold Coast and Lagos authorities to demonetise the dollar in 1880, though it remained in circulation for a few years. There is a full account in Ussher to Kimberley, 19 July 1880, C.O. 806/184.

98. Williams to Walkden, LBJW, 15 March 1882.

99. Williams to Walkden, LBJW, 29 August 1884.

Table 8.1. Isaac B. Williams: Trading Statement, 1882–1889 (£)

Year	Purchases	Duty (4%)	Total Cost	Turnover	Gross Profit (Total Cost + 15%)
1882	3,182	127	3,309	3,805	496
1883	5,193	208	5,401	6,211	810
1884	7,083	284	7,367	8,467	1,100
1885	5,664	227	5,891	6,775	884
1886	5,382	215	5,597	6,437	840
1887	4,856	194	5,050	5,807	757
1888	6,891	276	7,167	8,242	1,075
1889	3,986	159	4,145	4,767	622

Source: I. B. Williams, *Account Book with John Walkden, 1881–1919*.
Note: The duty paid had to be calculated on the basis of purchases plus freight and slightly overestimates the customs payments Williams made because duty was charged on the invoice value only.

'if you can let me have goods as cheap as possible I do not see why I should be roving here and there'.[100] He came near to defecting in 1886 but reaffirmed his loyalty at the end of the year. In 1887, he offered a statement of allegiance capped by a poorly disguised request: 'But rest assured that I can never forget an old friend. You are my old friend, but some things are very dear'.[101]

The lack of sales ledgers and balance sheets makes it impossible to say exactly how profitable the business was in the 1880s, but estimates that improve on guesswork can be derived from the figures for the purchases Williams made from John Walkden & Co., his sole supplier. Table 8.1 shows that Williams paid Walkden an average of £5,280 a year, which covered the cost of goods, freight, and insurance. He then paid an *ad valorem* duty of 4 per cent in Lagos, which amounted to an average of £211 per annum and raised the total annual average cost of his imports to £5,491.

The difficulty from this point is to know what markup Williams added to arrive at the retail price because it is hard to find precise information on this crucial matter either for Lagos or for comparable West Coast ports. Moreover, the import trade consisted of a wide range of products and the markup on each varied. Fortunately, however, clues can be found in estimates given by contemporary merchants, which suggests that the markup on goods imported from Europe in the 1880s ranged from 10 per cent to 20 per cent.[102] If the

100. Williams to Walkden, LBJW, 26 March 1885.
101. Williams to Walkden, LBJW, 18 August 1887.
102. Welsh to Holt, 17 February 1888, 23 March 1888, 17 May 1888, HP. G. A. Williams and S. H. Pearse suggested that 10 per cent was an upper limit in 1896, when trading

mid-point of 15 per cent is applied to Williams's annual turnover, it yields an annual average gross profit of £824 before deducting overhead costs. Overheads were relatively small because Williams had already bought his premises (in Martin's Street) from previous trading profits. The main residual expenditure was the salary of a clerk (Samuel Augustus Bright), who would have earned about £100 a year.[103] If a further £100 is deducted as a notional allowance for other, unspecified running costs, we can conclude that Williams's net profit in the 1880s averaged about £624 a year.[104]

At first sight, the figure seems too low to support the affluent lifestyle of one of the merchant princes of Lagos and was certainly less than the income of the high-risk and sometimes short-lived produce merchants, who stood at the top of the earnings league. Yet, all things being relative, Williams's net profit was sufficient for him to take his place comfortably among the Lagos elite. The *Oba's* stipend was only £250 a year between 1885 and 1894, book-keepers and head clerks earned about £100, skilled craftsmen were paid between £36 and £60, and unskilled labourers, only £10–£12.[105] It therefore seems that Williams's income was indeed sufficient for him to build Raymond House, buy a number of other properties, live well, employ sundry servants, and travel regularly to Europe.

Nevertheless, the fact that profit margins were narrowing also indicates how competitive the import-and-retail business had become after the steamship and submarine cable had opened it to low-cost entrants and the spread of silver had put paid to the barter trade. As Williams wrote in 1887:

> The state of trade now is not so much encouraging. Consequently, I am compelled to mention something which I have noticed for a long time. Indeed, for the past two years especially there are so many shops built here that it is very hard for each to effect sales as it was some time ago.[106]

His comment in the following year that 'business is not so encouraging now, it is *very small profit*', might be taken as a typical businessman's grumble, except that Williams had no record of complaints on this subject, and his comment fits what we now know of the slender profit margins on sales of imported

---

conditions were even worse than they had been in the 1880s. Evidence in João da Rocha v. Egerton Shyngle, LSCR, Civ. 18, 1896.

103. Bright was employed by the Lagos Warehouse Co. after Isaac Williams retired from business. Roberts v. Birtwistle, LSCR, Civ. 12, 1892.

104. It should be added that Williams claimed consistently that he never had any debts. The evidence indicates that this was indeed the case. Accordingly, it is safe to conclude that he had no repayments to make.

105. Information on book-keepers and clerks (for 1889) is in Moloney to Secretary of State, 28 Feb. 1889, CSO 8/7/1.

106. Williams to Walkden, LBJW, 11 August 1888.

goods.[107] These circumstances help to explain his preoccupation with the precise details of quality and price, his permanent search for cheaper prices from his supplier, his vigilant observation of his rivals, and his anxiety when trade was disrupted by political disputes on the mainland. In these matters, his business was a microcosm of the broader economic issues that were affecting European as well as African merchants in the late nineteenth century.[108]

In 1887, Williams notified Walkden that he would not be placing further orders with them. Walkden doubted his explanation that he was in poor health and needed a rest and suspected that he intended to transfer his business to one of their competitors. Ultimately, the orders were resumed, and good relations restored. In April 1889, however, Williams again wrote to Walkden, informing the firm that he was unwell and had decided to 'keep away from business for a few weeks'.[109] He followed this letter with another in June, saying:

> Really Mr. Walkden I am in need of a long rest, for the last 16 years I have not had a week's rest to myself, always busy, had it been that I have a trustworthy man that understood to manage my business I would have taken a trip to England, but as I have none I must manage the best way I can.[110]

Walkden still wondered if the explanation might be a cover for negotiations with other prospective business partners. Yet, whatever the cause of Williams's ill health, his claims had substance: his letters became less frequent and in October, he apologised for 'not writing as often as I ought'.[111] In February 1889, he wrote to Walkden saying that 'my late bereavement has cast me down a great deal'.[112] It was also true that Williams was thinking of disposing of his business, and in August he responded to Walkden's queries by referring to an 'arrangement' he was hoping to make.[113] By December, relations were again amicable. Williams thanked Mr Walkden for his 'kind and friendly letter' and promised to provide a full explanation of his plans for the business when he visited England in 1890.[114] For the moment, he said that he needed to free himself from business and expressed his regret that Walkden did not have 'a man here of your own who would have taken up my business when I am in need of rest'.[115]

107. Williams to Walkden, LBJW, 18 May 1888.
108. Hopkins, 'An Economic History of Lagos', ch. 4.
109. Williams to Walkden, LBJW, 8 June 1889.
110. Williams to Walkden, LBJW, 25 June 1889.
111. Williams to Walkden, LBJW, 11 October 1889.
112. Williams to Walkden, LBJW, 2 Feb. 1889.
113. Williams to Walkden, LBJW, 22 August 1889.
114. Williams to Walkden, LBJW, 3 December 1889.
115. Williams to Walkden, LBJW, 3 December 1889.

We now know that Williams had decided to sell his business to the Lagos Warehouse Co. Ltd., a Liverpool firm that had opened premises in Lagos in 1881 and subsequently expanded rapidly.[116] In 1891, Lagos Warehouse paid in customs duties the equivalent of 20 per cent of the entire revenue of Lagos, and in 1896 was said to be 'the first' British trading firm in the port.[117] The precise terms of the sale are not known, though it seems that Williams received a cash payment, joined the board, and held 1,300 £1 shares in the company. Early hopes were quickly followed by disappointing results. In 1895, Williams wrote expressing his sympathy for the directors, who 'lacked the capital to make the business successful'.[118] In 1898, he wrote to a nephew saying that the shares, which were fully paid, were now 'lost: there has been no dividend for the past five years and the company is losing money every year'.[119] The company, no longer the 'first firm' in Lagos, went into liquidation and was bought by John Holt in 1899.[120] Fortunately, Williams was able to rescue a good deal of his investment: he sold some shares in 1898 and converted the remainder after Holt took over the company.[121]

The sale of the business did not end Williams's connections with Walkden. After 1889, however, his purchases were almost entirely for his own use, though his wife imported some goods through the firm for her own small trading business.[122] Williams's long relationship with Walkden's combined competitive business dealings with genuine personal attachment. Christmas presents, wedding invitations (and wedding cake) were exchanged from an early date, and condolences were expressed on the occasion of the death of family members. There was substance behind these formalities: representatives of the Walkden family stayed with Williams in Lagos; he, in turn, stayed with the Walkdens in Manchester during his frequent visits to England. The final exchange of letters took place in 1919, when Isaac Williams wrote to Walkden as follows:

> All of us in Lagos both white and black were glad a few days ago when we heard that peace has been signed. And I now seize this opportunity to write this important letter to you so that you may know what I am

116. *Lagos Times*, 14 Sept. 1881.

117. Lagos Warehouse Co. to Knutsford, 18 February 1892, C.O. 147/88; Denton to Chamberlain, 23 November 1896, C.O. 147/107.

118. Williams to T. E. Tomlinson (agent of the Lagos Warehouse Company), LBMisc, 4 June 1895.

119. Williams to Pickering Jones, LBMisc., 15 May 1899; Williams to I. T. Palmer, 26 November 1898.

120. *Lagos Reporter*, 11 February 1899; *Lagos Weekly Record*, 15 July 1899.

121. Williams to Pickering Jones, LBMisc., 28 December 1917.

122. This was Isaac Williams's third wife, Marion (Taylor). Walkden opened its own branch in Lagos in 1890, became a private limited company in 1900, and remained a family business until 1917, when it was bought by Lever Brothers. Macmillan, *Red Book*, pp. 80–81.

doing. As my age is advancing very rapidly, I have decided to close up all my affairs as quickly as possible. Of course, you and I have been dealing with each other for the past forty-four years, and I feel very sorry indeed to put the above fact to you, and I should like you to do all that lies within your power to close my affairs with you finally by first opportunity.[123]

'My reason for writing this letter to you', he concluded, 'is that it is good for every man to set his house in order before the appointed time comes'.[124] Thomas Walkden's reply, one of the few in existence, reads as follows:

We quite understand your wish to get everything settled up. Still, we think you are only a comparatively young man and we do hope you will live for many years and we shall have the pleasure of seeing you once again in England. As you say, it is many years since we commenced business operations together and we think no small credit should be given to our late senior for the way in which at the commencement he managed the business on this side for you, and it has always been a rather sore point with us that this business should have gone into the hands of one of our competitors, and certainly we all thought that, when you contemplated selling the business, you might have given us the opportunity of purchasing same, as we considered that we had been the means of building up the business for you. Since you retired from business we have always given careful and special attention to your small personal orders, although we have certainly not made anything out of same. Still, we have done it for old friendship's sake. We shall be pleased to hear from you at all times and if you do come to England again we shall be pleased to see you.[125]

This was not the most gracious of farewells, though it captured the symbiotic relationship between business partners who needed to secure the best deal from each other without destroying the sense of trust that underpinned their interests. Walkden's specific complaint about Williams's action in disposing of his business in 1889 was overstated and unfair. The correspondence indicates that John Walkden was aware that Williams was contemplating alternative arrangements. Had the firm been serious about wanting to buy his business, it seems strange that there is nothing in the correspondence to indicate their interest, still less any sign of them making an offer. Indeed, as we have seen, Williams had written to Walkden at the time, expressing his regret that they did not have an agent in Lagos who could have taken over his business.[126] Isaac's

123. Williams to Walkden, LBJW, 5 July 1919.
124. Williams to Walkden, LBJW, 5 July 1919.
125. Walkden to Williams, LBJW, 29 July 1919.
126. Williams to Walkden, LBJW, 3 Dec. 1889.

reasons for selling his business seem to be those given in his correspondence: he had been unwell, and trading conditions were becoming more difficult as a result of increased local competition and the disruption to the Lagos market caused by political disputes in the hinterland.[127] When the right offer came along, he took it.

Despite some ill health, which his letters continue to record from time to time, Isaac Williams had nearly half of his life ahead of him after selling his business in 1889: he was forty-three in that year and seventy-nine when he died in 1925.[128] He continued to live at Raymond House, and to enjoy the lifestyle associated with membership of the elite, which in his case included frequent visits to England until 1914. He also had enough money to assist members of his family and to make substantial donations to various causes in Lagos. Notwithstanding these outgoings, Isaac's estate was still valued at the sum of £8,250 at his death.[129]

Property, Mortgages, and Rentals

The puzzle that now needs to be resolved is how Isaac was able to live so well for thirty-six years after selling his business, be a generous benefactor, and still leave substantial wealth upon his death. He had no visible sources of income after 1889, and past profits plus the proceeds of the sale of his business would not have been sufficient to cover his considerable outgoings. The answer, in a word, is property. Isaac's chief investment from the late 1870s, when he began to have money to spare, was in freehold land in the most rapidly developing area of Lagos around the Marina and Broad Street. The former was stocked with retail outlets and warehouses, which stored produce for trans-shipment and incoming goods awaiting distribution; the latter, just behind and parallel to it, was the main secondary centre for the sale of imported manufactures.[130]

At the close of the century, land on the Marina that had been acquired for virtually nothing in the 1860s had increased in value by between 500 per cent and 700 per cent, and the land market was well-established and active.[131] Isaac was not well placed, financially or socially, to secure crown grants on Marina sites in the 1860s. In 1866, he was only twenty years of age and had yet to enter business. During the 1870s, however, he acquired several properties

---

127. The cause of his illness is unknown, though he was also depressed by the death of his second wife. Williams to Walkden, LBJW, 24 January 1889.

128. For example, Williams to Walkden, LBJW, 9 January 1909, and Williams to Walkden, LBJW, 27 July 1909, reporting difficulties with his eyesight, which continued to deteriorate.

129. Extract from the will of I. B. Williams, dated 1924. LAP VI/346–54.

130. Egerton to C.O., 8 August 1907, C.O. 520/56.

131. Estimates in Denton to Chamberlain, 4 November 1898, C.O. 147/136.

nearby and added to them in the 1880s.[132] His strategy, which took time but was successful, was to assemble contiguous sites on the corners of Broad Street and Martin's Street going down almost to the Marina. In 1890, he completed the two blocks by buying properties from Zachariah Williams, whose fall from eminence had yet to reach the ground. He purchased Zachariah's property in Martin's Street adjoining his own property (Raymond House) for £300, a larger plot on the corner of Broad Street and Martin's Street for £1,000, and a smaller plot at the corner of Broad Street and Chapel Street for £200.[133] The investment paid off after the turn of the century when British rule was established and the railway line from Lagos reached Ibadan. As far as the records indicate, Isaac bought property but never sold it.

Crown grants were not free from ambiguity, even though they became treated as rights of freehold. As we have seen, families could and did contest claims to ownership, and the prospect of court action caused potential lenders, especially expatriate firms, to be selective in accepting land as security. These circumstances favoured intermediaries, such as Saro merchants, who were familiar with the Lagos property market and were well placed to judge its risks. Williams was fully qualified to become a lender and rentier. According to one source, his probity and credit rating were such that the Bank of British West Africa would accept a payment order on 'any piece of paper signed by him' in the same way that a cheque was negotiated.[134]

Isaac's property business had two branches: loans and rentals. The loan business consisted of cash advances, which varied in size, duration, and purpose, on the security of property in Lagos. He advanced money and held mortgage deeds on houses built on land registered as crown grants until the loan was repaid (with interest). In the majority of cases, the property was used by the mortgagor as security for commercial advances. In a few cases, Williams advanced money to enable a house to be bought and then held the deeds and received mortgage payments in much the same way as a mortgage company or building society does today, except that the mortgages he arranged were of short duration. It is likely that the minority of borrowers who wanted an advance to buy property turned to Williams for the shortfall rather than for the major part of the sum required. Had they needed a high proportion of the purchase price, it is unlikely that they would have been considered creditworthy borrowers. The reason for the short repayment term would seem to lie in the cost to the lender of receiving low repayments over many years and the commensurately extended risk of default. Despite the solidity of crown grants, lending remained a highly personal business. Williams ran his business as the

132. LLOR, Crown Grants Index, 1863–82, 28/117, 35/69, 37/162, 37/165, 1/292, 9/14, 10, 189, 10/204, 10/220, 15/117, 16/21, 14/48, 17/56.

133. Z. A. Williams, LLOR, 15/402, 16/74, 16/66.

134. Akinsanya, 'Dandies of the 1900s'.

sole proprietor: there was no one to take over if he fell ill or died. The management of a mortgage would then fall to others who lacked expertise and experience. Moreover, repayment could become problematic should the mortgagee become ill, and complicated if he died.

As seen from Raymond House, the loan market catered mainly to well-known Saro who needed money to fund commercial activities or to settle debts. Several eminent merchants whose businesses had collapsed in the 1880s turned to Isaac for financial help. One of the greatest merchants of the 1880s, Zachariah A. Williams, who was in desperate trouble in the late 1880s, was forced to sell assets to pay his considerable debts. Isaac Williams was among the purchasers.[135] Benjamin C. Dawodu, who was also struggling to survive, mortgaged a house in Bishop Street to Williams in 1891 for £500 at an interest rate of 12 per cent per annum.[136] Jacob S. Leigh, another Lagos merchant whose prosperity lay behind him, mortgaged property to Williams in Broad Street in 1896 for £600 at a rate of 3d. per pound per month repayable in 1898.[137] Leigh was unable to repay the debt and in 1902, G. B. Ollivant, a British firm trading in Lagos, took out a second mortgage on the property to pay the money owed to Williams and to secure the sum of £1,875 that Leigh owed them.[138] The issue became protracted. It seems that Williams eventually took possession of the property because in 1909, he wrote to Jacob Leigh's son advising him that the rent for the house occupied by his late father would be £4 a month.[139]

In 1899, Jacob K. Coker mortgaged a house to Williams at the corner of Broad Street and Market Street for an advance of £500, which was to be repaid in the following year with interest at the rate of 3d. per pound per month.[140] In 1903, Coker's father, Jacob Osolu Coker, mortgaged Rose Cottage, the family's main house in Lagos, to Williams to secure a loan of £360 at the same rate of interest.[141] Interest on the loan was paid but not the principal, which fell due in 1904. In that year, Jacob's son and heir-in-law, Jacob K. Coker, rearranged the mortgage to incorporate the balance outstanding on both properties. The new loan amounted to £660, which was to be repaid in 1905 (at the same rate of interest). In 1908, however, the debt was still outstanding and Williams had to remind Coker that, if the sum was not paid, he would have to 'exercise his powers of sale' over Rose Cottage.[142] Coker played a significant role in two costly, conjoined ventures at that time: the development of cocoa farming in nearby Agege and the

135. See n.130 above.

136. B. C. Dawudu, LLOR, 14/40.

137. J. S. Leigh, LLOR, 30/223.

138. J. S. Leigh, LLOR, 38/127.

139. LLOR, 30/223, 1896; Williams to J. S. Leigh, LBMisc., 23 December 1901; Williams to F. G. R. Leigh, LBMisc., 17 July 1909.

140. Jacob K. Coker, LLOR, 30/422.

141. Jacob K. Coker, LLOR, 30/422.

142. Williams to Coker, LBMisc., 7 January 1908.

expansion of the African Church.[143] He needed money for both: success with cocoa enabled him to finance the African Church and eventually to redeem his property in Lagos.[144]

It is surprising to find that small borrowers included many well-known names, the most prominent being the eminent lawyers, J. Egerton Shyngle and Kitoye Ajasa. The flamboyant Shyngle was being pursued for payment for an unspecified amount in 1901 and 1904.[145] In 1914, the highly visible and notably conservative Ajasa, who eventually acquired a knighthood, owed Williams the very modest sum of £15.[146] It is unclear why Ajasa needed such a small loan, but his financial difficulties appear to have been genuine because Williams had to send a stream of reminders throughout 1914. Ajasa finally responded in 1915 by asking for easier terms. Williams replied:[147]

> My Dear Mr. Ajasa,
>
> I am sorry I shall not be able to do as you requested. 3d. is my lowest charge and I can advise you to pay every month, as was agreed and as others are doing, then you will find that it will be easier for you.
>
> Yours faithfully,
(I. B. Williams)

Ajasa was unwilling or unable to change his ways. The reminders about non-payment and late payment continued through May 1916, which is when the letter-book ends.

Interest rates varied considerably during the last twenty years of the century, but Williams chose his borrowers carefully and charged about 10 per cent per annum on prime loans, with an upper limit of 12 per cent.[148] Higher rates were levied on riskier loans, which were paid monthly, but even in these cases the use of crown grants as security held the rate to a maximum of 15 per cent. By 1900, too, there were sufficient lenders to ensure that rates remained competitive. Admittedly, the bank rate in Britain stood at around 4 per cent

143. On Coker's career, see chapter 13.

144. Williams never bought land at Agege, but advanced money to another planter at Agege, Fred Williams, who borrowed £200 on the strength of land in Lemonu Street in 1908. Fred Williams, LLOR, 57/241.

145. Williams to Shyngle, LBMisc., 9 February 1901, 20 September 1904.

146. Williams to Ajasa, MB, 12 May 1914, and subsequently 21 Aug. 1914, 25 Aug. 1914, 11 Nov. 1914, 30 Dec. 1914, 12 Jan. 1915, 13 April 1915.

147. Williams to Ajasa, MB, 17 April 1915.

148. On interest rates, see A. W. Thomas v. Antonio Oke & Anor, LSCR Civ. 36, 1905. See also Mann, *Slavery and the Birth of an African City*, p. 147. 3d in the pound = 1.25 per cent per month, which equals 15 per cent per annum, if charged cumulatively on the sum contracted.

in the early 1900s, with mortgage rates somewhat higher than that, but Lagos was not London, and the discrepancy can readily be accounted for by the difference in the level of risk in the two centres.

As we have seen, rents from property had supplemented the incomes of successful merchants since the 1850s, though the market seems to have been on a modest scale until the 1880s. Williams appears to have been the first merchant to have made property and rentals his sole source of income. Blaize leased one property; Williams built rentals into his portfolio and generated a steady income from about half a dozen properties located in the prime business quarter. In 1895, he leased his property in Martin's Street (known as Liverpool House) and the store and outhouse at Raymond House to Lagos Stores, the British firm that had taken over his business, for rents of £80 and £99 per annum respectively.[149] Both leases were renewed in 1902, 1906, and 1915 for twenty-five years, when the rents were increased to £152 and £120 per annum, respectively. The trend towards long leases was new and reflected the expansion of the colony and the corresponding increase in confidence among the expatriate firms. Old Lodge, another house Williams owned in Martin's Street, was leased in the same year for an annual rent of £152.[150] In 1920, he leased land next door to Raymond House to the Nigerian merchant, Peter J. C. Thomas, for an annual rent of £192.[151] The main problem for the new landlords of Lagos was non-payment. The property leased to Lagos Stores (and subsequently to John Holt) was secure, but a handful of other houses were rented to Saro tenants who were sometimes in financial difficulties. Isaac's letters record his efforts, culminating on occasion in notices to quit, to secure payment from recalcitrant or impecunious tenants. Leasing property was to be the way of the future, but in 1895 the future could only be glimpsed.

It is hard to say very much about the size and profitability of Williams's rental business because no accounts have survived. One estimate suggests that, at the time of his death in 1925, Williams had a rental income of about £400 a year from five large houses in central Lagos.[152] This is probably an underestimate. By 1920, his three main properties, Raymond House, Liverpool House, and Old Lodge, were leased for a total of £424 per annum, and a fourth property adjoining Raymond House brought in £192, producing a total of £616. Prestwich House, and other properties, brought in additional rental income. The total can only be guessed, but is likely to have been at least £750 per annum.

149. I. B. Williams, LLOR, 27/336, 27/340, 40/450, 40/30.
150. All three leases were for twenty-five years. I. B. Williams, LLOR, 44/447, 48/362, 82/232, 82/237, 82/242.
151. LLOR, 129/403, 1920.
152. Mann, *Marrying Well*, p. 32. I am indebted to Kristin Mann for recording this fact, which had escaped me.

It is also impossible to calculate how much the loans side of the business brought in, though we know that the gross profit margin of a minimum of 10 per cent, rising to 15 per cent, was about the same as it was on his import business.[153] The scattered figures available suggest that Williams had at least £1,000 and probably much more, perhaps as much as £5,000, in outstanding loans at any one point between 1900 and 1914. Assuming, without any refinement, that he was earning at least 10 per cent a year on these amounts, his additional income would have ranged from £100 to £500 a year. If the midpoint of £2,500 is chosen to represent outstanding loans, the additional income would have amounted to £250 a year, bringing his total annual income to £1,000. This figure was higher than his gross income from trade (£624) in the 1880s. Overhead costs were broadly similar. Williams ran both businesses from Raymond House, where he 'lived above the shop'. He dispensed with a clerk and some labourers when he finished trading, but needed to employ a solicitor (Charles Forsythe) when it was necessary to take defaulters to court. These figures are entirely speculative and should be treated only as orders of magnitude. They also raise difficulties in comparing incomes in the 1880s with those in the 1920s, when real purchasing power had fallen. Nevertheless, they suggest that Williams's real income from his second business may have been higher than it was from his first and that he enjoyed added value from eliminating some of the hazards of commerce.

Family and Church

Isaac had two main financial commitments, apart from his own personal expenditure: one was to his brother, Jacob; the other was to the Wesleyan Church. Isaac gave Jacob substantial support, financing his training and ordination as a minister, giving him an allowance of £48 a year for sixteen years, and educating several of his children.[154] Isaac's support for his brother survived the fact that Jacob had abandoned the family's allegiance to the Wesleyans and joined the Anglican Church, and it continued after Jacob left the Anglicans for the African Church in 1901. Denominational differences came between the brothers only once, in 1899, when Isaac (who was taking care of Jacob's young children at the time), urged that his charges should be brought up as Wesleyans.[155] This was a claim too far: Jacob dissented, and the children were removed from Raymond House, though at least one of them (Isaac's favorite nephew, Jacob Olutunde Williams) later became a

153. As discussed earlier, the markup on imported manufactures was approximately 15 per cent; the "markup" (gross interest rate) charged on loans was 15 per cent (with a few charged at 10 per cent).

154. Webster, *African Churches*, p. 114.

155. I. B. Williams to J. S. Williams, LBMisc., 7 March 1899.

Wesleyan.[156] The episode was put behind them, and the brothers resumed their different lives in harmony. In this case, family ties and a shared affiliation with Christianity were sufficient to overcome differences of denominational doctrine and practice. Isaac himself remained a staunch and active Wesleyan. He donated an organ to the church in Olowogbowo at the cost of £600 and subscribed liberally to the church maintenance fund.[157]

Isaac was married three times but remained childless. His first wife, Mary, died at the age of twenty-nine in 1885. Two years later, he married Jane Beckley, the daughter of another Saro merchant, Thomas E. Beckley, and the grand-daughter of Thomas Joe, who was a prominent merchant in the 1860s and 1870s.[158] The wedding confirmed Isaac's status as one of the big men of the day. The ceremony in Tinubu Church in central Lagos was attended by the Lagos elite headed by Governor Moloney, who proposed the toast to the bride and groom.[159] Isaac's high standing received further recognition in 1898, when he was chosen to be a member of the colony's Legislative Council.[160] By then, however, his second marriage had ended with the death of his wife, Jane, in 1889. 'My late bereavement', Isaac confessed to Walkden, 'has cast me down a great deal'.[161] In 1894, he married Marion (also known as Mary) Amelia Taylor, who was to outlive him. The marriage, however, was not an immediate bonding of minds. In 1896, Isaac and his wife separated. One glimpse into this painful episode has survived: 'I cannot help it', Isaac wrote to Walkden, 'she is too strong for me'.[162] Time, however, appears to have softened the tensions sufficiently for them to resume married life. By the close of the century, the couple were travelling to England and meeting the Walkdens in Manchester. Mary Amelia then began trading with Walkden on her own account 'to prepare for the time', as Isaac put it, when he ceased to be the main provider. Isaac respected his wife's independence (and probably her strength too) and kept his distance from her business dealings.[163]

Isaac continued to manage his property business until his death in 1925, despite failing health. In his final years, he came to rely on his nephew, Jacob Olatunde Williams, who became the son he had never had. Isaac's will

156. I. B. Williams to J. S. Williams, LBMisc., 7 March 1899.

157. Adeshigbin, 'Almanack'; 'Outline of the Life'.

158. Thomas E. Beckley (1830–1905) was a repatriate who returned to Lagos in 1844 before settling in Abeokuta, where he became a teacher and then a trader dealing in raw cotton. *Lagos Standard*, 31 May 1905. His son, Joseph Ogunola Beckley (1862–1923), was a prominent farmer at Agege (see chapter 13).

159. A full report is given in the *Lagos Observer*, 25 August 1887.

160. Denton to Chamberlain, 28 September 1898, C.O. 147/135.

161. Williams to Walkden, LBJW, 2 Feb. 1889.

162. Williams to Walkden, LBJW, 3 Dec. 1896.

163. Isaac rarely felt bound to appeal to Walkden on her behalf. For one example, see Williams to Walkden, LBJW, 11 April 1909.

bequeathed £1,000 to the Lagos District Synod of the Wesleyan Church, a further £600 to create a fund to send candidates to England to be trained as ministers for the Lagos District, and the income from three houses (about £300 a year) to train African ministers for the Wesleyan mission in Lagos.[164] He also assigned three houses in Martin's Street and Broad Street for the use of the Lagos Wesleyan Synod. As for his family, his wife, Mary, received £300 and 'the use' of one of his properties, Prestwich House; his brother, Jacob, received £200; and his nephew, Jacob Olatunde, received the main prize: Raymond House. The marriage, though mended, seems not to have been close.

Raymond House survived into independence but has now been replaced by a seven-storey office block that, appropriately, became the headquarters of finance and property companies, including the United Bank for Africa and, today, Afriland Properties. The name lived on until 2018, when new owners renovated the building and changed the name to Afriland Towers. Today, Raymond House exists only in photographs and the fading memories of the few who can remember its existence. This is all the more reason why the record of the man who built Raymond House in 1886 should be remembered by his successors. Isaac Williams deserves to be known, not just as a merchant prince who disappeared in mid-career, but as the pioneer of the finance and property business that is so important to the economy of Lagos today.

Two Lives Compared

Previous chapters have drawn attention to the development of the understudied land market in Lagos and its contribution to the wealth of African merchants in Lagos. The present chapter has examined the careers of two merchants whose success in commerce was matched by their extensive property dealings. Richard Blaize combined the two, as did other wealthy Saro merchants. Isaac Williams followed them in sequence, beginning in trade and then shifting to property. The distinction between the two merchants is important because it marks a trend towards increased specialisation. Williams extended the familiar business of advancing money on the security of property to encompass leasing. In doing so, he showed that it was possible to live well as both a money lender and a rentier without also trading in goods. Others, such as Candido da Rocha, were to take the same route after the turn of the century. These unsung innovators pointed the way towards an important sector of the economy of what was to become Nigeria.

The careers of Blaize and Williams illustrate wider trends. Both merchants had to adapt to the new degree of dominance Britain established after 1892. Blaize struggled to reconcile relations of inequality with the universal ideals of his youth. Williams distanced himself from politics and adapted quietly to

164. Extract from the will of I. B. Williams, dated 1924. LAP, VI/346–54.

the new conditions. Both survived the difficulties of the 1880s, while other merchants, who were often their friends as well as their commercial rivals, struggled and some went out of business. Nevertheless, they were acutely aware that competition had grown and profit margins had been cut. Blaize was already wealthy and could supplement his income by directing some of his capital into his lending business. Williams, however, had entered trade later than Blaize, was not as wealthy as Blaize and, as his letters reveal, worried about his future in commerce. In selling his business to Lagos Stores in 1889, he decided, in effect, that his comparative advantage lay, not in competing with new entrants in the import trade, but in using his accumulated business skill and local knowledge to become a personal banker to the propertied community of Lagos. Demand for cash and credit, whether for investment or consumption, was unlimited; supply was made possible by the availability of landed security based on crown grants. In putting the two together, Williams was responding to shifting conditions that were reflected in the rate of profit attached to different business opportunities. In doing so, he also developed a new market in rental properties. If, as indicated here, Williams's second business was in some degree more profitable than his first and also reduced the uncertainties attached to trade, his decision to move from one niche to another was an entirely rational response to changing circumstances.

The careers of Blaize and Williams add complexity to judgements about the fortunes of Saro merchants in the nineteenth century because standard assessments omit their land transactions, which were an important component of their wealth and facilitated the growth of a capital market. The direction taken by Williams in particular illustrates how some merchants responded to adversity by extending established types of business in innovative ways. The adaptability shown by Lagos entrepreneurs in the late nineteenth century extended beyond Williams and beyond Lagos. A more radical adjustment, as chapter 9 will show, moved the town to the country and led to the foundation of the Nigerian cocoa-farming industry.

CHAPTER NINE

James Davies

THE FIRST OF THE COCOA FARMERS

JAMES DAVIES IS the only merchant to make two substantial appearances in this study. He featured in chapter 4 as the most prominent Saro merchant of the 1850s and 1860s, and one whose close relations with Daniel Taiwo showed the extent to which eminent returnees extended their commercial, political, and personal links beyond their own community. The sudden collapse of his business in 1873 and the subsequent humiliations he suffered after he was declared bankrupt could easily be interpreted as foreshadowing the losses sustained by other Saro merchants during the commercial difficulties that arose in the 1880s and 1890s. Yet, as noted in chapter 4, the collapse of Davies's business, dramatic though it was, preceded the challenging period that was to come and its cause was as much personal as contextual. More importantly, James Davies's career after 1873 extended far beyond his relatively modest commercial activities in the 1880s and 1890s, first with Christie & Co. and then as an auctioneer.[1]

The crucial early years of Nigeria's cocoa-farming industry passed virtually unrecorded in either official correspondence or the Lagos newspapers. The story has to be recovered from surviving personal papers and a variety of other sources in which scattered pieces of evidence appear in a seemingly unrelated and often unexpected manner. Inevitably, gaps and uncertainties remain. Nevertheless, enough of the record can be reconstructed to substantiate two claims: that Davies responded to the calamity he experienced in Lagos by directing his enterprising talents away from the town and into

---

1. I am most grateful to three of James Davies's grandchildren for their considerable help in reconstructing their grandfather's life: Mr John Romanes Adewale Randle (1893–1977), better known as Jack, Victoria Davies's son from her marriage with Dr John Randle, Mrs Catherine Olabisi Eshugibyi, and Mrs L. Beckley. Interviews in Lagos, 28 and 29 Jan. 1962, 12 April 1964.

the countryside; and that his venture into cocoa farming spread from modest beginnings to the much larger centre at Agege, and from there to other parts of Nigeria.[2]

Acquiring Woodland Estate

After he had been declared bankrupt in 1876, Davies had no option but to undertake a radical review of his future. As shown in chapter 4, he adapted by making an agreement to act as the Lagos agent of a London merchant, George W. Christie. This was a legitimate way of escaping the bankruptcy laws because Davies served as an employee, and was not trading in his own name. By the same token, it was not a position that offered much potential for expanding his earnings, and Davies was a man with high expectations and considerable commitments, especially the educational needs of his son and daughters, who were, or shortly would be, attending schools in England. More positively, his experience at sea and his visits to England had greatly broadened his conception of the world and its possibilities. He was not merely responding to influences that came upon him, but was also active in searching for creative opportunities that would deliver beneficial results. Given that his prospects in commerce were limited, he decided to enter the largest sector in the Yoruba economy: agriculture.

The first indication that Davies was turning his thoughts to pragmatic purpose appeared in 1879, when he bought £5 worth of coffee plants from the 'American' ship, *Casas*, which reached Lagos on 2 July.[3] The fate of this experimental purchase is unknown. Detailed evidence exists for his next move, however, which was to acquire land during the last three months of 1880 at a place known as Ijon.[4] The site he chose lay 15 miles (24 km) northwest of Lagos island, where the soil had lost the saline quality that characterised the coastline and was better suited to producing tree crops. The direct distance, however, was notional because there was no straight road between Ijon and Lagos at that time. Davies, a former sea captain, chose the site because it included an accessible landing place on the Owo River, which made its winding way down to the Lagos lagoon. Although travel by canoe took the greater

2. I first presented the elements of this story in 1978. The expanded version in this chapter is based on additional sources and has amplified, modified, and corrected, where necessary, the original outline statement. See Hopkins, 'Innovation in a Colonial Context', in Dewey and Hopkins, *The Imperial Impact*, pp. 83–96.

3. Jackson v. Jackson, LSCR, Civ. 2, 1879.

4. Until the 1840s, the area was referred to as Egan. The spelling was changed to Ijon in the late 1840s (though sometime rendered 'Ijan') to conform to the new rules for transforming unwritten languages into alphabetical form. See Elebute, *The Life of James Pinson Labulo Davies*, p. 93. Understandably, but also confusingly, some contemporaries referred to Davies's farm as being at Itele, which was the nearest settlement.

FIGURE 9.1. Ijon Village in 1964.

FIGURE 9.2. The Anglican Church and School at Ijon, 1964.

part of two days, it was the best route for transporting bulky produce. Davies may also have been influenced by the fact that Ijon was on the border but just inside British Territory, which gave him a measure of protection and access, if needed, to the colonial courts in Lagos.

Ijon occupied a small site in a swathe of borderland territories between Lagos to the south, Egba to the north, Dahomey to the west, and Ijebu to the east. The area had been a 'wilderness' since the start of the slave trade and was virtually uninhabited.[5] The absence of established political authority ensured that the region would be contested by competing neighbouring states, including Britain. In 1868, Governor Glover drew the northern boundary of the new Lagos Colony through Isheri, Ifako, Agege, Itele, and (by extension) Ijon, which he claimed was the limit of the territory previously controlled by King Dosunmu.[6] In bisecting these settlements, rather than running the boundary north or south of them, Glover intended to create a line of neutral settlements that would prevent predators from encroaching on British territory. The policy, however, produced a measure of ambiguity that gave the inhabitants some advantages in being both inside and outside British territory, but also exposed them to competing claims from other outside forces.[7] Disputes were either negotiated on the ground, sometimes forcefully, or were taken to court in Lagos, if they related to what was (or was held to be) British territory.[8] Davies experienced the consequences of this unsettled situation at first hand. Years after the event, he stated that he had acquired land at Ijon from 'all the native authorities who have any interest in it'.[9] The *Bale* of Isheri, who was Daniel Taiwo's agent, pointed out the boundaries and became a trusted ally. The 'King' of nearby Itele became 'a good friend' and supporter.

The site itself, however, was acquired through the agency of Chief Ojon, a Lagos White Cap chief who had connections with Ijebu, which had claims

5. Davies, evidence in Brimah Aduloju & Ors v. Davies & Ors, LSCR, Civ. 33 and 34, 1904.

6. Glover to Blackall, 17 Jan. 1869, C.O. 147/14.

7. For example, Otta, the Awori capital, was founded circa 1835 by refugees driven south by the conflicts that led to the foundation of the Egba capital at Abeokuta. One group founded Otta; another, Isheri. In 1841, the Egba conquered Otta, which then paid tribute to Abeokuta and was included in the Egba United Government in 1864. Isheri, Agege, Itele, and Ijon were also under Otta but lay on the borderline demarcated by Glover. These settlements were beyond Abeokuta's formal control but were subject to its informal influence as increasing numbers of Egba moved south. I am grateful to Chief *Alhaji* Shittu, *Seriki* of Otta, 24 May 1864, and to an unsigned and undated Intelligence Report that was probably written in 1936.

8. And in some cases, still is. See https://www.vanguardngr.com/2013/11/royal-family-forced-exile-itele-chief/.

9. Davies v. Olorunfemi & Ors, LSCR, Civ. 25, 1900. Also *Bale* of Ilogbo v. Davies, LSCR, Civ. 42, 1906.

on the area.[10] Davies secured traditional rights of use from Chief Ojon in exchange for several demijohns of rum and forty kola nuts, but did not extend the gifts to Ojon's successors. Why Davies, who bought and sold land in Lagos freely, did not try to obtain freehold tenure remains a mystery. He probably decided to tread carefully at the outset of his new venture, given the contested character of authority over the area. Equally, he might have reckoned that the novelty of freehold tenure, even if granted, was likely to provoke even greater challenges. Many years later, he asserted in court that his land at Ijon was (or had become) an absolute gift.[11] The court confirmed his right to farm there but did not pronounce on his more ambitious claim. For practical purposes, however, he was securely settled. He had powerful friends in the neighbour-hood and was recognised as a man of substance who could be a valuable ally in Lagos. As one witness stated in 1904: Davies was 'the master of all at Ijon'.[12] It was a small kingdom, but it was his own.

The land dispute in 1904 was the context for Davies's statement in court that '1880 was a remarkable year for me'.[13] As he looked back across a whole generation, it was evident to him that the novel and still obscure venture he started had delivered results that extended far beyond his initial aim. Yet, other influences also came together in 1880 to make the year a memo-rable one and help to explain his radical departure from the predictable path usually taken by educated Saro. One major event of immense personal sig-nificance was the death in August of his beloved wife, Sarah, who died from tuberculosis in Madeira, while on her way to England in the hope, ironi-cally, of improving her health.[14] What effect this loss had on Davies's deci-sion to take up farming is now a matter of guesswork, but it is reasonable to suppose that it gave him an additional incentive to rethink his future. The news may also have made it easier for him to establish a new base in Ijon because Sarah felt at home in Lagos, which provided a congenial outlet for her musical talents and literary interests. Davies still needed a base in Lagos, and in the same year he built a new house in Broad Street that became the family's town residence.[15] A rather different but equally significant event

10. Brimah Aduloju & Ors v. Davies & Ors, LSCR, Civ. 34, 1904. This is the best for-mulation I can suggest. I cannot trace a White Cap Chief of that name or title; nor is the Ijebu connection clear. When questioned in court, Davies was certain that Ijon was 'under Lagos', but was unable to explain why this was the case. Nevertheless, the evidence on these matters was not challenged. Glover's boundary line is the likely explanation for the author-ity of Lagos in the area.

11. Brimah Aduloju & Ors v. Davies & Ors, LSCR, Civ. 33 and 34, 1904.

12. Evidence in Brimah Aduloju & Ors v. Davies & Ors, LSCR, Civ. 33 and 34, 1904.

13. Evidence in Brimah Aduloju & Ors v. Davies & Ors, LSCR, Civ. 33 and 34, 1904.

14. Payne, *Payne's Lagos.*

15. Victoria Randle & Anor v. James George & Ors, LSCR, Civ. 61, 1911. The house was called Wood House (which is not to be confused with Woodland Estate).

also occurred in August: Davies, who had been deported from Lagos to stand trial in Accra for receiving money from his debtors while still remaining bankrupt, was acquitted.[16] Having avoided imprisonment, he returned to Lagos in September and was able to plan a future for himself as a free man. It was then that he began the negotiations that, before the end of the year, enabled him to establish his farm at Ijon. Necessity took him there; other circumstances eased his way.

The court records yield a further, unsuspected, piece of evidence about the creation of what became known as Woodland Estate. Davies was introduced to Chief Ojon by his cousin, Thomas Benjamin Macaulay, known as 'Smart' Macaulay, who was a Saro commission agent in Lagos.[17] As part of the deal, Davies and Macaulay made an agreement in January 1881 to work the farm jointly. Macaulay was to act as the 'resident superintendent', presumably to enable Davies to travel to and from Lagos while he was setting up his new business with Christie & Co. Davies, whose capital was limited, received help from his mother, Nancy Charlotte Davies, to fund the start-up costs.[18] There is enough evidence of the partnership to know that the farm was a going concern in 1881 because two Farm Books (now lost) were kept, one detailing daily transactions such as the work being done; the other recording items sent to and from Lagos. Although there is no information about the work undertaken in that year, it almost certainly involved some forest clearance and planting of food crops, though nothing can now be said about the presence of any export crops, including the coffee plants Davies bought in 1879.

The partnership lasted for just over one year and was dissolved acrimoniously in March 1882.[19] In June, Davies sent some of his 'Krooboys' to remove stock and provisions from the farm. Macaulay refused to co-operate; force was used; the matter ended in court. Christie & Co. (alias J.P.L. Davies) sued Macaulay for a debt of £697; Macaulay counter-claimed for his share of the stock; judgement was given to Christie for the sum the firm claimed. That was the end of Macaulay's involvement in experimental farming. From then on, Davies ran the farm himself with the assistance of his long-serving clerk and fellow Egba, William Alfred Allen.[20] Macaulay, though labelled 'Smart', continued to struggle. He shared with Davies the dishonour of being labelled bankrupt but, unlike his partner at Ijon, Macaulay failed to turn the status

16. See above, p. 156.

17. T. B. Macaulay was the eldest son of John Macaulay. David, one of his brothers, was the merchant who made the mistake of crossing D. C. Taiwo, as detailed in chapter 4.

18. Evidence in Brimah Aduloju & Ors v. Davies & Ors, LSCR, Civ. 33 and 34, 1904.

19. Christie & Co. v. Thomas B. Macaulay, LSCR, Civ. 5, 1882.

20. Allen worked for Davies from 1858 to 1863 and from 1869 to 1875. He joined Davies at Ijon in 1882 and remained there as his manager and clerk until the 1890s, when he took a post with the Egba government.

FIGURE 9.3. The Creek at Ijon Joining the River Owo, 1964.

FIGURE 9.4. Oldest Surviving Cocoa at Ijon, 1964.

into a successful career. He continued to run up debts in the 1880s and still owed money in the 1890s, while also lacking the means to pay his creditors.[21]

Developing the Estate in the 1880s

Davies commuted to Lagos from time to time to take care of his business interests there, but was far from being an absentee planter. Indeed, his commitment to the farm grew as it developed and as his business interests in Lagos diminished. His correspondence with Daniel Taiwo shows that he was often in Ijon, but still in touch with Lagos affairs.[22] It was from Woodland Estate, too, that he wrote his highly personal letter to Taiwo expressing his inconsolable loss at the sudden and unexpected death of his only son, Arthur.[23] A letter he sent to Taiwo in May 1883 said that he was 'feeling better' but had 'much to do', and gave the first details of produce on the farm.[24] He said that he had planted about 8,700 yams and hoped to reach a total of 10,000, with an additional 5,000 Aurora water yams. He had also transplanted 1,000 cocoa plants but was reluctant to add to the number because of the shortage of rain. He concluded his letter by saying that he had sent Taiwo a 'small present' of produce.

Although this is the first direct mention of cocoa at Ijon, it should not be a surprise that it occurred almost as an aside. Davies experimented, as the farmers at Agege were inclined to do, with a variety of possibilities, including coffee and kola, because at that time no one knew which, if any, of these would be profitable. It was clear to a small minority of shrewd and enterprising contemporaries, however, that palm oil and kernels were no longer novelties and that the former was experiencing setbacks in international markets. The originality of Davies's venture was not only that his main commitment was to farming rather than commerce but also that he decided to prospect for new export crops. Cocoa was the principal success story, but *nitida cola* (known locally as *Gbanja* kola), which Davies also pioneered, replaced cocoa as Agege's principal export crop during the inter-war period.[25]

Only scattered information is available to carry the story through the rest of the 1880s. At the close of 1886, Davies wrote to Taiwo reporting that he and his mother 'felt better' at Ijon, but that he had 'much and heavy work to do in

21. The details in LSCR, Civ. 2, 1880, Civ. 3, 1880–81, Civ. 9, 1889, Civ. 13, 1893.

22. See above, p. 146–51.

23. See above, p. 150.

24. Davies to Taiwo, May 1883, TP, Correspondence with J.P.L. Davies, 1870–94.

25. *Cola nitida* was imported from Sierra Leone and the Gold Coast before being planted in Ijon and Agege and exported, not overseas, but to northern Nigeria. Consumers preferred *cola nitida* to *cola acuminata*, which was indigenous to southwest Nigeria. See Agiri, 'The Yoruba'.

this place'.[26] Nevertheless, he found the estate congenial and wished he could stay 'for twelve months'. The farm was also becoming productive. At the beginning of 1887, his Lagos clerk, Samuel Sogunro Davies, wrote to him saying that he was 'glad that you have picked such a large quantity of cocoa this year'.[27] By then, Davies seems to have settled into his new home and way of life. Later in the year, he concluded a letter to Taiwo by saying that 'since my arrival here I feel better day by day and when I am well enough, I shall return to *cruel Lagos*'.[28] The two words he underlined provide a rare glimpse of the torment he had endured since disaster struck him in 1873 and the extent to which he no longer felt entirely at ease in the town that had seen him rise to exceptional heights of wealth and social status.

The first public comments on Davies's farm also appeared in 1887. Governor Alfred Moloney, who was a noted botanist, observed that before 1885 most of the cocoa imported into Britain from West Africa came from Fernando Po, but that attempts were now being made to promote the crop on other parts of the West Coast. In the case of Lagos, he referred explicitly to Davies's enterprise but to no others.[29] In the same year, the *African Times* provided a local view of what it termed Captain Davies's 'cocoa plantation'.[30] The paper estimated that it would take 'a good walker six hours to go through the plantation'. Brief and general though the report was, it indicated that the enterprise was substantial and that cocoa trees were especially prominent. Other sources record that by 1889, if not before, Davies was sending cocoa seeds and pods to his contacts elsewhere in Yorubaland.[31] An official who was touring the mainland border of the colony noted in June 1890 that 'near this village [Itele, with an estimated population of 350] Capt. Davies has a farm which I am informed is a success and upon which is cultivated coffee, cocoa, and kola'.[32] Of the towns the officer passed through, only Itele and Otta grew cocoa. Agege (population 200) was mentioned for farming and making palm oil but not for producing cocoa.

It was not until 1890, a decade after Davies had started his farm, that the first substantial account of Woodland Estate was recorded after Alvan Millson, the Assistant Colonial Secretary, toured the farm in August.[33] 'At Davies's farm', he wrote, 'I found a very encouraging example of enterprise and energy'.

26. Davies to Taiwo, 31 Dec. 1886, TP, Correspondence with J.P.L. Davies, 1870–94.

27. Samuel Sogunro Davies to J.P.L. Davies, 1 Jan. 1887, CP, 6/2.

28. Davies to Taiwo, 9 Aug. 1887, TP, Correspondence with J.P.L. Davies, 1870–94.

29. Moloney, *Sketch of the Forestry of West Africa*, p. 149.

30. *African Times*, 1 Oct. 1887.

31. William Allen (Abeokuta) to Davies, 1 Aug. 1889, CP, 6/2; J. W. Rowland to Davies, 2 July 1894, CP, 6/2.

32. Hadden Smith to Acting Inspector General of Constabulary, 2 June 1890, enc. in Moloney to Colonial Secretary, 30 Aug. 1890, CSO 8/7/3.

33. Millson to Denton, 24 Aug. 1890, enc in Denton to Knutsford, 10 April 1891, C.O. 147/79. Subsequent quotations in this paragraph are taken from this source.

Millson's report included valuable details that had previously been missing. He noted that there were 1,500 'full bearing' cocoa trees that were eight years old and 5,000 'young plants'. The trees were 10–15 feet high, disease free, and yielded an average of 55–60 pods per tree. In addition, Millson noted 'several hundred' kola trees and also some coffee, though the latter were 'less satisfactory' and required 'more personal supervision'. The coffee trees might have needed more than improved supervision. The farmers at the nearby settlement of Agege who followed Davies also began by planting large numbers of coffee trees, but they did not thrive and were gradually abandoned in favour of cocoa. Millson concluded by observing that 'a very handsome building with a life-sized marble statue in front of it completes the establishment'. He must have been referring to the granite obelisk that was Davies's memorial to his late wife, Sarah, and is still present on the site today.[34]

Acting Governor Denton, who visited Woodland Estate in the following year, was less enthusiastic.[35] The site was favourable but the 'lack of capital and skilled labour and experienced supervision' limited the 'success which will ultimately attend Captain Davies's efforts'. In particular, 'the dilapidated condition of the different buildings on the estate points to an absence of the funds necessary for the upkeep of what is undoubtedly a large undertaking for West Africa'. Denton was correct in identifying shortages of capital and labour that Davies himself was well aware of. Nevertheless, Denton was neither an agronomist nor a botanist and he may have been measuring Woodland Estate against an ideal drawn from neatly laid-out European plantations. Millson, like Moloney, was an official with considerable botanical expertise; his research on potential export crops had impressed the Director of Kew Gardens.[36] He also served as Commissioner for the Western District and his travels outside Lagos in that capacity enabled him to become familiar with African methods of cultivation.

Millson produced one more report on Woodland Estate, following a visit he made at the beginning of 1893.[37] His comments are worth extensive quotation because they contain detailed evidence that is not available in other sources.

'The next plantation I visited', Millson stated,

was that belonging to Captain J. P. L. Davies near Itele. This was the first one established in the Colony. Captain Davies introduced Cacao from

34. Elebute, *The Life and Times of James Pinson Labulo Davies*, p. 111, reproduces a photo of the obelisk.

35. Denton to Knutsford, 10 April 1891, C.O. 147/79.

36. Thistleton Dyer to Meade, 26 Nov. 1890, C.O.147/78. See also Millson, *The Yoruba Country*, and contributions to the *Journal of the Manchester Geographical Society*, 7 (1891), pp. 92–104, and 9 (1893), pp. 28–44.

37. Millson to Denton, enc. in Denton to Ripon, 14 Feb. 1893, C.O. 147/89.

Fernando Po some years ago, and has now about 10,000 trees planted out, many of which are bearing fruit. The land here is well suited for cacao as can be seen by the flourishing condition of the plants. The plantation is surrounded by low swampy ground from which there is a gradual rise to a low plateau. The principal plants grown are: Cacao, Kola, and a few Coffee plants. Several tons of Cacao are shipped annually from this plantation, the last consignment realising 62s. per cwt. I pointed out to Captain Davies that the trees required pruning. The pods produced were of a good size and the beans fully matured. A good plan, and one that answers well in planting Cacao, is being followed on this plantation. Roads are cut running parallel through the forest about three yards wide; and Cacao plants are then planted in the centre, the growth of trees on each forming shade under which the plants thrive well as they become established. The growth on the sides can be cut away when necessary. The plantation consists of 300 acres, and Captain Davies, who takes a great interest in it, would with more labour be able to keep it in a workable condition.

There is much that can be gleaned from Millson's observations. Although he was aware that several farmers in the vicinity of Lagos had begun planting cocoa and coffee by the early 1890s, he confirmed that Davies's farm was the first of its kind and was producing cocoa on what, at the time, was a large scale. Moreover, in stating explicitly that Davies introduced cocoa from Fernando Po, Millson solved a potentially crucial problem relating the type of cocoa grown at Ijon (and later Agege) to the subsequent spread of cocoa to other parts of Yorubaland. The cocoa grown on Fernando Po was almost exclusively of the Amelonado type, which had yellow pods. Davies grew Amelonado at Ijon, but Criollo cocoa, which had red pods, was present in some old trees at nearby Agege. If the Agege farmers grew Criollo cocoa in preference to Amelonado, they could not have obtained it from Ijon, nor could they have spread cocoa elsewhere because farmers in the rest of Yorubaland grew Amelonado rather than Criollo.

Joint detective work solved a mystery that could have severed the presumed links between Ijon, Agege, and other parts of Yorubaland that grew cocoa.[38] The suspect was eventually identified: it was the colonial government's Agricultural Department that planted Criollo at Ebute Metta and on a

38. I am greatly indebted here to the authority and generosity of the late Hille Toxopeus, who was attached to the Cocoa Research Institute of Nigeria at Moor Plantation, Ibadan, during the 1960s. Hille alerted me to the problem that red-podded cocoa presented for my initial hypothesis that cocoa spread from Ijon to Agege and from there to other parts of Yorubaland. Through correspondence and joint visits to the early farms near Lagos, he put me in a position to solve the puzzle. Without his intervention, I probably would have pursued my interpretation without being aware that it could have been refuted had Agege concentrated on Criollo rather than Amelonado.

small farm it acquired at Agege.[39] The Department was specific on this point: 'The variety cultivated at the Botanical Station is different from that cultivated generally locally. The latter has a yellow, thin pericarp when ripe; the former has a red, thick pericarp'.[40] The Department's experiment accounts for the appearance of Criollo on some of the African-run farms in and around Agege, where, nevertheless, Amelonado predominated. Moreover, the official trial of Criollo did not begin until the early 1900s, which was twenty years after Davies started his farm at Ijon and a decade after other pioneers from Lagos began to plant Amelonado cocoa at Agege. Criollo was rarely found beyond these initial sites. Although it produces high-quality cocoa, it is less prolific and requires greater care than Amelonado, which was good enough to meet the standards of the international cocoa market.

In forwarding Millson's report to the Colonial Office, Acting Governor Denton repeated his previous comment that the farm suffered from lack of capital and skilled labour, but that 'with these it should prove a very remunerative undertaking', adding that the farm produced 'very fair' cocoa.[41] The only other official comment on Woodland Estate worth mentioning from this time is a brief note by the Assistant Curator of the Botanic Station, who observed in 1895 that Captain Davies had 'the best and largest cocoa plantation in the Colony for sowing', adding that he also supplied the Botanic Station with cocoa pods.[42] This was a striking reversal of roles: the Botanic Station was supposed to act as a centre for the diffusion of novel crops and methods, whereas in this instance it was an African farmer who assisted the government's agricultural enterprise. This was not an isolated case. The Agege farmers frequently supported the official farms at Ebute Metta and Agege.

It was Governor Moloney's initiative in 1887 that led to the establishment of a Botanic Station at Ebute Metta, which was on the mainland just opposite Lagos.[43] Thoughtful commentators in the port had been advocating agricultural diversification since the early 1880s to reduce the dependence of Lagos on faltering staples, especially palm oil.[44] These ideas did not become official policy until Moloney became Governor and persuaded the Colonial Office to support his proposal.[45] Seeds from a variety of crops, including coffee, cotton,

39. Colony of Lagos, *Annual Reports, 1900–01: Botanic* (1901); Southern Nigeria, *Department of Agriculture, Annual Report*, 1911.

40. Colony of Lagos, *Annual Reports, 1900–01: Botanic* (1901); Southern Nigeria, *Department of Agriculture, Annual Report*, 1911.

41. Denton to Ripon, 14 Feb. 1893, C.O. 147/89.

42. *Lagos Gazette*, 12 Aug. 1899.

43. Moloney to C.O., 12 March 1887, C.O. 147/62. See also Omosini, 'Alfred Moloney'.

44. *Lagos Times*, 25 Oct. 1882; *Lagos Observer*, 16 March 1882; *Eagle & Lagos Critic*, 25 July 1885; *Lagos Observer*, 1 and 29 Oct. 1887.

45. There was 'no official information on botanical matters', before then. Griffith to Ussher, 1 April 1880, C.O. 147/40.

kola nut, arnotto (dye), and several fibres first became available for distribution in 1888. Cocoa was on the list too, but as a minor contributor.[46] In 1890, however, Moloney arranged a supply of cocoa seeds and plants from Fernando Po.[47] This promising start soon faltered. Early in 1891, Moloney was transferred to British Honduras; shortly after, Millson left to become Chief Assistant Colonial Secretary of the Gold Coast.[48] None of Moloney's successors shared his interest in botany or had the expertise to link it to wider issues of economic development.

It was clear as early as 1891 that the site at Ebute Metta was too small and the soil too sandy and saline.[49] Within a few years, Kew Gardens was expressing disillusion with the failure of successive governors to pursue Moloney's initiative.[50] In 1898, Kew judged that the station at Ebute Metta was 'of little use'.[51] Two years later, the Director of Kew concluded that the Botanic Station had 'drifted away from its original purpose. European vegetables were cultivated and as no one was prepared to buy them, they were distributed gratuitously'.[52] Numerous alternative sites were considered and rejected.[53] After the turn of the century, the Director of Kew felt obliged to add a touch of asperity to his habitual expressions of disappointment, writing in 1905 that 'Successive Governors have been more occupied in futile attempts to grow Eucalyptus and secure decorative plants for Government House than to promote the cultural industries of their colonies'.[54]

Although the Botanic Station should be credited with its efforts to diversify agriculture, its effectiveness was mainly confined to the first two or three years of its existence. By then, Davies had already demonstrated that cocoa farming could be profitable, and the industry had become self-propagating and self-supporting: African farmers distributed plants and seeds among themselves and to their labourers. Equally important, they performed a service that was not available at Ebute Metta: their own farms provided models of how to grow and process cocoa. The Botanic Station had a more direct role in supplying European plantations, which were started in West Africa during the 1890s.[55] But these ventures were no more successful than the government's Botanic

46. Moloney to C.O., 12 Nov. 1888, C.O. 147/59; Moloney to Knutsford, 25 Feb. 1889, C.O. 147/69; 16 May 1890, C.O. 147/75.

47. Moloney to Governor General, Fernando Po, 16 Aug. 1890, CSO, 8/5/6.

48. Millson's promising career was cut short in 1896, when he died from a 'fever' at the age of thirty-five while at sea off the coast of West Africa. *Geographical Journal*, 7 (1896), p. 668.

49. Thistleton Dyer to C.O., 31 Dec. 1897, C.O. 147/126.

50. Thistleton Dyer to C.O., 31 Dec. 1897, C.O. 147/126, 24 Aug. 1898, C.O. 147/139.

51. Thistleton Dyer to C.O., 24 Aug. 1898, C.O. 147/139.

52. Kew Gardens to C.O., 26 Nov. 1900, C.O. 147/153. Kew had noted the trend as early as 1897: Thistleton Dyer to C.O., 23 Feb. 1897, C.O. 147/126.

53. Denton to Chamberlain, 30 Oct. 1898, C.O. 147/135.

54. Thistleton Dyer to C.O., 22 May 1905, C.O. 147/177.

55. Denton to Ripon, 9 July 1895, C.O., 147/99.

Station, and their failure was even more complete.[56] Writing in 1914, the Director of Agriculture summarised the history of cocoa farming in Southern Nigeria as follows: 'All the plantations are owned by natives; those which were established by Europeans have been abandoned for various reasons'.[57]

The Estate Farm Book, 1896–1899

It would be impossible to say very much about Woodland Estate in the years between Millson's valuable report in 1893 and Davies's death in 1906 had it not been for the survival of a work diary or farm book that Davies kept from 1896 to 1899.[58] The information in the diary is limited. It contains no quantitative data of the kind Millson gathered and leaves several months of each year unrecorded. Nevertheless, the diary covers the cocoa 'season' and includes both main and minor crops. Taken as a whole, it provides a first-hand impression of the farming year as seen by those who were, literally, on the ground. No other known source provides this level of detail either about Ijon or any of the other pioneer cocoa farms in Nigeria before 1900.

The diary opens on 28 August 1896 with a simple entry: 'Arrived at the plantation on this day and found all well'.[59] The next day Davies walked around the estate and visited some of his local neighbours who were growing food crops (mostly corn). The afternoon, however, signalled a serious and persistent problem: 'the Iddo farm labourers refused to serve for more than seven months. I shall keep them and then send them away when I can get men'. Three days later, after his courier, Ojun, had arrived from Lagos 'with a bag of money and sundries', Davies was able to fix the pay of the thirteen labourers and send them 'into the field to work'. A dispute arose almost immediately. The men took from the farm 'what they ought not' and threatened to leave if they were not paid a higher wage. The matter was settled 'and they prostrated'. With this problem out of the way, at least temporarily, Davies and the men began to pick 'the ripe cocoa'. On the 1st of September, Davies travelled on foot and by canoe to the northern part of Ijon. He visited farms there and received presents of kola and a pig. The next day he was back on the estate inspecting coffee, yams, and cassava, and supervising the work of the sawyer. On the 4th, he was busy checking the performance of the labourers who had picked and opened cocoa pods, while dealing with 'the people of Isheri Idimu' who

56. See, for example, Austin, 'Mode of Production', in Clarence-Smith, ed., *Cocoa Pioneer Fronts since 1800.*

57. Johnson, 'Cocoa in the Southern Provinces', p. 190.

58. I am immensely grateful to Mrs Eshugbiyi, one of Davies's granddaughters, for permitting me to read and make notes on the diary. Igbobi College, Yaba, Lagos, 28 Jan. 1962 (and subsequent dates during that month).

59. The quotations in this and succeeding paragraphs are all taken from the dates of the diary entries given in the paragraph.

'came about their matter with Bakari'. The next day did not go well. 'The cocoa casked on Thursday' had not been 'properly fermented' and had to be taken out for further processing. Later in the day, he found time to send 'oranges and plantains' to his wife in Lagos.

The 20th of September began well: 'Up early as usual—set out all the cocoa for drying, the largest quantity ever done at a time and the best crop ever got'. On the 28th he was able to record with satisfaction that 'the cocoa turned out very well indeed'. Problems, however, were never far away. On the 29th, he discovered bugs under the mats used for drying cocoa, ordered the cocoa to be removed, and used salt to kill the insects. Evidently, this action did not go down well. The next day, 'the men gave some trouble and Ilori was stubborn and impertinent. It took some time before they began work'. The bugs persisted; so did the labour problems. At the start of October, Davies reported that the 'men worked most reluctantly and would not finish breaking the cocoa'. On 8 October he filled twenty bags of cocoa; on the 14th he 'bagged the fourth lot of cocoa and made preparations for loads to Lagos'; on the 16th he 'began picking the sixth lot of cocoa'. The next day, 'all hands picked cocoa in the afternoon. Went round the farm on 17th and discovered a heavy waste of cocoa as a result of some not being picked and some picked but not collected. Spoke strongly to the careless men'. Nevertheless, on the 19th he was able to load the canoe 'with 33 bags of cocoa and 5 bags of corn' before leaving for Lagos the next day.

Any time that remained from picking and processing cocoa was spent on routine tasks, such as making and mending fences, planting cassava and bananas, and weeding the corn farm. Some lucky labourers counted the kola trees, which on 13 October now 'number 430'; others, less fortunate, had to dig the well, which had reached a depth of thirty-two feet but was still unfinished. Work was unremitting. Nevertheless, Davies made sure that Christmas was a time of celebration for everyone. On Christmas Day 1896, he 'bought a pig for 10s. for the farm labourers and presented them with a yam and a pint of rice each. Jolly Christmas'. Local farmers reciprocated with presents for him. A few days later, however, Davies reported that 'the men refuse to work'. It took two more days for them to promise 'to do their work properly before they left'.

Davies had to deal with other obligations during this exceptionally busy time in the farming year. On 13 September, he was 'up early to hear the result of the examination with regard to the Iroko timber set on fire by the Iddo men'. Later in the day, he wrote letters and met 'one of Oseni's wives' who wanted to 'hear results of her complaints'. Davies told her that 'Oseni did not require her any more as a wife'. Summary justice was also speedy justice. Three days later, 'the King of Itele called at my invitation with two of his chiefs re the dispute they have with the corporal', who was stationed there as an agent of the Lagos government. In mid-October, Davies visited Itele and settled a dispute 'among the king and chiefs about repairs to the soldiers' house and the king's palace'. Two days later, 'the Balogun of Itele called with his son in the matter of Olowu's farmland and I advised him to give up his case'. With this settled, Davies resumed 'cleaning and drying the cocoa', but was again interrupted when 'Akande, the husband of Ramatu, lodged a complaint against the head farm labourer, Oje, for using indecent language against his wife'. The weariness in Davies's voice is almost audible as he wrote: 'I put off the case for Monday'.

Personal matters also required his attention. On 11 September, he received news from his wife, Catherine (neé Reffle), who reported that his daughter, Stella, was 'ill and unable to attend school'.[60] There was also a letter from Dr James Ojoye Coker, who was to marry Stella in 1898. More letters arrived from Lagos on the 27th, including one from Dr Coker's twin brother, Jacob, who had just begun to grow cocoa at Agege. The contents, unfortunately, are unknown. On 11 October, a messenger arrived from Lagos with an invitation for Stella to attend a dance given by the governor. 'Of course', Davies commented, 'I cannot give my consent'. Although Davies was Victorian in his attitude towards family matters, he was not grudging. However, he suspected that his other daughter, Victoria, who was ten years older than Stella and unhappily married to another doctor, John Randle, was concerned about her sister's prospective alliance. Randle had already complained to Davies that marriage to Victoria had made 'every waking hour miserable'.[61] The next day, Davies wrote to Stella, warning her of 'her sister's tricks'.

Victoria had an independent spirit that could easily turn into assertiveness. While in Sierra Leone in 1885, she had fallen in love with a successful lawyer named Samuel Lewis, who in 1896 became the first African to receive a knighthood.[62] The pair became engaged but overlooked the need (and wisdom) of informing Davies, who forbade the marriage. Adding his own mistake to his daughter's, he then pushed Victoria into marrying Randle. Victoria never forgave her father. By 1898, she was accusing Stella of allying with their father to support Randle and claimed that they had 'approved and emulated his cruelties and infidelities'.[63] It was every family's nightmare. In any event, Stella's marriage to James Coker, a remarkable physician, was a happy one until it was cut short by his early death in 1901.[64] Victoria's marriage ended in an acrimonious divorce.

No doubt Davies was keen to focus on his farm. His diary halts at the end of December 1896 and resumes in May 1897. On 20 May, Davies sent one of his workers to Oseni with 3,225 seeds of Ceara rubber. He then made a quick

60. Stella had started a school in Lagos in 1896, but ill health obliged her to close it.
61. Mann, *Marrying Well*, p. 85, for the quotation and the context.
62. Hargreaves, *A Life of Sir Samuel Lewis*, pp. 62–3, 82. Lewis's first wife had died in 1880; he married Edith Grant in 1892.
63. Quoted in Mann, *Marrying Well*, p. 85.
64. Both doctors had impressive careers, despite the fact that one ended prematurely: Adeloye, 'Some Early Nigerian Doctors'.

trip to Lagos and on his return found that the iron chest in his house 'had been disturbed'. The king of Itele sent his 'salutations' via his son and followed the greeting with presents. Afterwards, Davies 'went round the farm and was disgusted with the state of things'. The barn for storing yams had been badly constructed, the coffee plants had been neglected, a large number of cocoa trees had perished, and the 'passes [traces] had become overgrown'. Nevertheless, work continued. In June, 3,000 Ceara rubber seeds were planted in the nursery and fenced with wire netting, the men from Isheri-Idimu made heaps for 1,600 yams, and kola nuts were gathered. In the same month he planted 200 *Abata* kola and 50 *Gbanja*, planted more yams, put up a wire fence 'to prevent the goats from jumping into the verandah', and cleaned the sheepfold. In an intriguing aside, he ordered the 'bellows and anvil to be removed from the engine room'. By the middle of June, 5,000 yams had been planted. He then engaged men from Ijero to weed the cocoa and kola trees, and agreed to pay them £10, of which he advanced £1.

The next entry marked a big day: his sixty-ninth birthday on 14 August, when he took his wife and his daughter, Stella, and a party of fifteen guests to his estate for a celebration. Two days later, Davies was back patrolling the farm, noting that he 'inspected the job men's work and found it unsatisfactory'. He also had to deal with the matter of the disturbed chest, so he 'called the men together' on 19 August and found that 'Ojo was guilty of aiding the robberies and stealing the kola nuts, yams, etc'.. No record remains of what happened to the guilty party. Meanwhile, the men were busy gathering and processing cassava, weeding the yam heaps, and harvesting corn. On 29 August, Stella was still with her father because on that day, Sunday, 'she read the morning prayers' in the small church (which doubled as a school) that Davies had built. On 3 September, he left for Lagos, taking some corn with him but sending the 'bull and cow by land'.

He was back in Ijon in October. On the 23rd, the 'Isheri people arrived and went round the yam field and promised to work' on it. With this assurance, Davies 'saw no reason for employing the Idimu people as our men could do the work'. Although Idimu was nearby, Davies evidently preferred farm-workers from Isheri; no doubt his strong ties with Taiwo, the *Olofin* of Isheri, gave him confidence that this source would not disappoint him. At the end of the month, he 'loaded the canoe with plants ready to return to Lagos'.

The next entry is dated 23 April 1898, when Davies arrived at the estate from Lagos. Busy days returned immediately. Fields were inspected, palm nuts gathered, the 'wrecked engine house' was pulled down, and several local disputes settled, including an opaque instruction to local farmers that 'Akere could only return to the plantation if she behaved herself'. The main event of the year, though, was the shortage of rain, which led to the loss of many cocoa trees. On 4 May, Davies recorded that a total of 808 cocoa trees had died. The following day, 'Venn and myself began cleaning kola after tea about 960 kola'.

The next day he 'broke cocoa with Venn'. During the rest of the month, the men prepared the ground for yam heaps. The diary then moves to September 1898, when he was in Ijon supervising the cocoa harvest and expressing how 'disheartened' he was 'at the great loss of cocoa trees'. Cocoa-picking continued, nevertheless, and the men 'helped by the women, picked, broke and put the cocoa to ferment'. Corn was gathered and put in the barn, the coffee nursery was weeded, disputes at Itele sorted out, and 'the position of the sheep changed'. Work continued with 'all hands' breaking and preparing cocoa during October. On the 12th, Davies sent 'Ajayi with the cattle to Lagos', and followed him two days later.

Other matters continued to claim his attention: the Krooboys had to be organised to guard part of the estate where 'the hunters encroach'; Davies himself was 'up all night' on 29 May, 'to keep the leopard from the kids'. Presumably, he had some success because on the following day he put '8 sheep and 7 goats in the canoe for Lagos'. It seems that the elements of a shuttle service connected the settlements around Ijon to one another and to Lagos. On 24 April, Davies noted that 'the Ojo market canoes passed today'. Three days later a 'canoe from Itele called and took letters and yams, bananas, plantains, corn, and palm oil to Mrs Davies'. On 29 September, two unexpected events disturbed his routine. A fire had to be lit 'to frighten the squirrel which destroyed the cocoa'. Later on, burglars arrived 'at midnight'. Davies suspected 'some former employees now working with J. E. Shyngle', a Gambian lawyer in Lagos who had just started to farm at Ifako, one of the districts of Agege.[65] Amid the routine and the unexpected, Davies found time to prepare his 'last will' and write numerous letters, including (on 23 May) one to Jacob Coker, the prime mover behind the development of cocoa at Agege.

The entries resume in February 1899 and cease early in March. Davies arrived at Woodland Estate on 1 February with his wife and four children and began to receive visitors the next day. Among them was his son-in-law, Dr James Coker, who was now married to Stella. The diary ends on the 7th of March with a simple entry: 'loaded the canoe for Lagos'. This was not the end of the story; we know that cocoa continued to be produced on Woodland Estate and sent to Lagos for sale abroad.[66] It was, however, the end of detailed accounts of events on the farm between 1899 and 1906, when Davies died. From a very limited number of other sources, we know that Davies, who reached the age of seventy in 1898, began to suffer from an unknown (or at least an undisclosed) illness which lasted from about 1900 to his death.[67] It seems highly likely that he was unable to sustain the relentless pace of life on the farm. He appointed an estate manager and reduced his visits to Ijon.

65. Shyngle's family was from Ilesha, but his father made his career in the Gambia.
66. Tambaci to Davies, 5 Sept. 1900, CP, 6/2.
67. Davies v. Williams and Blaize, LSCR, Civ. 27, 1902.

Davies's wife, Catherine, inherited Woodland Estate but within a few years it passed into the hands of Jacob Coker, who had helped to manage it.[68] The connection between the two families lived on.

Ijon as a Centre of Innovation

These daily details yield several broad conclusions. Woodland Estate was clearly an innovative, frontier farm. Since cocoa was not indigenous to West Africa, Davies was taking a considerable risk in planting it and waiting several years before securing a return on his investment. Uncertainty about the outcome explains why he experimented with other potential exports, notably coffee and rubber, and invested in products for the domestic market, such as kola, food crops, and sheep, goats, and cattle. The focus on cocoa, which was ultimately successful, should not obscure the significance of these seemingly minor crops and livestock. In producing for the domestic market, Davies was anticipating the future, even if he was not aware of it. In the 1920s and 1930s, when cocoa at Ijon and Agege was in decline, the region adapted by becoming the leading market garden supplying quality foodstuffs to Lagos and selling kola nuts to a wider market, which stretched to northern Nigeria.

The production methods adopted on Woodland Estate were a further aspect of the experimental character of the enterprise, and also a measure of its success. There is no evidence of how Davies acquired the agronomic techniques he used to grow cocoa. The Gold Coast was not producing cocoa in the early 1880s; one or two farmers in the Oil Rivers and Calabar had also experimented with cocoa, which they obtained from Fernando Po, but there is no indication that Davies knew of them or their activities.[69] The evidence cited above states explicitly that Davies, too, obtained his cocoa from Fernando Po, in which case he probably copied the methods used there, though whether he visited the island or was given advice on cultivation from someone who was familiar with the methods employed there is unknown. Accordingly, Davies grew seeds in a nursery before transplanting them to cocoa groves, where they were shaded first by food crops and then by larger trees. The sequence that followed was recorded in his diary: pods were 'plucked', broken open, the beans cleaned and then dried, fermented, bagged, and shipped by canoe to Lagos.

This 'classic' procedure, as it might be called, was also adopted at Agege. Further north, especially around Ibadan, however, farmers varied the method of production by using the 'seed at stake' method, which dispensed with a nursery and transplanting. Instead, farmers put two or three seeds in a hole and relied on one of them to survive as a strong plant. Each method has

68. Confirmed by Chief Adekunle Coker, Jacob Coker's son, 23 Feb. 1962. Jacob Coker's draft will, dated 1911, left the farm at Ijon to the children of one of his wives.

69. See Howes, 'The Early Introduction of Cocoa', p. 172; Ayorinde, 'Historical Notes'.

advantages and disadvantages; both are sensible adaptations to local conditions. Davies's nursery benefitted from close proximity to water and his trees from his conscientious approach to weeding. He also spaced his trees to allow them room to grow and cut paths through the groves to provide easy access. The precise distance he allowed between the trees is now unknown and was in any case a matter of debate at the time. The opinion of the Director of Agriculture in Nigeria, who commented some years later and in general terms, was that 'the plants are put in far too closely together'.[70] His counterpart on the Gold Coast agreed, adding that the dangers of 'close planting' were the fault of the 'uneducated native'.[71] It seems reasonable to assume that Millson would have remarked on the spacing allowed by Davies had it been markedly at variance with what was thought of as best practice at the time. Whatever the defects of the enterprise at Ijon, Davies's trees produced significant quantities of cocoa from pods that Millson described as being 'disease-free' and of 'good size'. Davies, the farmer, was at least as capable as Davies, the sea captain.

The shortage of labour was a constant theme in Davies's diary and one he repeated in his evidence to the Commission on Trade in 1898. 'My great difficulty', he said, 'is the want of labour'.[72] Davies paid his labourers six pence a day plus food and added a bonus of cocoa seeds when they left the farm. Because there were no large settlements near Ijon, he used his extensive connections to secure workers. As he stated in 1898: 'I have been employing men who come from a long distance. Most of them are all planting cocoa for themselves now on their return home'.[73] He confirmed that 'they got the seeds from me'. Abeokuta, where he had relatives, was a particularly important source; Isheri, where Taiwo ruled, was another. It is evident that Woodland Estate was not sealed from the rest of Yorubaland but was a centre of diffusion that spread cocoa seeds over a wide catchment area.

Although Davies grumbled about the pay being too high and labourers being too idle, he also had a shrewd understanding of the underlying cause, which stemmed from the transformation of the labour market. The decline of internal slavery, which Davies dated from the beginning of colonial rule, had disrupted the large-scale production of palm oil and kernels, with the result that 'many of these large plantations are now deserted'.[74] Had the growing army of free workers lacked opportunities, labour would have been abundant and wage rates would have been driven down. Opportunities, however, were

70. Johnson, 'Cocoa in the Southern Provinces', p. 191.
71. Tudhope, 'The Development of the Cocoa Industry', p. 37.
72. Evidence in Denton to Chamberlain, 4 June 1898, C.O. 147/133; the Commission's Report is in Denton to Chamberlain, 25 May 1898, C.O. 147/59.
73. Evidence in Denton to Chamberlain, 4 June 1898, C.O. 147/133; the Commission's Report is in Denton to Chamberlain, 25 May 1898, C.O. 147/59.
74. Evidence in Denton to Chamberlain, 4 June 1898, C.O. 147/133; the Commission's Report is in Denton to Chamberlain, 25 May 1898, C.O. 147/59.

available. The main consequence was that 'small quantities of palm oil are now made by slaves who have deserted from their masters'.[75] In the late 1890s, too, there was a boom in exports of wild rubber. Existing trees could be tapped at very little cost and with an immediate return. There were other disincentives to taking employment at Ijon. Farm work for a 'master' was tainted by its association with slavery; it involved leaving home; and, as Davies's diary made clear, it was gruelling work.

Nevertheless, Davies was an innovative employer. By paying his workers in cash, he was transporting the idea of wage labour from Lagos into its hinterland. He remained resolute in his refusal to employ slaves of any description, and he appears not to have used the pawn system, whereby labour was offered as a means of repaying debt.[76] Davies was also enterprising in searching for ways of dealing with the labour shortage other than by raising wages, which, he feared, would make the farm unremunerative. Necessity combined with the technical training he had received during his time with the Royal Navy led him to experiment with labour-saving devices. He built an engine house for two sawmills and introduced shingle-making to replace thatch.[77] He may not have known that his reaction to the labour shortage was reproduced on a much larger scale in the United States, where the problem stimulated the widespread adoption of machinery in the nineteenth century. An additional response, which seems to have produced tangible results, was to employ the existing labour force more efficiently. 'Every year I improve', he said in 1898', 'and why because it is a necessity'.[78] 'Six men and myself do all the work', whereas formerly he used '20 to do the same amount of work'. It is unclear how the savings were made, though in 1898 he 'tried two women and found them better than the men in breaking and curing the pods'. By these means, Davies increased the estate's productivity and ensured that his enterprising venture remained viable.

Output and Profits

The important question of profitability, however, remains unanswered and is now unanswerable. No accounts have survived, and Davies's diary and other papers do not mention it. Only one estimate of his income from farming has survived and that was contained in evidence Davies gave in court in 1903, when he was being sued for the payment of a debt of £113.[79] He stated

75. Evidence in Denton to Chamberlain, 4 June 1898, C.O. 147/133; the Commission's Report is in Denton to Chamberlain, 25 May 1898, C.O. 147/59.

76. See chapter 4.

77. Brimah Aduloju v. Davies, LSCR, Civ. 33, 1904; Moloney, *Sketch of the Forestry of West Africa*, p. 149. The sawmills were more successful than the experiment with shingle.

78. The remaining quotations in this paragraph are taken from Davies's evidence to the Commission on Trade in Denton to Chamberlain, 4 June 1898, C.O. 147/133.

79. Thomas Jones as Assignee of Z. A. Williams v. Davies, LSCR, Civ. 29, 1903.

that he had found farming profitable and had cleared an average annual net profit of between £100 and £200 on cocoa sales during the last four years (1899–1902 inclusive). It is hard to know how to interpret this information. Although the figures come from the best source, it is possible that Davies was concerned to avoid giving his creditor the impression that he was doing very well. At first sight, the net profit appears to represent an indifferent return to the considerable effort that sustained the estate for twenty years. The only relevant additional evidence dates from 1896, when Davies had four thousand trees bearing cocoa and shipped about six tons before Christmas 1895 and an additional 1.2 tons between then and April 1896, making a total, in his estimation, of about 7.5 tons.[80] Moreover, the estate produced good-quality cocoa that fetched 'the best price in the market'.[81] Davies said he was 'doing well', in that year', and 'getting as much as £74 a ton'. His gross earnings from this shipment, which covered (approximately) both main and minor crops, would have been £555. His total income would have been higher because he was producing other crops for sale besides cocoa. These figures may not reflect conditions in 1899–1902; even if they do, the net return is a matter of guesswork.

Given the purchasing power of the pound sterling at the close of the nineteenth century and wage rates for other occupations at that time, it would seem that Davies was earning enough to maintain more than a façade of prosperity in Lagos, but that his net income undoubtedly fell far short of the level he achieved as a 'merchant prince' in the years before his downfall in 1873. This supposition receives some support from the Probate Office records, which show that the value of Davies's estate in 1906 was 'sworn at under £150'.[82] Although such declarations are unreliable guides to total assets, a wealthy person's executors would have had difficulty making a declaration as low as this. Moreover, the references in his will to his 'misfortunes' and struggles to educate his children make gloomy reading. In the end, there were few assets to distribute.

Uncertainty about the profitability of Davies's farming venture is matched by imprecision about the contribution his farm made to total exports of cocoa from Lagos. Although Alvan Millson, the most authoritative contemporary official, apart from Governor Moloney, clearly identified Davies as being the pioneer of cocoa farming, there is insufficient evidence to construct a time series relating the volume of cocoa he shipped to total exports.

Cocoa first appeared in the list of exports from Lagos in 1885 and remained there throughout the colonial period. The figures from that date to 1900, by which time cocoa farming had spread far beyond Ijon, are provided in table 9.1.

80. Davies evidence in Denton to Chamberlain, 4 June 1898, C.O. 147/133.
81. Davies evidence in Denton to Chamberlain, 4 June 1898, C.O. 147/133.
82. Lagos Probate Office Records, II, 407–415, 1906.

Table 9.1 Exports of Cocoa from Lagos, 1885–1900

Year	Pounds	Tons
1885	121	0.054
1886	2,751	1.22
1887	671	0.29
1888	3,738	1.66
1889	3,044	1.35
1890	13,657	6.09
1891	15,254	6.80
1892	15,820	6.81
1893	18,072	8.04
1894	39,177	17.48
1895	48,187	21.51
1896	27,968	12.48
1897	101,156	45.15
1898	76,965	34.35
1899	157,708	70.41
1900	256,234	114.39

Source: *Lagos Blue Books.*

The striking variations in export volumes prompted considerable debate among contemporary commentators. The consensus that emerged held that the prime cause was neither price fluctuations nor labour issues but lack of rainfall: drought in one year led to poor harvests in the next. Davies's diary supports this contention. It is also interesting to note that exports from Lagos preceded those from the Gold Coast, which did not record its first shipment of cocoa until 1891 (80 lbs valued at £4). The Gold Coast accelerated past Lagos in the late 1890s, and in 1901 exported 980 tons compared with 102 tons from Lagos. The difference reflects what is known about the early years of the two industries. Cocoa farming in the Lagos hinterland began slowly and was confined to a few planters. The port did not ship more than ten tons of cocoa annually until 1894. The Gold Coast made a late start but a rapid one: planting was speedily taken up by a multiplicity of small farmers. Lagos, however, quickly moved ahead of Central and Eastern Nigeria, where cocoa farming began on a small scale in the late 1870s following an initiative taken by Joseph Henshaw, who brought some pods back from Fernando Po.[83] The Western

83. This is well attested, though there are few details of the experiment. See Ayorinde, 'Historical Notes', pp. 18–23. I am grateful to Chief Emmanuel Daniel Henshaw, grandson of Joseph and eldest son of Daniel (who continued to work the farm) for adding to the available

and Eastern region (essentially Yorubaland) and the other regions exported comparable volumes during the 1880s and 1890s, when total shipments were on a small scale, but producers in Yorubaland sped ahead after the turn of the century: by 1910, they were exporting 2,547 tons compared to 385 tons from the two other regions combined.[84]

There is no direct evidence of the identity of the farmer who first exported cocoa in 1885. Although Davies began farming in 1880, he stated in 1898 that he did not plant cocoa until 1882. It is generally held that cocoa pods are not ready for harvesting until the trees are four or five years old, and Davies's trees were only three years old in 1885. However, the recommendation represents current thinking and may not have been applied in the early, experimental days of cocoa farming. Davies, like the farmers at Agege, began regular harvesting at four years rather than five, providing pods were ripe. Furthermore, in 1909, the Director of Agriculture on the Gold Coast reported that some cocoa trees there bore fruit less than a year after planting and produced a 'fair crop' when they were three to four years old.[85] Admittedly, conditions in the hinterland of Lagos were not identical to those on the Gold Coast. Nevertheless, they were similar and both countries grew the same type of cocoa. Accordingly, it is reasonable to suppose that Davies's trees produced some pods at three years. We also know that in 1885 he had 1,500 cocoa trees that were three years old.[86] This number could easily have produced the 121 pounds of cocoa exported in that year, even if the pods were picked selectively. Furthermore, Davies might well have made a trial shipment at the first opportunity to obtain an assessment of the quality of his cocoa and an estimate of the price it would fetch.

The evidence on this point is circumstantial and speculative. It is also conceivable that another farmer, or perhaps several farmers, had started planting at the same time as Davies or even earlier, and were beginning to ship cocoa from maturing trees. Such sources, however, remain unidentified and may not have existed in 1885. If other farmers had been growing cocoa on a considerable scale, like Davies, it is likely that their activities would have been recorded if they had made regular shipments after that date. Yet, Davies's farm at Ijon is the only one mentioned consistently during the 1880s. Moreover, his estate produced and exported cocoa continuously and in quantity from the mid-1880s.

---

information. Henshaw Town, Calabar, 25 March 1964. It seems that Joseph did not travel to Fernando Po to get cocoa but to see the British Consul about the trade dispute between the Efik of Duke Town and the Henshaws. Cocoa was a benign consequence of the visit.

84. The figures for the central and eastern regions are taken from Dudgeon, *Agricultural and Forest Products*, p. 107.

85. Tudhope, 'The Development of the Cocoa Industry', p. 37.

86. Millson to Denton, 24 Aug. 1890, enc. in Denton to Knutsford, 10 April 1891, C.O. 147/79.

As far as entrepreneurial innovation is concerned, who did it first matters less than who did it best. Davies qualifies as a prime mover because he set a successful example that encouraged others to follow. His stature in Lagos made him an 'opinion-leader'; his connections in the port and its hinterland created personal networks of diffusion. His friends asked him for pods and plants; his labourers took them to Isheri and Abeokuta. Davies also initiated what became the most important channel of distribution, which took cocoa from Ijon to Agege on a path he had cut.[87] Marriage joined Davies's daughter, Stella, to Dr James Coker, whose twin brother, Jacob, led the development of cocoa farming at Agege. Jacob visited Davies at Ijon and took pods and plants from there to Agege, which was only ten miles (16 km) away.[88] His story qualifies for inclusion in this study and will appear in chapter 13, because he, too, was a Lagos merchant who became a cocoa farmer.

The first of only three indications of the scale of Davies's enterprise dates from 1890, when Alvan Millson reported that the farm had 1,500 'full bearing' trees that were eight years old and produced an average yield of 55–60 pods.[89] Calculating pounds from pods is even harder than estimating output per tree, which varied from a low figure of 2 pounds per tree to a high figure of 8–12 pounds claimed by Jacob Coker, and an astonishing twenty pounds that Davies submitted in evidence in 1898.[90] If the figure of two pounds is applied to Davies's 'full bearing trees', they would have produced approximately 1.34 tons of dried and fermented cocoa. Since Millson was writing in August, when only the light crop had been harvested, the most appropriate comparison is with the calendar year 1889, when 1.35 tons were exported from Lagos. The estimate for marketed output from Davies's farm may be too high: much depends on the point in the production process at which the cocoa was weighed. Nevertheless, the figure is as realistic an estimate as is now likely to be achieved, and it indicates that, at the close of the 1880s, Davies was responsible for most of the cocoa exports leaving Lagos.

Millson's second report on the farm early in 1893 noted that, by then, there were ten thousand cocoa trees, 'many bearing fruit' with 'fully matured beans' that produced 'several tons' that were 'shipped annually'.[91] A more exact figure

87. Information from Ladipo Williams, son of one of the large Agege planters, Frederick E. Williams, who was a substantial farmer there. Iju, 16 Jan. 1967.

88. Interviews with Mr John Romanes Adewale Randle, 29 Jan. 1962, 12 April 1964; and Chief Adekunle Coker, Jacob Coker's son, 23 Feb. 1962, 16 May 1964, 24 May 1964.

89. Millson to Denton, 24 Aug. 1890, enc. in Denton to Knutsford, 10 April 1891, C.O. 147/79.

90. Evidence of Jacob Coker, T. B. Dawudu, and Frederick E. Williams in Re Public Lands Ordinance, Colonial Secretary v. Ogundimu, LSCR, Civ. 53, 1909; evidence of J.P.L. Davies in Denton to Chamberlain, 4 June 1898, C.O. 147/133. Initial high yields may have resulted from a lack of shading.

91. Enc. in Denton to Ripon, 14 Feb. 1893, C.O. 147/89.

cannot be derived from the data available because it is impossible to know how much to add to the tonnage produced by the 1,500 trees that were 'full bearing' three years earlier. If 'several' is taken to mean 'more than two', which is the conventional understanding, Woodland Estate was still producing around half or possibly more of the 6.81 tons of cocoa exported in 1892.

The final indicator comes from Davies's evidence to the Commission on Trade in 1898. In that year, Davies had four thousand trees bearing cocoa and shipped about 7.5 tons between what he referred to as 'before Christmas' 1897 and April 1898.[92] If the stated total represented the main crop in 1897 and the minor crop in 1898, it would have accounted for about 17 per cent of the 45.1 tons exported from Lagos in 1897. Although this was still a substantial proportion for one farm to supply, it is evident that by then a growing number of farmers had followed Davies's lead. The trend is consistent with what is known of the development of Agege, where cocoa farming began at the close of the 1880s and spread during the 1890s.

Final Years

Davies died without the 'son and heir' he had hoped for. He left two capable daughters, Victoria and Stella, from his marriage to Sarah Forbes Bonetta, and five younger daughters from his marriage in 1889 to Catherine Kofoworola Reffle, which followed Sarah's death in 1880.[93] His main asset, a fine residence in Broad Street called Wood House, became the subject of a dispute between the children of his second and third wives, and ended in court.[94] Davies had previously stated that he had bought the land for the house in 1880 in his mother's name. In 1911, the court ruled that the claim was a 'fraud on his creditors' executed with the aim of building a house that they could not seize. Nevertheless, the house remained in the family.[95] Davies's eldest child, Victoria, leased it after his death and paid rent to members of the family.

Victoria left her cheerless marriage to Dr John Randle in 1900 and lived in her own house in nearby Kose Street, though she spent most of her time in England, where she felt more at home than she did in Lagos. Unhappy memories of her life in Lagos kept her away; her privileged upbringing gave her a decided preference for societies that were organised by class and accompanying levels of status rather than by race. Her resources dwindled, however, because she had severed her ties with her father, and Randle offered her no

92. Davies evidence in Denton to Chamberlain, 4 June 1898, C.O. 147/133.

93. Catherine was the daughter of William Reffle, a Lagos merchant.

94. Victoria Randle & Anor. v. James George & Ors., LSCR, Civ. 61, 1911. There is a rare photo of the house in Elebute, *The Life of James Pinson Labulo Davies*, p. 146.

95. Further information on the history of the family can be found in two valuable sources: Mann, *Marrying Well*, pp. 30, 46–7, 85–8, 97–8, 99, 101; Elebute, *The Life of James Pinson Labulo Davies*, pp. 71–9.

support after they parted. She returned to Lagos in 1917 and opened a small shop. She never remarried. Her death in 1920 prompted a re-examination of the leasing arrangement for the old family house in Broad Street and to its sale for the sum of £1,800. The most prominent of Davies's grandchildren was Victoria's son, John Romanes Adewale Davies, who followed the family tradition of investing in both property and agriculture and became president of the Agege Cooperative Society.[96]

Stella shared her sister's admiration for England but allied it to a more accommodating personality. Nevertheless, she had also acquired her sister's snobbery, which extended not only to 'civilised' Africans, such as Richard Blaize, but also to many expatriates in Lagos, whom she categorised as 'the surplus who cannot make their way in England'.[97] In 1904, shortly after the death of her husband, Stella opened a girls' school, named after her mother, in Wood House.[98] Between 1909 and 1915, she lived with Herbert Macaulay in his house in Lagos. If she had hoped for marriage, she was disappointed. The relationship suited Macaulay, who had no intention of changing its status. Their partnership ended acrimoniously in 1915. Stella died in the following year. She had a son, Arthur, known as Kofi, who was born in 1900 from her brief marriage to James Coker. Kofi, who was what was then labelled 'a sickly child', may have had epilepsy. Given that Stella remained unmarried, she was exceptionally fortunate in being able to count on the support of Jacob Coker, her brother-in-law. Jacob's sense of family responsibility was fortified by the fact that he had been in love with Stella for many years. He had long wanted to marry her, but she was devoted to her school and, for a time, to Macaulay. Moreover, she had an Anglo-Christian view of marriage as being a monogamous institution, and Coker was polygamous. Nevertheless, Coker demonstrated the sincerity of his commitment to her by caring for Kofi during and after Stella's lifetime.

As noted earlier, Jacob Coker also managed Woodland Estate on behalf of the family for a while after Davies's death.[99] Little is known of his activities at Ijon, though he was sufficiently influential to turn the small Anglican church there into a branch of the African Church.[100] The farm appears to have prospered. A rare mention of the village in one of the Lagos newspapers advised

96. Onabolu, 'Mrs Randle', p. 8.
97. Newman, 'The Davies Chronicles', p. 75, quoting a letter from Stella to James Coker, dated 17 Sept. 1896.
98. The Bonetta Davies Memorial Ladies' School.
99. Interview with Mr John Romanes Adewale Randle, James Davies's grandson, Randle's Farm, Ikeja, 29 Jan. 1962, 12 April 1964. Mr Randle retained memories of the farm from his boyhood. Confirmed independently by Chief Adekunle Coker, Jacob Coker's son, 23 Feb. 1962.
100. Interview with Mrs Mary Anne Somefun, a resident of Ijon whose memories of the village covered the first half of the twentieth century, 12 April 1964.

readers in 1917 that, should anyone doubt 'the future of the cocoa industry in Nigeria, let that person take a holiday in Agege, foot it towards Ijon and Ipaja. The plantations are at present sights one will not easily forget. The fruits are numerous and healthy and the future full of promise'.[101] Optimistic forecasts dwindled during the inter-war period and with them the production of cocoa at Ijon. The village has now been incorporated into the port's ever-expanding metropolitan area, almost erasing the site, significance, and even knowledge of Woodland Estate.

A Full Life

Davies's career spans the two most important phases of Saro history in the nineteenth century. The first phase began in 1851, when Britain took forceful action to end the shipment of slaves from Lagos. The next thirty years were a time of opportunity for Saro returning to Lagos. The colonial government remained on the coast, was staffed by a small number of British officials, and relied on the returnees to help administer the colony, promote legitimate commerce, and advance the cause of Christianity. Abolitionist ideals continued to influence racial attitudes. Queen Victoria welcomed Sarah, encouraged her to play with the royal children, and later became godmother to Sarah's daughter, Victoria. Davies took his opportunities, became a wealthy merchant, followed the code of a Victorian gentleman, and was accepted in high society in London as well as in Lagos. His downfall in 1873 followed a sharp fall in the net barter terms of trade for both palm oil and kernels; the international banking crisis that ensued complicated his efforts to extricate himself from his difficulties. The direct cause, however, lay closer to home: Davies lost his property by investing with a Manchester firm that appeared to be sound, but swiftly went out of business. During the rest of the 1870s, he was preoccupied with his creditors and spent more of his time in court than in business.

The second phase began in the 1880s and continued, with various subdivisions, through the colonial period. The 'palmy days' of legitimate commerce ended, the British government moved inland, eventually to create Nigeria, and a rising tide of racism restricted opportunities, even for educated Africans. The year 1880 was also Davies's year of decision, when he committed most of his energy to his new farm at Ijon. Although Davies had lost most of his fortune, he had also read the signals of the time: increasing competition and diminishing profits during the 1880s indicated that the boom years lay in the past. He maintained a modest stake in Lagos commerce, but never returned to full-time business, even after he was discharged from bankruptcy in 1884. The way ahead, as he saw it, lay in developing new sources of income by diversifying agriculture away from the established staples. Woodland

101. *Nigerian Pioneer*, 21 Sept. 1917.

Estate became Nigeria's first model farm, a centre of innovation that led to the spread of cocoa farming to other parts of Yorubaland, and a signpost to similar initiatives that were to create the characteristic export economies of the colonial era.

Davies's motivation was primarily economic. He needed to find alternative means of maintaining his customary lifestyle and its weighty obligations. He remained a Victorian gentleman and carried the values of his generation of Saro into the countryside. His farm was named like an English estate; his labourers were paid wages. He built a small Anglican church that doubled as a school. He exemplified the mid-Victorian principles that joined the 'Bible and plough' in a happy and productive union. He enjoyed life at Ijon and did not treat it as a penance for financial failure. At the same time, he maintained his family house in Lagos, moved in lofty circles there, and wore his top hat on suitable occasions. Town and country were not in competition. Nevertheless, there are hints in Davies's personal papers, conveyed in his graphic phrase, 'cruel Lagos', that life in the big city had lost much of its shine.

Yet it would be a mistake to conclude that Davies was a Victorian clone whose admiration for the world the British were making was qualified by his own misfortunes. He was a Victorian from a generation that believed in and sought to propagate the 'civilising mission'. These beliefs guided his life and gave him a licence to reprove British representatives who, in his view, departed from it. His forthright opposition to Glover's assertive policies in the 1860s, his criticism of the new generation of CMS missionaries, and his belief in the capacities of Africans mark him as a precursor of the more militant opposition that some members of the Saro community promoted during and after the 1890s. Although there is no direct information about what he thought of the expansion of British rule and the growth of racial discrimination, he cannot have found such abrupt departures from attitudes he had imbibed as a boy either congenial or acceptable. When these changes began to make themselves felt, however, Davies was in his sixties and restrained by the weight of time and advancing ill health from joining the voices of active protest. A younger generation, as we shall see, had to devise an accommodation with colonial rule that was consistent with their own, African, values. It is in this wider sense that Woodland Estate was his refuge from a colonial order that had abandoned the once inspiring vision of co-operative development.

CHAPTER TEN

The Changing Economic
Environment, 1900–1914

THE SHOCK OF 1892 failed to produce the rapid response needed to resolve the problems that threatened the future of legitimate commerce. Prosperity remained elusive; consistent gains were limited to the colonial government, which greatly increased its revenues, and the German firms, which dominated the expanding trade in palm kernels. The 1890s ended, not with a boom, but with a major slump. It was not until after the turn of the century that the long-term ramifications of Governor Carter's intervention became apparent. The effective occupation of Yorubaland was complemented by similar advances inland from other parts of the coast and culminated in the creation of the Colony and Protectorate of Nigeria in 1914. Fundamental political change had far-reaching economic consequences that carried with it the prospect of creating a vast and united, or at least semi-united, market. On this occasion, too, political innovation was supported by a fortuitous and benign companion, the international economy, which began a revival that lasted for most of the period down to the First World War.

This chapter examines the consequences of these developments for entrepreneurial choice and performance. Although they followed the shock of 1892 and were results rather than departures, their far-reaching outcomes require a separate chapter. Moreover, the expanded colonial administration generated a library of new information, even though its eye was no longer fixed exclusively on Lagos. This, too, requires commensurate space. It is tempting to see the period as one that cemented the dominance of the European firms and confirmed the decline of African merchants. The story that unfolds in this chapter and those that follow is rather different and, I hope, more interesting.

Commercial Expansion and
Colonial Development Policy

One of the administrative consequences of political change was an alteration to the basis on which commercial statistics were compiled. In 1906, the Colony and Protectorate of Lagos was amalgamated with the Protectorate of Southern Nigeria to form the Colony and Protectorate of Southern Nigeria. Fortunately, commercial statistics relating to Lagos continued to be reported until 1910. Subsequently, however, the figures refer to Southern Nigeria as a whole and after 1914 to Nigeria, and it is no longer possible to identify those relating solely to Lagos.

Nevertheless, the main trends are clear.[1] Export volumes rose after 1890, as they did for British West Africa as a whole (figure 2.1 in chapter 2). In the case of Lagos itself, the increase in palm oil was slight until 1909, whereas the rise in kernels was marked. The value of the external trade of Lagos, though punctuated by poor years, was also on a broadly rising trend from the 1890s onwards. A marked increase occurred in 1902; between 1906 and 1910, the value almost doubled (from £2,103,692 to £4,045,609). Palm oil and kernels continued to dominate the export list, accounting for about 75 per cent of all exports between 1893 and 1910. The figures for palm produce disguise an important sub-trend: the faster growth of kernel exports, which averaged no less than 54 per cent of the value of all exports between 1906 and 1910, and the consequent reduction in the share taken by palm oil. The dominance of palm produce was interrupted briefly at the close of the 1890s, when rubber and timber enjoyed a sudden boom before fading after a few years. The generic entry, cotton goods, remained the leading import, accounting for 37 per cent of total imports between 1906 and 1910, but its share had been falling for some years as other goods either made their appearance or increased their

---

1. *Lagos Blue Books*, 1893–1905; *Annual Trade Reports of the Colony and Protectorate of Southern Nigeria*, 1906–1910. Although the figures suggest precision, they should be treated as approximations. They also contain discrepancies, as the Colonial Office pointed out (Minute by Ezechiel, 22 Jan. 1903 on MacGregor to Chamberlain, 13 Jan. 1903, C.O. 147/165). Values before 1896 were f.o.b., included transit trade, and excluded the movement of specie. Those between 1896 and 1905 excluded government imports, which expanded considerably as a result of the construction of the Lagos railway. The figures for 1906–10 were c.i.f. values but excluded government imports, specie, and the transit trade with Porto Novo. The change to c.i.f. values inflated the figures by about 10 per cent, but the exclusion of the transit trade with Dahomey reduced them by about the same amount. The value of the pound sterling remained stable during the 1890s and 1910s, and inflation was at consistently low levels. An additional complication is that imports for the period 1900–1914 also included substantial government purchases of materials for railway construction and harbour improvements. Several dedicated researchers will be needed to establish an appropriate and uniform time series. Olukoju, *The Liverpool of West Africa*, ch. 1, deals with specific years.

importance. Items that gained prominence were hardware (including corrugated iron for roofing), kerosene, richer fabrics such as silks, tobacco, kola nuts, and provisions (mostly tinned foods). The list will not support a firm conclusion but it is at least indicative that some consumers were able to afford goods that were above basic needs.

The net barter terms of trade for palm oil and kernels exported from Lagos rose from 1900 to about 1910 (see figure 2.2). Again, however, it is important to note the variations from the smoothed trend indicated by the broken lines, with peaks for palm oil in 1908–1910 and for kernels in 1912–1913. The most severe downturn, discussed in chapter 14, occurred during and after the first World War. When these trends are related to export volumes, it is evident that the income terms of trade also rose.[2] Taken as a whole, this was a time of prosperity for merchants engaged in West African trade and a welcome contrast to the gloomy years that preceded it.

The direction of trade extended the pattern established in the late nineteenth century. In the period 1906–1910, Britain and Germany received an average of 96 per cent of the value of Lagos's exports and supplied 87 per cent of the port's total imports.[3] Britain supplied 73 per cent of the imports into Lagos and accounted for nearly all the cotton goods shipped to the port. Germany dominated the export trade, taking 65 per cent of the total and increasing its share as the period advanced. The evidence also confirms that Britain was failing to match Germany in the expanding trade in palm kernels and even showed signs of slipping in the import trade, as German manufactures entered the market.[4] If colonies in Africa and Asia had served as a refuge for Britain's staple manufactures during the second half of the nineteenth century, there were indications that by 1914 these markets could no longer be preserved under conditions of free trade.

The data on imports and exports are consistent with qualitative assessments of the state of trade made by contemporaries. The generally sunny tone of the commentary in the 1900s contrasts with the end-of-the-world predictions that characterised the 1880s and 1890s. The reversal was the more impressive because Lagos merchants were quick to complain and slow to acknowledge prosperity, which might attract rivals and imply that there was scope for the government to increase taxation. In 1908, for example, Paterson Zochonis's agent admitted that, though competition in textiles was 'worse than ever' . . . , 'the general conditions of trade are better in Lagos than a decade ago'.[5] Local officials were also inclined to be circumspect in case unfulfilled optimism

2. Frankema, Williamson, and Woltjer, 'An Economic Rationale', table 7.3, p. 257, fig. 8, p. 258.

3. *Annual Trade Reports of the Colony and Protectorate of Southern Nigeria*, 1906–1910.

4. On the dominance of German firms in the kernel trade (and several other items), see Dennett, 'British and German Trade in Nigeria'.

5. Evidence, 9 July 1908, in Egerton to Crewe, 16 Dec. 1908, C.O. 520/68.

brought retribution from London. Nevertheless, in 1911, the Acting Governor felt sufficiently confident to comment that 'in Southern Nigeria Great Britain has a Colony and Protectorate advancing rapidly in all the essentials which lead to health, wealth and happiness'.[6] Going all in, he added that 'the town of Lagos itself has rightly earned the reputation of the "Liverpool" of British West Africa'.[7] His optimism was justified. The *Annual Reports* for Southern Nigeria record almost unbroken summaries of trade being 'prosperous', 'very prosperous', and even producing 'very great prosperity' in the years between 1906 and 1912, with the exception of 1908, when an international depression checked progress.

Lagos was well placed to participate in the revival of the international economy. The expansion of British rule created the prospect of a greatly enlarged market: the Lagos railway delivered the goods. Internal wars and the use of commerce as a weapon of policy were no longer possible once Britain had dismantled the sovereignty of Nigeria's independent states. Impediments to the ideal of completely free trade remained, notably in the system of internal tolls levied by Yoruba states.[8] The issue of abolition turned into a crisis in 1903, when the expatriate firms exerted pressure to end the system. Opposition came from African political leaders, who argued that eliminating tolls would undercut revenues, sovereignty, and chiefly authority.[9] Governor MacGregor, sensing that confrontation could produce a challenge to political control, moved cautiously.[10] A resolution was reached after a long wrangle. Tolls remained but were brought under the control of the colonial government. The number of toll gates was greatly reduced; half the proceeds were allocated to the provincial administration; chiefs received compensatory payments from the government, which also acquired the right to determine the level of legal duties. The result was that, by 1908, the Yoruba toll system had been shredded, free trade established, and previously independent states subordinated to the colonial government.[11]

The decision to build a railway from Lagos had even broader consequences. The Colonial Office recognised that Carter's invasion of Yorubaland implied greater British control and, in turn, the need for railways to make colonial rule effective and gain access to what dream-makers thought was the untold wealth of the interior.[12] In the late 1890s, several prospectors claimed that

6. Boyle to Harcourt, 31 May 1911, C.O. 520/103.

7. Boyle, 26 May 1911, enc. in Boyle to Harcourt, 31 May 1911, C.O. 520/103.

8. Denton to Chamberlain, 19 Nov. 1900, C.O. 147/151. The subject has been treated authoritatively by Falola, 'The Yoruba Toll System'.

9. *Lagos Weekly Record*, 4 July 1903.

10. MacGregor to Chamberlain, 5 Dec. 1902, C.O. 147/164, and 12 June 1903, 7 July 1903, 13 July 1903, C.O. 147/66.

11. Egerton to Elgin, 12 Sept. 1906, C.O. 520/37; Perham, *Lugard*, pp. 433–46.

12. The correspondence is in Lyttelton to Governors of Sierra Leone, Lagos, and the Gold Coast, 5 Dec. 1904, PP (1905), Cd. 2325, LVI, p. 23. A map of the Lagos hinterland

they had discovered extensive gold fields.[13] When analysis determined that they had found only fool's gold, the search for El Dorado shifted to other uncharted regions, often with the same results. Economic uncertainties, mixed with competing political interests, led to an extensive debate about the route, the cost, and the contractors. A key decision was made in 1895, when Lagos was confirmed as the starting point for a railway to run inland. This outcome was by no means inevitable.[14] Colonial officials in other parts of what became Nigeria lobbied strenuously for the locations they preferred.[15] Lagos, however, had a head start. It already conducted a substantial trade with the interior, and a railway would protect British interests against a possible eastward spread of French influence from neighbouring Dahomey.[16] Had an alternative site been chosen, Lagos might have withered. The railway line guaranteed its supremacy, not only as the leading port in Nigeria but also as the capital of the colony.[17] In 1901, and after a full review, the Colonial Office confirmed its support for the Lagos line and its extension beyond the Niger.[18]

Construction began in 1896. The line to Agege was opened in 1899, reached Abeokuta in the same year, and arrived in Ibadan, 61 miles (98 km) northeast of the Egba capital in 1900. On 4 March 1901, the railway was opened fully from Lagos to Ibadan, a distance of 125 miles (201 km). It was a considerable achievement and one appropriately celebrated. Several thousand people watched the departure of the first train from Lagos; an excited crowd of 20,000–30,000 inhabitants welcomed its arrival in Ibadan; ceremonial receptions for chiefs and other leading figures took place at intervening stops. Governor MacGregor, speaking in Ibadan, took advantage of the occasion to express his enthusiasm for extending the line even further. Adopting the 'colonial English' used at the time, MacGregor urged his audience never to be satisfied 'till your iron horse drinks the waters of Tchad'.[19] Although the governor had the bit between his teeth, the horse had run out of fodder. The construction of the railway had exhausted the government's financial resources; subsequent progress was slow. Nevertheless, in 1912, the line was opened to

---

showing a proposed railway line running through Abeokuta, Ibadan and unspecified points further north was prepared in 1894. See C.O. 147/114.

13. A. T. Lapworth to Rohrweger, 2 Oct. 1896, C.S.O. 8/2/1.

14. Crown Agents to Colonial Office, 31 Oct. 1895, C.O. 147/101; Colonial Office to Carter, 26 Nov. 1895, C.O. 147/101.

15. Report of the Niger Committee, 4 Aug. 1898, C.O. 446/3; Moor to Chamberlain, 17 Jan. 1901, PP (1905), Cd. 2787, pp. 35–9.

16. For further details, see Olukoju, *The Liverpool of West Africa*, pp. 14–18.

17. Even Lord Lugard, who suggested various alternatives, was unable to shift the weight of path dependency. See Bigon, 'Sanitation and Street Layout'.

18. Crown Agents to Colonial Office, 29 July 1901, C.O. 147/158.

19. MacGregor to Chamberlain, 23 March 1901, C.O. 147/154.

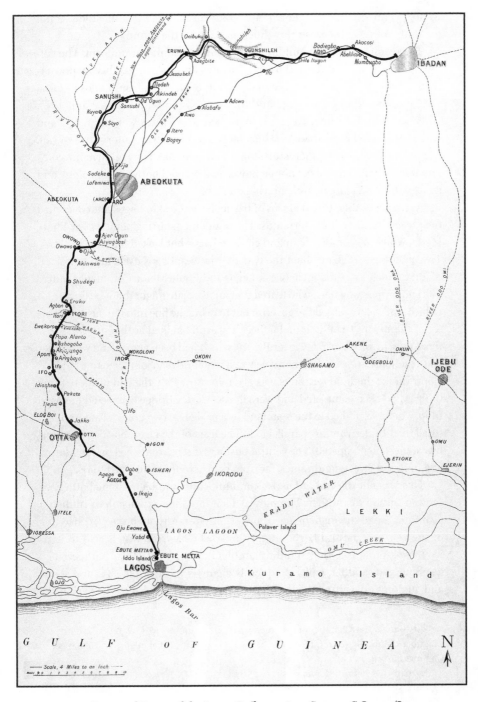

MAP 10.1. Proposed Route of the Lagos Railway, 1899. Source: C.O. 700/Lagos 22, with permission of the National Archives, U.K.

Kano, 711 miles (1,144 km) north of Lagos, symbolising the unification (if not the unity) of two otherwise very different parts of the country.

The results of railway-building were neither instant nor uniform. The volume of traffic was influenced by freight rates and the availability of alternatives. At the outset, rates on the first section of the line, from Lagos to Otta, were considered to be too high and the River Ogun remained a competitor, albeit an imperfect one. Demand increased when rates were adjusted and when the line reached Ibadan, which lacked a competitive alternative to rail. These qualifications do not disturb the conclusion that, by 1912, Britain's combination of political and economic power had created both a huge colony and an expanded and largely free internal market.

A chapter in this story that was of particular interest to Lagosians concerned the precise location of the terminus. The temporary starting point was at Ebute Metta, which was on the mainland close to Lagos but lacked harbour facilities. There followed a debate about the two alternatives: Lagos itself, and the island of Iddo, which was situated between Lagos and Ebute Metta. Commercial interests and property owners, who feared that another site might drain business and reduce land values, urged the government to bring the line into the business centre of the town.[20] The Colonial Office, however, baulked at the increased cost this would involve because Carter Bridge, which had been agreed and was under construction, had been designed solely as a road bridge to join Lagos and Iddo.[21] Approval for the Iddo terminus was given in 1897.[22] By the end of 1900, three bridges had been completed and were in use: Carter Bridge connected Lagos to Iddo, which was linked to the mainland by a bridge carrying the railway and by a small road-bridge running parallel to it. The fears of the Lagos business community were soon dissipated. The central business district remained on the Marina and in Broad Street; land values, far from being eroded, continued to rise.

This was not the end of Lagos's communication problems. One bottleneck drew attention to another. The railway facilitated the expansion of trade but also underlined the inadequacy of Lagos harbour. Although the port had one of the very few natural harbours on the West Coast, gaining access to it, as we have seen, was a long-standing problem because entry was hampered by a submerged sandbar, which frequently changed its position, size, and shape and, in doing so, shifted the location of the channel that led to the harbour.[23]

20. Manchester Chamber of Commerce to C.O. 17 June 1896, C.O. 147/110; Liverpool Chamber of Commerce to C.O. 23 Oct. 1896, C.O. 147/110; Petition enc. in Rohrweger to Chamberlain, 29 July 1896, C.O. 147/106.

21. Crown Agents to Colonial Office, 25 Jan. 1897, C.O. 147/122 and 9 Nov. 1899, C.O. 147/146. The Treasury also frowned on further expenditure: Treasury to Colonial Office, March 1903, C.O. 147/173.

22. Shelford, 'On West African Railways', p. 343.

23. As Burton, among others, had noted. Burton, *Wanderings in West Africa*, Vol. 2, pp. 204–6.

The hazard meant that only vessels of under 1,000 tons and drawing less than 12 feet of water could enter the harbour.[24] Although the limit allowed sailing ships to cross the bar, it was an obstacle for steamships, which had to anchor outside the harbour and transfer cargo and passengers to smaller craft. The operation was a dangerous one that even the indomitable Mary Kingsley found hard to forget.[25] One unsatisfactory solution was paired with another, which was to land goods at Forcados, a small port about 150 miles (241 km) east of Lagos, and trans-ship them to Lagos on small steamers that could negotiate the sandbar.[26]

Both solutions were time-consuming and increased costs. Having committed itself to the Lagos railway, the Colonial Office had to accept the imperative of improving the harbour. As always, cost was the stumbling block. In 1906, the process began with a dredger, which reduced the size of the sandbar.[27] Two breakwaters followed in 1908. In 1909, the Colonial Office approved a plan to extend the facilities of the harbour by developing a new site at Apapa, which was on the mainland opposite Lagos about half a mile away.[28] More work needed to be done, but by 1913 sufficient progress had been made for ocean-going steamships to enter the harbour for the first time.[29] Forcados, once advertised as a potential rival of Lagos, dwindled into insignificance.

The considerable expense incurred in building the railway and improving the harbour was met by raising loans on the London stock market.[30] This option became viable as the colony of Nigeria took shape. The size of its trade supplied the basis for servicing debt; its constitutional status provided an implied guarantee of last resort, because the British government could not allow one of its colonies to default. The initiative for what might be called state-sponsored development came from Joseph Chamberlain, who was Colonial Secretary from 1895 to 1903. In a departure that would have amazed a long line of his predecessors, Chamberlain called on colonial governors throughout the empire to submit a list of public works that would stimulate economic development.[31] Since ambitions far exceeded the funds available from current revenues, the required investment could be found only by borrowing. The main instrument

24. Egerton to Crewe, 17 May 1910, C.O. 520/93.

25. Kingsley, *Travels in West Africa*, Vol. 2, p. 208. See also Denton to Chamberlain, 7 July 1900, C.O. 147/150.

26. Denton to Chamberlain, 17 July 1900, C.O. 147/150. The practice began in the 1880s.

27. *Annual Report of the Marine Department*, 1907; Egerton to Elgin, 1 Feb. 1908, C.O. 520/58.

28. Egerton to Crewe, 22 Sept. 1908 and C.O. minutes by Antrobus, 20 Oct. 1908 and Crewe, 1 Nov. 1908, C.O. 520/59; Egerton to C.O. 28 Aug. 1909, C.O. 520/80; Egerton to Harcourt, 7 Feb. 1911, C.O. 520/101.

29. *Southern Nigeria Annual Report*, 1913.

30. The long-term costs of the port are charted by Olukoju, 'The Making of an "Expensive Port".

31. See, for example, Carter to Chamberlain, 18 April 1896 and C.O. minutes, C.O. 147/104.

was the Colonial Loans Act of 1899, though this measure had drawbacks that were formidably represented by what Lord Salisbury had called 'the Gladstonian garrison of the Treasury'.[32] As development costs rose, the Colonial Office turned to alternatives. In 1905, the Office raised a loan of £2 million on the open market at an interest rate of 3.5 per cent to be repaid within fifty years.[33] Similar loans followed, bringing Southern Nigeria's public debt to over £8 million by 1911.[34]

Chamberlain's well-known initiative deserves to be reappraised now that several new studies of colonial fiscal policy are available. For present purposes, however, it is sufficient to record that essential public infrastructure would not have been built without access to an external capital market. Whether economic development was encouraged or retarded by further export growth is an important issue, but not one that can be addressed here. What can be said is that loan service was met from revenues that came principally from import duties, which rose as trade expanded and as customs duties were increased. It is impossible at present to say how the burden of taxation was distributed between merchants, producers, and consumers. However, the fact that the level of customs duties did not become a political issue during the first decade of the century suggests that it was not seen to be particularly onerous. More positively, the enlarged borrowing capacity of the colony might be interpreted as an indication of increasing prosperity, as suggested by the terms of trade and contemporary opinion. The Colonial Office, which admittedly saw matters from London rather than from Lagos, seemed to think so. Contemplating the considerable public debt of £8 million, a senior official commented in 1911 that 'so far, the revenue has responded [so] well to a forward policy of development that we can face this without much apprehension'.[35] The gamble, of course, was that export revenues would continue to service the debt without producing a fiscal crisis and inflicting pain on taxpayers.

The New Commercial Environment

These developments altered the economic environment. By greatly reducing transaction costs, transport improvements made possible a considerable increase in the spatial extent of the market and the volume of transactions it was capable of supporting. Lagos merchants were quick to respond to new opportunities. They had powerful incentives to connect producers and consumers in largely untapped regions by advancing inland. Competition

32. Salisbury to Chamberlain, 13 Dec. 1896, quoted in Garvin, *The Life of Joseph Chamberlain*, Vol. 3, p. 177.

33. Crown Agents to Colonial Office, 3 March 1905, C.O. 147/177.

34. *Southern Nigeria Blue Books*, 1911–13; *Nigeria Blue Books*, 1914–15.

35. Minute by Fiddes (Assistant Under-Secretary of State for the Colonies), 4 April 1911, on Egerton to Harcourt, 23 Feb. 1911, C.O. 520/101.

increased in the late nineteenth century and continued into the new century.[36] Profit margins had been cut by a combination of adverse trading conditions, the end of barter, the use of British silver coin, the advent of the submarine cable, and the arrival of modern banking in the form of the Bank of British West Africa. A move inland offered an opportunity to increase turnover and the prospect of restoring profit margins.[37]

Like camp followers, most expatriate firms followed the construction of the railway line. Unsurprisingly, given their reputation for being ahead of the pack, Gaiser opened branches at Itori and Abeokuta in 1898, in anticipation of the line's arrival.[38] In 1900, Gaiser and Paterson Zochonis established premises in Ibadan.[39] By 1903, Lagos Stores and John Holt had joined Gaiser in Abeokuta and Ibadan; Witt & Busch were in Ibadan.[40] In 1906, eighteen of the nineteen expatriate firms in Lagos had branches or permanent representatives in a number of towns in the Western Province, though Abeokuta and Ibadan remained their main focus.[41] By the time the railway reached Kano in 1912, European firms had established a string of branches running north from Lagos. Gaiser again led the way, opening branches at Zaria in 1910 and Kano in 1911.[42] By 1912, to cite one example, Lagos Stores had established about twenty branches between Lagos and Kano.[43]

This development was accompanied by another of equal importance: the monetisation of the hinterland economy. In 1912, Matthew Brown, who had been in business in Lagos since 1894, stated that trade in the Western Province (which was approximately coterminous with Yorubaland) was conducted entirely in cash for both produce and goods.[44] The figures for the expansion of specie imports bear out his judgement.[45] Annual specie imports (essentially silver coin) did not breach the £100,000 mark until 1893. The subsequent increase was irregular. The years between 1900 and 1905 indicated that trade expansion had not yet taken a firm hold. Thereafter, however, the figures showed strong growth and in 1910, exceeded £500,000 for the first time. The

36. As consistently noted in the *Lagos* and the *Southern Nigeria Trade Reports*, 1899–1905 and 1906–12.

37. As Governor Egerton observed: Egerton to Lyttelton, 27 Jan. 1905, C.O. 147/174.

38. Hieke, *G. L. Gaiser*, p. 68.

39. *Annual Report on Ibadan*, 1900, C.I. 149/5.

40. MacGregor to Chamberlain, 7 July 1903, C.O. 147/166. Witt & Busch were in Ibadan but not Abeokuta.

41. *Annual Report on the Western Province*, 1907.

42. Hieke, *G. L. Gaiser*, p. 68.

43. Matthew Brown, Evidence to Committee on Lagos Trade, 8 Feb. 1912, PP (1912), Cd. 6427, pp. 94–7.

44. Matthew Brown, Evidence to Committee on Lagos Trade, 8 Feb. 1912, PP (1912), Cd. 6427, pp. 94–7.

45. *Lagos Blue Books*, 1876–1905; *Annual Trade Reports for the Colony of Southern Nigeria*, 1906–10; *Lagos Weekly Record*, 22 Jan. 1910.

net balance, which indicated the amount of silver coin retained in Nigeria, confirmed that local markets were becoming monetised. The railway made expansion possible; silver coin increased the facility and speed of transactions. The two together signified the emergence of a large and integrated market.

Expansion, however, was costly. Branches had to be established and staff numbers increased. Merchants needed access to additional capital, which involved borrowing from banks and paying interest, or raising money from shareholders and rewarding them with dividend payments. The advantage of size lay in the economies of scale it offered. A high volume of transactions enabled merchants to make savings by placing bulk orders for manufactured goods, negotiating reduced freight rates, and selling produce in quantities that commanded higher prices. If the right decisions were made, increased costs could be offset by increased turnover and improved profit margins. In these ways, the early twentieth century witnessed the foundation of commercial institutions that were to typify the colonial period.

Increased capital investment entailed risks that required protection. The expatriate firms responded by forming limited liability companies, if they had not done so already, and by making agreements to take some of the uncertainties out of the export trade. The initiative that led to joint action was prompted by the exceptionally challenging trading conditions at the close of the 1890s.[46] Eight firms that had exported about 88 per cent of all the palm kernels shipped from Lagos during the previous two years entered into an agreement in 1898, 'with a view to protecting and extending their trade and increasing the profits of their trade and of ending ruinous competition'.[47] Shares were allocated on the basis of past performance. The two leading German firms, Gaiser and Witt & Busch, which had shipped 57 per cent of the pool's total purchases in 1896 and 1897, received the largest allocation. A third German firm, Königsdorfer, received 8 per cent. These three firms exported almost two-thirds of the kernels shipped from Lagos, leaving just one-third in British hands. Evidently, in 1897 and 1898, African merchants had only a very limited stake in the direct export trade in kernels, though they were still acting as brokers, buying kernels from traders and selling them on to firms that shipped them. Although the pool did not attempt to fix prices directly, firms that bought more than their allotted share paid a penalty of £1 for every excess ton, which was passed on to members who had failed to buy their prescribed allocation.[48] The arrangement confirmed that the pool was a defensive organisation: its aim was not to expand trade but to steady the market by restraining competition.

46. Evidence of E. Holtmann, enc. in Denton to Chamberlain, 4 June 1898, C.O. 147/133.

47. Agreement, 31 Oct. 1898, HP 3/13; Pool Minutes, June 1899, HP 3/13.

48. Agreement, 31 Oct. 1898, HP 3/13; Gaiser to Holt, 27 April 1901, HP 3/13.

In 1901, some members of the pool wanted to widen its scope to include palm oil and spirits, but the proposal aroused too many discordant interests and was abandoned.[49] By then, adverse trading conditions and disputes about allocations had removed half the members of the pool, leaving only Gaiser, Witt & Busch, John Holt, and Lagos Stores, which between them bought about 67 per cent of the palm kernels shipped from Lagos in that year. Although Holt withdrew from the pool at the end of 1901, the remaining three members decided to continue it, despite competition from other firms.[50] At that point, however, detailed knowledge of its history comes to an end. Inside information depended on John Holt's correspondence, which ceased when his firm left the pool. All that can be said, unless new evidence is discovered, is that subsequent pooling arrangements were discontinuous. No pool seems to have been operating in 1905, when Miller Bros. entered the trade and reinvigorated competition. The established firms reacted to the challenge by forming a produce pool in 1907.[51] Once Miller Bros. had been accommodated, the incentive for retaining the pool diminished, and it was disbanded in 1909.[52] The *Lagos Weekly Record* printed an unflattering obituary: 'It was conceived in avarice', it intoned in 1910, 'and it died in despair'.[53] Life may have returned, however, though also briefly. In 1916, a representative of one of the Lagos firms stated that no fewer than six pools had been 'made and broken' since the close of the nineteenth century.[54]

The significance of the kernel pool exceeded its limited achievements. It provided a measure of assurance for its members, who were guaranteed an annual tonnage of kernels, but it had no appreciable effect on local produce prices.[55] Nevertheless, the pool marked the beginning of a trend towards combination that was to culminate in amalgamations after World War I. The risks facing large firms increased as Lagos trade expanded and investment needs mounted. A commercial downturn provided the incentive to join forces to limit the potential damage. Some firms viewed the situation as an opportunity to create a permanent organisation that would increase profits by driving out small competitors. The main advocate of this position was C. A. Birtwistle, the long-standing general manager of Lagos Stores who was soon to become the colony's first Commercial Intelligence Officer. His aim, enumerated in a detailed set of proposals in 1899, was to form a grand alliance of all the expatriate firms in Lagos,

49. Gaiser to Holt, 27 April 1901, HP, 3/13; Birtwistle to Holt, 9 Nov. 1901, HP 3/13.
50. Calculated from Birtwistle to Holt, 17 Aug. 1901, HP 3/13.
51. Hieke, *G. L. Gaiser*, pp. 73-4.
52. *Lagos Weekly Record*, 6 Nov. 1909.
53. *Lagos Weekly Record*, 12 March 1910.
54. Evidence of J. E. Trigge to Committee on Edible and Oil-Producing Nuts and Seeds, Cd. 8248 (1916), pp. 58-9.
55. A full account of the effects of the pool on prices and profits should begin with the evidence given to the Committee on Edible and Oil-Producing Nuts and Seeds, Cd. 8248 (1916).

if possible, and, if not, of all the produce firms.[56] His plans were discussed by members of the pool during the next two years and possibly later, but no agreement was reached.[57] As trade conditions improved, some members of the pool decided that independent action was a more effective way of increasing profits. As a result, pooling arrangements lost their attraction.

Yet, prosperity did not eliminate the underlying problem of insuring risk against future uncertainty. The continuous rise in produce prices after 1900 benefitted Lagos merchants and weakened the motives for combining with other firms. At the same time, increased prices for raw materials presented problems for manufacturers in Europe. It was this concern that prompted William Lever, the soap manufacturer, to explore the possibility of protecting his interests by investing in the production of palm oil and kernels.[58] Although the Colonial Office disallowed Lever's proposal to establish plantations in West Africa, he was welcomed by King Leopold, who was keen to attract investment into the Belgian Congo. In Lagos, Lever responded to his initial disappointment by pursuing vertical integration in a different form. In 1910, he bought the merchant firm, Charles McIver, and turned its premises into a kernel-crushing plant.[59] When the venture proved unprofitable, he converted it into a soap-making factory, which he promoted in 1910 by organising Nigeria's first soap-washing competition—a landmark in the extension of modern advertising.[60] Although this early effort at import substitution also lost money, Lever persisted. He moved the factory to new premises at Apapa and manufactured soap there throughout the difficult interwar years. The operation became profitable after 1945, when the revival of the economy boosted consumer demand. By then, Lever had successfully completed a gigantic act of horizontal integration in 1929 by forming the United Africa Company, which was intended to solve the problems that the Lagos kernel pool had first perceived in 1898.

Institutional Innovation

African merchants were well aware that organisational changes were needed if they were to keep pace with European firms. As always, it was easier to identify the problem than to devise a satisfactory solution. In 1899, the *Standard* suggested that the 'need of the hour for the Native . . . is the formation of co-operative business unions, joint stock companies and partnership concerns in which by uniting our capital we may gain and keep in our hands some of the business that is fast slipping away into foreign hands'.[61] The suggestion went

56. Birtwistle to Directors of Lagos Stores Ltd., 8 December 1899, HP 3/13.
57. Birtwistle to Holt, 9 Nov. 1901, HP 3/13.
58. Wilson, *History of Unilever*, Vol. 1, pp. 58, 69–72.
59. Fieldhouse, *Unilever Overseas*, pp. 341–60.
60. *Nigerian Chronicle*, 18 March 1910.
61. *Lagos Standard*, 21 June 1899.

beyond expansive rhetoric. A group of Saro merchants responded with an initiative that had far-reaching long-term consequences: they formed limited liability companies. The early ventures were not immediately successful; innovations of this kind usually involve trial, some resistance, and a good deal of error because they also affect the structure and values of the wider society. Nevertheless, these experiments deserve attention. They were the precursors of the limited companies that are an indispensable part of Nigeria's economy today, and their history has not been assembled before.

The first venture appears to have been the Lagos Wassaw & Ashanti Gold Mining Syndicate, which was formed in 1902, with the Lagos merchant, Josiah Doherty, as its Chairman to finance and manage a concession in the Gold Coast.[62] The enterprise took Doherty as close to gambling as his cautious instincts allowed. But the company was more restrained than many during the great 'Jungle Boom' of the time. The limit to its authorised capital of only £800 controlled the risk, and probably inhibited the company's development as well. Although the Syndicate seems to have disappeared, it retains some significance in likely being the first company in Lagos to attempt to raise money by issuing shares and, by implication, to limit the liability of shareholders.

The second undertaking was the Lagos Native Bank, which was formed a month later to issue loans on the security of property, furniture, and jewellery, and to purchase bills of exchange.[63] The headquarters were at the appropriately named Bonanza House on the Marina, which was owned by the financier, Candido da Rocha. Despite its name, the enterprise was not a bank in the full sense of the term but, with one exception, a lending operation of the kind already run by Richard Blaize, Isaac Williams, Alli Balogun, and da Rocha himself, who was both a director of the new bank and its manager. The exception was the facility of dealing in bills of exchange, which appear not to have been a prominent feature of established money lending businesses in Lagos. Nevertheless, the Bank was a novel venture that deserves to be recovered from its present state of oblivion. The structure of the Bank marked a departure from previous partnerships and associations that were already features of African businesses in Lagos. It brought together three notable but unrelated figures from the town's business community—Candido da Rocha, Josiah Doherty, and Seidu Williams—as directors, and aimed to raise money through a public share issue.[64] The authorised capital of £5,000 was divided

62. *Lagos Weekly Record*, 9 Aug. 1902, 15 Nov. 1902. It is unclear where or even whether this company was registered.

63. *Lagos Weekly Record*, 20 Sept. 1902. It is unclear if this company was registered.

64. Seidu Williams (c.1865–1948), though a prominent merchant, may have been included to appeal to the Muslim community. He was a younger brother of the (Christian) merchant, Jacob Williams. I am grateful to *Alhaji* Issa Williams, Seidu's son, for information about his father. Interviews, 20 Jan. 1962, 19 Feb. 1962. No records have been preserved.

into 500 £10 shares. The key statement in the prospectus was that 'the liability of shareholders is limited to the number of their shares'.[65] The bank issued several loans and continued to advertise until 1904, but failed to interest potential investors. The venture ended in that year when Candido and the other directors took J. P. Jackson, the auditor, to court for misappropriating funds and received judgement for £335.[66] The lending business continued, as it had done before 1902, under da Rocha's sole direction as the Lagos Agricultural Bank.

The third company, the Nigerian Shipping Corporation, which was formed in 1909, was an equally significant development because it, too, had the specific aim of becoming a limited liability company.[67] The wealthy auctioneer, Andrew Thomas, was Chair of the Board, and the directors included two prominent merchants, Josiah Doherty (again) and Samuel Pearse, among other well-known officers. The aim of the company, as set out in the prospectus, was to provide a shipping service for goods and passengers on the Niger, specifically between Forcados and Lokoja. The company had an authorised capital of £20,000 divided into £1 shares, of which ten thousand were offered for public subscription. The directors appear to have learned from the experience of the Bank of Nigeria because they not only reduced the cost of shares but also allowed payment to be made in instalments. Unlike many of the gold-mining companies being touted at this time, this was a respectable proposition and was backed by several of the most substantial and experienced figures in Lagos. The company, however, never managed to float, let alone have sight of the Niger. It responded to some initial scepticism by making what was reported to be a 'rational and feasible readjustment' and continued the promotion until 1911, when, so it appears, its main backers decided to abandon the ship and the project.[68]

In going under, the company nevertheless left a memorial, which has been as unnoticed as its own brief history. In 1911, the colonial government in Lagos considered a draft bill for the 'Corporation, Regulation, and Winding Up of Trading Companies', which was approved by the Board of Trade and passed as Ordinance 7 in 1912.[69] The measure was followed in the same year by the

65. *Lagos Weekly Record*, 20 Sept. 1902.
66. Candido da Rocha (as Manager) v. J. P. Jackson, Lagos Registrar's Minutes, LSCR, Civ. 19, 1903; da Rocha, & Ors v. Jackson (second case), Lagos Registrar's Minutes, LSCR, Civ. 19, 1903; *Lagos Weekly Record*, 27 Feb. 1904.
67. *Lagos Standard*, 13 Jan. 1909.
68. *Lagos Standard*, 20 Jan. 1909; *Lagos Weekly Record*, 17 July 1909. The *Lagos Standard* praised the standing of J. Bright Davies, the secretary of the company, but added an unhelpful comment hoping that 'selfishness' and 'sharp trick practices' would not appear.
69. Board of Trade to Colonial Office, 7 Nov. 1911, C.O. 520/108; Southern Nigeria, *Annual Report*, 1912. Parallel legislation regulating pawnbrokers and money lenders was also passed in 1912.

appointment of a Registrar of Companies and the creation for the first time of records dealing with limited liability in Nigeria.[70] From then on, it was possible to register limited liability companies in Nigeria instead of in London. The initiative for the legislation came from Christopher Sapara-Williams (1855–1915), an eminent Saro lawyer and a member of the Legislative Council. Sapara-Williams raised the matter explicitly at the request of the directors of the Nigerian Shipping Corporation, who claimed that their venture was handicapped by their inability to register the company locally.[71]

Sapara-Williams was well informed because he was also the company's official solicitor. He argued that potential investors would avoid companies registered in Britain because distance increased uncertainty and raised the risks of what could become an easy way of losing money.[72] At the same time, he pointed out that Nigerians who formed partnerships and firms styled as 'companies' had no protection in law. He cited a recent case in which the judge had ruled that a partnership was not a limited liability company and that the partners had to bear the full extent of the debts they had incurred. 'The time has come', Sapara-Williams concluded, 'when it is necessary for the Government to enact some useful legislation for the encouragement of local enterprise, and by beneficial regulations and measures to assist in promoting and enabling the efforts which native energy in the country is seeking to carry out in the direction of economic development and progress'.[73] He drew attention to several local initiatives, the most relevant being the Nigerian Shipping Corporation.

The Corporation left an enduring legacy: it opened the way for the creation of limited liability companies in Nigeria. A total of 226 companies were registered in the colony between 1912 and 1926.[74] Most expatriate firms were

70. As far as I am aware, the records of the Registrar of Companies have yet to be studied by historians. My own research was limited to a preliminary sampling of the possibilities.

71. Sapara-Williams to Governor, 8 June 1911, enc. in Boyle to Harcourt, 5 Aug. 1911, C.O. 520/105.

72. Sapara-Williams to Governor, 8 June 1911, enc. in Boyle to Harcourt, 5 Aug. 1911, C.O. 520/105. At least one company formed by Lagos merchants at this time was registered in London. This was 'Silva & Samadu', which was formed by Julio Borges da Silva (a junior brother of Lazaro Borges da Silva, who put up the money) and Thomas H. Jackson and registered in London in 1907. The venture had a short and unhappy history that kept the founders in the courts for many years: da Rocha v. da Silva and Jackson. LSCR, Civ. 51, 1908; Silva & Samadu Ltd. v. L. B. da Silva, LSCR, Civ. 53, 1909; J. B. da Silva v. Jackson, LSCR, Civ. 83, 1919; J. B. da Silva v. Jackson, LSCR, Civ. 91, 1921; Nigerian Daily Times, 15 June 1933.

73. Sapara-Williams to Governor, 8 June 1911, enc. in Boyle to Harcourt, 5 Aug. 1911, C.O. 520/105.

74. Calculated from the Registrar of Companies files, Lagos, Vol. 1 (1912–26) and 2 (1926–35).

already registered in Europe, so it was easy for them to add local registration. African businessmen, as we have seen, were experimenting with a novel institution and responded to the opportunity far more slowly. Approximately fifteen of the total of 226 were Nigerian and all except about two were based in Lagos. An additional 214 companies were registered between 1926 and the end of 1935, of which about fifty-five were Nigerian. By then, both the concept and the advantages of limited liability had begun to take hold. Unfortunately, the propitious conditions needed for success were not yet available, and did not appear until after World War II.

Limited liability encouraged enterprise in Nigeria, as it did in Britain. It opened the possibility of raising capital through share-issues, and it removed the prospect that debtors could lose all their personal assets and might also suffer imprisonment. However, there was more to the hesitation of Nigerian investors than the absence of local registration. The new legislation did not provoke an immediate rush into company formation. Nigerian businessmen were not inherently conservative, but they measured new institutions against existing alternatives and were understandably cautious. Business transactions are ultimately based on trust, as Adam Smith observed and modern economists have confirmed. Contracts formalise trust but can also be broken. Yoruba law prescribed measures for dealing with credit and debt; the extended family and its many associates provided ways of raising capital, issuing credit, and sanctioning those who failed tests of trustworthiness. The idea of raising funds from outside the family or lineage required investors to trust people who were beyond their immediate moral community. Early examples of limited companies in Nigeria alerted prospective investors to the chances of losing their money.[75] It would have been unreasonable for Nigerians to transfer from one system to another before the new institution had been allowed time to demonstrate its reliability and effectiveness.

As we have seen, impersonal transactions gained ground in Lagos when freehold property became acceptable security for borrowing money. Limited liability companies, however, had expansive ambitions that increased uncertainty and its companion, risk. At this stage of development, a capital market had only just begun to develop and few Africans had money to spare for novel, and hence risky, ventures. These considerations explain why the first experiments in company formation were on a modest scale and involved investors

75. For example, the Sierra Leone Deep Sea Fishing & Industries Co. Ltd., whose founder, John Eldred Taylor, disappeared from Lagos with over £1,000 of shareholders' money in 1909. Taylor's membership of a notable creole family in Sierra Leone inspired a misleading sense of confidence. Lagosians are still awaiting the trawler he promised to deliver. *Lagos Standard*, 17 April 1909; *Nigerian Times*, 7 Feb. 1911. Even the astute and wary Candido da Rocha was caught in 1908, when he invested in a new company, Silva & Samadu Ltd., which was registered in London in 1907, and discovered that the Bank of Nigeria had ceased to accept the company's cheques. See n.72.

who knew one another. Nevertheless, it was the initiative of Lagos entrepreneurs, not the colonial government, that led to the introduction of what was to become a key aid to economic development. Although the early history of company formation ought to have a place in the record of Nigeria's economic development, it must be acknowledged, nevertheless, that the story is largely one of failure, at least until the 1930s, and played no part in helping Lagos merchants to mobilise the capital they needed if they were to compete with the expatriate firms. Chapter 11 will show that African merchants matched European firms in establishing branches in the interior, but they did so by drawing on their own resources. Their own march into the hinterland was less visible but no less effective. They established formal branches, but they also employed low-cost travelling representatives, including that priceless asset of male merchants: their wives.

The possibility of complementary legislation dealing with bankruptcy was also considered during this period. The Privy Council's ruling in 1891 that the English Bankruptcy Act did, after all, apply to Lagos prompted considerable discussion and in 1898 led the *Lagos Weekly Record* to call for an Insolvency Act for Lagos modelled on the English Bankruptcy Act of 1883.[76] In the following year, the *Lagos Standard* added a series of essays in support of the proposal.[77] The aim was to give African merchants and traders the same rights that European firms already enjoyed. At present, the argument went, debtors were at the mercy of creditors. English firms were protected; African merchants were hounded and could not even use business losses to mitigate their position. The need was real but the timing was unfortunate. The adverse trading conditions at the close of the century had driven many firms, expatriate as well as African, out of business. A bill was drafted in 1899 but failed to become law.[78] The issue resurfaced in 1903, when BBWA sought redress from an African customer who had defrauded them of £2,500, but the proposal failed to achieve the support it needed.[79] The question was discussed again in 1912 with reference to the long-running struggle that had involved Child, Mills, CSM, and James Davies.[80] In 1921, the *Nigerian Pioneer* and the merchant, Samuel Pearse, gave the matter another outing but were as unsuccessful as their predecessors had been.[81]

At first sight, it seems strange that a measure offering protection for debtors failed to become law in Lagos. Limited liability ensured that investors had no financial responsibility beyond their share-holding. Yet, there were very few companies in Lagos before the 1920s and 1930s, and the majority of

76. *Lagos Weekly Record*, 11 June 1898, 14 Jan. 1899, 10 June 1899, 6 June 1903.
77. *Lagos Standard*, 15 Nov. 1899, 22 Nov. 1899, 29 Nov. 1899, 13 Dec. 1899.
78. *Lagos Standard*, 29 Nov. 1899.
79. Jones to Antrobus, 14 Dec. 1903 and C.O. minute, C.O. 147/168.
80. *Nigerian Chronicle*, 5 April 1912. See above, chapter 5.
81. *Nigerian Pioneer*, 6 May 1921, 20 May 1921, 17 June 1921, 1 July 1921.

commercial debtors were not shareholders of registered companies. Although the basis of opposition was not detailed either by the government or the press, it is clear that 'majority opinion', which presumably excluded the views of current and potential debtors, was against legislation.[82] The colonial government's position was not fixed; the expatriate firms did not press the matter with any enthusiasm. With the exception of Pearse, most African merchants were unconvinced.[83] The existing system, which relied on the ultimate sanction of imprisonment, was retained, possibly because local creditors thought that English bankruptcy law was too indulgent and might increase the incidence of indebtedness and default instead of reducing them. Whatever the explanation, scepticism about the merits of legislation remained throughout the colonial period. Even today, there are considerable difficulties in applying bankruptcy legislation in Nigeria.

Political Aspects of Entrepreneurial Motivation

In changing the balance of power, the shock caused by the invasion of Yorubaland also assaulted the assumptions that underlay the original concept of the civilising mission.[84] The world that had been shaped by mid-Victorian values was being transformed, and Africans were forced to revise their own expectations accordingly. The generation coming to maturity at the turn of the century was exposed to doctrines of 'scientific' racism, which eroded the universalism that had inspired Henry Venn and his protégés, who were faithfully represented by the Saro elite in Lagos. Discrimination was especially galling: in closing opportunities for Africans, racial prejudice also became a permanent and painful reminder of the inferior position of indigenous people in the revised hierarchy of human beings.

Racial bias made its first notable mark on Lagos in 1891, when Samuel Ajayi Crowther, the eminent Anglican Bishop of West Africa, died and was replaced by a European. Thereafter, discrimination became more common and more assertive. Governor McCallum led from the top, insisting in 1897 that 'native doctors' in official employment should be replaced on retirement by English appointees.[85] Details did not escape McCallum's keen eye:

82. Jones to Antrobus, 14 Dec. 1903 and C.O. minute, C.O. 147/168; *Nigerian Pioneer*, 24.6.21.

83. The Acting Governor commented in 1919 that there was no local bankruptcy law 'because the native traders do redeem their credit'. Boyle to Secretary of State, 20 March 1919, C.O. 583/73.

84. Vivian Beckford-Smith provides a helpful survey in 'The Betrayal of the Creole Elites, 1880–1920', in Philip D. Morgan and Sean Hawkins, eds., *Black Experience and the Empire* (Oxford: Oxford University Press, 2006), pp. 194–227.

85. McCallum to Chamberlain, 13 July 1897, and C.O. minute by Mercer, 23 Aug. 1898, C.O. 147/115. See also Egerton to Crewe, 6 Dec. 1909, and C.O. minutes, C.O. 520/83.

in 1897, he made sure that two cricket pitches were laid out in Lagos, 'one for the Europeans and one for the Natives'.[86] When a Saro, John Otunba Payne, the Chief Registrar of the Colony, retired in 1899, he too was replaced by a European.[87] The Lagos Chamber of Commerce became an all-European body in 1903.[88] By then, colonial racial policy had become a subject of frequent discussion, and dissent, in the Lagos press.[89]

After the turn of the century, assumptions of superiority became a regular feature of correspondence to and from the Colonial Office.[90] During the controversy over the system of tolls imposed by Yoruba states, James Hutton, the prominent Manchester merchant, wrote to the Colonial Office in 1903 expressing his belief that 'the black man is not the equal of the white and is therefore less trustworthy'.[91] The Colonial Office applied the same message in a more refined way, criticising Governor MacGregor's tendency to 'exalt the native rulers of Abeokuta and Ibadan and to treat them as friends and equals'.[92] A major step entrenching discrimination was taken in 1906, when Governor Egerton submitted proposals to build segregated residential housing, 'as advised for some time by medical opinion'.[93] Two years later, the governor forwarded a petition, signed by prominent Lagosians, including Saro merchants, opposing the policy.[94] The Colonial Office's minute on the despatch summarised the basis of their objection admirably: 'What is at the bottom of the agitation in Lagos is the feeling of the educated natives that segregation is a slur upon them'.[95] Nevertheless, the Colonial Office made it clear that there was to be no wavering on the issue of the 'colour bar' in West Africa. 'The administration of the West African colonies', Strachey wrote in 1909, 'is British, and as long as this is the case no Native African can expect to be appointed to any but subordinate posts'.[96] In 1913, Lugard noted with approval that the idea of segregation had taken a 'firm hold of the mind of the Colonial Office'.[97] Although the official mind was distracted by other matters during the war, action on implementing the policy resumed in 1918 and culminated in 1928,

86. McCallum to Chamberlain, 31 Aug. 1897, C.O. 147/116.

87. Denton to Chamberlain, 19 Dec. 1898, C.O. 147/136.

88. *Lagos Standard*, 28 June 1905; Hopkins, 'The Lagos Chamber of Commerce'.

89. For example, *Lagos Standard*, 14 Jan. 1903.

90. On this subject, as applied to Lagos and Dakar, see Bigon, *History of Urban Planning*, part II, ch. 2.

91. Hutton to C.O., 7 Oct. 1903, and enc. 5 Oct. 1903, C.O. 147/168.

92. Minute by Ezechial, 8 Oct. 1903 on MacGregor to Chamberlain, 14 Aug. 1908, C.O. 147/166.

93. Egerton to Elgin, 16 June 1906, C.O. 520/41.

94. Egerton to Elgin, 27 Jan. 1908, C.O. 520/58.

95. Minute by Antrobus, 22 Feb. 1908, on Egerton to Elgin, 27 Jan. 1908, C.O. 520/58.

96. Minute by Strachey, 10 Dec. 1909, on a Memo on 'the Colour Bar in West Africa', by Seely, 2 Dec. 1909, C.O. 520/87.

97. Lugard minute, 27 Jan 1913, on MB 4171/12.

when the first section of a large reservation for Europeans was opened on Ikoyi (at the eastern end of Lagos island).[98]

Discrimination had a direct and particular effect on educated Saro. As the Colonial Office had observed, it was a 'slur' upon them and one that also cut a deep wound. Far from having the status of co-partners in development, they found that they had been demoted not only on grounds of racial inferiority but also because of their education. The qualification that had once been an asset and assistance to the colonial government was now regarded as a conduit for subversive ideas. Official policy shifted towards alliances with 'traditional' authorities, whose conservative preferences provided a better fit with the new priority of maintaining settled colonial rule. This trend, coupled with the commercial challenges Saro faced, caused many of them to become progressively alienated from the state of subordination that had been thrust upon them.

Such radical departures from inherited expectations required a comparably far-reaching reappraisal of how progress was to be achieved if emulation, with its implied hope of equality, no longer brought its expected rewards. After the invasion of Yorubaland, and more evidently after the turn of the century, thinking among Saro began to shift away from a model based on imitation towards one that contained a larger African component. Signs of an emerging discussion of the issues appeared as early as 1881, when the *Lagos Observer* commented on the merits of exchanging English names and dress for their Yoruba equivalents and deployed heavy sarcasm to condemn the idea.[99] The spread of racism during and after the 1890s, however, accelerated the transition to alternative values. In 1890, a letter to the *Lagos Weekly Times* deplored 'this disposition of ours to ape the European', and urged that efforts be made to 'contrive a dress of our own'.[100] In supporting the proposal, the *Weekly Times* also reached a wider conclusion, namely that it was 'necessary to acquire an African identity'.[101] Some members of the elite began to adopt Yoruba names and dress. Others recorded Yoruba history and customs to 'lay a foundation', as one 'Native African' author put it, 'for others of my countrymen to build upon and improve for future generations'.[102] In 1896, the *Lagos Standard* felt able to remark that 'the days when the educated African aspired

98. Boyle to Secretary of State, 4 Oct. 1919, C.O. 583/68; Clifford to Milner, 2 April 1920, C.O. 583/85, and 19 May 1920, C.O. 583/87. The reservation was a considerable undertaking that involved reclaiming about 250 acres of swampland. Once completed, it housed the expatriate elite. Today, it houses the Nigerian super-elite and is the most expensive residential area in the country. Ikoyi is worth studying in its own right. Tim Livsey has reconstructed the area's history after 1935 in 'Late Colonialism'.

99. *Lagos Observer*, 31 Aug. 1882.

100. Letter from 'Salami' to *Lagos Weekly Times*, 26 July 1890.

101. *Lagos Weekly Times*, 26 July 1890.

102. J.A.O. Payne to Ripon, 12 July 1893, C.O. 147/93. See also S. O. Biobaku, ed., *Sources of Yoruba History* (London: Oxford University Press, 1973).

to European names are gone—or going'.[103] Ironically, the European version of 'scientific' racism prompted an African alternative: some commentators began to argue that imitating Europeans would 'enfeeble our manhood and destroy our race'.[104]

The effects of racism reverberated through the twentieth century. The Protestant churches paid an immediate price for promoting racial discrimination. One schism led to the creation of the United Native African Church in 1891; another of greater importance saw the foundation of the African Church in 1901. The implications for colonial rule unfolded less abruptly but had more expansive consequences. Opposition to rule without legitimacy shifted from constructive criticism to the formulation of alternatives that first found political expression in the National Congress of British West Africa (NCBWA).[105] The National Congress, which was founded in 1920, drew together ideas that had been discussed during the previous decade. The Lagos branch, which was established in the same year, had an unpromising history. Educated Saro were key supporters of the NCBWA. Yet the new political organisation experienced the same problems of achieving co-operation as the pioneers of limited companies faced. The Lagos branch was rescued from premature disintegration by a group of supporters led by Jacob Coker, though their intervention could not prevent the decline of the organisation during the 1920s. Yet, short-run failure, as with the efforts to form limited liability companies, was the precursor of subsequent achievements. The Nigerian National Democratic Party, which Herbert Macaulay founded in 1923, took much of its inspiration, and some of its founders, from the NCBWA, and achieved considerable success in local elections during the inter-war period.

The Port and Its Inhabitants

The growth of the town's population after the turn of the century was as impressive as the expansion of trade.[106] According to the census of 1911, the total population of the town itself had risen to 57,000, and reached 74,000 if the 'municipal area' was included.[107] The municipal area included Iddo, Apapa, and Ebute Metta, which had been brought under the authority of the newly created local administration. The population of the island had almost doubled in twenty years, and settlement on the nearby mainland had begun the process of urban sprawl that has continued to the present day. These figures should be taken as no more than orders of magnitude. The Lagos

103. *Lagos Standard*, 18 March 1896.
104. *Lagos Observer*, 2 and 16 April 1887. Quoted in Echeruo, *Victorian Lagos*, p. 38.
105. Olusanya, 'The Lagos Branch of the National Congress', remains a helpful guide.
106. For a valuable overview of the town's public utilities during this period, see Olu-koju, *Infra-Structure Development*, ch. 4.
107. *Census of the Colony of Southern Nigeria*, 1911.

population was highly mobile and fluctuated according to the trading seasons; it is also likely that many residents associated enumeration with taxation and took care to ensure that their presence was unrecorded. Nevertheless, it would have been surprising if the population of Lagos had not responded to the forces of 'push and displacement': the railway increased mobility; the growth of trade encouraged migration to Lagos.[108] Whatever the reality that greeted newcomers, Lagos was a magnet attracting the hopeful Dick Whittingtons of the day.[109] Expansion created problems of overcrowding and congestion. These considerations fed into Governor Lugard's wish to promote segregation. In 1913, he floated the idea of moving the capital 'about seven miles inland on the railway'.[110] In the following year, this idea was replaced with anther, namely, to Kaduna in the far north.[111]

Given that birth and death rates were more or less balanced, in-migration was the main cause of population growth. The result was that the cosmopolitan port increased its diversity still further. In 1911, about 20 per cent of the inhabitants of the Lagos Municipal Area came from regions outside the Western Province of Southern Nigeria. Some 'strangers', as newcomers were called, came from further afield. Traders from Northern Nigeria, who established their own quarter at Ebute Metta, were conspicuous among the newcomers.[112] They also represented another trend in Lagos: the spread of Islam, which in 1911 claimed the affiliation of about half the population of the town. Christian denominations accounted for approximately 30 per cent of the total but had progressed more slowly. Although figures of this kind record formal rather than effective support, in this case they underline the increasing importance of Islam, which was apparent in commerce as well as in religion. The corollary, as we have already seen, was the relative decline of the Saro, who lost visibility as other sections of society rose to greater prominence. The hallmark of port cities is their cosmopolitan character. Diversity places different experiences, values, and ideas in close proximity. Innovation is one of many outcomes.

The European population also increased in size and importance. In 1881, there were 117 Europeans in the town.[113] In 1901, the number was 301; in 1911, it reached 549. The majority lived on the island, but there were signs of a move to what were to become the suburbs of Lagos. In 1881, nearly all the Europeans were employed in trade; by 1911, about half were in the colonial administration, a shift that reflected not only the expansion of colonial rule

108. *First Annual Report on the Town of Lagos*, 1904.

109. This is a case of mythology rising above truth. Although Richard Whittington (1354–1423) achieved exceptional wealth and political influence, he came from an ancient and well-connected family.

110. Lugard to Harcourt, 11 Aug. 2013, C.O. 520/127.

111. *Lagos Weekly Record*, 14 Feb. 1914.

112. *Annual Medical Report on Ebute Metta*, 1903.

113. *Census of the Colony of Southern Nigeria*, 1911.

but also the discriminatory measures that prevented Africans from achieving senior positions in official employment. Nigeria remained part of what Hancock called the '"traders"' frontier' in West Africa, and never joined the settler colonies.[114] Nevertheless, advances in medicine, as well as colonial boundaries, had begun to alter the image of the 'white man's grave'. The regular use of quinine had already reduced the effects of malaria; Ross's discovery in 1897 of the connection between the anopheles mosquito and malaria marked a decisive advance in medical knowledge. By 1914, the previous rate of European mortality in West Africa had been greatly reduced and a more optimistic assessment of life expectancy installed instead.[115] Colonial rule and its 'mission', so it seemed, had an unlimited future.

The census of 1911 confirmed that commerce remained by far the largest single occupation.[116] This statement ought to be unexceptional but is worth emphasising because it questions the claim made by several sources in Lagos that the 'middlemen'—a poorly defined term—were in decline. Even making some allowance for the fact that the Municipal Area was larger than Lagos town itself, the number of traders had almost doubled in the thirty years since 1881. If sub-categories, such as mercantile clerks and shop assistants, are added to the total, almost half the occupied population of Lagos was directly engaged in commerce. Farming and fishing, the occupations that had engaged the island's first settlers, continued to decline, and in 1911 accounted for only about 4 per cent of the total employed population. What is more striking is that the census listed no fewer than ninety-five different occupations, apart from trading, as opposed to a mere ten recorded in 1881. Admittedly, the census of 1911 was more thorough than that of 1881. The key point, however, is that commercial expansion was accompanied by increased diversity. Only eight occupations had more than 1,000 members and sixty-two had fewer than 100. Some occupations, such as labourers and domestic servants, had been expanding since the 1880s. Others, such as engine drivers and a single electro-plater, had appeared only recently. The growing complexity of the economy has not been given the attention it deserved. As subsequent chapters will illustrate, African merchants both promoted diversification and gained from the opportunities it offered.

Unsurprisingly, the town itself filled up as well as filled out. As swampland was reclaimed, different sections of the town were joined together. The resulting increase in available residential space, however, did not keep pace with the inflow of new inhabitants. The consequence was overcrowding and increased rents.[117] The development of new suburbs provided an outlet but

114. Hancock, *Survey*, Vol. 2, part 2, ch. 2.

115. *Annual Reports of the Southern Nigeria Medical Department*, 1902–7.

116. *Census of the Colony of Southern Nigeria*, 1911.

117. Municipal Engineer to Lagos Municipal Board, 20 June 1900, MB 171/1900; Moseley to Lyttelton, 21 July 1904, C.O. 147/171; *First Annual Report on the Town of Lagos*, 1904; Municipal Engineer to Municipal Secretary, 26 Nov. 1912, MB 343/1912.

FIGURE 10.1. The Lagos Marina, 1909. Courtesy of edmondfortier.org.br, São Paulo, Brazil.

did not diminish the attraction of the island itself. Although the central business district had expanded, its focus remained the Marina and Broad Street. As if defying claims of their demise, African merchants such as Samuel Pearse (Elephant House), Josiah Doherty (Doherty House), Peter Thomas (Williams Street), and A. W. Thomas, the auctioneer (Ebun House), all built what were described as substantial and even 'palatial' residences between 1900 and 1914. Additionally, the 'Liverpool of West Africa' had something that Merseyside lacked: it was the capital city of a large state and commanded attention and personnel in its own right. The impressive solidity and spaciousness of Government House, built in 'colonial classical' style in 1896, was the most prominent of the public buildings erected following the invasion of Yorubaland, and symbolised the enhanced role and permanence of the colonial government. Ancillary buildings followed. By 1910, the colonial secretariat had its own establishment on the Marina close to Government House; the Supreme Court had relocated to Tinubu Square; the Police Court, Post Office, and Government Printer all had their own expanded premises.

The increased European presence, the adoption of the Chamberlain ethos, and the growth of revenues from trade led to a determined effort to improve public utilities.[118] The task was formidable. Reviewing the position in 1904, the evidently frustrated Director of Public Works commented that 'the task has been one compared to which the cleansing of the Augean stable was mere child's play'. 'Lagos', he concluded, is 'variously styled the "Liverpool" or the "Queen City of West Africa"'. 'To those who know her well there is a world of irony of a most painful character in these fanciful terms'.[119] All things being relative, however, Lagos was comparatively advanced. A visiting expert, Professor William Simpson, not only added to classical analogies in 1908, when he referred to the 'Sisyphean task' of improving sanitation, but also judged that Lagos was 'already the most progressive and advanced' port on the West African coast.[120] Moreover, the unenviable state of Lagos was similar to that in other large towns in Britain and the United States at that time.[121] Scientific knowledge of public health was still elementary, as was the means of applying it. Governor MacGregor, however, made public health one of his priorities. His qualifications as a doctor and his concern to raise welfare standards for those placed under his jurisdiction set him apart from 'military' governors like Carter and Lugard. During his time in Lagos (1899–1904), he set in motion reforms that were followed, if sometimes haltingly, by his successors.

118. Bigon, *History of Urban Planning*, part II, chs. 1–2.
119. Moseley to Lyttelton, 21 July 1904, enc. report by Director of Public Works, C.O. 147/171.
120. Brown, 'Public Health in Lagos', p. 337.
121. Brown, 'Public Health in Lagos', pp. 346–7, 352–3, 358, 360.

The provision of electric lighting was discussed in the late 1890s and made a flickering start on the Marina and Broad Street in 1898 and a more consistent appearance in Government House, where 'bright and soft' lights were installed in the following year.[122] Although progress was slow, most of the main streets were lit by 1910.[123] By then, too, some wealthy Lagosians had fitted electric lighting in their homes and business premises. A few had also acquired telephones, which had first appeared in government offices in 1900.[124] The supply and cost of lines inhibited the growth of the service, as it did with electric lighting. In 1914, most of the town's international business was still conducted by telegraph, which had been extended to Northern Nigeria by means of field cables.

Water supply was a more intractable problem. Lagos residents drew their water from public and private wells, all of which were 'highly polluted', with the result that dysentery was widespread.[125] In 1908, the government drew up a plan to divert water from the River Iju, which ran through Agege.[126] The plan was approved after much discussion, and construction was completed in 1915.[127] The plant became fully operative in 1916, when Lagos received pipe-borne water for the first time. Street fountains and fire hydrants followed. The result was a marked improvement, though one that failed to eradicate pollution completely.[128] The disposal of rubbish, which was thrown into the streets and the lagoon, was another health hazard of long standing. The stench was bad; the threat to public health even worse. In 1887, mounting frustration led to a suggestion, which was considered seriously, that three hundred buzzards should be imported to tackle the problem.[129] Practicalities intervened and the government resorted to a system of contracting the work to teams of scavengers. This, too, proved unsatisfactory, and in 1914, the Lagos Municipal Board decided to take direct control of the work.[130]

Improvements of a different kind left an immediate imprint on the character of the town. The first motor car made its appearance in 1902.[131] In 1906, the colonial government imported a car and another novelty: two motorcycles.[132] In the following year, the *Lagos Standard* claimed, with the exaggeration

122. *Lagos Weekly Record*, 26 Feb. 1898, 4 Nov. 1899.

123. *Lagos Standard*, 1 June 1910.

124. *Lagos Weekly Record*, 1 Sept. 1900.

125. *Lagos Weekly Record*, 15 April 1911; *Nigerian Chronicle*, 3 Feb. 1911.

126. *Lagos Weekly Record*, 31 Oct. 1980, 19 Dec. 1908, 17 April 1909; *Lagos Standard*, 1 Sept. 1909. A full account of the effects on Iju is in Lugard to Harcourt, 22 May 1913, C.O. 520/124.

127. *Nigerian Pioneer*, 3 March 1914.

128. See the perceptive remarks in Brown, 'Public Health in Lagos', pp. 342–6.

129. See Brown, 'Public Health in Lagos', p. 356.

130. Municipal Board minutes, 18 June 1914, 25 June 1914, MB 203/14.

131. Lovell, 'Lagos Present', p. 1.

132. *Lagos Weekly Record*, 12 May 1906.

that often attends novelty, that cars and motorcycles were 'common enough to cause problems' and were often driven 'at a reckless pace' that led to accidents.[133] By 1918, cars were familiar sights in Lagos and had become status symbols of the wealthy, which included the leading African merchants. The practical value of motor vehicles was limited because there were few roads that were robust enough to carry their weight. Nevertheless, motor cars had become the preferred advertisement of the town's Big Men, and a few women too, as horse-drawn carriages had been in the 1880s. Bicycles had already arrived. They were being advertised in Lagos in 1897 and were described two years later as 'the coming rage'.[134] When the 'rage' was transformed into speed, bicycles, like cars, produced accidents.[135] As the risks increased, the Municipal Authority felt obliged to make 'cycling furiously' an offence.[136]

Indications of improvements in public welfare have to be set against the low starting point and the problem of inequality, which increased as migrants from the hinterland joined the bulk of the population at the foot of life's ladder. Lagos itself was no longer divided by swampland but by its continuing inequalities, which were entrenched by the gulf between property owners and renters and between those who owned cars and those who looked at them. Modernity was making its appearance.

The Consequences of the Second Shock

The consequences of the second shock that struck Lagos in 1892 shaped much of the period of colonial rule that was to follow. Military advance was accompanied by the installation of colonial authority and the arrival inland of the expatriate firms. Taken together, they represented a form of compulsory globalisation spurred by imperialism. Constitutional change made a new country, Nigeria, a subsidiary of Britain; economic integration drew the two economies even closer together; political subordination and racial discrimination kept them apart. Seen from a narrow perspective, Lagos prospered from these developments. It became the capital of a large state; the railway made it the terminus of a vast hinterland; harbour improvements enabled it to retain its position as the largest port in West Africa.

Far-reaching changes involved more than instrumental adjustments to new circumstances. The fact that they took place not just in a port city but in a colonial port city had a deep influence on entrepreneurial motives and choice. The search for prosperity through profit remained a central concern, but it was accompanied by other sources of inspiration, especially a search for

---

133. *Lagos Standard*, 20 Nov. 1907; *Lagos Weekly Record*, 28 Oct. 1911.
134. *Lagos Weekly Record*, 1 May 1897, 14 Jan. 1899.
135. *Lagos Weekly Record*, 13 July 1907.
136. *Nigerian Pioneer*, 17 Nov. 1922.

self-respect, which had been damaged by the assertive advance of the new colonial order. This consideration helps to explain why business and politics shared an interest in the concept of 'co-operation', which a new generation of articulate colonial subjects mobilised during this period. Co-operation encapsulated their awareness of the need to combine in the face of the expanded power of the colonial government and the increasing size and ambition of the expatriate firms. In their different ways, leaders in business and politics saw co-operative action as a way of regaining self-respect. Roles that enabled them to be creative, whether in business or politics, allowed them a measure of independence in a situation of increasing subordination. Their positive reactions helped to generate the movements that eventually brought about the end of colonial rule.

CHAPTER ELEVEN

Accommodation and Diversification

THE CHANGES IN THE economic environment detailed in chapter 10 presented a new challenge for African merchants. They had survived the 1880s and 1890s, despite the economic and political crises that descended on them at that time. Their survival, however, might have postponed their fate instead of averting it. Many of the expatriate firms were already registered as limited companies and were able to raise the capital needed to move inland while also increasing the volume of trade they conducted. A few far-sighted African merchants recognised the problem and established limited companies to increase their capital resources. Although these ventures anticipated the future, their failure followed soon after their formation. The capital they required to take advantage of the enlarged hinterland market depended on established sources: accumulated profits and credit secured on property. A business structure that relied on sole ownership was becoming sub-optimal. A hypothesis pointing to this period as the one that submerged the surviving merchants seems promising. The evidence, however, suggests a different outcome: some merchants accommodated themselves to the new economic environment; others, more surprisingly, began to diversify the economy.

Mercantile Fortunes

Commentators in Lagos were well aware of the hazards facing African merchants. The Lagos newspapers had been raising concerns about the future profitability of the existing staples of 'legitimate' commerce since the 1880s. In 1891, the *Lagos Times* expressed the view that 'the individual will not be able to hold his own with large organisations' and declared that 'Native combination is needed to run the race with European combination'.[1] Depressing

1. *Lagos Times*, 13 June 1891.

predictions continued after the turn of the century, despite the revival of the economy. In 1910, the *Lagos Weekly Record* asked: 'What has become of the wealthy or rather the moneyed Native who we found here when we arrived nearly forty years ago? They dreamed of perpetuity. Where are they today?'[2] The *Record* gave an incomplete answer to its own question by noting, correctly, that 'the commercial class dating back to the eighties has disappeared for the greater part into the long home', a conclusion that led the paper to deplore the lack of continuity in African businesses.[3]

According to the *Lagos Weekly Record*, the end was nigh for the middlemen too. In 1910, the paper prepared an obituary notice: 'The role of the "middleman" which the Native of Lagos has filled from time immemorial has virtually been rendered extinct by the introduction of the railway which has carried foreign manufactures to the doors of the producer and dispensed with the necessity of an intermediary'.[4] Other commentators echoed this opinion.[5] Government officials were inclined to believe, instinctively, that 'middlemen' were surplus to requirements. The annual Trade Report for 1907 looked forward to replacing 'the influence of the middlemen . . . by more direct trade between the merchants and the consumers', thus giving 'further impetus' to trade.[6] The hope complemented the view that Lagos suffered from an 'unreasonable spirit of rivalry which has existed here for many years'.[7] This belief had inspired the scheme floated in 1899 to build a combination of European firms. The first assumption was mistaken because middlemen, far from being unproductive, were essential to the expansion of trade. Without them, the market would have been much smaller than it was. The second position was contrary to Britain's free-trade policy and, if implemented, would have been the means of controlling trade for the benefit of the few and to the disadvantage of the many.

The story of decline is a familiar one. It may also be correct. However, the hypothesis needs checking against contrary evidence before these gloomy conclusions are confirmed. It should be borne in mind, too, that the Lagos newspapers were mostly written by and for Saro and portrayed the world from a particular standpoint. Any assessment of the position of African merchants has to acknowledge that systematic data on the fortunes of African merchants during this period is lacking. The last objective account was Governor Moloney's list of contributors to the customs revenues derived from import duties, which showed that the leading eleven African importers accounted for a median value of 15 per cent of the total during the years 1881–1885

2. *Lagos Weekly Record*, 16 July 1910.
3. *Lagos Weekly Record*, 19 March 1910.
4. *Lagos Weekly Record*, 5 Nov. 1910.
5. *African Mail*, 23 Sept. 1910.
6. *Southern Nigeria Annual Report*, 1907.
7. *Lagos Annual Trade Report*, 1905, C.O. 149/5.

(inclusive).[8] This estimate, however, understated the total contribution made by African importers, which was in excess of 20 per cent. No comparable statement exists from that time until at least the 1930s.[9] Consequently, judgements have to be based on a few spot checks and estimates derived from qualitative evidence, and are necessarily provisional.

As chapter 7 showed, the depressed years from 1898 to 1900 removed many African and European businesses from the export trade. As trade recovered after the turn of the century, African exporters reappeared, though in limited numbers. In 1912, Matthew Brown, who represented Lagos Stores, thought that there were only 'about two' African merchants who were exporting produce directly to Europe.[10] Brown undercounted because Jacob Coker, Peter Thomas, Samuel Pearse, and several others were all exporting at that time, and continued to do so.[11] Nevertheless, it seems correct to conclude that only a handful of Africans were direct exporters, even though the trade had become profitable again. In 1916, an official estimate derived from the shipping and rail allocations imposed by war-time conditions showed that 'Native Firms' had been allotted 2,510 tons, which was about 13 per cent of all produce exports.[12] The allocation probably underestimated the total because it was based on railway freight and excluded produce ferried to Lagos across the lagoon. At the same time, it is likely that the allocation made in 1916 was higher than the share held by African exporters before the war because Africans took advantage of the expulsion of the German firms in 1914 to re-enter the export trade.

It seems fair to conclude that the stake of African merchants in the direct export trade remained below 10 per cent before 1914. This conclusion confirms a historical trend. The export trade had long been dominated by expatriate firms. In 1855, African exporters accounted for 20 per cent of the exports shipped from Lagos.[13] The substantial growth of trade since the mid-century suggests that the absolute value of exports shipped by Africans probably increased, but that their relative share continued to decline from already modest levels.

Imports, however, were a different story. As Matthew Brown confirmed in 1912, most African merchants focussed on the import trade. This trend, too, extended the pattern of the past.[14] The arrangements for importing goods,

8. See chapter 7 above.

9. And possibly beyond, though I may be corrected on this point.

10. Brown, Evidence to Committee on Lagos Trade, 8 Feb. 1912, PP (1912), Cd. 6427, pp. 94–7.

11. Boyle to Bonar Law, 31 Oct. 1916, C.O. 583/49.

12. Boyle to Bonar Law, 31 Oct. 1916, C.O. 583/49.

13. See chapter 3 above.

14. Brown, Evidence to Committee on Lagos Trade, 8 Feb. 1912, PP (1912), Cd. 6427, pp. 94–7.

however, had changed since the 1880s. According to Brown, 'native merchants' either paid cash for items they bought from European importers or ordered on consignment from Europe and redeemed their goods after paying the Bank of British West Africa (BBWA) in Lagos. Barter had disappeared and BBWA provided a facility that helped Africans while also giving European suppliers security. The import trade had several advantages for merchants whose capital was limited. Writing in 1902, E. A. Lovell, the Collector of Customs, observed that, thanks mainly to BBWA, 'the smallest trader can now order his goods direct from Europe through the various commission agents or merchants and this forms what is termed the Indent Trade'.[15]

Lovell estimated that 'about one quarter of the ad valorem goods are imported in this way'.[16] This was only an approximation and it applied just to one year. Nevertheless, Lovell was in a better position that anyone else to make such a judgement. The ad valorem tariff covered nearly all commercial imports, the most important exception being spirits, which accounted for just under 9 per cent of tariff revenue in 1902.[17] Since many African merchants also imported spirits, their share of total imports would have been higher than 25 per cent. Accordingly, it is reasonable to assume that African merchants had increased their share of the import trade from at least 20 per cent in 1881–1885 to a figure approaching 30 per cent in 1902. There is no way of arriving at an acceptable estimate of the share of total trade taken by Africans because the export figures for 1916 cannot legitimately be combined with those of imports in 1902. If the figure for 1902 (a minimum of 25 per cent), which is both conservative and reasonably well based, is added to a range of modest estimates below 10 per cent representing African merchants' share of exports, their share of total trade is not far below the figure for 1855.

African merchants had not been pushed out of the export trade: they had decided that imports were less risky than the produce trade and required less capital because consumer goods could be imported in relatively small quantities and still be traded profitably. In addition, the wide range of imported goods enabled merchants to create specialised niches for themselves. The

15. Lovell, 'Lagos Present', pp. 2–3. The view summarised here and referred to in subsequent paragraphs runs counter to the orthodox position, which is well expressed by Uche, 'Foreign Banks'. Uche emphasised the importance of the effective banking monopoly in limiting access to credit. The monopolist (the Bank of British West Africa), however, was owned by Elder Dempster, the shipping firm, which was keen to fill its ships and advanced credit to Africans who had adequate security, typically in the form of real estate.

16. Lovell, 'Lagos Present'.

17. Lovell's calculation excluded specie and government imports. It was not until 1908 that a committee investigated the matter and recommended switching from ad valorem to specific tariffs. Egerton to Crewe, 16 Dec. 1908, C.O. 520/68. Revisions were approved in 1909, though textiles were placed on the ad valorem list: Egerton to Crewe, 22 Oct. 1909, and C.O. minute, 11 March 1910, C.O. 520/82.

familiarity of Lagos importers with local society and markets enabled them to identify emerging patterns of demand that, combined with lower over-heads, gave them a competitive advantage over European firms. Given these conditions, it should not be surprising to find that some established merchants, such as Alli Balogun, continued to prosper, or that a new set of African importers appeared after the turn of the century, the most prominent being Josiah Doherty.

African merchants who traded directly with Europe were seen by contemporaries to have reached parity, at least in function, with the European firms. Their international connections and status placed them at the top of the commercial hierarchy. Status was a reflection of economic standing, which derived primarily from capital resources. Merchants who operated on a large scale were able to trade in bulk and negotiate cheaper freight rates. Their ability to mobilise substantial sums of capital beyond the limits of sole ownership awaited the formation of limited companies, which could draw on subscriptions from shareholders. Although African merchants had to rely on their own resources, they were greatly assisted by the facilities offered by BBWA, which helped them to remain competitive. Other potential advantages of scale were limited. Expatriate firms were unable to influence prices in Europe, and their lack of co-ordination in Lagos prevented them from controlling prices there too, as the history of the palm-kernel pool showed. A small number of individual exporters could both amass huge profits and incur spectacular losses. Both possibilities were symptoms of the high risks attached to what contemporaries sometimes referred to as gambling. There is little evidence to suggest that, before 1914, the small number of African direct importers and exporters added more value to the economy than brokers and other wholesalers.

The middlemen also defied predictions of their demise. They were still numerous in 1907, when the *Annual Trade Report* expressed the hope that they would be replaced.[18] In the following year, McIver's representative stated that most of his customers were 'middlemen', adding that 'Europeans rarely sell direct to the consumer'.[19] The agent of Lagos Stores agreed, noting that 'less than one per cent of his trade is done with the actual consumer'.[20] John Holt's manager confirmed both views, saying that goods 'pass through numerous middlemen before reaching the consumer'.[21] The representative of Paterson Zochonis concurred, saying that 'very little trade' was conducted with 'actual consumers'.[22] The Lagos census of 1911 reported that more than 21,000 inhabitants, about 46 per cent of the occupied population,

18. *Southern Nigeria Annual Report*, 1907.

19. Evidence of McIver, 30 June 1908, in Egerton to Crewe, 16 Dec. 1908, C.O. 520/68.

20. Evidence of Lagos Stores, 3 July 1908, in Egerton to Crewe, 16 Dec. 1908, C.O. 520/68.

21. Evidence, 7 July 1908, in Egerton to Crewe, 16 Dec. 1908, C.O. 520/68.

22. Evidence, 9 July 1908, in Egerton to Crewe, 16 Dec. 1908, C.O. 520/68.

entered 'trader' as their occupation.[23] This was easily the largest single occupational group and also one that had grown considerably during the last few decades. In the following year, Matthew Brown, the long-serving representative of Lagos Stores, provided detailed evidence of what was still a vibrant set of intermediaries, which he divided into three groups and four types.[24] Further down the commercial scale, the number of hawkers and petty traders in Lagos in 1910 was large enough to stimulate complaints, repeated two years later, that they were obstructing the streets and causing 'unfair' competition for European firms, which were obliged to maintain costly premises in the central business district.[25]

Women traders can scarcely be called 'middlemen', but they can be referred to as intermediaries who played a vital role in performing the same function as that described by the gendered term. They not only survived; they also organised. Signs of their opposition to government impositions date from at least 1908, when the proposed water rate generated opposition in Lagos. By the early 1920s, they had formed the Lagos Market Women Association under the dynamic leadership of Alimotu Pelewura (1871–1951), a fish trader, and thereafter mounted a series of protests against increases in the water rate, the imposition of market fees, and the prospect of paying income tax.[26] The Association co-operated closely with Herbert Macaulay and became a powerful agent of the Nigerian National Democratic Party (1923) throughout the inter-war period.

Evidently, middlemen in different shapes, sizes, and genders were present in force and showed no signs of disbanding. The explanation of their survival appears to be straightforward. The broad effect of the railway was to expand trade and increase the demand for intermediaries, who were needed to deliver supplies and distribute goods at stopping points on its long route to the north. Expansion undoubtedly had differential effects. Some existing markets benefitted; others were displaced. But this outcome was consistent with an increase in the total number of middlemen. Motor transport was at the outset of its career. It was not until after 1945 that cheaper vehicles and improved roads altered the 'middleman system', which is not to say that it was abolished, even then. This is another subject that lies beyond the scope of the present study and deserves detailed investigation.

23. *Census of the Colony of Southern Nigeria*, 1911.

24. Brown, evidence on the organisation of trade in Lagos, 8 Feb. 1912, in PP Cd. 6427 (1912).

25. Municipal Engineer to Lagos Municipal Board, 20 June 1910, LMB, 171/1910, and 26 Nov. 1912, LMB, 342/1912.

26. Johnson, 'Grass Roots Organising'; Afolabi, 'Lagos Market Women'; Somotan, 'Lagos Women in Colonial History'. From the standpoint of this study, it is unfortunate that studies of Alimotu Pelewura concentrate on her political activities and say little or nothing about her trading career.

Accommodating Colonial Rule

Most members of the merchant community had little option but to find a place within the economic environment that colonial rule had established. The survey that follows shows that this option remained viable as well as necessary, and allowed scope for a variety of responses. Living with colonial rule, however, did not mean agreeing with colonial policies. Most merchants found it possible to work within the colonial economy while also criticising the colonial government.

The cosmopolitan complexion of the merchant community reflected that of the wider Lagos population. Although Saro were still prominent among the leading merchants, their own numbers had not been reinforced by renewed inflows of migrants from Sierra Leone. Moreover, descendants of the first repatriates, who were in the second and third generations by 1900, rarely made a career in commerce their first choice, and few of those who followed parental footsteps were successful. The Saro continued to dominate the very small number of African merchants who featured as direct exporters. No doubt custom played a part in the decision to engage in exporting, but the more important influence was the familiarity of Saro with the English language and English ways, which enabled them to establish close relations with firms in Britain. The two leading Lagosians in the export trade between 1900 and 1920 were Samuel Pearse and Peter Thomas, whose volatile careers are given extended treatment in chapters 12 and 15. Jacob Coker, whose farming activities are detailed in chapter 13, also shipped produce to Europe. In addition, Saro were present as produce brokers (formerly known as barracooners).

David Taylor's career serves as an example of the way Saro merchants who were predominantly importers also traded in produce when market conditions seemed favourable.[27] David Augustus Taylor was born in Lagos in 1865. He was the youngest of three children, his seniors being Lavinia and Thomas. His father, Daddy Thomas Taylor, whose family name was Iwolode, was an Egba from Owu, who was captured, enslaved, and then freed in Sierra Leone.[28] He received some education there, adopted an English name and the Anglican religion, and began his adult life as a sawyer. He returned to Lagos with his wife, Mary, in 1858, and divided his time between Alakoro, where

27. I am grateful to the following for the invaluable information they kindly provided: three of David Taylor's sons, Frederick, Alfred, and Thomas, and two of his daughters, Mrs Elfreda Oni and Madame Bernice Taylor, Lagos, 9 Dec. 1961; Mr C. A. Taylor, David's nephew and son of his senior brother, Thomas, Lagos, 15 Jan. 1962. I am especially grateful to Thomas (Ola) Taylor for supplementary information and for permission to use some of his father's remaining papers, which are referred to here as the David Augustus Taylor Papers (DATP), Lagos, 14 Dec. 1961. Additional information, unless stated otherwise, is from: *Lagos Times*, 23 May 1891; *Lagos Daily News*, 29 April 1932; *Nigerian Daily Times*, 29 April 1932; Macmillan, *Red Book*, p. 108.

28. *Lagos Times*, 23 May 1891.

he had a house, Iddo, and Onigbongbo (near Ikeja), where he farmed. He was one of the founding members of St. Paul's Breadfruit and sent David to Breadfruit School and subsequently to the CMS Grammar School. On leaving school in 1880, David joined the firm of McIver as a clerk. In 1887, he moved from McIver to Blackstock and in 1891, having mastered the procedures and encountered the risks of Lagos trade, he started his own business at the age of twenty-six.[29]

Taylor began by mortgaging (with other family members) the land at Onigbongbo they had inherited from Daddy Thomas, who died in 1891.[30] Thomas had received the land, extending to about 11 acres, as a grant 'for ever' from Chief Fadu.[31] This is an early example of how the practice established in Lagos of using land as credit had begun to spread to the mainland. The mortgage, effectively a loan, secured an advance of £250 from Gaiser to help the new business get under way. In 1894, the same family group, having redeemed the mortgage in 1893, reassigned it as security for an advance of £200.[32] By then, David had become the sole proprietor, his senior brother, Thomas, having died in 1894. In that year, David moved from a modest house in Balogun Street to the Marina, where he rented larger premises in the central business district.[33] His business dealt almost exclusively in cotton goods, though, like many others, he also exported rubber during the boom at the close of the century. He ordered cottons on consignment directly from England and collected the shipment on arrival after paying the bank. His procedure with produce was different but also typical of that trade. He advanced cash to traders who bought rubber from producers in the hinterland; he then amalgamated purchases into bulk quantities, which he sold to merchants who shipped directly to Europe. In the evidence he gave before the Commission on Trade in 1898, he stated that his turnover on produce amounted to £8,000–10,000 in 1895, though the figure had dropped to £4,000 in the following year and competition meant that there was now 'very little profit' in the rubber trade.[34] His turnover on cotton goods was 'about' £10,000 in 1897; more recently, he said that he had lost money on his trade in imports.[35]

Evidently, an impressive turnover was an imperfect guide to profitability. Nevertheless, Taylor had done well enough, despite the depressing trading conditions at the end of the century, to purchase two properties on prime sites in the Marina, each flanking Caxton House, where Richard Blaize had

29. Lagos Stores v. Blackstock, LSCR, Civ. 26, 1901.

30. Last will dated 3 Jan. 1891, DATP.

31. LLOR, 14/355, 1891.

32. LLOR, 20/299, 1894.

33. The property in Balogun Street was leased to various tenants, including Blackstock & Co., who held it from 1913 to 1919 at a rent of £100 p.a.

34. Evidence in Denton to Chamberlain, 25 May 1898, C.O. 147/132.

35. Evidence in Denton to Chamberlain, 25 May 1898, C.O. 147/132.

his headquarters. Taylor bought the first property from James J. Thomas, for £3,750 in 1903, and the second from Victor Badou for £1,100 in 1904.[36] He also had a farm at Agege, inherited from his father, which in 1904 had 60 acres under cultivation.[37] The property he had acquired funded his business by serving as security for bank overdrafts and advances of goods from his European suppliers.[38]

The business continued to prosper until the First World War. In 1916, however, Taylor mortgaged his main Marina property (with use) to John Walkden & Co. to cover a loan of £2,000 that he had failed to pay on the due date.[39] The decision may have been an indication that the war had created difficulties for his business.[40] It may also have been connected to an agreement he made in that year with a London firm, the African Produce Trading Co. (APTC), to supply their Lagos agent with palm kernels.[41] Taylor probably realised that the elimination of the German firms created an opportunity to move into the kernel trade, which was being redirected to British ports. The agreement was tightly drawn. The London firm agreed to pay Thomas 10s. per ton above the Lagos price in exchange for a guaranteed supply of 100 tons of kernels each month. Penalties were imposed if the supply did not reach this figure. APTC also reserved the right to suspend the agreement should the Liverpool market collapse. Taylor became increasingly invested in the produce trade. In 1919, he leased his Marina property to the Colonial Bank and moved his import business to smaller premises in Breadfruit Street, while retaining a produce store in Alakoro.[42] The sale was not forced upon him: Taylor was attracted by the substantial rent of £720 p.a. that the bank was prepared to pay. Nevertheless, the move seems to have been connected to his decision to expand the produce side of his business.[43] There is no information about how profitable these decisions were, but it is clear that by the end of the war Taylor's fortunes depended on the prosperity of the produce trade.

When the slump replaced the short boom in 1920–1921, Taylor was caught with commitments he could not meet. In January 1922, Josiah Doherty

36. LLOR, 42/380, 1903; LLOR, 49/223, 1904.

37. McCallum to Chamberlain, 23 Sept. 1897, C.S.O. 1/1/19.

38. Marina property mortgaged to Walkden, LLOR, 49/223, 1907; Tinubu Square and Victoria Road property mortgaged to Bank of Nigeria, LLOR, 68/218, 1911; property at Balogun Street mortgaged to Walkden, LLOR, 81/400, 1913; Tinubu Square and Victoria Road mortgaged to BBWA, LLOR, 83/1, 1913; Marina property remortgaged to Walkden, LLOR, 83/303, 1914, and in 1916, LLOR, 98/133, 1916. Marina leased to Colonial Bank for fifty years at £600 p.a. for the first seventeen years, LLOR, 129/119, 1919.

39. Taylor to Walkden, LLOR, 98/133, 1916.

40. As suggested by the *Nigerian Daily Times*, 30 April 1932.

41. Agreement dated 1916 in DATP.

42. Marina leased to Colonial Bank for fifty years at £600 p.a. for the first seventeen years, LLOR, 129/119, 1919. The Colonial Bank (1917) became Barclays (DCO) in 1925.

43. Boyle to Bonar Law, 31 Oct. 1916, C.O. 583/49, and enclosure.

offered him an interest-free loan of £1,000, which secured his overdraft with the Colonial Bank and enabled him to remain in the produce business until the end of the season.[44] The relief expressed in Taylor's response indicated how precarious his position had suddenly become: 'I really cannot express my gratitude for this special favour', he wrote in his letter of acceptance.[45] He abandoned the produce trade, reduced his staple item, cotton goods, and took refuge in specialised items such as beads. His discomfort, however, had only just begun. The post-war slump, unlike most previous setbacks in Lagos trade, had a durable quality. In 1924, Taylor began lengthy negotiations with the Colonial Bank in an effort to raise money and offered to sell the Marina property they rented from him.[46] His starting price, £12,960, was refused; by 1927, he was prepared to accept £11,000. Meanwhile, he was being funded by Josiah Doherty, who supplemented his goodwill by obtaining mortgages on some of Taylor's properties.[47]

Matters deteriorated. In 1927, Taylor was forced to borrow £1,500 at the exceptionally high rate of 15 per cent per annum from the Scottish Nigerian Mortgage & Trust Company Ltd. in return for mortgaging the property on Iddo Island he had inherited from his father.[48] The slump of 1929 and the financial crisis of 1931 extinguished all optimism. Taylor was unable to service his debts. His death in April 1932 was accompanied by a financial settlement and foreclosures that left his estate bereft of assets.[49] His career was representative of many other Lagos merchants who had done well before the war but were ruined after it. His son, John, continued the business for a short while before branching out on his own and shipping produce to Europe. Unfavourable market conditions in the 1930s meant that the business was never very successful.

The Brazilians were in a similar position. By 1914, the decline and virtual elimination of direct commerce with Bahia had cut the lifeline that had carried returnees and trade to Lagos in the nineteenth century. Joaquim Francisco Branco (1852–1924), who had imported liquor and tobacco and exported kola nuts, shea butter, and pepper to Brazil since the 1880s, was typical in

44. Doherty to Taylor, 31 Jan. 1922, DATP.

45. Taylor to Doherty, 31 Jan. 1922, DATP.

46. Taylor to Colonial Bank, DATP, 10 Feb. 1925; Colonial Bank to Taylor, 20 Aug. 1925; Barclays to Taylor, 19 Sept. 1927; Taylor to Barclays, 8 Nov. 1927.

47. Doherty to Taylor, 31 Jan. 1922; Taylor to Doherty, 1 June 1925, mortgaging 30 Balogun Street; Barclays to Taylor, 3 Jan. 1927, informing him that Doherty had paid £500 into his account; Paying-in Slip, 3 Jan 1927, showing that Doherty had paid Taylor £1,000; all in DATP.

48. Indenture between Taylor and the Scottish Nigerian Mortgage & Trust Co. Ltd., DATP, 2 Nov. 1927.

49. For example, Peter Jones v. Taylor Family, Supreme Court Nigeria, Judgment 20 April 1932, DATP.

experiencing the decline of his business after the turn of the century.[50] He adapted by concentrating on his trade with Porto Novo and Cotonou. Other Brazilians were also obliged to adjust. Lourenço António Cardoso (1865–1940) had developed a specialised trade with Brazil, importing dried beef, tobacco, and brown sugar, and shipping rafia, black soap, and camwood, which he funded by bank overdrafts and mortgages.[51] When the Brazil trade declined, he adapted by establishing a large cocoa farm at Agege in 1909 while also becoming an auctioneer in Lagos. His story did not end well. In 1918, he mortgaged seven properties, including the farm, to Josiah Doherty to raise £5,000 for further expansion.[52] Like many others, he was caught out by the post-war slump and later by the crisis of 1929, found himself unable to service the debt, and in 1931 was forced to surrender the property.

By 1914, the Brazilians had made the biggest adjustment of all: they had become increasingly integrated with the land of their ancestors. A growing number spoke English as well as Portuguese and Yoruba. Marriage outside the community had ceased to be an unusual event. Cardoso's mother came from Ilesha; his son was educated at Cornell University; several of Branco's sons were educated in Britain before entering one of the professions; Moses, one of Candido da Rocha's brothers, studied in Edinburgh and qualified as a doctor. Although the community was small, it had expanded its horizons in unanticipated ways.

The import trade had a different character and trajectory. The Saro were not only more numerous in this branch of trade, but also produced the most successful of all the importers, Josiah Doherty, whose biography appears in chapter 12. The striking feature of the trade, however, was the increasing preponderance of Muslim traders, including some whose prosperity prompted a colonial official in Lagos to comment in 1908 that 'most of the large native traders are Mohammedans, many of them being very wealthy'.[53] Given that there had been a considerable increase in the proportion of Lagosians who were Muslims, it was only to be expected, other things being equal, that their

50. I am indebted to Mrs Edith Smith, Joaquim's eldest granddaughter, and to Mr F. P. Martins, his grandson-in-law, for information on the history of the family: interviews, Lagos, 7 Feb. 1962, 13 Feb. 1962. Additional information is from LSCR, Civ. 11, 1891; J. F. Branco to Municipal Secretary, 19 Oct. 1911, LMB, 328/1911; Last Will and Testament, LAP 6, 325/9; Egerton to Lyttelton, 30 Sept. 1904, 23 Oct. 1904, 29 Oct. 1904, C.O. 147/171; *Nigerian Pioneer*, 20 Sept. 1924.

51. I am indebted to Lourenço's son, Mr P. W. O. Cardoso, for information about his father. Interviews, Lagos, 14 Feb. 1962, 16 Feb. 1962. Additional information from: Macmillan, *Red Book*, p. 110; Thomas, 'News Diary', 5 Jan. 1938, pp. 261–3; 20 July 1938, p. 350; *Lagos Reporter*, 19 June 1899; overdraft of £300 with the Bank of Nigeria, LLOR, 68/1, 1910; overdraft of £400 with BBWA, LLOR, 81/137, 1912, repeated in 1914, LLOR, 83/286, 1914; Laotan, *The Torch Bearers*, p. 11.

52. Mortgage, LLOR, 123/122, 1918.

53. E. P. Cotton (Director of Surveys) to C.O. 19 Feb. 1908, C.O. 520/74.

share of the import trade would have grown too. This explanation, however, is incomplete. An important additional consideration followed from the opening of trade with the north, which gave Muslim traders both an opportunity to expand trade with Lagos and an advantage in doing so by connecting with co-religionists there. If the acquisition of freehold property is used as one index of prosperity, it is evident that Muslim names appeared with increasing frequency in the Lands Office records during the period 1900–1914.[54] The Muslim community, like its Brazilian counterpart, extended its reach in other ways, too, notably by adding Western education to Koranic scholarship.

Beyond these observations, it is difficult to add substantially to the jejune observation that the role of Muslim merchants has almost certainly been understated in this and other studies of Lagos history. Alli Balogun was by common consent the leading Muslim merchant of his day in Lagos and may even have been, as the *Nigerian Pioneer* claimed in 1933, 'the wealthiest African trader in Lagos'.[55] Moreover, his 'day' lasted a long time. He could have appeared at an earlier point in this study, but has been reserved for the period after 1900, when his flourishing career reached its highest point. Even so, it is hard to do justice to his distinction because so few records relating to his life have survived. The sketch that follows demonstrates how much of his career is known only in outline.[56]

Alli Balogun, like Daniel Taiwo, lived to an age so far beyond the norm that it was reckoned, variously, to have spanned between 100 and 130 years. The only certainty is that he died in 1933. The most informed obituary gave his date of birth as 1850, which would have made him eighty-three at his death.[57] There is no assured way of checking this. In 1909, Alli stated that he became a Muslim '50 years ago', that is, in 1859, which is a plausible approximation, assuming he was converted with other members of the family. Accordingly, 1850 is an acceptable date until a better alternative is produced. His father, Makanjuola, was an *Ibiga* (royal slave) of *Oba* Osinlokun who ruled Lagos from 1820–1821 to 1829.[58] Makanjuola was an intermediary in the slave trade who turned to legitimate commerce during the closing years of his life. Alli

54. As already noted in this study, the Lands Office records in Lagos remain an untapped source. My own assessment of Muslim property owners during this period must be classified as being 'preliminary' because the material on this subject would support several Ph.D. dissertations.

55. *Nigerian Pioneer*, 21 July 1933.

56. I am indebted to *Alhaji* Noah Alli Balogun, Alli's son, for providing information about his father's life and for confirming that Alli Balogun's papers were destroyed at his death. Interviews, 10 Jan. 1962, 16 Jan. 1962. Other information is drawn from Deniga, *Nigerian Who's Who*, *1919*, pp. 2–3, and the sources cited below. Dele Adeoti provides a short account (based on secondary sources) in 'The Career of Alli Balogun of Lagos, 1840–1933', in *Eminent Yoruba Muslims*, pp. 179–200.

57. *Nigerian Daily Times*, 14 July 1933.

58. I follow here the meticulous analysis of Law, 'The Dynastic Chronology of Lagos'.

began as a small-time trader selling iron bands in the lagoon markets and dealing in cattle.[59] In the 1870s and 1880s, he became a barracooner, supplying palm produce to Gaiser, Witt & Busch, and the African merchants, Zachariah Williams and Richard Blaize, and importing cotton goods, gunpowder, iron sheets, kerosene, and spirits.[60] By then, he was also operating a fleet of trading canoes for his own use and for hire, and had acquired the nickname Alli Oloko (Alli the boat-owner).[61] After the turn of the century, he added cocoa to the list of his exports, but also reduced his involvement with other exports and focussed on the import side of the business. He had a shop at Idumagbo, where he managed wholesale and retail trades and dealt in both cash and goods. He had received very little formal education apart from some instruction in Arabic. He was fluent in Yoruba but spoke no English and kept a business diary in Arabic. Like Daniel Taiwo, he employed clerks who kept accounts in English.

By the turn of the century, Alli had added a branch that was to become a predominant part of his business: money lending.[62] His shrewdness as a trader was matched by his astuteness as a property investor. Most of his business profits were channelled into property in Lagos. The Grantor Index in the Lands Office shows that he was one of the biggest property dealers in the town during the first thirty years of the century and easily the most important among the Muslim money lenders. Much of his property, moreover, was in prime locations. He was the only Muslim businessman to lease property on both the Marina and Broad Street to European firms.[63] What is even more striking is that, though his name recurs frequently in the Supreme Court records of civil cases, it is always as a creditor seeking a judgement for debts owed and never as a debtor himself.[64] The list of those who borrowed money from him ranged from notables, such as Samuel Pearse and Seidu Olowu, to

59. According to one source, Alli inherited his father's stock and contacts. *Nigerian Daily Times*, 14 July 1933. While he may have made use of his father's contacts, it is unlikely that, as the seventh son, he would have inherited his stock as well, as this would have been a departure from both Yoruba and Muslim law.

60. In 1904, he stated that he had been in the spirit trade for twenty years. Evidence in Egerton to Lyttelton, 23 Oct. 1904, C.O. 147/171; *Lagos Weekly Record*, 4 July 1903, and *Nigerian Pioneer*, 28 May 1909, give details of his trade in spirits.

61. See also Balogun v. Lana, LSCR, Civ. 86, 1919.

62. I am grateful to that most acute observer of the Lagos scene, the late Chief Theophilus Adebayo Doherty (1895–1974), who knew Alli Balogun, for confirming Alli's eminence in this field. Interviews on 31 Nov. 1961, 14 Dec. 1961, 22 Feb. 1962, 25 June 1964, and many other occasions.

63. For example, Balogun to British Colonial Trading Company (Marina), LLOR, 104/380, 1918; Balogun to Ashton Kinder (Broad Street), LLOR, 137/34, 1920; Balogun to African Association (Broad Street), LLOR, 82/188, 1914.

64. A few of many possible examples range from Balogun v. Willoughby LSCR, Civ. 22, 1899, to Balogun v. Oguntola Sapara, LSCR, Civ. 82, 1918.

FIGURE 11.1. *Alhaji* Alli Balogun. Copied by Paramount Photographers Lagos, with permission of Alhaji Noah Alli Balogun (son).

obscure Lagosians who had registered modest property far from the Marina and Broad Street as freehold.[65]

Little is known of Alli himself. In his prime, he was said to be 'tall and imposing in stature'.[66] He enjoyed an occasional drink, went to the races from time to time, but was too shrewd to bet his house on a horse, and was generous without being flamboyant.[67] Public evidence of his success is easily found. By 1900, he had built a fine house in Victoria Street (Makanjuola House), and acquired a rickshaw and two horses. In 1916, he added a car, which he bought from a colonial official for £310.[68] He had also attained prominence in public affairs. In 1897, he was a member of the Native Board of Trade, which had been formed to represent the interests of the 'non-Christian' merchants; in 1900 he was appointed to the Native Affairs Council formed by Governor MacGregor.[69] In 1908, he was asked to mediate a dispute between two families as to which had the right to nominate the successor to Daniel Taiwo as *Olofin* of Isheri. Alli's diplomacy included touches of statesmanship that ended the matter to the satisfaction of both parties.[70] His wealth was manifest in his substantial support for rebuilding the Central Mosque, which was opened in 1913 at a cost of nearly £13,000.[71]

Alli's position as one of the Big Men of the town drew him into politics. He was a founding member of the People's Union, which was formed in 1908 to urge the colonial government to pay more attention to the needs of ordinary Lagosians. Its cause and immediate focus was the proposed water rate, which, so the Union claimed, favoured the wealthy.[72] The Union mobilised considerable public support and sustained its campaign until 1916, when the government threatened the opposition with imprisonment and the forfeiture of personal property. The threat was too close to home, in every sense. The Union gave in and the water rate took effect. The retreat, which took Alli

65. Seidu Olowu borrowed £500 from him in 1910, using land at Idumagbo as security, LLOR, 68/87, 1911; Pearse borrowed £2,000 from Alli Balogun to finance his hotel but was forced to sell it to him for that sum in 1922, after the post-war slump struck.

66. *Nigerian Daily Times*, 14 July 1933.

67. *Nigerian Pioneer*, 28 May 1909.

68. *Nigerian Pioneer*, 20 July 1917; supplemented by information from *Alhaji* Noah Alli Balogun.

69. *Lagos Weekly Record*, 29 May 1897. It is unclear whether this organisation and the Egbe Olowo (Society for the Wealthy) were the same. They had the same joint presidents: Seidu Olowo and Fasheke Olukolu.

70. *Lagos Weekly Record*, 4 April 1908.

71. *Lagos Standard*, 23 July 1913. Animashaun, *The History of the Muslim Community*, p. 2. I am grateful to the late *Alhaji* Adamu Idrisu Animashaun, first General Secretary of the Jamat, Lagos, for discussing this issue with me and for kindly giving me a copy of his pamphlet. Lagos, 1 Feb. 1962.

72. *Lagos Weekly Record*, 20 Feb. 1909; *Nigerian Pioneer*, 26 March 1909. Alli Balogun also represented the Native Board of Trade on the issue.

Balogun with it, cost the Union and Alli much of their popular support. From being opponents of colonial policy, they found themselves in effect associated with it and displaced by the more intransigent Herbert Macaulay and his supporters. The outcome also split the Muslim community and led to a battle for power between what became known as the Jamaat Party, which remained critical of government policy, and the Lemonu faction named after the Chief Imam (also known as the Alli Balogun party), which favoured co-operation.[73] The conflict lasted until 1924, when the Supreme Court, in a ruling confirmed by the Privy Council, determined that the Central Mosque should be placed under the control of the Jamaat. A man of wealth, however, is not easily defeated. Alli's response to the judgement was to build his own mosque, which he did at a cost of nearly £10,000. The Wasinmi ('come and rest here') Mosque was opened in 1928 in Victoria Street close to both the Central Mosque and Alli's home.

Alli Balogun died in 1933, aged approximately eighty-three, and was buried in his own mosque. His will, which was 'sworn' at under £10,300, was a misleading guide to his total assets, most of which were contained in about fifty houses he owned in Lagos.[74] His trustees were instructed to pay his bequests, including pensions to his beneficiaries, principally his six surviving wives, six sons, and sixteen daughters, who received one or more houses each. He divided his stock into two parts. Half went to one of his sons, a quarter to his 'servant', and the remaining quarter, in further divisions, to his other sons. The eldest son, Busari Balogun, continued the business for about a year, at which point the family prevailed on him to close it and distribute the remaining stock. It was the end of a career that spanned the main phases of trade since the cession of Lagos: the rise of legitimate exports, the subsequent concentration on imports, and the final shift to money lending. The *Nigerian Daily Times* was correct in concluding that Alli Balogun survived 'almost alone of his generation and succeeding traders' and was 'least hit' by the 'ups and downs' of the produce trade.[75] It was a record shared only by Josiah Doherty.

If Muslim merchants have been under-represented in historical accounts of mercantile fortunes, women traders have been almost entirely bypassed, despite their indispensable contribution to Lagos trade. Their neglect may once have been a matter of prejudice but persists today because of the difficulty of recovering more than minimal information about their careers.[76]

73. There is a substantial assessment of the dispute in the *Lagos Weekly Record*, 26 July, 27 July, 2 Aug., 9 Aug., 30 Aug., 4 Oct., 22 Nov., and 13 Dec. 1919. Cole, *Modern and Traditional Elites*, ch. 3, remains a sure guide to this complex episode. See also Lawal, 'Islam and Colonial Rule in Lagos', pp. 66–80; Raifu, 'Intrigues', pp. 36–48.

74. LAP, VIII /234–47, 1933.

75. *Nigerian Daily Times*, 14 July 1933.

76. A valuable survey is Denzer, 'Yoruba Women'.

Wusamotu Shelle, Selia Jawandu, and Ireti will appear in chapter 12 because of their connection with Josiah Doherty's business. Two other traders will be entered here, not merely because they were distanced from Doherty's capacious embrace, but because their businesses departed from the standard specialisation in imported goods.

Samota Ikeolorun was born in Lagos around the year 1858.[77] Her father, Alufa Akidele, migrated from Addo-Ekiti as a young man and farmed at Idioroko (now in the Yaba area); her mother came from Ilesha. The pair met and married in Lagos in the late 1850s. While she was young, Samota lived in Idioroko and helped on the farm. She had no formal education, apart from elementary instruction in the Koran, and spoke no English. Around 1880, she married Alfa Iman Adamo and moved to Victoria Street in Lagos. Marriage was an opportunity that pointed to a necessity because she was then expected to earn her living. She began on a small scale, buying native cloth from centres such as Ilorin and Ogbomosho, and slowly built a thriving business. Once she was established, she bought cloth from itinerant traders who visited her shop in Victoria Street every nine days, and resold it either in bulk or in retail quantities. The trade was very varied, ranging from highly specialised cloth for important occasions to less exclusive styles that were within the range of customers who were not, or not yet, in the elite. As her business progressed, she developed an export trade employing Kroo and other agents to distribute cloth in Liberia, Sierra Leone, and the Gold Coast. She went on to add a mail-order business, using the Post Office to send orders to individual customers. The trade was conducted almost entirely in cash with the help of a clerk who kept accounts in English and moved money between Victoria Road and Barclays Bank. Business slackened during the inter-war depression, revived later, but contracted again as advancing age and increasing competition reduced profits.

Samota died in 1948.[78] Her wealth was distributed, as her will instructed, among her three children. Her son was educated at the Wesleyan Boys' High School and became a printer. In accordance with the custom of the time, Samota's daughters, Rabiatu and Sabitiyu, were not given the same opportunity, though Samota relented when it came to the next generation and educated many of her grandchildren. Her daughters maintained the family tradition of dealing in local cloth, though their businesses were entirely separate from each other as well as from that of their mother. Rabiatu was not only very successful but also became a prominent public figure as a result of her leading role in supporting the Nigerian National Democratic Party.[79] She invested her profits

77. I especially appreciated the opportunity of meeting *Alhaja* Rabiatu Iyalode, Samota's daughter, and Mrs Limota Alli Balogun, her granddaughter. Lagos, 13 Feb. 1962. See also *Nigerian Daily Times*, 8 Jan. 1948.

78. Her daughter, Rabiatu, had an impressive statue of Samota erected in Okesunna Cemetery.

79. Adeboye, Akinwumi, and Otusanay, 'Rabi "Also Oke" of Colonial Lagos'.

FIGURE 11.2. Samota Ikeolorun. Copied by Paramount Photographers Lagos, with permission of *Alhaja* Rabiatu Iyalode (daughter).

in Lagos property and in educating her children and grandchildren, some of whom studied in Britain. The family was accorded two rare distinctions: Samota was made *Iya Adinni* (head of the female Muslims) of Lagos; Rabiatu was made *Iyalode* (head of the market women) in the port.

Humuani Alake Thompson's parents were originally from Oyo but settled in Lagos, where she was born around 1873.[80] She acquired her English surname upon her marriage to Ailara Giwa Thompson, a Lagos trader.[81] His parents were former slaves who took the name Thompson after they had been freed in Sierra Leone. The name endured, but the religion associated with it proved to be transient: the family either were or became Muslims. Humuani had no formal education but began trading at an early age by hawking goods for her mother before starting her own business after her marriage. She traded exclusively in Nigerian-made cloth, which she bought from Abeokuta, Iseyin, Ilorin, and other centres. The business was partly wholesale and partly retail. Some of her stock was sold in Lagos; the remainder was shipped to Sierra Leone on the steamers that commuted regularly between Freetown and Lagos. Humuani kept the return trade irreducibly simple: she dealt entirely in cash and handled no other goods. The business had low overheads, being run from her house in Offin Road, though she employed a clerk who kept the accounts in English.

The business endured the difficulties of the interwar period and continued until Humuani's death in 1943. The accounts have not survived, so only indications of her wealth remain. She had several properties in Lagos, a large house at Ebute Metta, and a car. Her largest single investment outside her business was the Oladimeji Mosque, now flourishing in Surulere, which she commissioned in 1939 and financed to completion in 1940. As she was childless, her assets were distributed among other members of the family, though her house in Offin Road was placed in trust to provide a rental income for the upkeep of the mosque.

Diversifying the Economy

Standard discussions of the rise and decline of African commercial fortunes focus on trade with Europe. The existing literature omits important dimensions of mercantile enterprise: regional and coastal trade is one; new businesses arising from the diversification of the economy is another. Reference was made earlier to Taiwo's extensive cosmopolitan connections, which ran from the Niger to Bahia, and to Shitta Bey's commercial connections with the

80. I am grateful to *Alhaji* Iman Abdul Karimi Bello, first Iman of the Oladimejo Mosque, which Humuani had commissioned and built at her own expense. Interview, Lagos, 22 Jan. 1962.

81. Ayilara Thompson, 1861–1939, as given in Okesunna Cemetery.

northern emirates.[82] In general, however, it is much easier to write the economic history of external relations than it is to research local and regional trade, which accordingly has not received the prominence it merits. Innovations that began to diversify the economy, though similarly neglected, can be studied more easily because they grew in importance after the turn of the century, following the rapid expansion of the economy. The simultaneous increase in printed information, public and private, also provides some evidence about these new activities. The remainder of this chapter will show that Lagos entrepreneurs were pioneers of the diversification that began after 1900. The examples that follow have been chosen to indicate the range of these businesses, which stretched from construction to services. Additional illustrations can be found in subsequent chapters dealing with the careers of Josiah Doherty, Samuel Pearse, Peter Thomas, and Jacob Coker.

Regional trade in local products underwent considerable changes after the turn of the century. The extension of the railway line north of Lagos created novel possibilities for Lagos merchants, including undercutting the historic land route from the Gold Coast to Northern Nigeria. In 1909, Brimoh Igbo (c.1850–1946) took the opportunity of shipping kolas to Lagos and then transferring them to the railway.[83] He became known as *Baba Olobi* (father of the kola nuts), a title that fitted the organisation of the business, which was staffed by family members, especially his wives, who bought kola nuts in Winneba and sold them in Kano, Zaria, and Sokoto. Samuel Pearse became involved in the kola trade at about the same time, but was particularly active in buying kola nuts grown in Agege and selling them in Northern Nigeria during the interwar period.[84] Pearse also developed a return trade in cattle and hides before the war in competition with the Syrian immigrant, Michael Elias. The consequent growth of the market for meat, which was dominated by women, led the government to establish a new, expanded market at Iddo in 1910.[85]

In 1908, a colonial official noted, for the first time, the presence of Syrians and Indians among the street traders.[86] Some of these petty traders were to become major figures in the Lagos business world after World War I. Michael

82. See above, chapter 3.

83. I am grateful to Brimoh's son, Solomon Olayiwola Forrest, formerly Sule Brimoh Igbo, for information about his father. Interview, Lagos, 2 March 1962. For the record, I note that the gravestone in Okesunna Cemetery gives Igbo's first name as Buraimoh. The family prefers the spelling used here. I am not suggesting that Brimoh initiated the trade, which had its origins earlier in the century and was pioneered by Lagos Saro. See Babatunde Agiri, 'The Introduction of Nitida Kola'.

84. A longer account is given in chapter 13.

85. Thorburn to Crewe, 3 Oct. 1910, C.O. 520/95.

86. E. P. Cotton (Director of Surveys) to C.O. 19 Feb. 1908, C.O. 520/74. The term 'Syrian' was a generic applied to immigrants from the Middle East.

Elias was one of the few who made his mark before then.[87] His parents left Lebanon with their young son around 1880 with the aim of settling in South America. Like many others, they were unable to make the Atlantic crossing, found their way to West Africa instead, and eventually settled in Lagos in 1891. Michael began hawking goods when he was fourteen and progressed from there to develop the cattle trade. He was evidently an exceptional character, whose self-taught mastery of Yoruba and Hausa enabled him to make close connections in both Lagos and Northern Nigeria.[88] The firm of J. T. Chanrai, which specialised in textiles, was well established in India before it arrived in Lagos shortly before 1914.[89] The business was founded in Hyderabad in 1860 and from there spread to Bombay, Karachi, Malta, Gibraltar, Casablanca, the Canary Islands, and the main West African ports. The firm is a good example of how imperial subjects promoted globalisation. Chanrai not only extended its reach to Central and South America but also sourced fine-quality textiles from China and Japan as well as from India, Persia, and Egypt. The business prospered, adapted to changing economic and political times, and today remains one of Nigeria's most prominent companies.

Elements of what were eventually to become substantial import-substituting activities also appeared after the turn of the century. By 1919, Peter Thomas had established a tannery that processed hides brought down from the north by Pearse and others and produced leather for local shoemakers.[90] Thomas erected a flour mill at about the same time; shortly afterwards, Amos Shackleford, one of his former employees, founded what became the Nigerian bread industry.[91] Native cloth, as it was termed, won an expanded market in other parts of the West Coast following the initiatives taken, for example, by Samota Ikeolorun and Humuani Thompson, whose careers are referred to above. The local cloth industry adapted to foreign competition and the prospect of new markets by matching local designs to fit consumer preferences elsewhere in West Africa and by dyeing plain, imported cloth to meet the demand for cheap materials. The industry remained a large employer: in 1908, there were no fewer than 852 dyers in metropolitan Lagos.[92]

The local construction industry dominated the private sector and built most of Lagos. The expansion of the town increased demand; growth in incomes raised standards. Corrugated iron roofs replaced thatch; brick-built properties became more common. Much of Lagos during this period was built with bricks that were manufactured locally. In 1891, there were about 131

87. Macmillan, *Red Book*, pp. 102–3. A biography is much needed.

88. The family's business acumen is expressed today through his grandson, Elie Elias, who is Managing Director of Mayssa International (Nigeria) Ltd., a large construction company.

89. J. T. Chanrai to Secretary of State, 15 June 1914, C.O. 583/26.

90. For more information on Peter Thomas, see chapter 15.

91. Kilby, *African Enterprise*, ch. 2.

92. Egerton to Crewe, 16 Dec. 1908, C.O. 520/68.

brick-makers in the town.[93] One of the largest, Brimah Apatira (c.1830–1907), supplied Lagos from kilns on Ebute Metta.[94] The African American settler James C. Vaughan (1828–1893) added construction to his hardware business.[95] Brazilian artisans were already noted for their skilled design, as well as for their masonry and stone-work. Lazaro Borges da Silva and his foreman, Francisco Nobre, built the huge Holy Cross Cathedral, which was inaugurated in 1881; João Baptista da Costa was responsible for the mosque financed by the merchant Mohammed Shitta Bey, which was opened in 1894.[96]

After the turn of the century, however, the most important figure in the construction industry was Isaac A. Cole, who is almost unknown today. Cole was born in Lagos in 1862 and started work as a carpenter in 1883 before becoming an architect and builder.[97] As his business developed, he found that he needed more skilled labour than was available and decided to establish an institute to train apprentices in metal-work, carpentry, and associated skills. Cole's Technical Institute, which opened in 1905, was the first and only institute of its kind in Lagos.[98] By 1910, 'five or six' other workshops had followed his lead, but Cole, 'a self-made man', remained the 'leading mechanic' in Lagos.[99] By then, the Institute had eighty apprentices and fifteen journeymen.[100] In that year, too, Cole transferred the business to his 'large and commodious house' in Porto Novo Market Street, next door to his workshop.

Among Cole's notable achievements in the years down to 1920 were Elephant House, which he built for Samuel Pearse, a new parsonage for Holy Trinity Church in Ebute Ero, which he attended and to which he contributed generously, and a mortuary chapel for Jacob Ogunbiyi, Taiwo's long-time associate.[101] To these he added premises for expatriate firms, notably John Holt,

93. Duerkson, *Waterhouses*, p. 92. The page reference is to the manuscript, which Dr Duerkson kindly allowed me to cite.

94. I am grateful to *Alhaji* Gbadamosi Apatira, one of Brimah's sons, for this information. Interview, Lagos, 17 Feb. 1962.

95. Lindsay, *Atlantic Bonds*, pp. 150–52, 154.

96. I am grateful to Mrs Sophie Morelawa da Silva, Lazaro's daughter, for information about her father. Interview, Lagos, 7 Feb. 1962.

97. Macmillan, *Red Book*, pp. 110–11. I am grateful to Nozomi Sawada, who has some information on Cole in 'The Educated Elite', pp. 189–90, and also kindly supplied me with additional references from the Lagos press.

98. *Lagos Standard*, 25 Sept. 1909. The Institute received wide and favourable publicity in the Lagos press, especially on the annual anniversary of its founding. The event was attended by a representative sample of Lagos Big Men, and included a reception, the presentation of the annual report, and several speeches.

99. *Lagos Standard*, 19 Oct. 1910; *Nigerian Chronicle*, 6 May 1910; *Lagos Standard*, 11 May 1910.

100. *Nigerian Chronicle*, 6 May 1910; *Lagos Standard*, 11 May 1910; also Deniga, *Nigerian Who's Who, 1919*, p. 30.

101. *Lagos Standard*, 17 Nov. 1912; *Lagos Weekly Record*, 9 March 1912; *Times of Nigeria*, 29 Sept. 1914, 20 Oct. 1914.

Lagos Stores, the African & Eastern Trade Corporation, and Gaiser's 'massive and elegant' premises in Ebute Ero.[102] He was also commissioned by W. H. Lever to construct 'factories and dwellings' at Apapa to implement his plans for processing palm oil and manufacturing soap.[103] By 1921, Cole had become a developer and rentier as well as a contractor, offering plots for sale on the mainland and rental properties in Lagos.[104] Given the acknowledged importance of the construction sector in economic development, Cole's name deserves belated recognition and the sector itself needs to find its historian.[105]

Additions to the service sector suggested that at least some Lagosians had enough disposable income to support facilities that were either rare or nonexistent before 1900. Shortly after the turn of the century, Samuel Pearse, Candido da Rocha, and David Taylor established hotels and restaurants in central Lagos. In the 1920s, William Dawodu ran one of the first taxi services, Josiah Doherty turned his premises into a proto-department store, and Saka Laweni (Sakajojo, 1877–1949) opened one of the first cinemas in Lagos in 1922.[106] Printing and publishing services took advantage of the expansion of literacy. Rival newspapers, such as the *Lagos Weekly Record* and the *Nigerian Pioneer*, fought circulation battles while trying to capture the 'hearts and minds' of the reading public. A new generation of writers, such as Adeoye Deniga, Isaac B. Thomas, Jacob U. Egharevba, Eric A. Ajisafe Moore, T. Ola Avoseh, J. Olumide Lucas, and A. B. Laotan, were published by numerous small printing firms, some of which were financed by Lagos merchants.

Pioneers of Mechanisation

Three detailed examples occupy the rest of the chapter. The first two deal with very different types of mechanisation: sewing machines, which altered production in the household economy, and motor vehicles, which transformed public life for both individuals and companies. The third example reconstructs the early history of the financial sector.

Dada Adeshigbin's family came from Owu, Abeokuta.[107] His father, Mope, was a native doctor (*adahunse*); his mother, Adeola, was the eldest daughter

---

102. *Lagos Weekly Record*, 26 Aug. 1911.

103. *Lagos Weekly Record*, 26 Aug. 1911.

104. *Nigerian Pioneer*, 5 Aug. 1921.

105. The Institute continued to operate into the 1920s. Its subsequent history lies beyond the scope of this book and is not easily reconstructed. Some photographs of buildings in nineteenth-century Lagos have been preserved in Akinsemoyin and Vaughan-Richards, *Building Lagos*.

106. I am grateful to Mr B. A. Laweni, Sakjojo's son, for information about his father. Interview, Lagos, 7 May 1964. The name is also given as Lawani in some sources.

107. My appreciation goes to Olamide Adeshigbin (Lady Olamide Bank-Anthony, wife of Sir Mobolaji Bank Anthony), Dada's oldest surviving child, for information about

of Chief Layeni of Lagos. Dada, who was born in 1865, was their eldest son. The family moved to Lagos in 1878, when Dada was thirteen years of age. He received a primary education at St. Paul's School, Breadfruit, where he also became a devout Christian. On leaving school, he was apprenticed to Antoninus King, a noted master tailor, before starting his own tailoring business in the 1880s. By the 1890s, he had gained a reputation for quality that attracted official attention and led to orders for uniforms for government officers, including those in the prison service, and the inmates themselves. This connection led to another: in 1896, he was engaged to undertake work for a visiting detachment of West Indian soldiers.

Success posed a problem: existing methods of work, essentially by hand, could not cope with expanded output without raising the costs of collecting outwork and adding to administrative expenses. Dada needed a means of increasing output while also improving productivity. The sewing machine provided the solution. Exactly how Dada made the connection to manufacturers in the United States is uncertain, though family tradition suggests that it was through one of several foreign visitors who had purchased goods from him. Synergies of this kind were quick to appear in port cities. Dada ordered one Singer sewing machine as an experiment and was impressed with the results. He also discovered a demand among other tailors, so he ordered two more machines and quickly sold them. This was the motive for the agreement he made in 1896: Singer authorised Dada to be their sole agent in Lagos and a large area of the Nigerian interior and allowed him credit; he sold on his own account at prices he determined. Given Singer's dominance at the time, the contract gave Dada a near-monopoly of sewing machines in Nigeria.

Initially, Dada combined tailoring with his new business, but soon concentrated on selling rather than making. He began advertising in the late 1890s and kept his name and service before the public until the mid-1920s.[108] The business expanded during the next twenty years, as rising demand and an increasing range of machines kept sales buoyant. By 1910, he had become Dada Adeshigbin & Son, 'the noted sewing machine dealers', with headquarters in Broad Street, a store in Layeni Street (Abayomi Villa), and agencies in Abeokuta, Ijebu Ode, Ibadan, Oshogbo, Ilorin, Zaria, Kano, and Epe.[109] Success enabled Dada to acquire the familiar attributes of the Lagos wealthy:

her father, Lagos, 30 Nov. 1961; to Mr A. A. Adeshigbin, nephew, interview, Ikeja, 23 Nov. 1961; and to Mr B. O. Adeshigbin, nephew, interview, Lagos, 24 Nov. 1961. The business records have been destroyed. Additional information from: Dada Adeshigbin, *Almanack*, n.d.; Deniga, *Nigerian Who's Who, 1919*, pp. 6–7, and *1934*, p. 1; *Times of Nigeria*, 3–16 April 1915; *The Red S Review* (the official organ of the Singer Sewing Machine Company), April 1925.

108. For example, *Lagos Reporter*, 17 Oct. 1898; *Lagos Weekly Record*, 18 Jan. 1908.

109. *Lagos Weekly Record*, 2 April 1910; *Lagos Standard*, 30 March 1910; Adeshigbin, *Almanack*.

he completed the construction of a new country house, 'Bamidupe', at Ebute Metta in 1915, joined the car-owning elite a year or two later, and moved in circles that included invitations to events at Government House.[110] He was also a generous supporter of a range of 'good causes'. Yet, he was not the unqualified conformist these badges of status might suggest. By far his greatest commitment was to the African Church, which he joined as a founding member in 1901 and supported liberally for the rest of his life.[111] He was an ardent advocate of African rights and a well-known (and well-tailored) pioneer of Yoruba dress.[112] He also helped to fund the Tika Tore Press, an outlet for African opinion, which his brother, Akitunde, founded in 1910.[113]

Sales contracted during the war and in 1917 Dada altered his terms of business by discontinuing payment by instalments and accepting settlement in cash only.[114] The business survived the post-slump, but started to lose ground to a new generation of manufacturers who were beginning to compete with Singer. An effective response required improvements in the distribution network, but Dada lacked the capital to match the need. Limited liability, as the example of Peter Thomas will show in chapter 15, was still a novelty and the 1920s were not a favourable time for raising capital. Singer decided to terminate Dada's contract in 1924, when it was due for renewal. He was free to continue to sell Singer's machines but no longer enjoyed the benefit of sole agency. A few months later, in 1925, Dada died at his house in Layeni Street. The business continued under the direction of his brother, Oke Adeshigbin, who had left government service a few years earlier at Dada's request to assist in running the firm. Oke, however, was a surveyor, not a businessman. He operated the business to the best of his ability, but suffered from adverse conditions during the 1930s. When Oke died in 1942, the business ended too. By then, its great days lay well in the past.

By all accounts, Dada was a modest and congenial man who 'advertised his goods but not himself' and who maintained cordial relations with Singer throughout their long association.[115] Success in business, however, was accompanied by personal tragedy: his wife, Maryanne, died at an early age in 1902.[116] His eldest son, Alfred Ayodele, whose name was attached to the business, died in Freetown during the influenza pandemic of 1918 at the age of twenty-one.[117]

---

110. *Lagos Standard*, 24 April 1915; *Nigerian Pioneer*, 3 Dec. 1920.

111. Webster, *The African Churches among the Yoruba*, pp. 112, 180, 183, 185, 188–9; *Lagos Standard*, 30 March 1910; *Lagos Weekly Record*, 2 April 1910; *Times of Nigeria*, 6–13 April 1915.

112. Akinsanya, 'Dandies of the 1900s', *Sunday Express*, 27 Aug. 1961.

113. Deniga, *Who's Who in Nigeria, 1934*, pp. 6–7.

114. *Lagos Standard*, 7 Dec. 1917.

115. *The Red S Review*, April 1925.

116. *Lagos Weekly Record*, 5 April 1902.

117. *Nigerian Pioneer*, 13 Dec. 1918; *Lagos Standard*, 1 Jan. 1919.

Neither of the two remaining sons joined the business: one, Olufemi, who eventually qualified as a doctor, was still studying; the other, Folaranmi, was described by one of his cousins as a 'gentleman of leisure', a calling that many have aspired to but few have attained.[118] His daughters entered other occupations. Although Dada did not leave a will, his estate was settled amicably. His assets, which were mainly in property, supported his children, not least by funding their education. His daughter, Lady Olamide Bank Antony, provided him with a striking statue, carved in marble, which still stands in Ikoyi Cemetery today.

William Akinola Dawodu was a member of what the *Nigerian Daily Times* called 'one of the great families of Lagos'.[119] His grandfather, Mabinuori, who was born around 1800, originally came from Nupe and arrived in Lagos as a slave of one Ogunmade (also referred to as Ojumade), probably in the 1830s or 1840s.[120] Mabinuori was clearly upwardly mobile: in 1851, he owned about 200 slaves himself. During the upheaval that followed the bombardment of Lagos in 1851, he acquired land between what became the Marina and Broad Street and converted it into a crown grant in 1869.[121] Mabinuori traded successfully until 1862, when a fire destroyed his house, stock, and canoes. His business struggled from then on, though he was helped by his very capable eldest son, Fagbemi. When Mabinuori died in 1874, Fagbemi succeeded him as head of the family and restored its fortunes by trading successfully in the new items of legitimate commerce. Following the spiritual trend of the new times, he also converted to Christianity, adding Benjamin as his first name. In reporting his death in 1881, the *Lagos Times* commented that 'he was one of the successful aboriginal native merchants and had acquired wealth by dint of industry and perseverance'.[122]

Benjamin William Dawodu, named after his father, became the head of the family, and also its most publicised member.[123] He was born around 1860

118. Mr A. A. Adeshigbin, Folaranmi's cousin, Interview, Lagos, 23 Nov. 1961.

119. *Nigerian Daily Times*, 7 Jan. 1930. I am grateful to Mr S. O. Dawodu, William's son, for proving information about his father. Interview, Ibadan, 19 March 1962. I am equally appreciative of the help given by Mr A. Ajose-Adeogun, manager of W. A. Dawodu & Co., 1920-23, 1926-27. Interview, Lagos, 22 Jan. 1962. See also Macmillan, *Red Book*, pp. 101-2; Drummond-Thompson, 'The Rise of Entrepreneurs'. The family name was sometimes spelled 'Dawudu' in the nineteenth century. I have followed what has long been the preferred form: 'Dawodu'.

120. The early history of the family has been reconstructed mainly from the substantial evidence given in Lewis & Ors v. Banjoko & Ors, LSCR, Civ. 27, 1907, and Civ. 52, 1908.

121. LLOR, 1593.

122. *Lagos Times*, 9 Feb. 1881. Between 3,000 and 5,000 people attended his funeral.

123. I take this opportunity to deal with Benjamin Dawodu here because his name is often listed among those who were prominent merchants. As the sources show, however, prominence and success are not identical. I am grateful to Babalola Dawodu, Benjamin's son, for providing information about his father. Interview, Lagos, 22 Jan. 1962.

and was young and inexperienced when he inherited his father's responsibilities and most of his assets. He was entrusted with a considerable legacy that consisted of at least fourteen properties in Lagos and goods and cash worth £6,000. Benjamin followed the family tradition of trading in cotton goods and produce.[124] Unfortunately, he lacked his father's commitment and caution and, it seems, his shrewdness too.[125] His flamboyant inclinations earned him prominence in the new Lagos press; realities soon took him to the law courts. He received numerous judgements in the 1880s and 1890s for indebtedness, which he settled by selling many of the properties he had inherited.[126] When he died in 1900, he was far poorer at the end of his life than he had been when he became head of the family. Other members of the family had long objected to what they saw as Benjamin's mismanagement of Fagbemi's inheritance. In 1908, James, one of his brothers, declared that he was a 'spendthrift', a judgement that seems to be close to the mark.[127] Benjamin's death was followed by a dispute over the headship and rights of inheritance that ground on through the colonial period.[128]

William, who was born in 1879, was Benjamin's youngest brother. Benjamin assumed responsibility for the care and education of his siblings when he became head of the family. William, who was only two years old at that time, was given a good start: he received his primary education at the CMS Grammar School in Lagos and transferred to the Hussey Institute in the mid-1890s. It is impossible to say whether the move was at his brother's direction or of his own volition. What is clear, however, is that he showed a distinct aptitude for technical matters because around 1900 he was appointed to teach at the Institute, a position he seems to have combined with work for the Lagos railway. In 1905, he left to start his own business as a blacksmith with a side line repairing one of the novelties of the age: bicycles. Repairs required him to stock spare parts, which in turn led him to import bicycles for sale. As demand rose, he was able to secure sole agencies for Humber, Premier, Star, and Hobart cycles. His technical awareness ensured that he moved quickly when the next big

124. Additional information about Benjamin's business can be found in Ollivant v. Dawodu, LSCR, Civ. 8, 1888; Witt & Busch v. Dawodu, LSCR, Civ. 10, 1890; his own evidence to the Commission on Trade enc. in Denton to Chamberlain, 25 May 1898, C.O. 147/132.

125. It was probably not a good idea to go to England in 1886 and return with 'a European clerk, Mr Baker, aged 16'; Lagos Observer, 18 Sept. and 2 Oct. 1886.

126. Ollivant v. Dawodu, LSCR, Civ. 8, 1888; Witt & Busch v. Dawodu, LSCR, Civ. 10, 1890; Radcliffe & Durant v. Dawodu, LSCR, Civ. 11, 1891; Thomas v. Dawodu, LSCR, Civ. 12, 1892; Witt & Busch v. Dawodu, LSCR, Civ. 12, 1892; Benjamin Dawodu, evidence in James Dawodu v. Benjamin Dawodu, LSCR, Civ. 12, 1892.

127. James Dawodu, evidence in Lewis & Ors v. Banjoko & Ors, LSCR, Civ. 52, 1908. Benjamin spent of lot of time (and money) visiting England.

128. Evening Standard (London), 1962.

advance in transport, the motor car, appeared. By 1906, there were several cars in Lagos, the majority being owned by the government.[129]

Although the details of how William turned thought into action are lacking, we know that in 1907, he transferred his business from his small workshop on the Marina and established a substantial head office and service facilities in Daddy Alaja Street.[130] This is indicative but not conclusive evidence that he needed space for the new trade in motor vehicles. We also know that Governor Walter Egerton, who was in Lagos from 1904 to 1912, encouraged William to pursue his new venture.[131] An advertisement posted by Dawodu & Co. in April 1913 stated that the firm had stocked a range of Ford cars 'for some years'.[132] By that time, too, the business had evidently grown because branches had been opened in Bishop Street, Offin Road, and Balogun Street West.[133] The most plausible, though still necessarily provisional, conclusion is that the move to Daddy Alaja Street was prompted by the need for increased space to house motor vehicles and that the new business, the first of its kind in Nigeria, started in 1907. Given that William lacked the capital to launch the new import trade without support from other sources, it is also probable that the sole agency Ford granted him dates from that year. The Lands Office records show that he did not use property as security until 1913, when he opened an account with BBWA and secured an overdraft by mortgaging a house in Kossoh Street.[134] The exercise was repeated in 1916 and 1917 and extended in 1920, when he was allowed an overdraft of £5,000 on the security of property in Bankole and Bishop streets.[135]

Dawodu's business seems to have done well during the war, despite the shortage of both supplies and shipping. By 1918, Dawodu was selling lorries as well as cars. He held the agency for Dodge cars and Firestone tyres, and had opened additional premises in Egerton Square. Sales spawned additional services. Dawodu was busy servicing and repairing vehicles, as well as continuing to sell and repair bicycles.[136] The firm had also established a large branch in Oshogbo that employed about fifty men.[137] An assessment of the business in 1922 showed that it had achieved an average annual turnover of £26,000 during the past ten years and currently employed a total of 250 staff.[138] The

129. See above, p. 320–321.

130. Macmillan, *Red Book*, pp. 101–2.

131. Comment by C. T. Lawrence, 16 Aug. 1922, LTC (Lagos Town Council) Minutes 210/1922.

132. *Lagos Standard*, 16 and 30 April 1913.

133. *Lagos Standard*, 30 April 1913.

134. LLOR, 867/11, 1913.

135. LLOR, 109/25, 1916; LLOR, 116/188, 1917; LLOR, 132/239, 1920.

136. *Lagos Standard*, 18 July 1917, 28 Aug. 1918.

137. Macmillan, *Red Book*, pp. 101–2.

138. Egerton Shyngle forwarding a petition from W. A. Dawodu, 19 July 1922, LTC, Conf. 210/1922.

stock in hand in three Lagos stores was valued at £16,000 in September 1921 and £13,500 in June 1922. The post-war boom in 1919–1920 not only brought a sudden boost to the business, but also encouraged European competitors who had been restrained by the war economy and were keen to tap long-suppressed consumer demand. Around this time, William Lever, the soap magnate, offered to take over the business but retain William as the manager and also appoint him as a director. He refused. Like Peter Thomas, who received a similar offer, he wanted to remain independent.

The post-war slump that struck in 1920–1922 further increased competition and led to a price war. A Dodge car that had cost £425 in 1920 dropped to £300 in 1922.[139] William lost the Ford agency to Miller Bros., which became part of Lever's conglomerate. 'All this means', wrote an official at the close of 1922, 'that Dawodu is being squeezed out'.[140] By then, William had committed himself to two expensive building and refurbishing projects: a three-storey workshop in Balogun Street West, completed in 1923 at an estimated cost of £4,588, and the large building in Egerton Square, which was estimated to have cost £3,500.[141] He fought hard during the 1920s to retain his position. He introduced hire purchase instead of cash sales, ran a fleet of taxis with eight Dodge cars, and built motorised canoes, which he offered for hire. Without the credit attached to the Ford agency, William realised that he needed to increase his capital resources if the business was to remain competitive. He explored the prospect of forming a limited company, but his enquiries showed that there was no appetite for investing in a struggling company. His hope, shared by most of his contemporaries, was that the revival of the international economy would 'lift all boats'. The hope was disappointed. After 1923, the business ceased to make a profit, and by the end of the decade losses were mounting.[142]

By then, too, William was suffering from ill health. When he died in 1930, the business was closed.[143] The remaining assets, held mainly in property, passed to his son, Nathaniel Alabi, and were used to support William's family and their educational needs. He also had a farm in the Mushin area that he kept mainly for recreational purposes. His chief interest outside business was the African Church, which he joined partly through the influence of his elder brother, Thomas, who was Assistant Curator at the Botanic Station and one of Jacob Coker's close associates.[144]

---

139. John Holt, for example, introduced Willys-Knight cars in 1920, *Lagos Weekly Record*, 20 Nov. 1920. Comment by C. T. Lawrence, 16 Aug. 1922, LTC Minutes, 210/1922.

140. C. T. Lawrence, 27 Oct. 1922, LTC Minutes, 210/1922.

141. Town Engineer to Secretary, 24 April 1923, LTC Minutes, 210/1922.

142. Information from Mr A. Ajose Adeogun, manager of W. A. Dawodu, 1920–23, 1926–27. Interview, Lagos, 22 Jan. 1962.

143. He died intestate; his estate was 'sworn' at under £700. LAP, 12/207.

144. For Thomas Dawodu, see above, pp. 414, 417.

William shared with Dada Adeshigbin an interest in machinery as a means of improving productivity, as well as a commitment to the African Church. They were dissenters in the sense that they wanted religious expression and economic development to represent African values and achievements. They both suffered the fate of individual innovators whose insight and success drew in large, well-capitalised competitors. As the *Nigerian Pioneer* put it, William Dawodu was 'a self-made man'.[145] He was also, as a historian might put it, one whose modesty should not disguise his distinctive achievement as a risk-taking entrepreneur. His example encouraged other African entrepreneurs. Richard Blaize's daughter, Charlotte Obasa, introduced the first public bus service in Lagos in 1913; Jacob Coker operated the first commercial motor lorries, which began taking cocoa from Agege to Lagos in 1916.[146] A European official, writing in 1922, summarised Dawodu's achievement concisely by saying that he was 'the pioneer of the motor business in Lagos—long before the Europeans dared touch it'.[147]

Financial Innovation

The third example of innovation deals with the financial sector and specifically with the rise of a class of rentiers, who became one of the most important, and certainly the most neglected, economic interests in Lagos throughout the twentieth century and down to the present day. This transformative development, which affected the whole town, will be viewed through the life of Candido João da Rocha, who was one of the first of his generation of Brazilians in Lagos to move with ease beyond the Portuguese-speaking community in Lagos and who did more than any other Lagos 'man of money' to join the ownership of property to rent-paying tenants.[148]

145. *Nigerian Pioneer*, 10 Jan. 1930.

146. Charlotte Obasa's venture has already attracted attention from historians. The business lost money and eventually closed, though it showed the way for similar services that began to operate successfully in the interwar period. Its history can be traced through the following: *Lagos Standard*, 29 Jan. 2013, 10 Dec. 1913, 30 Aug. 1916; *Nigerian Chronicle*, 7 March 2013; *Times of Nigeria*, 29 Feb. 1916; *Nigerian Pioneer*, 20 Feb. 1920; Re R. B. Blaize (decd.), C.O. Blaize v. C.O. Obasa, LSCR, Civ. 84, 1919. Miller and others are incorrect in stating that the service closed in 1918, though it is curious that no reference to the complete closure of the Anfani business seems to have appeared in the newspapers of the time. Miller, 'The Beginnings of Modern Lagos', pp. 106–21, at p. 111. Jacob Coker's almost unknown lorry business is referred to in chapter 12.

147. Comment by C. T. Lawrence, 16 Aug. 1922, LTC Minutes, 210/1922.

148. As none of Candido's papers have survived, I have been especially fortunate in being able to consult two exceptionally well-placed sources: Candido's sister, Mrs Josephina Martins (interview, Lagos, 12 Feb. 1962), and his son, Alex (interview, Lagos, 10 Feb. 1962). I am also grateful to A. B. Laotan, the authority on the Brazilian community in Lagos (interview, Lagos, 23 Feb. 1962), and Theophilus Adebayo Doherty, one of Candido's closest

Candido's father, João, was born in Ilesha between 1820 and 1830, enslaved while he was still young, and shipped to Brazil.[149] Little is known of his early life in Brazil, except that he became a Catholic and that his master gave him the opportunity to earn his freedom by allowing him to take on extra work. João married Luiza Angelica, the daughter of one Pedro Noqueira; the couple had their first child, Candido João, in 1867.[150] João eventually earned his freedom by trading and returned to Lagos with his family in 1871. He was granted land in the Brazilian Quarter, where he built a substantial house in Kawaka Street in the distinctive Brazilian style. The house became known as Water House because it had two wells. Lagos was notoriously short of drinking water, and unpolluted water was a rarity. Whether by chance or through insight, João owned a site with some of the cleanest water available. He capitalised on the asset, lined the borehole, installed a pump, and sold water at 20 cowries a pot. He also opened a shop and store in Tinubu Street, supplying the Brazilian community (and its artisans) with building materials, hardware, provisions, tobacco, and cotton goods.[151] Laotan referred to him as being 'a prosperous merchant, perhaps the richest of his time'.[152] Although the second claim is probably an exaggeration, it is clear that at his death in 1891, João was both wealthy and debt-free.

Candido found himself in charge of the family at the age of twenty-three, his mother having died in 1885. His younger siblings (Moses, Joanna, and Josephina) were either of school age or still studying and needed support. The responsibility was greatly eased by his inheritance: in addition to two substantial properties, Water House and the 'Iron House' in Tinubu Street, Candido was able to take over his father's profitable business. Equally important, João, who had received almost no education, ensured that his children were given opportunities that had not been open to him. Candido and Moses went to St. Xavier Catholic School; their sisters attended St. Mary's School. Candido went on to the CMS Grammar School, finishing in 1885 as the first in his class and, more important for his career, with an excellent knowledge of English as well as Portuguese, Yoruba and French. João had hoped that his son would

---

friends (interview, Lagos, 22 Feb. 1962). A fuller account of Candido's life is in the *Sunday Express* (Nigeria), 25 Oct. 1959, 1 Nov. 1959, 8 Nov. 1959, 15 Nov. 1959, 22 Nov. 1959, 29 Nov. 1959. Dapo Thomas has provided an overview based on later oral testimony: 'Candido da Rocha: The Generous Capitalist', in *The News* (Nigeria), 3 Dec. 2016.

149. While it is always satisfying to provide an exact date of birth, it is often impossible to do so. Some sources say that João was aged seventy at his death; others assert that he was eighty years old. Neither claim can be verified.

150. I should add that there are variations on the date, which I have adopted because it fits other events, not least the date of his mother's birth. Pedro Noqueira (or Nogueira) died in Bahia in 1902. *Lagos Weekly Record*, 4 June 1901.

151. See, for example, Candido's evidence in Schuback v. Sant Anna, LSCR, Civ. 15, 1894.

152. Laotan, *The Torch Bearers*, p. 13.

FIGURE 11.3. Candido João da Rocha, 1913. Copied by Paramount Photographers Lagos, with permission of Mrs Josephine Martins (sister).

enter the business after he left school, but Candido asserted his independence by taking a job as a junior clerk with Witt & Busch. He joined his father a few years later, when his father's ill health and age made extra help necessary.

Candido assumed full control of the business after his father's death in 1891. In the absence of business accounts, there is only indirect evidence of his financial position in the 1890s. In 1896, he doubled the size of Water House by adding a storey to the ground floor, made his first land purchase, and sent his brother, Moses, to Edinburgh to study medicine.[153] He also had enough money to indulge in his only active pastime: the expensive sport of horse-racing. He was a skilled rider who rode one of his horses, Tempest, to victory at the Lagos Races in 1896.[154] It would seem that the business continued to be profitable, even though Candido may have been drawing on some of his inherited assets.

Candido was favoured by fortune as well as by his inheritance. Around the turn of the century, so the story goes, he was approached by some visiting foreigners who needed to sell gold worth about £5,000. Candido negotiated an advance from BBWA, bought the gold cheaply, and sold it on at a consider-able profit. According to one version of the story, the foreigners were Portu-guese sailors; another version holds that the gold was offered by a European prospector from the north of the country. Fabulous and often fabled stories of this kind frequently attach themselves to men of wealth. They usually have no means of proof, and invariably leave many obvious questions unanswered. The two best sources agree that the substance of the story is true, though they favour different accounts of who supplied the gold.[155] Candido himself never pronounced on the matter, at least in public. The stroke of luck, assuming that it happened, should be seen as a boost to Candido's fortunes but not as a turn-ing point: he had already become successful.

Candido continued to trade under the name João da Rocha, 'dealer in provisions, hardware, etc'. for some years after 1900.[156] Soon after the turn of the century, however, his business shifted decisively away from trade and into property, following the route taken by Isaac Williams. Candido, like Alli Balogun, realised that the growth of the town and the rise in property values that followed the expansion of British rule and the construction of the rail-way were opportunities to invest in real estate. A government official provided

153. He bought land at Ebute Metta from Seidu Olowu for £130. LLOR, 28/115, 1896.

154. *Lagos Weekly Record*, 7 Sept. 1895, 16 May 1896, 15 Aug. 1896, 24 Nov. 1900.

155. Alex da Rocha, Candido's son, believed the first version; Theophilus Adebayo Doherty, one of Candido's closest friends, favoured the second. If forced to choose, I would accept the second version. Doherty (1895–1974) was a businessman, like Candido, and a close friend who visited him every Sunday for many years and acted as one of his executors. Interview, Lagos, 22 Feb. 1962.

156. Receipt made out to David Taylor, DATP, 3 Jan. 1901; *Lagos Weekly Record*, 29 Nov. 1902.

an accurate summary of the potential in 1908: 'the value of land in Lagos has increased very rapidly. It is the ambition of every Lagos man to own land in Lagos and money saved is at once invested in land'.[157] Calculations of the rate of return in relation to the degree of risk favoured property rather than trade. Although the general level of property prices fell during the inter-war period, prime sites, such as the Marina, retained most of their value, whereas profits from trade were whittled almost to a vanishing point. The entry threshold, however, limited access. Property dealers needed either to have accumulated sufficient capital or to have enough security to cover bank loans. Candido had both, though he seems not to have mortgaged property that he owned. Like Alli Balogun, he also never had a court case filed against him to recover debt.

Candido ran the business himself with only minimum assistance from a clerk, who mostly worked part-time, and an agent who bid for property at auction. Candido knew the market well and had the capital to enter quickly and decisively, often buying before bidding began. The business made its public appearance in 1901 with the formation of the Lagos Native Bank, which was notable for being one of the first attempts to create a company in Lagos that raised capital from shareholders while limiting their financial liability.[158] After the venture failed, Candido used a variety of other names, including the Lagos Agricultural Bank, the Lagos Finance Company, and finally da Rocha Properties (1949).[159] It is unclear why he changed the name of a going concern that continued to focus on Lagos property and remained under his sole control. It is evident, however, that his experience with the Lagos Native Bank made him wary of being involved with other shareholders, not least because his business could remain self-financed and still be prosperous. His disappointment, however, did not deter him from initiating other ventures related to property. In 1897, he converted the Iron House, Tinubu Street, into the Restaurant de Rocha, one of the first of its kind, offering 'excellent cuisine and wines', 'furnished rooms', and private suites for 'dinners, dancing and meetings'.[160] A few years later, after the failure of the Lagos Native Bank, he turned 37 Marina into a hotel and moved his own business to Water House. He also developed property as well as buying and leasing it. In 1911, for example, he built premises in Custom Street for an expatriate firm, the Bank of Nigeria, which had recently arrived in Lagos.[161]

It would take a separate study and a thorough investigation of the Lands Office records to reconstruct a full account of Candido's property dealings during the course of half a century. A few representative examples, however, will illustrate the nature of his business, which took two forms. One dealt with

157. Thorburn to Crewe, 14 Jan. 1908, C.O. 520/77.
158. See chapter 10.
159. File BN 676, Registrar of Companies Department, Lagos.
160. *Lagos Weekly Record*, 26 April 1898; 16 Oct. 1897.
161. Candido da Rocha to Municipal Secretary, Lagos, 29 Aug. 1911, LMB, 287/1911.

traditional mortgages, as the term was used in Lagos, which Candido accepted as security for cash advances. These could be modest, as in the cases of Adolphus Brimah Martins, who received a loan of £100 (at 5 per cent p.a.) on security of land at Ebute Metta in 1906, and Jacob Coker, who mortgaged land at Bamgbose Street in 1911 in return for an advance of £150 (at 4.5p. a month).[162] There were also larger contracts, notably the series of loans Candido made to Jacob Coker on the security of Rose Cottage, his Marina property. These began in 1912, with a loan £1,000 at 10 per cent per annum, which was increased to £1,250 in 1913, also at 10 per cent, extended in 1914 at 15 per cent because the principal had not been repaid on time, and renegotiated in 1919 to raise £1,600.[163] Given that Coker was the most important of the pioneering farmers at Agege, and owed his financial position largely to the possession of Rose Cottage, it is apparent that Candido made an important, if indirect, contribution to funding the development of cocoa at Agege, and possibly the African Church too.

The other branch of Candido's business purchased property for rent. The portfolio was assembled partly from foreclosed mortgages and partly from outright purchases. Candido made his first major purchase of a prime site in 1901, when he bought 37 Marina (originally a crown grant issued to Daniel Taiwo in 1863) from Witt & Busch for £1,300.[164] He renamed the property Perseveranza House and leased it to a succession of expatriate firms, beginning with Tin Areas of Nigeria at a rent of £200 per annum. In 1947, in a sign of changing times, the National Bank of Nigeria leased Perseveranza House for fifty years at £600 annually, having also paid seven years' ground rent in advance. Candido was in the rare position of having capital to invest during the 1930s. In 1932, he bought 44 Marina (originally owned by the Crowther family), for £4,000, leased it in 1939 to J. T. Chanrai & Co. for £400 for a period of five years, and renewed the lease in 1945 at an annual rent of £625 for the remainder of his life.[165] In 1938, he completed his trio of Marina properties by buying 38 Marina (owned by the Robbin family since 1863) for £5,000, and leasing it to Shell for sixty years at a rent of £400 a year, which repaid the purchase price in just under thirteen years.[166] All three properties remained in Candido's hands and formed part of his estate after his death in 1959.[167] The distinctive feature of these three properties was that they were all long leases. Isaac Williams had pioneered the leasing business, but his typical contracts were for relatively short terms. Candido operated in a

---

162. LLOR, 49/192, 1906; LLOR, 68/300, 1911. In 1905, Candido stated that he charged 'up to 10 per cent' and that the precise rate was determined by the 'nature of the security offered'. Evidence in A. W. Thomas v. Antonio Oke & Anor. LSCR, Civ. 36, 1905.

163. LLOR, 83/142, 1913; 86/197, 1914; 124/218, 1919.

164. LLOR, 1535.

165. LLOR, 2854.

166. LLOR, 0219.

167. LLOR, 77/425, and the rest of the file in LLOR, 1535.

changed commercial environment in which colonial rule over the whole of Nigeria gave expatriate firms a sense of confidence in their future.

Although Candido was exceptional in the scale of his operations, and unique in owning three prime sites on the Marina, he also represented the rise of a class of Lagos rentiers who have long been hidden from view. African ownership of sites on the Marina remained long after the families who had once lived there had moved elsewhere. The Marina provides a robust test of continuous ownership because property there was virtually a requirement for expatriate firms, which had the capital needed to buy out local owners. If African proprietors could survive there, where competition was fierce, it is reasonable to suppose that their position was far stronger in other parts of the town. Of course, some African owners sold their Marina properties, whether by choice or to deal with financial exigencies. What is remarkable, though, is the tenacity families showed in holding on to property that had often been inherited from original crown grants issued in the 1860s.

A sample of twenty-eight properties on the Marina shows that about two-thirds remained in African hands for almost the whole of the colonial period and in some cases well beyond it, and that only about nine were transferred to expatriate owners.[168] An exceptional degree of continuity characterised several families referred to in this study, including the Mabinuori clan (W. A. Dawodu), Daniel Taiwo, James George, Richard Blaize, Jacob Coker, Henry Robbin, Peter Thomas, Zachariah Williams, and Josiah Doherty, as well as Candido da Rocha. Moreover, families that sold property also did very well: James George's family sold 145 Broad Street to McIver & Co., for £16,000 in 1920; the Robbin family sold 52 Marina to Ollivant for £7,000 in 1935; Zachariah Williams's family sold 50 Marina to Nigerian Properties Ltd. for £10,000 in 1936; Daniel Taiwo's family sold 40 Marina to Nigerian Properties for £19,500 in 1946.[169] Given the currency values of the time, these were very considerable sums. Families that took the long view did even better because rents rose with property values, which increased throughout the colonial period, apart from a dip during the 1930s.

By all accounts, Candido was a very private person. He safeguarded the interests of his two sisters, Joanna and Josephina, and supported his younger brother, Moses, during the many years he was studying in Edinburgh. When Moses finally qualified as a doctor in 1913, Candido made his first trip to Britain to celebrate the event before returning with him to Lagos.[170] Moses took his time, not because he was indolent but because he was committed to the emerging nationalist cause.[171] He was also an intellectual who wrote thought-

168. Principally from 37–58 Marina (where the record is clear) with an additional five properties formally assigned to Broad Street but extending to the Marina.
169. LLOR, 2202; LLOR, 3222; LLOR, 039; LLOR, 1412 and 1209.
170. *Sunday Express* (Nigeria), 1 Nov. 1959.
171. Deniga, *Nigerian Who's Who, 1934*, p. 24.

fully on a wide range of subjects.[172] In 1914, when Moses had settled in Lagos, Candido arranged the long-postponed distribution of his father's estate. He bought Water House for £10,000, half of which he gave to his unmarried sister, Joanna, and retained the Iron House in Tinubu Street.[173] Candido's introverted character, which was so different from his brother's, made him few close friends outside his immediate family. Josiah Doherty and his son, Theophilus, were among the principal exceptions. Indeed, Candido never married, though he had children from three women. He fell out with his first son, Alex, in 1920 and refused to see him again. Alex then left Lagos with his mother, who came from the Gold Coast, became a pharmacist and stayed there until shortly before his father's death in 1959.

Candido had modest pleasures. He attended the Lagos races, owned a car, and made frequent trips to Brazil. He was also a staunch supporter of the Catholic Church.[174] He was persuaded to make one conspicuously unsuccessful venture into Lagos politics, which confirmed that his personality had not fitted him for life in the public eye.[175] The family's Yoruba origins gave him a particular interest in Ilesha; his wealth and position led the *Owa* to confer the title of *Lodofi* on him in 1938, at which point he exchanged European clothes for African dress for the first time.[176] He continued to run the business until his death, but as he aged he was content to manage his existing portfolio rather than seeking to augment it. He also spent an increasing amount of time at his farm at Agege, where he could relax away from the noise and pace of the town.[177] He continued to live in Water House, where in his last years he sat at his upstairs window in the evening, reading and gazing at the bustle below.

Was Candido Nigeria's first millionaire or perhaps even its first billionaire, as some sources have claimed?[178] There is no definitive answer to this question. His estate was 'sworn' at under £37,662. This was a misleading guide to his wealth, which consisted mainly of property, but may also have been invested in company shares.[179] He left £500 to the Holy Cross Cathedral but was not otherwise especially noted for his charitable contributions.[180] The rest

172. See, for example, *Lagos Weekly Record*, 22 Aug. 1896, 31 July 1897, 9 Oct. 1897, 5 Feb. 1898, 16 Dec. 1905, 25 Jan. 1919; *Lagos Standard*, 19 May 1915, 9 Aug. 1916.

173. Candido da Rocha v. Moses, Joanna, and Josephine da Rocha, LSCR, Civ. 87, 1919; *Daily Express* (Nigeria), 8 Nov. 1919.

174. Laotan, *The Torch Bearers*, p. 13.

175. *Sunday Express* (Nigeria), 22 Nov. 1959.

176. *Sunday Express* (Nigeria), 15 Nov. 1959.

177. *Sunday Express* (Nigeria), 15 Nov. 1959.

178. Although these are mostly online items without sources, they cannot be dismissed because fables repeated eventually become 'facts', or rather honorary facts.

179. LAP, 18/459–61, 1959.

180. This comment is not intended to denigrate Candido but rather to make the uncontroversial point that not all rich men are equally generous and that standards of philanthropy in Lagos among the wealthy were impressively high. Some sources claim, for

of the estate was distributed among his children and grandchildren, with the striking exception of Alex, who was not mentioned. Water House remained in the family and is one of the very few houses of the great merchants from the early colonial period to be standing today. Predictably, given that Candido was both unmarried and had several children, the will was contested by Alex and two of his siblings. Court action was started, but the family reached a settlement before legal fees began to drain the estate. The terms included an allocation of property to Alex and the considerable sum of £5,000 for the erection of a suitably monumental tombstone for Candido.

Was the exceptionally expensive tombstone an indication of great wealth that might have been associated with the estate of a millionaire? Candido's own words would seem to refute the possibility. In 1939, he commented that 'the wealthiest African solicitor, doctor, or merchant can never be called a millionaire because at death, his estate would only be about five figures and only very few may reach this'.[181] His judgement was probably accurate, but it is impossible to know for certain whether he was revealing a truth about himself or disguising reality.[182] Candido remained an enigma throughout his life.

Bouncing Back

The available evidence, incomplete though it is, shows that African merchants did not suffer a reversal of fortune during the period 1900–1914. Although their share of the export trade declined, it had never been large and had been shrinking slowly since the 1850s. Their position in the import trade, however, remained sizeable and almost certainly strengthened before 1914, while the much-criticised 'middlemen' also increased both their numbers and their reach. Nevertheless, African entrepreneurs of all kinds had to reposition themselves if they were to survive and take advantage of the newly enlarged market. Merchants and brokers needed to expand their credit to deal with an increased volume of produce and create agencies in the hinterland. Importers also needed access to substantial credit facilities, and faced the challenge of establishing outlets inland and extending the intermediaries they needed to cover a market that had increased in both size and extent. Contrary to accepted opinion, the BBWA supported these ambitions. Although sole ownership remained the predominant business structure, Lagos merchants recognised the need to move from informal to formal means of co-operating

example, that Candido volunteered one of his properties on the Marina for government use during the Second World War. The only reference I can find, however, is to 37 Marina, which the government requisitioned in 1941, while also paying Candido a rent of £550 p.a. LLOR, 597/1, 1941, 607/59, 1942.

181. *Sunday Express* (Nigeria), 8 Nov. 1959.

182. *Sunday Express* (Nigeria), 8 Nov. 1959. The paper concluded that he was a very rich man but not a millionaire.

and began experimenting with limited companies. Although the early ventures failed, they were important in pointing the way to a future that was to be realised after 1945.

Many African merchants were able to prosper within the import and export trades. Others, however, began to diversify the colonial economy by developing opportunities outside the established commercial staples. They were joined in this initiative by entrepreneurs like Dada Adeshigbin, William Dawodu, and Isaac Cole, who had received technical training. Changes in the political and economic context after 1900 prompted Lagosians to reassess their comparative advantage. Opportunities in the internal economy favoured those with local knowledge and limited capital resources. The innovations detailed here were the product of African enterprise. The expatriate firms rarely ventured beyond their established interests except to take over novelties like sewing machines and motor vehicles, which Africans had introduced. The colonial banks expanded the number of their customers and size of their deposits but remained wary of investing directly in the complex property market, which financiers like Alli Balogun and Candido da Rocha were able to negotiate with confidence. Out of their enterprise came the class of rentiers whose invisibility has long disguised their importance to the economy.

Orthodox theory holds that export-led growth transmits development through a series of multiplier effects that raise demand for additional goods and services. Although the argument holds in the present case, too, it is also incomplete. There is room for allowing a degree of reverse causation, whereby internally driven demand for local goods and services generated incomes that were partly spent on imported consumer goods. The evidence presented in this chapter suggests that these developments need full consideration before reaching conclusions about the history of Lagos merchants and wider issues of colonial development.

CHAPTER TWELVE

Negotiating Colonial Rule

JOSIAH DOHERTY AND SAMUEL PEARSE

DOHERTY AND PEARSE WERE both born in 1866 and were the sons of repatriates rather than repatriates themselves. They started work when they reached adulthood in the 1880s and began their own businesses around the time Governor Carter's invasion of Yorubaland took place. Consequently, they spent most of their adult lives under the new conditions imposed by the expanded colonial state. Seen from this perspective, their careers provide insights into both the economic effects of colonial rule on indigenous enterprise and the political dilemmas it posed for the Saro community. The two 'merchant princes' were not of course identical. Among other differences, Doherty was an Egbado who retained ties to his homeland through his family, who were farmers; Pearse was an Egba, whose values were largely urban-based and influenced by those of his father, an Anglican minister. The main difference between the two merchants, however, lay in their business interests. Pearse concentrated on the export trade in produce; Doherty specialised in imported consumer goods. Between them, they offer an understanding of how commercial success could be achieved during a period of transformative change. The fortuitous survival of some of their business records and personal correspondence provides an incomplete but still invaluable insight into their acumen and aspirations.[1] Definitions of their 'success' require further consideration, which is given in the concluding section of the chapter.

The Doherty Family: Beginnings

Although the name Doherty is far less common than many other Saro family names, such as Williams and Thomas, not all the Lagos Dohertys are related. Consequently, the research needed to reconstruct the history of the family

1. Their records are abbreviated in the notes as follows: JHDP and SHPP.

presents its own unexpected uncertainties.[2] The first member of the family to appear in the historical records was William Doherty, who was sold into slavery early in the nineteenth century, freed by the Anti-Slavery Squadron, and taken to Sierra Leone in 1826. William's exact date of birth is unknown. According to one source it was 1793, but this would have made him 110 at his death in 1903 and is almost certainly an exaggeration. We know that William married in Sierra Leone, had a son, who was named Samuel, and that the family returned to Lagos in 1855. This would suggest, though imprecisely, that he was born at some point during the first quarter of the nineteenth century. The family's arrival in Lagos was related to the creation of the British Consulate there and the renewed stimulus it gave the Christian missions. William was appointed to be the first CMS agent at Isaga (which was first transcribed as Ishagga) in Egbado country.

The match between William and the location was appropriate because the family came from Ilaro, the Egbado capital, and Isaga was in Ilaro country. It was also a risky decision because Isaga was some forty miles (65 km) northwest of Lagos and well beyond British protection. Exposure to danger delivered a second, possibly unique, slice of bad luck: William, who was known in the locality as Oshotan, was seized by Dahomeyan raiders in 1862 and remained in captivity until 1867, when the British government negotiated his release. He returned to his work as a CMS catechist serving at Isaga, Ebute Metta, and Abeokuta until he retired in 1894. Some two thousand people attended his funeral in Abeokuta in 1903.

Shortly after William arrived in Lagos in 1855, he adopted a 'close relation', possibly a nephew, and brought him up with his own children.[3] Far from being unusual, adoptions of this kind were a common means of holding families together in the face of the disruption inflicted by predatory states. The newcomer, who was born in 1837 and named Henry Theodore Doherty, joined William's three sons. One, Samuel, began as a catechist in Abeokuta in the early 1870s before being ordained in 1882 and becoming a well-known minister in Lagos and Abeokuta; another, Frederick, later joined the business started by Henry's son, Josiah. William hoped that Henry would follow the family tradition and enter the ministry. Sons, however, often surprise fathers by having minds of their own. In the 1870s, Henry was described variously as a trader and catechist but seems to have combined the latter with farming, which became his main occupation.[4]

2. I am especially grateful to the late Chief Theophilus Adebayo Doherty (1895–1974) for his considerable help with the history of the family and for many insightful and stimulating conversations on the 'merchant princes' of Lagos. Interviews on 31 Nov. 1961, 14 Dec. 1961, 22 Feb. 1962, 25 June 1964, and numerous other occasions. Sources used in this paragraph include: SHDP; Payne, *Payne's Lagos*; *Lagos Times*, 8 June 1881; *Lagos Standard*, 18 March 1903; *Lagos Standard*, 18 Sept. 1907; *CMS Gazette*, March 1912, p. 79.

3. I am indebted to Chief Theophilus Adebayo Doherty for establishing this connection, which could not otherwise be made with any conviction. See n. 2 above.

4. LLOR, 14/185, 1871; 25/420, 1877.

In the 1890s, he acquired two farms at Iju (Agege), one of 74 acres in 1895 and the other of 134 acres in 1897.[5] In 1911, he converted occupancy to ownership by paying small sums (£10 and £30 respectively) that reflected the 'many gifts' he had made since beginning to farm the land. Once he settled in Agege, it was inevitable that Henry would get to know Jacob Coker; it was through the influence of the Agege planters that he joined the African Church and invested in cocoa farming. In 1904, he had 30,000 young cocoa trees on his two farms.[6] At his death in 1912, he was identified as Henry Doherty 'of Iju plantations'.[7]

Despite this possible hint of affluence, Henry was not wealthy. Deniga, writing in 1919, referred to Josiah as being 'of poor parents', an impression that is shared by members of the family.[8] In 1863, Henry married Eleanor Ariwoola (née Fatoregun), who came from Ijero Ekiti.[9] The couple had several children, one of whom was Josiah Henryson Doherty, the second and only surviving son, who was born in 1866.[10] Josiah began his education in Lagos at the school attached to St. John's Church, Araloya, before entering the CMS training institution in 1880 in accordance with his father's wish that he should follow the family tradition of Christian service.[11] Josiah's training was well advanced when, in 1885, he was expelled after a quarrel with a fellow student. He then found himself out of work before he was even in it. The intercession of a friend, however, gave him a start with a prominent Lagos merchant, Seidu Olowu, who conducted a substantial business during the 1880s and 1890s in both produce and imported goods. Seidu, who was illiterate, employed several clerks, of whom Josiah was one, to keep accounts and conduct correspondence.[12] After six years with Seidu Olowu, Josiah had mastered business procedures and become familiar with the various influences that affected commercial fortunes. Josiah remained close to Seidu throughout his life and helped him financially after his business declined.[13]

5. Oniye & Anor to Henry Doherty, LLOR, 72/131, 1911; Dada Agunwa to Henry Doherty, LLOR, 72/135, 1911.

6. Moseley to Lyttelton, 11 June 1904, C.O. 147/170.

7. *Nigerian Chronicle*, 21 Oct. 1912, 15 Nov. 1912.

8. Deniga, *African Leaders*, p. 22.

9. *Lagos Standard*, 31 March 1897.

10. This is the date favoured by the family and by Deniga, *African Leaders*, p. 22. It is worth noting, however, that the cover of a Day Book in Doherty's records is inscribed: 'Mr Doherty's birthday 16 July 1865'.

11. The chronology in what follows differs from that in Deniga, *African Leaders*, pp. 22–3, which states that Josiah joined Seidu Olowu in 1888, and stayed with him for about six years before starting on his own in 1891. Clearly, at least one of these dates is incorrect. I have preferred the source given in n.14, below, which implies that Josiah took employment with Seidu Olowu in 1885.

12. Seidu Olowu, evidence in Olowu v. Ekere, LSCR, Civ.10, 1890.

13. *African Mail*, 18 Aug. 1921. Another friend, Richard Blaize, also offered Seidu financial help. *Nigerian Pioneer*, 19 Aug. 1921. Seidu Olowu died in 1921, by which time he was 'almost penniless', *African Mail*, 2 June 1921.

Josiah Doherty Founds His Own Business

In 1891, Josiah left Seidu Olowu's employment to start his own business.[14] His meagre capital resources, which amounted to just £47, were far exceeded by his exceptional personal assets: commitment allied to ambition tempered by shrewdness.[15] Josiah began in partnership with his cousin, Frederick, in a modest, rented property in Alakoro in the Olowogbowo district of Lagos. Their business, like Seidu Olowu's, dealt in produce and imported manufactures, though in 1892 Josiah stopped dealing in spirits in deference to his family's strongly held Christian principles. At about that time, Frederick left the partnership to start his own business, though without achieving much success.[16] Meanwhile, Josiah prospered. He established a relationship with the German firm, Gaiser, which began by allowing him credit of £120 a month and eventually extended it to £4,000 a month. In 1897, Josiah gave a large party to celebrate the opening of his new house, named Doherty Villa, at the corner of Campos Square and Bamgbose Street.[17] The *Lagos Standard* called it a 'grand villa', which was appropriate, given that it cost the considerable sum of £1,200.[18] The cost would have been much higher had the house not been built on swampland, which Josiah had bought cheaply and reclaimed. Two years later, he opened a new, large store in Alakoro. By then, he was being referred to as 'a young merchant prince', whose 'best years so far', in 1893, 1894, and 1895, had enabled him to 'make his fortune'.[19]

One fragment of Josiah's business at this time has survived: a cash book covering the financial year April to March for 1898–1899, 1899–1900, and 1900–1901.[20] The book lists monthly cash receipts for the three years without giving further details of the transactions. Total receipts for each year amounted to £57,968, £50,915, and £37,343. The downward trend was not an indication of a failing business but a reflection of the exceptional trading conditions at the end of the century, when several prominent merchants, including Seidu Olowu, found themselves in debt and in court.[21] It is likely that the surviving cash book recorded most of the business because in the late 1890s Josiah greatly reduced his produce dealings and concentrated on imports. Only limited conclusions can be drawn from this single piece of evidence. The most obvious is the impressive scale of the business, which had average receipts of almost

14. Day Book for 1893: 'business starts May 1891', JHDP.

15. Macmillan, *Red Book*, pp. 98–9.

16. Frederick later returned to Josiah's firm and was sent to Lokoja as an agent, but under strictly worded conditions.

17. *Lagos Standard*, 31 March 1897.

18. *Lagos Standard*, 31 March 1897.

19. *Lagos Standard*, 31 March 1897.

20. JHDP.

21. See above, chapter 6.

FIGURE 12.1. Josiah Henryson Doherty, c.1920. Copied by Paramount Photographers Lagos, with permission of Chief Theophilus Adebayo Doherty (son).

£49,000 annually during the three years. An estimate of profitability would require evidence about the invoice value of stock, overhead, and running costs, and information about the company's debts, none of which is available. Contemporary merchants estimated that net profits on imports had declined during the mid- and late 1890s to between 5 per cent and 10 per cent. If an average of 7.5 per cent is applied to Josiah's average gross receipts of £49,000, it produces an annual average net income of £3,657. This figure can be no more than a 'ballpark' approximation, but it nevertheless indicates that the business was performing well during exceptionally difficult times.

Evidence for the period after 1900, though sketchy, confirms that Josiah's business remained, or perhaps became, highly profitable. By about 1904, the firm had opened six branches in Lagos and begun to expand inland. By 1914, Josiah's business was established in Abeokuta, Epe, Ibara, Ibadan, Oshogbo, Ikirun, Warri, Kano, Zaria, Lokoja, Port Harcourt, and Duala in the Cameroons.[22] The head office in Alakoro kept in touch with the branches and issued instructions by cable. Doherty's name had also been noted in high places. In 1911, the colonial government regarded him as 'the leading native trader in Lagos in imported textiles', and a suitable candidate for membership of the Legislative Council.[23] The spread of the firm beyond Lagos was made possible by two developments: the extension of the railway, which reached Kano, a distance of 712 miles, in 1912; and the construction of the land telegraph, which by 1912 had connected Lagos to all the major towns in northern Nigeria.[24] Improvements in infrastructure, however, facilitated commercial expansion without guaranteeing it. The decision to advance beyond the immediate hinterland of the port was a major departure for Lagos merchants and a matter of entrepreneurial choice. Doherty moved carefully, sending agents on low-cost ventures to survey market potential before deciding whether and where to establish a permanent presence. It is already known that the expatriate firms expanded inland after 1900; Doherty was among the African merchants of Lagos who moved with them.

A further indication of Doherty's growing success at this time can be seen in his new-found ability to raise and lend money. In 1908, he mortgaged Remo House on the Marina (which he had bought from Joseph Haastrup) to BBWA to secure an overdraft of £2,000.[25] Two years later, he mortgaged the same house and a property in Davies Street to BBWA to cover an advance of £4,000.[26] In the same year, he leased Remo House to Rylands for five years

22. In 1918, Doherty was said to be one of 'the three gentlemen in Lagos who are the largest owners of land in Ibadan', the other two being J. W. and B. C. Vaughan. *Lagos Weekly Record*, 27 July and 4 Aug. 1918.
23. Egerton to Harcourt, 21 Sept. 1911, C.O. 520/106.
24. Scott-Keltie, *The Statesman's Year Book, 1912*, p. 234.
25. LLOR, 57/369, 1908.
26. LLOR, 66/68, 1910.

at an annual rent of £350.[27] In 1913, he took out a second mortgage on Remo House to cover an overdraft to John Walkden & Co., and added two properties (in Campos Square and Kosoko Street) to secure advances of goods valued at up to £20,000.[28] By then, as is evident, his credit was second to none. He seems to have confined his own lending activities to a limited number of relatively substantial sums. In 1908, for example, he advanced £700 to Jacob Coker on the security of Coker's main asset, Rose Cottage on the Marina, and renewed the loan in 1912 to cover an advance of £1,000.[29] In 1918, he issued a loan of £5,000 to Lourenço Cardoso on the security of seven properties, of which three were in Lagos, two in Mushin, and two in Ipaja.[30] By then, the Lagos custom of mortgaging property had spread to the mainland.

Doherty was also aware of the need for institutional change if African merchants were to keep pace with the expatriate firms. As chapter 10 showed, he was involved in several of the early limited liability companies, the most important being the Nigerian Shipping Corporation, which was formed in 1909. It was this company that opened the way for the registration of limited liability in Nigeria in 1911. By the 1920s, experience allied to age made Doherty reluctant to turn his own business into a limited company, and it was left to his son, Theophilus Adebayo Doherty, to effect the transformation and also link economic co-operation to its political counterpart in Herbert Macaulay's nationalist movement. Nevertheless, Josiah Doherty should be recognised as one of the pioneers of a major change in business organisation: the shift from sole to joint ownership.

Feeling the Strain, 1914–1928

It is well known that World War I disrupted international trade and was followed by a sudden boom and an equally deep collapse. The post-war years, which offered misleading glimpses of recovery that became a long depression, have also been charted with appropriate solemnity. It is rare, however, to see these major events from the perspective of a Nigerian businessman. The survival of some of Josiah Doherty's correspondence for the period 1914–1928 provides an insight into the experience of a merchant who had to grapple with the challenges of the time on a daily basis.[31]

Doherty, like other Lagos merchants, had to pick his way through profound changes over which he had no control. The outbreak of war led to the expulsion of the German firms and the loss of markets in continental Europe.[32] British companies reacted to the sudden loss of their powerful competitors

27. LLOR, 62, 401, 1910.
28. LLOR, 81/236, 1913; 83/237, 1913.
29. LLOR, 57/750, 1908; 75/382, 1912; and 83/147, 1913, reconveying the property.
30. LLOR, 123/122, 1918.
31. As detailed in n. 1 above.
32. These issues are elaborated in chapter 14.

by forming a combine to control produce prices and manage the allocation of the limited shipping space available. Doherty, who had conducted a substantial business with Gaiser, tried to compensate for their absence by opening or expanding accounts with Walkden, Pickering & Berthoud, Ollivant, Rylands, and Blackstock. His strategy was to order a variety of goods, from textiles to provisions, and to import minor lines, like gunpowder, according to availability and demand. Exceptionally, he also ventured into produce in 1917, exporting palm kernels to Britain after crushing mills had been opened in Liverpool.[33] The allocation of shipping space, however, limited the trade of African merchants and led to complaints that were taken up and publicised by the early nationalists.[34]

Doherty's correspondence provides evidence of difficulties that lasted throughout the war. In 1916, he wrote to his agent in Warri asking him to close the business and sell the stock.[35] At the end of 1917, J. H. John, his manager in Lagos, reported that turnover in all the branches in Nigeria was 'exceedingly low' and that underemployed sales staff had been redeployed to focus on debt collection.[36] A month later, John submitted another report.[37] Sales were 'very, very low and discouraging', and the market for palm kernels was so 'dull' that he had ordered branches to halt purchases. In October 1918, Doherty wrote to his supplier, Blackstock, saying that while the war continued, he intended to sell his 'large stock and await an opportunity of good business'.[38] Meanwhile, he intended to 'lay by sufficient cash to do a cash on the nail trade'.[39]

Doherty's opportunity came sooner than he expected. A month later, on 11 November, the war ended. Doherty's letters expressed optimism he had not felt for four years. As he wrote to Blackstock, 'I expect we shall be able to do a large business together', adding that he wanted his orders to be dealt with 'as soon as possible' and without his trade being 'exposed to others', and assuring them in return that he would always 'pay the bank promptly'.[40] Nevertheless, he was soon taken aback by the news that Blackstock's prices had increased more than four times in the course of the war and said that he was 'inclined to wait at present and see that things are easier' before placing an order.[41] By April 1919, however, he had become more confident and began to order a range

33. In 1916, he was described as a merchant 'not directly interested in produce'. Boyle to Bonar Law, 31 Oct. 1916, C.O. 583/49.

34. J. H. John (Doherty's manager in Lagos) to Elder Dempster, 21 Nov. 1917; John to Doherty, 28 Nov. 1917, JHDP. More generally on this subject, see Yearwood, *Nigeria*, pp. 146–52.

35. Doherty to da Souza, 15 Aug. 1916, JHDP.

36. John to Doherty, 28 Nov. 1917, JHDP.

37. John to Doherty, 13 Dec. 1917, JHDP.

38. Doherty to Blackstock, 29 Oct. 1918, JHDP.

39. Doherty to Blackstock, 29 Oct. 1918, JHDP.

40. Doherty to Blackstock, 18 Nov. 1918, 6 Dec. 1919, JHDP.

41. Doherty to Blackstock, 8 Feb. 1919, JHDP.

of textiles, haberdashery, beads, metal goods, and numerous sundry items.[42] Elements of pre-war trade were quickly re-established. In 1919, Blackstock was already ordering velvets and beads from Germany on his behalf; in 1921, Doherty was placing orders directly with Gaiser and asking them to ensure that their prices were lower than those offered by the British firms.[43] Doherty's surviving correspondence with Blackstock ends at the close of 1919: 'I note all your remarks on this [market]', he wrote in his final letter, 'and that prices are not coming down. I wonder where it will end'.[44]

He did not have to wait long for an answer. In 1920, the boom ended and gloom returned. Doherty's reaction can be traced through a letter book containing his correspondence with a different set of agents (Latham & Co.) in Britain. His first letter, written in January 1921, summarised the changed conditions of trade admirably. 'Produce is a great failure out here now and most produce buyers are simply rolling in debt. As long as produce prices are low, prices of all goods will be low in proportion'.[45] There followed a series of funereal statements. In January he wrote that 'trade is very, very bad here and firms are selling goods at any price simply to get money'.[46] Matters deteriorated further in February: 'some firms are staggering and I am almost sure they will fall unless they can get finance'.[47] Consequently, as he remarked to Harold Hopwood, 'I dare not order any goods now till things are settled down'.[48] In April, he commented that: 'I do not think prices will ever jump up as people are predicting. I am almost sure the past boom is finished forever and the great slump will not be cured for some time'.[49] In August, he wrote to Paul Meyer, saying that the slump had 'discouraged' him and that, having lost money, he was 'trying to reduce his trade'.[50] In October, he confirmed that he did not want 'to touch produce again'.[51] The tone of his letters continued to match the state of trade throughout 1922. In 1923, he was pressing his debtors for payment.[52] The last letter in the book, dated September 1923, repeated a familiar refrain: 'trade is particularly bad now'.[53]

42. Doherty to Blackstock, 25 April 1919, 22 May 1919, 19 Sept. 1919, JHDP.

43. Doherty to Blackstock, 22 May 1919, 19 Sept. 1919; Doherty to Gaiser, 19 Aug. 1921, JHDP.

44. Doherty to Blackstock, 24 December 1919, SHDP.

45. Doherty to Messrs A. Latham & Co., 8 Jan. 1921, JHDP.

46. Doherty to Bentley & Holden, Ltd., 22 Jan.1921, JHDP.

47. Doherty to Bentley & Holden, Ltd., 5 Feb. 1921, JHDP.

48. Doherty to Hopwood, 5 Feb. 1921, JHDP.

49. Doherty to Hopwood & Son, 3 April 1921, JHDP.

50. Doherty to Meyer, 18 Aug. 1921, JHDP.

51. Doherty to Meyer, 28 Oct. 1921, JHDP.

52. Doherty to J. Lasile, Freetown, 19 July 1923, JHDP. One of the largest debtors was the merchant and farmer, Lourenço Cardoso, who owed Doherty £6,000. Cardoso was unable to pay and eventually forfeited most of his property in Lagos.

53. Doherty to J. Lasile, Freetown, 13 Sept. 1923, JHDP.

The prospect of renewed prosperity retreated as the decade advanced. Doherty's correspondence with family members during the second half of the 1920s continued a familiar theme. In 1925, he wrote to his son, Richard, that 'trade is dull and one has to be careful to avoid a collapse'.[54] In the following year, the General Strike in England slowed trade by raising the cost of goods imported into Lagos.[55] In September, he wrote to another son, Henry, saying: 'I have repeatedly told you that my business is not what it used to be and if I am not very careful I shall not be able to educate any more of the younger members of the family'.[56] He had already been 'obliged to give up the education of some boys' who were not members of the family but had benefitted from his generosity.[57] In the last of these letters, written in October 1926 to his daughter, Adebisi, he reported that trade continued to be 'very bad' in Lagos.[58] Some allowance has to be made for the tendency of businessmen to be as vociferous about their difficulties as they are reticent about their wealth. Doherty also had an understandable inclination to restrain the expenditure of those of his children who were being educated, expensively, in England. Nevertheless, his correspondence during the 1920s reflects the mood of the times as attested by sources unconnected with his own affairs, notably the correspondence of Peter Thomas, which is cited in chapter 15.

The Man in the Merchant

Doherty was a remarkable businessman. In a career lasting nearly thirty years, he took advantage of the booms and negotiated the slumps with what became practised adroitness. His son, Adebayo, who disagreed with his father over some key issues relating to the structure of the firm, nevertheless called him a 'business genius'.[59] The qualities that made him distinctive, however, are not easily identified. Hard work and integrity, two attributes that contemporaries recognised in him, were necessary causes of his success, but by no means sufficient. His decision to focus on the trade in imported goods, with only occasional ventures into produce, eliminated one large risk that had the potential to turn prosperity into debt without warning. The uncertainties associated with the export trade, however, meant that the import trade was crowded and exceptionally competitive.

Yet Doherty was very successful, despite eschewing the lucrative trade in spirits. His close connection with Gaiser, though not exclusive, was undoubtedly advantageous. Gaiser, the leading expatriate firm in Lagos, offered credit

54. Doherty to Richard Doherty, 26 March 1925, JHDP.
55. Doherty to Adebisi Doherty, 18 June 1926, JHDP.
56. Doherty to Henry Doherty, 10 Sept. 1926, JHDP.
57. Doherty to Joseph Doherty, 10 Sept. 1926, JHDP.
58. Doherty to Adebisi Doherty, 8 Oct. 1926, JHDP.
59. Interview with Theophilus Adebayo Doherty, Lagos, 31 Nov. 1961.

facilities that were more generous than those offered by the British firms and supplied imports at prices that were lower than those of their rivals. Moreover, Doherty always repaid his cash advances and settled his credits promptly, and was never taken to court to settle a debt. On the contrary, the court action he took was always to seek repayment from his own debtors.[60] In a highly competitive market, where details could make the difference between profit and loss, Doherty's keen eye prompted him to adjust his orders to match both need and fashion, while his acute sense of timing enabled him to place orders at the first hint of consumer demand for particular items. Additionally, he was prepared to take risks, providing they fell below the level of gambling. His readiness to establish branches inland ahead of most of his competitors is one example; his willingness to experiment in introducing limited liability into Lagos is another.

Doherty also developed an effective form of advertising though his wives and their associates, who traded independently but did so partly and sometimes exclusively with goods he supplied. These mobile and highly personal agents promoted Doherty's name and products while expanding their own trade. Doherty knew how valuable these links were. He reciprocated through acts of conspicuous expenditure, acting as patron of the Lagos Native Beads Sellers' Association, supporting various local charities, and funding the education of children who were not family members. The examples that follow rescue three traders from undeserved obscurity, and add substance to generalisations about the contribution made by women to the commercial life of the town. They also show how much more needs to be done to record oral testimony while it is still possible to do so, and to preserve records that are all too easily and too frequently destroyed.

One of Doherty's wives, Wusamotu Shelle (1879–1939), became one of the most notable female traders of her time.[61] Wusamotu's father, Bakare, was the first son of Sumonu Alapafuja, the *Aremo* of Oyo. Little is known of Wusamotu's mother, except that she was from Nupe and made her living as a trader. It appears that Bakare was expelled from Oyo, following a reversal of the family's political fortunes. He made his way south, pausing in Ibadan, Abeokuta, and Porto Novo before eventually settling in Lagos. Both parents traded between Lagos and Porto Novo in produce and consumer goods. Bakare opened a shop in Bishop Street before moving to Offin Road, where he dealt in ivory, timber, cotton goods, and coral beads. He remained in business until he died in 1895.

60. For example, Doherty v. Tepowa, LSCR, Civ. 75, 1915; Doherty v. Salami and Seliya, LSCR, Civ. 76, 1915; Doherty v. Ithiel Doherty, LSCR, Civ. 79, 1917; Doherty v. Jacob Thomas, LSCR, Civ. 81, 1918.

61. The date of birth is taken from the tombstone in Ikoyi Cemetery. Some members of the family have an alternative date: 1875. I am grateful to Mr Akanni Shelle, Wusamotu's Shelle's brother, and to Mrs A. Jokotade and Mrs E. Adeshigbin, her daughters, for some of the information presented here. Interviews, Lagos, 22 Jan. 1962, 1 March 1962.

As was typical for daughters of families outside the elite, Wusamotu received no formal education and started trading at an early age as a small-scale seller of local beads. Her marriage to Doherty marked a turning point: he introduced her to Gaiser and other European firms; she also converted from Islam to Christianity to fit in with his religion, taking the Christian name, Sarah. Wusamotu (as she was still generally known) began trading in conjunction with her husband. She managed the distribution of goods to his other wives who were trading with him, but kept her own account separate from his and ordered many of her goods directly from Europe.[62] Her main shop in Balogun Street was eventually supplemented by five branches in Lagos, which were managed by literate clerks. She stocked a variety of consumer imports but her specialty was local and imported beads.[63] She did a cash trade and kept accounts with the Colonial Bank and then with its successor, Barclays.

The business did well until the setbacks of the 1920s and 1930s, when some branches had to be closed and the scale of operations reduced.[64] Wusamotu was assisted from 1929 by her brother, Akanni Shelle, who was literate in English as well as in Yoruba. She invested some of her profits in property, bought a farm on the mainland as a refuge from the town, operated several motor lorries, kept a car for her own use, and put the rest into educating some of her brothers and sisters and her children, one of whom became a doctor. Her eldest daughter continued the business after her mother's death in 1939, and ran it successfully for many years.[65]

Selia Jawando had access to Doherty's business through one of her sisters, who was married to him.[66] She was born in Lagos around 1855 but spent much of her early life in Ibadan, where her husband, Disu Animashaun (also known as Jawando), traded. Nevertheless, the connection with Lagos remained vital for her own business: she bought cottons from Doherty and later from other merchants as well, and transported them to Ibadan, initially employing canoes and porters and subsequently using the railway. Around 1940, she returned to Lagos, closed the business, and lived off the rents from four houses she had acquired (three in Lagos and one in Ibadan) until her death in 1950. According

62. Her full name was Sarah Ajibola Wusamotu Shelle, LAP, 14/295, 1939; Shelle v. Martins, LSCR, Civ. 100, 1923.

63. Shelle v. Martins, LSCR, Civ. 100, 1923.

64. The court records (civil cases) indicate that the business was experiencing difficulties in the 1920s. See for example, Jaeckel v. Shelle, LSCR, Civ. 110, 1925 (e for £754). She also claimed that some of her staff had deceived her. See Shelle v. Martins, LSCR, Civ. 100, 1923.

65. This was Madame A. Jokotade. The business was still a going concern in 1962.

66. I am grateful to *Alhaja* Lamalutu Ajobi, Selia Jawandu's granddaughter, and Dr J. Akanni Doherty, her nephew, for much of what follows. Interview, Lagos, 24 Jan. 1962. Selia's date of birth is no more than a best guess. I have adopted the date given in Okesunna Cemetery. The obituary in the *Daily Times*, 31 July 1950, contains some errors.

FIGURE 12.2. Wusamotu Shelle. Copied by Paramount Photographers Lagos, with permission of Mr Akanni Shelle (brother).

to her family, Selia was 'only moderately wealthy', but that made her typical of many other female traders and more successful than most of them.

Dorcas Folashade Macaulay, popularly known as Ireti (her trading name), was even further removed from Doherty than Selia Jawando was, but was introduced to his firm by a mutual friend.[67] Her father, who was from Ilesha, took the name Johnson upon becoming a Christian and settled in Lagos, where he was a trader and money lender. He did well enough to send Dorcas, who was born in 1887, to St. Paul's School, Breadfruit. On leaving school at the age of fifteen, she began working as a seamstress but soon established her own dress-making business. After marrying Milton Macaulay in 1910, she established a store in their house in Bamgbose Street and started importing textiles, which is when her link with Josiah Doherty was established but also soon supplemented. Ireti had an artistic eye and produced her own designs, which she sent to Europe, ordering both directly and through intermediaries in Lagos. By the early 1920s, she had five shops in Lagos and branches in Ibadan and Calabar. The business suffered during the world slump and Ireti was forced to close all her outlets in and outside Lagos between 1929 and 1932, apart from one shop in Martin's Street.

Ireti's story, unlike many others at this grim time, did not end unhappily. The business revived during World War II, when she was one of the few traders to be granted a licence to import cotton goods. She continued the business until shortly before her death in 1955. Her unfettered philanthropy, coupled with her generous support for both Anglican and Wesleyan Churches, consumed much of her wealth, but she was still able to educate her four children. One son became a barrister, another a high-ranking official, and the third a successful businessman. Her daughter trained as a teacher but joined the business before her mother's death and steered it successfully into the new era of Nigerian independence.

It should be added that Doherty distanced himself from one of the great sources of capital haemorrhage in Lagos: politics. He was sympathetic towards the position taken by contemporaries, such as Herbert Macaulay and Jacob Coker, who were promoting African rights and culture. Nevertheless, as Isaac Thomas noted in his obituary notice, 'Josiah Henryson Doherty, who had stood clear from the squabble of Lagos politics, was a good friend of all and an enemy of none in the old political muddle of Lagos'.[68] Similarly, he did not join the Lagos Chamber of Commerce when it agreed to admit African members in 1921 because he believed it to be an unproductive 'talking shop'.[69] All the

67. I am grateful to Mrs M. Y. Ladeinde, Ireti's daughter (who carried on the business), for information about her mother's life. Interview, Lagos, 9 Feb. 1962.

68. Thomas, *Life History of Herbert Macaulay*, caption to a photo of Doherty facing p. 38. See also *Nigerian Spectator*, 31 March 1928.

69. Theophilus Adebayo Doherty, Interview, Lagos, 14 Dec. 1961.

same, he was an active figure in the public sphere. He contributed generously to a range of 'good causes', provided a new site for Eko Boys' High School, and supported Christchurch Cathedral, the church he attended.

Doherty placed his considerable family commitments above other tempting expenditures. When he died in 1928, the *Nigerian Spectator* paid tribute to 'one of the most outstanding citizens of Lagos' who had built up 'one of the most successful trading firms an African had ever established' in the town.[70] The paper went on to refer to Doherty's 'complex' social and religious life, noting that, though he attended Christchurch 'regularly', he was 'a native in his marriage habits'. This was an oblique reference to the fact that Doherty had seven wives and 'at least' forty-two children.[71] Doherty was far from alone in being both polygamous and a member of the Anglican Church. As argued earlier, polygamy was not the central issue that led to the creation of African Churches.[72] To the extent that polygamy was an issue in the secession from Anglicanism, it was as a matter of principle, not practice. Members of the African Churches were uncomfortable being polygamous while also remaining in denominations that opposed the practice on theological grounds.

The family commanded Doherty's attention and made considerable claims on his resources. Evidence of his commitment appears in letters written to some of his children who were being educated in England during the 1920s.[73] Unexceptionally, the tone of the letters to sons and daughters alike was one of concern that they should work hard to achieve success while being careful with the money he sent them. Such injunctions are universal. Individuals received specific advice. Writing to Richard in 1924, Doherty gave his opinion that 'the study of economics will not benefit you here at all'.[74] 'Adebayo', he added, 'has done a lot in it and has since found that it will not bring money to his pocket out here'. 'What can you do with a B.A. or a B.Com.? The country is not ripe enough to give you any material benefit with those qualifications'. Doherty suggested that his son should try medicine, lawyers being 'too plentiful here now'. Another son, Joseph, was enjoined to make a verse from Colossians his 'watchword': 'Set your mind on things above, not on earthly things'.[75] Flora was offered similar advice phrased more directly: 'One should be very careful in spending money and I want you to know that I shall only send you a limited amount'.[76]

70. *Nigerian Spectator*, 31 March 1928.
71. Lagos High Court Records, LAP, 7/188–97, 1928.
72. See chapter 13.
73. The surviving correspondence in JHDP is with this group of children. Numerous letters to his other children must also have been written.
74. Doherty to Richard Doherty, 4 Jan. 1924, JHDP.
75. Doherty to Joseph Doherty, 14 Feb. 1924, JHDP. The biblical refence is Col. 3:2.
76. Doherty to Flora Doherty, 31 Jan. 1924, JHDP.

Doherty's requests for economy continued in 1926, with an added touch of asperity in the case of Henry: 'I have repeatedly told you that my business is not what it used to be and if I am not very careful I shall not be able to educate any more of the younger members of the family'.[77] A similar letter was sent to Joseph, with the additional information that Doherty had been to obliged 'give up the education of some boys whom I have been privately financing'.[78] The litany of instructions and homilies might suggest that Doherty had a Scrooge-like attitude towards expenditure, but this was hardly the case. He was exceptionally generous and supportive, but he had taken on formidable obligations to ensure that he gave his children, and others, opportunities that had not been open to him. It was also true, as we have seen, that business conditions remained difficult during the 1920s. Given the circumstances, it was remarkable that Doherty continued to do so much for so many.

Doherty died in 1928, just before the world slump depressed business even further and well before any prospect of economic recovery was in sight. His estate was substantial but his lack of ostentation and concern with unnecessary waste were both evident in the final provision of his will, which stated that his funeral was not to exceed £300. The estate, which was 'sworn at under £58,000', a very considerable sum, was nearly all tied up in a portfolio of Lagos property that Doherty had accumulated to supplement his income at times of business difficulty and increase his resources in the future.[79] He bequeathed £100 and a pension to each of his seven wives, £500 to each of his sons, and £250 to each of his daughters. The will was complicated and required trustees to administer the income from the estate. Yet disputes were limited until 1954 and 1964, when they came to court. In 1964, the trustees were managing forty-two properties that yielded an annual income of about £50,000, which provided for the needs of Doherty's thirty-six remaining children and funded the education of the younger children and other relatives.[80] Fortunately, these disputes did not jeopardise Doherty's priority, which was to foster education. Among his sons and daughters were lawyers, doctors, accountants, surveyors, and teachers, as well as members of other professions.

Doherty instructed his executors either to continue the business or to sell it. They decided to keep it going, principally on the initiative of Josiah's second son, Theophilus Adebayo, who was emerging at this time as a prominent figure in his own right. Adebayo, who was born in 1895, was educated in Lagos at the CMS Grammar School and King's College before studying law at the London School

77. Doherty to Henry Doherty, 10 Sept. 1926, JHDP.

78. Doherty to Joseph Doherty, 10 Sept. 1926, JHDP.

79. Lagos High Court Records, Letters of Administration and Probate, LAP, 7, 188–97, 1928.

80. Theophilus and Henry Doherty v. Richard Doherty, Nigerian Supreme Court, Case FSC 219/1964.

of Economics. He was admitted to the Middle Temple in 1918, called to the bar in 1921, and returned to Lagos, where he began his career as a lawyer.

Adebayo's interests extended well beyond the law.[81] His relevance to the present study, however, mainly concerns his commercial activities. In particular, he formed a bridge between sole ownership, which was typical of the firms run by Lagos merchants between 1850 and 1930, and limited liability companies, which followed and had the potential to increase the scale of operations. Adebayo, who was one of the trustees of his father's estate, took the lead in introducing important changes, which together pointed towards a future that was to be realised after World War II. In 1930, he turned J. H. Doherty into a limited liability company, making him the first member of one of the great merchant families in Lagos to do so. During the 1930s, he closed many up-country branches, created a much larger store in Lagos, reduced traditional lines of merchandise, such as Manchester piece goods and beads, and stocked a range of items that appealed to a new generation of consumers. To some extent, these changes were reactions to the continuing economic crisis, but they also reflected Adebayo's perception of global developments, notably the rise of the department store. In this respect, J. H. Doherty Ltd. anticipated the much larger Kingsway Stores, owned by the United Africa Company, which opened its doors in 1948.

Adebayo was also politically active. He was a prominent member of the fledgling Nigerian National Democratic Party and was elected to the Nigerian Legislative Council in 1928 and again in 1933. As suggested earlier, the idea of co-operation formed a link between business and politics. Limited liability, which brought shareholders together, was to economic development what political unity, which aimed at organising the populace, was to national aspirations. Other ventures that Adebayo helped to promote also gave co-operation an influential voice. He helped to bring the Nigerian Association of African Importers & Exporters into being in 1941, and in the same year was one of the organisers of a new Chamber of Commerce that represented African interests. The aim in both cases was to increase the influence of African merchants with the expatriate firms and the colonial government. Adebayo's most significant innovation, however, was the National Bank of Nigeria, which he founded with six other subscribers in 1933. The National Bank became the first successful indigenous bank in the country.[82] It outlasted colonial rule and, despite encountering a series of difficulties, survived into the twenty-first century. Adebayo capped his career in 1960 by becoming one of the founders of the Lagos Stock Exchange, which became the Nigerian Stock Exchange in the following year and has recently celebrated its sixtieth birthday.

81. Much of what follows is taken from the interviews detailed in n. 1 above.

82. See also chapter 14. The history of the bank down to 1954 is covered by Newlyn and Rowan, *Money and Banking*, pp. 99–122.

Adebayo Doherty's Rolls Royce Silver Cloud II (1960) with its black chassis and silver bonnet, roof, and boot, was a familiar site in Lagos during the 1960s and early 1970s. It inspired both awe and, one might reasonably guess, aspiration, as it made its stately progress along the town's main streets. Its appearance in 1960 marked the culmination of both Adebayo's career and the achievement of Nigerian independence. The co-operation the early nationalists sought had finally triumphed. The vehicle remained in the hands of the family for some years after Adebayo's death before its 'second owner' offered it for sale at an auction held in Brussels in 2016.[83] The car was one of an edition that was limited to a total of 299. It had 'a long chassis', 'driver separation', 'colonial springing', and—a final touch—was 'completely tropicalised'. The guide price was estimated at £50,000–70,000. The Doherty family remained shrewd investors to the end.

Samuel Pearse: The Great Survivor

Samuel Pearse's family were Egba from Abeokuta, where his grandfather was head of the Itosi quarter.[84] Members of the family were enslaved in the 1820s but liberated and then settled in Sierra Leone, where Pearse's father was born around 1830. Like many other former slaves who had been freed, the family adopted English names after they had been baptised. Nevertheless, the family's original name, Awoboh, was carried forward and later gained publicity as the title of Samuel's publishing house. Pearse's father, who was also named Samuel, was educated at CMS schools in Freetown before entering the service of the mission in 1848.[85] He was transferred to Lagos in 1856, where he served as a catechist and school teacher under the guidance of the senior missionary, the redoubtable Charles Gollmer. In 1859, he was placed in charge of the mission station at Badagry, where he remained for twenty years before becoming pastor of the Anglican church at Ebute Ero on the northern tip of Lagos island. He was ordained in 1880 and stayed at Ebute Ero for the rest of his career. On retirement, he remained in Lagos until he died in 1902.

Samuel Herbert Pearse was born in Badagri in 1866, the first and only son of the marriage between his father, Samuel, and Betsy Jemima Pearse, though

83. https://www.bonhams.com/auctions/23262/lot/410/#/!

84. I am most grateful to Samuel Pearse's son, Dr Samuel Herbert Abiodun Pearse, and his daughter, Mrs Remilekun Jones, for interviews on 6 Dec. 1961, 7 Dec. 1961, 11 Dec. 1961, and 18 Dec. 1961; to Mrs Jones for permission to use her autobiographical notes dated 29 May 1958; and to Mrs Silva (granddaughter) for permission to use Samuel Herbert Pearse's remaining papers, cited here as SHPP. The early history of the family is also drawn from evidence given by Samuel Pearse Snr. In the Matter of the Estate of Hotonu, LSCR, Civ. 9, 1889.

85. See Kopytoff, *A Preface to Modern Nigeria*, p. 296.

he also had an older and a younger sister.[86] He was educated at the CMS Grammar School in Lagos between 1879 and 1883 and was then apprenticed briefly to the English firm of McIver & Co., which had a branch in Lagos. With savings from his first wages, he bought his father a clock, which he later inherited and hung in his own house throughout his lifetime. At the end of 1883, Pearse joined the African firm of Williams Bros., which was managed by the senior partner and prominent merchant, Zachariah Williams.[87]

In 1888, Pearse left Williams Bros. to start his own business as principal of a partnership with a Sierra Leonean named Thompson, about whom little is known.[88] Pearse & Thomson made a bold start, presumably with borrowed money, and took premises on the Marina and in Leadenhall Street in the City of London, where Thompson represented the firm. The partnership, which focussed on buying and shipping palm oil, had made sufficient progress by 1891 to be elected to membership of the Lagos Chamber of Commerce. The firm continued, seemingly in good health, until 1894, when the *Lagos Weekly Record* reported that the town was 'somewhat startled' by the news that Pearse had 'suddenly disappeared from the Colony'.[89] In September, Pearse wrote to the Chamber of Commerce from the Canary Islands, resigning his membership and saying that he intended to return to Lagos in 1895.[90] It is impossible to say whether the success of the firm was apparent rather than real or whether it was brought down by bad luck or mismanagement. Allegations of deception by Thompson were made but not taken to court. Unlike Pearse, Thompson did not reappear in Lagos; indeed, he seems to have disappeared entirely. Pearse was left to deal with the consequences. It was not the last time he found himself facing disaster.

Pearse kept his word: he returned to Lagos in October 1894, before his predicted time, as a commission agent for the African & Gold Coast Trading Corporation. Little is known of this short-lived Liverpool firm. Pearse was introduced to them by his agents, Taylor & Co., while he was in Liverpool, and made sufficient impression to be taken on as an employee.[91] The post was a modest one: in 1895, Pearse was earning about £12 a month.[92] By 1896, he had moved on and up: he was acting as a commission agent for several firms and earning £20–25 a month.[93] He was also engulfed in claims from his previous firm's creditors. As the senior partner, Pearse had accepted responsibility

86. A separate article could be written on Samuel Herbert Pearse's date of birth. In summary, three dates, 1865, 1866, and 1867, appear in various sources. I have preferred 1866, which is the date given by Samuel Pearse's son, Abiodun, and his daughter, Remi.

87. Macmillan, *Red Book*, p. 97. On Z. A. Williams, see chapter 7.

88. Deniga, *Who's Who in Nigeria, 1934*, pp. 23–4.

89. 23 June 1894.

90. *Lagos Weekly Record*, 8 Sept. 1894; Holt & Welsh v. Williams, LSCR, Civ. 16, 1895.

91. Taylor & Co. remained Pearse's Liverpool agents throughout his career.

92. Pearse's evidence in Falano & Ors v. Pearse, LSCR, Civ. 16, 1895.

93. Pearse's evidence in Shongotola v. Pearse, LSCR, Civ. 16, 1896.

FIGURE 12.3. Samuel Herbert Pearse, c.1905. Copied by Paramount
Photographers Lagos, with permission of Mrs Remilekun Jones (daughter).

for Thompson & Pearse's liabilities, which kept him in court during the late 1890s. Judgements in an incomplete selection of seven important cases totalled about £3,000, which Pearse paid by surrendering a property in Lagos and assigning some of his monthly income to his creditors.[94] Repayment took time: Pearse was not free from his pursuers until about 1902.[95]

Resilience, however, might have been Pearse's motto. He was never short of ideas or the courage needed to test them. His financial difficulties gave him a powerful incentive to generate an income well above his earnings as a commission agent. Moreover, in 1897 he married Cassandra Lydia Decker, the eldest daughter of J. P. Decker, one of the first African Police Inspectors in Lagos.[96] The family was socially well placed, if not noticeably wealthy. Members of the Decker family were scattered along the West Coast and were related to the Willoughbys, who were represented in Lagos by the notable Isaac Willoughby, the long-serving Superintendent of Police. While paying off his debts, Pearse also needed to provide a suitable home for his new bride. With a Reverend as his father and senior police officers among his in-laws, Pearse knew where his duty lay.

Calabar and the Ivory Boom

In 1897, Pearse made a typically ambitious decision: he shifted his commercial activities to a less developed frontier, Old Calabar, while also exploring opportunities on the lower Niger. The new venture was undertaken in partnership with Edwin O. Williams, a Lagos commission agent who had also accumulated a series of debts during the 1890s.[97] When Williams left Lagos for Calabar in 1897, he acknowledged that he still owed 'about £1,000', had little income, and no property.[98] This might appear to be a partnership without a future, but it should be remembered that produce was accepted as being a high-risk trade and that debt was a commonplace. Merchants would sue one another, as Williams sued Pearse in 1894, yet still remain friends. In 1897, the pair rented a house in Duke Town, Calabar, and added a store and landing pier in the

94. Edwin O. Williams v. Pearse, LSCR, Civ. 15, 1894; Walkden & Co. v. Pearse, LSCR, Civ. 15, 1894; Radcliffe & Durant v. Pearse, LSCR, Civ. 15, 1894; Falano & Ors v. Pearse, LSCR, Civ. 16, 1895; Shongotola v. Pearse, LSCR, Civ. 16, 1896; Alli Balogun v. Pearse, LSCR, Civ. 17, 1896. I have added to these cases the sum of £360 owed to the Bank of British West Africa: BBWA to Pearse, 10 Sept. 1995, SHPP.

95. Letters from creditors confirming the settlement of debt: Falana and Bakare to Pearse, 15 Aug. 1901, SHPP; Pearse to W. E. George, 1 July 1902, SHPP; Receipt from C. A. Thompson, 10 July 1902; Receipt from Walkden, 7 Aug. 1902, 24 Sept. 1902, SHPP; Receipt from J. O. George, 25 Nov. 1902, SHPP.

96. The couple married in Calabar; their first daughter, Remilekun, was born there in 1903.

97. Tomlinson & Co. v. Williams, LSCR, Civ. 9, 1890; Walkden & Co. v. Williams, LSCR, Civ. 15, 1895; Holt & Welsh v. Williams, LSCR, Civ. 16, 1895.

98. Holt & Welsh v. Williams, LSCR, Civ. 20, 1898.

following year.[99] In January 1899, however, Williams died, the partnership was dissolved, and Pearse was left to continue the business on his own.[100]

In 1898, the firm was shipping palm oil, rubber, and ivory, importing a range of consumer items, including gin, soap, salt, and iron rods, and allowing local traders credit on the security of property in Old Calabar.[101]The half-yearly account for 1898 valued the assets at £849 and liabilities at £156.[102] Williams was entitled to a half share of the net assets (or liabilities), which in January 1899 amounted to £221.[103] The figures were scarcely impressive, but at least they were moving in a direction that neither Pearse nor Williams had seen for some time. In 1900, Pearse signed an agreement with the African Association whereby he undertook to consign to them all 'his direct trade with England' for a period of two years.[104] The Association undertook to sell the firm's produce for a commission of 2.5 per cent, to supply goods to him through their agent on advantageous terms, and—a final touch—to allow him to use their 'crane and wharf'.[105]

These details are insufficient to allow an assessment of Pearse's business at this time. What can be said, however, is that the partnership, or rather Pearse, was finally on the brink of a bonanza: ivory. Although small quantities of ivory had long been exported from the region, shifting consumer tastes in Victorian England boosted demand to unprecedented levels.[106] The piano keys, cutlery handles, combs, and billiard balls that colonised the homes of middle-class England were all made of ivory. Elephant tusks being in finite supply, the trade shifted from exhausted to untapped sources, of which the hinterland of Calabar was one.

In October 1897, Williams & Pearse bought their first 'elephant gun' in response to a request from three hunters, who employed a clerk to make the following proposition:[107]

> Sir,
>
> We the undersigned do hereby beg to any Agent in the River to give us a Helping hand to get a gun for the purpose of going to the bush to hunt Elephant.[108] And whoever may give us a help, we shall always be placing the ivory at the disposal of the agent.

99. Agreement with Chief Ephraim Adam, 30 June 1897, SHPP; Agreement with Mrs E. Ballantyne, 1 Sept. 1898, SHHP.

100. *Lagos Reporter*, 11 Feb. 1899.

101. For example, the Pledge made by Sailu Oshegbe, 3 Aug. 1897, SHPP.

102. Williams & Pearse, Statement of Account, 4 April 1898, SHPP.

103. Statement of Account, Jan. 1899, SHPP.

104. Agreement between the African Association and Pearse, 1 March 1900, SHPP.

105. Agreement between the African Association and Pearse, 1 March 1900, SHPP.

106. The best study of the region at this time is Latham, *Old Calabar*.

107. Anon. to Williams & Pearse, 15 Oct. 1897, SHPP.

108. Cole, Tucker and Fry to Williams & Pearse, 12 Oct. 1897, SHPP; Anon. to Williams & Pearse, 15 Oct. 1897, SHPP.

We remain,
Gentlemen,

> Your Obedient Servant,
> James Cole X
> John Tucker X
> John Fry X

On the margin of the letter, Pearse noted: 'engaged 16 October 1897. Half shares'. Unfortunately, this promising evidence of the opening of Pearse's trade in ivory is not continued in his surviving papers. There is just one further reference, which appeared in the following year, when Miller Bros. asked if Williams & Pearse had made arrangements to ship 55 pounds of ivory they had in store.[109] The statement of account that followed Williams's death listed ivory among many other items of stock but without indicating its importance. Nevertheless, the general understanding among Pearse's informed contemporaries, and indeed Pearse himself, was that ivory was responsible for generating the degree of wealth that allowed him to take his place among the merchant princes of Lagos.

From 1897 to 1904, Pearse divided his time between Lagos and Calabar. He was frequently on the move after 1904, too, even though he had settled in Lagos by then. He sealed the decision in 1905, when he appointed a manager for his 'commercial and auctioneering business' in Calabar.[110] By the end of 1902, the profits from his trade in Calabar had enabled him to pay off the debts he had inherited from Pearse & Thompson and to reorganise his business in Lagos. He leased his Broad Street premises to a series of tenants, starting with Sasche & Co. in 1904 and continuing with Peter Thomas in 1909.[111] In exchange, he rented new premises at the corner of Balogun Street in 1904, and properties in Kakawa Street in 1906 and Oke Olowogbowo in 1908.[112] It is indicative of Pearse's improved circumstances that, from the early 1900s, he was lending money rather than borrowing it and buying property rather than selling it. Nevertheless, Pearse seems to have been exceptional among his peers in not acquiring a substantial portfolio of properties.[113] By this time, his business appears to have been largely self-financing. The loans he made were generally on a small scale.[114] Kitoyi Ajasa and

109. Miller Bros. to Williams & Pearse, 25 Aug. 1898, SHPP.

110. Agreement between Pearse and Lawrence Kasumu Bajulaye of Lagos, 31 Jan. 1905, SHPP.

111. Lease to Sasche, 18 Oct. 1904; Lease to P. J. C. Thomas, 20 May 1909, SHPP.

112. Lease from Brimah Ajoro to Pearse, 1 April 1904; lease from J.A.O. Payne, 12 Dec. 1906; lease from J. A. Williams, 18 May 1908, SHPP.

113. Apart from those mentioned in this chapter. It is possible, however, that I have overlooked some transactions outside the Marina and Broad Street.

114. For example: Loan Agreements with Belo and Alli Dawodu, 15 Oct. 1903; with A. Widicombe, 10 June 1903; with Rebecca Cole, 20 May 1909; with Sani Aro, 6 May 1918, SHPP.

Egerton Shyngle, both wealthy lawyers, were constantly short of cash and often borrowed trifling sums from Pearse and Isaac Williams, among others.

Pearse's business remained focussed on exports of produce, notably ivory, palm oil, palm kernels, and cocoa, which he consigned to his agent, Taylor & Co., in Liverpool. In 1910, he added a new product: hides.[115] He made a separate agreement with Kraus & Co., a European firm, to ship at least 10,000 hides annually to them.[116] This innovative trade was made viable by the extension of the railway to the cattle country in the north of what was shortly to become Nigeria. Pearse's import trade, which dealt with cottons, hardware, and other dry goods, was on a far smaller scale. Pragmatism rather than principle lay behind his decision not to stock alcohol.[117] His experience in Calabar, where he did sell spirits, led him to conclude that the profitability of the trade was insufficient to justify continuing to stock it. He also thought that prohibition would have the effect of promoting alternative alcoholic drinks.

Pearse had a nose for opportunities and a compulsion to follow their scent. Numerous novel and speculative ventures surrounded his core business. The trade in hides was just one example. In 1903, while still paying off his debtors, he bought shares in three gold-mining companies on the Gold Coast.[118] Two years later, he put £150 into another Gold Coast mining company, Gamelsoo Concessions Ltd., which went out of business shortly afterwards.[119] In 1906, he tried his hand at road building in the Cross River area, but with little success.[120] In 1911, with hope still springing eternal, he joined the Lagos Venture Syndicate, which intended to exploit a concession in Bauchi on the Jos Plateau.[121] At about the same time, he began supplying Kru labourers for Lagos firms. A more promising enterprise was the Nigerian Shipping Corporation, which was formed in 1909 to offer a regular steamship service on the Niger between Forcados and Lokoja.[122] The venture had the backing of two prominent and wealthy Lagosians: the merchant, Josiah Henryson Doherty, and the auctioneer, Andrew Wilkinson Thomas, who were not known for wasting their money. Yet, as we have seen, the enterprise soon disappeared from public view and slowly withered.[123] As far as can be judged, Pearse did not strike gold with any of these activities. Given his adventurous nature, however, it is no less important to record that none reduced him to penury either.

115. For an overview of the trade as a whole, see Adebayo, 'Production and Export'.
116. Contract between Pearse and Kraus, 8 Oct. 1910, SHPP.
117. Pearse's evidence to the Liquor Commission: *Nigerian Chronicle*, 20 Aug. 1909.
118. Bannerman Martin to Pearse, 2 March 1903, SHPP.
119. Note of share purchase, 17 July 1905, SHPP.
120. Note in SSPH, 1906.
121. Deed of release and receipt, 21 June 1911, SHPP.
122. *Lagos Weekly Record*, 13 Jan. 1909; *Lagos Standard*, 26 May 1909.
123. See p. 306–11.

Two businesses of greater substance deserve to be mentioned. In 1907, Pearse opened the grandly titled Hotel de l'Europe, which occupied 36 Kakawa Street.[124] This was not quite the first hotel in Lagos, as is sometimes claimed. That accolade should be awarded to the Lagos Hotel, which was opened by a European named H. M. C. Carroll in 1883.[125] But the Hotel de l'Europe was the second hotel in the town, and its relationship to the first could not have been closer because Pearse bought, refurbished, and renamed the Lagos Hotel. The new hotel had electric lights, a billiard room, and a tennis court, and was placed under the 'genial and courteous management' of an experienced European.[126] Pearse's own knowledge of hotel management appears not to have exceeded his attempt to start a bread-making business in the late 1890s, when he was trying to get out of debt. On this occasion, however, his assessment of new possibilities was shrewd and far-sighted, and his accumulated business experience enabled him to hire professionals and operate the hotel successfully. The Hotel de l'Europe remained in Pearse's hands until shortly after the war, by which time it had undergone a change of name to fit the times and had emerged as the Grand Hotel.

The other venture worth noting was Pearse's entry into publishing. In 1920, the *Lagos Weekly Record* reported what it called 'a gigantic undertaking': Pearse had just bought the 'largest printing machinery' in West Africa and had plans for producing a 'brilliant' West African journal and a daily newspaper.[127] The postwar slump obliged Pearse to curtail his ambitions. Although the publications failed to appear in the form Pearse had initially envisaged, the press survived as the Awoboh Printing Press and had an illustrious history in providing an outlet (with Tika Tore Press) for new Nigerian voices. Awoboh published a newspaper, the *African Messenger*, from 1921 to 1925 and its successor, the *Nigerian Daily Times*, in 1926.[128] Both papers were edited by Ernest Ikoli, whose nationalist stance placed him some distance from Pearse's own views.[129]

The years between 1900 and 1914 were generally kind to Pearse, as they were to many other traders who took advantage of the favourable commercial conditions that characterised the period. In default of business accounts for the period, there is one signature development that serves as an unusual but illuminating proxy for Pearse's increasing wealth and status: the construction in Broad Street of what became one of the most distinctive buildings in Lagos, known

124. I have compiled the story from various undated notes in SHPP and advertisements in the Lagos press, as well as with help from members of the family.

125. *Lagos Observer*, 29 March 1883, 12 April 1883.

126. *Lagos Standard*, 20 Jan. 1909.

127. *Lagos Weekly Record*, 20 March 1920; Campbell v. Pearse, LSCR, Civ. 91, 1921.

128. The *Nigerian Daily Times* is still being published, though it has experienced many changes since 1926.

129. On the press during this period, see Barber, 'Experiments with Genre', in *African Print Cultures*, ch. 6.

FIGURE 12.4. Elephant House, 214 Broad St. (1904; renovated 1919). Copied by Paramount Photographers Lagos, with permission of Mrs Remilekun Jones (daughter).

throughout the town by its name: Elephant House. The house was designed and constructed by Isaac Cole, one of the most prominent builders of the time.[130] The property was originally part of Isaac Willoughby's estate. Although Willoughby died in 1890, a family dispute delayed the distribution of his assets until 1898, by which time the house, which was built of wood, was in a poor condition.[131] In 1901, Pearse's wife, Cassandra (who was also Willoughby's cousin), bought the property with funds earned from her own trading business.[132] Cassandra's resources were limited because she had just settled one of her husband's

130. See above, pp. 344–45.

131. *Lagos Weekly Times*, 26 July 1890; Willoughby v. Willoughby, LSCR, Civ. 121, 1898.

132. Autobiographical notes written by Pearse's daughter, Mrs Remilekun Jones (born 1903), dated 29 May 1958 and cited with her permission.

debts with the financier, Alli Balogun.[133] Nevertheless, she took a chance: the location was a prime position in Broad Street, and the price was within reach because the condition of the house discouraged prospective buyers.

The gamble succeeded. After 1902, Pearse had the necessary funds and the state of the house compelled him to spend them. He hired contractors, rebuilt the house in stone and brick, and in 1904 moved the family from Phoenix Lane into what became their family home. The house had become a mansion. It had three floors, spacious rooms, and a roof garden, and was furnished in the fashionable style prevailing in Edwardian England. The front of the house sported a black-painted wooden elephant that proclaimed the origins of the owner's wealth. Elephant House was extensively renovated in 1919, at which point it had electric lighting and a ballroom.[134] The wooden elephant, which had weathered over the years, was superseded by a more durable replica in stone. The 'handsome and palatial' property became the headquarters of Pearse's business (with the telegraphic address 'Awoboh') and a social centre, as well as a family home. It was one of the few private houses in Lagos with the space for dancing to the music of a full orchestra, which was provided by 'a large orchestrion operated by electric power'.[135] Elephant House became popular among members of the elite who gathered there to attend balls, dinners, soirées, wedding receptions, and meetings of various organisations. From 1904 until well into the 1920s, the house was rarely out of the Lagos newspapers.

These events enhanced Pearse's status and gave him valuable connections with influential figures in the colonial government and Lagos society. Within a few years, he had bought a Ford car and a farm at Agege, which he used as a country retreat. He became a prominent member of numerous societies, and a secretary, trustee, or patron of such varied organisations as the Lagos Auxiliary of the Anti-Slavery & Aborigines Protection Society, the Glover Memorial Hall, the Lagos Town Hall, the Sarah Bonetta Davies Memorial Ladies' School, and the management board of the Lagos Race Course, as well as being a generous supporter of Christchurch, the Anglican church patronised by the Lagos elite.[136] Pearse also commended himself to the colonial authorities. In 1907, they employed him to report on the rubber resources of Benin; in 1913, he provided evidence in London to the Royal Commission on Native Land Tenure.[137] Parallel developments confirmed that he was moving up the ladder of social progress. In 1907, the *Lagos Standard* reported that Pearse had been elected Worthy Master of St. John's Masonic Lodge.[138] In the same year, 'our esteemed

133. Alli Balogun to Mrs S. H. Pearse, 16 Aug. 1900, SHPP.
134. Photographs of the renovated property are reproduced in Macmillan, *Red Book*, pp. 97–8.
135. Macmillan, *Red Book*, pp. 97–8.
136. Macmillan, *Red Book*, pp. 97–8.
137. Deniga, *The Nigerian Who's Who, 1934*, pp. 23–4.
138. *Lagos Standard*, 26 June 1907.

and enterprising townsman' was elected a Fellow of the Royal Geographical Society and the Royal Colonial Institute.[139] Pearse reached the highest rung in 1915, when he was appointed to be a member of the Nigerian Legislative Council and entitled to prefix his name with the abbreviation 'Hon'..[140] Public distinctions do not tell the whole story. Pearse was well known for his informal contributions to charitable causes, which included redeeming several children from slavery and bringing others from Calabar to be educated in Lagos.[141]

Pearse's nomination to the Legislative Council provides an indication of his political views. Membership was not offered to critics, especially those who had expressed dissent before the war and became vociferous during and after it. On the contrary, the colonial authorities were keen to align themselves with elite Africans whose loyalty could be relied on and who would act as a counterweight to dissidents. The Colonial Office had already identified Pearse as a 'distinctly able man', adding that 'for a native' he was 'broadminded'.[142] Pearse had proclaimed his allegiance during the war in declaring that 'our duty as loyal subjects is to support the empire in its time of need'.[143] Many others shared his opinion, including some, like Jacob Coker, who were not natural advocates of colonial rule.

Pearse earned his appointment for an additional and more precise reason: he was a critic of Herbert Macaulay and his nationalist programme. His record was not pristine: in 1908, he had joined a protest against the government's proposal to purchase African property and build houses that would be restricted to white occupants.[144] But time had passed and Pearse's status had risen. In 1915, and continuing in the following year, there was a much larger protest in Lagos, this time against the imposition of a water rate.[145] On this occasion, Pearse stood with those who supported the government.[146] His stance allied him to an elite group of conservatives, notably Kitoyi Ajasa, Peter Thomas, and Bishop Isaac Oluwole, who, with Joseph Egerton Shyngle and Candido da Rocha, were among his closest friends. In 1917, Pearse combined business acumen with loyalty by investing £10,000 in War Bonds and adding

139. *Lagos Standard*, 20 Feb. 1907.

140. *Nigerian Pioneer*, 7 May 1917. Pearse's appointment ended in 1921.

141. Receipt dated 18 April 1899, in Family Notes, SHPP; *Nigerian Chronicle*, 20 Nov. 1914.

142. Memo on the West African Lands Committee delegation, 7 June 1913, C.O. 520/130. The memo also stated, incorrectly, that he had given up trading and turned to money lending.

143. *Nigerian Chronicle*, 11 Aug. 1916.

144. *Lagos Standard*, 4 Dec. 1907; *Lagos Weekly Record*, 1 Jan. 1908.

145. The most recent account of this episode is in Yearwood, *Nigeria and the Death of Liberal England*, pp. 153–6.

146. In 1917, Pearse was criticised for his 'attitude of inglorious silence' when Eric Moore asked the Legislative Council to apply the principle of representation to the Town Council's Ordinance, which was then under consideration. *Lagos Weekly Record*, 28 April 1917.

£2,450 in Victory Bonds in 1921.[147] He was 'the first to subscribe an ample sum' to the government's fund for building aeroplanes and 'gave largely' to another fund to benefit the Red Cross.[148]

The War and Its Aftermath

Pearse's business was at its height during the decade before the outbreak of war. The war years brought upheaval and uncertainty. Some produce prices, such as cocoa, rose sharply; others, such as palm kernels, suffered from the closure of markets in Germany, where the main source of demand was located. European commercial firms combined to control prices to the disadvantage, so critics alleged, of those outside the group. Shortages and consequent high prices reduced the size of the import trade. All overseas commerce was adversely affected by a lack of shipping. Although Pearse exported palm oil and kernels, it is impossible to know how important the trade was to his business as a whole.[149] A larger problem, which was independent of the war, was that supplies of ivory from Nigerian sources had essentially petered out. Although Pearse's business undoubtedly suffered during the war, he was still wealthy at the end of it.

Pearse's status survived with his business. He was one of only two Lagosians to be elected to the Lagos Chamber of Commerce in 1921, when the committee voted to readmit Africans.[150] He went on to become Vice President on several occasions and President in 1931–1932.[151] Invitations to Government House and other grand events continued.[152] In 1923, the *Alake* of Abeokuta installed Pearse as *Oluwo* of Itesi Ake, and in 1929 added the title of *Odofin*, which had once been held by his grandfather.[153] In 1936, Pearse was awarded an MBE (Member of the British Empire) in recognition of his loyalty to Britain.[154] Throughout this time, Cassandra, Pearse's wife, ran her own independent business in imported textiles, and helped her husband when called on to do so. Their resources enabled them to educate their four adult children in England during the 1920s and assist their entry into independent lives. Two of his daughters attended Ryford Hall Ladies' College, where their

147. Receipt dated 30 March 1917; BBWA to Pearse, 13 April 1921, SHPP. See also *Lagos Weekly Record*, 19 July 1919.

148. *Lagos Weekly Record*, 19 July 1919.

149. Receipts from Royal Niger Company to Pearse for 480 tons of palm kernels, 3–10 Sept. 1917, SHPP; H. S. Peters (produce buyer) to Pearse, 18 May 1919, SHPP.

150. *Nigerian Pioneer*, 7 Oct. 1921. The Chamber became an entirely European body in 1903. Hopkins, 'The Lagos Chamber of Commerce', p. 246.

151. *West Africa*, 14 Nov. 1931.

152. *Lagos Weekly Record*, 3 Jan. 1920; Lagos Chamber of Commerce, Banquet Menu, 21 Jan. 1926, SHPP.

153. *Nigerian Pioneer*, 19 April 1929; Evidence of Samuel Pearse Snr. In the Matter of the Estate of Hotonu Deceased, LSCR, Civ. 9, 1889.

154. *Nigerian Daily Times*, 26 June 1936.

musical talent became apparent.[155] The marriage of his eldest daughter, Evangeline Ayodele Pearse, to the Rev. S. C. Phillips in 1922 was followed by a lavish reception for 300 guests.[156] Pearse's son, Samuel Herbert Abiodun Pearse, attended Dulwich College from 1922 to 1928 and progressed to St. Thomas's Hospital, where he qualified as a doctor. This was not the original plan. Abiodun wanted a career in commerce, but his father warned him against following his own route because of the high risks attached to business in Lagos. On this subject, Pearse undoubtedly spoke with authority.

Behind the public face of affluence, Pearse faced an uphill struggle during the interwar period as he waited, with his contemporaries, for signs of economic revival to become permanent. Sustained recovery, as we now know, did not arrive until after World War II. Pearse was undoubtedly damaged by the devastating post-war slump, which struck suddenly in the middle of 1920, even though (unlike Peter Thomas) he survived it. He greatly reduced his trade in produce, as did many other African merchants. In 1921, he was forced to sell securities to the value of £11,750 to cover his overdraft with the BBWA.[157] In the following year, he sold the Grand Hotel to the eminent merchant-financier Alli Balogun for £2,000. Yet Pearse was by no means finished. He increased his commitment to the export trade in rubber, which showed promise in the mid-1920s. In 1926, he was able to buy shares in BBWA, in the African & Eastern Corporation, and in its successor, the United Africa Company, in 1929.[158] If you cannot beat them, he might have reflected, you might as well join them. The worldwide slump of 1929, however, ruined hopes that prosperity would return. Rubber prices fell sharply and in the 1930s, Pearse was again selling securities to cover his overdraft.[159]

In the midst of these pressures, Pearse remained true to form in exploring commercial opportunities with his customary vigour. In 1920, he was importing corrugated iron sheets; later in the decade he was selling wool and beads; during the 1930s, he imported silver for local silversmiths and developed a promising trade in stockfish; in the early 1940s, he started to import salt.[160] Two lines of business, kola nuts and cattle, were successful. Both, significantly, were responses to internal demand. Consumer purchasing power in Nigeria was still related to the health of international trade, but superior connections, knowledge of local customs and languages, and lower costs gave

155. *Nigerian Pioneer*, 31 Aug. 1917. See also Mann, *Marrying Well*, p. 98.

156. *Nigerian Pioneer*, 20 Jan. 1922. Ayodele (Ayo) had a fine voice: she was one of the soloists in a performance of Mendelssohn's *Elijah* in 1921. *Lagos Weekly Record*, 17 Dec. 1921.

157. BBWA to Pearse, 13 April 1921; Pearse to BBWA, 5 Sept. 1921, SHPP.

158. Pearse Receipt from BBWA, 1 May 1929, SHPP.

159. Pearse to BBWA, 4 Dec. 1939; BBWA to Pearse, 6 Jan. 1941, SHPP.

160. I am grateful to Mr A. Gbadamosi, Pearse's clerk, 1930–55, for information on this period: interview, 19 Dec. 1961; also A. O. Thomas to Pearse, 16 March 1920, SHPP; Agreement between Sadiko Lawani and Pearse, 28 Jan. 1928, SHPP.

African merchants advantages in developing the internal market. Pearse was also able to ride on the back of the 'iron horse', after it reached Kano. The railway did not create an entirely new trade: kola nuts and cattle had long been exchanged between southern and northern Nigeria, and a larger overland trade had carried kola from the Gold Coast to the north. The railway, however, was much faster and safer than travel by caravan. It cut transport costs and also raised purchasing power in the north by facilitating the expansion of groundnut exports. Pearse ran the business from Elephant House with the assistance of four clerks in Lagos, another stationed at Apapa to check arrivals and departures, and twelve or more other employees distributed along the railway line and in Kano and Zaria.[161] Between them, they handled both cattle and kola trades.

Pearse's business received a boost in 1912, when the colonial government imposed a tariff on kola imports from the Gold Coast to augment its revenue.[162] The measure encouraged the Agege farmers to increase their commitment to kola; the post-war slump and the decline of cocoa prices accelerated the trend. These developments enabled Pearse to draw on a local and high-quality source of supply. He shipped kola nuts to the north, where his agents oversaw their distribution and employed debt collectors (who worked on commission) to gather money he was owed.[163] Pearse had developed the cattle trade before the war but expanded his stake in it considerably during the 1920s and 1930s. He was probably the most important of the Lagos merchants engaged in the trade at this time.[164] His closest competitor was the Syrian immigrant, Michael Elias, who had also entered the trade shortly before the First World War.[165] Pearse appointed specialised agents in the north to buy cattle on his behalf. One of these, *Alhadji* Tukuru, who was employed to buy cattle, rams, and sheep in the area between Nguru and Kano, was paid a small salary of £1 a month and a more substantial commission of 2s. per head of cattle and 1s. for each ram.[166] Some hides were sold in Lagos; others were shipped by Elder, Dempster & Co. and consigned to Taylor & Co. in Liverpool. The other product, meat, was sold for local consumption. In the 1930s, cattle arrived in Lagos at a total cost of about £15 a head and were sold for about £20, out of which Pearse had to pay expenses. The business was not a gold mine, but it was profitable.

161. Information supplied by Mr A. Gbadamosi, Pearse's clerk, 1930–55, 19 Dec. 1961.

162. *Lagos Weekly Record*, 16 March 1912. Imports from the Gold Coast 'collapsed'. *Lagos Weekly Record*, 15 June 1912.

163. Agreement between Pearse and I. S. Shanusi, 1 Jan. 1935; Pearse, Power of Attorney to E. T. A. Daniel, 7 March 1936; Agreement between Pearse and Atiku Pedro, 28 July 1937, SHPP.

164. Mr A. Gbadamosi, Pearse's clerk, claimed that Pearse had a larger allocation of railway freight than Elias had. Interview, 19 Dec. 1961.

165. See above, pp. 342–43. Also Macmillan, *Red Book*, pp. 102–03.

166. Contract between Pearse and Tukuru, 26 Feb. 1928, SHPP.

Final Years

The year 1941 was not a good one for the family. Cassandra, Pearse's wife of forty-four years, died; Pearse himself had a serious fall on the stairs in Elephant House, was partly paralysed, and was confined to the house from then on. By that point, too, his business was in decline and he relied increasingly on his savings and rental income from his property in Lagos. He died in 1953 aged eighty-seven, having been born just after the Colony of Lagos was established and having survived almost the whole of the colonial era.[167] Although he was not wealthy at his death, he had the satisfaction of knowing that he had put his money not only into his own life but also into that of his children and the many good causes he supported. He instructed his executors to ensure that his funeral 'should be as simple and as inexpensive as possible'.[168]

Advanced age encourages the desire to bestow a personal legacy that is more than a memory. In the hope that some of his own past would be carried into the future, Pearse gave his eldest daughter, Ayodele, 'my brass bed, big silver tea horn, big glass case in the Drawing Room, my photo taken when forty years of age, washstand, two silver dishes inside the glass case in the Drawing Room, one framed mirror and its stand, now a furniture in the Drawing Room, my spring sofa with its mattress, my silver tray, Sir Kitoye's photograph, my bath tub, and what remains of my orchestra'.[169] Elephant House outlasted its owner and probably the remains of his orchestrion as well. In 1981, however, the once famous landmark was demolished and its material artefacts crushed by the machines of modern construction. Today, the house is hardly a memory outside members of the family. The name alone lives on, detached from its origins and surviving to embellish the facade of 214 Broad Street, which is now a seventeen-storey block of offices and apartments owned, perhaps appropriately, by the Bank of Nigeria.

Two Kinds of Success

The careers of two merchant princes cannot be treated as proxies for the wider commercial community. Nevertheless, they show that it was possible for astute businessmen to prosper during a time that is generally thought to have signalled the decline of indigenous commercial enterprise. Both took advantage of the expansion of the market that followed the extension of the railway and its sponsor, British rule. Doherty did so as an importer; Pearse as one of the risk-takers in the export trade. Doherty was one of the first Lagos merchants to establish branches inland and to adapt his stock to the needs of a larger and more varied market. Pearse developed the ivory trade from Calabar and later

167. *Daily Service* (Nigeria), 8 Jan. 1953.
168. Will dated 1948, LAP, 18/301–6, 1955.
169. Will dated 1948, LAP, 18/301–6, 1955.

promoted the rubber trade. The two men came together briefly in an effort to introduce limited liability companies in Nigeria. The chronology of their success was similar: they made their fortunes between the late 1890s and 1914, when international trade was, in general, buoyant. Similarly, they both faced considerable difficulties during the upheaval brought by World War I and the depressed state of commerce that followed. While both can be regarded as merchants tied to the forces of international trade, their businesses reflected the growth of the internal market as well. Although this is most obvious in the case of Doherty, it also applied to Pearse, who promoted the cattle and kola trades and in a further departure established a hotel and an influential printing press, both of which responded to needs that pointed to the future rather than the past.

In matters of political choice, their diverse responses to the expansion of colonial rule illustrated a dilemma the whole Saro community faced: how to adjust to subordination and discrimination. Doherty sympathised with the views advanced by Jacob Coker and Herbert Macaulay; Pearse became an empire loyalist of the kind epitomised by Kitoyi Ajasa. In practice, both had to pick their way through compromises imposed by colonial rule. The dilemma was not resolved until after World War II, when a negotiated settlement culminated in the independence of Nigeria in 1960.

Doherty was the more successful of the two, at least in the long run. He carefully assembled a portfolio of property that supported his business during the difficult war years and the 1920s, and remained intact at his death. Pearse's business, like his personality, was more volatile and depended to a greater degree on a series of 'lucky strikes' rather than on steady accumulation. The absence of limited liability companies and the standard accounting procedures that accompanied them, means that success is not easily measured, especially when accounts of any kind are no longer readily available. The issue, however, is one of conception as well as measurement. The evaluation of businesses that are highly personal must also take account of the ambitions of their owners. Doherty and Pearse were not primarily concerned with perpetuating the enterprises they had founded but with investing their wealth in ways that would benefit their own families and the wider society. Judged by this measure, they were both successful in funding numerous good causes and in promoting the priority they shared: education. They realised that education was the best of all long-term investments, and the one that has been indispensable to creating the advanced economy that exists in Nigeria today. Their achievements demonstrated to sceptical expatriates that African entrepreneurs could survive and prosper, even within an enveloping colonial context. This, too, must be counted a success.

CHAPTER THIRTEEN

Jacob Coker and the New Farming Frontier at Agege

THE STORY OF THE survival of African merchants and their pioneering efforts to diversify the urban economy after 1900, though striking, is incomplete. Diversification of an even more radical kind occurred at this time and involved a group of Lagos merchants returning to the land, not to retreat into subsistence but to create a new export economy based on cocoa farming. Their story is an extraordinary one by any measure. It turns on the initiative of one man, Jacob Coker, who displayed the heroic qualities that Joseph Schumpeter identified with entrepreneurship.

Like so many Lagos Saro, Jacob Kehinde Coker belonged to an Egba family.[1] His father, Ajobo, was born in Sierra Leone in 1838 to two freed slaves from Abeokuta. His mother, Dotunmu, arrived later, having been enslaved in Egba country and taken to Freetown after the intervention of the British Naval Squadron. Ajobo became a Christian and took the name James Osolu Coker, though his original name remained in common use. He married Dotunmu in Sierra Leone

---

1. I am grateful to two of Jacob Coker's sons for providing information about the history of the family: Oyebade Coker, interviews, 9 Nov. 1961, 5 Feb. 1962, 23 Feb. 1962, and Adekunle Coker, interviews, 16 May 1964, 24 May 1964, 8 Jan. 1967. Daniel Otun, who first came to Agege in 1919 as one of Jacob Coker's labourers, guided me through some of the intricacies of cocoa farming. Interview, 19 Jan. 1967. I have added to what is known of the family's early history by drawing on Phillip Coker and Anor v. Daniel Coker & Anors., LSCR, Civ. 67, 1913.

I expressed my considerable debt to James Bertin Webster in the preface. It was thanks to Bertin's generosity that I was able to use the Coker Papers (hereafter abbreviated as CP), which he had located and remained uncatalogued. This explains why some of the references that follow lack the identification that was attached to them when the papers were placed in the Nigerian National Archives housed by the University of Ibadan. Bertin published a short note on the subject of this chapter in Webster, 'Agege Plantations and the African Church'.

FIGURE 13.1. Jacob Kehinde Coker. From
James B. Webster, *The African Churches among
the Yoruba, 1888–1922* (Oxford: Clarendon
Press, 1964).

and the couple returned to Lagos, probably in the late 1850s, but stayed only
briefly before moving on to Abeokuta, where they settled. Ajobo became a large-
scale farmer, producing cotton in association with the scheme sponsored by CMS
and employing domestic slaves to do so. He also became a substantial trader, and
in 1870 extended his business from Abeokuta to Lagos. His success earned him
the chiefly title of *Jaguna* of Iporo township. Dotunmu is known for the part she
played in encouraging other Egba to return home. Formally, the pair can be classified as Saro. In practice, missionary influence appears to have been limited to
Ajobo's conversion and involvement in the cotton project and did not extend to
his education; Dotunmu was in Sierra Leone only briefly. But it was their decision to return to Abeokuta that placed them in Yoruba society rather than in the
British world that the Saro elite in Lagos inhabited. The difference was to be
significant in shaping the outlook of their son, Jacob.

Ajobo took several wives and had numerous children, one of whom, Jacob Kehinde, was born in Abeokuta in 1866, the third son of Ajobo's 'lawful native marriage' to Efuyoye.[2] As noted earlier, Jacob's (slightly) older twin brother, James Ojoye, became one of the first Nigerian doctors and married James Davies's daughter, Stella.[3] Jacob was educated at Ake school in Abeokuta and later at Breadfruit School, Lagos, which was sponsored by St. Paul's Church. Jacob gave serious consideration to entering the ministry before deciding on another career in Lagos. The most important formative influence on him beyond his family came from the noted cleric, Rev. James Johnson, who was one of his teachers in Abeokuta and later moved to Lagos. It was there that Johnson's inspirational preaching in the mid-1880s added commitment to Jacob's Christianity. Jacob, who was only nineteen in 1885, was at the outset of his career and was particularly open to new ideas. Johnson's emphasis on the need for Christianity to take account of African societies, their values, and their capacity for innovation, shaped Jacob's own views. Johnson became, and remained, his life-long hero.[4]

From Commerce to Farming

In 1885, Jacob began his career in Lagos as a clerk for the Lagos Warehouse Company, which was one of the leading English firms in Lagos. Very little is known about this phase of his life, apart from the fact that he left the firm in 1892 to begin trading independently.[5] He may have been helped by his father, who had at least three properties in Lagos, including 48 Marina, known as Rose Cottage, which served as the family home in the port. It may also be an indication of Ajobo's regard for Jacob that he placed him 'in possession' of Rose Cottage in 1896.[6] The premises gave him an opportunity to develop his own business, which imported manufactured goods and dealt in produce.[7] Jacob used property in Lagos to borrow money for his business, but did not feature either regularly or prominently in court cases concerning debt. In

2. I have also used a brief and incomplete autobiography written in c.1911–12 and now deposited with the Coker Papers in Ibadan University. An alternative date of birth, 1865, is given in two sources: Webster, *African Churches Among the Yoruba*, p. 161, though without a reference; and *Nigerian Daily Times*, 5 Jan. 1945. The family, however, prefer 1866, which is also on the graveyard tombstone, and given in Macmillan, *Red Book*, p. 114. All the sources listed are reputable but open to error, as is my own judgement, which is to prefer 1866.

3. See above, p. 291.

4. Johnson had a small farm at Agege that Coker managed until Johnson's death in 1917.

5. Macmillan, *Red Book*, p. 114. Evidence that Coker was trading in 1895 is in Coker v. O'Connor Williams, LSCR, Civ. 16, 1895.

6. Phillip Coker and Anor v. Daniel Coker & Anors., LSCR, Civ. 67, 1913. James Osolu Coker, Jacob's father, had bought the property from William Lewis in 1887. It was originally a crown grant issued to Mary Lewis in 1863. LLOR, 38/303, 1903 and 43/262, 1904.

7. Coker v. Somefun, LSCR, Civ. 27, 1902.

1896, he mortgaged land at the corner of Broad Street and Market Street to the Lagos Warehouse Company to secure 'advances of up to £600 in goods'.[8] He repeated the operation in 1899, though this time to borrow £500 from Isaac Williams, and in 1900 to secure his trading account with John Holt.[9] All three mortgages were repaid and the property reconveyed. There appears to be only one example where Jacob was brought to court, and that involved a modest sum of £139 owed to the British firm, Rylands, in 1899.[10] The debt was paid. It is hard to read anything either way from this meagre record. Jacob's business seems to have been at least moderately successful, if also on a relatively small scale. He made no appearance in contemporary records of the large or rising African merchants of the time. But it must be remembered that in 1900 he was still a young man with a long career ahead of him.

Although Jacob had acquired a small farm at Agege in 1893, it remained an adjunct to his Lagos business.[11] In 1896, he asked a friend, Moses Somefun, who was from the same township in Abeokuta and a former employee of Ajobo, to manage the farm for him so that he could concentrate on his mercantile business.[12] Coker paid for Somefun's services by making cash advances that were to be repaid when the farm became profitable. As the arrangement lasted until 1901, it is clear that, at the close of the century, Jacob was set on becoming a merchant rather than a farmer.

In 1903, Jacob changed his mind, devoted himself to farming, and became the most important of the cocoa farmers at Agege, which emerged as the leading centre of diffusion for the new export crop between 1900 and 1920.[13] This sudden change of course requires an explanation. One clue is provided by the history of the family, which was dominated at this time by the ailing health of the patriarch, Ajobo, who died on 4 February 1904, leaving a complex estate, a

8. LLOR, 25/315, 1896.

9. LLOR, 30/422, 1899; 43/262, 1904.

10. Rylands & Sons v. J. K. Coker, LSCR, Civ. 22, 1899. Rylands claimed £195 for 'goods sold and delivered', but were awarded £139 plus costs of £2.11s.

11. Webster, 'Agege Plantations and the African Church', p. 125, notes that Coker had bought land at Agege in 1885. Oyebade Coker, one of Jacob Coker's sons, supplied similar information, which I have been unable to confirm. This does not mean, of course, that it is incorrect. Although Coker referred once to 1890 as being the date he started farming, he stated on three other occasions that the correct date was 1893: Coker draft affidavit for Coker v. Holt, Suit 93, Lagos Supreme Court, 1906; Evidence in Re Public Lands Ordinance: Colonial Secretary v. Ogundimu, LSCR, Civ. 53, 1909; A. W. Shitta v. M. F. Shitta, LSCR, Civ. 1914.

12. Coker v. Somefun, LSCR, Civ. 27, 1902. I am grateful to Mr J. B. Somefun, Moses Somefun's son, for information about the history of the family. Interview, 16 Jan. 1967.

13. Coker's evidence in Re Public Lands Ordinance: Colonial Secretary v. Ogundimu, LSCR, Civ. 53, 1909. What follows is a modified, more detailed, and (I hope) more satisfactory account of the main argument first set out in Hopkins, 'Innovation in a Colonial Context', ch. 5.

large number of children who were still minors, and some unspecified debts.[14] Ajobo's brother, Harry, who became head of the family, died a few months later; he was succeeded by Joseph, the eldest surviving son, but he too died within a year of Ajobo's death. It was then that Jacob qualified to take on his father's formidable obligations and needed the money to do so.[15] In 1903, he raised £1,250 by selling a property at the corner of Broad Street and Market Street to a prominent merchant named Disu Ige. In the following year he mortgaged Rose Cottage to secure an advance of £300 from Isaac Williams.[16] Having just committed himself to his farm at Agege, Jacob found that he also had to spend time in Abeokuta dealing with his father's affairs. Evidently, some delegation was called for because Jacob could not manage Ajobo's farm at Abeokuta, his own farm at Agege, and the business in Lagos simultaneously. He resolved the problem by appointing one brother, Ben, to oversee operations at Abeokuta, and another brother, John, to take charge of his affairs in Lagos.[17]

The arrangement with Ben worked well; the plan for Lagos, however, quickly ran into difficulties. John, who was in sole charge of the Lagos business from October 1903 to December 1905, incurred debts amounting to £2,100 during this short period. The creditors, who were some of the leading European firms, initiated a series of court cases in 1906 and 1907 that tied Jacob into repaying the money he owed from produce shipments.[18] In 1907, Jacob wrote to John Holt saying that he had no money left and 'did nothing in trade at present'.[19] In the following year, he was forced to remortgage Rose Cottage, this time to the rising merchant Josiah Doherty, who advanced £700 at the exceptionally high rate of 15 per cent per annum, which reflected the risks attached to Jacob's affairs at the time.[20] Reviewing the episode a few years later, Jacob had no doubt that John had 'ruined' the business and drained his resources.[21] The disaster had multiple causes, including heavy losses on palm kernels arising from new rules for inspecting produce, robbery, and mismanagement.[22] It took Jacob six years to clear the debt before he

14. Jacob Coker, to Rev. D. Coker, 6 June 1907, CP.

15. Phillip Coker and Anor v. Daniel Coker & Anors., LSCR, Civ. 67, 1913. I would like to thank Chief Adekunle Coker for clarifying the succession to the headship of the family after Ajobo's death.

16. LLOR, 43/262, 1904.

17. Ben Coker to Jacob Coker, 8 July 1904, 28 Dec. 1904, CP. Jacob gave John full authority to manage the business in Lagos on his behalf and confirmed the arrangement later in a power of attorney executed on 17 March 1906, CP.

18. Miller Bros v. Coker, LSCR, Civ. 44, 1906; John Holt v. Coker, ditto, McIver v. Coker, ditto; Paterson Zochonis v. Coker, LSCR, Civ. 48, 1907.

19. Coker to Holt, 7 Nov. 1907, CP.

20. LLOR, 57/75, 1908.

21. Coker to Disu Ige, 10 June 1912, CP.

22. Coker to Paterson Zochonis, 24 April 1907, 8 May 1907; Coker to McIver, 19 June 1907, CP.

could look forward in 1912 to redeeming the mortgage on Rose Cottage from the proceeds of the next cocoa harvest, which he managed to do.[23]

The juxtaposition of commercial debt and export crops might suggest a causal relationship: debt in Lagos led to farming in Agege. A closer look at the chronology, however, suggests otherwise. In September 1903, Jacob settled his Lagos trading account, apart from a small debt of £75 owed to Gaiser, which he paid soon afterwards, and turned the business over to his brother, John. At this point, he had already decided to focus his energies on farming by developing his interest in Agege. His arrangement with John was a consequence of that decision. The debts subsequently incurred by John were an important source of motivation, not because they prompted Jacob to take up farming but because they committed him to continuing it.

Why, then, did Jacob, who seemed set on a mercantile career in 1900, turn to farming in 1903? At this point, the evidence becomes speculative and inferential rather than robust and direct. Two contextual influences can be identified. First, Jacob's business in Lagos was still on a modest scale and conditions for expansion were not propitious, especially at the close of the century, when widespread concern led Governor McCallum to appoint a Commission of Enquiry into the state of trade in Lagos.[24] The *Lagos Weekly Record* summarised the mood of the times in 1897, when it recommended that 'a resort to agriculture offers the only and surest means of livelihood for the community in the future. The keen competition in trade is fast closing this pursuit to native enterprise'.[25] The *Record* did not flinch from exaggeration and on this occasion its generalisation conformed to its norm.[26] Nevertheless, if commercial conditions were not incentives to abandon commerce, they did suggest that the 'palmy days' had passed and that alternatives should be explored. Agriculture had additional merits. According to the *Record*, it was both 'natural' and a means of restoring economic independence.[27] It was also the route to development as exemplified by the United States, which had begun as the 'granary of the world'.[28]

The second influence can be cited with greater confidence. By 1901, Jacob had become one of the leading lay members of St. Paul's Church, Breadfruit, which was the most energetic and innovative of the Anglican churches in Lagos. As Peoples' Warden, he was at the centre of the controversy that led about 800 members of the congregation to secede in 1901 and form their own

23. Coker to Disu Ige, 10 June 1912, CP 2/1; LLOR, 57/75, 75/382, 1912.

24. Denton to Chamberlain, 25 May 1898, C.O. 147/132; and chapter 7 above.

25. *Lagos Weekly Record*, 17 April 1897. The report mentioned the names of a few agricultural pioneers, including James Davies.

26. For a similar statement see *Lagos Standard*, 17 Jan. 1900.

27. *Lagos Weekly Record*, 28 May 1904; *Lagos Weekly Record*, 26 Sept. 1896, *Lagos Standard*, 23 May 1900.

28. *Lagos Weekly Record*, 28 May 1904.

church, which became known as the African Church.[29] The link between secession and farming is not as remote as it may seem at first sight. The founders of the African Church were motivated by matters of government more than by matters of doctrine. In their view, the Anglican mission under the ultra-conservative leadership of Bishop Herbert Tugwell, an expatriate, had failed in its duty to promote Christianity in Africa. The mission's understanding of African societies was limited; its interpretation of biblical truth was inflexible. Consequently, paganism remained largely untouched while Islam was spreading rapidly.

The larger picture, which was clear to the founders of the African Church, was that church and state had disowned the pact that Venn and others had made with the Saro and other converts, whereby the Christian mission in Africa, like the aspiration to achieve economic development, was to be a joint effort undertaken on the basis of equality. Governor Carter's invasion of Yoruba country in 1892 had broken one arm of the compact; the failure to appoint an African successor to Bishop Samuel Ajayi Crowther after his death in 1891, and the subsequent humiliation of the Rev. James Johnson, Coker's hero, broke the other.[30] Assertive racism doused church and state alike and completed the sense of alienation felt by many members of the younger generation of Saro, prominent among them being Jacob Coker.

Reactions among Saro and other converts varied. Some conformed to the new order; others compromised; others still, like Richard Blaize, tried, but failed, to formulate a way of bringing different cultures together.[31] Coker found a route through the dilemma facing educated Saro: he created a society at Agege that was both Christian and African and was committed to economic development without the enterprise becoming a mere subsidiary of the European firms. His solution sprang from his roots in agriculture, which was the basis of the Egba economy; his inspiration derived from his ambition to show that Africans could participate successfully in the modern world on terms that harnessed their own institutions. The venture at Agege was designed to preserve as much independence as possible within an expanding colonial order that was intent on creating subordinate colonial subjects. The inaugural service of the new Church was held at Rose Cottage, the Coker family's residence, in 1901. The text chosen for the sermon, taken from the

29. I follow here Webster, *African Churches among the Yoruba*, p. 77. It should be noted, however, that four years after the event, Jacob Coker stated in court that five to six hundred members had seceded out of a congregation of eight hundred. Evidence in Coates v. Thomas, LSCR, Civ. 41, 1905. See also Akebiyi, 'Jacob Keinde Coker', in J. *Makers of the Church in Nigeria*, pp. 98–115.

30. These matters are fully covered in Webster, *African Churches among the Yoruba*, part 2.

31. See chapter 8.

Song of Solomon, provided an eloquent summary of the motives of the secessionists:

'Look not on me because I am black . . . they made me the keeper of the vineyards; but mine own vineyard I have not kept'.[32]

In 1901, Coker was still only thirty-five years of age. He had a life to make and time to make it. He was no longer in tune with a Church that discriminated against Africans or a government that treated them as inferior subjects rather than as equal participants. He also needed to accumulate enough capital to finance his ambitions. Farming, and on a large scale, was to be the way forward.

The Agege Plantation Complex

Agege lies some 15 miles (24 km) north of Lagos. In the late nineteenth century, it was still a village, though one large enough to give its name to a district that encompassed several even smaller settlements. The area covered by the plantations was contained within an approximate 10-mile (16 km) radius of the town and consisted of seven sub-divisions, the most prominent being Ifako, but included others, notably Adiyan, Akute, Hausa, Iju, Isheri, and Oke Aro, that also produced export crops.[33] Contemporaries commonly used the generic term 'Agege' to apply to the whole district. The precedent will be followed here, though today what might now be called 'old Agege' has been swallowed by the ever-expanding Lagos metropolitan area and would be unrecognisable to the pioneers who colonised the area more than a century ago.

Migrants from Lagos were not the first to settle in Agege. The district, like Ijon, was part of the uncertain borderlands that lay north of Lagos and south of Egba territory. Similarly, some migrants and refugees who represented 'collateral damage' from the Yoruba wars and the predations inflicted by Dahomey had made their homes at Ebute Metta after the *Ifole* in 1867; others settled at Ikeja, a few miles north of Ebute Metta, in the 1870s.[34] Agege was the next stop north from Lagos. The area was not only thinly settled but also, in its way, cosmopolitan: one source claimed that Agege had been founded by Popos, whose territory lay far to the west of Lagos beyond Ouidah, whose motive was also to escape the grip of Dahomey; a number of 'Hausas' from

32. Song of Solomon, i. 6, quoted in Webster, *African Churches among the Yoruba*, p. 77.

33. The settlements listed are those recognised by the Agege Planters Union (APU) as being the seven sub-districts within the orbit of Agege. APU minutes of meeting, 16 Oct. 1908; *Lagos Standard*, 14 Nov. 1908. The list of districts evolved with the passage of time.

34. Manoel Antonio v. Matamuni, LSCR, Civ. 10, 1890; Akisoje v. Jeremiah Sowenimo, LSCR, Civ. 20, 1897.

the distant north had settled in the area too.[35] A handful of Saro from Lagos moved into Agege in the 1870s or even earlier, the first to settle in Ifako being Daddy George Turner.[36] Peter Davies added another dimension to the already diverse community. He was originally from Ekiti, but returned from slavery in the West Indies, and in 1874 was given land at Ifako.[37] The early settlers harvested palm produce and kola nuts, and grew food crops for local consumption. Export crops came later.

Authority over land at Agege was clearer than it was at Ijon. It was generally accepted that the district came under the jurisdiction of Otta, which lay about thirteen miles (21 km) north of Agege in Egba territory. Rights in the borderlands, however, were frequently contested. Some local farmers, for example, asserted that Ifako and Ogba were under Isheri, where Taiwo ruled, but the Lagos court decided that the claim was unfounded.[38] The majority of Saro farmers who acquired land at Agege in the late 1880s and during the 1890s (including Jacob Coker) did so with the permission of Obawole, *Bada* of Otta, or through one of his subordinates.[39] The terms accorded with Yoruba custom: use rights were granted in exchange for presents, which ranged from cases of gin to bags of salt, and an annual gift, typically of corn and yams.[40] Such payments were tokens rather than commercial rents, but were important in acknowledging the continuing rights of the authorities in Otta and their agents in Agege to reassign the land if the occupants departed from the norms of 'good behaviour'.

The terms on which land was held at Agege began to change in the mid-1890s. Relativities shifted, at least for some Lagosians. As commercial difficulties in Lagos continued, agriculture became more attractive: it not only provided security, but also offered the prospect of earning an income from new export crops. Moreover, the Colonial Office had made a key decision in 1895 to build a railway from Lagos to Otta, Abeokuta, and Ibadan

35. *Lagos Weekly Record*, 18 Sept. 1909; Evidence of Peter Davis in Ashade v. Brimah Bashorun, Osho v. Odu, Osho v. Somefun, LSCR, Civ. 17, 1896. 'Hausas' were also farming nearby at Erege: Awudi v. Ashade of Ogba, LSCR, Civ. 19, 1897.

36. Peter Davies, Evidence in Ashade v. Brimah Bashorun, Osho v. Odu, Osho v. Somefun, LSCR, Civ. 17, 1896; evidence of Osho in this case.

37. Peter Davies v. Akidele & Ors, LSCR, Civ. 14, 1894. Peter Davis and James Davies were unrelated. Additional names are given in *Lagos Standard*, 14 Nov. 1908.

38. Evidence of Obawole Bada Ashade v. Brimah Bashorun, Osho v. Odu, Osho v. Somefun, LSCR, Civ. 17, 1896; and Chief Justice Rayner's judgement in Evidence of Obawole Bada Ashade v. Brimah Bashorun, Osho v. Odu, Osho v. Somefun, LSCR, Civ. 18, 1896.

39. Evidence in Ashade v. Brimah Bashorun, Osho v. Odu, Osho v. Somefun, LSCR, Civ. 17, 1896.

40. Evidence in Ashade v. Brimah Bashorun, Osho v. Odu, Osho v. Somefun, LSCR, Civ. 17, 1896.

FIGURE 13.2. The Drive to J. K. Coker's Farm at Ifako in 1964.

FIGURE 13.3. J. K. Coker's Estate House at Ifako (c.1914) in 1964.

FIGURE 13.4. J. K. Coker's Church at Ifako in 1964.

FIGURE 13.5. Samuel A. Jibowu's Estate House at Agege (renovated in the 1930s) in 1964.

in preference to joining Lagos to Ijebu Ode.[41] The attractions of the Agege complex grew commensurately. As the number of newcomers multiplied, land ceased to be abundant and boundary disputes became common.[42] Scarcity increased the value of farms at Agege with the result that, by the turn of the century, land sales had become common. In 1910, the Commissioner of Lands reported that: 'In Lagos itself and the adjoining territory absolute gift, mortgage and sales of land are continually in progress'.[43] Moreover, he added, 'already good farm land with a few miles of Lagos has passed from the original overlords'.[44] In 1913, a further report on land tenure confirmed the trend and showed that monetisation had begun to transform annual gifts into rents. The position was summarised by Dada Oke, a farmer at Agege, in the following way:

> In my part of the country between Agege and Isheri, a lot of cocoa is grown by Aworri and by Lagos people. The latter have asked the Aworri usually for permission to cultivate in the neighbourhood which I know best and pay an annual monetary rent. Some, however, have bought their land outright and we recognise that the purchasers have a right to hold the land they have bought for ever. This is not the proper native custom but it is the result of the white man coming to our country.[45]

Jacob Coker, who gave evidence to the same enquiry, stated that he had first acquired land in 1893 'as was customary, there being no selling in those days'.[46] When buying and selling were introduced, 'since 1898 approximately', he 'preferred to get documentary evidence' and had a deed of sale executed. Land sales had far-reaching implications for customary rights and rules of inheritance.[47] Chiefs lost much of their authority because new landowners were able to entail their land and offer it as security, if they wished. Freehold tenure, assuming the land was retained, enlarged inheritance prospects: land could still be assigned to the deceased's elder brother, but could be

41. Crown Agents to Colonial Office, 31 Oct. 1895, C.O. 147/101; Colonial Office to Carter, 26 Nov. 1895, C.O. 147/101.

42. Evidence of Herbert Macaulay, in Rosanna Coker v. Jacob Coker, LSCR, Civ. 51, 1908.

43. Egerton to Harcourt, 30 May 1911, C.O. 520/103, and report dated 4 Nov. 1910.

44. Commissioner of Lands, 4 Nov. 1910, in Egerton to Harcourt 30 May 1911, C.O. 520/103.

45. The report is in Lugard to Harcourt, 6 March 1913, C.O. 520/123, as is Dada Oke's evidence.

46. This and the subsequent quotation are from Coker's evidence in Lugard to Harcourt, 6 March 1913, C.O. 520/123.

47. Evidence of Frederick Williams and Joseph Odunburu, in Lugard to Harcourt, 6 March 1913, C.O. 520/123.

inherited instead by the first son or daughter (if there were no sons). The trend increased with the influence of Saro farmers, who brought practices that were already established in Lagos to rural communities in Agege.

The process can be followed in detail through the Lands Office records in Lagos, though there is room here to cite only a few examples. A typical conveyance was executed in 1910, when Ige Egun Oniye and others, 'farmers, hunters and representatives of the house of Iyanru', transferred 54 acres of 'good farmland' to Jacob Beckley, a planter from Lagos.[48] The family's representatives, who stated that the land had belonged to their house 'from time immemorial', conveyed the land 'in fee simple' for just over £7 in recognition of Beckley's 'many and several gifts over the years'. The pace of sales increased after the turn of the century, when it became clear that cocoa farming was highly profitable. Large farmers, like Frederick Williams and Jacob Coker, acquired contiguous farms of different sizes through a series of purchases, though the home farm, where the family house was located, was usually on a sizeable piece of land. The market was exceptionally busy in the years preceding the outbreak of war in 1914. In 1911, Fred (as he was known) Williams, acquired at least six plots ranging from 19 to 578 acres. The former was transferred free 'in consideration of the many gifts he has made since 1895'; the latter cost him only £60, a price that took account of the 'several valuable' gifts he had made 'from time to time'.[49] Williams continued to buy land in 1915.[50] The large planters were accompanied by the appearance of increasing numbers of small farmers. When Dada Okin sold 7.5 acres to Isiah Ogundeji for £10 in 1911, his example was one of many that could be cited.[51]

It is impossible to plot changing land values during this period with any precision. Prices and areas can be matched, but the resulting index would exclude considerations of location, soil quality, the value of existing trees and crops, and the indefinable allowance made for existing personal relationships expressed in the 'many gifts' the early purchasers had often made. What can be said is that land rights at Agege were transformed in twenty years: in the early 1890s customary rights were the norm; by the early 1910s, land there had become fully monetised. Before 1900, sales were mostly under £10; by 1914, payments of this order were still common because many newcomers were buying small plots. Simultaneously, though, some substantial payments began to appear in the

48. LLOR, 63/276, 1910.

49. Ige Egun Oniye and Oriyomi Balogun to Williams, LLOR, 72/106, 1911; Owotan and Akilabe to Williams, LLOR, 72/106, 1911; Ogundimu Akereshe & Ors to Williams, LLOR, 72/112, 1911; Ogundimu Akereshe to Williams, LLOR, 72/117, 1911; Dada Ogunwa to Williams, LLOR, 72/128, 1911; Ogunji Aferebiekun to Williams, LLOR, 72/126, 1911.

50. See LLOR, 92/172, 92/203, and 95/216, 1915.

51. LLOR, 73/219, 1911.

records: £100 for 50 acres at Ifako in 1911 and £260 for 18.5 acres at Iju in 1915.[52] What emerged was a patchwork of farms and a hierarchy of farmers. The large farmers, who referred to themselves as 'planters', pioneered the sale of land beyond Lagos and dominated Agege. The small farmers, however, pointed the way to the future. The typical cocoa farm in the twentieth century was smaller than ten acres and depended on household labour.

Agege commended itself because its soils, like those at Ijon, were more suitable for tree crops, such as coffee and cocoa, than were the sandy soils closer to the coast. Moreover, Agege occupied a plateau that was crossed by several streams but also retained water, which enabled tree crops to survive during periods of drought. The Iju River, a small tributary of the Owo, and other streams meandered down to the Lagos lagoon. They were not ideal waterways, but canoes had advantages for transporting bulk produce, as they did at Ijon. The Otta Road, the old caravan route that joined the port to the far north and ran through some of the Agege farms, was also used. In 1897, however, the Lagos railway was opened to Agege on a trial basis and cut the travel time to thirty-five minutes.[53] The advantages were not realised immediately because freight rates were too high to attract bulk traffic, but the potential was undeniable.[54] Political connections were also a consideration. Otta came under Egba jurisdiction and many of the early planters from Lagos were Egba with family members in Abeokuta.[55] Although Governor Glover denied that the Egba had rights to Otta, he never pressed the point. Instead, he created a border that made Agege, like Ijon, a neutral zone.[56] In practice, the settlers could combine the advantages of having links with Abeokuta with access to British law in Lagos. As a last resort, they could also call on the colonial government for support. This option was solidified after 1892, when Governor Carter subdued Ijebu and took effective control of most of Yoruba country. By the close of the century, Agege had become more accessible and more attractive to newcomers.

The Farming Community

Other planters from Lagos had already decided to make Agege their principal base before Jacob Coker committed himself fully to farming in 1903. During the 1890s, the first planters, including Coker, experimented with several export crops, as did James Davies at Ijon during the 1880s, while giving priority to

---

52. John Olawunmi George to James Karunwi, LLOR, 73/286, 1911; Idowu Afagidi to Adolphus Martins, LLOR, 95/216, 1915.

53. *Lagos Standard*, 23 June 1897.

54. The problem had not been resolved in 1905. C.A. to C.O. 7 Nov. 1905, C.O. 147/177.

55. I am grateful to Chief *Alhaji* Shittu, *Seriki* of Otta, for confirming and amplifying aspects of Otta's history in the nineteenth century. Interview, Otta, 24 May 1964.

56. As drawn by Governor Glover in 1867. Glover to Blackall, 17 Jan. 1868, C.O. 147/14.

coffee and cotton.[57] After the turn of the century, however, and in response to international prices and competition, they made cocoa their principal product, a position it retained for the next twenty years.[58] In 1904, a survey of Ifako, one of Agege's main sub-districts, showed that eleven farmers there had 158,000 cocoa trees and 132,000 coffee trees between them.[59] Other crops, such as kola (8,850) and rubber (8,400), were far behind; cotton occupied 595 acres. Although Coker did not appear on that list, we know that by 1907 he had planted 30,000 cocoa trees and that 6,500 of these were bearing fruit in 1908.[60] The only farmer who owned a larger number was Rufus Wright, with 40,000 trees. The other important omission from the list was maize, which was grown for export as well as for sale in local markets and was far more remunerative than cotton was.[61] Gerald Dudgeon, the head of the Forestry and Agriculture Department, recognised the distinctive position of this group of farmers in 1906, when he noted that by then there were 'several small cocoa plantations in the southern part of the Protectorate, the best being at Agege'.[62]

The survey of Ifako in 1904, though incomplete, is valuable because there are few systematic attempts to correlate planters, acres, and crops in Agege. The principal planters there can be identified only by using a range of sources that combine broad accuracy with unavoidable imprecision. On this basis, a small group, headed by Jacob Coker, occupied the top of the hierarchy. Although Coker had been farming at Ifako since 1893, it was only after 1903 that he emerged as the leading figure there. He added to the modest thirty-five acres he already had at Ifako by buying land at Ajokoro, Iju, Alakasi, Agbado, and Ifo, where he founded Coker Market. By 1914, he owned more than 1,000 acres in the district.[63]

It is revealing to see how Coker managed to assemble these acquisitions, given that most of the proceeds from his sales of export crops were assigned to his creditors. Although land was still cheap, capital costs, such as clearing forest land and building a farmhouse, had to be found, and running costs, especially wages for labourers, had to be met. Jacob was in a much better position than most of the Agege planters because he had property in Lagos, notably Rose Cottage, which was on a prime site on the Marina, and could be offered

57. *Lagos Standard*, 14 Nov. 1908

58. Thorburn to Elgin, 28 June 1907, C.O. 520/47, and Thorburn to Crewe, 25 May 1909, C.O. 520/79, describe the decisions that led Agege to settle on cocoa as its main export. See *Lagos Standard*, 14 Nov. 1908.

59. Moseley to Lyttelton, 11 June 1904, C.O. 147/170.

60. Coker's evidence in Public Lands Ordinance: Colonial Secretary v. Ogundimu, LSCR, Civ. 53, 1909.

61. *Lagos Weekly Record*, 22 Oct. 1904.

62. G. C. Dudgeon to Under-Secretary of State, 28 April 1906, CSO, 12/25/34.

63. This information is drawn mainly from the Lagos Lands Office records and from information supplied by Mr Oyebade Coker, Jacob Coker's son.

as security.[64] In 1903, he used Rose Cottage to raise a loan of £360 from the Saro financier, Isaac Williams. He mortgaged Rose Cottage again in 1908, this time borrowing £700 at 15 per cent from the Saro merchant, Josiah Doherty, and repeated the exercise in 1912, this time securing an advance of £1,000 at a rate of 10 per cent. In 1913, he used the same security to borrow £1,250 from the 'Brazilian' financier, Candido da Rocha, at 10 per cent, and in 1917 he borrowed £1,000 from BBWA, also at a rate of 10 per cent. Jacob also mobilised two less valuable properties in Lagos: in 1911, he raised £150 on the security of land in Bamgbose Street and leased property in Oke Olowogbowo to Miller Bros for five years at a rent of £36 per annum.[65] The most interesting contract was agreed in 1912, when Jacob mortgaged his small Ifako farm 'with all rights, buildings, crops' to Miller Bros. to secure a loan of £200 at 6 per cent.[66] This is one of the first examples of a British firm being willing to advance money outside Lagos and on farmland owned by an African. Agege's credit rating had definitely risen.

By 1910, Jacob Coker's own credit rating had also improved. In the years immediately after 1903, he was raising money to keep his commercial affairs afloat and dealing with his obligations as Ajobo's successor, and had limited funds to help finance other activities at Agege. As his burden of debt eased, however, he was able to expand export production, assist other Agege farmers, and promote the African Church. As his assets grew and his repayment record attested to his reliability, lenders reduced the interest rates they charged. A few other Lagos planters, such as Fred Williams, raised money on property in Lagos, but they were unable to mobilise finance on the scale that Jacob could because none owned property in one of the town's prime sites.[67] The clearest indication of Jacob's new-found prosperity came in 1912, when a family meeting agreed to divide Ajobo's estate.[68] Jacob submitted a claim against the estate of £1,954, which included the cost of maintaining and educating Ajobo's children, but compensated the family by offering inflated prices for the assets: £2,000 for Rose Cottage (value £1,640), £150 for the property at Olowogbowo (£125), £600 for Adatan House, Abeokuta (£160), and £800 for Kemta House, also in Abeokuta (£225). The net balance of £1,800 was to be shared equally among Ajobo's children. The offer was accepted. Jacob was not only head of the family but had also become a Big Man, and the biggest in Agege.

The scale, ambition, and affluence of the Agege farmers on the eve of World War I are attested by the now rare visual record of their estates in figures 13.2–13.5. Jacob Coker's own house was long past its best in 1964, when

64. The following examples are all taken from the file on 48 Marina: LLOR, LO 2447. 38/303, 57/75, 75/382, 83/142, 86/297, 120/26, 104/420.

65. LLOR, 74/174, 75/187.

66. LLOR, 75/187.

67. For Williams, see LLOR, 57/241, 81/428.

68. Minutes of family meetings, 5 Sept. 1912, 10 Oct. 1912, CP 1/10.

the photo was taken, but its size and substance are evidence of how it must have looked during the prosperous years before the war, when it was built. Visitors approaching the house on the long driveway flanked by kola trees would surely have been impressed when they arrived. Fortunately, the survival of Samuel Jibowu's estate house in good condition enables historians to add realism to conjecture. The Agege farmers continued to devote resources to maintaining the churches on their estates, despite the region's declining fortunes in and after the 1920s. The African Church on Jacob Coker's farm was one among several that were still well attended and in fine condition in the 1960s. In this case, religion outlasted capitalism.

There was more to Coker's predominance than his access to finance. Contemporary accounts show that he was blessed with qualities that would have made him stand out in other times and places. His abilities exceeded his education. His publications revealed a capacity to analyse as well as to record; his speeches demonstrated skill in holding an audience; his public debates displayed mental agility and astuteness.[69] He was an innovator who was always looking for fresh ideas. He had a keen interest in industrial education that would encourage diversification, in machinery that would reduce processing costs, and in novelties like motor vehicles that would cut transport rates. He gave substance to his commitment in 1916 by founding an Industrial Institute at Agege, which offered training in mechanical as well as agricultural skills. The colonial government soon regarded him as the 'go to' person where agricultural affairs were concerned, and sought his advice on wider issues relating to Yoruba life and values.[70] If this were not enough for one person, Coker had an engaging as well as a commanding presence, unlimited energy, and a degree of generosity that added popularity to his influence.

Coker stood at the head of an assorted farming community. A small number of planters with varied but sizeable farms formed Coker's inner circle. His closest associates were headed by Frederick Ephraim Williams (1867–1918), and included Joseph Ogunola Beckley (1862–1923), Samuel Alexander Jibowu (1862–1928), and Moses Odeyinka Somefun (1862–1929). The members of this group were all Egba, who came either from Iporo Ake (as did Coker) or the adjacent township of Ijeun, and were born within a few years of each other in the 1860s. Coker, Beckley, Jibowu, and Somefun were all educated at Ake school, Iporo. Williams was educated in Lagos because his family moved there after the

---

69. Several of Coker's papers, including 'Polygamy Defended' (1915), are reproduced in Dada, *Jacob Kehinde Coker*. Coker also wrote an incomplete 'History of the African Church' (1941), which is deposited with the Coker Papers in the National Archives, University of Ibadan.

70. For example: Colonial Secretary to Coker, 13 Dec. 1907, inviting him to join a committee charged with preparing samples of production for the Franco-British Exhibition, CP; Coker to Governor General (draft paper, 1913) on the difference between pawning and *iwofa*.

Ifole in 1867. All of them were Christians and members of the Anglican Church; all of them joined the African Church when it was formed in 1901 or shortly afterwards. Many of them increased these affiliations through ties of marriage.[71]

Coker and his associates from Abeokuta were also Egba patriots who found themselves compelled to adjust to political upheaval in their homeland.[72] The Egba had managed to hold on to their independence after the colonial government invaded the Ijebu in 1892. However, there was a price to be paid. The British insisted on reforms that resulted in the creation of the Egba United Government (EUG) in 1898.[73] From one perspective, the new structure was an attempt to unite established and progressive elites behind a policy of cautious modernisation that would uphold independence and keep the British at bay. From another viewpoint, by increasing centralisation and elevating the power of the ruler (the *Alake*), the EUG altered the internal balance of power and provided a mechanism that allowed the British to exercise a degree of indirect rule over the Egba state. The period after 1898 was one of tension and occasional crises shaped by an internal struggle for power and external pressure, real and imagined, from the British. In 1914, the British stepped in, abolished the EUG, and incorporated the Egba into the new colony of Nigeria.[74] The loss of independence left many Egba patriots, including leading figures at Agege, with feelings of disaffection and distrust at what they regarded as Britain's arbitrary exercise of power. The world envisaged by Henry Venn and his contemporaries had already receded: Lugard drove it out of sight.

Although no other group in Agege was tied together by comparable layers of overlapping connections, most farmers had some ties with Coker or members of his inner circle. One self-selecting cluster were clergy of the new African Church, who farmed, typically on a small scale, to supplement their incomes. Samuel A. Coker, a curate at St. Paul's Church who was one of the leaders of the schism in 1901, was one; Joseph Fanimokun, who acquired farms at Agege in 1901 and 1902, was another.[75] Other clergymen who farmed at Agege included

71. For example, Daniel Sasegbon's sister, Bernice, married Jacob Coker.

72. One of them, Samuel Jibowu, was appointed Supervisor of the Customs Department with the EUG in 1907. Clerk of Council, Abeokuta to Jibowu, 31 Jan. 1907, CP. I am grateful to Mrs S. Peters, Samuel Jibowu's daughter, for help with the history of the family. Interview, Lagos, 23 Feb. 1962.

73. Pallinder-Law, 'Aborted Modernisation'; and the author's full account in her still unsurpassed Ph.D. dissertation, which I had the privilege of examining: 'Government in Abeokuta'.

74. On the colonial government's satisfaction with the outcome, see the telling quotation in Pallinder-Law, 'Government in Abeokuta', p. 93.

75. The range of Cokers can baffle outsiders. Samuel A. Coker was unrelated either to Jacob Coker or to the merchant Samuel A. Coker, who helpfully presented himself as S. Alfred Coker to avoid confusion. On Fanimokun, see J. S. Williams v. Owoshebi & Anor, LSCR, Civ. 79, 1917. Archdeacon J. Olumide Lucas informed me that Fanimokun lost his job as a teacher because he spent too much time on his farms. Interview, Lagos, 5 Feb. 1962.

David Hughes, an Egba who was a founder member of the UNA, which, in doctrinal terms, was only a short step away from the African Church.

A much larger cohort of small farmers were connected to Coker and Williams by their need for working capital. Some, like Odedeyi Olowu, who farmed 24 acres, were already established in the area. He was baptised, joined the African Church after Coker became fully resident in Agege, and was instructed by Fred Williams in how to grow cocoa.[76] Others, like Joseph Odunburo, were refugees from the hinterland wars who had few resources. They acquired small plots, often with Coker's help, and tended to follow the lead of the Big Men in becoming members of the African Church and planting cocoa.[77] Others, still, had developed connections with members of important families as a result of long service. Fred Williams helped James Akinduro, his head labourer, who was also a member of the African Church, to establish his own farm. Similarly, Jacob Coker settled Ismail Abatan, a 'Hausa' and one of his father's former slaves, on land that was then transferred to him.[78]

Finally, there was a miscellaneous group who were friends with Coker and his circle but were largely independent of them. Rufus Wright (1856–1907), who held nearly one thousand acres at Ifako, began as a part-time farmer in 1891 but made it his principal occupation after the turn of the century.[79] His family came from Ijeun, Abeokuta, and settled in Lagos, where Rufus was born and educated. His father was the Anglican vicar of St. Peter's Broad Street. Rufus, too, remained a committed Anglican. Daniel Sasegbon (1870–1955) was from Abeokuta and was related to Jacob Coker by marriage, but spent most of his career in the colonial service as a customs officer. He did not settle in Agege until 1918, long after the pioneers.[80] He was a small farmer, but he had the distinction of bringing the Anglican Church to Agege. David Taylor (1865–1932), an Egba from Owu and an Anglican, was a successful merchant in Lagos who had inherited a farm at Ifako after the death of his father in 1891.[81] He ran the farm as a business rather than as a weekend retreat, and in 1904 was listed as being among the eleven most important farmers there.[82] Similarly, Josiah Doherty,

---

76. Information supplied by Odedeyi Olowu's son, Mr J. T. Odedeyi, Iju, Agege, 15 Jan. 1967.

77. Information supplied by Chief Adekunle Coker, Lagos, 8 Jan. 1967.

78. Information supplied by Chief Adekunle Coker, Lagos, 8 Jan. 1967. 'Hausa' was a term used generally to refer to northerners who were (typically) Muslims.

79. I am grateful to Mrs J. O. Smith, Rufus Wright's daughter, for information about her father. Ibadan, 23 March 1962, 9 May 1962. See also *Lagos Weekly Record*, 2 Feb. 1907.

80. I am grateful to Dr A. O. Sasegbon, Daniel's son, for information about the family. Ikeja, 27 April 1964.

81. *Lagos Times*, 23 May 1891; McCallum to Chamberlain, 23 Sept. 1897, CSO 1/1/19, enc. 1.

82. Moseley to Lyttelton, 11 June 1904, C.O. 147/170. A sketch of Taylor's career is given on pp. 329–32 above.

whose family came from Ilaro in Egbado territory, inherited two farms from his father and maintained them with the help of a manager.[83]

Thomas Dawodu (1871–1920) possessed a special quality that made him a valuable contact for Coker and other farmers: he had received training in tropical agriculture at Kew Gardens and in Jamaica. Dawodu, who came from a prominent Lagos family, spent his career as a government employee.[84] He entered the colonial service in 1890, following Governor Moloney's initiative to promote tropical agriculture, and became Assistant Curator at the Botanic Station. He held the position until resigning in 1910 to become a full-time farmer. Dawodu acquired a small farm at Agege in 1902 and joined the African Church in 1905.[85] He exchanged advice and seeds with Coker for more than twenty years.[86]

One other member of this group of independent farmers deserves particular mention because his presence at Agege represented a trend in land use that was very different from that of Coker and his circle. Joseph Egerton Shyngle (1861–1926) was an eminent lawyer who also became a prominent politician.[87] His family, which was originally from Ilesha, followed a route that was familiar in taking them from slavery to Freetown, but unusual in that they then moved to the Gambia, where Joseph was born. The family were Methodists, as was Joseph: the African Churches did not tempt him. He was educated in Sierra Leone, Oxford, and London. He was called to the Bar in 1888 and decided to practise law in Lagos, where he settled in 1892.[88] He established a farm called 'Gambia Plantation' at Ifako at the close of the 1890s, and by 1904 had planted twenty thousand cocoa trees and five thousand coffee trees on about 250 acres.[89] Egerton Shyngle was an outlier: he was a familiar figure in Lagos high society and an absentee planter who took up farming as

83. Information from Josiah Doherty's son, Theophilus Adebayo Doherty, Lagos 14 Dec. 1961; Moseley to Lyttelton, 11 June 1904, C.O. 147/170.

84. *Lagos Weekly Record*, 29 May 1920; A. W. Shitta v. M. F. Shitta & Ors., LSCR, Civ. 73, 1914; Moloney to Knutsford, 8 July 1890, C.O. 147/75; Thorburn to Crewe, 4 March 1909, C.O. 520/78; Thorburn to Crewe, 31 May 1909, C.O. 147/79; Egerton to Crewe, 29 March 1909, C.O. 520/92.

85. African civil servants were allowed to take part-time employment outside the colonial service to compensate for the low pay they received.

86. Valuable details of Dawodu's career are listed in a memo written by the Assistant Colonial Secretary, Lagos, dated 22 Jan 1910 and contained in C.S.O. 12/29/8.

87. Egerton Shyngle became Leader of the Nigerian Bar and was the first President of the Nigerian National Democratic Party. Deniga, *Nigerian Who's Who, 1919*, pp. 14–15; *Nigerian Pioneer*, 19 March 1926. I am grateful to three of Joseph's children, Miss G. Shyngle, Mrs B. A. Byass, and Mr George Egerton Shyngle, for helping me with some of the details of their father's life. Interview, Lagos 1 March 1962.

88. Shyngle v. Shyngle, LSCR, Civ. 101, 1923. I have preferred the date from this source to the one given by Deniga (1892) in the previous note.

89. Moseley to Lyttelton, 11 June 1904, C.O. 147/170. He was also growing smaller amounts of kola, rubber, and cotton. Wotton v. Shyngle, LSCR, Civ. 94, 1921.

a hobby, employed a manager (from Abeokuta) and visited the farm occasionally at weekends. His lifestyle and purpose were very different from those of
Coker's group.[90] Yet, in an unplanned way, he too was an innovator. He was
instrumental not only in promoting freehold tenure in Agege but also in starting a trend for acquiring weekend retreats there.[91] As Lagos expanded and
affluence increased, rising numbers of relatively wealthy Lagosians acquired
conveyances for 'country places' in Agege.

The more diverse the Agege farmers are seen to be, the harder generalisations about them become. The distinction drawn here between opinion leaders and followers, innovators and imitators, has identified the close ties that
united the pioneers and gave them a degree of coherence and effectiveness that
they would otherwise not have possessed. It is possible to go further than this
and suggest a characteristic that extended beyond Coker's immediate circle. A
majority of the early Lagosian farmers at Agege were educated Christians whose
values and aspirations had been shaped by the progressive ethos of Victorian
England, yet whose achievements fell short of their expectations. Individual circumstances, as always, enter the explanation, but structural considerations are
needed to account for the fortunes and the motives that characterised many of
the early farmers. The most important contextual influences were formed by the
adverse commercial environment of the 1890s, and the subsequent expansion
of colonial rule, which made it harder for Africans to achieve senior positions in
Church or state.[92] These circumstances were not fixed throughout the colonial
period, but they applied at a moment when a whole generation of young, educated Africans were hoping to build successful careers.

Jacob Coker's experience illustrates the argument; other farmers supplemented it. Fred Williams had an unhappy start as a clerk for Voigt & Co. In
1888, he was charged with embezzlement, acquitted, and then dismissed![93]
He ran his own business during the 1890s but, like many others, was badly
affected by the downturn in trade at the close of the century. A series of court
judgements between 1898 and 1902 showed that he had accumulated debts
of nearly £1,000 to four European firms.[94] Williams had begun to farm at
Agege in 1893, but it was only after his commercial setbacks that he became

90. Except, arguably, that he was a polygamist.
91. On the former, see Fred Williams's evidence in A. W. Shitta v. M. F. Shitta, LSCR,
Civ. 73, 1914.
92. For a succinct statement of these changes, see Mann, *Marrying Well*, pp. 23–4.
93. Voigt v. Williams, LSCR, Civ. 8, 1888. I am grateful to Mr Ladipo Williams, Frederick's son, for assistance with the history of the family and of Iju. Interview Iju, 16 Jan. 1967.
See also *Lagos Weekly Record*, 5 May 1917, 2 and 30 Nov. 1918; *Lagos Standard*, 13 and 27
Nov. 1918.
94. Witt & Busch v. Williams, LSCR, Civ. 20, 1898; Rylands & Sons v. Williams, LSCR,
Civ. 21, 1898; Pickering & Berthoud v. Williams, LSCR, Civ. 26, 1901; M. D. Elliot v. Williams,
LSCR, Civ. 27, 1902.

a full-time farmer.[95] Rufus Wright was in a similar position.[96] In the early 1890s, he was the Lagos agent for Cornelius Moore, the Egba merchant in Abeokuta.[97] He then transferred to Ollivants, an English firm, but was replaced by an English agent in 1899. Between 1900 and 1902, he incurred debts amounting to £2,503, and had to sell large parcels of land on Ebute Metta to help settle with his creditors.[98] Wright started farming at Agege in 1889, but like Williams, made it his full-time occupation after the turn of the century.

Moses Somefun, who was a clerk for the German firm, Gaiser, in the early 1890s, left in 1896 to manage Jacob Coker's farm at Agege, as well as his own.[99] The arrangement proved to be unsatisfactory. In 1901, when the contract ended, Jacob won an action for debt against Moses.[100] It was then that Moses concentrated fully on his own farm, which he had first acquired in 1890. Lourenço Cardoso, one of the few 'Brazilians' who took up cocoa farming, did so in 1908 in response to the decline of trade between Lagos and Latin America.[101] Another rarity was Mohammed Bello Fashola, a substantial Muslim trader who gave up his business in Lagos and bought several farms in Agege in 1914 to compensate for the expulsion of Gaiser, which had been his main commercial contact in Europe.[102]

David Hughes, Joseph Beckley, Samuel Jibowu, Thomas Dawodu, and Daniel Sasegbon occupied a different category. They were not aspiring merchants who had run into difficulties, but men who experienced frustrations in searching for purposeful careers. Hughes's hopes of a career in teaching ended when he was dismissed by the CMS.[103] He became a clerk for the merchant, Zachariah Williams, in the mid-1880s, when that business was in rapid

95. See his evidence in A. W. Shitta v. M. F. Shitta, LSCR, Civ. 73, 1914.

96. I am grateful to Mr J. B. Somefun, Moses's son, for help with the family's history. Interview, Lagos, 16 Jan 1967.

97. Wright v. Z. A. Williams & John Walkden, LSCR, Civ. 11, 1891.

98. BBWA v. Olubi and Wright, LSCR, Civ. 21, 1898; Ollivant v. Wright, LSCR, Civ. 25, 1900; I. B. Williams v. Wright, LSCR, Civ. 25, 1901; Rylands v. Wright, LSCR, Civ. 27, 1902; C. B. Moore v. Wright, LSCR, Civ. 27, 1902. His land sales and those of his wife, Felicia, between 1906 and 1912 can be followed in the Lands Office records.

99. Coker v. Somefun, LSCR, Civ. 27, 1902; Interview with Mr J. B. Somefun, Moses's son, Lagos, 16 Jan. 1967.

100. Coker v. Somefun, LSCR, Civ. 27, 1902.

101. Information from Lourenço Cardoso's son, Mr P. W. O. Cardoso. Lagos 14 Feb. 1962, 16 Feb. 1962; Macmillan, *Red Book*, p. 110; Thomas, 'News Diary', 5 Jan. 1938, pp. 261–3; 20 July 1938, p. 350.

102. I am grateful to Mohammed Fashola's sons, Mr Shaffi Fashola and Mr Sadike Fashola, for this information. Lagos, 9 June 1962.

103. I am grateful to David Hughes's son, Mr W. Hughes, for information about his father. Interview, Ebute Metta, 24 Feb. 1962. See also evidence in Wright v. Z. A. Williams and John Walkden, LSCR, Civ. 11, 1891; Williams v. Hughes, LSCR, Civ. 17, 1896; Ashade v. Brimah Bashorun & Ors, LSCR, Civ. 17, 1896; *Nigerian Daily Times*, 8 Aug. 1936.

decline, before becoming a commission agent for the planter Fred Williams in the 1890s. None of these positions appeared to produce a future worth working for, but Hughes found his purpose by becoming a founder member of the UNA in 1891 and the means of achieving it by converting the small farm he acquired in the early 1890s to cocoa in the early 1900s. Beckley became a produce buyer in Lagos for Jacob Coker in the 1890s. When Coker moved to Agege in 1903, Beckley saw a chance to improve his own prospects and followed him there in 1906. With Coker's help, he was able to buy his own farm, where he made cocoa the chief crop. Jibowu was close to both Beckley and Coker.[104] He, too, became a produce buyer in Lagos before becoming Supervisor of the Customs Department at the EUG in 1907. Mounting tensions within the EUG caused him to resign in 1910 and devote himself to the small farm in Agege he had bought with Coker's help. Jibowu's ambitions were fulfilled by his cocoa farm and, exceptionally, by music. He was a noted organist whose skills were in demand among the churches that sprang up on the Agege plantations.

Thomas Dawodu and Daniel Sasegbon were civil servants whose ambitions were limited by a policy that reserved the most senior posts for Europeans. Dawodu remained an Assistant Curator throughout his career, which saw the formation and expansion of Forestry and Agricultural Departments in Nigeria. In 1910, he refused to be transferred to Calabar on the grounds that the request breached his terms of service.[105] The governor's office responded by recommending that he be dismissed. The Secretary of State rejected the request and instructed Lagos to suspend Dawodu for four months with loss of pay. The governor then attempted to transfer Dawodu permanently, at which point he responded by asking to be allowed to retire without loss of pension. To its considerable credit, the Colonial Office reviewed the case, censured the Lagos officials, and allowed Dawodu's request. Antrobus minuted: 'This is persecution. The right is wholly on Dawodu's side'.[106] It was then that Dawodu became a full-time farmer. Sasegbon remained Assistant Chief Clerk in the Customs Department for most of his career. While on leave, he had a dispute over his salary in 1912 that went as far as the Secretary of State, who ruled against him.[107] It is impossible to say how far this episode, and perhaps others, dented Sasegbon's hopes of promotion. We do know, however, that he was

104. I am grateful to Mrs J. Peters and Mrs C. O. Bright, two of Samuel Jibowu's daughters, for providing information about their father. Interviews, Lagos, 23 Feb. 1962. Clerk of Council, Abeokuta to Jibowu, 31 Jan. 1907, CP.

105. Thorburn to Crewe, 4 March 1909, C.O. 520/78 and 31 May 1909, C.O. 520/79; Egerton to Crewe, 29 March 1910, C.O. 520/92.

106. Antrobus minute, 26 April 1910, on Egerton to Crewe, 29 March 1910, C.O. 520/92.

107. Boyle to Harcourt, 19 Sept. 1912, C.O. 520/1116. Governor Clifford later commended his 'loyal and faithful service'. Clifford to Secretary of State, 6 Jan. 1920, C.O. 583/84.

a committed Christian who found fulfilment in managing his small farm at
Agege and bringing Anglicanism to the area.[108]

The Agege Planters' Union

The continuing difficulties facing staple exports in the 1890s prompted the
colonial government to revive Governor Moloney's initiative, which had led to
the foundation of the Botanic Station in 1887. At the close of the 1890s, agriculture, forestry, and botanical matters were covered by one small department.
In 1903, the government supplemented the existing institution by sponsoring
an Agricultural Union, which was given the task of fostering new products and
improving existing ones.[109] Jacob Coker and Rufus Wright were among those
nominated to be members of the council of the Union. The Agege farmers
already had the best possible contact in the Botanic Station, where Thomas
Dawodu was Assistant Curator. They also had specific needs that were not
covered by the Agricultural Union. Consequently, in 1907 the planters decided
to form their own organisation, the Agege Planters' Union (APU).[110] They
continued to be represented on the council of the Agricultural Union and
added to the pressure to form a separate Department of Agriculture, which
was established in 1908. In supporting the proposal, Governor Egerton drew
attention to the 'great interest which the planters in the country have been taking in scientific agriculture in recent years'.[111] The new department acted as a
complement to the APU, which remained the principal body co-ordinating the
activities of farmers in Agege.

There were compelling reasons for seeking cooperative solutions to fundamental issues arising from mobilising land, raising capital, attracting labour,
and improving entrepreneurial skills. The leading farmers took the initiative in
forming the APU and held the main offices: David Hughes was elected chair and
subsequently president; Jacob Coker held the key position of secretary. Other
pioneer farmers, headed by Fred Williams, backed the initiative and remained

108. Sasegbon began farming in 1911. He had about 28 acres at Agege and about the
same at Abori (six miles from Agege). He remained in the Customs Department until 1927,
when he retired and devoted himself to his farm and the church he had built on his land at
Agege. I am indebted to Dr A. O. Sasegbon, Daniel's son, for this information. Interview,
Ikeja, 27 April 1964.

109. McGregor to Chamberlain, 30 Nov. 1903, C.O. 147/167; *Lagos Weekly Record*, 28
Nov. 1903; *Lagos Annual Reports, 1899–1905* (Agricultural Supplement No. 1), C.O. 149/5.

110. The history of the APU can be told, not through official documents, but from its
own surviving records, which are in the Coker Papers. See above n. 1. The APU continued
to be represented on the council of the Agricultural Union.

111. The Departments of Agriculture and Forestry. Egerton to Crewe, 16 June 1908,
C.O. 520/61. In formal terms, the APU was incorporated into the Agricultural Union,
though without compromising its independence. Henry Carr to J. K. Coker, 9 June
1908, CP.

among the APU's most consistent and active supporters.[112] Yet, the APU was also an inclusive organisation: in 1908, it had 298 members drawn from the seven main districts of Agege; in 1909, the number had risen to 308.[113] It was also democratic: the constitution gave members equal voting rights and made the Union's officers accountable by requiring them to be elected (or re-elected) annually.[114] co-operation depended on consent; sanctions were limited and had to be agreed and not imposed from above. Moreover, the variety of the membership is striking: there was no discrimination among Christian denominations; numerous 'Hausas' (Muslims) and others were also members.[115] The only qualification required was to be a farmer in the Agege district.

To some extent, inclusivity was instrumental: to be effective, the APU needed to be representative. But there was more to the policy than that. Coker and his allies aimed to build a new community, not to create a privileged enclave. Accordingly, he and the APU assisted farmers who were not members of the African Church to secure land, helped with or suspended the membership fee of those who were struggling, and offered small loans at low or zero interest rates. Additionally, the APU accepted social responsibilities, raising money for funerals, helping to settle disputes, and supervising the farms of members who were temporarily ill or absent. It was also willing to confront the government, as it did in 1908, when a scheme for using the Iju River to create supply of fresh water for Lagos caused alarm among some Agege farmers who feared that their land would be expropriated.[116]

Land continued to be acquired by seeking permission from the local authorities. The difference between the 1890s and the 1900s, as has been shown, was that land values had risen and customary tenure was being replaced by freehold grants.[117] The APU assisted newcomers not only by introducing them to existing land-holders but also by helping them financially. The purchase price of land, however, was only one component of the financial requirements of cocoa farming. Working capital was also required to ease liquidity problems arising from the need for cash at the beginning of the season to pay the labour force, while export earnings were received only when the harvested crop was delivered for sale. In 1905, Sir Alfred Jones, the Liverpool shipping magnate, suggested forming an agricultural bank that could advance cash to farmers.[118] Frederick Lugard, then High Commissioner of the

112. Minutes of the first meeting held to discuss the formation of the APU, 5 July 1907; minutes of first committee meeting, 20 July 1907; minutes of committee meeting, 17 Aug. 1907, all in CP.

113. List of members, 16 Oct. 1908, CP; *Lagos Standard*, 1 Sept. 1909.

114. APU 2nd annual report, *Lagos Standard*, 1 Sept. 1909.

115. There were fifty 'Hausa' members of the APU in 1912.

116. *Lagos Standard*, 1 Sept. 1909.

117. Lugard to Harcourt, 6 March 1913, C.O. 520/123.

118. A. L. Jones to Under-Secretary of State, C.O. 147/176.

Northern Nigeria Protectorate, opposed the idea, saying that it was neither 'feasible nor desirable'.[119] In his opinion, loans would lead to increased debt and be 'frittered' on consumer goods. The military mind was not well attuned to issues of economic development.

Self-finance was the only option. The APU itself had no independent sources of finance and continued to rely on funding from the large farmers, especially Coker and Williams. As noted earlier, Coker had the unequalled advantage of owning a valuable property on the Marina that he mortgaged, in the event continuously, to fund his activities at Agege. This source made him the community's principal financier. The link between Lagos property and the development of Agege was crucial both to the expansion of cocoa farming and to Jacob Coker's personal dominance of the farming community. He stood at the head of an intricate network of finance, lending money he had borrowed to smaller farmers and easing the acute liquidity problems they all faced. All bets were placed on the cocoa harvest to settle cash advances. There was a constant exchange of small sums to ease cash-flow problems. Coker himself was often short of money for immediate purposes. In 1909, for example, Joseph Beckley, who was usually a borrower, sent Coker £2 to help him out of a short-term difficulty.[120] In 1913, Jacob wrote to Fred Williams thanking him for lending money to Beckley, Jibowu, and himself during a year 'when you have yourself borrowed for your very pressing needs'.[121]

To understand the precarious finances of even the large farmers, it should be remembered that several of them were also building spacious churches on their farms, helping to finance the schools associated with them, and supporting the African Church's travelling missionaries. In 1913, Jacob Coker wrote to Rev. Coates stating, with regret, that 'I find that I am greatly short of money and as such I shall fail to give you any money till the end of November. I am much drained by church building expenses and cocoa has not come out to help me'.[122] The Agege farmers were constantly farming their way out of debt and hoping that the combination of harvest and price would generate a return that exceeded their obligations. Without the security provided by property in Lagos, large-scale plantations would have faced insuperable obstacles. Without access to start-up finance, funds for running costs, and savings accrued by negotiating bulk shipments, Agege's farmers would have been confined to small-scale operations. Their main advantages were that they were first in the field and close to the port of shipment. When competition developed from Ibadan and other regions, Agege's early start ceased to protect its product. The

119. Lugard to Elgin, 19 May 1906, C.S.O. 12/25/34. In 1913, Jones tried again, this time through his bank, the BBWA, but Lugard remained unmoved and the matter was dropped.

120. Beckley to Coker, 14 April 1909, CP. This is just one of many possible examples.

121. Coker to Williams, 30 Jan. 1913, CP.

122. Coker to Rev. Coates, 6 Oct 1913, CP. 3/1.

Lagos railway reached Ibadan in 1901. By 1905, the region accounted for about 60 per cent of the expanding acreage under cocoa in Western Nigeria (which approximated to the whole of Yorubaland); by 1910, the figure had risen to 66 per cent.[123] The production model based on plantations did not travel with the techniques and cocoa seeds the Agege farmers generously distributed. Elsewhere, as noted earlier, small-scale farming using household and extra-household labour became the norm.

The difficulty of securing labour was at least as great as the problem of paying for it. The shortage of labour was one of the most important issues the APU discussed.[124] James Davies encountered the same problem in the 1880s and 1890s.[125] The explanation of the bottleneck was the same then as it was in the early years of the new century: the supply of labour was determined by available alternatives, and in this case land could be taken up and new export crops grown by households as well as by planters. There was no immediate solution to the problem, apart from paying high wages. By 1909, the average wage had risen from 10s. a month in the mid-1890s to 15s. plus extras in the form of crops, food, and often accommodation.[126]

The APU mobilised family and commercial networks in Egba country and elsewhere to secure sufficient labourers; some who came stayed on as independent farmers. Although the government recognised the limits on supply, the only solution suggested by R. E. Dennett, the new Director of Agriculture, was that the farmers should 'make more children', to which the President of the APU replied that it would be better to have appropriate machinery.[127] Nevertheless, a belief formed, and persisted, that the African churches favoured polygamy for exactly this reason. The connection is appealing but mistaken. The attitude of the African Church was that Christians should have the right to choose monogamy or polygamy.[128] Moreover, as Jacob Coker put it, wives in a polygamous relationship were 'helpers in partnership' and not 'slaves or servants', and their children were not bound to the land.[129] The African Church brought teaching and practice together. Many Anglicans in Lagos

123. Calculated from Sara S. Berry, *Cocoa, Custom, and Socio-Economic Change in Rural Western Nigeria* (Oxford: Clarendon Press, 1975), appendix 3, table 2, p. 222. This is a book that can truly be said to be irreplaceable. During the 1920s, the centre of growth shifted again, this time from Ibadan to Oyo and Ondo, with Ondo becoming predominant in the 1930s and 1940s. During the 1940s, the acreage under cocoa in Ibadan had returned to the levels of the early 1900s.

124. *Lagos Standard*, 1 Sept. 1909.

125. See chapter 9.

126. *Lagos Standard*, 1 Sept. 1909.

127. Meeting of APU with Director of Agriculture, Agege, 16 June 1909, CP.

128. Coker to 'Cousin', 16 July 1913, CP.

129. Coker to 'Cousin', 16 July 1913, CP. In a later statement, Coker advanced the view that polygamy was needed to deal with the high death rate in Nigeria. His argument was challenged by Obi T. George, *Lagos Weekly Record*, 13 March 1920, 1 May 1920.

were polygamists who remained in the Church, even though principle and practice were at variance.

Far from drawing on 'free' labour from polygamous households, the planters were the first to promote wage labour in Yoruba agriculture.[130] There are very few recorded references either to *iwofa* or to pawning (both means of repaying debt), or to sharecropping on cocoa farms, though labourers might be given harvested crops as gifts rather than as part of their contract.[131] In a lucid statement prepared for the governor of the colony in 1913, Jacob Coker distinguished between *iwofa*, in which labour was employed under controlled conditions to repay debt, and pawning, which Coker described as 'a form of slavery'.[132] *Iwofa* was used to supplement wage labour but did not suit the planters because the creditor was entitled to no more than one-third of the debtor's labour time in any single month. Pawning was contrary to the Christian principles espoused by Coker and his fellow planters. Wages were a necessary incentive in conditions of labour scarcity and were preferred by farm-hands because money conferred freedom of choice. Given that freedom of choice allowed labour mobility, the APU took care to define categories of work and appropriate rates of pay, and to draw up conditions that prevented farmers from poaching labourers while they were still under contract.[133]

Labour shortages also explain why the APU, like James Davies, took a keen interest in machinery. In 1909, the Union organised a demonstration of a machine invented by a teacher at Abeokuta Grammar School that extracted palm oil from the fruit.[134] In the following year, they compared the performance of a machine designed to crack palm kernels with that of Ibadan's champion female kernel-cracker and found that the machine had no decisive advantage.[135] The Agege farmers adopted specialised picking and pruning tools because they were cost-effective, and even considered using ploughs but judged them, correctly, to be inappropriate.

Given the limits to cutting production costs, the APU focussed on achieving pecuniary economies, which were realised not only by reducing the cost of capital, as has been seen, but also by cutting transport and related transaction charges. A railway from Lagos to the north had been much discussed and long awaited. The first section, from Lagos to Agege, was opened fully in 1899; the extension to Otta entered service in 1901.[136] A few years later, the

130. Agiri, 'The Development of Wage Labour'.

131. The context is given in Toyin Falola, 'Slavery and Pawnship'; and Lovejoy, 'Pawnship, Debt, and "Freedom"'.

132. Jacob K. Coker to Governor General, n.d. but 1913, CP.

133. Minutes of meeting of APU, 17 Aug. 1907, CP.

134. J. K. Coker to Egba Farmers' Association, 23 Oct. 1909, CP.

135. Coker to Birtwistle, 18 Jan. 1910, CP.

136. *Lagos Standard*, 2 Aug. 1899; Denton to Chamberlain, 11 June 1898, C.O. 147/133; MacGregor to Chamberlain, 4 March 1901, C.O. 147/154.

APU persuaded the government to open a small station at Iju, Agege.[137] At a stroke, the journey between Lagos and Agege was cut to 30 minutes. Previously, as Jacob Coker recalled, 'there was only a narrow path (unsafe and dangerous) for caravans from up-country going to and from Lagos. The advent of the railway station has brought many traders and farmers to reside here from different places of origin'.[138] The next step was to reduce the cost of carrying produce to the station. In 1909, the APU agreed to support a newly formed 'cartage company', though the firm appears to have had a short life.[139]

In 1912, the planters became the first farmers in Nigeria to back a more promising development: motor transport.[140] The APU persuaded the government to construct a motor road from Ebute Metta and Agege, and in return agreed to build suitable roads within Agege and invest in motor vehicles.[141] In 1916, the APU formed the APU Motor Transport Company to 'buy and run a lorry for the convenience of members'.[142] Later in the year, the first Albion motor lorry arrived. Unfortunately, the experiment disappointed expectations, principally because the early lorries were too heavy for unmetalled roads. The APU had seen the future clearly but was defeated by being too far ahead of its time.[143]

In the absence of cost-effective machinery, the APU concentrated on improving the quality of Agege's cocoa. The strategy was a way of improving the skills of rural entrepreneurs with the ultimate aim of increasing the prices paid for their produce. Accordingly, the APU distributed cocoa pods and seeds, advised newcomers about best practice, circulated information about crop diseases, and experimented with possible new crops, including Chinese oil bean, nutmeg, rubber, kola, and varieties of corn.[144] In 1912, the APU requested, and secured, an official produce inspector with specific responsibilities for

137. Photos of the original station, in reality a large shed, are available online.

138. Speech made by Jacob Coker on behalf of the APU at the opening of new market in Agege, 1922, CP.

139. Minutes of a committee meeting of the APU, 11 Sept. 1909, CP. I have been unable to find further information about the venture, which was run by Sylvanus Turlo (who later changed his name to Adeniyi Olugbile). Turlo was employed by Josiah Doherty between 1902 and 1919 and was probably acting for him in running the 'cartage' company. He was also a founder member of the African Church. Deniga, *The Nigerian Who's Who for 1934*.

140. J. K. Coker, report to APU, 9 March 1912, CP.

141. Commissioner of Lands to J. K. Coker, 11 May 1912, CP; minutes of a meeting of the APU, 14 Oct. 1916, CP.

142. Minutes of a committee meeting of the APU, 14 Oct. 1916, CP.

143. In 1918, Kitoyi Ajasa stated that 'the only road that the colony can boast of is that leading from Ebute Metta to Agege; and when you get to Agege you have to depend on privately-made roads'. Statement to the Nigerian Council reported in Lees to Secretary of State, 18 Feb. 1918, C.O. 583/65.

144. Coker to members of APU, 15 Nov. 1907, about the improper preparation of cocoa, CP; Coker to Carr, Secretary of the Lagos Agricultural Union, n.d. but 1907, CP.

Agege.[145] The policy of improvement and quality control was pursued in co-operation with the Botanic Station at Ebute Metta. As tropical agronomy was a new science, both parties needed each other. The APU exchanged cocoa, kola, and other seeds with Ebute Metta, shared advice on techniques of cultivation, and discussed methods of controlling disease.[146]

By 1910, Agege cocoa fetched the highest price on the Lagos market and had become a standard in the trade, being ranked with 'best Accra'.[147] In 1917, it commanded 'a special market and an enhanced price'.[148] High-quality cocoa, consistently delivered, enabled the APU to organise bulk shipments, which improved the price paid to producers, reduced freight rates, and ben-efitted small as well as large farmers.[149] Coker and his fellow planters usually shipped their produce through contracts with the expatriate firms in Lagos, such as McIver and John Holt, though they sometimes risked shipping on consignment in the hope that the landing price of cocoa in Liverpool would be higher than that prevailing locally.[150] The aim, however, was not only to secure the best price but also to obtain a grade mark for Agege cocoa so that, as Coker explained to McIver, 'you may be able to sell our cocoa on forward shipments'.[151] Coker and the APU were, in effect, promoting a futures market that would give them a degree of security and, above all, ease the acute cash-flow problem that plagued them throughout the year.

Within a few years of its foundation, the APU was winning most of the prizes at the agricultural shows sponsored by the government and setting quality standards for other farmers.[152] By 1910, Agege had become, in Gover-nor Egerton's words, 'the chief agricultural centre in the colony'.[153] Its reputa-tion spread far beyond the colony. The Director of Agriculture in French West

145. Coker to Colonial Secretary, Lagos, 12 April 1912, CP; Controller of Customs, Southern Nigeria, to Coker, 25 July 1912, CP.

146. Forestry Department to APU, 14 July 1909, CP; Farquharson to Coker, 17 May 1912; Director of Agriculture to Coker, 14 Nov. 1913, CP; Assistant Superintendent of Agriculture to Secretary of APU, 4 Sept. 1914, CP (asking for 4,000 *Gbanja* Kola seeds for the Department of Agriculture). *Gbanja* was the Yoruba term for cola nitida, which was preferred in northern Nigeria. See Agiri, 'The Yoruba and the Pre-Colonial Kola Trade'. It is worth noting that, while colonial officials criticised African farmers for 'close planting', Coker's cocoa trees were 12 feet apart, which was the ideal recommended by the experts of the day. Holt to Coker, 23 Dec. 1907, CP.

147. *Lagos Standard*, 1 Sept. 1909; minutes of a meeting of the APU, June 1910, CP; Coker to McIver, 13 Dec. 1911, CP 3/1; Coker to Rose Hewitt, 5 March 1915, CP; *Lagos Weekly Record*, 27 Nov. 1915.

148. *Lagos Weekly Record*, 15 Dec. 1917.

149. Coker to McIver, 18 Nov. 1980, CP; Coker to Central Secretariat, 1 March 1918, CP.

150. McIver to Coker, 5 July 1910, CP.

151. Coker to McIver, 13 Dec. 1911, CP 3/1.

152. *Lagos Standard*, 11 Nov. 1908; minutes of a meeting of the APU, June 1910, CP; Dawodu to Coker, 7 March 1914, CP.

153. Egerton, 15 Feb. 1910, quoted in *Lagos Weekly Record*, 23 April 1910.

Africa visited Agege in 1909; his compatriot, Auguste Chevalier, the eminent botanist and explorer, had already toured the district.[154] A representative from Cadbury's followed in 1912.[155] Agege served as a large and appealing model farm, attracting farmers from many regions of Yorubaland who came to acquire plants and seeds and learn techniques of cocoa farming, and sending representatives to advise farming communities in Egba, Ijebu Ode, and Ibadan on best practice.[156] As opinion leaders, the Agege planters had a clear advantage over expatriate officers in the Agricultural Department because they could relate to their compatriots and win their confidence without having to cross cultural and linguistic barriers.[157] The best model farm in Nigeria was the one Africans had established.

These substantial claims should not be overstated. Agege made a vital contribution to the Nigerian cocoa-farming industry in its early stages. As the success of the experiment became known, however, other farmers began to specialise in cocoa, even if they had already been growing it on a small scale. The Agege farmers spread 'the gospel' of cocoa farming through their numerous connections, through labourers returning to their homes, through enquiring travellers on the caravan road to Lagos, which passed near Coker's Ifako plantation, and through the African Church's missionaries. But there were increasing numbers of others who carried the message beyond Agege's reach independently of its direct influence. Sara Berry's invaluable research has traced the spread of cocoa farming in Ibadan, Ondo, and Ilesha, where Anglican Christians were particularly influential in delivering the message that God and Mammon could be reconciled through cocoa farming.[158] The CMS had finally realised that it needed

154. Meeting of the APU with Director of the Department of Agriculture and Director of Agriculture in French West Africa, Agege, 16 June 1909, CP. Auguste Chevalier (1873–1956) wrote the first scientific study of cocoa in West Africa: *le Cacaoyer dans l'Ouest Africain*.

155. Henry Carr to Coker, 3 May 1912, CP.

156. See, for example, Coker, report to the APU, 1911, 9 March 1912, CP; Superintendent of Agriculture, Lagos, to Director of Agriculture, Ibadan, 12 Dec. 1912; the encouragement was given to farmers to 'see the more advanced methods of agriculture' practised at Agege. *Lagos Weekly Record*, 5 March 1910.

157. Assistant Superintendent of Agriculture to Coker, 24 May 1912, asking for cocoa pods in connection with the government's plan to establish a model fermenting house at Agege. Coker to Colonial Secretary, Lagos, 7 July 1912, CP, suggesting that officials in the Department of Agriculture should visit Ifako to be shown methods of planting and curing cocoa that could be passed on to others.

158. Berry, *Cocoa, Custom, and Socio-Economic Change*, ch. 2, and the biographical information in appendix 1, pp. 211–15, and appendix 2, pp. 216–20. It is relevant to note that Bishop Phillips knew Jacob Coker and the Agege community, and that the colonial government established its own model farm (of 390 acres) at Olokomeji (twenty-five miles west of Ibadan) in 1903. Olokomeji had ten thousand cocoa plants ready for distribution in 1905. Lagos *Annual Reports, Agricultural Supplement* No. 6, 1899–1905, C.O. 149/5.

to compete with the African Churches or risk being marginalised.[159] Cocoa was introduced to Ijebu Ode principally by Joseph Odunmosu, a committed Anglican and noted 'country' doctor, in the early 1900s.[160] The APU did not control the secrets of cocoa farming; nor did it seek to do so. On the contrary, it was eager to see cocoa flourish throughout Yorubaland.[161] Its purpose was not to monopolise profits but to spread the idea that Africans could retain their self-respect and shared values under colonial rule while also participating in the global economy.

Costs and Benefits

The importance of estimating the profitability of the enterprise displayed at Agege is as evident as it is difficult. Jacob Coker's records contain information about income and expenditure, including labour and shipping costs, but lack a series of balance sheets. It might be possible to deduce a statement of net profits from the available material, but to do so would require a separate and substantial research project. The only previous calculation, made by Webster, suggested that Coker's gross income averaged £5,000 a year before 1914 and £20,000 a year just after 1914, when World War I started.[162] Webster's figures are a valuable start but were intended to be no more than indicative. My own estimate suggests that Webster was correct in drawing attention to an increase in Coker's income, which coincided with the expansion and rising price of cocoa exports, though his figures for gross income may be on the high side. Averages also disguise sudden and potentially crippling falls brought about by the hazards of the harvest and international conditions. Periods of drought caused a sharp drop in output; incomes fell unless prices compensated. The war also instigated a series of crises following the closure of markets on the continent of Europe and a persistent shortage of shipping space. The main difficulty, however, is that gross income needs to be set against expenses to arrive at net profits. Coker's list of outgoings may not include all his running costs and rarely refers to capital expenditure. A further complication is that before 1912, Coker was repaying money he owed through produce sales, and a systematic analysis would need to specify how these payments were accounted for.

159. See also Webster, *African Churches among the Yoruba*, part 2, for competition among the various missions and the spread of cocoa as the railway line extended north of Lagos.

160. Interview with Chief Odubanjo Odutola, *Olotufore* of Ijebu Ode and son of Joseph. Ijebu Ode, 3 May 1964. See also *Nigerian Times*, 19 Sept. 1911; *Lagos Standard*, 20 Sept. 1911; *Lagos Weekly Record*, 23 Sept. 1911. Joseph Odutola knew Jacob Coker and other merchants and farmers in Lagos and Agege, including Daniel Sasegbon, who built the first Anglican church at Agege.

161. For the enthusiasm with which the Agege farmers created competing farmers, see *Lagos Weekly Record*, 5 Oct. 1910.

162. Webster, 'Agege Plantations and the African Church', p. 126.

The figures for the years after 1914 and into the 1920s are more detailed than those for the earlier period. The first complete sales figures run from 1 October 1904 to 30 September 1905 and show a gross return of £2,053, comprised of palm kernels (£1,415), cocoa (£369), corn (£206), and coffee (£63).[163] The distribution of earnings among different crops reflects the fact that large plantings of cocoa were just beginning to bear fruit, having been planted three or four years earlier. The first complete statement of income and expenditure, after cocoa became the principal crop at Agege, covers the calendar year January to December 1918, when export prices were high. Coker's income then stood at £9,759 and expenditure at £9,983, resulting in a formal deficit of £224.[164] It is hard to know how to interpret these figures, given that the document was not a full balance sheet but a simple list of monthly income alongside monthly expenditure. It may suggest what other evidence indicates, namely that Coker was operating at increasing levels of income and expenditure. He remained reliant on credit in the form of advances against sales of cocoa, which meant the business also had a shadowy companion: debt. This interpretation would fit with what is known of Coker's ambition, which was not to die rich but to amass a fortune that would enable him to finance the expansion of the African Church, the education of his and several other children, and the various 'good causes' he supported during his own lifetime.

By 1918, Coker was undoubtedly very wealthy. He had extended his holdings at Agege to some two thousand acres, owned several houses in Lagos in addition to Rose Cottage on the Marina, and in 1916 possessed one of the small number of motor cars seen in Lagos at that time.[165] One public illustration of Coker's standing occurred at the close of World War I, when his annual income was substantial enough to enable him to engage fully in that most costly of activities: politics. As noted earlier, Coker and his Egba compatriots at Agege had long taken a keen interest in political developments in Abeokuta. In 1919, Coker's wealth and public profile had led to his election as the head (*Olori-Parakoyi*) of the commercial community in the capital, an achievement that involved some expense. More was to come. The death of *Alake* Gbadebo I in 1920 was followed by intense competition among the contending parties. Coker, Jibowu, and others supported what became known as the Church party, which favoured Ladapo Ademola and opposed the candidate favoured by Adegboyega Edun,

163. Sales data of Coker's farms at Ifako, Agege and Otere, CP. 3/2, Box 2. A word of caution: it is possible that Coker had additional farms at this date, in which case the figures quoted would underestimate total output.

164. CP. 3/2.

165. Webster, 'Agege Plantations and the African Church', p. 126. Information about the motor car, which he lent frequently, is in a note following Coker to 'Dear Bro', 9 March 1916, CP.

the long-standing Secretary of the EUG.[166] Edun had become a controversial figure in Egba politics; Coker and others held him partly responsible for the loss of Egba's independence in 1914.[167] Coker, who was already the chief executor of *Alake* Gbadebo's estate, increased his influence in 1920 by agreeing to pay the considerable expenses of the late *Alake*'s funeral. There was even talk that Coker himself might become *Alake*. Ultimately, his preferred candidate, Ladapo Ademola, won the contest and ruled as Gbadebo II from 1920 to 1962. Imperfect though the measurement is, it can be said that the high point of Coker's finances coincided with the high point of his political influence.

Chapter 14 provides an outline of what happened to Jacob Coker and Agege after 1920. By then, the great days of cocoa farming in the area were already in the past. Yet, Agege's story retains interest and importance: it adapted to changing circumstances and continued to be a centre of innovation.

From Davies to Coker

A series of extraordinary innovations gave Agege a significance that extended far beyond its own confines.[168] In promoting a new export crop, Coker and his fellow pioneers were the first to introduce freehold land sales outside Lagos and greatly expanded the use of wage labour, which had been introduced by James Davies. In doing so, they demonstrated that education and farming could be productive partners rather than being confined to the work of slaves and others of low status. As a result, Agege became the single most important centre of diffusion for cocoa farming in Nigeria. The explanation of this transformative development requires a degree of subtlety. Part of the problem can be understood by showing how planters responded to shifting opportunities signalled by price incentives. The commitment made by Jacob Coker, like that made by James Davies, was strongly influenced by the need to deal with commercial indebtedness in circumstances in which farming seemed to be the most promising of limited alternatives. Several of Coker's associates also took up farming as a result of business difficulties. While this reaction might qualify as a necessary condition in the case of some of the leading pioneers, it is far from being sufficient because it excludes other important contextual influences. Moreover, this analysis will not account for the motives of many

166. Boyle to Secretary of State, 10 May 1919, C.O. 583/95; *Lagos Weekly Record*, 26 June 1920.

167. The issues were debated in the press. For one example of support for Coker's position against Edun, see the letter from Akiwunde Savage, in the *Lagos Weekly Record*, 22 May 1920.

168. My stress on the innovative activities of the Agege farmers is in line with Sara S. Berry's analysis, 'The Concept of Innovation and the History of Cocoa Farming in Western Nigeria', *Journal of African History*, 15 (1974), pp. 83–95.

other Lagosians who farmed at Agege. They were not merchants in trouble but government employees who were dissatisfied with their career prospects.

At this point the merits of seeing Lagos as a colonial port city come into view. A common theme applied to both groups of pioneer farmers, whether they were victims of commercial indebtedness or former government employees: they were frustrated by what they saw as shrinking opportunities for advancement in commerce, government, and the Church. Nearly all of them belonged to a generation of young, educated Africans of Saro origin who saw their ambitions being blocked by the new colonial order. Cocoa farming offered a new opportunity to generate income; the APU maximised pecuniary economies by acting as a conduit for supplies of capital and by organising bulk shipments to reduce transaction costs. The enterprise as a whole was organised to give Agege farmers as much autonomy as was consistent with colonial status. The African Church complemented the farming economy by giving its ministers independent status and a large measure of internal self-government in religious affairs. The leading farmers were also politically active, especially in opposing Britain's encroachment into Egba territory, where many of them had strong family connections. Accordingly, Agege was much more than a large model farm for potential cocoa producers; it was also a centre of diffusion for a way of life that was both resolutely African and committed to the modern world of international development. In providing a new source of income, Agege delivered an even higher return: self-respect and a degree of independence in a situation of overall subordination.

Support for this explanation can be found by comparing the motives that influenced James Davies and Jacob Coker. Although Davies conformed in many ways to the archetype of the Saro Victorian gentleman, the image should not be turned into a caricature. Davies held strong beliefs about African rights and challenged the colonial government when he thought that it had shifted, without justification, from cooperative to assertive policies. He was also impressed by the Rev. James Johnson, Coker's mentor, and sympathised with his reforming ambitions.[169] Yet, he remained an Anglican, built a small Anglican Church on his farm, retained his English name, and continued to dress like a Victorian gentleman. His position is not to be explained by a lack of nerve or verve, but by generational change. Davies was seventy-three in 1901, when the African Church was founded; he was also ill and did not regain good health before he died in 1906. His reaction to the far-reaching changes that affected the fortunes of Lagos and the Saro at the close of the century is not on record. It is apparent, however, that he found life as a working farmer fulfilling rather than a penance. When these qualifications have been included, it is nevertheless the case that Davies's farming venture was instrumental in being primarily a means of restoring his income and his position in Lagos. He

169. Herskovits, *A Preface to Modern Nigeria*, pp. 239–40, 255.

maintained his house and his presence among the elite in the capital, even though it had lost some of the attractions it had held in his younger and highly prosperous days.[170] His values were formed earlier in the century under Venn's influence. They remained with him, as did his gratitude to those who had rescued his family, and his wife, Sarah, from slavery.

Coker's position was very different. He was born in Abeokuta, not Freetown, educated there and in Lagos and greatly influenced in his youth, and indeed throughout his life, by the Rev. James Johnson, the Christian reformer and Yoruba patriot. In 1901, moreover, Coker was only thirty-five, half Davies's age. His future lay ahead; Davies's was mostly behind him. By the 1890s, Venn's ideas of co-operation and equality had been put aside and Africans of Coker's age had to reassess and even rescue their own values in the face of the advance of colonial rule. It was then that 'Westernised' Africans began to adopt indigenous dress and revert to their original family names. Coker took to the former but retained his English name, as does his family today. Farming for Coker was instrumental, as it was for Davies: he, too, needed an income to repay debt. But Coker had a more spacious purpose: he saw cocoa and the African Church as the means of disseminating his vision of an Africa that could both retain its values and harness them to achieve economic development. This ambition explains why Coker and the APU were missionaries for both the Church and cocoa. Davies gave advice and plants willingly but did not feel a compulsion to spread the message throughout Yorubaland. Coker and his fellow planters were, in effect, creating competitors for their own pioneering industry. They succeeded, but Coker regarded the outcome as fulfilment, not as defeat.

The increasing uncertainties among the Saro about how to respond to life under colonial rule began to find political expression in the early years of the twentieth century. One of the most overt signals of the trend occurred in what became known as the 'Eleko Affair'. Governor Hugh Clifford's decision to suspend recognition of Eshugbayi Eleko, the *Oba* of Lagos, in 1919 produced an immediate, fierce, and very public controversy that pitted a group of pro-government conservatives, headed by the lawyer Kitoyi Ajasa, against proto-nationalists, led by Herbert Macaulay.[171] Coker was already playing an important and previously little-known part in keeping the fledgling and flagging National Congress of British West Africa alive.[172] He then defended the *Oba* in the pages of the *Lagos Weekly Record*, which supported Macaulay's faction.[173]

Ajasa took aim through the newspaper he founded, the *Nigerian Pioneer*, which was the main outlet for the government's supporters.[174] His attack on

170. See above p. 150, for his reference to 'cruel Lagos'.
171. The complexities of the affair are unpacked by Cole, *Modern and Traditional Elites*, ch.5.
172. *Lagos Weekly Record*, 10 July 1920.
173. *Lagos Weekly Record*, 22 Nov., 29 Nov. 1919.
174. *Nigerian Pioneer*, 5 Dec. 1919.

the 'ravings' of this 'obscure person from Abeokuta' touched a point some way below normal levels of personal abuse. The article claimed that Coker had been unable to write his letter 'unaided' and deplored the figure he 'cut at Government House when he gave us the impression of a chimpanzee at the zoo trying to make a speech; his antics were most painful to behold'. Ajasa went on to urge Coker to stick to farming and avoid matters of politics, which were beyond him. The *Weekly Record* and correspondents jumped to Coker's defence.[175] Coker was not a 'government-made man', said one correspondent, nor was he 'a regular attender of Government House balls, concerts, lodge rooms, race meetings', but moved among 'the people, mostly the poor and suffering ones'.[176]

The significance of this episode for present purposes is that it dramatises the changes that had overtaken the Saro community since the mid-nineteenth century. The sense of commonality that had characterised the first generation of returnees, like James Davies, became strained at the close of the century and politicised after it. Coker's initial ambitions were not political; in 1914, he joined many other Saro in declaring his support for the British war effort. As we will see in the next chapter, however, the shock delivered by World War I sharpened dilemmas that had been latent and made them both public and political.

175. *Lagos Weekly Record*, 13 Dec. 1919.
176. Letter from O. T. Somefun, *Lagos Weekly Record*, 13 Dec. 1919.

PART III

The Shock of 1914

War and Its Consequences

THE THIRD PART OF this book describes the shock that occurred in 1914 and its effect on the mercantile community down to the economic crisis of 1929–1931. The closing stages of the careers of Josiah Doherty and Samuel Pearse have already provided an indication of the hardships that were to mark the inter-war period.[1] Yet, the war had consequences that were far wider than these biographies can encompass. An adequate account of the period requires another book rather than the chapter offered here. At the same time, it would be unsatisfactory to halt in 1914 without providing some signposts to the future. Accordingly, the first half of the chapter deals with the upheaval brought by World War I, the post-war boom of 1919–1920, and the slump that followed in 1920–1922. The war and, even more decisively, the failure of the peace settlement, limited the scope for economic recovery and culminated in the global economic crisis that began at the end of the decade. The second half of the chapter examines the effects of these developments on the African mercantile community as a whole. By the close of the 1930s, economic adversity had found effective political expression. World War II accelerated the movement that led to independence, but its origins lay in the inter-war years.

Paradoxically, information relating to Lagos merchants in colonial records becomes increasingly scarce, even as the volume of official documentation reaches daunting dimensions. The amalgamation of different administrations that produced the Colony and Protectorate of Nigeria in 1914 obliged officials in Lagos to focus on issues that extended far beyond the port. Policies of racial discrimination altered the relationship between rulers and ruled that had characterised the second half of the nineteenth century. The world inhabited by Chief Daniel Taiwo and Governor Glover was much smaller and far more intimate than that presided over by Governor General Frederick Lugard and

---

1. See chapter 12.

his successors.[2] Moreover, Lugard detested Lagos and its educated elite.[3] His successors, though more tolerant, continued to work within the structures he had done so much to create. Official documents and newspapers do, of course, provide general guides to the shock of 1914 and its immediate consequences.[4] Statistical returns, however, reflected activities in the expanded colony with the result that data relating specifically to Lagos are no longer available.

Accordingly, details of how the turbulent conditions between 1914 and 1931 buffeted African merchants and affected their fortunes depend largely on unofficial records and private sources. The family papers cited here are only samples of a much larger number that no longer exist; similarly, the oral testimony referred to can no longer be replicated. Despite their limited number, these sources provide an illuminating and generally consistent insight into the individual consequences of general trends. The discussion in this chapter is followed by a detailed example, that of Peter Thomas, whose story, told in chapter 15, relies almost entirely on the survival of a substantial part of his business correspondence.

The Fortunes of War

The immediate shock, following Britain's declaration of war in August 1914, was felt through the disruption of international trade. Established markets were severed; shipping was requisitioned or diverted. Lagos was severely affected because about half the value of produce shipped from the port went to Germany and a sizeable share of the shipping tonnage was handled by the German firm, Woermann Linie. In 1913, 75 per cent of the value of Nigeria's palm kernels, 53 per cent of its groundnuts, 46 per cent of its cocoa, and significant proportions of other agricultural produce, were shipped to Germany.[5] Although Britain dominated the import trade, Germany had a strong position in specific lines of business, notably varieties of textiles, hardware, and beads. During the war, however, imports from all sources were in short supply and consequently were available only at increasingly high prices.

Figure 2.2 in chapter 2 traces the net barter terms of trade for palm oil and kernels exported from Nigeria during this period.[6] Decline in both cases set

2. Lugard (1858–1945), Nigeria's first governor general, held office from 1914 to 1919.
3. Few in Lagos regretted his departure. *Lagos Weekly Record*, 12 July 1919.
4. Historians are fortunate in having Olukoju's book at their disposal: *The Liverpool of West Africa*, which draws together many decades of thorough research on this period. A more specialised study by Peter J. Yearwood also contains relevant information: *Nigeria*.
5. Nigeria: *Annual Report*, 1914; Lugard to Secretary of State, 20 Oct. 1914, C.O. 583/19.
6. Tribute should be paid here to Gerald Helleiner's pioneering work, which was the first to describe the main trends in Nigeria's barter and income terms of trade: Helleiner, *Peasant Agriculture*, pp. 494 (table IV-A-2), and 500 (table IV-A-6). Helleiner's data vary in

in just before the outbreak of war and became precipitous during the inter-war period, despite a brief and, in the event, deceptive rise in the mid-1920s. As in previous periods, the broken lines in figure 2.2 indicate marked short-term variations that gave merchants unpredictable roller-coaster rides. As figure 2.1 in chapter 2 shows, export volumes (from British West Africa) rose at the same time, apart from the early years of the war. It seems clear that the increase was intended to compensate for falling export prices. It is unlikely that it did so: Helleiner's data for Nigeria indicate that the income terms of trade also declined, apart from a brief boost at the close of the 1930s.[7] It is impossible to say very much at present about the distribution of the returns from the export trades. Existing producers worked harder; others, commensurate with population growth, took up land for the first time. In the absence of significant improvements in productivity, export producers suffered a fall in real incomes during the period under review. The boost provided by the railway had been absorbed; motor transport did not have a significant effect on transaction costs until after 1945. In general, the quantitative data add precision to what is already well known: this was a testing time for producers and all other Lagosians engaged in overseas trade.

A closer look at the war-time commercial environment will identify the obstacles and opportunities merchants faced, while also illustrating the familiar proposition that war can make as well as destroy fortunes.

The Changing Commercial Environment

Imperial commercial policy during this period can be summarised as orthodoxy modified by temporary intervention. The Colonial Office and the governor-general adhered to inherited free-trade principles. In their view, a competitive market would deliver economic efficiency and fair prices for all parties. The colonial government benefitted because competition was the best means of expanding trade and hence revenues, which relied on customs duties. Similarly, competitive principles implied opposition to monopolies and the obligation to ensure that small merchants, who were mostly African, were treated fairly.[8] The British firms, however, regarded the expulsion of their German rivals as an opportunity to establish a combine that would enable them to control prices in local markets. The ensuing struggle between the surviving

---

detail from Frankema's at some points, because they have chosen different base dates and have a slightly different mix of exports.

7. Helleiner, *Peasant Agriculture*, table 2, p. 20. This finding is consistent with figure 2.2 in this text. The broken lines in the graph show that there was a brief revival in the late 1930s.

8. See, for example, Lugard to Secretary of State, 4 June 1916, C.O. 583/45; C.O. minutes on House of Commons, 19 Oct.1916, C.O. 583/52; C.O. minutes on Lugard to Secretary of State, 30 Aug. 1916, C.O. 583/48.

commercial firms intersected with the British government's judgement that national priorities during war-time called for an exceptional and temporary degree of intervention into economic affairs.

This position remained unchanged throughout the war. Lugard's assessment of post-war economic policy, presented in 1917, confirmed the need to maintain an open door and free competition with the primary aim of developing Nigeria's agricultural resources and helping Britain's recovery.[9] No consideration was given to diversifying the economy. By 1919, however, even Lugard had begun to waver. Increases in the price of both imports and domestic foodstuffs prompted him to advocate the development of import-substituting manufactures. His appeal to British firms in Nigeria produced 'no results'.[10] It would be more satisfactory, he added, 'if Natives would embark on these ventures and keep the money and the industry in the country'.[11] This was a hope, not a policy. Moreover, immediate pressures subdued initiative: import-substituting manufactures had the disadvantage of reducing government revenues, which depended heavily on import duties. In 1919, Lugard left Nigeria to ruminate further in retirement. The advent of peace was seen not as an opportunity to change traditional policy, but to reaffirm it.

The only practical reference to support for new manufactures in Nigeria appeared shortly before the outbreak of war, when a British firm applied for protection to establish a brewing plant.[12] A Colonial Office official commented that there was 'no point in giving the brewery protection unless it is desired to test the validity of Mill on "infant industries"'.[13] Officials had no enthusiasm for putting Mill to the test, though the company, the West African Brewery Syndicate, showed remarkable persistence in pressing its case until at least 1919.[14] The only other distinctive proposition put to the Colonial Office during the war came from a group of South African entrepreneurs who took advantage of the war-time emergency to promote a form of mercantilism aimed at creating a protectionist empire. The group first appeared as the Empire Resources Development Committee (ERDC) in 1917 with an ambitious scheme, not to diversify West Africa's economy, but to accelerate

9. Lugard to Secretary of State, 31 Jan. 1917, C.O. 583/55.

10. Address to the Nigerian Council, reported in *West Africa*, 22 March 1919.

11. Address to the Nigerian Council, reported in *West Africa*, 22 March 1919.

12. Lugard to Secretary of State, 25 May 1914, C.O. 583/14.

13. Baynes minute on Lugard to Secretary of State, 25 May 1914, C.O. 583/14. As noted already, Mill's qualified support for infant industries (as they became known) first appeared in his *Principles of Political Economy* (1848), which became a standard text during the second half of the century.

14. West African Brewery Syndicate to C.O., 16 Jan. 1919, C.O. 583/82. Brewing and other water-based products are typically among the early import-substituting industries because they can use local water and economise on international transport cost. Nigeria conformed to this pattern after 1945.

the development of its agricultural resources. The ERDC proposed to acquire extensive concessions for plantations and ranches that would be owned and run by expatriates, generate increased revenues, and help to repay Britain's war debt.[15] The project was as poorly considered as it was ambitious. It provoked opposition from African leaders, the Colonial Office, and British commercial firms who feared that the ERDC would eat into their established interests.[16] The promoters continued to press their case but they faded at the end of the war, when the return to normality confirmed that free trade remained official policy.

Prevailing economic orthodoxy ensured that African merchants received no special treatment and had to find their own way through the far-reaching changes brought by the war. The expulsion of the German firms was a particularly serious setback. Several of the most prominent merchants in Lagos, such as Josiah Doherty and Alli Balogun, had benefitted from the advantageous credit and keen prices the German firms offered.[17] The superiority of the German firms was long established and detailed in reports by successive governors from the 1860s onwards. A new set of official comments followed their expulsion. Shortly after the outbreak of war, Lugard remarked on the 'amazingly low' prices of imports from Germany; two years later, he judged the absence of the firms to be a 'calamity'.[18] In 1917, the *Board of Trade Journal* praised German firms for the range and cheapness of their goods and their excellent relations with African customers.[19] In 1920, with his eye on the developing peace rather than the completed war, the Controller of Customs extolled the wide range of products, managerial expertise, and excellent customer relations that had characterised the German firms.[20] African merchants spoke for themselves. A deputation visited London in 1916 to voice various frustrations, including the exclusion of the German firms, which had given Africans 'better treatment'.[21]

The loss of the German kernel market eliminated the most profitable of the export trades; the removal of German imports obliged Lagos merchants to stock higher-priced, less profitable British goods. Formal restrictions imposed on the foreign markets Lagos firms were allowed to access reinforced their

15. Killingray, 'The Empire Resources Development Committee'.

16. See, for example, *West Africa*, 6 Oct. 1917, 22 Dec. 1917, 12 Jan. 1918, 19 Jan. 1918, 4 Feb. 1918, 9 Feb. 1918, 16 Feb. 1918, 30 March 1918, 6 April 1918, 18 Jan. 1919, 22 Feb. 1919. *Lagos Weekly Record*, 28 April 1917, 2–9 Feb. 1918.

17. Moorhouse to Secretary of State, 8 Feb. 1919, C.O. 583/73.

18. Lugard to Secretary of State, 4 Oct. 1914, C.O. 583/20. Lugard to Secretary of State, 20 Oct. 1914, C.O. 583/19, and 8 April 1916, C.O. 583/45. The Report of the Committee on Edible and Oil-Producing Nuts and Seeds, Cd. 8247 (1916), endorsed these views.

19. Quoted in *West Africa*, 4 Jan. 1918.

20. Reported in *West Africa*, 11 Dec. 1920.

21. Enclosed in British Cotton Growing Association to C.O., 12 Sept. 1916, C.O. 583/53.

dependence on the British market. Export duties were imposed in 1916 to compensate for the loss of revenue from spirits, which were in short supply during the war.[22] The main consequence for Lagos and its hinterland was to reduce the incomes, and hence the purchasing power, of producers.[23] Britain, however, was able to capture Nigeria's export trade. In 1913, Britain took about 50 per cent of Nigeria's exports; by 1918, the figure had jumped to 90 per cent.[24] Moreover, the barriers to alternative markets protected Britain's infant kernel-crushing industry. In 1913, only two mills in Britain were capable of handling palm oil and kernels; by 1918, capacity was sufficient to deal with most of Nigeria's exported palm produce.[25] One reaction, which African merchants pioneered, was to develop trade with the United States, a friendly country that had been omitted from Britain's list of exclusions. In 1916, Jacob Coker and Peter Thomas combined to charter a ship to transport cocoa to New York. By the end of the war, the United States had become a significant market for cocoa and had replaced Germany as the second-largest importer into Nigeria.[26]

British firms in Lagos treated the elimination of their German rivals as an exceptional opportunity to fill the large gap that had suddenly appeared in the market. Discussions in 1915 led to the formation in the following year of a combine of eight Liverpool firms that traded extensively with Lagos.[27] The combine had three aims: to control prices in Lagos; to negotiate favourable freight rates; and to act in concert to buy German property, which the colonial government had requisitioned and intended to sell. Opposition was immediate and vociferous.[28] Firms outside the combine listed their objections; African merchants and their agents in London protested; Lugard feared that the low produce prices offered by the combine would depress imports and reduce customs revenue; the Colonial Office waved a flag for free trade. There followed a long wrangle about the effect of the combine on the prices of both imports and exports. The combine was represented by the Association of West African Merchants (AWAM), which was formed in 1916. Although the name was new, in the eyes of the Colonial

22. These issues receive extensive treatment in Olukoju, *The Liverpool of West Africa*, pp. 85–92, and Yearwood, *Nigeria*, pp. 104–5, 115–22, 177, 235–6.

23. *West Africa*, 22 Nov. 1919, 6 Aug. 1921; C.O. minutes on Clifford to Secretary of State, 31 Oct. 1919, C.O. 583/78.

24. *Lagos Weekly Record*, 19 and 26 Oct. 1918.

25. *West Africa*, 15 Dec. 1917; *Lagos Weekly Record*, 19–26 Oct. 1918.

26. *West Africa*, 13 Oct. 1917, 5 Oct. 1918, 4 Oct. 1919.

27. Lugard to Secretary of State, 8 April 1916, C.O. 583/45; West Africa, 22 Nov. 1919, 31 Jan. 1920; *Lagos Weekly Record*, 30 Oct. 1920.

28. African Association to C.O., 3 and 7 Nov. 1916, C.O. 583/53; Association of West African Merchants to C.O., 20 Sept. 1916, C.O. 583/53; *Lagos Weekly Record*, 7 Aug. 1916, Lugard to Secretary of State, 8 April 1916, C.O. 583/45; Boyle to Secretary of State, 31 Oct. 1916, C.O. 583/49.

Office it was 'just the old mob in a new grouping'.[29] AWAM admitted that British firms had made 'good profits' in 1915 but denied that these were 'excessive' because they bore heavier costs and paid higher taxes than African firms did.[30] Increased profits still delivered a return of only 7.2 per cent on capital, which was 'surely not very excessive'.[31] Lugard and the Colonial Office were unconvinced.[32]

It is impossible to deliver a definitive judgement on these issues, given the uncertainty surrounding the term 'excessive' and the absence of relevant evidence. It is clear, however, that the firms in the combine were able to control prices paid for produce in Lagos while also maintaining healthy profits. Their grip on the market fell short of being a monopoly. In paying low prices for produce, they created opportunities for merchants outside the combine and those operating on low costs to enter the market. By 1915, there were reports that 'several native traders have now entered the field as shippers of produce' because they could offer prices that were slightly higher than those paid by the combine.[33] By 1917, more than seventy Africans were exporting produce from Lagos compared to nine before the war.[34] The newcomers did not disturb the hold exerted by the combine because they lacked the capital to secure more than a small share of the market. Nevertheless, their increased presence as exporters confirms that African merchants had not been eliminated and were capable of taking advantage of market opportunities, despite facing considerable obstacles.

With regard to freight rates, there was undoubtedly a fear that Africans might suffer discrimination.[35] Elder Dempster's advertised rates remained the same for everyone. Large firms, however, could negotiate discounts for bulk shipments, as they had done before the war. Africans focussed their complaints on the space allocated to them rather than on the rates they were charged. Their problem was that, with a few exceptions, their businesses were too small to benefit from the discount offered for large orders. The large firms also co-ordinated their purchases of enemy property, which was auctioned in 1916, and raised a total of £383,674.[36] A senior official in the Colonial Office commented: 'It has been glorious victory for the ring and Elder Dempster'.[37]

29. Yearwood, *Nigeria*, pp. 106–7.

30. AWAM to C.O., 4 Oct. 1916, C.O. 583/53, 10 Oct. 1916, C.O. 583/53.

31. AWAM to C.O., 9 Nov. 1916, C.O. 583/53.

32. Lugard to Secretary of State, 8 April 1916, C.O. 583/45; C.O. minutes on Lugard to Secretary of State, 30 Aug. 1916, C.O. 583/48.

33. *Nigeria: Annual Report*, 1915, p. 8.

34. *West Africa*, 9 Nov. 1918, drawing on the *Nigerian Trade Report* for 1917.

35. Olukoju, 'Elder Dempster'; also Yearwood, *Nigeria*, p. 78.

36. This is the figure for Nigeria. Eleven sites in Lagos sold for £268,500. Lugard to Secretary of State, 1 Aug. 1916, C.O. 583/47, 26 Oct. 1916, C.O. 583/49, and 16 Dec. 1916, C.O. 583/52.

37. Harding minute on Burrowes to Colonial Office, 15 Nov. 1916, C.O. 583/54.

Although Africans were allowed to bid, few did so. The only sizeable purchases were made by Peter Thomas, who paid £5,000 for property at the corner of Market Street and Williams Street and £2,100 for a site in Kano.[38]

The most persistent difficulty throughout the war was the shortage of shipping space.[39] The loss of Woermann Linie reduced the available tonnage and left Elder Dempster as the sole supplier. Many of their ships were requisitioned for war service; some were sunk, especially during the last two years of the war, when submarines were deployed for the first time. Inevitably, the lack of tonnage produced a long-running dispute over the allocation of space on Elder Dempster's ships. Officials in Lagos attempted to produce a degree of order and certainty into the trade by allocating freight space according to the shares taken by shipping firms before the war. The combine firms were allocated 60 per cent; firms outside the combine and everyone else (including African merchants) were offered 40 per cent.[40] The fundamental problem, however, remained. In 1918, the shortage of shipping prevented much of Nigeria's cocoa crop from being exported. Local prices fell sharply; most of the crop rotted.[41] According to A. G. Boyle, the Acting Governor, the result was a serious risk of over-production.[42]

Inevitably, the decision produced an acrimonious debate. African merchants claimed that the allocation took no account of the trade they had conducted with Woermann before 1914 and ignored the share of the trade they had won since the start of the war by undercutting the combine.[43] AWAM responded by saying that the shipping shortage affected them disproportionately because their members conducted far more business than African merchants, and added that the latter had more tonnage than they could use.[44] Admittedly, representatives of African shippers were not above making exaggerated claims.[45] Yet, in 1916, one of the London firms handling consignments of produce for African merchants stated that their 'customers cannot get the space' they needed.[46] In the following year, the Agege Planters' Union had more cocoa to ship than its allocation permitted.[47] Colonial officials

38. Burrowes to Colonial Office, 23 Oct. 1916, C.O. 583/54. A complete list of purchases is given in Yearwood, *Nigeria*, pp. 269–73.

39. Olukoju, 'Elder Dempster'.

40. *Lagos Weekly Record*, 29 April, 5 May, 24 June, 1 July, 15 July 1916; Rose Hewitt to C.O., 25 Sept. 1916, C.O. 583/54; Lugard to Secretary of State, 13 Dec. 1917, C.O. 583/61.

41. *West Africa*, 9 Feb. 1918.

42. Boyle to Secretary of State, 3 Jan. 1918, C.O. 583/72.

43. Dransfield and Price to C.O., 9 Sept. 1916, enc. memo from African merchants, C.O. 583/54.

44. AWAM delegation to C.O., 4 Oct. 1916, C.O. 583/53; AWAM to C.O., 23. Oct. 1916, C.O. 583/53.

45. Yearwood, *Nigeria*, p. 244.

46. Taylor & Co. to C.O., 7 Aug. 1916, C.O. 583/54.

47. Coker to Elder Dempster, 20 Aug. 1918, CP 1//3/7.

also expressed concern that the combine could organise the distribution of tonnage among the component firms to ensure that their full allocation was used.[48] Complaints about discrimination in the allocation of freight space continued in 1918.[49]

The evidence suggests that Elder Dempster and the combine firms had 'a good war' and that non-combine firms and African merchants had difficulty securing the shipping space they needed.[50] Business records kept by Jacob Coker and Peter Thomas confirm that they experienced many difficulties in securing the freight space they needed.[51] Moreover, the fact that the criticisms coming from African merchants and their supporters were not matched by complaints from British firms in the combine indicates that they were satisfied with their allocation. The frustration African merchants felt led them to explore alternatives. As mentioned above, Jacob Coker and Peter Thomas began chartering ships to serve New York, which had become a major market for cocoa.[52] Another group formed the British & African Produce Supply Company in 1916 with the aim of securing an increased allocation.[53] In 1918 a consortium, headed by Josiah Doherty, Jacob Coker, and David Taylor, considered forming a cooperative to counter the British combine and to secure additional shipping space.[54] In the following year, another set of merchants founded the West African Federation of Native Shippers, which aimed to charter vessels for its members and provide freight for Marcus Garvey's Black Star Line.[55] None of these plans advanced much beyond good intentions, but they were all indicative of the problems African merchants faced in shipping produce. They also had wider significance as manifestations of a growing awareness that the commercial world was producing increasingly large firms with monopolistic aspirations and that Africans needed to co-operate if they were to avoid being overwhelmed.

The Armistice agreed in November 1918 was greeted with relief and rejoicing in Lagos, as it was throughout the empire. Lagos had an additional cause for celebration because the news came as the fearful influenza epidemic was receding.[56] Governor-General Lugard sent his 'hearty congratulations

48. Boyle to Secretary of State, 31 Oct. 1916, C.O. 583/49.

49. *Lagos Weekly Record*, 21 July, 4 Aug. 1918.

50. Olukoju, 'Elder Dempster', pp. 268–9.

51. See chapter 15.

52. *West Africa*, 5 Oct. 1918.

53. Josiah Doherty and others enc. in Dransfield & Price to C.O., 9 Sept. 1916, C.O. 583/54.

54. This episode is discussed in chapter 15.

55. *Lagos Weekly Record*, 11 Dec. 1920.

56. See *Lagos Standard*, 2 Oct. 1918, 25 April 1918, *Nigerian Pioneer*, 11 Oct. 1918, 18 Oct. 1918, 23 Oct. 1918; Boyle to Secretary of State, 21 Jan. 1919, C.O. 583/74. As far as I am aware, only one of the entrepreneurs studied in this book died as a result of influenza.

to the people of Nigeria who have faced all difficulties and privations with never wavering loyalty'.[57] The *Nigerian Pioneer* was so stunned by the 'stupendous and far reaching' news that it had difficulty grasping the fact that the war had really ended.[58] The *Lagos Weekly Record* had no such issue. In a wide-ranging essay, the paper drew attention to the changing contours of Europe, the rise of Japan and the United States, and the 'future political status of subject races', given President Wilson's endorsement of the principle of self-determination, the foundation of the League of Nations, and current discussions about forming an imperial parliament.[59] As the government planned to return to normality based on free trade, minimal state intervention, and a strong empire, Africans looked forward to a reformed empire that incorporated the progressive principles galvanised by the war.[60] Japan had shown that there were diverse paths to development; India was beginning to follow; Nigeria did not want to be left behind. Herbert Macaulay had begun to organise nationalist sentiment into a movement that would enable Nigeria to join the route to liberation. In both politics and the economy, 'the spirit of a New Age' had appeared, and would remain.[61]

Boom and Bust

The optimism stimulated by the end of the war was accompanied by a trade boom that began in the second half of 1919 and lasted until the middle of 1920. Looking back on the event from the vantage point of 1923, Nigeria's Governor, Hugh Clifford, referred to the period as being marked by 'recklessness' that had few historical parallels.[62] The 'excited and feverish' mood he observed was certainly exceptional, but it was not unique. There was a similar boom following the end of the French Wars in 1815, and there was to be another after 1945. The underlying causes were similar. Markets that had been closed (in this case in Germany and Austria) reopened; reconstruction fuelled the demand for tropical produce and consumer goods; restrictions on prices and volumes were lifted; the reappearance of firms from Allied and neutral

---

This was Frederick Williams, who died in November 1918, aged fifty-one. Williams was a prominent planter and close ally of Jacob Coker. *Lagos Weekly Record*, 30 Nov. 1918.

57. *Nigerian Pioneer*, 22 Nov. 1918.

58. *Nigerian Pioneer*, 22 Nov. 1918.

59. *Lagos Weekly Record*, 25 Jan. 1919.

60. For further statements covering increased representation, the importance of a charter of rights, improvements in education, and the need to combine to achieve economic independence, see *Lagos Weekly Record*, 14, 21, 28 Oct. 2016; 4, 25, Jan. 1919, 1, 3, 31 May 1919.

61. The title of a leader in *West Africa*, 24 May 1919.

62. Quoted in Olukoju, *The Liverpool of West Africa*, p. 131. Clifford (1866–1941), governor of the Gold Coast (1912–99) and Nigeria (1919–25).

countries increased competition; shipping services began to return to civilian duty.[63]

These developments were neither instantaneous nor simultaneous. Several war-time difficulties lingered. Complaints about inadequate shipping space continued in 1919 and 1920.[64] The scarcity of consumer goods raised prices and limited effective demand.[65] Currency problems also constrained market growth. The lack of silver restricted the volume of token currency in circulation. The attempt to promote currency notes met resistance, not because of innate conservatism but because paper currency was better as a medium of circulation than as a store of value.[66] In 1919, the government contributed to the problems merchants faced by imposing a differential duty of £2 per ton on exports of palm kernels. The levy was remitted on consignments entering Britain.[67] The aim was to protect the British kernel-crushing industry against the anticipated revival of its German competitors after the war. Government policy gave practical application to Mill's argument in favour of supporting nascent industries, but did so in Britain rather than in Nigeria.

Whether the conditions needed to support the milling industry in Nigeria were present at that time is another question, but it was not one the government chose to pursue.[68] Although the differential duty was abolished in 1922, the export duties imposed in 1916 were retained, despite opposition from both expatriate and African merchants, who pointed out that they were a direct cost to the producer and resulted in reduced purchasing power and diminished demand for consumer imports.[69] The duty also had the unintended effect of providing an incentive for the German firm of Gaiser to look elsewhere for palm kernels. In 1920, when Gaiser returned to West Africa, it chose Liberia as the location for 'the newest palm-kernel crushing machines' and the 'best packing on facilities'.[70] More impressively still, by the close of the 1920s, Gaiser had made considerable progress in recovering its pre-war position in

63. For further details, see Olukoju, *The Liverpool of West Africa*, pp. 131–5.

64. *West Africa*, 27 Dec. 1919, 26 June 1920.

65. Lugard, Address to the Nigerian Council, reported in *West Africa*, 22 March 1919; *Lagos Weekly Record*, 24 Jan 1920; *West Africa*, 26 June 1920.

66. *West Africa*, 3 Jan. 1920, commenting on the Report of the West African Currency Board for 1919; *West Africa*, 20 March 1920.

67. *West Africa*, 31 Jan. 1920; *Lagos Weekly Record*, 30 Oct. 1920.

68. In 1919, the Colonial Office discussed a request from W. H. Lever, who had established two kernel mills at Opobo and Apapa, and applied to have kernel oil and cake exempted from export duties on the grounds that they were infant industries. C.O. minutes on Clifford to Secretary of State, 31 Oct. 1919, C.O. 583/78.

69. Clifford wanted to increase them. Clifford to Secretary of State, 31 Oct. 1919, C.O. 583/78. Tariff issues are thoroughly covered in Olukoju, *The Liverpool of West Africa*, pp. 83–100.

70. *West Africa*, 14 Feb. 1920; *Lagos Weekly Record*, 5 Nov. 1921.

Nigeria's export trade.[71] It is tempting to see Gaiser's history in Nigeria as a microcosm of the productivity problems that were emerging in Britain and are present even more visibly today.

Despite these qualifications, the economy boomed. By some measures, recovery was under way even before 1919.[72] The volume of major exports was higher between 1917 and 1920 than it was during the years of pre-war prosperity between 1910 and 1913. Both export and import values experienced a marked rise towards the end of the war. These indicators need to be handled with care. Values given in current rather than constant prices ignore changes in exchange rates and are inadequate measures of purchasing power. In this case, they fail to incorporate the fall in the value of sterling during the course of the war. In 1919, the purchasing power of sterling had dropped to about one-third of its pre-war value.[73] Similarly, the rise in import values was partly explained by rising prices. Nevertheless, when these complications have been accounted for, it is clear that the net barter terms of trade rose in 1919, just as contemporary commentary suggested they should have done (see figure 2.2).

In January 1920, the *Lagos Weekly Record* noted that produce prices, driven by scarcity, were at 'unprecedented levels'.[74] In the months before the outbreak of war in 1914, Lagos prices for palm kernels averaged £17 per ton; in February 1920, they reached a peak of £36 per ton. Similarly, palm oil prices averaged £23 per ton shortly before the war; in December 1919, they rose to just over £62.[75] The boom of 1919–1920 favoured established and therefore well-placed merchants. Those who had 'done well' out of the war bought motor cars and enjoyed increased property values and the rents they were able to charge.[76] The boom also drew in a horde of newcomers who were keen to try their luck in the same way that day-traders do in our own time. In 1920, an official calculation reckoned that the number of 'native' shippers had reached the record total of 362.[77] This was an extraordinary transformation when compared not only to the count of nine in 1913 but also to the position in 1917, when there were said to be 'over 70 native shippers in Lagos'.[78] It is unclear how these small, part-timers were able to get a foot into exporting. Friends may have banded together;

71. Olukoju, *The Liverpool of West Africa*, pp. 154–8.
72. Olukoju, *The Liverpool of West Africa*, pp. 62–3, 91; Yearwood, *Nigeria*, p. 245.
73. Boyle to Secretary of State, 21 Jan. 1919, C.O. 583/72.
74. *Lagos Weekly Record*, 31 Jan. 1920.
75. These examples are taken from Olukoju, *The Liverpool of West Africa*, p. 131. Some adjustment to these figures is needed to take account of the falling value of sterling during these periods.
76. Olukoju, *The Liverpool of West Africa*, pp. 132–4; 105 motor cars were imported into Lagos in 1917. *West Africa*, 9 Nov. 1918.
77. *Nigerian Trade Statistical Abstract* for 1920 and comments by the Liverpool Chamber of Commerce, reported and updated by the *Lagos Weekly Record*, 19 Nov. 1921.
78. *West Africa*, 9 Nov. 1918.

modest savings may have been mobilised. An informed comment in *West Africa* added another possibility. In 1919, the journal rejected accusations that the expatriate banks discriminated against Africans and claimed that, 'if anything they have a slight bias towards Africans'.[79] Whatever the explanation, it seemed that 'good times' had arrived for everyone. Since effortless profits breed euphoria, it was easy to believe that the transient had become permanent.

Disillusion was sudden and complete. By mid-1920, gloom had descended and euphoria had dissolved. In January, the combine had paid £70 per ton for palm oil and £35 for kernels; in July, prices had fallen to £30–31 and £20–21 respectively.[80] Cocoa offered at £90–95 per ton in June fetched only £30 in October.[81] In July, when prices still had some way to fall, *West Africa* noted that the slump had 'caused uneasiness' and hoped, though without conviction, that 'normality' would soon return.[82] Export volumes of palm oil, kernels, and cocoa fell by nearly 50 per cent between 1919 and 1920.[83] By October, all prospects of recovery had vanished. The *Lagos Weekly Record*, reporting on the 'current stagnation', found the outlook 'very depressing'.[84] The volume of currency in circulation, having expanded rapidly in 1919, began to contract early in 1920.[85] Export prices were now so low that the 'native producer has practically gone on strike'.[86] Import prices, however, had risen sharply. According to one estimate, domestic and imported food prices were 300 per cent higher than they had been before the war and had far outstripped the rise in wages.[87] As the market for imports shrank, some firms were forced to sell consumer goods at 50–60 per cent below cost to secure the cash needed to meet their liabilities.[88] Reductions, even on this scale, failed to revive demand. Faced with falling real wages, railway workers went on strike in January 1920.[89] At the same time, the National Congress of British West Africa increased its pressure on the colonial government to allow Africans larger representation in the councils of state.[90]

79. *West Africa*, 15 March 1919.

80. *Lagos Weekly Record*, 10 July 1920.

81. *Lagos Weekly Record*, 2 Oct. 1921.

82. *West Africa*, 24 July 1920.

83. Yearwood, *Nigeria*, p. 251.

84. *Lagos Weekly Record*, 30 Oct. 1920.

85. *West Africa*, 2 April 1921, commenting on the *Report of the West African Currency Board* for the year that ended on 30 June 1920.

86. *West Africa*, 2 April 1921, commenting on the *Report of the West African Currency Board* for the year that ended on 30 June 1920.

87. *Lagos Weekly Record*, 24 Jan. 1920. Domestic and imported food prices had been rising since at least 1919: *Lagos Weekly Record*, 7 June 1919, 9 Aug. 1919, 3 Nov. 1919, 17 April 1920.

88. *Lagos Weekly Record*, 11 Dec. 1920.

89. *Lagos Weekly Record*, 31 Jan. 1920.

90. *Lagos Weekly Record*, 1 Jan. 1921.

The sequence that followed was to become a familiar response to what Governor Clifford called 'recklessness'.[91] In 1920, the Bank of England raised interest rates to what at the time was the formidable level of 7 per cent. The deflationary consequences were felt from the middle of 1921.[92] Commercial banks called on customers to repay the credit they had received; businesses were placed in acute difficulty.[93] Some firms had contracted to buy produce at prices that were far higher than those currently on offer; others had bought consumer goods at prices that could no longer be realised locally. The 'mushroom gentlemen', as they were called, disappeared as quickly as they had grown. By the close of 1920, the number of Africans exporting produce had shrunk from 362 to 102; by the end of 1921, that figure had been reduced to 'about a dozen'.[94] These numbers should be regarded as approximations. The *Nigerian Handbook*, for example, reported that there were 121 African exporters in 1921.[95] The figures are not necessarily contradictory because the periods they covered were not identical. The trend, however, is clear: the good times had come to an end, taking with them the brief experience of mass participation in the export trade.

The immediate cause of the collapse was the saturation of international markets once the most pressing needs of post-war reconstruction had been met. Britain had brought its war-time purchases to a close; Germany, Austria and France were devoid of purchasing power; the declining value of sterling not only assisted exports to the United States but also raised the cost of imports.[96] Previous depressions had been followed by recovery. This one was different. In August 1921, after the bank rate had been cut to 5.5 per cent, there were hopes of a revival; some observers thought that 'normality' was again 'in sight'.[97] All such expectations were disappointed. The 1920s promised far more than they delivered; the 1930s were disastrous. As over-production in the tropical colonies met inadequate demand in the developed world, thoughtful commentators on both sides began to consider an alternative future.

John Maynard Keynes had claimed that a punitive peace would be a lost peace.[98] His argument was influential at the time, but has been criticised since.[99] The leaders of Europe and the United States should be allowed a substantial measure of free will in the way they directed events during the inter-war period. Nevertheless, Keynes's claim that a 'Carthaginian Peace' would

91. See n. 63.

92. *Lagos Weekly Record*, 27 Aug. 1921.

93. *Lagos Weekly Record*, 8 Jan. 1921.

94. *Nigerian Trade Statistical Abstract* for 1920 and comments by the Liverpool Chamber of Commerce, reported (and updated) by the *Lagos Weekly Record*, 19 Nov. 1921.

95. *Nigerian Handbook* (London: West African Publicity, 1936), pp. 187, 275.

96. *West Africa*, 2 April 1921.

97. *Lagos Weekly Record*, 27 Aug. 1921, 24 Sept. 1921.

98. Keynes, *The Economic Consequences of the Peace*.

99. *Lagos Weekly Record*, 8 Jan. 1921, supported Keynes's argument.

FIGURE 14.1. Aerial View of the Marina Looking North, 1929.
Source: C.O. 1069/62, with permission of the National Archives, U.K.

stall recovery was sound. The failure of the victorious powers to promote policies that would rebuild devasted countries retarded economic growth in continental Europe. It took the experience of another world war to persuade a new generation of leaders to apply Keynes's recommendation.

The Mercantile Community

The changes that shook established trading patterns after 1914 had far-reaching consequences for the Lagos business community. The expatriate firms were buffeted by the same storms that struck African merchants and experienced comparable rates of attrition. Of the 197 expatriate companies operating independently in Nigeria at some point between 1921 and 1936 (inclusive), only fourteen traded continuously while also retaining their autonomy.[100] The expansion of trade after 1900 increased commercial opportunities

100. The figures cover all commercial firms except those involved in mining. Perham, ed. *Mining, Commerce, and Finance*, pp. 47–53. The contributions to this book, though rarely cited today, have not been surpassed.

and concomitant risks; unpredictable fluctuations provided an incentive for insuring against them. In 1898, as we have seen, a group of expatriate firms formed the first of several 'pools' to control local palm-kernel prices.[101] Following the expulsion of the German firms in 1914, their British rivals used the opportunity to create an informal combine with the aim of managing other produce prices, as well as kernels. The hectic post-war boom and the sudden slump that followed added impetus to these tendencies.

In 1919, a group of British firms, led by Miller Bros. and F. & A. Swanzy, joined with the African Association to form the African & Eastern Trade Corporation (AETC), which was bought by W. H. Lever in 1920.[102] The company struggled during the 1920s before merging with the Niger Company (which Lever had acquired in 1920) to create a sprawling conglomerate, the United Africa Company (UAC), in 1929.[103] The motives were mixed: vertical integration opened the prospect of joining mercantile operations with export production; horizontal integration offered the possibility of controlling local prices. One clear result was to eliminate the high rate of loss companies experienced during the 1920s and provide surviving firms what they most wanted: security.[104] Profits, however, remained elusive and disappeared entirely in the early 1930s, when the new company had to be bailed out by its parent, Unilever.[105]

Big may not have been beautiful in the eyes of African merchants, but small had revealed its weaknesses. No African merchant escaped unscathed from the upheaval caused by the war and the post-war slump. The most successful of the surviving merchants was Josiah Doherty (whose career was surveyed in chapter 12), though even he found conditions during the 1920s taxing. Samuel Pearse showed resolve in searching for new items of trade, but his best years were behind him. The few others who retained both prosperity and eminence, such as Alli Balogun, Isaac Williams, and Candido da Rocha, had moved from commerce to money lending before the start of the war and to this extent were shielded from the direct ravages of the post-war depression.

One businessman who flourished during hard times was Andrew Wilkinson Thomas, the leading auctioneer in Lagos.[106] Thomas was born in Oyo in

101. See above, pp. 304–6.

102. For some contemporary discussion, see *West Africa*, 2 Oct. 1920; *Lagos Weekly Record*, 30 Oct. 1920.

103. The Standard Account of UAC is Fieldhouse, *Merchant Capital*.

104. An analysis in *Fortune* (1948) showed that in the decade after the First World War, the companies that constituted UAC had returned an average of 5 per cent on capital and that UAC faced losses of £3 million in its first two years of operation (1929/31).

105. Wale, 'Changing Activities'.

106. I am grateful to Jacob O. Thomas, Andrew's son, for interviews on 21 and 31 Dec. 1961, and to Mrs Ayo Coker, daughter, for a lengthy interview on 7 June 1964. Thomas's name was originally Andrew Obalaye Thomas, but Wilkinson was a nickname that stuck. Other sources include: Macmillan, *Red Book*, pp. 103–4; Deniga, *Nigerian Who's Who, 1919*, pp. 31–3; LAP, 6/202–8 (1924); *Nigerian Pioneer*, 7 Jan. 1924.

1856 and educated in Ibadan and Lagos. He entered government service as a clerk, and became Deputy Registrar of the Colony in 1886. Promotion was an indication of Thomas's exceptional ability; his sharp eye for opportunities, however, prompted him to exercise his talents outside government service. The commercial difficulties of the time had led to business failures that created an opening for specialists who could deal with the debris. Thomas resigned his post in 1899 and took out an auctioneer's licence in the following year. He never looked back. In 1913, he built a five-story mansion in Odunfa Street in Brazilian-Gothic style; by then, he had also acquired a substantial portfolio of properties in Lagos.[107] He was a familiar figure in high society and was known as one of the best dressed (and most flamboyant) men in town.[108] His chief interest outside business was the African Church; his financial contributions were the main support of the Bethel branch of the Church. Predictably, Thomas did well out of the war. He was appointed to oversee the sale of German property; he then handled a large share of the property and stock that became available as a result of the post-war slump.

When Thomas died in 1924, the business was still prosperous, but the succession was not entirely straightforward. Initially, the firm was run by Andrew's chief clerk, who was supervised by one of his daughters, Mrs Ayo Coker. In 1934, however, Thomas's son, Jacob (also known as Mosalawa) Thomas, took over and carried the firm into the 1960s. A. W. Thomas & Co. and Josiah Doherty were the only two African businesses in Lagos to have survived from the late nineteenth century into Nigeria's period of independence.

The main story, as in the case of the expatriate companies, concerns the high rate of failure among African firms following the post-war slump. According to the *Nigerian Handbook*, the number of African exporters fell from 121 in 1921, to 22 in 1925, 21 in 1929, 13 in 1933, and 8 in 1936.[109] There is no indication that declining numbers were offset by the increasing size of the surviving firms. The trend is clear, though it is worth noting that the number of survivors in 1936 was very similar to the number of African exporters just before the war.

Thomas Johnstone provides a striking example of a 'mushroom gentleman' whose sudden appearance was exceeded only by the speed of his departure.[110] Others could be cited.[111] Johnstone originally came from Lagos but settled in

107. The house was destroyed by fire in the 1980s.

108. Akinsanya, 'Dandies of the 1900s'.

109. *Nigerian Handbook* (London: West African Publicity, 1936), pp. 187, 275.

110. Macmillan, *Red Book*, pp. 105–6. I am grateful to the late Chief Adebayo Doherty for his shrewd assessment of Johnstone (and many of his contemporaries, including the two who follow).

111. Samuel W. Duncan, was born in the Gold Coast, became a cashier for H. B. W. Russell in Lagos in 1908, and started his own business there in 1915. He made money in produce before losing it in 1919 and returning to the Gold Coast. Macmillan, *Red Book*, p. 109;

Britain before being sent to West Africa in 1916 to buy produce for the Fantee Planters and Mining Owners Company. Once established in Lagos, he began trading on his own account. By 1919, he had built an extensive business described by the *Red Book* as being 'one of the largest native undertakings in West Africa'.[112] The *Red Book* was probably unaware that the edifice was built on credit and extravagant promises to deliver an agreed volume of produce at a fixed price by a specified date. From his head office in Apongbon Street, Johnstone presided over twenty-eight staff, including a European head clerk, and employed managers who oversaw branches in Warri, Sapele, and Accra. He also had numerous agencies along the railway line. Life was good while it lasted, but it did not last long. Johnstone's façade began to slip in 1919, even before the slump had descended. Between 1919 and 1921, creditors won a series of court cases for breach of contract.[113] Eleven of these delivered judgement against Johnstone for a total of £23,952 (plus costs). By then, he had long disappeared, leaving his creditors to pick over the remnants of his short stay in Nigeria. It is unclear what happened to his racehorse.

Established merchants rarely fell so swiftly. The most dramatic exception was Peter Thomas, whose career is examined in detail in the next chapter. Thomas was drawn into the boom and suffered irreversible damage during the slump that followed. Where Peter Thomas led the way, a parade of other exporters followed. All were tempted into the produce trade by irresistible prices and suffered the consequences, if not on the scale experienced by Thomas. Many of these merchants have been discussed at some length in previous chapters. The summary of their fortunes presented next brings a selection of them together to illustrate the widespread consequences of the post-war crisis.

David Taylor, who had built up a successful business in the 1890s, did well down to the war, when he, like Thomas, was tempted to place a large bet on the produce trade.[114] The post-war slump exposed the fragility of a business built on excessive credit; Taylor spent the 1920s negotiating with the Colonial Bank. The slump of 1929 eliminated all hope of revival. After he died in 1932, the business was closed and almost all his assets were sold to pay his creditors.

Duncan v. Glover, LSCR, Civ. 55, 1909; Duncan v. Duncan, LSCR, Civ. 92, 1921; LSCR, Civ. 101, 1923; Keef Bros v. Samuel Duncan, LSCR, Civ. 104, 1924. Samuel Oke Bamgbose (trading as S. O. Bangbose & Bros.), who appeared in 1915, achieved prominence briefly and disappeared rapidly during the post-war slump. Macmillan, *Red Book*, p. 1. Delo Dosunmu was a teacher who dabbled in commerce during the war and ended being sued for debt. Macmillan, *Red Book*, pp. 107, 117; Niger Company v. Amos Olusanya Delo Dosunmu, LSCR, Civ. 101, 1923. Interview with Adebayo Doherty, 22 Feb. 1962.

112. Macmillan, *Red Book*, p. 105.

113. The cases are in LSCR, Civ. 85 (1919), Civ. 86 (1920), Civ. 89 (1920), Civ. 90 (1920), Civ. 90 (1921).

114. The examples that follow in this paragraph refer to longer accounts of these merchants given in previous chapters.

James George & Son (1864), the longest established partnership in Lagos before 1945, ran into difficulties during and just after the war and survived only by selling valuable property in the 1920s. In the 1930s, the business existed in name more than in function. George Will George (the third generation of Georges) retired in 1935; the business closed when he died in 1940. Brimoh Igbo, who had helped to develop the kola trade from the Gold Coast to Northern Nigeria via Lagos after the turn of the century, avoided the post-war produce boom but suffered from the general decline in purchasing power and even more from the death in 1933 of his wife, Rabiatu Koshemani, who was his key agent in the Gold Coast. The business never recovered its former prosperity and ended shortly after Brimah's death in 1946. In 1909, Lourenço António Cardoso adapted to the decline of trade with Brazil by taking up cocoa farming at Agege. In 1918, he mortgaged seven properties to cover an advance of £5,000 to finance further expansion. The post-war slump took him by surprise; the economic crisis in 1929 completed his downfall. He was unable to service his debts and was forced to surrender his property in 1931.

Several other cocoa farmers suffered similarly. Even the largest of them, Jacob Coker, struggled during and after the post-war slump. Coker was being pressed by creditors in 1921 and was never fully clear of difficulties during the inter-war period.[115] In the calendar year 1918, his income and expenditure almost balanced at just under £10,000; in the year ending in May 1933 his income had fallen to just under £800 and his net profit was no more than £275.[116] Coker's generosity towards the African Church and his costly involvement in Egba politics ensured that he would never die a rich man; nor was that his ambition. His problems, however, and those of Agege, extended far beyond personal preferences. The prices paid for cocoa during the inter-war period offered no incentive for producing it. By the 1920s, too, the main areas of production had moved north to Ibadan and Ondo, where competitive small farmers predominated. Their calculations of costs and returns did not require them to include finance for churches and schools. Various agronomic problems also came to the fore: disease was one; close planting near kola trees was another. Adversity brought depressing consequences. During the 1930s, Agege farmers cut down their cocoa trees to make way for other crops, especially kola.[117] In 1918, the Agege Planters' Union had 'over 200 members';

115. See, for example, London & Kano Trading Co. Ltd, v. J. Ade Williams, J. K. Coker, and J. Beckley, LSCR, Civ. 89 (1920); Coker to Noye (London), 12 Dec. 1921, CP 3/1; Coker to H. B. W. Russell, 25 July 1923; Irving & Bonnar to Coker, 24 Nov. 1923; Candido da Rocha to Coker, 2 Jan 1924; H. B. W. Russell to Coker 8 March 1924, all in CP 2/1.

116. Account Books, CP 3/1. The figures for outgoings in 1932/33 may not have included all accountable expenditure. Accordingly, the figure cited here may not have been net profit.

117. Exports of kola from Agege and Otta to Northern Nigeria rose from 100 tons in 1922/23 to 5,307 tons in 1932/33. Agiri, 'The Introduction of Nitida Kola', p. 8.

in the 1930s, it became moribund.[118] Jacob Coker fulfilled his ambition: far from becoming a rich man, he owed £1,817 at the time of his death in 1945.[119] Coker's achievements, however, survived him. His role in developing the Nigerian cocoa-farming industry is unsurpassed; his advocacy of African rights, expressed in his political values and through the foundation of the African Church, entitles him to a place in the top rank of Nigeria's early nationalist leaders.[120]

African import merchants were too numerous to be assigned a precise number. They also occupied a range of gradations that ran from major figures like Josiah Doherty to more modest importers who managed one shop. Aside from the substantial merchants who have been referred to above, few of the many other importers rose to the point where they could be classified as being outstanding. It is also hard to do justice to their contribution to the Lagos economy because of the fragmentary quality of the surviving information.

Two exceptional figures, who were both importers and pioneers of diversification, were in rapid retreat after World War I.[121] Dada Adeshigbin and William Dawodu were hit by the post-war slump but even more by competition from British and American firms. Both fought to retain the businesses they had built up before the war, but were overtaken by foreign companies that had the capital to buy in bulk and were able to finance expansion in what had become a large market. Adeshigbin lost the franchise for Singer sewing machines in 1924 and died a few months later. His brother, Oke, tried to keep the business going but was defeated by adverse conditions in the 1930s. When he died in 1942, the business was wound up. Similarly, Dawodu's agency for Ford cars was reassigned to Miller Bros. soon after the war. By the end of the 1920s, the business was operating at a loss and was closed in 1930, shortly after his death.

The remaining examples are selected from about thirty-five importers who were trading actively in 1920. The broad impression is that those who survived the adverse years that followed the First World War did little more than stay afloat; no one appears to have become rich during this period. The most buoyant were merchants who were able to draw on wealth they had accumulated before the war. As only sketchy information about most of these merchants has survived, commentary is necessarily brief.

David Akerele (1876–1943) began his career as a clerk in government employment and did not enter trade until 1909.[122] He started in what had

118. T. B. Dawodu to Elder Dempster, 12 April 1918, CP 1/3/7; interview with Oyebade Coker, Jacob's son, 23 Feb. 1962.

119. Information from Oyebade Coker, 23 Feb. 1962. There is an obituary in the *Nigerian Daily Times*, 8 Jan. 1945.

120. The African Church currently has about two million members.

121. See chapter 11.

122. I am indebted to David Akerele's son, Dr Flavius Abiola Akerele, for information about his father: interview, 19 June 1964. Additional sources include: Macmillan, *Red Book*,

become the standard way by mortgaging several modest properties in Lagos to cover advances of goods.[123] His import business prospered, and he opened several branches in the Lagos hinterland and in Duala and Victoria before being tempted into the produce trade. The slump that followed the brief post-war boom left him heavily in debt and compelled him to make a much-reduced living as a government contractor. Unlike many of his contemporaries who were affected by the slump, Akerele had already made enough money to educate most of his children. He also took care to direct them away from an unpredictable life in business and towards the professions. Of seven children who survived to adulthood, two (including a daughter, Elizabeth Abimbola) became doctors and two became barristers. As we have seen, this route was followed by the children of many other successful Lagosian merchants.

Badaru Abina (1875–1937) was a large trader in cotton goods who avoided the produce trade and appears to have kept going steadily until his death in 1937.[124] Sanni Adewale (1866–1944), who also specialised in textiles (especially damask and velvet), had to close two branches after the war but continued to run his main business in Balogun Street until his death. At that point, the business was wound up and the assets distributed among members of his family.[125]Another successful Muslim merchant, Abibu Oke (?1849–1935), traded in a variety of imports before concentrating on cotton goods.[126] His prominence in the Muslim community was recognised in 1919, when he was made *Balogun* of the Jamat Muslims. His business survived the post-war slump but faltered in the 1930s, by which time he was in his eighties and had been confined to his house for several years. Like David Akerele, however, his finances were bolstered by money made before the war, which he invested in property. Although the business ended at his death, profits from the prosperous years enabled many of his children to be educated and qualified some of them to enter the professions. Idris Olaniyan (1856–1926) made money before

p. 114; Lagos Supreme Court records: LSCR, Civ. 71, 1914, Civ. 75, 1915, Civ. 80, 1917, Civ. 83, 1919, Civ. 90, 1920, Civ. 94, 1922, Civ. 98, 1922, Civ. 99, 1922, Civ. 101, 1923; *Nigerian Daily Times*, 13 Dec. 1943.

123. Land at Moloney Street to John Holt (£50), LLOR, 66/276, 1910; land at Oil Mills Street to Walkden (£125), LLOR, 68/127, 1910; land at Bamgbose Street to Holt (£600), LLOR, 68/423, 1912.

124. I am grateful to Mr M. B. Abina, Badaru's son, for information about his father. Interview, 26 Jan. and 3 Feb. 1962; *Nigerian Daily Times*, 5 May 1937. According to Mr M. B. Abina, the date of birth given in Ikoyi Cemetery (1867) is incorrect.

125. Interview with Tijani Sanni Adewale, Sanni's son, 2 Feb. 1962; evidence in John Walkden & Co. Ltd., v. J. A. Oshodi and anor., LSCR, Civ. 101, 1923; Deniga, *Who's Who in Nigeria, 1919*, p. 2.

126. I am grateful to Mr M. Oke, Abibu's son, for interviews on 12 Jan. 1962, 19 January, 24 Jan. 1962, and for making notes on the history of the family available. See also *Nigerian Daily Times*, 27 July 1935.

the war trading in cotton goods.[127] He survived the war, was a creditor after it, and was still prosperous at his death. James Asani Disu (1881–1950) was one of the very few merchants in the sample to enter business during the inter-war period. He began as an 'office boy' for Ashton Kinder and progressed to become their sole agent in Lagos. When Ashton Kinder left Lagos in 1924, Disu started his own business in imported goods and traded until his death, when the firm was closed.[128]

The list of merchants whose businesses either failed or were much reduced is sizeable. Mohammed Bello Fashola (c.1845–1930) was hit twice: in 1914, he left trade for farming after the German firms, who were his main suppliers, were expelled; he was then battered by the slump in cocoa prices in the 1920s. He survived because he could draw on rents from property he had bought during the prosperous pre-war years.[129] Mohammed Laweni Kekereogun (d. 1942) was another importer whose trade suffered from the post-war slump and even more from the economic crisis of 1929.[130] *Alhaji* Abdul Ramonu Olorun Nimbe (1879–1948) was a merchant whose import business contracted during the 1930s but who had made enough money by then to educate some of his sons and daughters in England.[131] One son, Ibiyinka, became a doctor and later the first mayor of Lagos (1950–1952).

Philip Henryson Williams (1872–1946) began as a clerk for Claudius Oni in 1889 and started on his own in 1903 as an importer of cotton goods and hardware. He experienced a setback in 1916, when the court found that he owed £2,419 for goods supplied by Gaiser. He turned to the produce trade in 1919, but soon lost money. Although he continued to trade in imported goods until he died, the business struggled during the slump of the 1930s and never recovered.[132] Seidu Williams (?–1948) was an import merchant who began trading in 1889 and did well enough to open a branch in Ibadan shortly after

127. I am grateful to *Alhaji* Ismail Aremu Laniyan, first grandson, for information about his grandfather. Interviews, 32 Jan. 1962, 5 Feb. 1962; date of birth is given in Oke-sunna Cemetery; Disu Laniyan v. J. A. Davies, LSCR, Civ. 93, 1921.

128. Information kindly supplied by Mr A.R.A. Disu, James's son, 17 May 1964, 24 May 1964. Disu was a Muslim; 'James' was an acquired name dating from his time with Ashton Kinder; *Nigerian Daily Times*, 27 Dec. 1950.

129. I am grateful to two of Mohammed's sons, Shaffi and Sadike Fashola, for information about their father. Interview, 9 June 1962; also *Alhaji* Shittu Fashola, 26 Feb. 1962, and Adebayo Doherty, 15 Feb. 1962.

130. I am grateful for information provided by Mohammed's son, Mr R. A. Kekereogun, 31 Jan. 1962.

131. Interview with Dr Ibiyinka Olorun-Nimbe, Abdul's son, 13 Feb. 1962; *Nigerian Daily Times*, 19 Aug. 1948.

132. I am grateful to Philip's daughter, Mrs Alapa Philips, for information about her father. Interview, 2 March 1962; Macmillan, *Red Book*, p. 115; Receiver of G. L. Gaiser v. P.H. Williams, LSCR, Civ. 77, 1916 and Civ. 79, 1917; Randall v. Williams, LSCR, Civ. 96, 1922; *Nigerian Daily Times*, 2 May 1946.

1900 and other branches subsequently.[133] Like many others, he was tempted into the produce trade during the war and lost money on cocoa in 1920–1921. After this reversal, he abandoned the produce trade and concentrated on imports. The slump in the 1930s damaged the business and forced him to close his remaining branches. Like others whose good times lay behind them, Seidu was helped through his difficulties by his ability to draw an income from properties he had acquired before the war.

The concentration of Muslim merchants on the import trades, especially textiles, was far from being new. Their numbers almost certainly expanded during the inter-war period because their share of the Lagos population had grown. Their absence from the export trade can be explained partly by their wariness of the Anglo world, which the Saro had embraced. Concentration on imports had the benefit of shielding merchants from the considerable risks that accompanied that trade while withholding the windfall profits that tempted others into it. Nevertheless, the Muslim community had started to make selective adaptations to the culture sponsored by colonial rule. During the inter-war period, an increasing number of Muslim merchants sent their children to Western and predominantly Christian schools, thus creating a generation that was literate in English and equipped to play a much broader part in the economic and political life of the port. Other customs, however, retained their hold. Businesses lacked continuity because assets were realised at death and distributed among the family.

If, as Schumpeter argued, economic crises follow booms, declining mercantile fortunes ought to have stimulated innovation. There were undoubtedly signs of creative reactions amidst the landscape of stagnating or failing businesses. The examples that follow, though no more than indicative, suggest that preliminary efforts were being made to adopt new economic institutions and to find innovative ways of restoring profitability.

Co-operation and Innovation

African businessmen and politicians had already advertised the importance of what they termed 'co-operation'. It was their pressure that led in 1912 to the ordinance that enabled businessmen to register limited companies locally.[134] The increase in registrations that followed expanded after the war, when about fifty-five African-owned limited companies were catalogued between 1926 and the end of 1935, most of them operating in Lagos. Although the rate

133. Interviews with Seidu's sons, *Alhaji* Issa Williams and Mr A. O. Williams, 20 Jan.1962, 19 Feb. 1962; Lagos Stores v. Blackstock, LSCR, Civ. 26, 1901; Receiver of P. Meyer v. Seidu and Brimah Williams, LSCR, Civ. 79, 1917. Seidu traded with this brother, Brimah, for some years under the name S & B. Williams.

134. See chapter 13.

of failure was correspondingly high, at least two important companies survived the world slump and the world war that followed. The charismatic Theophilus Adebayo Doherty (1895–1974) was a formative influence on both. After Josiah Doherty died in 1928, his second son, Adebayo (as he was known), took over the business, and with the agreement of the executors converted it into a limited company in 1930.[135] Josiah had wanted his son to join the business before then, but Adebayo, who qualified as a lawyer in 1921, declined because his father was unwilling to make the change to limited liability.[136] The second firm, the National Bank of Nigeria, which was registered in 1933, resulted from the initiative of three founders, of whom Adebayo Doherty was the wealthiest and had the most business experience.[137]

It was Winifried Tete Ansa (1889–1941), however, who devised the most ambitious cooperative scheme that appeared in Lagos during the inter-war period.[138] Tete Ansa was a businessman who originated in the Gold Coast but had travelled widely before he arrived in Lagos in 1925. He combined a mercurial personality with exceptional presentational gifts that joined economic and political aspirations in a winning partnership. Following the lead given by the National Congress of British West Africa, Tete Ansa planned to make co-operation a reality. If Africans were to compete with foreign firms and create the unity needed to achieve independence, they had to pool their resources, form limited liability companies, and assert control of both production and marketing. He began by founding West African Cooperative Producers Ltd., which was inaugurated in Accra in 1925, registered in Nigeria in 1928, and began to ship produce in 1929. By 1930, Tete Ansa had won the support of forty-five of the leading farmers' associations that were responsible for producing about 60 per cent of the cocoa exported from West Africa. This unprecedented achievement met only part of Tete Ansa's ambitions. In 1924, he acquired a defunct company, the Industrial & Commercial Bank Ltd., which he transferred to Nigeria in 1928.[139] The Bank's main aim was to mobilise local savings and provide financial help to African farmers and traders, particularly those associated with the Cooperative. A third company, the West African American Corporation, was incorporated in the United States in 1930 to provide a marketing outlet for West African Cooperative Producers. The omens were promising. Not only had the United States become the largest consumer of cocoa, but there was also the prospect of tapping the savings of African American sympathisers.

135. Interview with Adebayo Doherty, 31 Nov. 1961; 25 June 1964; RCL, 325/29, 1930.

136. Josiah Doherty's experience with limited liability companies before the war may have made him hesitate; advancing years may also have been a consideration.

137. Newlyn and Rowan, *Money and Banking*, pp. 99–101; Chukwu, 'Economic Impact'.

138. Hopkins, 'Economic Aspects of Political Movements in Nigeria', ch. 5; Harnett-Sievers, 'African Business'.

139. See Chukwu, 'Economic Impact'; Chukwu, 'Indigenous Banks in Colonial Nigeria'.

Tete Ansa's breadth of vision was unsurpassed. His three companies aimed to achieve a degree of vertical and horizontal integration that would enable Africans to compete with the large expatriate combines. He looked beyond Nigeria to a form of pan-African commercial corporatism that encompassed the United States. His concept of racial unity identified a political force that could be mobilised to challenge colonial rule. The limited liability company was the means of harnessing economic power; the energy produced by racial unity would realise its liberating potential. Unfortunately, the seductive appeal of Tete Ansa's companies was not matched by their performance. Ambition leapt beyond reality. All three firms were significantly under-capitalised. Economic hardship had helped to generate a favourable response to Tete Ansa's plans; the same hardship limited the capital his companies were able to attract. Unity formed in idealism fragmented when solutions failed to appear. Inexperience, mismanagement, and an element of fraud made their contributions. The Industrial & Commercial Bank closed its doors in 1930 and was wound up in 1935. The Cooperative crumbled at the same time. The West African American Corporation ended its short life without having conducted any business. Tete Ansa, however, was not quite finished. In an illustration of hope triumphing over experience, he registered two new companies: the Nigerian Mercantile Bank in 1931, and the West African Producers Co-operative Society Ltd., in the following year. Both were short-lived. By 1936, Tete Ansa's career in Nigeria had come to a definitive end.

Tete Ansa's spectacular failures, combined with the high rate of attrition among limited companies of more modest ambitions, suggest a dispiriting conclusion. A longer view, however, points to a different interpretation. Profound institutional transformation of the kind required by a shift from finance based on personal trust to a system based on impersonal relations has challenged every country that has experienced it. The ability to use property as security was a step away from purely personal business relations. Limited companies, however, though impersonal organisations, still required investors to believe that their money would not be wasted. Confidence in the unknown was understandably limited. Moreover, to introduce a change of this order during a period of poor trade interspersed by a world slump was an additional obstacle that was insurmountable. Nevertheless, Tete Ansa's bold experiment assisted the learning process of his successors. It is no coincidence that the successful National Bank of Nigeria (1933) confined itself to banking in one country, made modest claims, and had the experienced hand of a prominent local businessman, Adebayo Doherty, on the steering wheel. Nigeria's political leaders drew the additional conclusion that African businessmen had only limited ability to influence the shape and direction of the colonial economy. From this perspective, fundamental economic change depended on first securing political control. This was the lesson applied after World War II.

Developments that currently remain obscure may also have had considerable significance for the future. The declining terms of trade during the inter-war years ought to have stimulated the internal market (assuming that the economic environment was favourable). Early signs of adaptation were found in the palm-produce industry, where low prices for exports of palm oil encouraged the growth of the domestic market.[140] Increased quantities of palm oil were consumed locally and also sent to Northern Nigeria. Similarly, a growing proportion of palm kernels was redirected to import-substituting manufactures, such as soap, lamp oil, and other products. The Agege farmers adapted to the low prices and declining yields of cocoa first by expanding the production of kola to serve the northern market and then by becoming the principal source of vegetables and poultry for Lagos. Outside agriculture, as we have already seen, Peter Thomas started a tannery just after the war to make shoe leather from hides produced in Northern Nigeria.[141] He also opened a flour mill that enabled a former employee to found the Nigerian bread industry. Samuel Pearse and Michael Elias harnessed the railway to expand the trade in cattle: a proportion of the hides arriving in Lagos entered local tanneries; the meat market catered to the needs of the expanding population.[142] The local cloth industry, far from declining, incorporated the sewing machines imported by Dada Adeshigbin, and found new markets not only inland but along the West Coast. The construction industry, pioneered by Isaac Cole, continued to build houses for the town's growing population.

One of the most striking adjustments, also noted earlier, was the expansion of the finance and service sector. Property in Lagos was the foundation of credit and the fount of a developing money market. Merchants had long advanced money on the security of freehold property, but after the turn of the century they became more specialised. The careers of Isaac Williams and Candido da Rocha chart the shift from trade to finance and illustrate the expanding importance of the mortgage market and of rental incomes. The growth of the service industry is evident in the initiative of Lagos merchants who imported the first motor vehicles, opened the first hotels and restaurants, operated the first cinemas and taxis, expanded the publishing industry, and anticipated, as Josiah Doherty did, the concept of the department store.

At present it is impossible to know how extensive initiatives of this kind were or how far some of them were temporary adjustments that receded when economic conditions changed. Their importance in the present context is that they reveal a dimension of the bleak inter-war years that is easily overlooked, largely because it remains uncharted. Even the story of the substantial financial sector, which not only survived the inter-war period but also expanded after World War II to become the gigantic industry it is today, remains known

140. I am indebted here to Olukoju, *The Liverpool of West Africa*, pp. 149–50.
141. This example and those that follow are drawn from chapter 11.
142. The remainder was exported to Britain by Thomas and Pearse among others. Lugard to Secretary of State, 22 Nov. 1915, C.O. 583/38.

only in outline. Taken as a whole, the history of diversification needs to be told if the link between the colonial era and Nigeria's present economy is to be understood.

The Outcome

World War I threw international trade into disarray. Hostilities realigned trade relations; commercial priorities were altered to meet war-time demands; shortages of shipping and consumer goods limited the volume of trade. The shocks of 1851 and 1892 had provided a stimulus to Lagos trade. The shock of 1914 was different. Despite a brief but heady post-war boom in 1919–1920, and fleeting signs of revival in the mid-1920s and mid-1930s, external trade was depressed for the greater part of the period 1914–1945. The terms of trade moved against primary producers. The growth in export volumes during the 1930s was largely an attempt to compensate for falling prices; productivity, however, remained static. Depressed conditions applied throughout the colonial world; Lagos was among many other port cities that experienced the adverse consequences of this grim and gloomy period.

A closer look at these generalisations reveals a more varied picture. The frequent fluctuations that characterised the war opened and closed opportunities in unpredictable ways. The expulsion of the German firms was a gift to the British companies who reacted by combining to enlarge their share of trade without using the opportunity to improve their productivity or their relations with their African customers. The removal of the Germans had a differential effect on African merchants. This was not only a setback to the numerous African import merchants who had traded with them, but it also created a gap that enabled other Africans to enter the export trade. Sudden variations in prices of imports and exports were hazardous for everyone. On balance, however, African merchants survived the war, and some did very well out of the post-war boom that followed. It was the post-war slump that finished many of them. A few disappeared almost overnight; some ceased to trade when the founder died; many limped along hoping for better times, which failed to arrive. The most active continued to trade without being able to expand their businesses. The majority of those whose businesses remained even moderately prosperous had built a solid foundation from years of shrewd trading before the war and were able to rest on the cushion provided by their accumulated property.

The sample used in this chapter has important limits. It was chosen to cover the period from 1851 to 1931. Accordingly, it traces the fortunes of merchants who were established before World War I, not those who began careers in business after it. Chronology as well as enterprise explains why some of them had been able to accumulate property during the prosperous pre-war years. The passing of time also accounts for the high death rate among the merchants surveyed; many of them were middle-aged or older when the slump descended in 1920; hardly any were still active in 1939. The provisional findings advanced here should be treated as an advertisement for a thorough account, complementary in depth to this study, that will carry the story through the interwar period and down to the end of colonial rule.

An analysis of the causes of the unfavourable commercial conditions that prevailed during the inter-war years extends beyond the scope of this book. For contextual purposes it is sufficient to identify two related influences: one political, the other economic. Although the war was won in 1918, the peace was lost. Commenting in 1920 on the 'current stagnation', the *Lagos Weekly Record* observed that, if the defeated powers were driven into bankruptcy, the rest of the world would follow.[143] The lack of a Marshall Plan and the rise of economic nationalism in Europe were large obstacles to recovery. Economic adversity produced unrest. Colonial subjects protested against falling levels of income; political organisations arose to express their discontent. Developments in Lagos were one manifestation of a trend that was found throughout the Western world and its empires. The underlying influence stemmed from the structure and performance of the colonial economy. The long boom in primary products that culminated in 1914 not only raised export volumes but also increased competition among colonial suppliers and cut their profit margins. By the 1930s, supplies of many staple exports were exceeding effective demand. It was at this point that far-sighted economists began to reconsider orthodox assumptions about the link between export growth and economic development. Colonial rule was largely a gamble on the continued success of international trade. By 1939, the bet had been lost, even if some of the players continued to hope that their luck would turn.

143. *Lagos Weekly Record*, 30 October 1920.

CHAPTER FIFTEEN

Peter Thomas

FROM METEOR TO FALLING STAR

BEYOND HIS IMMEDIATE FAMILY, Peter Thomas's name is known today only to a small group of specialists who draw principally on one source, Allister Macmillan's *The Red Book of West Africa*, which was published in 1920.[1] Macmillan provided valuable portraits of numerous Lagos notables. Although he did not specify his sources, his accounts of contemporaries, such as Samuel Pearse, Josiah Doherty, and Peter Thomas, could only have come from them or from close family members. Each entry is accompanied by photographs of the subject and in some cases his house and business premises as well. Thomas received lavish treatment. He appears resplendent in a frock coat and with top hat in hand; members of his staff, with a European manager in the centre, are presented separately. The *ensemble* is undoubtedly impressive.

The problem with Macmillan's informative study is that most of the material was gathered in 1919 at the height of the post-war boom. By the time the *Red Book* was published, the boom was about to be overtaken by a deep and disastrous slump and, as we now know, by a long period during which sustained recovery, though fervently hoped for, failed to materialise. In an unpremeditated way, the *Red Book* presents Thomas at the apex of his career. His history before that point remains sketchy; the inter-war years, however, can be reconstructed from records preserved by his family.[2] Taken as a whole, the

---

1. With a substantial subtitle: *Historical and Descriptive, Commercial and Industrial Facts, Figures & Resources* (London: Collingridge, 1920). A preliminary version of this chapter appeared in Hopkins, 'Peter Thomas (1873–1947)', in *Les Africains*, Vol. 9, pp. 297–329.

2. I am immensely grateful to Mr E. A. Peter Thomas (son of Peter Thomas, for an interview on 1 Feb. 1962), Dr Irene Thomas (daughter, for an interview on 20 Feb. 1962) and Mrs Lucretia Nylander (cousin), who gave me permission to use the family records cited here as Peter John Claudius Thomas Papers (PJCTP).

evidence presents a familiar trajectory: prosperity before the war; hardship after it. Thomas's private correspondence is probably unique in revealing his own comments on his aspirations and his increasingly desperate attempts to realise them amid difficulties that were far beyond his control.

The Making of a Civil Servant

Peter John Claudius Thomas was born in Freetown, Sierra Leone, in 1873.[3] The early history of his family and his own upbringing are known only in outline and mainly from oral testimony. His parents belonged to different sub-groups of the Yoruba. His father, John, came from Ilesha; his mother, Jane, who was born in 1828, was an Egba.[4] At some point in the 1840s, John and Jane (as they were to become) were sold into slavery and shipped from Lagos for a destination in the Americas. As in many other cases reconstructed in this study, the vessel taking them across the Atlantic was intercepted by the Royal Navy's Anti-Slavery Squadron and the captives taken to Sierra Leone, where they were released and placed in the care of British missionaries. It was there that John and Jane became Christians of the Wesleyan faith and adopted English names. They met and married in Freetown, where their three children were born. In addition to Peter, there was an elder brother, Stephen, who was born in 1870, and a daughter named Laetitia Rebecca, who was born in 1865.[5] Peter's father, a farmer, remained in Sierra Leone, where he died in 1881; so, too, did his mother, who died in 1907.[6] Laetitia, who married a local man named King, also spent her life in Freetown.

Much later, Peter recalled with a mixture of realism and affection his early days as 'a tail-shirt boy of an unlettered father and a four-penny-a-month village elementary school mother'.[7] In the circumstances of the time, however, all three children were given a rare start: they were educated at a mission school and there acquired the values and skills that were to influence them throughout their lives.

Peter's first employer in the late 1880s was a prominent British merchant in Freetown, John Broadhurst, who taught him the elements of commerce.[8] In 1890 or 1891, Peter's brother, Stephen, left Freetown for Lagos, where his qualifications in spoken and written English enabled him to become a clerk in the expanding colonial administration. His favourable reports on his new job encouraged Peter to join him in Lagos, where in 1894 he began the first stage

3. See n. 2 above.
4. Thomas to Laetitia King (his sister), 20 June 1918, PJCTP.
5. *Sierra Leone Weekly News*, 16 March 1907.
6. *Sierra Leone Weekly News*, 16 March 1907.
7. Thomas to C. J. F. Macfoy, 11 Oct. 1946, PJCTP.
8. Thomas to C. J. F. Macfoy, 11 Oct. 1946, PJCTP. Christopher Fyfe has some information on Broadhurst in his *History of Sierra Leone*, pp. 339, 383, 417, 438.

in a career that was to keep him in Nigeria for the rest of his life.[9] Peter had a successful career in government service. He spent several years in the Customs Department in Old Calabar before transferring in 1906 to Lagos, where he became chief clerk (second in command) in the Financial Commissioner's Office in the newly constituted government of Southern Nigeria.[10] Two years later, he moved to the Treasury Department at the same rank. By 1911, his salary was £300 a year, a considerable sum in those days. In terms of promotion, he had achieved all that an African could hope for within the colonial service, which reserved the most senior positions for expatriates. In 1912, he retired with a pension as a result of ill health which affected his eyesight. Fortunately, the disability turned out to be temporary.[11] Nevertheless, Peter found himself unexpectedly out of a secure job at the age of thirty-nine, with much of his life ahead of him and with large ambitions to occupy his future.

From Government Official to Merchant

By the time Thomas's career as a government official had come to an end, two other important events had taken place. The first was the premature death of his brother, Stephen, who died at sea in 1903, having left for Freetown to get married. The brothers had a close personal relationship. They worked in the same Department, and they had also begun trading together in Old Calabar in a small way and on a part-time basis, wholesaling fish, salt beef, and biscuits to traders who sold them to labourers in the town. This activity was within the rules: African civil servants were allowed to have limited paid activities to supplement their relatively low salaries. Many years later, when Peter Thomas registered the name of his business, he gave the date of its foundation as 1903 and called the firm S. Thomas & Co. in memory of his brother. The business was not registered, but the suffix was widely adopted at the time as a way of impressing potential customers. The second event was a much happier one: in 1907, Peter married Josetta Cole, a Saro of Yoruba ancestry who was a member of a well-known Lagos family.[12] Peter's marriage not only strengthened his ties with Lagos but also provided him with valuable help in his business because Josetta acted as his cashier and clerk after Stephen's death.

It is impossible to know whether Thomas would have committed himself fully to the hazards of business had illness not forced him to give up the security of government service. Circumstantial evidence suggests that he might

9. *West Africa*, 4 Oct. 1919.

10. Thomas's progress in the colonial administration can be followed through the *Lagos Blue Books* for the period. There is relevant information in Deniga, *Nigerian Who's Who, 1919*, pp. 14–15, though some of it is unreliable.

11. Thomas later said that it was a cataract. *West Africa*, 4 Oct. 1919.

12. Josetta was born in 1887. Thomas to Laetitia King, 30 Dec. 1946, PJCTP. I have been unable to determine which of several possible Cole families she belonged to.

FIGURE 15.1 Peter Thomas, 1921. Copied by Paramount Photographers Lagos, with permission of E. A. Peter Thomas (son) and Dr Irene Thomas (daughter).

well have done. There was neither challenge nor reward left for him as a colonial administrator. As will become clear later on, Thomas was ambitious and an idealist: he wanted to show that Africans were capable of being creative and independent. Furthermore, by 1912 Thomas's plans had to take account of his children, some of whom would soon be approaching school age. Like most of his Saro contemporaries, Thomas regarded Western education as a passport to moral and material fulfilment. To enter higher education meant, at that time, a period of study in England, which was a costly undertaking. To motive can be added opportunity: Thomas already had a certain amount of business experience, and he saw, correctly, that prospects for further expansion in the years before the First World War were encouraging.

Thomas joined the limited but important set of African merchants who entered the produce trade after 1900. He focussed on cocoa, palm produce, and hides and added a range of imported goods, except spirits, which as a Wesleyan he refused to stock. As the export trade was buoyant, the business grew rapidly. Although Thomas had already begun buying property, rising profits enabled him to increase his purchases. In 1913, he bought a site on the Marina from Herbert Macaulay for £2,300, and assigned it as security for an overdraft of £1,800 from the Bank of British West Africa.[13] The advance enabled Thomas to expand his produce-buying business. He soon followed Samuel Pearse, Josiah Doherty, and others in moving inland. In 1912 he opened an agency in Abeokuta; in the following year he established a branch in Kano.[14] In 1914, he opened a general store in Lagos specialising in sales of imported manufactures.

The Exigencies of War

The First World War delivered a shock that was transmitted as a crisis for businesses throughout the world, including port cities, and especially those, like Lagos, that were colonies of warring empires. Survival required agility; profits depended on marrying risk and luck; disaster lay in wait. The strong demand for tropical raw materials translated into high produce prices; achieving them, however, was made difficult by the shortage of commercial shipping and the closure of markets in continental Europe. Thomas held his nerve. He kept a close eye on the produce market, offered prices that were fractionally better than those of his British competitors, and was adroit in managing the shipping quotas imposed by the government. He also took advantage of the good luck that followed the expulsion of the German firms from Nigeria. Their removal left a large gap in the market and gave British and local firms an opportunity to fill it. In 1915, the government appointed Thomas to draw up an account of German and other enemy property in Lagos.[15] The post gave him a privileged insight into the condition of some of his main competitors. In 1917, he was the only African to bid (or perhaps even to compete) in the auction of enemy property and was successful in buying the premises of

13. LLOR, 85/42,1913, 86/41, 1913. The property was rented to G. B. Ollivant in 1914 for five years at £150 p.a. LLOR, 82/99, 1914.

14. Evidence of A. V. Johnson, in Johnson v. S. Thomas & Co., LSCR, Civ. 84, 1919.

15. Deniga, *Nigerian Who's Who, 1919*, pp. 14–15.

J. W. Jaeckel & Co. in Williams Street for the considerable sum of £5,000.[16] In the following year, he moved from Broad Street into his 'new and palatial offices'.[17] His war had been a prosperous one.

Surviving correspondence between Thomas and one of his main suppliers of cocoa, Jacob Coker, provides an insight into the unremitting attention to detail the rapidly shifting uncertainties of the war demanded. Thomas would advise Coker (and other suppliers) of current prices, which were relayed by cable and then transmitted by telegraph and telephone, comment on prospects, and arrange loading and shipment. The price Thomas offered Coker depended mainly on the amount of cocoa he supplied. In 1916, Thomas wrote: 'we were not going to allow you £45 a ton because you have not given us the support we expected. We were going to advance you only £600. However, we send you the £675 and will continue at that rate'.[18] Later in the year, Coker wrote to his brother advising him that Thomas's price for cocoa was fractionally better than that offered by Dyer & Wintle, his English agents, and that they should accept it.[19] In a reference to the British combine, Thomas informed Coker in 1917 that 'we can also arrange to do regular business on a fixed basis above the pool price from time to time according to circumstances'.[20]

As we have seen, the expulsion of the German firms, far from increasing competition among their British rivals, encouraged them to combine.[21] The resulting produce pool held down local producer prices and gave African merchants unanticipated opportunities to offer prices that were slightly higher. In addition, Thomas's overhead costs were lower than those of his rivals and he may also have been prepared to accept a more modest rate of return. Samuel Pearse was able to undercut the price for cocoa offered by the combine for similar reasons.[22] Coker also praised Thomas's attention to detail, saying that he seemed to know 'all things' that were needed to ensure that the rail link between Lagos and inland producers ran smoothly.[23] Thomas certainly took great care to ensure that the railway delivered the waggons Coker required and gave him detailed instructions about loading and trans-shipping procedures.[24]

Thomas also needed to negotiate his way through and around the allocations of tonnage the government had authorised to deal with the shortage of shipping space. The arrangement became contentious because Thomas

16. Boyle to Secretary of State, 22 Jan. 1919, C.O. 583/73. See also LLOR, LO 3026.
17. *Nigerian Pioneer*, 15 March 1918.
18. Thomas to Coker, 25 Jan. 1916, PJCTP.
19. Coker to Jonathan Coker, 28 Sept. 1916, PJCTP.
20. Thomas to Coker, 17 April 1917, PJCTP.
21. See chapter 14. Also Olukoju, *The Liverpool of West Africa*, pp. 56–63.
22. Pearse to Coker, 7 Dec. 1914, CP.
23. Coker to Jonathan Coker, 9 March 1916, CP.
24. Thomas to Coker, 20 July 1916, 24 July 1916, PJCTP.

and other African shippers, like Coker, claimed that it put producers at a disadvantage.[25] Coker supplied cocoa on behalf of the APU as well as himself. Sometimes he fell short of his allocation, but more often he had more cocoa than space, while Thomas's allocation often fell short of the tonnage he could have exported.[26] Moreover, freight rates rose sharply during the war, partly because of increased risk and partly because the British firm Elder Dempster had acquired a virtual monopoly of shipping following the expulsion of the Woermann Linie, which had supplied about 40 per cent of the tonnage entering Lagos before the war.[27] Smaller shippers were penalised because those with substantial allocations could negotiate discounts on freight charges.

Thomas moved as adroitly as he could, filling allocations from other sources when his main supplier fell short and distributing excess tonnage to other shippers if they had space available.[28] The twin problems posed by the war and the combine, however, led to a search for a permanent solution that would enable Africans to compete successfully once peace returned. As Coker summarised the problem in 1916, 'It appears that a pool of European combined firms have managed to push us out of shipping'.[29] In response, he revealed that 'we' [the Agege Planters Union and several Lagos merchants] are 'sending Mr Duncan to England to discuss the matter' and that 'the Africans' can manage a chartered ship once a month to take 1,500–2,000 tons of cocoa.[30] Peter Thomas was one of the Lagos merchants; another was Josiah Doherty, who helped to pay for Duncan's trip to London. The immediate solution, which Coker and Thomas devised in combination, was to charter a ship and send their cocoa directly to the United States.[31] The idea was first mentioned in correspondence between them in February 1916, when Thomas said that he would pay an advance of £40 per ton against the consignment, adding that it would be 'risky'.[32] Coker responded by asking Thomas to confirm that he thought the experiment would be profitable.[33] Presumably, the answer was encouraging because by July the pair were shipping cocoa to New York.[34] By

25. Olukoju, *The Liverpool of West Africa*, pp. 67–8. See chapter 14.

26. See Coker's complaint to Elder Dempster, 20 Aug. 1918, CP 1/3/7; also Elder Dempster to Coker, 1 July 1917, CP 1/3/7; Coker to Central Secretariat, Lagos, 1 March 1918, CP 1/2/7.

27. Olukoju, *The Liverpool of West Africa*, pp. 69–72; Yearwood, *Nigeria*, pp. 72, 78–9.

28. This matter was the subject of some urgent exchanges. See Coker's telegram to 'Ekabo' (Thomas), 11 Aug. 1916; Thomas to Coker, 22 Aug. 1916, 28 Aug. 1916, PJCTP.

29. Coker to Rose Hewitt, 24 July 1916, CP.

30. Samuel Duncan was originally from the Gold Coast. In 1915, he extended the British & African Produce Supply Co. to Lagos. The firm had been founded by his father, W. T. Duncan, in the 1890s. See Yearwood, *Nigeria*, pp. 146–7, 152, 165–6, 184–5.

31. Coker to Rose Hewitt, 24 July 1916, CP.

32. Thomas to Coker, 18 Feb. 1916, PJCTP.

33. Coker to Jonathan Coker, 19 Feb. 1916, PJCTP.

34. Thomas to Coker, 20 July 1916, PJCTP.

then, Thomas had established a new set of connections that enabled him to compare prices there and in London and advise Coker accordingly.[35]

The link with New York, which rapidly became a major market for cocoa, was a development of great significance. It signalled the advance of the United States as a global commercial and financial power and enlarged the breach in the wall of established custom that joined the colony to the imperial centre. In forming a combine to deal with the exigencies of war, the British firms stimulated their African competitors to search for alternative markets that were to remain important after peace was restored.

The British combine prompted a second and equally unforeseen reaction, which was expressed in renewed attempts by Lagos merchants at collective action. Similar efforts had been made before the war with the formation of the first limited liability companies.[36] The war, however, galvanised what became a movement that aimed to transform cooperative ideals into effective instruments. Some of the resulting ventures remain obscure; others attracted widespread publicity. In 1916, Thomas wrote to Coker saying that he hoped that they could 'come to an arrangement to control prices'.[37] In the following year, the pair discussed a 'scheme' to counter the combine by mobilising African producers and merchants.[38] Also in 1917, Thomas, Pearse and 'others' were prepared to come together 'to form a limited company' because 'they realised its uses'.[39] In 1918, David Taylor, Josiah Doherty, Jacob Coker, and two other Lagos businessmen met to discuss a proposal put forward by M. J. Hughes for creating a co-operative association.[40] Although Thomas appears not to have been formally associated with this particular scheme, its aims fitted his own sentiments and interests.

Hughes was asked to develop a plan that would bring farmers and merchants together. The preamble captured the inspiration behind the final proposal, which was circulated in 1920:[41]

> What do we propose to do to safeguard our commercial interests in the face of rapid encroachments of foreign commercial houses swarming our coast towns and hinterlands, establishing business houses and relations with inter-produce sellers? Shall we continue to remain inactive and allow the wealth of our country to slip from our hands to those of foreigners?

35. Thomas to Coker, 17 July 1916, PJCTP.

36. See above, pp. 306–11

37. Thomas to Coker, 25 Aug. 1916, PJCTP.

38. Thomas to Coker, 10 May 1917, PJCTP.

39. J. Bright Davies to Coker, 17 Aug. 1917, CP 1/3/7.

40. Minutes of meeting, 26 March 1918. I have been unable to identify Hughes or trace his possible connection with David Hughes, the first president of the APU.

41. M. J. Hughes to Countrymen, 4 March 1920, CP 1/9/box 3.

Hughes then referred to the 'Afro-Americans of the USA', who have 'learned to work together' and had formed a shipping company known as the Black Star Line. The publicity achieved by this venture, Hughes said, ought to inspire comparable action by Africans. He suggested the formation of a company consisting of about seven investors to provide freight for the Black Star Line.[42]

> It would be a means of investing your wealth and securing it firmly for the benefit of your successors, thereby remaining an everlasting asset which will be handed from generation to generation and a help towards the development of your country. It would save the scattering of everyone's wealth to the wind after death, many examples of which are still fresh in our memories.

The example set by the Black Star Line turned out to be one to avoid rather than follow. Marcus Garvey and his colleagues in the Universal Negro Improvement Association, who founded the line in 1919, closed it in 1922 with substantial losses.[43] Duncan's venture also failed the test of long-term survival, as did Hughes's ambitious proposal to create an effective African cooperative. Yet, as argued earlier, none of these, or similar, schemes should be dismissed.[44] They have an important place in the still unwritten history of company formation in Nigeria, and in Africa as a whole. An expanded and increasingly complex economy required co-operation that extended beyond the family, first to include friends and then to encompass large numbers of shareholders who were unknown to the founders of the business. Structural change of this order depended on a shift in attitudes towards risk, which in turn meant trusting those who could not be policed by the family hierarchy. It is scarcely surprising that a change of this magnitude took time, or that the early ventures failed. What is significant, though, is that the first efforts marked a course that others were to take during the inter-war period, when, amid continuing failures, a small number of successful companies were formed.

Life at the Top

At the end of the war, Thomas's position seemed unassailable. By 1919, he had five stores in Lagos, twenty-one branches inland, stretching to Kano in the north, an agency in Zaria, several factories, and a fleet of motor lorries.[45] He planned to expand to Calabar, the Cameroons, the Gold Coast, and Sierra Leone. In 1918, his annual expenditure on salaries, wages, and rent (excluding

42. M. J. Hughes to Countrymen, 4 March 1920, CP 1/9/box 3.
43. This subject has produced a large literature. Essentially, the venture failed because of poor management and the hostile intervention of the US federal government.
44. See chapter 10.
45. Macmillan, *Red Book*, p. 96.

his own house and family outgoings) amounted to about £18,000.[46] In 1919, he had more than three hundred employees, including eight Europeans. His chief clerk was a Scot, Stewart Chalmers, whom Thomas regarded as 'very hard working and most conscientious'.[47] Another of his employees between 1918 and 1921 was Amos Shackleford, a Jamaican who later pioneered the Nigerian bread industry.[48] In 1919, Thomas felt confident enough to rent Jacob Coker's main property, Rose Cottage (48 Marina) for forty years at £500 per annum. It is scarcely surprising to find that he visited his up-country branches in a 'special coach' and was given 'every facility' to stop 'at all intermediate stations'.[49]

The most telling indication of Thomas's wealth and standing, however, was contained in his property portfolio. He had been buying property on a large scale between 1917 and 1919, and by the close of 1920 had amassed no fewer than thirty-seven houses in Lagos itself and an additional twenty on nearby Ebute Metta. The combined total of fifty-seven properties was valued at £91,691.[50] This was not all. In 1919, he also had property in Kano worth £8,000, and several large houses in central Freetown, including one for his own use that later became the City Hotel.[51] A haul of this size was unprecedented. Even Daniel Taiwo and James Davies, the two greatest property magnates of the nineteenth century, would have been impressed.

Thomas also began to diversify. As we have seen, he built a tannery for the production of shoe leather, a mill for grinding flour from local corn, and in 1920 purchased one of the few printing presses in Lagos from Isaac Williams.[52] In addition, he joined the growing number of wealthy Lagosians who bought farms in the Agege area. He had about 150 acres at Ifo and engaged an African American manager to oversee experiments in the production of corn, vegetables, casava, fruit, sugar cane, poultry, and even sheep.[53] In 1921, there were 23 labourers on the farm, each earning 30s. per month. Although Thomas used Ifo Farm, as it was known, primarily as a retreat, the produce grown there was to characterise Agege in the era that followed its decline as a centre of cocoa production. He hoped that the trustees of his estate would maintain the farm as a site of experimentation because the 'products of West Africa should instead of being exported in their raw state be partly or wholly manufactured or dealt with in West Africa'.[54]

46. Thomas to his sister, Laetitia King, 19 June 1918, PJCTP.
47. Thomas to Laetitia King, 24 Jan. 1920, PJCTP.
48. Kilby, *African Enterprise*, ch. 2.
49. *Nigerian Pioneer*, 24 April 1920.
50. Valuation dated 30 Oct. 1920, PJCTP.
51. John v. S. Thomas & Co., LSCR, Civ. 84, 1919; *Sierra Leone Weekly News*, 21 March 1925.
52. Note on Printing Press, 1921, PJCTP.
53. Note on 'Ifo Farm', 1921, PJCTP.
54. Thomas, last will, dated 1919, LAP, 15/231–41, 1947.

Thomas is remembered as a gentleman in the British idiom. In 1961, *Oba* Samuel Akinsanya recalled that, when at his office, Thomas was 'always fully dressed in lounge suit, with vest coat, vest slip, collar, tie, etc., no matter what the temperature'.[55] Photographs of him confirm the accuracy of the recollection.[56] His tailors in London maintained his appearance by supplying him with new suits every other month.[57] In 1919, the weekly journal, *West Africa*, which at that time catered mainly to a European readership, devoted considerable space to Thomas, describing him as 'something of a phenomenon in the life of Nigeria', and his career as 'one of the romances of latter-day West Africa'.[58]

The image of the Afro-English gentleman is easily mocked today, when current styles of dress are entirely different (and may themselves be mocked in the future). Apart from the need to resist making anachronistic judgements, it is important to remember the significance of dress as being, in this case, a badge of standing and probity. Thomas had to conduct business with Europeans, many of whom had imbibed racist beliefs about superior and inferior peoples. Thomas was intent on showing that Africans had the capacity to match, and even exceed, the standards set by British opinion. Dress that seemed to some observers to be an inferior imitation of the original served the purpose of making African merchants recognisable and hence potentially trustworthy to British businessmen and bankers. Advertising began with the image of the owner of the business. In Thomas's judgement, his style of dress showed that Africans were on an evolutionary course that would eventually lead to their full emancipation.

Thomas's aspirations were formed at the outset of his career and remained with him throughout his life. It was his 'earnest conviction that my fellow countrymen are destined at some time to take a great and good part in the world, and to add their part to the happiness and well-being of man'.[59] For this to happen, several conditions had to be met: the creation of 'a sound public opinion'; the presence of a 'class of Africans ready and able to devote themselves to the welfare of their fellows'; and 'the encouragement of technical education', which included 'farmers, engineers, woodworkers, contractors'. Meanwhile, Thomas saw his 'chief aim in life' as bringing about 'a better understanding between Africans and Europeans' because each needed the other.[60] This position required him to see two points of view. He affirmed that he was 'a loyal British subject' because the British had brought Christianity, Western education, and a 'love of

55. *Oba* Samuel Akinsanya, 'Gentlemen of Fashion', *Sunday Express* (Nigeria), 3 Sept. 1961.

56. Macmillan, *Red Book*, pp. 95–6.

57. Akinsanya, 'Gentlemen of Fashion'.

58. *West Africa*, 4 Oct. 1919.

59. This and the following quotations are taken from the preamble to Thomas's will, dated 1919, in LAP, 15/231–41, 1947.

60. *West Africa*, 4 Oct. 1919.

freedom' to Africa.[61] At the same time, as he declared to the Pan-African Congress in London in 1921, he exercised the right to hold the British to account whenever they departed from their own ideals.[62] Some years later, he addressed the National Congress on the subject of achieving economic independence.[63]

Thomas thought that departures from proclaimed values had become increasingly common. He was particularly critical of the 'Northern System' Lugard had installed while Governor of the Northern Nigeria Protectorate.[64] In a candid interview published in *West Africa* in 1919, Thomas offered some striking examples from his own experience.[65] When he applied for a first-class ticket to visit his branch in Kano in 1913, he was kept waiting for several weeks, then told he could not travel first class, and finally allowed to take the journey in the electrician's compartment. On arriving in Kano, he was informed that he could not stay in any of the three European residential and trading sites that he owned and had to travel some distance to find appropriate accommodation. Thomas dismissed the argument that residential discrimination was a measure taken to control disease. Separation, he claimed, did not prevent disease from spreading from African to European communities. The solution, he argued, was to have one policy to safeguard health and apply it to both communities. Thomas concluded that racially-based policies were a potent source of disaffection that would generate a sense of injustice and eventually produce hostility towards colonial rule. His was not a lone voice, but the thought was not one that resonated in Government House.

Thomas practised what he preached. In 1919, the Niger Company offered to buy his business 'on advantageous terms'.[66] When Thomas refused to sell, the Niger Company proposed to 'take him on as an associated company'.[67] Thomas again declined, not from 'conceit', as he put it, but because his business was still 'a pioneering work developing day by day'.[68] He wanted S. Thomas & Co. 'to be an entirely African business even though we found it necessary to engage European assistance in its development'.[69] This statement fitted his evolutionary view of economic development. European staff had a part to play until a new generation of suitably-trained Africans could take their place. He deferred forming a limited liability company for the same reason. He recognised the advantages of attracting

61. *Nigerian Pioneer*, 30 Sept. 1921. The second quotation is from *West Africa*, 4 Oct. 1919.

62. *West Africa*, 4 Oct. 1919.

63. Reported in *West Africa*, 5 Sept. 1931.

64. 1912–1914, and confirmed during his tenure as Governor General of Nigeria in 1914–1919.

65. *West Africa*, 4 Oct. 1919.

66. Thomas to Couper (General Manager, BBWA, London), 12 Oct. 1923, PJCTP.

67. Thomas to Couper (General Manager, BBWA, London), 12 Oct. 1923, PJCTP.

68. Thomas to Couper (General Manager, BBWA, London), 12 Oct. 1923, PJCTP.

69. Thomas to Auntie Agnes, Freetown, 24 Jan. 1947, PJCTP.

shareholders and limiting losses, but he wanted his firm to be 'really established before getting others to join. It would have been a major setback to the African cause if others had invested and then lost their savings'.[70] The opportunity would not recur.

Thomas also expressed his beliefs through philanthropy, which was strongly motivated by his Christian commitment. The following examples, which are no more than illustrations of a lifetime of generosity, also demonstrate the continuing importance of his long-standing connection with Sierra Leone. In 1908, while still in government service, he raised money in Lagos for Aaron Sibthorpe, the pioneering historian of Sierra Leone, who was then living in poverty.[71] In 1918, he asked his sister in Sierra Leone to 'give a few shillings each to any poor neighbours or friends whom you know would be thankful to God for an unexpected few shillings from a distant countryman . . . who has thought of others at a time like this. Tell them that this money is not sent by me but in a message of God's love to them through the agency of His creature, man'.[72] In 1919, he founded the John and Jane Thomas Fund, which supported 'several boys in training in Lagos and Sierra Leone'.[73] During a visit to Freetown in 1921, he entertained two hundred 'poor people' in his capacity as Patron of the Sierra Leone Friendly Society.[74] Thomas kept his eye on wider causes too. In 1917, he contributed £100 guineas to the Red Cross Fund; two years later he gave 200 guineas to the Liverpool School of Tropical Medicine.[75] It is even more impressive to learn that he continued to assist 'the poor' in Lagos in 1926, after his business had virtually collapsed following the slump of 1920.[76] He was still donating 7.5 per cent of his gross income to charity in 1942–1943, when his total income had shrunk still further.[77]

Politically, Thomas's views no longer resonated with a growing body of African opinion. His standpoint, which was similar to that adopted by his friends, Samuel Pearse and Kitoyi Ajasa, was in line with that of James Davies and other Saro, who in the 1860s appreciated the benefits that followed from emancipation and education while also criticising policies that departed from the ideals of co-operation and equality. What was once mainstream, however, was becoming a minority taste. The expansion of colonial rule at the close of the nineteenth century, and the rise of racism associated with it, opened the way for

70. Thomas to Couper (General Manager, BBWA, London), 12 Oct. 1923, PJCTP.

71. *Sierra Leone Weekly News*, 17 Oct. 1908. Aaron Belisarius Como Sibthorpe (?1829–1916), a long neglected figure, wrote the first *History of Sierra Leone* (London: Elliot Stock, 1868). See Fyfe, 'A. B. C. Sibthorpe: A Tribute'.

72. Thomas to Laetitia King, 21 Oct. 1918, PJCTP.

73. Deniga, *Nigerian Who's Who, 1919*, p. 15.

74. *Nigerian Pioneer*, 21 Feb. 1920; *Sierra Leone Weekly News*, 22 Oct. 1921.

75. *Nigerian Pioneer*, 9 Nov. 1917; *Sierra Leone Weekly News*, 1 Nov. 1919.

76. *Sierra Leone Weekly News*, 18 Sept. 1926.

77. Thomas Tax Return, 1942/43, PJCTP.

more radical views. By the 1920s, Thomas and those who shared his views were regarded as conservatives. Whether as a consequence of his position or for other reasons, Thomas left the Wesleyans for the Anglicans (and for Christchurch in particular) in 1931. The political future lay with the advocates of colonial nationalism, who promised benefits now rather than in an unspecified future. Thomas realised that he and others like him were being left behind. In 1926, he stood for election to the Legislative Council and lost to Herbert Macaulay's Nigerian National Democratic Party (NNDP)—as he knew he would.[78]

Philanthropy, like the ideals that inspired it, began at home. Thomas and his wife, Josetta, had seven children (four daughters and three sons) who reached adulthood. All were well educated and went on to some form of advanced education, except for one, Margaret, who married early and became a well-known journalist. The remaining six had notable careers. Two sons entered the law: Peter became a solicitor, Stephen a judge. Of the three daughters, Irene became one of the first female doctors in Nigeria, and Stella became the first female barrister. The remaining son, Emmanuel, was given only a glimpse of his adult life. He volunteered for service in 1941, was the first African to be commissioned in the RAF, and was killed in 1945, when the end of the war was in sight.[79]

It is an extraordinary record by any measure. Yet, it is also a story with a variation on a familiar theme. The common ambition among successful Lagos merchants was to invest in educating their children so that they could access occupations that were less risky than commercial life. Thomas made it clear in his will (written in 1919) that he wanted his children, daughters as well as sons, to have opportunities of 'following a profession or a vocation'.[80] But he added that the trustees of his estate should 'admit to the business' any son who 'shows business aptitude', and that he should become a director of the business if it 'becomes a limited company'. As it turned out, all the adult children worked in the business at various times, but the inter-war years provided little incentive for educated Lagosians to choose careers in business. Thomas's own firm was in decline; the limited company never materialised; alternative occupations were far more attractive. His children chose wisely.

The Long Descent

Reversals of fortune can be swift or slow. Thomas's fate combined the two: a precipitous fall followed by a prolonged and unavailing struggle to regain the heights he had occupied previously. In 1919, just as the post-war boom reached

78. Thomas to Abel Smith, 7 May 1926, PJCTP.

79. Emanuel Peter John Adeniyi Thomas, born 1914, was Peter Thomas's youngest child. He had planned to enter the law after the war.

80. Thomas, will, dated 1919, LAP, 15/321–41, 1946.

its peak, Thomas struck a wholly exceptional deal with BBWA, which granted him credit of up to £150,000 against produce in store and hypothecated to the bank.[81] In exchange, Thomas deposited the title deeds of property valued at £100,000 as security for payment 'on demand' of a total sum of £200,000, and agreed to mortgage the property, if called on to do so. Given that Thomas's fifty-seven properties in Lagos and Ebute Metta were valued at £91,691 in 1920, the deal had some solid backing—provided that produce and property prices remained high.

An arrangement on this scale was unprecedented in Lagos during the previous seventy years, even allowing for changes in the value of the pound sterling. It eclipsed its nearest competitor, the agreement James Davies made in 1872, mortgaging his Lagos property to cover an advance of £60,000.[82] Yet, both deals had a common feature: they were made by outstandingly successful merchants whose years of prosperity encouraged them to think that the good times were permanent. The illusion is a recurring one that beguiles experienced investors, as well as novices, today. Because the international economy was more tightly integrated in 1919 than it was in 1872, Thomas's experience was replicated throughout the world's produce markets.

The mirage of permanence dissolved in 1920. The boom had seen astonishing increases in the prices of produce shipped from Lagos and a corresponding rise in the volumes exported. When the transition to a peacetime economy experienced difficulties, the boom collapsed. Industrial production contracted; demand for tropical produce shank; deflation and falling prices took hold. The produce Thomas had agreed to supply to BBWA was suddenly worth far less than had been estimated in the euphoric days of 1919. During the second half of 1920, the price paid for cocoa in Europe was only about one quarter of the price paid in the year from March 1919 to April 1920. The precipitate fall was calamitous for Thomas and many others in Lagos and elsewhere who could meet their commitments only by accepting huge losses. Thomas confronted reality in 1921, when he was obliged to reach a new agreement with the bank.[83] In essence, BBWA arranged for him to settle a debt of £60,000 to his creditors in England by making an immediate and greatly reduced payment of 4s. in the pound, and advanced £10,000, secured on his property in Kano, to enable him to do so. The arrangement still left his debt to the bank itself and a further sum of £8,000 owing to creditors (presumably British firms) in Lagos.

Thomas's correspondence for 1922 has not been preserved, but the issue reappeared in 1923 and can be followed through an invaluable set of exchanges

81. Memo of Agreement between BBWA and Thomas, 15 Oct. 1919.
82. See above, pp. 151–54.
83. Memo of Agreement between BBWA and Thomas, 1 Sep. 1921, PJCTP; Indenture with London Creditors, 5 Sept. 1921, PJCTP. The arrangement included some complexities that lie beyond what is needed for present purposes.

with Arbuthnot Latham, his merchant-bankers in London.[84] Although the correspondence refers to matters of business, it also hints at the drama and poignancy of Thomas's struggle. The letters are fraught with tension and at times despair, yet also express friendship and optimism. They provide a rare insight into Afro-European business relations, and in doing so underline the human consequences of world events as they affected one merchant in one colonial port city.

In August 1923, Arbuthnot Latham wrote encouragingly about a proposed arrangement that they were helping to negotiate with BBWA, hoping that it 'will not merely relieve you wholly from a very severe burden of debt, but will enable you to recover to some extent your former position'.[85] A few days later, they confirmed their support, adding that 'it is because of our strong belief in you that we consider any trouble and time given to considering your affairs worth the while'.[86] They followed their letter with news of the proposed deal. BBWA was considering giving up its claim, which at one time had stood at 'over £100,000', in return for an immediate cash settlement of £50,000.[87] Arbuthnot Latham noted that Thomas was exploring the possibility of forming a limited company as a means of raising the necessary sum. Thomas was heartened by the news. 'Well, I really should like to pull through if I can possibly keep the strain going because it will not only rejoice the hearts of my friends but will be a very great achievement helping on my race by an example they had not had hitherto'.[88]

Unfortunately for Thomas, BBWA withdrew its generous offer, probably because Thomas could not find the required £50,000. In September, Arbuthnot Latham wrote to say that they had 'interceded with BBWA, who had modified their proposals'.[89] The bank had already forgone the interest on the debt since 1920 and now proposed to reduce the capital sum owing, which at one time was 'over £100,000', to £95,000. Arbuthnot Latham advised Thomas to accept the terms, which they judged to be 'lenient', and take the opportunity to trade his way out of debt.[90] The alternative was for BBWA to exercise its legal rights and annex the assets that Thomas had pledged. Arbuthnot Latham thought that Thomas could continue to manage the business provided he

---

84. Arbuthnot Latham, founded in 1833, began as merchants before becoming both private and commercial bankers. They also acted as brokers for Thomas's shipments of produce. The family's interest in the firm ceased in 1981 and the name survives today only as a nameplate for a global corporation, as is the case with most of the old merchant banks in the City.

85. Arbuthnot Latham to Thomas, 7 Aug. 1923, PJCTP.

86. Abel Smith to Thomas, 21 Aug. 1923, PJCTP.

87. W. R. Arbuthnot to Thomas, 22 Aug. 1923, PJCTP.

88. Thomas to Abel Smith, 31 Aug. 1923, PJCTP.

89. Abel Smith to Thomas, 4 Sept. 1923, PJCTP.

90. Abel Smith to Thomas, 4 Sept. 1923, PJCTP.

recognised the need to make economies and 'conduct and organise your business in less expensive surroundings. It is a matter of having to cut one's coat
in accordance with the cloth available, and of recognising that things cannot
be run on the large scale that was possible in boom days, which are unlikely to
re-occur [*sic*] for many a year'.[91]

Thomas's reply expressed his appreciation of their efforts on his behalf and
acknowledged that, without their help, he 'would not be able to carry on'.[92] He
was keeping his spirits up, he added, sustained by the thought that, 'whatever
happens', he had made 'a personal contribution to an undertaking from small
beginnings but with high ideals to a standard unprecedented in West Africa
amongst my own people, and which I have been trying to save, caught in an
unprecedented world trade disaster'.[93] A few days later, Thomas wrote to confirm
that 'you will not find me lacking in spirit to save a business which I have made a
life work, and not in any personal sense but something which I had hoped would
be an incentive to my race'.[94] More ominously, Thomas also noted that 'trade has
been worse than it has ever been', adding that he was again thinking of forming a
limited company, which 'may be the answer'.[95] The thought never materialised.
The prospects of raising capital in Lagos at a time of continuing recession were
less than minimal, as Thomas eventually came to accept. As for cutting his coat,
Thomas decided that it was more like cutting his throat. He resolved to maintain
his branches 'in case a revival occurs suddenly'.[96] A smaller business would not
enable him to pay his debts or to regain his former position.

In retrospect, we know that the revival did not happen, but it was reasonable for Thomas to suppose that the transition to a post-war economy
might save him if he could manage to stay afloat while awaiting rescue. In the
absence of an infusion of capital, he had to place his bet on the recovery of the
international economy. He kept his spirits up by hoping that his luck would
take a turn for the better.

In the event, nothing turned up. In October 1923, Thomas wrote an
eighteen-page letter to BBWA about the settlement of his affairs. He pleaded
with the bank to take the long view. 'I have tried to carry on hoping that my
labours may be educative'. He urged BBWA to think ahead: 'your bank can be
of no real service to Africa until you can build up an African business' ... and
'this will be the task of years'.[97] The current desire to recover recent losses, he
argued, was short-sighted because it would lead to race hatred and doctrines
of 'Africa for the Africans'. If the bank decided to treat him harshly, he added,

91. Abel Smith to Thomas, 4 Sept. 1923, PJCTP.
92. Thomas to Abel Smith, 13 Sept. 1923, PJCTP.
93. Thomas to Abel Smith, 13 Sept. 1923, PJCTP.
94. Thomas to Abel Smith, 28 Sept. 1923, PJCTP.
95. Thomas to Abel Smith, 13 Sept. 1923, PJCTP.
96. Thomas to Scriven Bros. & Co., 28 Sept. 1923, PJCTP.
97. Thomas to Couper (General Manager, BBWA, London), 12 Oct. 1923, PJCTP.

it will make his life's work a failure and discredit his philosophy of co-operation. He referred at this point to the recent elections to the Legislative Council, which resulted in a victory for members of the NNDP, who were 'not the sort of men' to 'trust with your affairs'. The popular view that expatriate firms are 'exploiters' will only be changed 'when the native sees African businessmen succeed'. Thomas concluded his letter with a proposal of his own. His debt to BBWA stood at the intimidating figure of £95,756 and the number of mortgaged properties had risen to sixty-four. He urged the bank to value the portfolio at £80,000 instead of (as at present) £60,000 and asked to be allowed to use some of the property 'on reasonable terms'.

Arbuthnot Latham expressed their disappointment with Thomas's proposal.[98] In their view, his plea to be allowed to retain some of the most valuable properties showed that he had still not grasped the need for economy. Nevertheless, they continued to allow him credit until the end of year, when they could review his balance sheet and decide what action to take. BBWA followed with an uncompromising letter that snuffed out Thomas's hopes.[99] 'You are well aware', the general manager wrote, 'that both myself and my directors have been very sympathetic towards your aims and aspirations for your race'. Nevertheless, he concluded, he could not justify making any further concessions.

In December 1923, Thomas, now 'very depressed' about what he called his 'nightmare', made a final appeal.[100] In expressing his disappointment with the bank to Arbuthnot Latham, he explained that he needed to retain key premises in Lagos to provide accommodation for his family and also because some branches there were profitable. The shop in Tinubu Street had made £749 in 1922–1923, the wholesale store in Williams Street had made £1,900, and the estate agency (which he had founded just after the war) had made £342. These examples showed, Thomas claimed, that he was adapting by developing lines of business other than produce. If he were to succeed, he must not be seen to be discredited, as would be the case if he were 'turned out' of his property. Nevertheless, he was obliged to report a 'very bad trading year' following losses on exports of produce: £1,757 on cocoa, £161 on goatskins, £98 on palm kernels, and £6 on maize. The total net loss of £2,022 was only just offset by a profit of £2,455 on his import trade, leaving a final net profit of £433. By the end of 1923, just three weeks away, he had agreed to pay BBWA a final settlement of £93,757.[101] It was a bleak Christmas.

Unwelcome realities descended heavily in 1924. In January, Thomas was obliged to accept a final agreement with BBWA whereby he surrendered

98. Arbuthnot Latham to Thomas, 12 Nov. 1923, PJCTP.
99. Couper to Thomas, 13 Nov. 1923, PJCTP.
100. Thomas to Abel Smith, 7 Dec. 1923, PJCTP.
101. Thomas to BBWA (Lagos), 28 Dec. 1923, PJCTP; Thomas to BBWA (Couper in London), 16 Jan. 1924, PJCTP.

almost all of the sixty-four properties he had mortgaged to cover his debt, which now stood at the fractionally lower sum of £93,288.[102] Thomas made a final appeal in a letter to Abel Smith, in which he restated his philosophy of business.[103] 'It is not possible for my race to get along by itself today, as when it had not come into contact with the onward march of Western development'. The need for co-operation, his familiar theme, was essential at present, 'even though the African may find it humiliating and may be misunderstood by his own people for doing so'. A rupture with the bank, he concluded, would destroy the ideals he stood for. Matters, however, had gone too far. The bank refused to make further concessions; sales of Thomas's mortgaged property began in 1924 and continued throughout the following year.[104]

A second letter in January 1924 came from Abel Smith, writing on behalf of Arbuthnot Latham, who said that he was keen to see Thomas get started again but that the disappointing balance sheet meant that credit could not be granted without security.[105] In a further comment, Abel Smith observed that Thomas's assets exceeded his liabilities by about £7,500 and that he needed to secure payment from his numerous debtors.[106] In the light of these facts, Abel Smith would only allow him credit on the security of his property in Kano, which was valued at £8,000.[107] Their decision, he added, was because of their confidence in him personally rather than being based on the strength of the balance sheet. Thomas had already taken some of his debtors to court. In 1922, he had obtained judgement against the permanently indebted lawyer, Egerton Shyngle, who was ordered to repay a loan of £488.[108] In the following year, Thomas won a case against James Aboderin for the sum of £2,885.[109] Aboderin had received the money to buy produce but had failed to deliver it. As creditors knew well, however, securing judgement was different from securing payment. Shyngle was notoriously dilatory in obeying court orders; Aboderin died in 1945 still owing Thomas a substantial sum, which his family undertook to pay.[110] Thomas had even less control over his balance sheet,

102. Thomas to BBWA (Lagos), 15 Jan. 1924, PJCTP.

103. Thomas to Abel Smith, 18 Jan. 1924, PJCTP.

104. LO 181: 174/352/3975/392/400/543/553/680/690; 182: 280/301; 183: 211; 184: 132/140/157; 186/22. These references are indicative only. It would require a separate article to detail the disposals fully.

105. Abel Smith to Thomas, 1 Jan. 1924, PJCTP.

106. Abel Smith to Thomas, 22 Jan. 1924, PJCTP; Thomas to Abel Smith, 24 Jan. 1924, PJCTP.

107. Abel Smith to Thomas, 22 Jan. 1924, PJCTP; Thomas to Abel Smith, 24 Jan. 1924, PJCTP.

108. Thomas v. Egerton Shyngle, LSCR, Civ. 96. 1922.

109. Thomas v. Aboderin, LSCR, Civ. 102, 1923.

110. The P. J. C. Thomas Papers includes a large file containing several hundred letters dealing with his efforts to secure payment.

which was influenced primarily by prevailing conditions in the international economy.

Thomas rallied in March and wrote more cheerfully to Abel Smith, saying that his resolve had not weakened.[111] In again thanking Arbuthnot Latham for their support, Thomas said that he had put the past behind him and was working hard to rebuild the business. The exchanges retained their optimistic tone for the next few months.[112] At the end of August, however, Thomas had to deliver some bad news.[113] He reported that sales of produce, principally cocoa, to the end of September 1923 showed a net loss of £4,193 and that profits on imported goods for the nine months to the end of June 1924 amounted to only £736. It was very hard work, he added, perhaps unnecessarily, 'to make ends meet'. Thomas also complained that Arbuthnot Latham bore some responsibility for the loss incurred on sales of hides.[114] William Arbuthnot responded by saying that they looked after his affairs 'as if they were their own' and that he was free to move his business elsewhere if he was dissatisfied. Abel Smith sent a mollifying supplementary letter explaining that they were unable to deal on Thomas's behalf when he had reached his credit limit, which was governed by his balance sheet.[115] A patch was put on the disagreement. At the close of the year, Thomas wrote a friendly personal note to Mrs Abel Smith, who was godmother to his daughter, Margaret. The omens, however, were not favourable.

The correspondence resumed in March 1926, when Abel Smith wrote a long review of the state of Thomas's business.[116] He set the tone in his opening remarks: 'we do not feel satisfied with the manner in which the business has been conducted recently'. Thomas's failure to provide a balance sheet and other necessary documentation had 'endangered confidence'. The produce side of the business seemed to have contracted considerably. News that Thomas was beginning to export rubber raised concerns because he had 'no experience' with the product. They were also aware that he had sold hides and skins through other agents. Thomas responded with concessions and explanations, one of which was to claim that he did have experience of exporting rubber.[117] He agreed that the profit on cocoa was not good enough and that he would have to reduce shipments if there were losses.[118] He admitted that he was very close to making a loss. His net profit on cocoa in 1924–1925 was only £358 on total purchases of £31,419. He added, dejectedly, that he was exhausted. Later

111. Thomas to Abel Smith, 13 March 1924, 28 March 1924, PJCTP.

112. Thomas to Abel Smith, 10 April 1924; Abel Smith to Thomas, 13 May 1924, 23 May 1924, PJCTP.

113. Thomas to Abel Smith, 29 Aug. 1924, PJCTP.

114. W. R. Arbuthnot to Thomas, 19 Sept. 1924, PJCTP.

115. Abel Smith to Thomas, 26 May 1924, PJCTP.

116. Abel Smith to Thomas, 30 March 1926, PJCTP.

117. Thomas to Abel Smith, 23 April 1926, PJCTP.

118. Thomas to Abel Smith, 7 May 1926, PJCTP.

in the year, Thomas sent an eleven-page statement admitting that he had been slow to respond to Abel Smith's letters, which he blamed on 'overwork and 'despondency'.[119] He repeated his appreciation of Arbuthnot Latham's support in 1921, when he was 'on the point of winding up' his company, and said that he hoped to attract more funds next year by forming a limited liability company.

The limited company, as Abel Smith guessed, lay beyond Thomas's reach. Abel Smith was more concerned with immediate realities, which suggested that the credits Arbuthnot Latham had advanced were not fully covered by the security Thomas had provided.[120] Thomas's next letter, written in February 1927, increased the anxiety felt in London.[121] He was obliged to deliver more bad news. The balance sheet for the twelve months that ended on 30 September 1926 showed a gross profit of £7,973 and a loss of £10,601, producing a net loss of £2,629. Alarm bells started ringing in Arbuthnot Latham's office. Abel Smith told Thomas that the balance sheet confirmed that the business was 'unhealthy'.[122] Thomas had no option but to agree that turnover and profits were inadequate to meet overheads. He continued to believe, however, that he needed to keep the organisation intact 'for the return of better times'.[123] At this point, the London firm had spent its reserves of patience and poured cold water on Thomas's illusions. Abel Smith wrote an uncompromising letter telling Thomas that he should liquidate unprofitable assets, such as the Kano properties and some cocoa depots, and undertake a 'drastic' reduction in overhead costs.[124] Given the state of the present balance sheet, he added, it would be 'useless' to form a limited company because there was no prospect of attracting fresh investment.

Thomas was evidently dismayed by news he had hoped to avoid. After nearly three months without a reply, Abel Smith wrote, expressing his surprise and disappointment, informing Thomas that confidence in him was ebbing, and suggesting that he should close his account and transfer to another firm.[125] It took Thomas five months to reply in February 1928. His response was sombre.[126] He had ceased buying cocoa and was concentrating on exports of hides. One European employee had left, and he was 'working 18 hours a day' with a 'depleted' staff, but still hoping to 'turn the corner'. That was the last exchange in the series and probably, so it would seem, the end of Thomas's connection with Arbuthnot Latham.

119. Thomas to Abel Smith, 19 Nov. 1926, PJCTP.
120. Abel Smith to Thomas, 21 Dec. 1926, PJCTP.
121. Thomas to Abel Smith, 11 Feb. 1927, PJCTP.
122. Abel Smith to Thomas, 14 March 1927, PJCTP.
123. Thomas to Arbuthnot Latham, 6 May 1927, PJCTP.
124. Abel Smith to Thomas, 5 July 1927, PJCTP.
125. Abel Smith to Thomas, 27 Sept. 1927, PJCTP.
126. Thomas to Arbuthnot Latham, 10 Feb. 1928, PJCTP.

The Final Phase

Only fragmentary details of the rest of Thomas's career have survived. There is enough evidence, however, to show that the corner was never turned.[127] The recovery Thomas was waiting for failed to materialise. Adverse trading conditions deepened the problems he and other Lagos merchants faced. The world slump struck in 1929; the financial crisis followed in 1931. A hint of hope appeared later in the 1930s but was obscured and then eliminated by the international crisis that led to World War II. Against the trend, Thomas somehow managed to retain 45 Marina, which he had bought from Herbert Macaulay in 1923, when he still had plans for expansion.[128] He was forced to mortgage the property in 1930 and take a second mortgage in 1938, but was able to discharge both mortgages in 1944. Nevertheless, survival became the priority of the day; prosperity lay in the past; the future could only be guessed at.

Thomas's trading position deteriorated during the 1930s. In 1930, he still maintained two stores in Lagos and eleven branches inland.[129] But as losses on produce mounted, staff began leaving and branches were closed. Stewart Chalmers, the chief cashier, returned to England in 1936. By the end of the decade, Thomas had ceased to export produce to markets in Europe, had closed his up-country branches, apart from Kano and Ibadan, and retained only his main store and shop in Williams Street in Lagos. The year 1931 was one of several low points. He was forced to write a four-page letter to the Town Council asking for time to pay £25 for a half-year spirit licence 'because of bad trade conditions'.[130] Evidently, his need for income had obliged him to discard his objections to alcohol. In the following year, he had to give up the lease he had contracted in the heady days of 1919 to rent 48 Marina (Rose Cottage) from Jacob Coker.[131] The terms, by which he agreed to pay £500 a year for forty years, were now far beyond his means.

These discouraging developments stimulated innovation. One initiative, which led to the development of 'country trade', involved shipping local products, notably groundnuts, shea butter, benniseed, and 'native' cloth, to coastal ports in West Africa, especially Freetown. Another departure involved making mattresses in Kano from local materials, importing iron bedsteads from

127. At this point, I am particularly grateful for information supplied by Mr E. A. Peter Thomas and Dr Irene Thomas, both of whom worked in the business at various times during the 1930s and early 1940s. See n. 2 above.

128. He paid £2,300 for the property. LLOR, LO 4827.

129. Information submitted by Thomas to the Registrar of Companies, Lagos, 23 Jan. 1930, PJCTP.

130. Thomas to Lagos Town Council, 10 Oct. 1931, PJCTP. His change of heart about selling spirits may also be related to his transfer from the Wesleyans to the Anglicans.

131. LLOR, LO 104/420,1919; LO 305/59/60 1932.

Birmingham, putting the two together, and selling them in Lagos as complete sets. Unlike the great but brief post-war boom, these lines of business did not generate exceptional wealth. They also lacked the public prominence and prestige of the great import and export trades and their association with European firms and markets. Nevertheless, they should not be dismissed as being inconsequential activities. They represented a diversification of trade away from established staples, made use of local inputs, and showed that effective demand, at least in Lagos, was able to support purchases of new types of consumer goods. In these respects, the adaptations Thomas promoted pointed towards the post-war economy.

Thomas's status as a merchant prince survived the drop in his income. He was elected President of the Lagos Chamber of Commerce in 1929 and again in 1930.[132] He also retained sufficient stature to be appointed Chief *Lokoyi* of Ilesha in 1936.[133] The title offers an insight into a little-known feature of Thomas's interests and shows that his sense of commitment extended beyond Lagos (and Freetown) to include his homeland. He was active during the 1930s in rejuvenating the Ekitiparapo Society, which aimed at fostering joint Ijesha–Ekiti interests.[134] It was a worthy but frustrating task.[135] There was little enthusiasm for paying membership fees at a time of hardship; attendance at meetings was poor and unpunctual. Moreover, the existing Ijesha Union was wary of co-operating because it feared that the Ekitiparapo Society would attract recruits from its own members.[136]

The impasse produced a discussion of the historical similarities and differences between the Ekitiparapo and the Ijesha. Members of both societies reached the conclusion that the two were distinct but had joined forces temporarily to resist attacks from Ibadan.[137] Consensus produced compromise, which was expressed in 1935 in the formation of the Ijesha–Ekitiparapo Society, which took as its motto 'Unity is Strength'.[138] However, the Society was soon forced to make concessions to diversity. By 1940, there were at least twelve Ijesha societies in Lagos alone, and efforts to merge them had failed.[139] A further compromise was reached in 1938 with the formation of a Central Council, which consisted of representatives from each of the Ijesha–Ekiti

132. Minutes of the Lagos Chamber of Commerce, 2 Oct. 1929, PJCTP.

133. *Owa* of Ilesha to Thomas, 29 March 1936, PJCTP.

134. Minutes of a Meeting of Ekitiparapo Society, 11 June 1935; J. Rosiji Turton to Thomas, 25 Sept. 1935, PJCTP.

135. Minutes of Meetings of the Ekitiparapo Society, 18 June 1935, 9 July 1935; Thomas to General Secretary of the Society, 26 Aug. 1936, PJCTP.

136. Minutes of Meetings of the Ekitiparapo Society, 25 June 1935; Lagos Ijesha Union to Ijesha–Ekitiparapo Society, 14 Dec. 1936, PJCTP.

137. Minutes of a Meeting of Ekitiparapo Society, 9 July 1935, PJCTP.

138. Lagos Ijesha Union to Ekitparapo Society, 14 Dec. 1936, PJCTP.

139. Lagos Ijesha Union to Thomas, 24 June 1940, PJCTP.

groups in Lagos.[140] Although this is an obscure story, it is possible to see in it some of the elements that led ultimately to Nigeria's federal system of government.

Thomas 'ceased to do business in any appreciable manner a few years before he died' in 1947.[141] Although the initiatives he took to diversify the business were promising, commercial conditions remained unfavourable and the outbreak of war in 1939 added another layer of adversity. Evidence contained in Thomas's tax returns charts the contraction of his income from business and the extent to which he had become reliant on rental income from his remaining and recovered property.[142] In 1938–1939, his total gross income amounted to no more than £1,089, most of which came from rents. In the following year, his gross income was almost the same at £1,181, his trade profit was only £75, and rents again accounted for almost the whole of his income. In 1940–1941, his gross income fell to £479. In 1941–1942, it recovered to reach £2,034, and in 1942–1943, it was £1,949, of which business profits contributed £222.

By then, however, time was also against him. His health began to fail soon after he reached the age of seventy in 1943. In 1946, he confided to his aunt in Freetown that he was doing 'almost no trade now' as a result of 'failing health and loss of quota'.[143] After his death on 30 December 1947, the business was discontinued. One of his obituary notices referred to him as a 'merchant prince', but could not conceal the fact that his days of fame lay far behind him.[144] As *Oba* Samuel Akinsanya astutely commented: he 'saw too much and attempted to do too much'.[145]

Thomas's vision, however, lived on. In his will, drafted in 1919, he looked forward to the time 'when my country will be a great manufacturing, a great producing centre. Its wealth made and possessed by Africans—governed by African statesmen—the people prosperous, honourable, God-fearing—then shall the African hold up his head throughout the world, honouring his superiors and being honoured. He shall have his literature—his art—such is my vision and to this end I wish to make my humble effort asking that it may please God to further it'.[146] Although Thomas was unable to sustain his own

140. Lagos Ijesha Union to Thomas, 24 June 1940, PJCTP.
141. A. G. Nylander (executor) to Registrar of Business Names, 19 March 1948, PJCTP.
142. Income Tax Returns, for 1938/39, 1939/40, 1940/41, 1941/42, PJCTP. Most of Thomas's property was leased to expatriate firms. 45 Marina, which he had bought from Herbert Macaulay, was leased to K. Chelleram & Sons in 1939. The lease was renewed in 1952 and again in 1962, when it was extended for twenty-five years at a rent of £600 p.a. LLOR, LO 4872, 1962.
143. Thomas to Auntie Agnes (Freetown), 21 Dec. 1946, PJCTP. One of his problems was that his sight was deteriorating. Another was that the quota system imposed during the war limited his business prospects.
144. *Nigerian Daily Times*, 30 Dec. 1947, 9 Jan. 1948.
145. *Sunday Express* (Nigeria), 3 Sept. 1961.
146. Thomas, last will, dated 1919, LAP, 15/231-41, 1947.

effort, he did enough to show that African enterprise could, and eventually did, produce the 'great manufacturing' and 'producing' centre he dreamed would become a reality.

A Vision Postponed

Thomas was one of the few African merchants to feature prominently in the export trade of Lagos during the years when Nigeria was coming into existence. Several others scaled lesser heights before falling back. Only Samuel Pearse approximated Thomas's stature. The less risky trade in imports had more numerous representatives. Even so, few if any import merchants matched the status of Josiah Doherty. Evidently, Thomas's achievements, like those of Pearse and Doherty, were partly the result of personal qualities. Many others tried and failed where they succeeded. Thomas was known to be astute, energetic, efficient, industrious, and well connected, not only in Lagos but also in Europe. He applied these qualities at a propitious time. International trade was generally buoyant in the years before the war, when he decided to leave the civil service and enter business on a full-time basis. The war itself presented serious challenges, but Thomas was nimble as well as lucky. Produce prices rose as the conflict proceeded, and Thomas ended the war more prosperously than he began it. The post-war boom then carried him to unprecedented levels. In 1919, it seemed that nothing could stand in his way. His success brought him closer to realising his great ambition than even he had imagined: demonstrating to sceptics the potential of Africans and of their continent.

The rest of the story has elements of tragedy in which the failings of the main character are the cause of his downfall. Thomas, like James Davies before him, turned success into excess. He failed to see that the boom might end, still less that it might collapse suddenly and without warning. Like many others before and since, he thought that this time it really would be different. Unlike Doherty or Pearse, Thomas was a recent entrant into the business world, had not encountered a slump before 1919, and was unable to heed warnings from personal experience. His own errors, however, need to be set against the power of uncontrollable forces in the international economy. The tsunami that struck the world in 1920 did not distinguish between colonists and colonised, even though the consequences were not evenly distributed. Many European firms collapsed too; some were rescued by the process of amalgamation that eventually produced the United Africa Company in 1929. The tidal wave also had political consequences in stimulating nationalist feelings across the colonial world, as the widening political divisions within the Saro community in Lagos illustrate. No individual could resist shocks of this magnitude.

The aftermath can be followed through Thomas's exchanges with his London bankers and brokers. The surviving correspondence is more detailed than any comparable records in Lagos found so far for the period 1900–1940, including those relating to Josiah Doherty and Samuel Pearse. The letters trace the slow submergence of a once eminent merchant who continued to cling to his ideals as realities closed over him. It is a story of distress that is also distressing to read. There are residues, however, that are worth holding on to. Like Doherty and Pearse, Thomas found that he had to innovate to survive. This explains his interest in processing locally some of the products from his farm and in developing import-substituting manufactures. Although these were scarcely dramatic departures, they deserve to be identified as pioneers of innovations that were to alter the structure of Nigeria's economy after the Second World War. If Thomas fell short of being Schumpeter's ideal heroic innovator, he and some of his peers nevertheless can be seen as precursors of a new age and not just as residues of the old one.

CHAPTER SIXTEEN

A Conclusion, a Conundrum, and a Speculation

Conclusion: Capitalists and the Spread of Capitalism

This book has dealt with a universal theme: the global spread of capitalism. It aims to revive some of the larger questions that were once central to historical research and attract the attention of a new generation of historians to a subject that has a future and not just a past. Issues relating to the 'rise of capitalism' are already present in the debate over the 'transition' in West Africa during the nineteenth century and the claimed 'crisis of adaptation' that accompanied it.[1] Current assessments of the role of entrepreneurs in this process can discard some of the key assumptions that guided earlier work. Far from lacking initiative and energy, West Africa produced an abundance of commercial capitalists, vibrant markets, and a system of exchange that was driven primarily by the profit motive. A distinction needs to be drawn, however, between capitalists as individuals who promoted trade in goods and services, and capitalism as a socio-economic system.[2] The present study has contributed to the existing literature by tracing the way Lagos capitalists developed and diffused some of the key institutions of capitalism, notably freehold property rights, wage labour, and a market for capital that served third parties. It has also followed their initiative in carrying these institutions from the town to the mainland, applying them to export agriculture, and demonstrating, through

---

1. Hopkins, *An Economic History of West Africa*, ch. 4; Law, ed., *From Slave Trade to 'Legitimate' Commerce*, and other sources too numerous to be listed here.

2. I am indebted to Morten Jerven and Gareth Austin for their clear exposition of the distinction. See Jerven, 'The Emergence of African Capitalism', in *The Cambridge History of Capitalism*, Vol. 1, pp. 301–47; Austin, 'Comment: The Return of Capitalism as a Concept', in *Capitalism*, pp. 207–34.

cocoa farming, the benefits of postponing immediate consumption to secure higher returns from long-term development.

Lagos merchants, like others in the West Coast ports, were trying to find their way in the midst of the changes they were helping to introduce while also acting as the vanguard of Britain's global development plan. Their immediate environment was shaped by the island that became a port city and, in particular, a colonial port city. The former gave Lagos qualities of cosmopolitanism and mobility; the latter added foreign rule and racial discrimination. These attributes explain the main characteristics of the port and enable it to join comparisons that currently survey the Atlantic and Asia but bypass Africa. An analysis of entrepreneurship that fits the merchants who were the principal agents of capitalism, however, is not easily found. The considerable literature on entrepreneurial theory has been developed to explain the performance of advanced industrial economies and has little applicability to colonial economies of the kind prevailing in tropical Africa during the colonial period. A return to principles of entrepreneurship that were devised in the eighteenth century to apply to pre-industrial economies provides a more appropriate starting point and one that can readily be extended to economies of the kind typified by port cities with substantial international connections.

Cantillon held that entrepreneurs were essential to maintaining what he referred to as the 'circular flow' of economic life. Without their initiative, he argued, society would soon revert to a primitive state. Three hundred years later, Schumpeter devised his own model of circular flow that emphasised the innovative role of entrepreneurs in forming what he called 'new combinations'. Their actions in upsetting one state of equilibrium and creating another were the key to understanding the booms and slumps that constituted the business cycle. Cantillon and Schumpeter had different ideas of entrepreneurship. For Cantillon, entrepreneurs were members of society who did not benefit from fixed incomes and accordingly were found in many walks of life. Schumpeter restricted the term to the talented few who could engineer the 'creative destruction' needed to shift the economy from one state to another. Nevertheless, both writers agreed on the importance of entrepreneurs in influencing the economy at the macro level as well as at the micro level populated by individual businesses.

The purpose of this study has not been to grapple with the giants of the subject but to use their authority to reaffirm the centrality of entrepreneurship in understanding long-run economic development. In the case of tropical Africa, admirable research has reconstructed trade and traders in the precolonial era. Detailed accounts of individuals and groups of merchants have contributed to our knowledge of the nineteenth century, though few studies have extended into the period of full colonial rule. This book has sought to build on the existing literature by reconsidering some established views of the period between 1851 and 1931. The analysis rests on a detailed examination of the careers of 116 African entrepreneurs (of whom 100 were merchants) who were active during this period. The sample is larger than others so far available and the period is long enough to assess how Lagosian merchants negotiated the upheaval brought by the expansion of colonial rule.

The analysis of port cities and entrepreneurs has been set in motion by dividing the period into three chronological parts, each signalled by an external shock that was manifested in military action but had powerful economic causes and consequences. The first shock, in 1851, witnessed the bombardment of Lagos by the British Navy and the suppression of the external slave trade. The second shock, in 1892, saw Britain invade Yorubaland, an act that turned out to be a prelude to the creation of Nigeria. The third shock, the start of the First World War in 1914, threw established commercial relations into disarray and had reverberations that extended far into the inter-war period. Each shock altered the economic environment and with it opportunities available to African entrepreneurs and the way they made (and sometimes lost) their fortunes.

The shock of 1851 led to the establishment of a consulate in Lagos, which was converted into a colony ten years later. This was the era in which informal influence was added to formal rule as a means of extending Britain's global power. Informality was consistent with a short, sharp shock of the kind experienced by Lagos and, as the British also demonstrated, in China too. The purpose in both cases was not to acquire territory but to establish compliant polities that would follow the rules of free trade. This aim could also be achieved through diplomacy, as in the case of the Ottoman Empire and the newly emancipated Latin American republics, among other examples. Lagos, however, did not have a ready-made political alternative to the slave-trading regime. The result was a state-led revolution that installed the British as protectors of a new and uncertain *Oba* and his followers.

The abrupt shift of power that followed the arrival of the British presented an opportunity for a new generation of African merchants to establish themselves in the town. The advance guard was formed by freed slaves from Sierra Leone, known locally as Saro, who returned to their homeland once their security was guaranteed. Most of them had received education, converted to Christianity, and taken European names. Yet, they also spoke Yoruba and re-established ties with their homelands. They were ideal intermediaries, as both the colonial government and the Yoruba states well understood. These events, which set the business scene down to 1892, have attracted more attention than any other as far as Lagos merchants, particularly the Saro, are concerned. The period is widely regarded as a 'Golden Age' characterised by prosperity derived from international trade. It has also been seen as the prelude to a long era of declining influence and diminishing visibility.

It is undoubtedly the case that before 1892 the first generation of Saro immigrants enjoyed a degree of prominence that they were unable to sustain subsequently. They had embraced the universal ideals of the mid-Victorian period. Race was not the obstacle to advancement it was to become: suitably qualified Africans could unite with Europeans in a partnership that would civilise the world while also developing its resources. Some Saro joined the colonial service, others entered the Church, another group pioneered the new export trade. Success was measured not only by prosperity derived from substantial businesses but also by demonstrating a high degree of acculturation to Western influences through education, religious observance, and social customs, including dress. What became known as 'legitimate commerce' was an innovative activity that produced a generation of substantial Big Men. James Davies, the acknowledged king of the merchant princes, is one example. Daniel Taiwo, a converted slave-trader who retained African dress and customs, showed how 'traditional' institutions could be adapted to new circumstances.

The creation of the Colony of Lagos transformed entrepreneurial opportunities and business structures in ways that have not been fully appreciated. The promotion of legitimate commerce not only inspired new values but also called for new business organisations. Lagos slave-traders had kept their operations 'in house'. Taiwo's business was specialised and profit-oriented, like those of a firm, but the structure was that of a large household. His network of traders stretching into the hinterland remained essential to the new trade. Taiwo offered his followers employment, accommodation, and security. Loyalties based on the power and reputation of a Big Man created social cohesion and reduced transaction costs by resolving, at least partly, the principal-agent problem. These attributes were well worth preserving. Taiwo added to them by using the new colonial court system to chastise debtors who could not be managed informally and to reinforce his political standing. Similarly, he was quick to take advantage of new freehold rights to amass more property than anyone else in Lagos during this period. Characteristically, he used landed assets for dual purposes: securing trading credits, and rewarding and housing followers. Taiwo's example was followed by others. Networks of traders who linked merchants and brokers to the hinterland survived, even if none matched Taiwo's status as the 'head of all the markets in the Colony'. His business was a hybrid: neither purely a household nor a firm, it is perhaps best categorised as a quasi-firm.

Saro had no ready-made networks and depended on brokers who did. Their skills and opportunities lay in connecting Lagos to the international economy and their businesses met the criteria that qualified them to be referred to as firms. They were specialised and profit-seeking but did not have or require extensive households to manage their affairs. On the contrary, they had relatively few employees. Some were family members; the majority earned wages. Moreover, Saro had no para-military force at their disposal, as Taiwo had. They delegated protection costs to the colonial government and relied on the courts to deal with debtors and settle business disputes. Saro merchants led the revolutionary changes that occurred in the 1850s and 1860s. They were the main advocates and beneficiaries of new property rights, which became the basis of credit and of mercantile fortunes. They promoted and installed a second novelty: wage labour. Considerable fortunes were made during this period; even so, the available evidence indicates that, at the outset of their 'Golden Age', Saro merchants accounted for no more than about one-fifth of the value of the port's total overseas trade.

The second shock struck Lagos in 1892, when Governor Carter extended Britain's reach by invading the hinterland. This singular event was part of a series of assertive actions by European powers, the United States, and Japan that extended foreign rule across the world, transforming the lives of millions of people by turning them into colonial subjects. In the case of Lagos, the invasion of the independent Yoruba states had its origins in the early 1880s, when declining terms of trade reduced profits and caused relations with the hinterland states to deteriorate. At the same time, competition increased following the shift from barter to cash transactions, the completion of the undersea telegraphic cable, and the reduction in freight rates brought by improved steamship services. Faced with threats to legitimate commerce and everything it stood for, the Colonial Office abandoned its traditional policy of combining informal influence with minimal government and authorised the Lagos government to take control of the hinterland. Military action, however, lacked the power to improve the terms of trade. There was no immediate recovery; the closing years of the century were some of the worst on record.

The late nineteenth century is commonly seen, and not only in Lagos, as marking the end of the great days of Saro prosperity and prominence. The decline thesis draws further support from developments after the turn of the century, when the advance of British rule into the far north of the country, accompanied by the new railway line, appeared to favour expatriate firms that had the capital resources to establish branches inland. Nevertheless, these developments did not mark the first steps of a journey from eminence to obscurity. The decline thesis rests on a limited number of examples of success and failure that tend to exaggerate both the rise and the fall of African merchants during the second half of the nineteenth century. Additionally, a distinction needs to be drawn between the decline of the Saro as a group and the specific fortunes of its mercantile component. There is no doubt that the increased size of the Lagos population reduced the relative position of the Saro and that the growth of racial discrimination during the 1890s, and especially after 1900, closed the door to senior positions in Church and state. Business, however, was not disadvantaged to the same extent: merchants could still prosper if market opportunities remained favourable.

Quantitative evidence of the share of overseas trade handled by African merchants during this period is limited. An assessment of customs duties paid to the colonial government indicated that they accounted for a median value of 15 per cent of imports between 1880 and 1885. The calculation, however, understated the total contribution of African import merchants by excluding those who were not 'native gentlemen' and those who imported goods such as spirits. It is impossible to say what the full contribution of African importers was, but it is reasonable to suppose that it exceeded 20 per cent. The next set of reliable data shows that in 1902 African merchants accounted for about 25 per cent of imports of ad valorem goods. The estimate excluded spirits, which were not on the ad valorem list in that year but accounted for nearly 9 per cent of customs duties. A cautious guess suggests that African importers were responsible for nearly 30 per cent of imports in that year. Accordingly, it appears that African merchants increased their share of imports during the 1880s and expanded it further after the turn of the century.

Comparable data on exports are missing. Although African merchants continued to ship produce to Europe, qualitative evidence suggests that their share of the export trade contracted during the period 1880–1914, though by an amount that cannot be specified. Incomplete data allow only a provisional conclusion. Although the value of overseas trade handled by African merchants relative to European firms probably experienced a modest reduction between 1851 and 1914, the decline was from a level that was already low in 1855, when the first survey was made. Consequently, it is unlikely that Lagos merchants suffered a dramatic reversal of fortune. Reports of their demise are premature.

This trend merits further consideration. It is tempting to infer from the data that Africans reduced their share of direct exports and expanded their share of imports during the last quarter of the century because European firms were squeezing them out of the export trade. As we have seen, however, the expatriate firms were not seizing control of an especially profitable branch of trade. They were also struggling (and many were failing) in the adverse conditions of the time. It is more likely that African merchants made a rational choice in deciding to reduce their participation in the export trade. The decline of barter from the 1880s allowed greater specialisation. Imports were less risky than the produce trade during the late nineteenth century and required less capital because consumer goods could be imported in relatively small quantities and still be traded profitably. Moreover, African merchants adapted to changing conditions more easily than Europeans did because they knew local languages, markets, and consumer tastes. Put in the most general terms, it can be said that Africans were able to capitalise on their comparative advantage in developing the consumer market. The same principle applied to the initiatives they took to diversify the economy after 1900. The European firms could not perceive or grasp these opportunities either so readily or at all. They adjusted to adversity by trying to control the export market through pooling arrangements and, later, by forming combines.

An equally important consideration is that assessments of mercantile fortunes that count failures ignore the high rate of turnover among small businesses everywhere. Constant mobility allows newcomers to fill gaps left by the fallen. This was the case in Lagos. The return of generally prosperous years between 1900 and 1914 provided incentives for African merchants as well as for expatriate firms. New figures, who made their mark after the turn of the century, started modest businesses in the 1890s, including the greatest merchant of the time, Josiah Doherty, and others such as Alli Balogun, who represented the growing visibility of the Muslim community. Doherty, Samuel Pearse, and Peter Thomas were among the Lagosians who moved quickly to set up branches inland. These and other African merchants took advantage of the consignment system introduced by the Bank of British West Africa in 1894. Merchants put down deposits, the bank placed orders on their behalf and received full payment when the goods arrived. The orthodox view is mistaken: expatriate banks did not discriminate against Africans, at least not in Lagos during the period covered by this study.[3] Elder Dempster, the shipping firm that owned the Bank, was keen to fill its ships. In this instance, capitalism was colour-blind. Freehold property was sound security, no matter who owned it. Many fortunes were made during these years.

The long-standing focus on the import and export trades has allowed a development of great significance to be overlooked: the innovative enterprise of Lagosians, especially merchants, in diversifying the economy during this period. Schumpeterian 'heroes' are readily found. It was James Davies, whose career was thought to have ended with his bankruptcy, who started the first successful cocoa farm near Lagos in 1880. Jacob Coker, another merchant (who was related to Davies by marriage), took the idea to Agege, 10 miles away, at the turn of the century. He created a vast plantation complex there that not only produced the best quality cocoa in Nigeria but also spread cocoa farming to the rest of Yorubaland. 'Agege quality' became a recognised standard that allowed the Agege Planters' Union to sell ahead of the harvesting season, thus easing liquidity problems and pointing the way towards a futures market. As is well known, during the colonial period Nigeria became the second most important producer of cocoa in the world after the Gold Coast.

Innovation, however, stretched well beyond supplying new agricultural exports. Between 1900 and 1914, Lagosians, with some of the great merchants among the innovators, devised new lines of business in ivory, cattle, kola, and local cloth, introduced motor vehicles and sewing machines, founded the construction industry that built the town, started tanneries and flour mills, opened the first hotels and restaurants, established publishing houses, and developed the finance sector to the point where it supported a new and permanent class of rentiers. Isaac Williams may have been the first merchant to abandon trade in

3. In 1925, a collusive agreement between BBWA and Barclays raised rates and other charges but did not discriminate specifically against African customers, who increased their business with both banks. See Austin and Uche, 'Collusion and Competition', pp. 1–26.

favour of property in 1889, and to have developed a rental business. The career of the greatest of his successors, Candido da Rocha, spanned the first half of the twentieth century and even flourished during the dark years of the 1930s.

The return of prosperity after 1900 suggests that these pioneering examples of diversification were generated by export-led growth. Although this hypothesis has undeniable plausibility, it is worth considering the possibility of a degree of reverse causation: the extent to which internal growth derived from trade in foodstuffs, handicrafts, and other items added to demand for imported consumer goods. The records of Lagos merchants from Taiwo onwards are full of references to trade in items other than the staples of legitimate commerce and to extensive connections with markets in Africa and even beyond it. The range and scale of this trade have yet to be charted. The subject is well worth pursuing because of its insight into larger questions of long-run development.

Most of these activities took place within business structures founded in the 1850s and 1860s and characterised by sole ownership. Capital resources were accumulated from past profits; credit was advanced on the security of landed property, which had either been acquired as a crown grant or purchased from business profits. Before about 1900, sole ownership did not place African merchants at a relative disadvantage because most expatriate firms were also run by individuals or partnerships. The structural differences that did exist were insufficient to give expatriate firms an advantage: their rate of failure between 1880 and 1900 was similar to that of their African competitors and in some respects might have been worse: only two expatriate firms lasted for the whole period. At the same time, Lagos merchants were well aware of the need for institutional change. It was their almost unknown initiative that led to the first experiments in company formation in Nigeria and specifically to the Ordinance of 1912 that allowed limited companies to be registered in the colony.

This was undoubtedly a traumatic time for the Saro community, even though the merchants among them had promising opportunities. The onward march of colonial rule, which was accompanied by assertive racism in state and Church, undermined the universal ethos that had inspired the development programme based on the civilising mission and inter-racial co-operation. Cosmopolitan ideals were replaced by hierarchical principles in which a clear distinction was drawn between superior races who ruled and inferior races who became subjects. The outcome divided the Saro between those who favoured continuing co-operation and those who sought an alternative way forward.

Peter Thomas, one of the leading merchants during the 1910s, was driven by the hope that principles of equality and co-operation could still operate under colonial rule. In 1919, he had 300 employees including eight Europeans, and had amassed a portfolio of sixty properties. In the same year, the Niger Company offered to take over his firm and make him a director of the company, but Thomas refused, saying that he wanted to show that Africans could run large companies successfully. His ambition expressed the belief that development was an evolutionary process that required a partnership between Europeans and Africans.

Jacob Coker took an entirely different position. He abstracted himself as far as possible from the racial order that was so evident in Lagos. Thomas stayed in Lagos and held on to his top hat; Coker retained his house on the Marina, but moved to Agege and adopted African dress. An analysis of the farmers who left Lagos to join him at Agege shows that discrimination was a common motive in their decision to create a new life under colonial rule. Coker's innovative agricultural venture was dedicated to the principle that capitalism was consistent with African social institutions and values. His ambition was to spread this vision throughout Yoruba country, even though he knew that he was creating competitors for his own business. Coker was also a devoted Christian who was the prime mover in founding the African Church in 1901 in protest against the discriminatory policies of the Anglican Church and its failure to compete with the rapid spread of Islam.

The leading merchants of Lagos, whether they came from established families or were recent arrivals, were by definition men of standing and 'good repute'. Their positions gave them privileges but also duties. Men like Taiwo and Oshodi Tapa were obliged to support large followings and to look after 'their people', whether or not they contributed to their businesses. Saro, such as James Davies, Richard Blaize, Isaac Williams, Jacob Coker, Peter Thomas, and many others, were philanthropists who supported their churches, fostered education, dispensed charity to the poor, and assisted children who had been freed from slavery. The great Muslim merchants like Muhammed Shitta Bey and Alli Balogun embraced the same values. They all recognised that reputation generated confidence and benefitted business. Reputation, however, was not simply an instrumental resource expended for economic gain. Its value was expressed in a much wider sense of obligation to society that imposed burdens of cost and time but also generated psychic income in the form of status and admiration. The quest for status as an expression of eminence achieved in honourable ways was a motive that inspired all successful merchants. If these motives pass unrecognised or are treated as mere refinements, explanations of decision-making will be shorn of essential components that account for both the causes of actions and their timing.

These characteristics were both timeless in upholding the Yoruba tradition of generosity and specific in being moulded by the colonial context. The first generation of Saro, personified by James Davies, expressed mid-Victorian values. Members of the next generation, exemplified by Jacob Coker, reacted to British dominance and its companion, racism, by founding a model community, in which capitalist means were harnessed to preserving African values in the world created by colonial rule. Both generations, however, continued to be guided by their Yoruba inheritance. Josiah Doherty's letters written during the lean years of the 1920s convey the difficulties he faced in trying to keep his extensive obligations. He repeatedly urged his adult children studying in Britain to limit their expenditure while he was also continuing to support children outside the family and manage his business during a time of adversity. Jacob Coker offered land and financial help to small farmers at Agege. Peter Thomas gave generously and anonymously to 'the poor' and was still donating 7.5 per cent of his gross income to charity in 1942–1943, even though his income was only a small fraction of what it had been before the post-war slump of 1920–1921.

Western economic theory has been slow to incorporate extra-pecuniary values into standard concepts of rationality. The notion of bounded rationality, for example, suggests that information may be incomplete and constraints of time may modify optimal decisions, leading to what Simon called 'satisficing' behaviour.[4] Nevertheless, this account falls short of the broader assessment of decision-making that Joseph Schumpeter advocated.[5] Yet, the pattern of behaviour described here was neither peculiar to Lagos nor a relic of semi-modern societies. On the contrary, it is a familiar feature of entrepreneurial motivation and expenditure in the United States, where Big Men gain status and preserve the memory of their achievements by attaching their names to universities, hospitals, and schools. Large family-run businesses in Japan and Korea (the zaibatsu and chaebols) recognise similar obligations, which are still consistent with high-performing companies.

Nigeria continues to preserve the connection between business success and philanthropy today. Aliko Dangote, who is reputedly the wealthiest individual in Nigeria, graduated from trade to manufacturing cement, sugar, and flour, and acquired interests in oil. He has established one of the most substantial charitable foundations in Nigeria. Folorunsho Alakija, who is one of Nigeria's richest female entrepreneurs, made her fortune from fashion, real estate, and oil, and is a noted philanthropist. Temie Giwa-Tubosun, who was only thirty-seven at the time of writing, is perhaps the most interesting of Nigeria's currently successful entrepreneurs because her business unites profitability with social welfare. Inspired by her experience in giving birth to her first child, she founded a company to increase awareness of donating blood and to speed its transmission. She is currently upgrading existing methods of transport from motorbikes and boats to drones. Given the evidence of this study and the continuing vitality of Nigeria's entrepreneurs, it is extraordinary to think that modernisation theory assumed that indigenous societies were backward and needed to be thoroughly overhauled before development could begin. Extended families had to be cut down to Western sizes; aspirations had to be reformed to eliminate sloth and

4. Simon, *Models of Man*.
5. Schumpeter, *The Theory of Economic Development*, pp. 90–4.

fatalism. The moral is a sobering one for policy-makers who are persuaded that the latest idea is also the best. Simple theories of a complex world have immediate appeal but rarely have staying power.

The third shock, which began with the declaration of war in 1914 and had ramifications that extended into the inter-war period, marks the culmination of this study. The war dislocated international commerce and presented African merchants with unprecedented challenges. Nevertheless, though buffeted, they survived. The expulsion of the German firms was a blow to many merchants who had traded with them, but their absence opened opportunities, especially in the export trade, which African merchants began to fill. They also experimented with plans for forming cooperatives that could compete with the British combine, and devised alternative shipping arrangements to overcome the shortage of freight space. The peace initiated a destabilising boom in 1919 and a correspondingly dislocating slump in 1920–1921. The effects on Lagos were replicated throughout the world. Fortunes quickly made were quickly lost. The subsequent clear-out deprived many African entrepreneurs of their businesses and left them with weighty debts. Expatriate firms suffered too; the survivors sought safety in amalgamations that reduced their number and increased their size and market power. The inter-war years offered little remission and even less hope. The global depression that began in 1929 and the financial crisis that followed in 1931 extinguished all prospects of recovery.

The chapter dealing with the war ends on a note of gloom that reflects the mood of the time. Old ideals were shaken; expectations were shattered. The hardships of war and the failure of peace to restore prosperity gave impetus to mounting criticisms of colonial rule. This was the moment when Mohandas Gandhi, Mao Tse-tung, and Ho Chi Minh appeared on the world stage. Figures like Manuel Quezon and Sergio Osmena in the Philippines and Albizu Campos in Puerto Rico, though less well known, were equally important in their own countries. Herbert Macaulay emerged to lead the embryonic nationalist movement in Nigeria. The Bolsheviks had already pronounced judgement on imperial Russia; Leon Trotsky and Vladimir Lenin were the first to advocate the principle of self-determination. New ideals and expectations made their appearance. As Chateaubriand predicted in 1841, ideas have wings that cannot be clipped. The great imperial dialectic was beginning to unfold: the forces that generated colonial expansion produced a reaction that set in motion the chain of events that eventually led to decolonisation.

Conundrum: The Missing Years

The long-run consequences of these events are directly relevant to understanding not only the vitality of the mercantile community but also the history of Nigeria's economic development during the remainder of the colonial period. The main issue can be put in the form of a conundrum, which is easily stated: what happened to African merchants after the 1920s? The question arises because, in the absence of the necessary research, the response has to be conjured out of fragmentary evidence and presented as tentative hypotheses. The resolution of the problem is self-evidently important because it determines whether the expansion of the Nigerian economy after 1945 drew on previous entrepreneurial initiatives or whether it marked a completely new start. The former makes a case for long-run continuity in Nigeria's economic development; the latter places the emphasis on discontinuity and leads to a wider discussion of the post-war period, including the conversion of colonial policy to make development a priority, the changing strategy of the expatriate firms, the growing influence of nationalist demands, the consequences of independence, and the ever-present conditions set by international trade.

The hypothesis that immediately suggests itself is that the post-war slump, combined with the world economic crisis that descended in 1929–1931, either eliminated Africans from the staple import and export trades or reduced the proportion of trade they handled to trivial levels. The slump of 1920–1921 undoubtedly found many merchants, European as well as African, overextended and resulted in numerous business closures. Previous commercial crises had ended with a recovery, however partial. The 1920s, however, promised a revival that never came and were followed instead by a global slump during the next decade, when Nigeria's GDP contracted.[6] The detailed evidence in this study is limited to the history of those merchants whose careers extended into the interwar period. Their stories tend to support the hypothesis of decline. Peter Thomas's extensive correspondence is a depressing record of a permanent struggle against adversity sustained by hopes of a recovery that failed to materialise. Even the great Josiah Doherty, whose business and property portfolio were in a far better condition than Thomas's, had to reduce the number of his branches and curtail some of his expenditure during the 1920s.

If this hypothesis is substantiated, the present study will have shown that African merchants suffered a reversal of fortune, but one that occurred during the inter-war period rather than at the close of the nineteenth century. Given the current uncertainty about the fate of African entrepreneurs between 1918 and 1945, however, the jury needs to deliberate further before passing judgement. African merchants continued to compete with the United African Company in the import trade; a handful, numbering seven in 1936, still exported produce directly to Europe, though on a small scale.[7] A much larger contingent remained brokers or traded in the vast domestic market. Evidence cited

6. Broadberry and Gardner, 'Economic Growth in Sub-Saharan Africa', pp. 18–19, 26.
7. *The Nigerian Handbook* (London: West African Publicity, 1936). Very few African firms (Odutola Brothers and the Union Development Trading Co. among them) were allocated export licenses during the Second World War. The two firms referred to here were judged to be 'rather unimportant' by Mars, 'Extra-Territorial Enterprises', in *Mining, Commerce, and Finance*, pp. 56–7.

in previous chapters and summarised here also drew attention to innovations during the prosperous years between 1900 and 1914 that were outside the staple import and export trades.

The Odutola brothers, Adeole (1902–1995) and Jimoh (1905–2010), deserve to be mentioned at this point, even though their careers lie beyond the scope of this study.[8] They were born in Ijebu Ode, which remained their base, though they later established a second headquarters in Lagos. The brothers began trading during the unpromising interwar years. First, they retailed cotton goods and other household items before forming a partnership in 1932, after which they added produce to the business. Against the expectations of the time, the business was successful: in 1935 it had thirty-five employees and a turnover of £54,000.[9] The partnership survived the war and was well placed to take advantage of the post-war boom. The firm was one of the leaders of a new wave of innovations that established a wide range of manufacturing businesses during the 1950s. The partnership ended in 1948, when the brothers established separate businesses, but they continued to prosper after Nigeria became independent in 1960. Their example may be exceptional, but it may also point to more modest initiatives about which little is known at present.

There are glimpses of innovation prompted by the adversity that followed the First World War. Difficult trading conditions obliged Josiah Doherty and his son, Adebayo, to reduce the firm's up-country branches in the 1920s and concentrate the Lagos business in a way that anticipated the department stores that appeared after 1945. Peter Thomas devised an ingenious scheme for combining imported bedsteads with mattresses made in Northern Nigeria. The farmers of Agege adapted to falling cocoa prices by exporting kola nuts to Northern Nigeria and becoming market gardeners serving the ever-swelling Lagos market. Yoruba cloth, far from dying out, was widely traded, as the examples of prominent female traders, Wusamotu Shelle, Samota Ikeolorun, and Humuani Alake Thompson, make clear.[10]

One sector, however, that not only survived but also prospered was finance, which was represented at the time by property development and money lending. The inter-war years witnessed the emergence of a class of rentiers

8. There is no business history of the Odutola Brothers. There is a brief study of one brother by Abati, *The Biography of T. Adeola Odutola*. Additional examples are given in Kilby, 'Manufacturing in Colonial Africa', in *Colonialism in Africa*, Vol. 4, pp. 513–16. See also Forrest, *The Advance of African Capital*, pp. 60–63.

9. I am indebted to Prof. Ayodeji Olukoju for this information.

10. See chapter 11, p. 338–41. A qualification should be added to these promising examples. Some innovative activities during the 1930s may have been examples of a shift towards self-sufficiency rather than illustrations of increasing productivity and of value added to the economy. Palm oil producers, for example, benefitted from diverting part of their output from exports to domestic consumers.

who drew rental incomes from properties they had acquired during the pre-war years, when trade had been buoyant.[11] This development has been overlooked because it is virtually invisible. By the 1930s, for example, many properties on the Marina sported the names of European firms, which appeared to be an evident sign of a change of ownership. As we have seen, however, by then only about nine of a sample of twenty-eight properties in prime positions had been transferred to expatriates. Two-thirds were still owned by Africans and remained in their hands for almost the whole of the colonial period and in some cases well beyond it. Substantial property portfolios provided the basis for developing a capital market that was impersonal and capable of exceeding the limits of personal trust and other forms of security that preceded the creation of freehold land.

The puzzle is to discover what happened to the profits from capital gains and rental incomes. A full answer will have to wait until a dedicated team of researchers writes the history of property in Lagos. No doubt some income was spent on 'high living' and some just on living. The indications emerging from the research undertaken for this study, however, are that much, if not most, of it was invested in education and increasingly in higher education. As we have seen, few of the children of successful merchants entered commerce themselves. Their aim was to join the professions, which offered higher status, greater security, and often larger incomes, too. The origins of the lawyers, doctors, pharmacists, teachers, accountants, surveyors, insurers, and eventually the scientists and engineers who populate Lagos today and are indispensable to Nigeria's economic development are to be found in the colonial period and specifically in the property revolution that began with freehold crown grants in the 1860s. Arthur Young's well-known phrase applied beyond the eighteenth century and outside Europe: 'the magic of property turns sand into gold'.[12]

Rentiers have long received bad press, being perceived as drawing incomes without exhibiting enterprise or incurring significant production costs. The first Saro settlers in Lagos who obtained costless crown grants in what, subsequently, became prime sites exemplify the principle of economic rent, though it should be added that they took considerable risks in staking their future on an uncertain polity and an experimental form of commerce. Nevertheless, they should be credited with adding value to the economy. The merchant families of Lagos made an indispensable contribution to economic growth by investing in human capital. By funding the education of their children from rents derived from property, they created what has been called a 'market for talent'

11. The Lagos market discussed here was self-regulated and orderly. Lower down the social scale, the unregulated activities of money lenders led to charges of exploitation that increased in volume during the hardship brought by the 1930s. Government intervention in 1938 to regulate the industry had only a limited effect. Toyin Falola, '"My Friend the Shylock"', pp. 403–23.

12. *Travels, During the Years 1787, 1788, and 1789.*

that produced the professionals who played a key part in the development of the economy after 1945. The rise of the rentiers, though scarcely known, deserves far more attention than it has received. They were the founders of the financial sector that is so important in Lagos today. They also illustrate a route to economic development that has still to receive the appreciation it merits.[13]

These examples of initiatives that occurred during the inter-war years suggest that this unpromising period deserves more attention than it has received from economic historians. If, as Schumpeter claimed, innovation arises to shift the economy from one state of equilibrium to another, further investigation might reveal unknown initiatives in the midst of adversity: green shoots that were to develop when favourable conditions returned after 1945.[14]

Speculation: Development in the Long Run

The argument so far has not attempted to refute the hypothesis that African merchants experienced a decline in their fortunes after the First World War, but to set out alternative possibilities that change the way the subject has traditionally been approached. The speculative remarks that follow consider how four variables—colonial policy, the expatriate firms, the business structure of African firms, and the international economy—influenced the opportunities and performance of Lagos merchants during the period under review.

Government action was undoubtedly crucial in altering the economic environment, as the three shocks Lagos experienced clearly show. Beyond that point, however, economic policy conformed to free-trade policies, which offered little or no support for African merchants. Although Joseph Chamberlain's initiative in borrowing to invest in infrastructure was a marked departure from the Treasury's maxim of local self-sufficiency, it was not the prelude to other significant innovations in economic policy. Nigerian governors were not economists. Lugard's military mind made him especially wary of innovations that might corrupt or even disturb the placid acceptance of colonial rule he aimed to achieve. This concern prompted his opposition to the formation of an agricultural bank and his fear that imported consumer goods would encourage Africans to value trivialities. It was not until the upheaval brought by the First World War that signs of novelty entered Colonial Office thinking. Tentative references to John Stuart Mill's argument in favour of protecting

13. Cain and Hopkins have argued that finance and commercial services, summarised in the phrase 'gentlemanly capitalism', are the key to understanding the economic modernisation of Britain: Cain and Hopkins, *British Imperialism, 1688–1990*. Similarly, Richard Sylla has stressed the role of the financial sector in the early history of the US economy: Sylla, 'Financial Systems and Economic Modernization'.

14. On the dynamism of Nigerian entrepreneurs after 1945, see Forrest, *The Advance of African Capital*.

what he had termed 'infant industries' appeared briefly and vanished with comparable speed.[15]

Towards the end of the war, when the increasing cost of imports and domestic foods began to worry the colonial authorities, even Lugard started to speculate about the merits of import substitution. The thought, however, was transient. The end of the war brought a bonfire of controls and the reassertion of free-trade policy.[16] This was the orthodoxy of the day that applied to Britain as well as to its colonies. It survived until the world economic crisis of 1929–1931. The Ottawa Conference in 1932 breached free trade by imposing imperial protection in ways that favoured British goods. At the same time, colonial policy enforced austerity as a means of balancing budgets. These measures did not solve the economic problem. They were, however, very effective in stimulating political unrest.

Put another way, colonial policy was based on the assumption that the route to economic development was best reached through export growth, and that agricultural (and mineral) exports were the most effective means of reaching the destination. International specialisation in the nineteenth century drew economies throughout the world into exchanges based on the principle of comparative advantage. The result was the well-known division of enterprise between countries that exported manufactures and those that exported primary products. The policy drew support from history. The developing countries in the Western world all started from an agricultural base. The United States, a former colony, exported cotton and wheat in the nineteenth century before it developed modern industries. Parts of the empire, like Canada, South Africa, Australia, and New Zealand, which had acquired dominion status by 1914, had also begun to build manufacturing sectors on the basis of primary exports. The trend accelerated during the 1930s, when adverse terms of trade for primary producers and increasing protectionism in Europe (and the United States) further encouraged import- and export-substituting industries.

The colonial government combined free-trade principles with a bias towards the British firms that had the advantage of access to Parliament and the Colonial Office.[17] During the First World War, officials expressed sympathy with African merchants over the allocation of shipping space and regarded the new combine the British firms had formed as a self-evident attempt to rig the market. The issue went as far as the cabinet but no action was taken, partly because Britain had no anti-trust legislation and partly because the exigencies of war trumped the interests of equality. The amalgamations that occurred in 1919, followed by the formation of UAC in 1929, consolidated the power of

15. See Irwin, *Against the Tide*, ch. 8.
16. The classic statement is Tawney, 'The Abolition of Economic Controls', pp. 1–30.
17. Olukoju, 'Anatomy of Business–Government Relations'.

the British companies and increased their influence in the colony.[18] UAC was unable to dictate economic policy, but the Colonial Office was obliged to consider the combine's representations carefully because of the colony's dependence on revenue from customs duties. Colonial policy remained unchanged for most of the 1930s. This was a time for retrenchment, not for departing from established policies and relationships.

Nevertheless, the role of the expatriate firms should not be reduced to a stereotype. They suffered a high rate of attrition during the 1880s and 1890s and experienced a high rate of turnover after World War I, irrespective of whether they were single ownerships, partnerships, or limited companies. UAC's defensive reaction to adverse commercial conditions produced a policy of horizontal integration that limited opportunities for African merchants and traders.[19] Size, however, did not generate immediate profits. Even the largest expatriate firms bowed before the forces of international trade. UAC suffered losses of £3 million during its first two years of operation (1929–1931) and had to be rescued by Unilever, its parent company.[20] Taken as a whole, the expatriate firms were unadventurous and confined themselves to trade in the established staples. Their principal innovation, plantation agriculture, failed completely. Their main aim, attested by produce pools and efforts to create combines after 1900, was not to stimulate market competition, but to control it. As we have seen, innovation came from African entrepreneurs who began to diversify the economy before 1914. Commercial conditions remained difficult throughout the decade. UAC began to change its policy only at the close of the 1930s, when it established a small textile factory in Lagos employing local workers and tailors who used their own sewing machines.[21] Until this trend expanded after 1945, UAC's strategy is best summarised by John Hicks, who observed in 1935 that 'the best of all monopoly profits is a quiet life'.[22]

Neither government policy nor the expatriate firms promoted diversification during this period, and the need to protect the colony's revenues may even have inhibited official support for import-substituting manufactures. Other constraints, however, may have had a greater influence on the prospects for diversification. There is a case for questioning whether the consumer market in Nigeria was large enough and per capita incomes high enough in the 1930s to justify the cost and risk of establishing substantial import-substituting industries. If this proposition has merit, structural economic change had to await the revival of prosperity and the expansion of purchasing

18. Mars, 'Extra-Territorial Enterprises', pp. 61–3.

19. Specific examples are given in Olukoju, 'The Impact of British Colonialism', p. 194.

20. Reported in *Fortune*, Jan. 1948.

21. van den Bersselaar, 'UAC Between Developmentalists and Anti-Revolutionaries', in *Perspektiven auf eine globale Konstellation*, p. 219.

22. Hicks, 'Annual Survey', pp. 1–20 (at p. 8). The wider implications of this thought are considered in Hirschman, *Exit, Voice, and Loyalty*, ch. 5.

power after 1945. The position regarding export processing was rather different. The potential for investing in factories to process exports locally was limited because the colonial government had declared its support for indigenous producers and denied William Lever, who had the necessary capital, the opportunity to establish plantations in British West Africa. These propositions remain hypothetical. Future research on the likely probabilities should add to current understanding of Nigeria's development potential during the inter-war period and provide a secure base for evaluating long-standing arguments about the costs and benefits of colonial rule.

These considerations lead to a reappraisal of the structure of African businesses. It is often said that the difficulties indigenous merchants faced after World War I were caused by their failure to transform firms with single owners into limited companies that would be able to raise capital, curtail personal risk, and guarantee continuity. The literature on this question is paradoxical: from one perspective Africans were too 'communal' to allow individual initiative to thrive; from another, they were too 'individual' to pool their resources in cooperative enterprises. Both approaches fail to recognise that transferring from personal to impersonal business structures is not 'the work of a night', but takes time. As we have seen, singly-owned businesses remained efficient and innovative at least before 1914. Of course, the welfare of the Lagos mercantile community would have been greatly enhanced had it developed companies that could have matched UAC, and had colonial policy provided financial support, for example, for infant industries. These possibilities may point to a plausible truth, but they also need pass the test of historical realism and discount the risk of anachronism.

By 1929, it was clear that African merchants lacked the firepower to compete with the new commercial giant, UAC. At this point, the singly-owned, family firm, British or African, had clearly become sub-optimal as far as the direct import and export trades were concerned. This was far less the case in other fields of business, where single ownership prevailed, and still does. After 1900, African merchants were well aware of the need to pool resources of capital and information. It was their initiative that led to the Ordinance that allowed limited companies to be registered locally. The opportunity was taken up: the number of companies registered in Nigeria climbed steadily throughout the inter-war period. The necessity for structural change had been recognised and acted on. Unfortunately, this was not a favourable time for calling on hard-pressed fellow citizens to part with their money, especially when the promoters were often inexperienced and over-ambitious.[23] Consequently, the failure rate was high.

Yet, the record should not be regarded as a demonstration of entrepreneurial inadequacy. The shift from personal to impersonal methods of raising

---

23. Broadberry and Wallis, 'Growing, Shrinking'.

money and managing businesses involved a leap of faith that made many hesitate and caused some who jumped to fall. Such wariness was not confined to Nigeria. The introduction of limited liability into Britain during the second half of the nineteenth century was also accompanied by scepticism that was bolstered by graphic examples of mismanagement and fraudulent activity. Dickens and Trollope were among the authors who recorded memorable illustrations of the disasters that followed the failure of some of the early limited companies. Moreover, the story has a positive aspect to it. The first successful companies in Nigeria were formed in the depths of recession. Adebayo Doherty turned his father's firm into a limited company in 1930 and was one of the prime movers behind the formation of the National Bank of Nigeria in 1933. Both companies survived into the era of independence. Doherty capped his entrepreneurial career by becoming one of the founders of the Lagos Stock Exchange in 1960. Joseph Schumpeter might regard the first two examples as illustrating his thesis joining innovation to the search for a new equilibrium in conditions of adversity, and the third as an example of prosperity that followed recovery.

This appraisal allows the familiar critique that African businesses lacked continuity to be considered afresh. It has been argued that the failure of founders to entail their businesses meant that trade was discontinued after their deaths, assets were distributed, and valuable knowledge was lost.[24] The evidence confirms that continuity was indeed rare. Muslim merchants followed established principles and distributed their assets at the death of the founder. There are only two examples of long-run continuity among the sample of one hundred merchants deployed in this book. Both relate to Saro families that had accepted the principle of primogeniture, or a variation of it, that enabled a son to continue the business. James George started his business in the 1850s and formed a partnership with his son, Charles, in 1864. Charles continued the business until 1906, when he died, and his son, Charles Will George, took over. Charles Will continued to run the business, but prosperity took leave during the interwar years and closure followed his death in 1940. Josiah Doherty began as an independent trader in 1891. Adebayo Doherty, Josiah's second son, continued the business after his father's death in 1928. As noted earlier, he converted it into a limited liability company in 1930. The business continued after Adebayo's death in 1974 and remains active today. Lack of continuity is not a specifically African phenomenon: it is a feature

---

24. Olukoju, 'The Impact of British Colonialism', in *Black Business and Economic Power*, p. 194. Prof. Olukoju kindly quotes my Ph.D. dissertation at this point. That dissertation, however, was written sixty years ago and the judgement rested on the limited evidence I was able to gather at that time. My assessment today is based on additional research and fuller reflection than was possible then, which is not to say, of course, that it is necessarily any better.

of family businesses everywhere.[25] Seen from this angle, the story is less one of failure than of persistent initiatives that achieved success in the 1950s and 1960s.

Little can be inferred from a sample of two. The example of the George family, however, suggests that entailing a business guarantees continuity but not prosperity. This proposition is summarised in the Lancashire proverb 'clogs to clogs in only three generations', a prediction that is found in various forms throughout the world.[26] The claim is that the founder possesses ability and commitment, the next generation manages more than it innovates, and the third generation, having inherited wealth and being far removed from the ethos of the founder, tends to spend its inheritance. Problems of samples and measurement make it hard to evaluate the proposition. A careful study of wealth in three generations of British business families, however, has supported the idea that the third generation does not perform as well as comparators who are newcomers.[27] Absence of continuity, however, could also be a matter of choice rather than an indication of personal or structural weaknesses. African merchants who were still able to draw on capital resources after World War I invested in education and directed their children into occupations that offered greater stability and higher status than business did.

The foregoing influences on mercantile fortunes need to be placed in the wider context formed by the performance of the international economy. This variable, which lay beyond political control and commercial lobbying, has been the central theme of this study. The evidence for the period from the 1850s to the 1930s shows that mercantile opportunities, decisions, and rewards were linked more closely to fluctuations in international trade than they were to any other causal influence. Buoyant produce prices during the 1850s, 1860s, and 1870s, combined with institutional change in the shape of new land rights, produced prosperity and the first merchant princes. Declining terms of trade and increasingly competitive conditions during the last twenty years of the century reduced profits and caused many businesses, expatriate as well as African, to fail. Improved conditions between 1900 and 1914 provided opportunities for a new generation of merchants and encouraged initiatives that began to diversify the economy. Favourable circumstances ended with the First World War, which was followed by a period of grim commercial conditions that lasted until 1945.

These alternating booms and slumps might suggest a history of random oscillations. After 1914, however, the international market for tropical produce

25. Wagstyl, 'The Struggle Between Success and Succession'.
26. The Japanese have a pithy saying: 'The third generation ruins the house'.
27. Nicholas, 'Clogs to Clogs in Three Generations?'. The analysis is subtler than my summary. The specific finding is that poor performance was marked among high-status families whose children had considerable opportunities for alternative employment and expensive tastes.

underwent a significant change. Buoyant exports had helped the United States and some of the dominions to begin the process of diversifying their economies in the nineteenth century. Nigeria's entrepreneurs entered on the same path after 1900, but were still at a very early stage in a long process. The possibilities of further structural change in Nigeria, as in other countries at the same point of development, were retarded by the adverse terms of trade that eroded capital resources and consumer purchasing power during the interwar period. There was an important difference, however, between late-start countries during this period and those that had been able to diversify on the basis of primary exports in the nineteenth century. The experience of the 1920s and 1930s showed that the terms of trade of primary producers were subject not just to short-term fluctuations but to long-term decline. The success of the imperial powers in 'opening up' underdeveloped countries in the late nineteenth century had increased supplies of raw materials. Intense competition among countries producing the same items or substitutes for them ensured that inefficiencies were squeezed out of production and that profit margins, where they existed, were slim. In these circumstances, increases in incomes of the kind needed to support structural economic change depended on a sustained revival in the terms of trade of producers. This long-awaited event was postponed until after World War II.

Adverse conditions did eventually produce significant changes. The searing experience of the 1930s caused economists to rethink assumptions inherited from the nineteenth century. Under the pressure of changing realities, including rising nationalist agitation built on continuing hardship, imperial policy was reviewed and reconsidered.[28] Lord Hailey's *African Survey* made the case for change in 1938. The Colonial Development & Welfare Act of 1940 created the basis for a new economic policy that made explicit provision for education and health.[29] The Treasury was appalled. The Act, it thundered, would put the colonies 'on the dole from henceforth and forever'.[30] The damage to orthodoxy did not stop there. In 1942, the Beveridge Report laid out policies that formed the basis of the welfare state. The deprived in Britain, as well as those in the colonies, were offered glimpses of a post-war world that paired reform with hope.

If this interpretation has substance, it ought to be relevant to developments that followed the Second World War. After 1945, three stars came into benign alignment. The revival of the international economy raised purchasing power in Nigeria, despite the heavy hand of the marketing boards. Government policy entered the field of development on a large scale for the first time in an attempt to demonstrate that a reformed empire could still claim the loyalty

---

28. Ochonu, 'Conjoined to Empire'; Olukoju, 'Nigeria or Lever-ia?'.
29. Lord Hailey, *An African Survey*; revised 1956.
30. Quoted in Bowden, 'Development and Control in British Colonial Policy', p. 103.

of its subjects. The expatriate firms adjusted their policy by reducing some of their wholesale and retail functions and developing import-substituting manufactures.[31] The post-war recovery had allowed Africans (and others) to enter the market. In 1949, Nigerian merchants were responsible for only 5 per cent of imports; by 1963, their share had risen to 20 per cent—almost the same figure as at the beginning of the century.[32] Faced with renewed competition and the costs of repelling it, the expatriate firms gave ground. Instead, they turned to manufacturing, where they had a clear competitive advantage. By producing goods in Nigeria instead of importing them, they hoped to retain their market share and gain kudos with the nationalist movement.[33] A future beyond colonial rule was about to embrace everyone. New cards were about to be dealt; diplomacy was needed in playing them.

This account of the history of Lagos merchants suggests that the bourgeoisie and its sprinkling of Schumpeterian heroes has indeed 'played a most revolutionary part' in the history of the port and its wider hinterland.[34] Indigenous entrepreneurs were not shot down soon after taking flight. As capitalists, they were effective in spreading capitalism within and beyond the port. They adjusted creatively to the expansion of colonial rule by diversifying the economy and responded to the challenging inter-war years as adroitly as conditions allowed, not least by creating a market for talent that facilitated the structural economic change that was to occur after 1945. Even if the interpretation advanced here fails to be persuasive, common agreement may be found in the less ambitious proposition that the history of Nigeria's economy after 1945 will be missing several chapters until the story I have tried to tell has been completed.

31. Wale, 'Changing Activities', pp. 131–3; and, more generally, Decker, *Postcolonial Transition*.

32. Kilby, 'Manufacturing in Colonial Africa', p. 494.

33. Decker, 'Africanisation', shows that the adaptation did not always end well, especially for UAC.

34. Marx and Engels, *Manifesto of the Communist Party*, p. 46.

Epilogue

THE FUTURE OF Lagos was decided in the early 1900s, when it became the terminus of the railway to the north, the beneficiary of harbour improvements, and the crowned capital of Nigeria in 1914. Thereafter, as Lagos grew, its competitors receded. The expansion of population and the colonisation of space now appear to be inexorable laws of nature. What was a small fishing village on an obscure island has become a megacity, the capital of a metropolitan area with a population that is close to 25 million, and an appetite that has devoured stretches of forest extending more than twenty miles inland.[1] Although Lagos remains a major port, the largest in West Africa and one of the largest in Africa, it has also become the financial and industrial centre of tropical Africa. The congestion at Christmas, though only slightly greater than at other times of the year, has reached the point where all remedies retreat before the advancing battalions of traffic.

The wheels of progress have turned the artifacts of the past into dust and concrete. The Marina and Broad Street, the commercial centres of Lagos for much of the nineteenth and twentieth centuries, have retained their names and locations but have otherwise been transformed. The premises of the great merchants, which could still be seen in the 1960s and 1970s, have been pounded into oblivion.[2] In their place stand business offices and banks that are now just part of a much larger Central Business District. Trade has migrated to other areas of the town. Retail outlets are found in large markets, such as Idumota and Balogun, and gathered in modern shopping malls. In recognition of its demotion from the

1. For the wider setting, see Howard W. French, 'How Coastal West Africa Will Shape the Coming Century', *The Guardian*, 27 Oct. 2022.
2. Water House, the home of the da Rocha family in Kakawa Street (behind the Marina off Broad Street), is the only great house to have survived and has now been declared a national monument.

position it had long held, the Marina has also lost its waterfront. It was reclaimed from the lagoon in the 1860s to improve access to the piers that were needed to land imported goods and load barrels of palm oil. Today, there is an Outer Marina separating the original Marina from the waterfront. This, too, is built on reclaimed land and provides a broad carriageway running parallel to the Marina and topped by a flyover that snakes along the same route. Society, as well as commerce, has emigrated. Until well into the twentieth century, Lagos merchants lived and entertained in their houses on the Marina and Broad Street. It was here that horses and carriages set out to impress the populace and the first motor cars coughed their way towards progress. Today, the separation between business and pleasure is complete. Successful entrepreneurs live on Ikoyi and Victoria Island and enjoy their social life there too. These former white reservations have become the most expensive residential areas in Nigeria.

Change in the commercial capital of Nigeria is to be expected. The complete transformation of the countryside, however, is nothing less than astonishing. In the 1960s, Ijon, the site of the first successful cocoa farm in Nigeria, was a tiny, unknown hamlet that could be reached only through forest and with some difficulty. Today, Ijon is unrecognisable. Most of the forest has been cleared, the cocoa trees have long disappeared, and nothing is left of James Davies's house or the small church he built on his estate. Even someone who knew the original village would be unable to identify its exact location had not one durable signpost survived. This is the granite obelisk James Davies erected to commemorate the death of his wife, Sarah, in 1880, the year he started his farming enterprise. Although plant growth laps at its plinth, the memorial stands tall and upright, just as Davies hoped it would. Ijon itself still exists and is larger than it was in the nineteenth century. It has now rearranged itself along either side of an improbably wide dual carriageway, which halts at Ijon as if baffled, there being no obvious purpose for its presence at this point.[3] Here, if nowhere else, light traffic moves freely. Today, the residents trade, fish in the nearby Owo River, and look for work. The only remaining extensive greenery lies on the other side of the Owo, where the bush, in alliance with the river, still resists the advance of the town.

None of these changes, however, can compare with the fate of Agege. It is impossible to believe that this crowded outer suburb of Lagos was created in the early 1900s by pioneering farmers from Lagos who tamed the forest, established extensive plantations, produced the finest quality cocoa, and spread their knowledge and seeds to many other parts of Yorubaland. Under Jacob Coker's leadership, they also made Agege the headquarters of the African Church and carried its message to inland towns and villages. None of these innovations can be discerned today. The impressive driveways flanked by kola trees have lost their one-sided battle with bulldozers; the fine estate houses have been demolished; the plantations have been excised. Even the sizeable and carefully tended churches that dotted the estates of the large planters have

3. Lack of funds have halted further advance towards Otta. See *This Day*, 12 April 2018, 22 Jan. 2023.

been taken down. Only one tenuous memento remains: the church and school in Agege that bear Jacob Coker's name. These, however, are relatively recent foundations that have no connection, other than a celebrated name, with the exceptional enterprise that made Agege such a striking centre of innovation. Past glories have not just faded: they have been obliterated.

During the 1920s, when cocoa exports declined, the Agege farmers turned to kola, sending the nuts north to centres of demand in Kano and other large towns. After World War II, they adapted again, becoming market gardeners supplying Lagos with vegetables, fruit, and chickens. The innovative ingenuity of the farming community, however, was unable to compete with the rising price of the land needed to house Lagos's swelling population. Today, Agege provides low-cost housing for immigrants whose hopes are not for riches but for jobs—of any kind.[4]

This epilogue, however, is not a lament for the past but an expression of regret that so much of it has been removed from the historical record. Change is inexorable, and may bring progress, though the two are not synonymous. A separate study is needed to examine whether the developments referred to here are manifestations of rising per capita incomes and welfare, or are no more than indications of persistent poverty spread over an increasing population. What is incontestable is that these changes, being so extensive, have had a direct effect on historical studies. The people and places discussed in this book have been erased from visual memory, despite their eminence and contribution to economic development. Lagosians who look around will find only two remaining memorials: Daniel Taiwo's tomb in Broad Street, which was erected in 1905 and is still watched over by the family compound nearby; and Sarah Davies's obelisk, which is in an obscure and unprotected location in Ijon. Everything else has been swept away.

Despite these unpromising precedents, everyone who values Nigerian history must hope that the current guardians of the Lagos past will preserve the evidence better than their predecessors managed to do. Low-cost initiatives, such as collecting photographs, business and private papers, and modest artifacts, could produce a collection that, suitably housed, would become a public legacy.[5] If we forget our past, we cannot understand our present. If we leave a void, it will be filled by those who prize opinions above evidence.

4. Agege's complex politics in the post-colonial period have been studied by Olukoju, 'Actors and Institutions'.

5. I am glad to be able to conclude this depressing catalogue on an optimistic note. The Lagos State Record and Archives Bureau (LASRAB), which began operations in 2008, appointed a new Director General, Mrs Bilikiss Adebiyi, in 2019. A meeting between Mrs Adebiyi, Professor Ayodeji Olukoju (Department of History, University of Lagos), and myself, held on 6 December 2022, established a common interest in preserving records of the kind referred to in this paragraph and agreed to increase communication between LASRAB and the Department of History to ensure that records discovered by members of the Department and its postgraduate researchers will be made known to the Bureau. Beyond this modest aim, there is also the prospect of a team effort to locate the private papers of individuals and companies and ensure that they are properly housed, and, above all, not destroyed.

APPENDIX

Lagos Entrepreneurs, 1851–1931

THE FOLLOWING LIST is divided into three parts: merchants (100), finance and services (6), and planters (15). The total (121) includes five entrepreneurs whose careers spanned two occupations: either commerce and finance or commerce and farming. If the five are counted once rather than twice, the total number on the list is reduced to 116.

Merchants

Abina, Badaru (c.1867–1937)
Adewale, Sanni (1866–1944)
Affini, Buramoh (1843–1914)
Agbete, Alfa Bakare (?–1918)
Ajai-Ajagbe, Caroline Ayoola, aka Araoti (1884–1946)
Ajao, Buraimoh, aka Abibu Oke (1849–1935)
Akerele, David Evaristo (1876–1943)
Akitoye, Alfred Ibikunle (1871–1928)
Alayaki, Abdul Kadiri (c.1829–1919)
Animashaun, Sumanu (c.1810–1895)
Apatira, Braimah (c.1830–1907)
Ariyo, Muhammed Salu (c.1833–1923)

Balogun, Alli, aka Alli Oloko, *Alhaji* (1850–1933)
Blaize, Richard Beale (1845–1904)
Branco, Joaquim Francisco Devode (1852–1924)
Britto, Benedicto Antonio (c.1845–1910)
Bucknor, Joseph Samuel (1840–1890)

Campbell, Alfred Cope (c.1850–1914)
Campos, João Angelo (c.1850–1904)
Cardoso, Lourenço António (1865–1940)
Coker, Jacob Kehinde (1866–1945)
Coker, Samuel Alfred Akinwande, aka S. Alfred Coker (1865–1917)
Cole, James William (1844–1897)
Cole, Thomas Francis, aka Daddy Alade (c.1812–1890)
Crowther, Josiah (1839–1910)
Crowther, Samuel Jr. (1829–1900)

Davies, Abdul Salami Bakare, *Alhaji* (1863–1935)
Davies, James Pinson Labulo (1828–1906)
Davies, Samuel Sogunro (?–1911)
Dawodu, Benjamin, aka Fagbemi (?–1881)
Dawodu, Benjamin Charles (1860–1900)
Disu, James Asani, *Alhaji* (1881–1950)
Doherty, Josiah Henryson (1866–1928)

Fashola, Mohammed Bello (1845–1930)

George, Charles Joseph (1840–1906)
George, Charles Will (1867–1940)
George, John Olawunmi (c.1850–1914)
George, James, aka Osoba (?–1876)
Giwa, Sanni, *Alhaji* (1860–1942)

Haastrup, Joseph Pythagoras (1852–1903)
Hoare, Thomas George (1824–1889)

Igbo, Brimoh (?1850–1946)
Ige, Idirisu (1861–1920)
Ikeolorun, Samota Ike (1858–1948)
Iyorinde, Jinadu, aka Kabiawun (c.1835–1898)

Jawandu, Selia (c.1855–1950)
Joe, Thomas (c.1810–1880)
Johnstone, Thomas Baker (c.1885–?)
Jones, Tom (c.1852–1917)

Kekereogun, Mohammed Lawani (c.1850–1942)
Kotun, Kariumu, *Alhaji* (1881–1958)

Layeni, Oluyode (c.1810–1891)
Leigh, Jacob Samuel (1837–1907)

Macaulay, David (1842–1914)
Macaulay, Dorcas Folashade, aka Ireti (1887–1955)

Macaulay, Thomas Benjamin, aka 'Smart' (c.1838–?)
Martins, Adolphus Buramoh (1874–1918)
Misinhun, Bakare (c.1845–1935)
Moore, Cornelius Bartholomew (1841–1906)
Mustapha, Mohammed, *Alhaji* (1869–1958)

Nimbe, Abdul Ramonu Olorun, *Alhaji* (1879–1948)

Ogunbiyi, Jacob (c.1805–1886)
Olaniyan, Idris (1866–1926)
Olowu, Seidu (c.1840–1921)
Olukolu, Fasheke (c.1825–1906)
Olusesi, Abdul Ramonu (c.1880–1945)
Oni, Claudius Ayodele (1861–1932)
Oshodi, 'Tapa', aka Landuji (c.1800–1868)

Pearse, Samuel Herbert (1866–1953)
Pratt, Harry (?–1886)

Robbin, Henry (1835–1887)
Rocha, João Esan da (1821–1891)

Sant Anna, Manoel Joaquim de (?–1896)
Savage, Josiah Alfred (1849–1920)
Shelle, Sarah Ajibola Wusamotu (1875–1939)
Shepherd, Nathaniel Thomas Babington (1830–1909)
Shitta (Bey), Mohammed, aka 'William' (1824–1895)
Siffre, Walter Paul (?–1923)
Silva, Lazaro Borges da (1856–1928)

Taiwo, Daniel Conrad (1814–1901)
Taylor, David Augustus (1865–1932)
Tete-Ansa, Winifried (c.1889–1935)
Thomas, Andrew Wilkinson (1856–1924)
Thomas, James Jonathan (1850–1919)
Thomas, Peter John Claudius (1873–1947)
Thompson, Humuani Alake (?1873–1943)
Tinubu, Efunroye, aka Efunroye (c.1810–1887)
Turner, James Moses (c.1830–1909)

Vaughan, Burrel Carter (1870–1926)
Vaughan, James Churchill (1828–1893)
Vaughan, James Wilson (1866–1923)

Williams, Abdul Ramanu 'Aranmoletiesho' (c.1859–1931)
Williams, Edwin Oshunkon (?–1899)
Williams, Isaac Benjamin (1846–1925)

Williams, Jacob 'Aleshinloye' (1830–1893)
Williams, Jacob Taiwo (1859–1911)
Williams, James O'Connor (1843–1906)
Williams, Philip Henryson (1872–1946)
Williams, Seidu Jabita (?–1948)
Williams, Zachariah Archibald (1851–1912)

Finance and Commercial Services

Adeshigbin, Dada (1865–1925)
Cole, Isaac A. (1862–?1935)
Dawodu, William Akinola (1879–1930)
Laweni, Saka Francis, aka Sakajojo (1877–1949)
Rocha, Candido João da (1867–1959)
Williams, Isaac Benjamin, ex-merchant (1846–1925)

Planters

Beckley, Joseph Ogunola (1862–1923)
Coker, Jacob Kehinde, ex-merchant (1866–1945)
Davies, James Pinson Labulo, ex-merchant (1828–1906)
Dawodu, Thomas Bankunbi (1872–1920)
Doherty, Henry Theodore (1837–1912)
Egerton Shyngle, Joseph (1861–1926)
Fashola, Mohammed Bello, ex-merchant (1845–1930)
Hughes, David Ayodele (1856–1936)
Jibowu, Samuel Alexander (1862–1928)
Obadina, Alfred Adeshina (1878–1934)
Sasegbon, Daniel Taiwo (1870–1955)
Somefun, Moses Odeyinka (1862–1929)
Taylor, David Augustus, ex-merchant (1865–1932)
Williams, Frederick Ephraim (1867–1918)
Wright, Rufus Alexander (1856–1907)

SOURCES

Manuscript Sources

NATIONAL ARCHIVES, LONDON

Slave Trade, FO 84/816–1141 (1850–1861)
Lagos, C.O. 147/1–179 (1862–1906)
Africa West Supplementary Correspondence, C.O. 537/10–16 (1884–1909)
Lagos Legislative Council and Annual Reports, C.O. 149/1–7 (1872–1906)
Southern Nigeria Legislative Council and Annual Reports, C.O. 592 (1906–1912)
Southern Nigeria, C.O. 520/35–131 (1906–1913)
Nigeria, C.O. 583/1–205 (1913–1935)

NIGERIAN NATIONAL ARCHIVES, IBADAN

Central Secretary's Office, C.S.O. 1–12 (1862–1914)
Badagry Divisional Office, Badadiv 1–7 (1865–1914)
Epe Divisional Office, Epediv, 4–7 (1889–1913)
Jacob K. Coker Papers: Coker 1–3 (1901–1951)
Comcol 1 (1886–1958) Administrative Records of the Officers of the Colony Forestry
    Department Records, 1904–
Department of Agriculture Records, 1912–

LAGOS GOVERNMENT

Chief Magistrate's Court and Vice-Admiralty Court, 1863–1868
Supreme Court Civil Cases 1–146 (1877–1934)
Judge's Notebooks, 1876–1916
High Court Records, Letters of Administration and Probate (including Wills), Vols. 1–18
    (1888–1960); Vols. 11–21 (1921–1962)
Land Registry:

    Dosunmu's Land Grants, 1853–1861
    Crown Grants Index, 1862–1882
    Grantor and Grantee Indexes: Mortgages and Conveyances, 1862–1921 (includes crown
        grants from 1882)

Municipal Board of Health Records, MB 1/1902–1/1917
Registrar of Companies Records, Vol. 1 (1912–1926); Vol. II (1926–1935)
Lagos Town Council Records, 1919–1930

OTHER ARCHIVES

Church Missionary Society, University of Birmingham, CA2, G3.A.2 Yoruba Mission
    (1852–1934)
John Holt Papers (Liverpool) Series 1–2 (1886–1915). Now in Rhodes House Library, Oxford

PRIVATE RECORDS, LAGOS

Jacob K. Coker Papers. Now in the National Archives, Ibadan
James P. L. Davies Papers. In the possession of the family
Josiah H. Doherty Papers. In the possession of the family
Samuel H. Pearse Papers. In the possession of the family
Daniel C. Taiwo Papers. In the possession of the family
David A. Taylor Papers. In the possession of the family
Peter J.C. Thomas Papers. In the possession of the family
Isaac B. Williams Papers. In the possession of the family

UNPUBLISHED PRIMARY SOURCES

Confidential Prints (Now C.O.879)

C.O. 806/3. West African Trade, 1874
C.O. 806/12. Enquiry into the West African Settlements, 1865
C.O. 806/184. Currency of West African Colonies, 1879–1882
C.O. 806/274. West Africa: Salmon's Ideas for Expanding Trade, 1885–1886
C.O. 806/334. Lagos. Millson's Visit to the Interior, 1889–1891
C.O. 806/357. Lagos: Stoppage of Trade Routes, 1891–1893
C.O. 806/362. West Africa: Proposed Railway Construction, 1879–1893
C.O. 806/455. Lagos: Interior Expedition, 1892
C.O. 806/592. West Africa: Currency Matters, 1892–1899
C.O. 806/616. West Africa: Report of the Currency Committee, 1900
C.O. 806/635. West Africa: Botanic and Forestry Matters, 1889–1901
C.O. 806/647. Nigeria: Railway Construction, 1897–1901
C.O. 806/661. West Africa: Botanic and Forestry Matters, 1901–1904
C.O. 806/845. Nigeria: Railway Construction, 1906–1908
C.O. 806/982. Southern Nigeria: Railway and Wharfage, Lagos, 1910–1911

PUBLISHED PRIMARY SOURCES

Annual Reports, Lagos Colony (1862–1905)
Annual Reports, Southern Nigeria (1905–1914)
Annual Reports, Nigeria, (1914–1930)
Blue Books, Lagos Colony, C.O. 151 (1862–1905)
Blue Books, Southern Nigeria, C.O. 473 (1905–1913)
Blue Books, Nigeria, C.O. 660 (1913–1930)
Bulletin of the Imperial Institute, selected years
Customs and Trade Journals, Nigeria, C.O. 659/1–3 (1911–1916)
International Congress of Tropical Agriculture, 1905–1914, 1930–1931
Kew Bulletin, selected years
Lagos Customs and Trade Journals, C.O. 659/1–3 (1911–1916)
Lagos Official Handbook, 1897–1898
Nigeria Handbook, 1917–1936
Southern Nigeria Handbook, 1911, 1912
Trade Supplements, Nigeria, C.O. 658/23–42 (1917–1938)

Parliamentary Papers

Cd 4668, XLVII (1909) Report on Shipping Rings
Cd 4670, XLVII (1909) Minutes of Evidence for Cd 4688
Cd 4685, XLVIII (1909) Minutes of Evidence for Cd 4688
Cd 4906, LX (1909) Report into the Liquor Trade in Southern Nigeria
Cd 4907, LX (1909) Minutes of Evidence for Cd. 4906
Cd 6426, XLVIII (1912) Report into the Currency of British West African Colonies
Cd 6427, XLVIII (1912) Minutes of Evidence for Cd. 6426
Cd 6561 (1912–1913) Correspondence on Lever's Application to Extract Palm Oil
Cd 6771 (1913) Reports on British Trade with West Africa
Cd 8247 (1916) Report on Edible and Oil-Producing Nuts and Seeds
Cd 8248 (1916) Minutes of Evidence on Cd 8247

NEWSPAPERS

African Times, 1862–1902
Anglo-African, 1863–1865
The Comet, 1933–1944
Daily Service, 1951–
Eagle & Lagos Critic, 1883–1888
Iwe Irohin Eko, 1888–1891
Lagos Observer, 1882–1888
Lagos Reporter, 1898–1899
Lagos Standard, 1895–1930
Lagos Times & Gold Coast Advertiser, 1881–1883, 1890–1891
Lagos Weekly Record, 1891–1930
Lagos Weekly Times, 1890
The Mirror, 1887–1888
Nigerian Chronicle, 1908–1915
Nigerian Daily Times, 1930–1948
Nigerian Pioneer, 1914–1934
Nigerian Times, 1910–1911
Times of Nigeria, 1914–1920
The Wasp, 1900
West Africa, 1917–1933
West African Pilot, 1951–

Books, Articles, Dissertations

Abati, Reuben. *The Biography of T. Adeola Odutola* (Abeokuta: Alf Publications, 1995).
Adebayo, A. G. 'The Production and Export of Hides and Skins in Colonial Nigeria, 1900–1945,' *Journal of African History*, 33 (1992), pp. 273–300.
Adeboye, Olufunke, Tunde Akinwumi, and Tosin Otusanay. 'Rabi "Also Oke" of Colonial Lagos: A Female Textile Merchant Commemorated in a Yoruba Proverb', *JENdA: A Journal of Culture and Women Studies*, 16 (2010), pp. 85–102.
Adedeji, J. A. 'The Church and the Emergence of the Nigerian Theatre, 1866–1914', *Journal of the Historical Society of Nigeria*, 6 (1971), pp. 25–45.
Adeloye, Adeola. 'Some Early Doctors and Their Contribution to Modern Medicine in Nigeria', *Medical History*, 18 (1974), pp. 275–93.

Adeoti, Dele. 'The Career of Alli Balogun of Lagos, 1840–1933', in Siyan Oyewesi, ed. *Eminent Yoruba Muslims of the Nineteenth and Early Twentieth Centuries* (Lagos: Rex Charles, 1999), pp. 179–200.

Afolabi, Abiodun S. 'Lagos Market Women During the Inter-War Years: The Water Rate Agitation, 1932–1941', *Journal of the Historical Society of* Nigeria, 25 (2016), pp. 102–18.

Agiri, Babatunde A. 'The Yoruba and the Pre-Colonial Kola Trade', *Odu*, 25 (1975), pp. 55–68.

Agiri, Babatunde A. 'The Introduction of Nitida Kola into Nigerian Agriculture, 1880–1920', *African Economic History*, 3 (1977), pp. 1–14.

Agiri, Babatunde A. 'The Development of Wage Labour in Agriculture in Southern Yorubaland, 1900–1940', *Journal of the Historical Society of Nigeria* 12, (1983–4), pp. 75–107.

Ajayi, J.F.A. 'Henry Venn and the Policy of Development', *Journal of the Historical Society of Nigeria*, 1 (1959), pp. 331–42.

Akebiyi, Peter Awelewa. 'Jacob Keinde Coker', in J. Akinyele Ajowo, ed. *Makers of the Church in Nigeria* (Lagos: CCS Bookshops, 1995).

Akinsanya, Oba Samuel. 'Dandies of the 1900s', *Sunday Express* (Lagos), 27 June 1961, 27 Aug. 1961.

Akinsemoyin, Kunle and Alan Vaughan-Richards. *Building Lagos* (Jersey: Pengrail, 2nd ed., 1977).

Akintan, E. A. *Epetedo Lands: Historical Survey of the Settlement* (Lagos: Yoruba Printing Press, 1929).

Akintan, E. A. *Awful Disclosures on Epetedo Lands* (Lagos: Tika Tore Press, c.1936).

Akyeampong, Emmanuel, Robert Bates, Nathan Nunn, and James A. Robinson, eds. *Africa's Development in Historical Perspective* (Cambridge: Cambridge University Press, 2014).

d'Almeida-Topor, Hélène. 'Les termes de l'échange du Dahomey, 1890–1914', in G. Liesegang, H. Pasch, and A. Jones, eds. *Figuring African Trade* (Berlin: Reimer, 1986), pp. 345–62.

Amin, Samir. *Le monde des affaires sénégalais* (Paris: Editions de Minuit, 1969).

Amrith, Sunil S. *Migration and Diaspora in Modern Asia* (Cambridge: Cambridge University Press, 2011).

Animashaun, Adam I. *The History of the Muslim Community of Lagos and the Central Mosque* (Lagos: Hope Rising Press, 1939).

Animashaun, Bashir Olalekan. 'Benin Imperialism and the Transformation of Idejo Chieftaincy in Lagos, 1603–1850', *Journal of the Historical Society of Nigeria*, 25 (2016), pp. 37–52.

Anon, 'Port Cities', *Economic Geography*, 11 (1935), n.p.

Austin, Gareth. 'Mode of Production or Mode of Cultivation: Explaining the Failure of European Cocoa Farmers in Competition with African Farmers in Colonial Ghana', in William Gervase Clarence-Smith, ed. *Cocoa Pioneer Fronts since 1800* (London: Macmillan, 1996), pp. 154–75.

Austin, Gareth. 'African Business in the Nineteenth Century', in Alusine Jalloh and Toyin Falola, eds. *Black Business and Economic Power* (Rochester: University of Rochester Press, 2002), ch. 4.

Austin, Gareth. 'The "Reversal of Fortune" Thesis and the Compression of History: Perspectives from African and Comparative Economic History', *Journal of International Development*, 20 (2008), pp. 996–1027.

Austin, Gareth. 'Comment: The Return of Capitalism as a Concept', in Jürgen Kocka and Marcel van der Linden, eds. *Capitalism: The Reemergence of a Historical Concept* (London: Bloomsbury, 2016), pp. 207–34.

Austin Gareth. 'African Business History', in John F. Wilson, Steven Toms, Abe de Jong, and Emily Buchnea, eds. *The Routledge Companion to Business History* (London: Routledge, 2017), pp. 141–58.

Austin, Gareth, Carlos Davila, and Geoffrey Jones. 'The Alternative Business History: Business in Emerging Markets', *Business History Review*, 91 (2017), pp. 537–69.

Austin, Gareth and Chibuike Ugochukwu Uche. 'Collusion and Competition in Colonial Economies: Banking in British West Africa', *Business History Review*, 81 (2007), pp. 1–26.

Avoseh, T. Ola. *A Short History of Badagri* (Lagos: Ife-Olu Press, 1938).

Ayandele, E. A. *Holy Johnson: Pioneer of African Nationalism, 1836–1917* (London: Cass, 1970).

Ayorinde, J. A. 'Historical Notes on the Introduction and Development of the Cocoa Industry in Nigeria', *The Nigerian Agricultural Journal*, 3 (1966), pp. 18–23.

Barber, Karin. 'Documenting Social and Ideological Change Through Yoruba Oriki: A Stylistic Analysis', *Journal of the Historical Society of Nigeria*, 10 (1981), pp. 39–52.

Barber, Karin. 'Experiments with Genre in Yoruba Newspapers of the 1920s', in Derek R. Peterson, Emma Hunter, and Stephanie Newell, eds. *African Print Cultures: Newspapers and Their Publics in the Twentieth Century* (Ann Abor: University of Michigan Press, 2016), ch. 6.

Barghardt, Andrew F. 'A Hypothesis about Gateway Cities', *Annals of the Association of American Geographers*, 61 (1971), pp. 269–85.

Barnes, Trevor T. 'Notes from the Underground. Why the History of Economic Geography Matters: The Case of Central Place Theory', *Economic Geography*, 88 (2012), pp. 1–26.

Barry, Boubacar and Leonhard Harding, eds. *Commerce et commerçants en Afrique de l'Ouest: Le Sénégal* (Paris: L'Harmattan, 1992).

Basu, Dilip K., ed. *The Rise and Growth of Colonial Port Cities in Asia* (Lanham: University Press of America, 1985).

Beckert, Sven. *Empire of Cotton: A New History of Global Capitalism* (London: Penguin, 2014).

Beckert, Sven and Christine Desan, eds. *American Capitalism: New Histories* (New York: Columbia University Press, 2018).

Beckert, Sven and Seth Rockman, eds. *Slavery's Capitalism: A New History of American Economic Development* (Philadelphia: University of Pennsylvania Press, 2016).

Beckert, Sven and Dominic Sachsenmaier, eds. *Global History, Globally: Research and Practice around the World* (London: Bloomsbury, 2018).

Berquist, An-Kristin. 'Renewing Business History the Era of the Anthropocene', *Business History Review*, 92 (2019), pp. 3–24.

Berry, Sara S. 'The Concept of Innovation and the History of Cocoa Farming in Western Nigeria', *Journal of African History*, 15 (1974), pp. 83–95

Berry, Sara S. *Cocoa, Custom, and Socio-Economic Change in Rural Western Nigeria* (Oxford: Clarendon Press, 1975)

Bersselaar, Dimitri van den. 'UAC Between Developmentalists and Anti-Revolutionaries: A Multinational Enterprise Makes Sense of Post-Independence Africa', in Steffan Fiebrig, Jürgen Dinkel, and Frank Reichherzer, eds. *Perspektiven auf eine globale Konstellation* (Berlin: De Gruyter Oldenbourg, 2020), pp. 210–39.

Bickford-Smith, Vivian. 'The Betrayal of Creole Elites, 1880–1920', in Philip D. Morgan and Sean Hawkins, eds. *Black Experience and the Empire* (Oxford: Oxford University Press, 2006), pp. 194–227.

Bigon, Liora. 'Sanitation and Street Layout in Early Colonial Lagos: British and Indigenous Conceptions, 1851–1900', *Planning Perspectives*, 20 (2005), pp. 262–3.

Bigon, Liora. *History of Urban Planning in Two West African Colonial Capitals: Residential Segregation in British Lagos and French Dakar (1850–1930)* (New York: Edwin Mellen, 2009).

Bigon, Liora. 'The Former Names of Lagos (Nigeria) in Historical Perspective', *Names: A Journal of Onomastics*, 59 (2011), pp. 229–40.

Billows, H. C. and H. Beckwick. *Palm Oil and Kernels, 'The Consols of the West Coast'* (Birchall: Liverpool, 1913).

Biobaku, Saburi O. *The Egba and their Neighbours, 1842–1872* (Oxford: Clarendon Press, 1957).

Blyden, Edward W. *West Africa Before Europe* (London: Phillips, 1905).

Bosa, Miguel Suárez, ed. *Atlantic Ports and the First Globalisation, c.1850–1930* (Basingstoke: Macmillan, 2014).

Bowden, Jane H. 'Development and Control in British Colonial Policy with Reference to Nigeria and the Gold Coast' (University of Birmingham Ph.D. thesis, 1981).

Broadberry, Stephen and Leigh Gardner. 'Economic Growth in Sub-Saharan Africa, 1885–2008', LSE: *Economic History Working Papers* 296 (2019).

Broadberry, Stephen and J. Wallis. 'Growing, Shrinking and Long Run Economic Performance: Historical Perspectives on Economic Development', *National Bureau of Economic Research Working Paper* No. 23343 (2017).

Broeze, Frank. 'Port Cities: The Search for an Identity', *Journal of Urban History*, 11 (1985), pp. 209–25.

Broeze, Frank, ed. *Brides of the Sea: Port Cities of Asia from the 16th–20th Centuries* (Honolulu: University of Hawai'i Press, 1989).

Broeze, Frank. 'The Ports and Port Systems of the Asian Seas: An Overview with Historical Perspective from c.1750', *The Great Circle*, 18 (1996), pp. 73–96.

Broeze, Frank, ed. *Gateways of Asia: Port Cities in the 13th–20th Centuries* (London: Kegan Paul, 1997).

Brooks, George E. *The Kru Mariner in the Nineteenth Century* (Newark: University of Delaware Press, 1972).

Brown, Chris and Mark Thornton. 'Entrepreneurship Theory and the Creation of Economics: Insights from Cantillon's Essay', *Quarterly Journal of Austrian Economics*, 16 (2013), pp. 401–14.

Brown, Jonathan and Mary B. Rose, eds. *Entrepreneurship, Methods and Modern Business* (Manchester: Manchester University Press, 1993).

Brown, Spencer H. 'Public Health in Lagos, 1850–1900: Perceptions, Patterns and Perspectives', *International Journal of African Historical Studies*, 25 (1992), pp. 337–60.

Burton, Richard Francis. *Wanderings in West Africa*, Vol. 2 (London: Tinsley Bros, 1863).

Cain, P. J. and A. G. Hopkins. *British Imperialism, 1688–1990* (London: Longman, 1993; 3rd ed. Routledge, 2016).

Cantillon, Richard. *Essaie sur la nature du commerce en général* (Paris: Fletcher Gyles, 1755).

Cassis, Youssef and Ioanna Pepelasis Minoglou, eds. *Entrepreneurship in Theory and History* (Basingstoke: Macmillan, 2005).

Casson, Mark C. *The Entrepreneur: An Economic Theory* (Cheltenham: Edward Elgar, 2nd ed., 2005).

Casson, Mark C. *Entrepreneurship: Theory, Networks, History* (Cheltenham: Edward Elgar, 2010).

Castillo, Lisa Earl. 'Mapping the Nineteenth-Century Brazilian Returnee Movement: Demographics, Life Stories, and the Question of Slavery', *Atlantic Studies*, 13 (2016), pp. 51–2.

Chaplin, Julia Elizabeth. 'The Origins of the 1885/6 Introduction of General Limited Liability in England' (University of East Anglia Ph.D. thesis, 2016).

Chapman, S. D. 'Agency Houses: British Mercantile Enterprise in the Far East, c.1780–1920', *Textile History*, 19 (1988), pp. 239–54.

Chevalier, Auguste. *le Cacaoyer dans l'Ouest Africain* (Paris: Challamel, 1908).

Christaller, Walter. *The Central Places in Southern Germany* (1933; English translation, Englewood Cliffs: Prentice Hall, 1966).

Chukwu, Dan O. 'Economic Impact of Pioneer Indigenous Banks in Colonial Nigeria, 1920–1960', *Journal of the Historical Society of Nigeria*, 19 (2010), pp. 93–109.

Coker, B. A. *Family Property among the Yorubas* (London: Sweet & Maxwell, 1958; 2nd ed. 1966).

Cole, Gibril. *The Krio of West Africa: Islam, Culture, Creolization and Colonialism in the Nineteenth Century* (Athens: Ohio University Press, 2013).

Cole, Patrick. *Modern and Traditional Elites in the Politics of Lagos* (Cambridge: Cambridge University Press, 1975).

Collier, Paul. *The Bottom Billion: Why the Poorest Countries Are Failing and What Can Be Done about It* (Oxford: Oxford University Press, 2007).

Coquery-Vidrovich, Catherine. *Histoire des villes d'Afrique noire: des origines à la colonisation* (Paris: Albin Michel, 1993).

Coret, Celia, Roberto Zaugg, and Gérard Chouin, eds. 'Les villes en Afrique avant 1900', Special issue of *Afriques*, 11 (2020).

Curtin, Philip D. *Disease and Empire: The Health of European Troops in the Conquest of Africa* (Cambridge: Cambridge University Press, 1998).

Dada, S. A., ed. *Jacob Kehinde Coker, Father of African Independent Churches* (Ibadan: AOWA, 1986).

Darch, John H. 'The Church Missionary Society and the Governors of Lagos. 1862–72', *Journal of Ecclesiastical History*, 52 (2001), pp. 313–33.

Darwin, John. 'Imperialism and the Victorians: The Dynamics of Territorial Expansion', *English Historical Review*, 112 (1997), pp. 614–42.

Darwin, John. *Unlocking the World: Port Cities and Globalisation in the Age of Steam, 1830–1930* (London: Allen Lane, 2020).

Davies, P. N. *The Trade Makers: Elder Dempster in West Africa, 1852–1972* (London: Allen & Unwin, 1973).

Davies, P. N. *Sir Alfred Jones: Shipping Entrepreneur Par Excellence* (London: Europa, 1978).

Decker, Stephanie. 'Africanisation in British Multinationals in Ghana and Nigeria, 1945–1970', *Business History Review*, 92 (2018), pp. 691–718.

Decker, Stephanie. *Postcolonial Transition and Global Business History: British Multinational Companies in Ghana and Nigeria* (London: Routledge, 2022).

Decker, Tunde and Adeyemi Balogun. 'Landuji Oshodi Tapa in the Eye of History', in Siyan Oyeweso, ed. *Eminent Yoruba Muslims of the Nineteenth and Early Twentieth Centuries* (Lagos: Rex Charles, 1999), ch. 7.

Deniga, Adeoye. *African Leaders Past and Present*, Vol. 2 (Lagos: Tika Tore, 1915).

Deniga, Adeoye. *African Leaders* (Lagos: Tika Tore, 1919).

Deniga, Adeoye. *The Nigerian Who's Who, 1919* (Lagos: Tika Tore, 1919).

Deniga, Adeoye. *Notes on Lagos Streets* (Lagos: Tika Tore, 1921).

Deniga, Adeoye. *The Nigerian Who's Who for 1934* (Lagos: Awobo Press, 1934).

Dennett, R. E. 'British and German Trade in Nigeria', *United Empire*, 5 (1914), pp. 883–96.

Denzer, LaRay. 'Yoruba Women: A Historiographical Survey', *International Journal of African Historical Studies*, 27 (1994), pp. 1–39.

Dixon-Fyle, Mac. *A Saro Community in the Niger Delta, 1912–1984* (Rochester: University of Rochester Press, 1999).

Drayton, Richard. 'The Globalisation of France: Provincial Cities and French Expansion, c.1500–1800', *History of European Ideas*, 34 (2008), pp. 424–30.

Drummond-Thompson, Philip. 'The Rise of Entrepreneurs in Nigerian Motor Transport: A Study in Indigenous Enterprise', *Journal of Transport History*, 14 (1993), pp. 46–63.

Dudgeon, Gerald C. *The Agricultural and Forest Products of British West Africa* (London: Murray, 1922).

Duerkson, Mark. *Waterhouses: Landscapes, Housing and the Making of Modern Lagos* (Athens: Ohio University Press, 2023).

Dumett, Raymond E. 'African Merchants of the Gold Coast, 1860–1905: Dynamics of Indigenous Entrepreneurship', *Comparative Studies in Society & History*, 25 (1983), pp. 661–93.

Ebner, Alex. 'Schumpeterian Entrepreneurship Revisited: Historical Specificity and the Phases of Capitalist Development', *Journal of the History of Economic Thought*, 28 (2006), pp. 315–32.

Echeruo, Michael J. C. *Victorian Lagos: Aspects of Nineteenth Century Lagos Life* (Basingstoke: Macmillan, 1977).

Elebute, Adeyemo. *The Life of James Pinson Labulo Davies: A Colossus of Victorian Lagos* (Lagos: Prestige Publishers, 2013; 2nd ed. 2017).

Elias, T. Olowale. *Nigerian Land Law and Custom* (London: Routledge & Kegan Paul, 1951).

Ellis, Alfred B. *The Land of Fetish* (London: Chapman and Hall, 1883).

Ellis, Stephen and Yves-A. Fauré, eds. *Entreprises et entrepreneurs africains* (Paris: Karthala, 1995).

Engel, Alexander. 'Buying Time: Futures Trading and Telegraphy in Nineteenth-Century Global Commodity Markets', *Journal of Global History*, 10 (2015), pp. 284–306.

Everill, Bronwen. *Abolition and Empire in Sierra Leone and Liberia* (Basingstoke: Palgrave Macmillan, 2013).

Falola, Toyin. *The Political Economy of a Pre-Colonial State: Ibadan, 1830–1900* (Ile-Ife: University of Ife Press, 1984).

Falola, Toyin. 'The Yoruba Toll System: Its Operation and Abolition', *Journal of African History*, 30 (1989), pp. 69–88.

Falola, Toyin. 'The Yoruba Caravan System of the Nineteenth Century', *International Journal of African Historical Studies*, 24 (1991), pp. 111–32.

Falola, Toyin. '"My Friend the Shylock": Money Lenders and Their Clients in South-West Nigeria', *Journal of African History*, 34 (1993), pp. 403–23.

Falola, Toyin. *Pioneer, Patriot and Patriarch: Samuel Johnson and the Yoruba People* (Madison: African Studies Program, University of Wisconsin–Madison, 1993).

Falola, Toyin. 'Slavery and Pawnship in the Yoruba Economy in the Nineteenth Century', *Slavery & Abolition*, 15 (1994), pp. 221–45.

Falola, Toyin and Emily Brownell, eds. *Africa, Empire and Globalization: Essays in Honor of A. G. Hopkins* (Durham, NC: Carolina Academic Press, 2011).

Falola, Toyin and Matt D. Childs, eds. *The Yoruba Diaspora in the Atlantic World* (Bloomington: Indiana University Press, 2004).

Falola, Toyin and Matt D. Childs, eds. *The Changing World of Atlantic Africa: Essays in Honor of Robin Law* (Durham, NC: Carolina Academic Press, 2009).

Falola, Toyin and Dare Oguntomisin. *The Military in Nineteenth-Century Yoruba Politics* (Ile-Ife: University of Ife Press, 1984).

Falola Toyin and Dare Oguntomisin. *Yoruba Warlords of the Nineteenth Century* (Trenton: Africa World Press, 1999).

Faluyi, Keinde. 'Migrants and the Socio-Economic Development of Lagos from Earliest Times to 1880', *Lagos Historical Review*, 1 (2005), pp. 68–83.

Ferreira, Manuel P., Nuno R. Reis, and Rui Miranda. 'Thirty Years of Entrepreneurship: Research Published in Top Journals: Analysis of Citations, Co-Citations and Themes', *Journal of Global Entrepreneurial Research*, 5 (2015), pp. 1–22.

Fieldhouse, D. K. *Unilever Overseas: The Anatomy of a Multinational, 1895–1965* (London: Croom Helm, 1978).

Fieldhouse, D. K. *Merchant Capital and Economic Decolonization: The United Africa Company, 1929–1897* (Oxford: Clarendon Press, 1994).

Folarin, Kola. 'Egbado to 1832: The Birth of a Dilemma', *Journal of the Historical Society of Nigeria*, 4 (1967), pp. 15–33.

Forrest, Tom. *The Advance of African Capital: The Growth of Nigerian Private Enterprise* (Edinburgh: Edinburgh University Press, 1994).

Fourchard, Laurent. 'African Urban History: Past and Present Perspectives', *Lagos Historical Review*, 5 (2005), pp. 1–21.

Fourie, Johan. 'The Data Revolution in African Economic History', *Journal of Interdisciplinary History*, 47 (2016), pp. 192–212.

Fox, Edward Whiting. *History in Geographic Perspective: The Other France* (New York: Norton, 1971).

Frankema, Ewout and Marlous van Waijenburg. 'Bridging the Gap with the "New Economic History of Africa"', *Journal of African History*, 64 (2023), pp. 1–24.

Frankema, Ewout, Jeffrey Williamson, and Pieter Woltjer. 'An Economic Rationale for the West African Scramble? The Commercial Transition and the Commodity Price Boom of 1835–1885', *Journal of Economic History*, 78 (2018), pp. 231–67.

Fredona, Robert and Sophus A. Reinert. 'The Harvard Research Center in Entrepreneurial History and the Daimonic Entrepreneur', *History of Political Economy*, 49 (2017), pp. 267–314.

Fujita, Masahisa and Paul Krugman. 'The New Economic Geography: Past, Present and the Future', *Papers in Regional Science*, 83 (2004), pp. 139–64.

Fyfe, Christopher. *A History of Sierra Leone* (Oxford: Oxford University Press, 1962).

Fyfe, Christopher. 'A. B. C. Sibthorpe: A Tribute', *History in Africa*, 19 (1992), pp. 327–52.

Gallagher, J. 'Fowell Buxton and the New African Policy, 1838–1842', *Cambridge Historical Journal*, 10 (1950), pp. 36–58.

Garvin, J. L. *The Life of Joseph Chamberlain*, Vol. 3, 1895–1900 (London: Macmillan, 1934).

Gavin, Robert J. 'Palmerston's Policy Towards East and West Africa, 1830–1865' (Cambridge University Ph.D. thesis, 1958).

Gipouloux, François, Jonathan Hall, and Diana Martin, eds. *The Asian Mediterranean: Port Cities and Trading Networks in China, Japan and Southeast Asia, 13th to 21st Centuries* (Cheltenham: Edward Elgar, 2011).

Gleave, M. B. 'Port Activities and the Spatial Structure of Cities: The Case of Freetown', *Journal of Transport Geography*, 5 (1997), pp. 257–76.

Glover, Lady Elizabeth Rosetta. *Life of Sir John Hawley Glover* (London: Smith, Elder & Co., 1897; facsimile ed. Alpha Editions, 2019).

Goerg, Odile. 'La destruction d'un réseau d'échange précolonial: l'exemple de la Guinée', *Journal of African History*, 21 (1980), pp. 467–84.

Greaves, Ron. *Islam in Victorian Britain: The Life and Times of Abdullah Quilliam* (Markfield: Kube, 2010).

Green, Nile. 'Maritime Worlds and Global History: Comparing the Mediterranean and Indian Ocean through Barcelona and Bombay', *History Compass*, 11 (2013), pp. 513–23.

Hagedorn, John. 'Innovation and Entrepreneurship: Schumpeter Revisited', *Industrial and Corporate Change*, 5 (1996), pp. 883–96.

Hailey, Lord. *An African Survey* (London: Oxford University Press, 1938; revised 1956).

Hancock, W. K. (Sir Keith). *Survey of British Commonwealth Affairs, 1918–1939*, Vol. 2, Part 2 (London: Oxford University Press, 1940).

Harding, Leonhard and Pierre Kipré, eds. *Commerce et commerçants en Afrique de l'Ouest: La Côte d'Ivoire* (Paris: Harmattan, 1992).

Hargreaves, John D. *A Life of Sir Samuel Lewis* (London: Oxford University Press, 1958).

Hargreaves, John D. *Prelude to the Partition of West Africa* (London: Macmillan, 1963).

Harnelt-Sievers, Axel. 'African Business, Economic Nationalism and British Colonial Policy: Southern Nigeria, 1935–1954', *African Economic History*, 23 (1995), pp. 79–128.

Hein, Carola, ed. *Port Cities: Dynamic Landscapes and Global Networks* (London: Routledge, 2011).

Helleiner, Gerald K. *Peasant Agriculture, Government, and Economic Growth in Nigeria* (Homewood: Irwin, 1966).

Hicks, J. R. 'Annual Survey of Economic Theory: The Theory of Monopoly', *Econometrica*, 3 (1934), pp. 1–20.

Hieke, Ernst. *G. L. Gaiser: Hamburg-Westafrika. 100 Jahre Handel mit Nigeria* (Hamburg: Hoffmann & Campe, 1949).

Hirschman, Albert O. *Exit, Voice, and Loyalty* (Cambridge, MA: Harvard University Press, 1970).

Hogendorn, Jan S. *Nigerian Groundnut Exports: Origins and Early Development* (Ibadan: Oxford University Press, 1978).

Hogendorn, Jan S. and Marion Johnson. *The Shell Money of the Slave Trade* (Cambridge: Cambridge University Press, 1986).

Hopkins, A. G. 'An Economic History of Lagos, 1880–1914' (University of London Ph.D. thesis, 1964).

Hopkins, A. G. 'The Lagos Chamber of Commerce, 1888–1903', *Journal of the Historical Society of Nigeria*, 3 (1965), pp. 241–8.

Hopkins, A. G. 'The Currency Revolution in South-West Nigeria in the Late Nineteenth Century', *Journal of the Historical Society of Nigeria*, 3 (1966), pp. 471–83.

Hopkins, A. G. 'Economic Aspects of Political Movements in Nigeria and the Gold Coast, 1918–1939', *Journal of African History*, 7 (1966), pp. 133–52.

Hopkins, A. G. 'The Lagos Strike of 1897: An Exploration in Nigerian Labour History', *Past & Present*, 35 (1966), pp. 133–55.

Hopkins, A. G. 'Economic Imperialism in West Africa: Lagos, 1880–1892', *Economic History Review*, 21 (1968), pp. 580–606.

Hopkins, A. G. *An Economic History of West Africa* (London: Longman, 1973; 2nd ed. Routledge, 2020).

Hopkins, A. G. 'Innovation in a Colonial Context: African Origins of the Nigerian Cocoa-Farming Industry', in Clive Dewey and A. G. Hopkins, eds. *The Imperial Impact: Studies in the Economic History of Africa and India* (London: Athlone Press, 1978), pp. 83–96.

Hopkins, A. G. 'Peter Thomas (1873–1947): un commerçant nigérian à l'épreuve d'une économie coloniale en crise', in Charles-André Julien et al., eds. *Les Africains*, Vol. 9 (Paris: Jeune Afrique, 1978), pp. 297–329.

Hopkins, A. G. 'Property Rights and Empire-Building: Britain's Annexation of Lagos, 1851', *Journal of Economic History*, 40 (1980), pp. 777–98.

Hopkins, A. G. 'The New Economic History of Africa', *Journal of African History*, 50 (2009), pp. 155–77.

Hopkins, A. G. *American Empire: A Global History* (Princeton: Princeton University Press, 2018).

Hopkins, A. G. 'Fifty Years of African Economic History', *Economic History of Developing Regions*, 34 (2019), pp. 1–15.

Hopkins, A. G. *Africa, Empire and World Disorder* (London: Routledge, 2021).

Howes, F. N. 'The Early Introduction of Cocoa to West Africa', *Tropical Agriculture*, 23 (1946), pp. 152–3.

Hutchinson, T. J. *Impressions of Western Africa* (London: Longman, 1858).

Irwin, Douglas A. *Against the Tide: An Intellectual History of Free Trade* (Princeton: Princeton University Press, 1998).

Jerven, Morten. 'The Emergence of African Capitalism', in Larry Neal and Jeffrey G. Williamson, eds. *The Cambridge History of Capitalism*, Vol. 1, *The Rise of Capitalism from Ancient Origins to 1848* (Cambridge: Cambridge University Press, 2014), pp. 301–47.

Jing, S., Z. Qinghua, and H. Landström. 'Entrepreneurship Research in Three Regions—the USA, Europe and China', *International Entrepreneurship and Management Journal*, 11 (2015), pp. 861–90.

Johnson, Cheryl. 'Grass Roots Organising: Women in Anti-Colonial Activities in Southwestern Nigeria', *African Studies Review*, 25 (1982), pp. 137–57.

Johnson, Linda Cooke. *Shanghai: From Market Town to Treaty Port, 1074–1858* (Stanford: Stanford University Press, 1993).

Johnson, Samuel. *The History of the Yorubas* (Lagos: CMS Bookshops, 1921).

Johnson, W. H. 'Cocoa in the Southern Provinces and Colony of Nigeria', *Transactions of the Third International Congress of Tropical Agriculture*, 1914, Vol. 2 (London: Bale, 1917), pp. 189–99.

Keynes, John Maynard. *The Economic Consequences of the Peace* (London: Macmillan, 1919).

Kilby, Peter. *African Enterprise: The Nigerian Bread Industry* (Stanford: Hoover Institution, 1965).

Kilby, Peter. *Industrialization in an Open Economy: Nigeria, 1945–1966* (Cambridge: Cambridge University Press, 1969).

Kilby, Peter. 'Manufacturing in Colonial Africa', in Peter Duignan and L. H. Gann, eds. *Colonialism in Africa*, Vol. 4 (Cambridge: Cambridge University Press, 1973), pp. 513–16.

Killingray, David. 'The Empire Resources Development Committee and West Africa, 1916–20', *Journal of Imperial and Commonwealth History*, 10 (1982), pp. 194–210.

Kingsley, Mary. *Travels in West Africa* (London: Macmillan, 1897).

Knight, Franklin and Peggy K. Liss. *Atlantic Port Cities: Economy, Culture and Society in the Atlantic World, 1550–1850* (Knoxville: University of Tennessee Press, 1991).

Kocka, Jürgen and Marcel van der Linden, eds. *Capitalism: The Reemergence of a Concept* (London: Bloomsbury, 2016).

Konvitz, Josef W. 'The Crises of Atlantic Port Cities, 1880–1920', *Comparative Studies in Society & History*, 36 (1994), pp. 293–318.

Koolman, G. 'Say's Conception of the Role of the Entrepreneur', *Economica*, 38 (1971), pp. 266–86.

Kopytoff, Jean Herskovits. *A Preface to Modern Nigeria: The Sierra Leonians in Yoruba, 1830–1890* (Madison: University of Wisconsin Press, 1965).

Laboratoire Connaissance du Tiers-Monde. *Actes du colloque entreprises et entrepreneurs en Afrique noire*, 2 vols. (Paris: L'Harmattan, 1983).

Laotan, A. B. *The Torch Bearers or the Old Brazilian Colony in Lagos* (Lagos: Ife-Olu Press, 1943).

Latham, A.J.H. *Old Calabar, 1600–1891* (Oxford: Clarendon Press, 1973).

Latham, A.J.H. 'Palm Produce from Calabar, 1812–1887', in G. Liesegang, H. Pasch, and A. Jones, eds. *Figuring African Trade* (Berlin: Reimer, 1986), pp. 265–96.

Law, R.C.C. 'The Dynastic Chronology of Lagos', *Lagos Notes & Records*, 2 (1968), pp. 46–54.

Law, R.C.C. 'The Chronology of the Yoruba Wars of the Early Nineteenth Century: A Reconsideration', *Journal of the Historical Society of Nigeria*, 5 (1970), pp. 211–22.

Law, R.C.C. 'Trade and Politics Behind the Slave Coast: The Lagoon Traffic and the Rise of Lagos, 1500–1800', *Journal of African History*, 24 (1981), pp. 321–48.

Law, Robin, ed. *From Slave Trade to 'Legitimate' Commerce* (Cambridge: Cambridge University Press, 1995).

Law, Robin. *Ouidah: The Social History of a West African Slaving 'Port', 1727–1892* (Oxford: James Currey, 2004).

Law, Robin. 'Yoruba Liberated Slaves Who Returned to West Africa', in Toyin Falola and Matt D. Childs, eds. *The Yoruba Diaspora in the Atlantic World* (Bloomington: Indiana University Press, 2004), ch. 17.

Law, Robin. 'The "Crisis of Adaptation" Revisited: The Yoruba Wars of 1877–1893', in Toyin Falola and Emily Brownell, eds. *Africa, Empire and Globalization: Essays in Honor of A. G. Hopkins* (Durham: Carolina Academic Press, 2011), ch. 6.

Law, Robin, Suzanne Schwarz, and Silke Strickrodt, eds. *Commercial Agriculture, the Slave Trade and Slavery in Atlantic Africa* (Woodbridge: James Currey, 2013).

Lawal, Olakunle A. 'Islam and Colonial Rule in Lagos', *American Journal of Islamic Social Science*, 12 (1995), pp. 66–80.

Lindsay, Lisa A. '"To Return to the Bosom of Their Fatherland": Brazilian Immigrants in Nineteenth-Century Lagos', *Slavery & Abolition*, 15 (1994), pp. 22–50.

Lindsay, Lisa A. *Atlantic Bonds: A Nineteenth-Century Odyssey from America to Africa* (Chapel Hill: University of North Carolina Press, 2017).

Lindsay, Lisa A. 'Biography in African History', *History in Africa*, 443 (2017), pp. 11–26.

Livsey, Tim. 'Late Colonialism and Segregation at the Ikoyi Reservation in Lagos, Nigeria', *Journal of African History*, 63 (2022), pp. 178–96.

Losi, John B. *History of Lagos* (Lagos: Tika Tore, 1914).

Lovejoy, Paul E. 'Pawnship, Debt, and "Freedom" in Atlantic Africa during the Era of the Slave Trade: A Reassessment', *Journal of African History*, 55 (2014), pp. 33–78.

Lovell, E. A. 'Lagos Present', *Proceedings of the Lagos Institute* (Lagos, 1902).

Low, Murray B. and Ian C. MacMillan. 'Entrepreneurship: Past Research and Future Prospects', *Journal of Management*, 14 (1988), pp. 39–61.

Lucas, J. Olumide. *Lecture on the History of St. Paul's Church, Breadfruit, Lagos* (Lagos: CMS Press, 1947).

Lynch, Hollis R. *Edward Wilmot Blyden, Pan-Negro Patriot* (London: Oxford University Press, 1967).

Lynn, Martin. 'Consuls and Kings: British Policy, the Man on the Spot, and the Seizure of Lagos, 1851', *Journal of Imperial & Commonwealth History*, 10 (1982), pp. 150–67.

Lynn, Martin. *Commerce and Economic Change in West Africa: The Palm Oil Trade in the Nineteenth Century* (Cambridge: Cambridge University Press, 1997).

Lynn, Martin. 'British Policy, Trade and Informal Empire in the Mid-Nineteenth Century', in Andrew Porter, ed. *The Oxford History of the British Empire*, Vol. 3 (Oxford: Oxford University Press, 1999), pp. 101–22.

Mabogunje, A. L. and J. Omar-Cooper. *Owu in Yoruba History* (Ibadan: Ibadan University Press, 1971).

Macmillan, Allister. *The Red Book of West Africa: Historical and Descriptive, Commercial and Industrial Facts, Figures & Resources* (London: Collingridge, 1920).

Maier, Donna J. E. 'Precolonial Palm Oil Production and Gender Division of Labor in Nineteenth-Century Gold Coast and Togoland', *African Economic History*, 37 (2009), pp. 1–32.

Mann, Kristin. *Marrying Well: Marriage, Status, and Social Change among the Educated Elite in Colonial Lagos* (Cambridge: Cambridge University Press, 1985).

Mann, Kristin. 'The Rise of Taiwo Olowo: Law, Accumulation and Mobility in Early Colonial Lagos', in Kristin Mann and Richard Roberts, eds. *Law in Colonial Africa* (Portsmouth: Heinemann, 1991), pp. 92–3.

Mann, Kristin. *Slavery and the Birth of an African City: Lagos, 1760–1900* (Bloomington: Indiana University Press, 2007).

Mann, Kristin. 'African and European Initiatives in the Transformation of Land Law in Colonial Lagos (West Africa), 1840–1920', in Salilha Belmessouss, ed. *Native Claims: Indigenous Law Against Empire, 1500–1920* (Oxford: Oxford University Press, 2012), pp. 223–47.

Mars, J. 'Extra-Territorial Enterprises', in P. A. Bower A. J. Brown, C. Leubuscher, J. Mars and A. Pim, eds. *Mining, Commerce, and Finance in Nigeria* (London: Faber, 1948), pp. 43–136.

Marx, Karl and Frederick Engels. *Manifesto of the Communist Party* (Moscow: Progress Publishers, n.d.; originally published in 1848).

Masashi, Haneda, ed. *Asian Port Cities, 1600–1800: Local and Foreign Cultural Interactions* (Singapore: National University of Singapore Press, 2009).

McPhee, Allan. *The Economic Revolution in British West Africa* (London: Routledge, 1926).

McPherson, Kenneth. 'Port Cities as Nodal Points of Change: The Indian Ocean, 1890s–1920s', in Leila Tarazi Fawaz and C. A. Bayly, eds. *Modernity and Culture from the Mediterranean to the Indian Ocean* (New York: Columbia University Press, 2002), pp. 75–95.

Miller, N. S. 'The Beginnings of Modern Lagos', *Nigeria Magazine*, 69 (1961), pp. 106–21.

Millson, Alvan. 'The Yoruba Country, West Africa', *Royal Geographical Society Proceedings*, 13 (1891), pp. 577–87.

Millson, Alvan. 'Notes on the Preparation of Lagos Palm Oil', *Kew Bulletin of Miscellaneous Information*, 69 (1892), pp. 203–8.

Moloney, Cornelius Alfred. *Sketch of the Forestry of West Africa* (London: Low, Marston, Searle, and Rivington, 1887).

Moloney, Cornelius Alfred. 'Cotton Interests, Foreign and Native, in Yoruba, and Generally in West Africa', *Journal of the Manchester Geographical Society*, 5 (1889), pp. 255–76.

Moore, E. A. Ajisafe. *The Laws and Customs of the Yoruba People* (Abeokuta: Ola Falola, 1924).

Murphy, Antoin E. *Richard Cantillon: Entrepreneur and Economist* (Oxford: Oxford University Press, 1986).

Nafziger, E. Wayne. *African Capitalism: A Case Study of Nigerian Entrepreneurship* (Stanford: Hoover Institute, 1977).

Neal, Larry and Jeffrey G. Williamson, eds. *The Cambridge History of Capitalism*, Vol. 1, *From Ancient Origins to 1848* (Cambridge: Cambridge University Press, 2013); Vol. 2, *1848 to the Present* (Cambridge: Cambridge University Press, 2014).

Newbury, Colin W. *The Western Slave Coast and its Rulers* (Oxford: Oxford University Press, 1961).

Newbury, Colin W. 'Credit and Debt in Early Nineteenth-Century West African Trade', *Journal of African History*, 13 (1972), pp. 81–95.

Newlyn W. T. and Rowan, C. *Money and Banking in British Colonial Africa* (Oxford: Clarendon Press, 1954).

Newman, Kenneth R. 'The Davies Chronicles: An African Merchant Family in Victorian Lagos' (Dalhousie University M.A. thesis, 1983).

Nicholas, Tom. 'Clogs to Clogs in Three Generations? Explaining Entrepreneurial Performance in Britain Since 1850', *Journal of Economic History*, 59 (1999), pp. 688–713.

Nigeria, *The Epetedo Lands: Representations of the Oshodi Chieftaincy Family Submitted to the Commissioner, Lagos Land Inquiry* (Lagos: Hope Rising Press, 1939),

Nwabughuogu, Anthony I. 'From Wealthy Entrepreneurs to Petty Traders: The Decline of African Middlemen in Eastern Nigeria, 1900–1950', *Journal of African History*, 23 (1982), pp. 365–79.

Nwamunobi, C. Onyeke. 'Incendiarism and Other Fires in Nineteenth-Century Lagos (1863–88)', *Africa*, 60 (1990), pp. 111–20.

Nzemeke, A. D. 'Local Patronage and Commercial Enterprise in Lagos, 1830–1861', *Africa*, 47 (1992), pp. 105–14.

Ochonu, Moses E. 'Conjoined to Empire: The Great Depression and Nigeria', *African Economic History*, 5 (2006), pp. 103–45.

Ochonu, Moses E., ed. *Entrepreneurship in Africa: A Historical Approach* (Bloomington: Indiana University Press, 2018).

O'Flanagan, Patrick. *Port Cities of Atlantic Iberia, c.1500–1930* (Aldershot: Ashgate, 2008).

Ojo, Olatunji. 'The Organization of the Atlantic Slave Trade in Yorubaland, 1777–1856', *International Journal of African Historical Studies*, 48 (2008), pp. 77–100.

Oke, G. A. *A Short History of the U.N.A., 1891–1903* (Lagos, 1918).

Olaoba, Olufemi Bamigboyega and Oluranti Edward Ojo. 'Influence of British Economic Activity on Lagos Traditional Markets, 1900–1960' *Journal of the Historical Society of Nigeria*, 23 (2014), pp. 111–30.

Olukoju, Ayodeji. 'Elder Dempster and the Shipping Trade of Nigeria during the First World War', *Journal of African History*, 33 (1992), pp. 255–71.

Olukoju, Ayodeji. 'The Making of an "Expensive Port": Shipping Lines, Government and Port Tariffs in Lagos, 1917–1949', *International Journal of Maritime History*, 6 (1994), pp. 141–59.

Olukoju, Ayodeji. 'Anatomy of Business–Government Relations: Fiscal Policy and Mercantile Pressure Group Activity in Nigeria, 1916–33', *African Studies Review*, 38 (1995), pp. 23–50.

Olukoju, Ayodeji. 'The Impact of British Colonialism on the Development of African Business in Colonial Nigeria', in Alusine Jalloh and Toyin Falola, eds. *Black Business and Economic Power* (Rochester: University of Rochester Press, 2002), pp. 176–98.

Olukoju, Ayodeji. 'Nigeria or Lever-ia? Nationalist Reactions to Economic Depression and the "Menace of Mergers" in Colonial Nigeria', *Journal of Third World Studies*, 19 (2002), pp. 173–94.

Olukoju, Ayodeji. *Infra-Structure Development and Urban Facilities in Lagos, 1861–2000* (Ibadan: IFRA, 2003).

Olukoju, Ayodeji. *The Liverpool of West Africa: The Dynamics and Impact of Maritime Trade on Lagos, 1900–1950* (Trenton, NJ: African World Press, 2004).

Olukoju, Ayodeji. 'Actors and Institutions in Urban Politics in Nigeria: Agege (Lagos) since the 1950s', *Afrika Zamani*, 13–14 (2005), pp. 153–78.

Olukoju, Ayodeji. 'The Port of Lagos, 1850–1929: The Rise of West Africa's Leading Seaport', in Miguel Suárez Bosa, ed. *Atlantic Ports and the First Globalisation, c.1850–1930* (Basingstoke: Macmillan, 2014), ch. 6.

Olukoju, Ayodeji. 'Which Lagos, Whose (Hi)Story?', *Lagos Notes & Records*, 24 (2018), pp. 140–67.

Olukoju, Ayodeji and Daniel Castillo Hidalgo, eds. *African Seaports and Maritime Economics in Historical Perspective* (Basingstoke: Palgrave Macmillan, 2020).

Olusanya, G. O. 'The Lagos Branch of the National Congress of British West Africa', *Journal of the Historical Society of Nigeria*, 6 (1968), pp. 321–33.

Omenka, Nicholas. 'The Afro-Brazilian Repatriates and the Religious and Cultural Trans-formation of Colonial Lagos', *Abia Journal of the Humanities and Social Sciences*, 1 (2004), pp. 27–45.

Omosini, Olufemi. 'Alfred Moloney and his Strategies for Economic Development in Lagos and its Hinterland, 1886–91', *Journal of the Historical Society of Nigeria*, 7 (1975), pp. 657–72.

Omu, Fred I. A. 'Journalism and the Rise of Nigerian Nationalism: John Payne Jackson, 1848–1915', *Journal of the Historical Society of Nigeria*, 7 (1974), pp. 521–39.

Onabolu, A. Olu. 'Mrs Randle: Child of Queen Victoria', *Daily Service*, 4 Feb. 1956.

Oyeweso, Siyan. *Across Three Centuries: The Life and Times of Mohammed Shitta Bey, 1824–1895* (Lagos: Free Enterprise Press, 2001).

Pallinder-Law, Agneta. 'Government in Abeokuta, 1830–1914 with Special Reference to the Egba United Government, 1898–1914' (University of Göteborg Ph.D. thesis, 1973).

Pallinder-Law, Agneta. 'Aborted Modernisation in West Africa: The Case of Abeokuta', *Journal of African History*, 15 (1974), pp. 65–82.

Park, A.E.W. 'The Cession of Territory and Private Land Rights: A Reconsideration of the Tijani Case', *Nigerian Law Journal*, 1 (1964), pp. 38–49.

Payne, J.A.O. *Payne's Lagos and West African Almanack and Diary*, 24 vols. (London: J. A. Johnson, 1874–1902).

Pearson, Michael N. *Port Cities and Intruders: The Swahili Coast, India and Portugal in the Early Modern Era* (Baltimore: Johns Hopkins University Press, 1998).

Pearson, Scott R. 'The Economic Imperialism of the Royal Niger Company', *Food Research Institute Studies*, 10 (1971), pp. 69–88.

Peel, John. 'Olaju: A Yoruba Concept of Development', *Journal of Development Studies*, 14 (1978), pp. 139–65.

Perham, Margery, ed. *Mining, Commerce, and Finance in Nigeria* (London: Faber, 1948).

Perham, Margery. *Lugard: The Years of Authority, 1898–1945* (London: Collins, 1960).

Phillips, Earl. 'The Egba at Ikorodu, 1865: Perfidious Lagos?', *African Historical Studies*, 3 (1970), pp. 23–35.

Pines David. 'New Economic Geography: Revolution or Counter-Revolution?', *Journal of Economic Geography*, 1 (2001) pp. 139–46.

Raifu, Isiaka Okunola. 'Intrigues and Twists in the Imamate Crisis of Lagos Central Mosque (Jama'atul Muslimeen Council), 1841–1947', *International Journal of Arts and Humanities*, 5 (2016), pp. 36–48.

Reynolds, Ed. 'The Rise and Fall of African Merchants on the Gold Cast, 1830–74', *Cahiers d'études africaines*, 54 (1974), pp. 253–64.

Rönnbäck, Klas. 'Climate, Conflicts, and Variations in Prices on Pre-Colonial West African Markets for Staple Crops', *Economic History Review*, 67 (2014), pp. 1065–88.

Rönnbäck, Klas. 'The Business of Barter on the Pre-colonial Gold Coast', *Economic History of Developing Regions*, 35 (2020), pp. 123–42.

Rosenfeld, Susan A. C. 'Apparitions of the Atlantic: Mobility, Kinship and Freedom among Afro-Brazilian Emigrants from Bahia to Lagos' (UCLA Ph.D. thesis, 2020).

Salma, Steven J. and Toyin Falola, eds. *The History of African Cities South of the Sahara* (Rochester: University of Rochester Press, 2005).

Saupin, Guy. 'The Emergence of Port Towns in Pre-Colonial Sub-Saharan Africa, 1450–1850', *International Journal of Maritime History*, 32 (2020), pp. 172–84.

Sawada, Nozomi. 'The Educated Elite and Associational Life in Early Lagos Newspapers' (Unpublished Ph.D. thesis, University of Birmingham, 2012).

Say, Jean-Baptiste. *Traité d'économie politique* (Paris: Horace Say, 1803).

Schumpeter, Joseph A. *The Theory of Economic Development* (Boston: Harvard University Press, 1934).

Scott-Keltie, J., ed. *The Statesman's Year Book, 1912* (London: Macmillan, 1912).

Seeman, Albert L. 'Seattle as a Port City', *Economic Geography*, 11 (1935), pp. 20–32.

Shelford, Frederick. 'On West African Railways', *Journal of the African Society*, 1 (1902), pp. 339–54.

Shoorl, Evert. *Jean-Baptiste Say: Revolutionary, Entrepreneur, Economist* (London: Routledge, 2013).

Silva, Filipa Ribeiro da. 'The Slave Trade and the Development of the Atlantic Port System (c.1400–c.1800)', *International Journal of Maritime History*, 29 (2017), pp. 138–54.

Simon, Herbert. *Models of Man, Social and Rational: Mathematical Essays on Rational Human Behavior in a Social Setting* (New York: Wiley, 1957).

Singleton, Brent D. '"That Ye May Know Each Other": Late Victorian Interactions between British and West African Muslims', *Journal of Muslim Minority Affairs*, 29 (2009), pp. 369–85.

Sivasundaram, Sujit. *Islanded: Britain, Sri Lanka, and the Bounds of an Indian Ocean Colony* (Chicago: University of Chicago Press, 2013).

Sivasundaram, Sujit. *Waves Across the South: A New History of Revolution and Empire* (London: Collins, 2020).

Smith, Adam. *The Wealth of Nations* 1776 (New York: Random House, 1937).

Smith, Robert S. *The Lagos Consulate, 1851–1861* (Basingstoke: Macmillan, 1978).

Smith, Robert S., ed. *Memoirs of Giambattista Scala* (Oxford: Oxford University Press, 2000).

Somotan, Halimat T. 'Lagos Women in Colonial History: A Biographical Sketch of Alimotu Pelewura', *Vestiges: Traces of Record*, 4 (2018), https://www.vestiges-journal.info/2018/somotan_2018.html.

Sorensen-Gilmore, Caroline. 'Badagri, 1784–1863: The Political and Commercial History of a Pre-Colonial Lagoonside Community in South-West Nigeria' (University of Stirling Ph.D. thesis, 1995).

Sylla, Richard. 'Financial Systems and Economic Modernization', *Journal of Economic History*, 62 (2002), pp. 277–92.

Tawney, R. H. 'The Abolition of Economic Controls, 1918–21', *Economic History Review*, 13 (1943), pp. 1–30.

Thomas, Isaac B. *Life History of Herbert Macaulay, C.E.*, 3rd ed. (Lagos: Tika-Tore Press, 1946).

Thünen, Johan Heinrich von. *The Isolated State in Relation to Agriculture and Political Economy* (Hamburg: Perthes, 1826. First published in German; English translation, 1966).

Tijani, Hakeem Ibikunle. 'The Lagos-Awori Frontier: Nineteenth-Century History, Migrations and Transformation of an African Community', *Journal of the Historical Society of Nigeria*, 16 (2005), pp. 141–55.

Tudhope, W.S.D. 'The Development of the Cocoa Industry in the Gold Coast and Ashanti', *Journal of the Royal African Society*, 9 (1909).

Uche, Chibuike. 'Foreign Banks, Africans, and Credit in Colonial Nigeria, c.1890–1912', *Economic History Review*, 52 (1999), pp. 669–91.

Uche, Chibuike. 'Indigenous Banks in Colonial Nigeria', *International Journal of African Historical Studies*, 43 (2010), pp. 476–87.

Verhoef, Grietjie. *The History of Business in Africa* (Berlin: Springer, 2017).

Wadhwani, R. Daniel and Christina Lubinski. 'Reinventing Entrepreneurial History', *Business History Review*, 91 (2017), pp. 767–99.

Wagstyl, Stefan. 'The Struggle Between Success and Succession', *Financial Times*, 31 Oct. 2020.

Wale, Judith. 'The Changing Activities of British Trading Companies in Black Africa', *Société française d'histoire d'outre-mer* (2001), pp. 119–44.

Webster, James Bertin. 'Agege: Plantations and the African Church, 1901–20', West African Institute of Social and Economic Research, *Conference Proceedings, 1962* (Ibadan: NISER, 1963), pp. 124–30.

Webster, James Bertin. *The African Churches among the Yoruba, 1888–1922* (Oxford: Clarendon Press, 1964).

Whitford, John. *Trading Life in Western and Central Africa* (London, 1877; 2nd ed. with an introduction by A. G. Hopkins. London: Frank Cass, 1967).

Wilson, Charles. *History of Unilever: A Study in Economic Growth and Social Change*, Vol. 1 (London: Cassell, 1954).

Yearwood, Peter J. *Nigeria and the Death of Liberal England: Palm Nuts and Prime Ministers, 1914–1916* (Cham: Palgrave Macmillan, 2018).

Yemitan, Oladipo. *Madame Tinubu: Merchant and King-Maker* (Ibadan: University of Ibadan Press, 1987).

Young, Arthur. *Travels, During the Years 1787, 1788, and 1789* (London: Dent, 1792).

A NOTE ON THE TYPE

———◆———

THIS BOOK has been composed in Miller, a Scotch Roman typeface designed by Matthew Carter and first released by Font Bureau in 1997. It resembles Monticello, the typeface developed for The Papers of Thomas Jefferson in the 1940s by C. H. Griffith and P. J. Conkwright and reinterpreted in digital form by Carter in 2003.

Pleasant Jefferson ("P. J.") Conkwright (1905–1986) was Typographer at Princeton University Press from 1939 to 1970. He was an acclaimed book designer and AIGA Medalist.

The ornament used throughout this book was designed by Pierre Simon Fournier (1712–1768) and was a favorite of Conkwright's, used in his design of the *Princeton University Library Chronicle*.